Behavioral Finance, Individual Investors, and Institutional Investors

CFA® PROGRAM CURRICULUM • VOLUME 2

LEVEL III
2011

Mexico City   Munich   Paris   Cape Town   Hong Kong   Montreal

ISBN 10: 0-558-52194-0
ISBN 13: 978-0-558-52194-3

Mixed Sources
Product group from well-managed forests, controlled sources and recycled wood or fiber
www.fsc.org   Cert no. SW-COC-002985
©1996 Forest Stewardship Council

CONTENTS

STUDY SESSION 5   PORTFOLIO MANAGEMENT FOR INSTITUTIONAL INVESTORS

READING 20

READING 21

HOW TO USE THE CFA PROGRAM CURRICULUM

Congratulations on passing Level II of the Chartered Financial Analyst (CFA®) Program. This exciting and rewarding program of study reflects your desire to become a serious investment professional. You are participating in a program noted for its high ethical standards and the breadth of knowledge, skills, and abilities it develops. Your commitment to the CFA Program should be educationally and professionally rewarding.

The credential you seek is respected around the world as a mark of accomplishment and dedication. Each level of the program represents a distinct achievement in professional development. Successful completion of the program is rewarded with membership in a prestigious global community of investment professionals. CFA charterholders are dedicated to life-long learning and maintaining currency with the ever-changing dynamics of a challenging profession.

The CFA examination measures your degree of mastery of the assigned CFA Program curriculum. Therefore, the key to your success on the examination is reading and studying the CFA Program curriculum. The remaining sections provide background on the Candidate Body of Knowledge (CBOK™), the organization of the curriculum and tips for developing an effective study program.

Curriculum Development

The CFA Program curriculum is grounded in the practice of the investment profession. Utilizing the Global Body of Investment Knowledge (GBIK) collaborative website, CFA Institute performs a continuous practice analysis with investment professionals around the world to determine the knowledge, skills, and abilities that are relevant to the profession. Regional panels and targeted surveys are conducted annually to verify and reinforce the continuous feedback. The practice analysis process ultimately defines the Candidate Body of Knowledge (CBOK). The CBOK consists of four components:

▶ A broad topic outline that lists the major knowledge areas

▶ Topic area weights that indicate the relative exam weightings of the top-level topic areas

▶ Learning Outcome Statements (LOS) that advise candidates as to what they should be able to do with this knowledge (LOS are provided in candidate study sessions and at the beginning of each reading)

▶ The curriculum of material that candidates receive upon exam registration and are expected to master

A committee made up of practicing charterholders, in conjunction with CFA Institute staff, designs the CFA Program curriculum to deliver the CBOK to candidates. The examinations, also written by practicing charterholders, are designed to allow you to demonstrate your mastery of the CBOK as set forth in the CFA Program curriculum. As you structure your personal study program, you should emphasize mastery of the CBOK and the practical application of that knowledge. For more information on the practice analysis, CBOK, and development of the CFA Program curriculum, please visit www.cfainstitute.org/toolkit.

Organization of the Curriculum

The Level III CFA Program curriculum is organized into 10 topic areas. Each topic area begins with a brief statement of the material and the depth of knowledge expected.

Each topic area is then divided into one or more study sessions. These study sessions—18 sessions in the Level III curriculum—should form the basic structure of your reading and preparation.

Each study session includes a statement of its structure and objective, and is further divided into specific reading assignments. The outline on the inside front cover of each volume illustrates the organization of these 18 study sessions.

The reading assignments are the basis for all examination questions, and are selected or developed specifically to teach the CBOK. These readings are drawn from CFA Program-commissioned content, textbook chapters, professional journal articles, research analyst reports, and cases. Readings include problems and solutions as well as appendices to help you learn.

Reading-specific Learning Outcome Statements (LOS) are listed at the beginning of each reading. These LOS indicate what you should be able to accomplish after studying the reading. We encourage you to review how to properly use LOS, and the descriptions of commonly used LOS "command words," at www.cfainstitute.org/toolkit. The command words signal the depth of learning you are expected to achieve from the reading. You should use the LOS to guide and focus your study, as each examination question is based on an assigned reading and one or more LOS. However, the readings provide context for the LOS and enable you to apply a principle or concept in a variety of scenarios. The candidate is responsible for the entirety of all of the required material in a study session, the assigned readings as well as the end-of-reading questions and problems.

Features of the Curriculum

▶ **Required vs. Optional Segments** - You should read all of the pages for an assigned reading. In some cases, however, we have reprinted an entire chapter or article and marked those parts of the reading that are not required as "optional." The CFA examination is based only on the required segments, and the optional segments are included only when they might help you to better understand the required segments (by seeing the required material in its full context). When an optional segment begins, you will see an icon and a solid vertical bar in the outside margin that will continue until the optional segment ends, accompanied by another icon. *Unless the material is specifically marked as optional, you should assume it is required.* Keep in mind that the optional material is provided strictly for your convenience and will not be tested. You should rely on the required segments and the reading-specific LOS in preparing for the examination.

▶ **Problems/Solutions** - *All questions and problems in the readings as well as their solutions (which are provided directly following the problems) are part of the curriculum and required material for the exam.* When appropriate, we have included problems within and after the readings to demonstrate practical application and reinforce your understanding of the concepts presented. The questions and problems are designed to help you learn these concepts and may serve as a basis for exam questions. Many of the questions are adapted from past CFA examinations.

For your benefit, we have also made available the last three years' LIII essay questions and solutions. Please visit www.cfainstitute.org/toolkit to review these resources.

▶ **Margins** - The wide margins in each volume provide space for your note-taking.

▶ **Two-Color Format** - To enrich the visual appeal and clarity of the exhibits, tables, and text, the curriculum is printed in a two-color format.

▶ **Six-Volume Structure** - For portability of the curriculum, the material is spread over six volumes.

▶ **Glossary and Index** - For your convenience, we have printed a glossary and index in each volume. Throughout the curriculum, a **bolded blue** word in a reading denotes a term defined in the glossary.

▶ **Source Material** - The authorship, publisher, and copyright owners are given for each reading for your reference. We recommend that you use this CFA Institute curriculum rather than the original source materials because the curriculum may include only selected pages from outside readings, updated sections within the readings, and has problems and solutions tailored to the CFA Program.

▶ **LOS Self-Check** - We have inserted checkboxes next to each LOS that you can use to track your progress in mastering the concepts in each reading.

Designing Your Personal Study Program

Create a Schedule - An orderly, systematic approach to examination preparation is critical. You should dedicate a consistent block of time every week to reading and studying. Complete all reading assignments and the associated problems and solutions in each study session. Review the LOS both before and after you study each reading to ensure that you have mastered the applicable content and can demonstrate the knowledge, skill, or ability described by the LOS and the assigned reading. Use the new LOS self-check to track your progress and highlight areas of weakness for later review.

You will receive periodic e-mail communications that contain important study tips and preparation strategies. Be sure to read these carefully.

CFA Institute estimates that you will need to devote a minimum of 10–15 hours per week for 18 weeks to study the assigned readings. Allow a minimum of one week for each study session, and plan to complete them all at least 30–45 days prior to the examination. This schedule will allow you to spend the final four to six weeks before the examination reviewing the assigned material and taking online sample and mock examinations.

At CFA Institute, we believe that candidates need to commit to a *minimum* of 270–300 hours reading and reviewing the curriculum and end-of-reading questions and problems. Many candidates have also incorporated the online sample examinations into their preparations during the final weeks before the exam. This recommendation, however, may substantially underestimate the hours needed for appropriate examination preparation depending on your individual circumstances, relevant experience, and academic background. You will undoubtedly adjust your study time to conform to your own strengths and weaknesses, and your educational and professional background.

You will probably spend more time on some study sessions than on others, but on average you should plan on devoting 15 hours per study session. You should allow ample time for both in-depth study of all topic areas and additional concentration on those topic areas for which you feel least prepared.

Candidate Preparation Toolkit - We have created the online toolkit to provide a single comprehensive location with resources and guidance for candidate preparation. In addition to in-depth information on study program planning, the CFA

Program curriculum, and the online sample and mock examinations, the toolkit also contains curriculum errata, printable study session outlines, sample examination questions, and more. Errata that we have identified in the curriculum are corrected and listed periodically in the errata listing in the toolkit. We encourage you to use the toolkit as your central preparation resource during your tenure as a candidate. Visit the toolkit at www.cfainstitute.org/toolkit.

Online Sample Examinations - CFA Institute online sample examinations are intended to assess your exam preparation as you progress toward the end of your study. After each question, you will receive immediate feedback noting the correct response and indicating the relevant assigned reading, so you'll be able to identify areas of weakness for further study. The 120-minute sample examinations reflect the question formats, topics, and level of difficulty of the actual CFA examinations. Aggregate data indicate that the CFA examination pass rate was higher among candidates who took one or more online sample examinations than among candidates who did not take the online sample examinations. For more information on the online sample examinations, please visit www.cfainstitute.org/toolkit.

Online Mock Examinations - In response to candidate requests, CFA Institute has developed mock examinations that mimic the actual CFA examinations not only in question format and level of difficulty, but also in length. The three-hour online mock exams are intended to be taken after you complete your study of the full curriculum, so you can test your understanding of the CBOK and your readiness for the exam. To further differentiate, feedback is provided at the end of the exam, rather than after each question as with the sample exams. CFA Institute recommends that you take these mock exams at the final stage of your preparation toward the actual CFA examination. For more information on the online mock examinations, please visit www.cfainstitute.org/toolkit.

Tools to Measure Your Comprehension of the Curriculum

With the addition of the online mock exams, CFA Institute now provides three distinct ways you can practice for the actual CFA exam. The full descriptions are above, but below is a brief summary of each:

End-of-Reading Questions and Problems - These are found at the end of each reading in the printed curriculum, and should be used to test your understanding of the concepts.

Online Sample Exams - Available in Fall 2010, online sample exams are designed to assess your exam preparation, and can help you target areas of weakness for further study.

Online Mock Exams - In contrast to the sample exams, mock exams will be available in Spring 2011. Mock exams are designed to replicate the exam day experience, and should be taken near the end of your study period to prepare for exam day.

Preparatory Providers - After you enroll in the CFA Program, you may receive numerous solicitations for preparatory courses and review materials. When considering a prep course, make sure the provider is in compliance with the

CFA Institute Prep Provider Guidelines Program. Just remember, there are no shortcuts to success on the CFA examinations; reading and studying the CFA curriculum is the key to success on the examination. The CFA examinations reference only the CFA Institute assigned curriculum—no preparatory course or review course materials are consulted or referenced. For more information on the Prep Provider Guidelines Program, visit www.cfainstitute.org/cfaprog/resources/prepcourse.html.

SUMMARY

Every question on the CFA examination is based on specific pages in the required readings and on one or more LOS. Frequently, an examination question is also tied to a specific example highlighted within a reading or to a specific end-of-reading question and/or problem and its solution. To make effective use of the curriculum, please remember these key points:

1. All pages printed in the Custom Curriculum are required reading for the examination except for occasional sections marked as optional. You may read optional pages as background, but you will not be tested on them.

2. All questions, problems, and their solutions - printed at the end of readings - are part of the curriculum and required study material for the examination.

3. You should make appropriate use of the CFA Candidate Toolkit and the online sample/mock examinations.

4. You should schedule and commit sufficient study time to cover the 18 study sessions, review the materials, and take sample/mock examinations.

5. **Note:** Some of the concepts in the study sessions may be superseded by updated rulings and/or pronouncements issued after a reading was published. Candidates are expected to be familiar with the overall analytical framework contained in the assigned readings. Candidates are not responsible for changes that occur after the material was written.

Feedback

At CFA Institute, we are committed to delivering a comprehensive and rigorous curriculum for the development of competent, ethically grounded investment professionals. We rely on candidate and member feedback as we work to incorporate content, design, and packaging improvements. You can be assured that we will continue to listen to your suggestions. Please send any comments or feedback to curriculum@cfainstitute.org. Ongoing improvements in the curriculum will help you prepare for success on the upcoming examinations, and for a lifetime of learning as a serious investment professional.

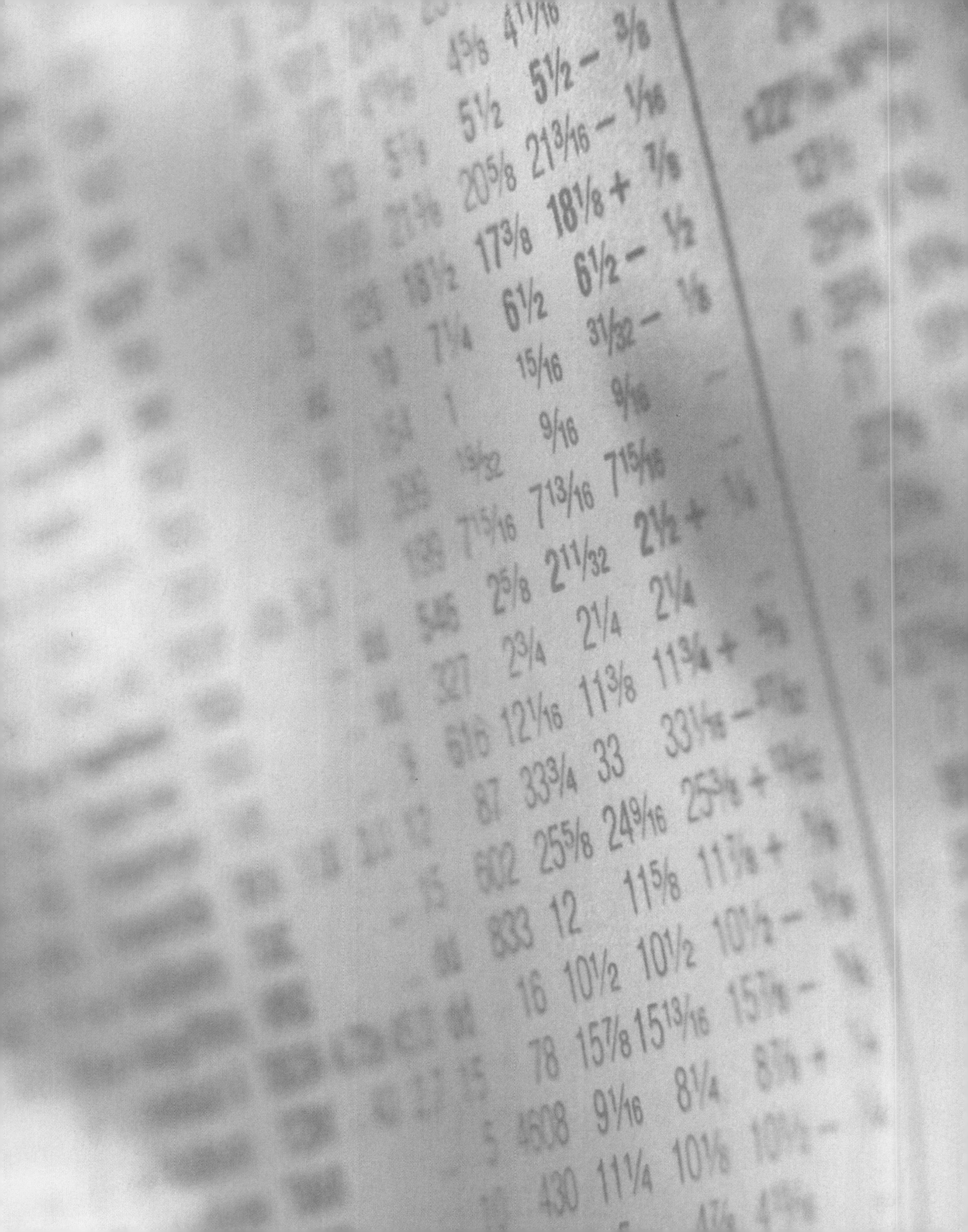

4⅝ 4¹¹/₁₆

5½ − ⅜

5½ 5½

20⅝ 2¹³/₁₆ − ⅛

17⅜ 18⅛ + ⅞

18½

7¼ 6½ 6½ − ½

15/16 3¹/₃₂ − ⅛

9/16 9/16

1⁵/₃₂

7¹⁵/₁₆ 7¹³/₁₆ 7¹⁵/₁₆

2⅝ 2¹¹/₃₂ 2½ +

2¾ 2¼ 2¼

6½ 12¹/₁₆ 11⅜ 11¾ +

87 33¾ 33 33¹/₁₆ −

502 25⅝ 24⁹/₁₆ 25⅜ +

833 12 11⅝ 11⅞ +

16 10½ 10½ 10½ −

78 15⅝ 15¹³/₁₆ 15⅞ −

4508 9¹/₁₆ 8¼ 8⅛ +

430 11¼ 10⅝

PORTFOLIO MANAGEMENT

STUDY SESSIONS

This volume includes Study Sessions 3–5.

TOPIC LEVEL LEARNING OUTCOME

The candidate should be able to construct an appropriate investment policy statement and asset allocation; formulate strategies for managing, monitoring, and rebalancing the investment portfolio; and interpret performance relative to benchmarks and present investment returns in a manner consistent with Global Investment Performance Standards (GIPS®).

STUDY SESSION 3
BEHAVIORAL FINANCE

Behavioral finance is introduced in the first study session on portfolio management because an understanding of the psychological factors that affect investment decision making is relevant for the management of both private wealth and institutional assets. Behavioral finance provides practical insight to investors' perceptions and preferences regarding financial risk, making it a valuable aid to understanding client goals and concerns. The analysis of investment decision making from a behavioral finance perspective may also provide an explanation for certain market inefficiencies and suggest investment strategies to exploit them.

READING ASSIGNMENTS

Reading 7   Heuristic-Driven Bias: The First Theme
              Beyond Greed and Fear: Understanding Behavioral Finance and the Psychology of Investing, by Hersh Shefrin

Reading 8   Frame Dependence: The Second Theme
              Beyond Greed and Fear: Understanding Behavioral Finance and the Psychology of Investing, by Hersh Shefrin

Reading 9   Inefficient Markets: The Third Theme
              Beyond Greed and Fear: Understanding Behavioral Finance and the Psychology of Investing, by Hersh Shefrin

Reading 10   Portfolios, Pyramids, Emotions, and Biases
              Beyond Greed and Fear: Understanding Behavioral Finance and the Psychology of Investing, by Hersh Shefrin

Reading 11   Investment Decision Making in Defined Contribution
              Pension Plans
              Pensions

Reading 12   Global Equity Strategy: The Folly of Forecasting: Ignore All
              Economists, Strategists, and Analysts
              Global Equity Strategy, by James Montier

Reading 13   Alpha Hunters and Beta Grazers
              Financial Analysts Journal

Note:
Some of the behavioral concepts presented in this study session are developed across multiple readings. Candidates should consider the readings as a whole in mastering the Learning Outcome Statements.

3

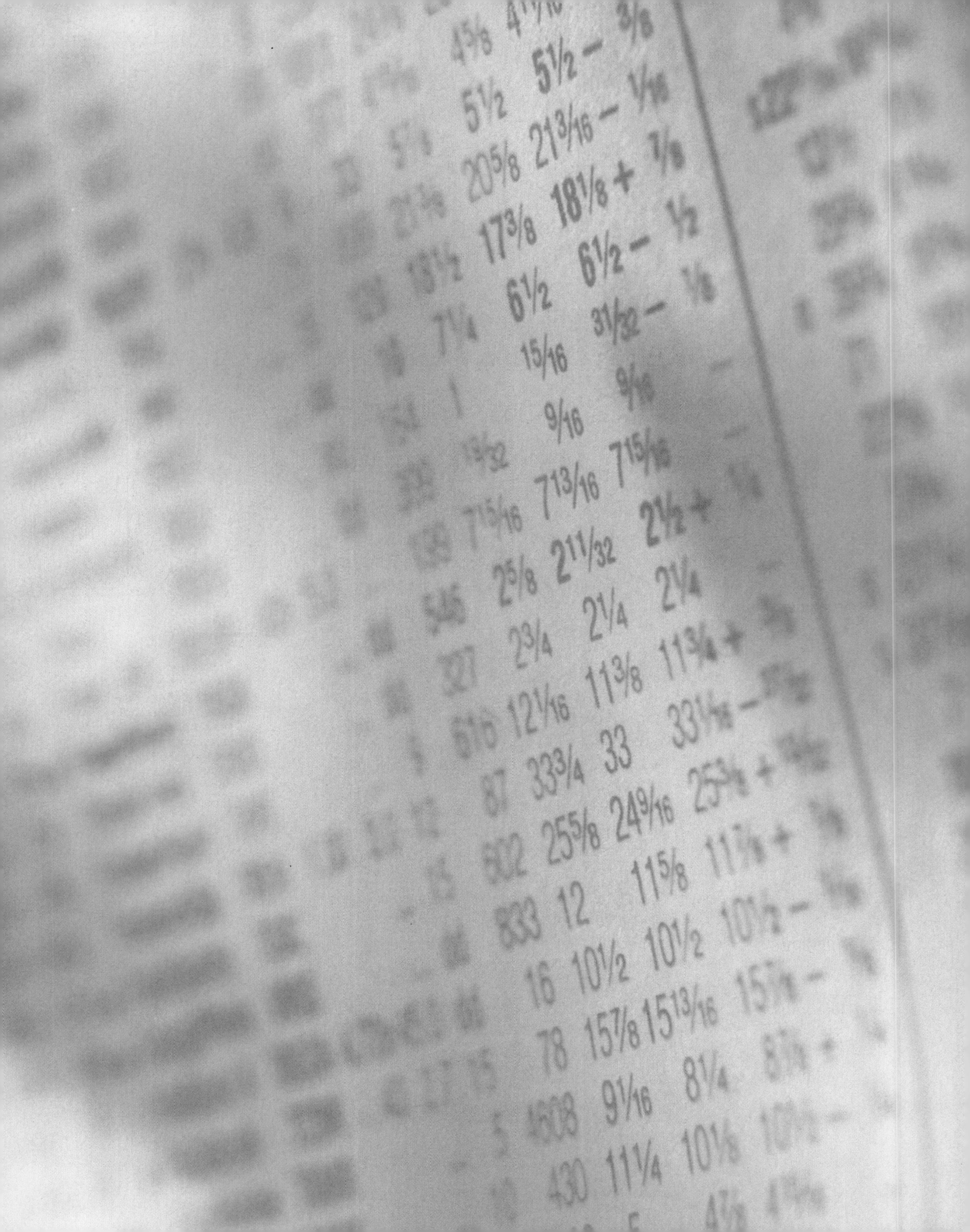

4⅝	4⅛	**⅜**
5½	**5½** −	
5½	21³⁄₁₆ − ⅛	
20⅝	**18⅛** + ⅞	
17⅜	6½ − ½	
6½	**6½** −	
7¼	31⁄32 − ⅛	
	15⁄16	9⁄16
	9⁄16	
1⁄32	7¹³⁄₁₆	7¹⁵⁄₁₆
7⁵⁄₁₆	**2½** +	
2⅝	2¹¹⁄₃₂	
5⁄16	2¾	2¼
827	2¾ 2¼ 2¼	
6⅛	12¹⁄₁₆ 11⅜ 11¾ +	
87	33¾ 33 33⅛ −	
502	25⅝ 24⁹⁄₁₆ 25⅜ +	
833	12 11⅝ 11⅞ +	
16	10½ 10½ 10½ −	
78	15⅞ 15¹³⁄₁₆ 15⅞ −	
4508	9¹⁄₁₆ 8¼ 8⅛ +	
430	11¼ 10⅜ 10½	

HEURISTIC-DRIVEN BIAS: THE FIRST THEME
by Hersh Shefrin

LEARNING OUTCOME

The candidate should be able to evaluate the impact of heuristic-driven biases (including representativeness, overconfidence, anchoring-and-adjustment, aversion to ambiguity) on investment decision making.

Mastery ☐

INTRODUCTION

The dictionary definition for the word *heuristic* refers to the process by which people find things out for themselves, usually by trial and error. Trial and error often leads people to develop rules of thumb, but this process often leads to other errors. One of the great advances of behavioral psychology is the identification of the principles underlying these rules of thumb and the systematic errors associated with them. In turn, these rules of thumb have themselves come to be called *heuristics*.

AN ILLUSTRATIVE EXAMPLE   1

Consider this question: Which is the more frequent cause of death in the United States, homicide or stroke? How do most people go about answering this question? The majority rely on recall, that is, by seeing how many events of each type come readily to mind. If people more readily recall instances of homicide than of stroke, then they will answer "homicide." This simple rule conforms to the principle known as *availability*—the degree to which information is readily available. A rule based on this principle is called an *availability heuristic*.

Heuristics are like back-of-the-envelope calculations that sometimes come close to providing the right answer. But heuristics may involve *bias*, meaning they may tend to be off target in a particular direction, and this can apply to an availability heuristic also. Most people rely on the media for their information about homicides and strokes. Suppose that the media tends to report one cause of death more than the other, because one is newsworthy and the other is not. Then people who rely on an availability heuristic may recall instances related to one type of death more readily than the other. Therefore, media coverage biases a rule based on recall.

What about error? Which is the more frequent cause of death, homicide or stroke? The answer is stroke. In fact, strokes occur *eleven* times as often as homicides (Slovic, Fischoff, and Lichtenstein 1979). People who rely on an availability heuristic tend to be amazed by this fact.

Let's look at these steps from a broader perspective:

▶ People develop general principles as they find things out for themselves.

▶ They rely on heuristics, rules of thumb, to draw inferences from the information at their disposal.

▶ People are susceptible to particular errors because the heuristics they use are imperfect.

▶ People actually commit errors in particular situations.

Taken together, these four statements define *heuristic-driven bias*.[1]

2 REPRESENTATIVENESS

One of the most important principles affecting financial decisions is known as *representativeness*. Representativeness refers to judgments based on stereotypes. The principle of representativeness was proposed by psychologists Daniel Kahneman and Amos Tversky (1972), and analyzed in a series of papers reproduced in the collection edited by Kahneman, Slovic, and Tversky (1982).

Consider an example involving admissions officers in universities. One measure of successful admission decisions is that students who are admitted perform well scholastically. Therefore, imagine a situation where an admissions officer is attempting to predict the grade point average (GPA) of some prospective students based upon their high school GPA levels.

Here are some actual data for undergraduates at Santa Clara University, based on students who entered the university in the years 1990, 1991, and 1992.[2] During this period, the mean high school GPA of students who entered as freshmen and graduated was 3.44 (standard deviation was 0.36). The mean college GPA of those same students was 3.08 (standard deviation 0.40). Suppose you are given the task of predicting the graduating GPA for three undergraduate students, based solely on their high school GPA scores. The three high school GPA scores are 2.20, 3.00, and 3.80. What are your predictions for the college GPAs of these students upon graduation?

In administering this question to large groups, I have obtained very consistent mean responses. Table 1 contains the mean predictions along with the

---

[1] In case it's not clear: *Availability* is the principle; judging the frequency of occurrence by the number of instances that come readily to mind is the *heuristic rule of thumb;* being predisposed to ease of recall resulting from distortions in media coverage is the *bias;* and judging homicide to be a more frequent cause of death than stroke is the *error.*

[2] I thank Barbara Stewart, Santa Clara University, for providing these data.

TABLE 1	Actual GPAs Are Closer to the Mean than Predicted GPAs	
High School GPA	Predicted College GPA	Actual College GPA
2.20	2.03	2.70
3.00	2.77	2.93
3.80	3.46	3.30

actual results. The average predictions for the question are 2.03, 2.77, and 3.46, whereas the actual results are 2.70, 2.93, and 3.30, respectively. Notice that at both the low end and the high end, the predictions are too far from the mean of 3.08. That is, both the low (2.20) and high (3.80) high school GPAs result in college GPAs that are much closer to the mean than the predictions. These responses illustrate that people do not appreciate the extent to which there is *regression to the mean*.

Representativeness is about reliance on stereotypes. The simplest example based on this principle is to predict that college GPA will be the same as high school GPA. Now most people do not use as simple a rule as this one. But they do base their predictions on how *representative* a student appears to be. Thus a student with a high GPA in high school is seen as representative of a good student. Notice that they are especially hard on students with low high school GPAs. What most people fail to appreciate is that students with the lowest high school GPAs may have experienced bad luck, and consequently will, on average, do better in college.[3] So, the heuristic involves bias; representativeness can be misleading. Again, people fail to recognize regression to the mean. Therefore, they are predisposed to making errors when they predict the future GPA of particular individuals.

A financial example illustrating representativeness is the winner–loser effect documented by Werner De Bondt and Richard Thaler (1985, 1987). De Bondt and Thaler find that stocks that have been extreme past losers in the preceding three years do much better than extreme past winners over the subsequent three years. De Bondt (1992) shows that the long-term earnings forecasts made by security analysts tend to be biased in the direction of recent success. Specifically, analysts overreact in that they are much more optimistic about recent winners than they are about recent losers.

Do you recognize any similarities with the GPA question above? De Bondt and Thaler base their argument on the misapplication of representativeness. In effect, I suggest that investors treat past losers like high school students with low GPAs, and past winners as high school students with high GPAs. Notice that the predictions are particularly pessimistic when it comes to the low GPA students. People tend to predict that student with a low high school GPA will end up with an even lower college GPA, indicative of a "kick 'em when they're down" perspective.[4] As we shall see in the reading on inefficient markets, the same phenomenon also appears to be at work when it comes to stocks. The returns to past losers are exceptionally high, suggesting that investors become unduly pessimistic about the prospects of these stocks.

---

[3] Keep in mind that the question pertains to those who graduate college.

[4] Readers will see that representativeness plays a major role in many of the issues discussed in this volume. Some of the most important applications are predicting the market, picking stocks, choosing mutual funds, selecting money managers, and investing in initial public offerings (IPOs) and seasoned equity offerings (SEOs).

Before leaving representativeness, let us consider one more example show-ing that although financial professionals may recognize regression to the mean, they may not apply it properly. Below is an excerpt from an interview that appeared in the August 18, 1997 issue of *Fortune* magazine, with global strategist Barton Biggs of Morgan Stanley and senior investment adviser Robert Farrell of Merrill Lynch (Armour, 1997). This interview occurred after two-and-one-half years of spectacular stock market returns. I have divided the excerpt into two parts. The first part sets the stage for a discussion about regression to the mean. Here is the first part of the excerpt:

> **Biggs:** My view is that we're at the very tag end of a super bull market. That means the prudent person who's thinking ahead toward retirement should assume that over the next five to ten years the total return from his equity portfolio is going to be in the 5%- to 6%-a-year range.
> **Fortune:** Not the 15% to 20% we've come to love and expect?
> **Biggs:** Right. It's very late in the game.
> **Farrell:** Trouble is, it's looked that way for a long time.
> **Biggs:** Yes, but it's never looked as much that way as it does right now.

We will come back to the "late-in-the-game issue" a little later. For now, con-sider regression to the mean.

> **Farrell:** It's been better to have been a novice than a professional the past few years, because people with the most experience have been the most cautious. But markets do regress back to the mean {return to their long-term average performance}, and I agree we are late in the ball game. This is the longest period we've ever had with such high returns from equities, and I can't believe it's a new era that will just keep going forever. I don't know if returns going forward will be 7% or 8%, but I'm pretty sure they will be below average.

This interview raises a number of very important issues. Look first at the last three sentences in Robert Farrell's remarks, where he predicts below-average returns. What's his rationale? Well, he says markets "regress back to the mean" and points out that this "is the longest period we've ever had with such high returns."

Is a prediction of below-average returns appropriate? Take another look at Table 1, the GPA example. Would we predict that the student with the 3.80 high school GPA would end up with a college GPA *below* the mean of 3.08? I don't think so. Regression to the mean suggests that future returns will be closer to their historical average. But it doesn't say they will be *below* their his-torical average.[5]

Farrell's error, too low a prediction, stems from *gambler's fallacy*. If five tosses of a fair coin all turn out to be heads, what is the probability that the sixth toss will be tails? If the coin is fair, the correct answer is one-half. Yet many people have a mental picture that when a fair coin is tossed a few times in a row, the resulting pattern will feature about the same number of heads as tails. In other words, the representative pattern features about the same number of heads and tails. So, after a run of five heads, people tend to predict tails on the sixth toss, because of the representativeness heuristic. From their perspective, "a tail is due." But this reasoning is wrong, just as below-average returns are no more likely after "the longest period we've ever had with such high returns."

---

[5] There is a technical issue about predicting autocorrelated time series. Is the autocorrelation positive or negative? Most economic and financial series feature positive autocorrelation, whereby above-average performance tends to be followed by above-average performance; likewise, below-average performance tends to be followed by below-average performance.

Gambler's fallacy arises because people misinterpret the law of averages, technically known as the "law of large numbers." They think the law of large numbers applies to small samples as well as to large samples. This led Tversky and Kahneman (1971) to facetiously describe gambler's fallacy as the "law of small numbers."

Let's go back to Farrell's remarks about future returns. Notice that he tells us he is "pretty sure they will be below average." Time will tell if he ultimately is right. I say ultimately because in the twenty-one months that followed the *Fortune* magazine interview, the S&P 500 returned more than 41 percent. But his statement that he is "pretty sure" leads us to the next issue—*overconfidence*.

OVERCONFIDENCE · 3

Here is a question for you.

> The Dow Jones Industrial Average closed 1998 at 9,181. As a price index, the Dow does not include reinvested dividends. If the Dow were redefined to reflect the reinvestment of all dividends since May 1896, when it commenced at a value of 40, what would its value have been at the end of 1998? In addition to writing down your best guess, also write down a low guess and a high guess, so that you feel 90 percent confident that the true answer will lie between your low guess and your high guess.

Ready? The answer to the preceding question is found in the title of a paper by Roger Clarke and Meir Statman (1999): "The DJIA Crossed 652,230 (in 1998)." If people were well calibrated, then 90 out of every 100 would find that the correct answer lay between their low and high guesses. But when I ask this question as part of a survey, virtually nobody finds that the true answer lies between his or her low and high guesses. For most, their high guesses are much too low. So most people are not well calibrated. Instead, they are overconfident.

When people are overconfident, they set overly narrow confidence bands. They set their high guess too low (and their low guess too high). Hence, they get surprised more frequently than they anticipated. Consider the Wall Street strategists who, in the course of reviewing their predictions in the light of actual events, speak about being "humbled." In other words, they were overconfident in their predictions.

ANCHORING-AND-ADJUSTMENT, CONSERVATISM · 4

Next is a textbook problem in probability, designed by psychologist Ward Edwards (1964) that provides some insight into analysts' earnings revisions.

> Imagine 100 book bags, each of which contains 1,000 poker chips. Forty-five bags contain 700 black chips and 300 red chips. The other 55 bags contain 300 black chips and 700 red chips. You cannot see inside either bag. One of the bags is selected at random by means of a coin toss. Consider the following two questions about the book bag.
>
> 1. What probability would you assign to the event that the selected bag contains predominantly black chips?

2. Now imagine that 12 chips are drawn, with replacement, from the selected bag. These twelve draws produce 8 blacks and 4 reds. Would you use the new information about the drawing of chips to revise your probability that the selected bag contains predominantly black chips? If so, what new probability would you assign?

This problem is analogous to the tasks faced by financial analysts. The bag is like a company that in the future may operate in the black or in the red. So in accordance with generally accepted accounting colors, black chips stand for good future earnings, red for poor future earnings. Analysts start out with information that leads them to form their initial beliefs. In this case, beliefs concern the probability that the bag contains predominantly black chips. The most frequent answer given to the first of the two preceding questions is 45 percent. So, the bag of chips is like a company that appears more likely to generate poor future earnings than good future earnings.

The second question is a lot more difficult than the first. The drawing of 8 black chips and 4 red chips is akin to a positive earnings announcement. So now the question is how to react to a positive earnings announcement made by a company that has not been performing all that well.

When I administer these questions, I find that the two most frequent responses to the second question are 45 percent and 67 percent—the two most *salient* numbers in the problem—with 45 percent being the number of bags containing predominantly black chips, and 67 percent the fraction of black chips drawn with replacement.

Those who respond with 45 percent essentially do not know how to incorporate the new information. So, they stick with their initial beliefs. Since the "earnings announcement" is favorable, they *underreact.*

People who answer 67 percent (or thereabouts) focus on the fact that two thirds of the chips drawn with replacement are black. They ignore their prior information, in accordance with the representativeness heuristic. Do they overreact, underreact, or get it just right?

The correct answer to the second question is 96.04 percent. About 55 percent of those responding choose either 45 percent or 67 percent; the remaining responses are scattered. But most are well below 96 percent. In fact, most are below 75 percent. In other words, most people respond too *conservatively* to the new information in this problem. Perhaps they get anchored on to 45 percent and do not adjust sufficiently to the new information.

This is how security analysts react to earnings announcements: They do not revise their earnings estimates enough to reflect the new information. Consequently, positive earnings surprises tend to be followed by more positive earnings surprises, and negative surprises by more negative surprises. Of course, the unexpected surprises in store for analysts are also a manifestation of overconfidence because overly narrow confidence bands mean people get surprised more frequently than they anticipate.

5   AVERSION TO AMBIGUITY

Imagine that I offered you the choice between accepting a sure $1,000 or an even gamble in which you either win $0 or $2,000. When I pose this question in MBA classes, about 40 percent of the students say they would take the gamble.

I describe this choice to students by telling them that there is a bag containing 100 poker chips, 50 black chips and 50 red chips; they can choose a sure

$1,000, or a lottery ticket that pays $2,000 if a black chip is drawn at random from the bag but $0 if a red chip is drawn.

Now consider this variation. Imagine the bag contains 100 colored chips that are either red or black, but the proportions are unknown. Many people who are willing to gamble when the odds are even prefer to play it safe and take the sure $1,000 when the odds are unknown. This phenomenon is known as the *aversion to ambiguity*. People prefer the familiar to the unfamiliar.

Remember the Wall Street proverb about greed and fear? I note that the emotional aspect of aversion to ambiguity is fear of the unknown. The case of Long-Term Capital Management provides an apt example of this phenomenon. On September 23, 1998, a $3.6 billion private rescue of LTCM was arranged. The Federal Reserve Bank of New York orchestrated this plan because of a concern that the failure of LTCM might cause a collapse in the global financial system. The November 16, 1998, issue of the *Wall Street Journal* describes the scene as the participants departed the meeting at which the deal was struck. The article attributes an interesting remark to Herbert Allison, then president of Merrill Lynch, a remark that typifies aversion to ambiguity as fear of the unknown. "As they filed out, they were left to ponder whether all this was necessary, and whether a collapse would really have jolted the global financial system. 'It was a very large unknown,' Merrill's Mr. Allison says. 'It wasn't worth a jump into the abyss to find out how deep it was.'"[6]

EMOTION AND COGNITION

6

The issues discussed in this reading involve cognitive errors, that is, errors that stem from the way that people think. But in describing aversion to ambiguity in terms of fear of the unknown, I suggest that some phenomena involve a combination of cognition and emotion. Of course, both involve mental processes, and may be physiologically linked, as opposed to being separate from each other. Scholars have produced ample evidence that emotion plays an important role in the way people remember events. So, phenomena involving the availability heuristic may reflect both cognitive and emotional elements. Here is an example.

In 1972, the Dow closed at 1,020. In 1982 it closed at 1,047, just 27 points higher than the value achieved a decade earlier. In between, it gyrated wildly, recording four years of negative growth. During this period, inflation reduced the purchasing power of a dollar by over 66 percent. A 1995 article in the *Wall Street Journal* quotes Russell Fuller, president of RJF Asset Management (now Fuller & Thaler Asset Management) in San Mateo, California, as follows: "'People like myself, who have been in the business since before the 1973–74 crash, we were terrified by that crash,' says Mr. Fuller, the money manager. 'That's a very low probability event. But many of the people in this business have spent the last 20 years worrying about that happening again.'"[7]

---

[6] Michael Siconolfi, Anita Raghavan, and Mitchell Pacelle, "All Bets Are Off: How the Salesmanship and Brainpower Failed at Long-Term Capital," *Wall Street Journal*, 16 November 1998.

[7] Jonathan Clements, "Getting Going: Behavioral Specialists Put Investors on Couch," *Wall Street Journal*, 28 November 1995.

SUMMARY

This reading described the first theme of behavioral finance, heuristic-driven bias, and introduced some of the main heuristics upon which financial practitioners rely: representativeness, anchoring-and-adjustment, overconfidence, availability bias, and aversion to ambiguity. These heuristics surface in many different contexts, such as analysts' earnings forecasts, investors' evaluation of mutual fund performance, corporate takeover decisions, and the types of portfolios selected by both individual and institutional investors. Because of their reliance on heuristics, practitioners hold biased beliefs that render them vulnerable to committing errors. In addition to the heuristics described in this reading, readers will come across a host of others, such as excessive optimism, the illusion of validity, hindsight bias, the illusion of control, and self-attribution error. There are many examples of such errors throughout this volume.

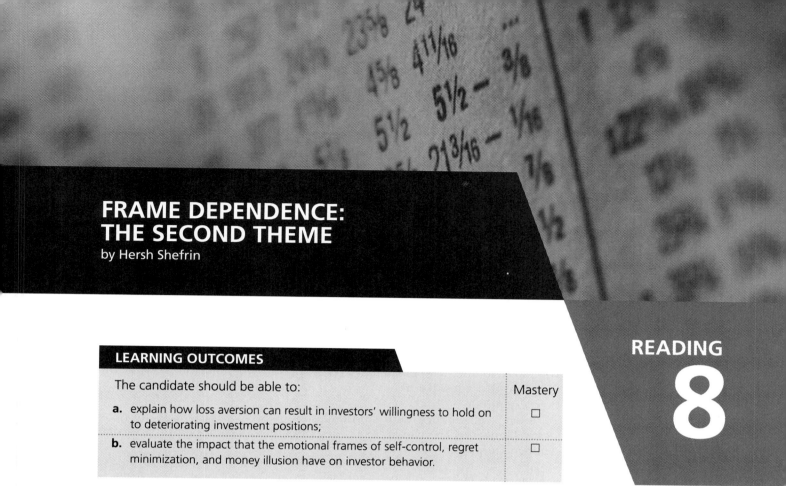

FRAME DEPENDENCE: THE SECOND THEME
by Hersh Shefrin

LEARNING OUTCOMES

The candidate should be able to: Mastery

a. explain how loss aversion can result in investors' willingness to hold on   ☐
to deteriorating investment positions;

b. evaluate the impact that the emotional frames of self-control, regret   ☐
minimization, and money illusion have on investor behavior.

INTRODUCTION

Frame *independence* lies at the heart of the Modigliani–Miller approach to corporate finance. Merton Miller has a succinct description of frame independence. When asked to explain, in twenty-five words or less, the essence of his contributions with Franco Modigliani, he said: "If you transfer a dollar from your right pocket to your left pocket, you are no wealthier. Franco and I proved that rigorously."[1]

It is a matter of form whether a person keeps a dollar of wealth in the right pocket or in the left pocket. The form used to describe a decision problem is called its *frame*. When I speak of frame independence, I mean that form is irrelevant to behavior. Proponents of traditional finance assume that framing is *transparent*. This means that practitioners can see through all the different ways cash flows might be described. Yet many frames are not transparent but rather are *opaque*. When a person has difficulty seeing through an opaque frame, his decisions

---

[1] Miller made this statement at the University of Chicago conference on behavioral finance in October 1986, on the day the Nobel Prize committee announced that Franco Modigliani was to receive the prize for that year.

typically depend on the particular frame he uses. Consequently, a difference in form is also a difference in substance. Behavior reflects frame dependence.

1

LOSS AVERSION

In their landmark work on prospect theory, a descriptive framework for the way people make choices in the face of risk and uncertainty, Daniel Kahneman and Amos Tversky (1979) provide evidence of frame dependence. The starting point in their work is the role of "loss," an issue explored by Harry Markowitz (1952b). Kahneman and Tversky studied how people respond to the prospect of a loss. Here is one of their examples. Suppose you face a choice between 1) accepting a sure loss of $7,500, or 2) taking a chance where there is a 75 percent chance you will lose $10,000 and a 25 percent chance you will lose nothing. The expected loss in both choices is $7,500. Would you choose to take the guaranteed loss or take a chance? Most people opt for the latter. Why? Because they hate to lose! And the uncertain choice holds out the hope they won't have to lose. Kahneman and Tversky call this phenomenon *loss aversion*. They find that a loss has about *two and a half times* the impact of a gain of the same magnitude.[2]

It is not difficult to find real-world illustrations of loss aversion. In a manual for stockbrokers, Leroy Gross (1982) describes the difficulties investors face in coming to terms with losses.

> Many clients, however, will not sell anything at a loss. They don't want to give up the hope of making money on a particular investment, or perhaps they want to get even before they get out. The "get-evenitis" disease has probably wrought more destruction on investment portfolios than anything else. . .
>
> Investors who accept losses can no longer prattle to their loved ones, "Honey, it's only a paper loss. Just wait. It will come back." (p. 150)

Some people learn about "get-evenitis" the hard way. Take the case of Nicholas Leeson. In 1995, Leeson became famous for having caused the collapse of his employer, 232-year-old Barings PLC. How? He lost over $1.4 billion through trading. In 1992, Leeson began to engage in rogue trading in order to hide errors made by his subordinates. Eventually, he incurred losses of his own, and "get-evenitis" set in. He asserts that he "gambled on the stock market to reverse his mistakes and save the bank."[3]

"Get-evenitis" also afflicts corporate executives' ability to terminate losing projects. For example, 3Com's popular Palm Computing products, the handheld organizers that access data with a stylus, had a predecessor—Apple Computer's

---

[2] Loss aversion implies that people have a *predisposition* toward avoiding a certain loss. But I note that loss aversion can be counterbalanced by panic. In an interview with *Forbes* magazine titled "Management, Strategies, Trends: Living with the Bull, Preparing for the Bear," fund manager Martin Zweig compared his own behavior with that of Warren Buffett, stating: "I could never do what he does. He buys things and holds forever—correctly, because he recognizes that if you sell and pay taxes, it cuts your return. But my problem is, I can't sit through bear markets. Buffett says, if you can't afford to see your stock go down 30% or 40%, you shouldn't be in it. I can't take the pain. I built my technique based on what I can handle personally. This means I have to be in and out a lot. My main thing is, I want to survive. I want to be there, and when the big bear market comes, I don't want to get chewed up" (Brimelow 1998).

[3] "Today's Rogue Traders Just Want to Save Face," *Associated Press,* 13 September 1995.

more sophisticated Newton.[4] Apple CEO John Sculley was thoroughly committed to the Newton, and made it the center of his personal vision for the computer industry. He coined the term "personal digital assistant" to describe the concept and argued that it would be a pivotal step in the convergence of three industries: computing, communications, and entertainment.[5]

Development of the Newton began in 1987, and the product was launched in 1993. But at $1,000, it was much too expensive for the mass market. Moreover, because of initial failures in its handwriting recognition capability, cartoonist Gary Trudeau lampooned the Newton in his comic strip *Doonesbury*. Given the size and demographics of Gary Trudeau's readership, think about the impact the availability heuristic had on Newton's potential market.

By January 1994, it was apparent that sales were disappointing and the Newton was a losing project. But Apple did not terminate it. The company was committed to personal digital assistants. A year later, in January 1995, Apple had added enhanced features, and the year after that it came out with a backlit screen, but to no avail. In March 1997 Apple spun the Newton off into its own division, but this did little good, and six months later Apple folded the division back into its own organization. Through all this, the Newton remained a loser.

CEOs may come and go, but losing projects stay on. John Sculley "went"; he was replaced by Gil Amelio, who also came and went. In a dramatic comeback, Steve Jobs, Apple's cofounder and first CEO, replaced Amelio. Years before, Sculley had ousted Jobs. In January 1998, about ten years after its inception, CEO Jobs announced his decision to terminate the Newton project.

CONCURRENT DECISIONS   2

Here is another Kahneman-Tversky decision problem:

> Imagine that you face the following pair of *concurrent* decisions. First examine both sets of choices, then indicate the option you prefer for each.
>
> *First decision.* Choose:
>
> A. a sure gain of $2,400, or
>
> B. a 25 percent chance to gain $10,000 and a 75 percent chance to gain nothing.
>
> *Second decision.* Choose:
>
> C. a sure loss of $7,500, or
>
> D. a 75 percent chance to lose $10,000 and a 25 percent chance to lose nothing.

The way that people respond to this problem tells us a lot about their approach to making decisions. Consider your own responses. Choosing A in the first decision would be the risk-averse choice. Most people find a sure $2,400 difficult to pass up. Although $10,000 is a lot more than $2,400, the odds of collecting it are only one in four. Hence, the expected value of B is $2,500, considerably less than $10,000. In fact, $2,500 is just a tad more than the guaranteed $2,400 offered in A.

---

[4] I thank Bob Saltmarsh, who was treasurer at Apple during this period, for sharing his insights about the Newton with me.

[5] Jim Carlton, "Apple Drops Newton, an Idea Ahead of Its Time," *Wall Street Journal,* 2 March 1998.

Did you recognize the second decision? We encountered it before, in the previous section. Did you respond the same way as before? In my own experience, about 90 percent choose *D* in the second decision problem. They want the chance to get even.

The two decision problems together constitute a concurrent "package." But most people do not see the package. They separate the choices into *mental accounts*. And that brings us to frame dependence.

Suppose you face a choice. You can take a 75 percent chance you will lose $7,600 and a 25 percent chance you will win $2,400. Or you can take that same chance and accept an additional $100. Which choice would you make? A no-brainer, right? It should be: This decision frame is transparent.

But sometimes the frame is opaque. Consider the decision problem at the beginning of this section. When I administer this problem to my MBA students, about half choose *A & D: A* in the first decision problem and *D* in the second. People who choose *A & D* end up facing a 25 percent chance of winning $2,400 and a 75 percent chance of losing $7,600. However, they could do better: They could choose the *B & C* combination, which would offer them a 25 percent chance of winning $2,500 and a 75 percent chance of losing $7,500. But most people don't see through the opaque frame. Therefore, they act as if they don't value $100. The opaque frame makes for a "brainer" instead of a no-brainer.

3 HEDONIC EDITING

In his stockbroker manual, Gross (1982) implicitly raises the issue of frame dependence within the context of realizing a loss. His essential point is that investors prefer some frames to others, a principle known as *hedonic editing*. Consider Gross's advice to stockbrokers:

> When you suggest that the client close at a loss a transaction that you originally recommended and invest the proceeds in another position you are currently recommending, *a real act of faith has to take place*. That act of faith can more easily be effected if you make use of some transitional words that I call "magic selling words."
>
> The words that I consider to have magical power in the sense that they make for a more easy acceptance of the loss are these: "Transfer your assets." (p. 150)

Why are "transfer your assets" magic selling words? Because they induce the client to use a frame in which he or she reallocates assets from one mental account to another, rather than closing a mental account at a loss.

Thaler and Eric Johnson (1991) propose a theory of hedonic editing for mental accounts. As part of a study, they administered a series of choice problems to subjects. You will find two of these problems below. Read the first problem, record your answer, and then move on to the next problem.

1. Imagine that you face the following choice. You can accept a guaranteed $1,500 or play a stylized lottery. The outcome of the stylized lottery is determined by the toss of a fair coin. If heads comes up, you win $1,950. If tails comes up, you win $1,050. Would you choose to participate in the lottery? Yes or no? Yes means you take your chances with the coin toss. No means you accept the guaranteed $1,500.[6]

[6] Because their studies used students, Thaler and Johnson employed stakes that were smaller by a factor of 100.

2. Imagine that you face the following choice. You can accept a guaranteed loss of $750 or play a stylized lottery. The outcome of the stylized lottery is determined by the toss of a fair coin. If heads comes up, you lose $525. If tails comes up, you lose $975. Would you accept the guaranteed loss? Yes or no? Yes means you accept a $750 loss. No means you take your chance with the coin toss.

Let's consider how people usually respond to these questions. In the first choice problem, the majority prefer to take the guaranteed $1,500 over the gamble where they might get less. This could be viewed as a typical risk-averse response, because the average payoff to the lottery ticket is $1,500, the same amount involved in the riskless option. However in the second choice problem, many people choose the lottery over the guaranteed loss. This is decidedly a risk-seeking response, in that the expected payoff to the coin toss is a $750 loss, the same amount involved in the riskless option.

There is a lesson here: People are not uniform in their tolerance for risk. It depends on the situation. Some appear to tolerate risk more readily when they face the prospect of a loss than when they do not.

It is common for financial planners and investment advisers to administer risk tolerance quizzes in order to determine a degree of risk that is suitable for their clients. However behavioral finance stresses that tolerance for risk is not uni-dimensional. Rather it depends on several factors, one being recent experience facing risk. Here are two more examples developed by Thaler and Johnson that bring out the complexity of these issues.

3. Imagine that you have just won $1,500 in one stylized lottery, and have the opportunity to participate in a second stylized lottery. The outcome of the second lottery is determined by the toss of a fair coin. If heads comes up, you win $450 in the second lottery. If tails comes up, you lose $450. Would you choose to participate in the second lottery after having won the first? Yes or no?

4. Imagine that you have just lost $750 in one stylized lottery, but have the opportunity to participate in a second stylized lottery. The outcome of the second lottery is determined by the toss of a fair coin. If heads comes up, you win $225 in the second lottery. If tails comes up, you lose $225. Would you choose to participate in the second lottery after having lost in the first? Yes or no?

Now that you have recorded your yes or no answers, compare your response to choice 3 with your response to choice 1. From a dollar perspective, choices 1 and 3 are equivalent. In the framework of standard finance, people should respond the same to both. Yet in practice, many "switch" their choices. When replicating the Thaler-Johnson study I have found that about 25 percent of the respondents are more willing to take the gamble in choice problem 3 than they are in the dollar-equivalent choice problem 1. Why?

Thaler and Johnson suggest that the answer involves hedonic editing, the way people organize their mental accounts. In choice problem 3, if people lose $450 they combine it with the $1,500 gain and experience the net position of $1,050—exactly the situation they are presented with in choice problem 1. But if they win, they do not net their two gains; instead, they savor them separately. According to Thaler and Johnson, the added attraction of experiencing gains separately inclines people to be more willing to gamble.

Thaler and Johnson found that in choice problem 2, over 75 percent chose to gamble rather than accept a sure $750 loss. However, although example 4 is dollar-equivalent to choice problem 2, almost 50 percent switch their choice from taking a gamble in example 2 to playing it safe in choice problem 4. Thaler and Johnson suggest an explanation based on the way people experience losses. They note that people seem incapable of netting out moderately sized losses of similar magnitudes. So, a loss of $225 coming on top of a prior loss of $750 is especially painful. The added pain leads people to shy away from taking the gamble as framed in choice problem 4, relative to the frame in choice problem 2.

4   COGNITIVE AND EMOTIONAL ASPECTS

People who exhibit frame dependence do so for both cognitive and emotional reasons. The cognitive aspects concern the way people organize their information, while the emotional aspects deal with the way people *feel* as they register the information.

The distinction between cognitive and emotional aspects is important. For example, the main cognitive issue in choice problem 3 is whether people ignore having just won $1,500 when deciding whether or not to take an even chance on winning or losing $450. Some do ignore the $1,500, whereas others see themselves as being $1,500 ahead. The cognitive and emotional aspects operate together, in that those who ignore the $1,500 *feel* a $450 loss as just that, a $450 loss. But those who begin by seeing themselves as $1,500 ahead instead experience a $450 loss as a smaller gain of $1,050. This difference affects behavior: Because of loss aversion, people who ignore having just won $1,500 are much less prone to accepting the gamble than those who see themselves as $1,500 ahead. Thaler and Johnson call this a "house money" effect.[7]

The term *frame dependence* means that the way people behave depends on the way that their decision problems are framed. Hedonic editing means they prefer some frames to others. That is the main insight to be gleaned from studying how people chose in the four preceding choices. In a financial context, hedonic editing offers some insight into investors' preference for cash dividends. When stock prices go up, dividends can be savored separately from capital gains. When stock prices go down, dividends serve as a "silver lining" to buffer a capital loss. Remember Merton Miller's succinct description of frame independence? Some investors prefer to keep dividends in their right pocket.

The following excerpt, taken from a *Forbes* magazine interview with closed-end fund manager Marty Zweig, describes how he came to realize the importance of dividends. It began with the fact that his fund was trading at a deep discount relative to net asset value (NAV), the value the shares would trade for if the fund were open-ended instead of being closed.

> Then in 1986 we did a closed-end fund. . . . I always worried about discounts on closed-end funds. . . . The first nine months out of the gate, we were at a 17 percent discount. I was mortified. I sat down and did a lot of thinking. Bond funds at the time were selling at about parity. Stock funds were all at discounts. It didn't make sense, because stocks do better than bonds in the long run. And I realized bond funds pay interest. People like the certainty of an income stream. So I said, "Well, we're going to pay the dividend, whether we earn it or not." And we went to this 10 percent dividend policy. . . . The discount narrowed immediately. (Brimelow, 1998)

---

[7] So called because gamblers who receive a gift of chips from the house tend to be more tolerant of risk, since they begin by seeing themselves ahead.

SELF-CONTROL   5

Self-control means controlling emotions. Some investors value dividends for self-control reasons as well as for reasons that stem from hedonic editing.

Marty Zweig talks about paying a dividend whether earned or not because people "like the certainty of an income stream." What does a reliable dividend have to do with self-control? Meir Statman and I (Shefrin and Statman 1984) argue that the answer involves the "don't dip into capital" heuristic. Older investors, especially retirees who finance their living expenditures from their portfolios, worry about spending their wealth too quickly, thereby outliving their assets. They fear a loss of self-control, where the urge for immediate gratification leads them to go on a spending binge. Therefore, they put rules into place to guard against the temptation to overspend.

"Don't dip into capital" is akin to "don't kill the goose that lays the golden eggs." But if you don't dip into capital, how do you finance consumer expenditures—Social Security and pension checks alone? Not necessarily—this is where dividends come in. Dividends are labeled as income, not capital. And investors tend to frame dividends as income, not capital. Again, this is frame dependence. Investors feel quite comfortable choosing a portfolio of stocks that feature high dividend payouts and spending those dividends.

REGRET   6

Imagine someone who makes a decision that turned out badly and engages in self-recrimination for not having done the right thing. *Regret* is the emotion experienced for not having made the right decision. Regret is more than the pain of loss. It is the pain associated with feeling responsible for the loss.

For example, imagine someone who has a regular route to work. One day, for the sake of variety, she decides to try a different route. That particular day she winds up in an accident. Now, even if the odds of an accident were no different on the two routes, how will that person feel? Will she chastise herself, thinking "If only I had done what I always do and taken my regular route!" If so, she is experiencing the frustration of regret.

Regret can affect the decisions people make. Someone who feels regret intensely, does not have a strong preference for variety, and thinks ahead, may follow the same route to work every day, in order to minimize possible future regret.

Here is a financial example. Consider the choice of equity-fixed income allocation in a defined contribution retirement plan. In the January 1998 issue of *Money* magazine, Harry Markowitz explains what motivated his personal choice about allocation. As the Nobel laureate recognized for having developed modern portfolio theory, was he seeking the optimum trade-off of risk and return? Not exactly. He said, "My intention was to minimize my future regret. So I split my contributions fifty-fifty between bonds and equities" (Zweig 1998, 118). In other words, had Harry Markowitz selected a 100 percent equity allocation, and had stocks subsequently done terribly, it would have been too easy, in hindsight, to imagine having selected a more conservative posture—and this would give rise to considerable self-recrimination, meaning regret.

Regret minimization also leads some investors to use dividends, instead of selling stock, to finance consumer expenditures. Those who sell stock to finance a purchase, only to find that shortly thereafter the stock price soars, are liable to feel considerable regret. That is often at the heart of expressions such as "this is my half-million-dollar car."

7 ◢

MONEY ILLUSION

Frame dependence also impacts the way that people deal with inflation, both cognitively and emotionally. This is the issue of *money illusion*. Let us examine the following questions from a study by Eldan Shafir, Peter Diamond, and Amos Tversky (1997).

> Consider two individuals, Ann and Barbara, who graduated from the same college a year apart. Upon graduation, both took similar jobs with publishing firms. Ann started with a yearly salary of $30,000. During her first year on the job, there was no inflation, and in her second year, Ann received a 2 percent ($600) raise in salary. Barbara also started with a yearly salary of $30,000. During her first year on the job, there was 4 percent inflation, and in her second year, Barbara received a 5 percent ($1,500) raise in salary.
>
> a. As they entered their second year on the job, who was doing better in economic terms, Ann or Barbara?
>
> b. As they entered their second year on the job, who do you think was happier, Ann or Barbara?
>
> c. As they entered their second year on the job, each received a job offer from another firm. Who do you think was more likely to leave her present position for another job, Ann or Barbara?

Most people indicate that Ann is better off, Barbara is happier, and Ann is more likely to look for another job. Now this is somewhat perplexing. If Ann is better off, why is she less happy and more likely to look for another position? Shafir, Diamond, and Tversky suggest that although people can figure out how to adjust for inflation, it is not a natural way for them to think. The natural way is to think in terms of nominal values. Therefore people's emotional reaction is driven by the nominal values, and those appear more favorable for Barbara than they do for Ann.

SUMMARY

This reading presents the second theme of behavioral finance, frame dependence, which deals with the distinction between form and substance. Framing is about form. In short, frame dependence holds that differences in form may also be substantive. It reflects a mix of cognitive and emotional elements. The cognitive issues pertain to the way that information is mentally organized, especially the coding of outcomes into gains and losses. There are several emotional issues, the most fundamental of which is that people tend to feel losses much more acutely than they feel gains of comparable magnitude. This phenomenon has come to be known as loss aversion. Therefore, people prefer frames that obscure losses, if possible—and engage in hedonic editing. People tend to experience losses even more acutely when they feel responsible for the decision that led to the loss; this sense of responsibility leads to regret. Regret is an emotion. People who have difficulty controlling their emotions are said to lack self-control. Some people use framing effects constructively to help themselves deal with self-control difficulties.

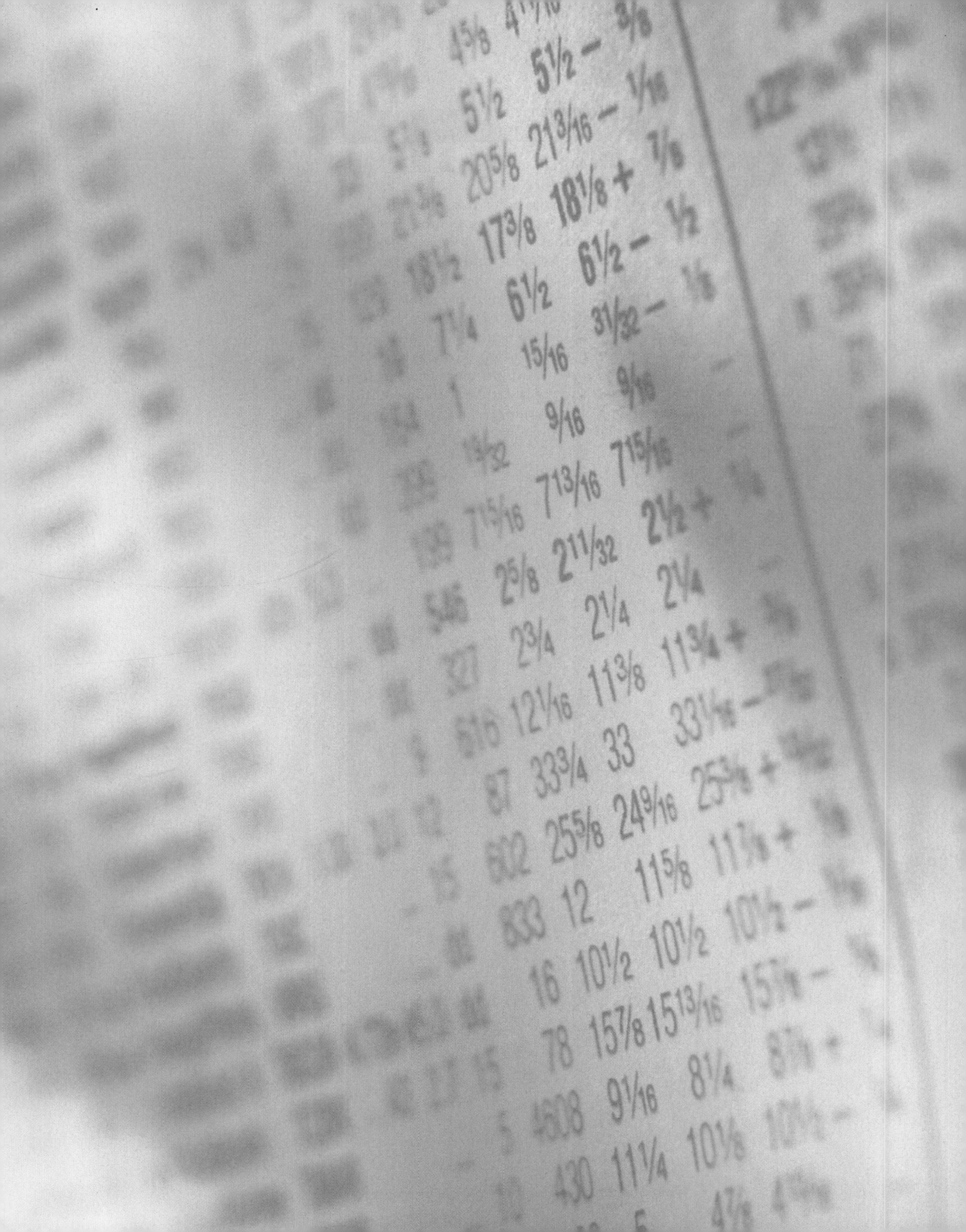

4⅝ 4 1/16 — ⅜

5½ 5½ — ⅜

5½ 2 13/16 — 1/16

20⅝ 21 13/16 — 1/16

17⅜ 18⅛ + ⅞

18½ 6½ 6½ — ½

7¼ 6½ 31/32 — 1/16

15/16

9/16 9/16

1 13/32

7 15/16 7 13/16 7 15/16

2⅝ 2 11/32 2½ +

2¾ 2¼ 2¼

12 1/16 11⅜ 11¾ +

6½

87 33¾ 33 33 1/16 —

602 25⅝ 24 9/16 25⅜ +

833 12 11⅝ 11¾ +

16 10½ 10½ 10½ —

78 15⅞ 15 13/16 15⅞ —

4608 9 1/16 8¼ 8⅝ +

430 11¼ 10⅛

INEFFICIENT MARKETS: THE THIRD THEME

by Hersh Shefrin

LEARNING OUTCOMES

The candidate should be able to:	Mastery
a. evaluate the impact that representativeness, conservatism (anchoring-and-adjustment), and frame dependence may have on security pricing and discuss the implications for market efficiency;	☐
b. discuss the implications of investor overconfidence when trading.	☐

CAUSE AND EFFECT　　　1

One of the most fiercely debated questions in finance is whether the market is efficient or inefficient. Remember the hedge fund Long-Term Capital Management (LTCM)? How did it advertise itself to investors? LTCM members promoted their firm as an exploiter of pricing anomalies in global markets. In this regard, consider the following heated exchange between Myron Scholes, LTCM partner and Nobel laureate, and Andrew Chow, vice president in charge of derivatives for potential investor Conseco Capital. Chow is quoted as saying to Scholes, "I don't think there are that many pure anomalies that can occur"; to which Scholes responded: "As long as there continue to be people like you, we'll make money."[1]

That last remark might not be the best way to win friends and influence people. But Scholes is correct about cause and effect—investors' errors are the cause of mispricing. Is the market efficient?

The fact is that from 1994 through 1997, LTCM claims to have successfully made leveraged bets—bets that exploited mispricing identified by the option

---

[1] Michael Siconolfi, Anita Raghavan, and Mitchell Pacelle, "All Bets Are Off: How Salesmanship and Brainpower Failed at Long-Term Capital," *Wall Street Journal*, 16 November 1998.

Beyond Greed and Fear: Understanding Behavioral Finance and the Psychology of Investing, by Hersh Shefrin. Copyright © 2002 by Oxford University Press. Reprinted with permission of Oxford University Press, Inc.

pricing theory for which Scholes and Merton jointly received the Nobel prize. In this regard Merton Miller, another Nobel laureate, is quoted as having said, "Myron once told me they are sucking up nickels from all over the world. But because they are so leveraged, that amounts to a lot of money."[2] "Sucking up nickels" is indicative of inefficiency. Of course, then came LTCM's 1998 fiasco, but more on that later.

2 EFFECTS STEMMING FROM REPRESENTATIVENESS

Let's begin with the De Bondt–Thaler winner–loser effect. De Bondt and Thaler (1985) argue that investors who rely on the representativeness heuristic become overly pessimistic about past losers and overly optimistic about past winners, and that this instance of heuristic-driven bias causes prices to deviate from fundamental value. Specifically, past losers come to be undervalued and past winners come to be overvalued. But mispricing is not permanent; over time the mispricing corrects itself. Then losers will outperform the general market, while winners will underperform.

De Bondt and Thaler (1989) present evidence in support of their claim. Figure 1 displays the returns to two portfolios, one consisting of extreme losers and the other of extreme winners. In both cases, the criterion used to judge

FIGURE 1   Cumulative Average Residuals for Winner and Loser Portfolios of 35 Stocks (1–60 Months into the Test Period)

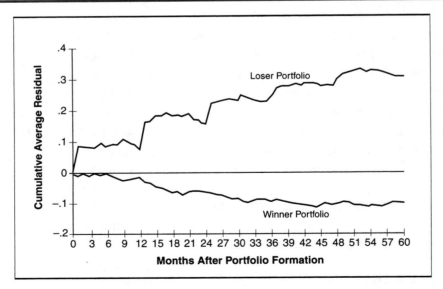

Cumulative abnormal returns for two portfolios, one consisting of past losers and the other consisting of past winners. Past losers subsequently outperform, while past winners subsequently underperform.

---

[2] Ibid.

performance is past-three-year returns. Extreme losers are the stocks that lie in the bottom tenth percentile, while the stocks that lie in the top tenth percentile are the extreme winners.

Figure 1 shows cumulative returns to the two portfolios for the sixty months after formation, relative to the overall market. Notice that the cumulative returns are indeed positive for losers, about 30 percent, and negative for winners, about −10 percent. De Bondt and Thaler suggest that this pattern signifies a correction to mispricing.

In traditional finance, the pattern depicted in Figure 1 would reflect compensation for risk. That is, losers would be associated with higher returns because they are riskier than the average stock; the opposite holds for winners. But De Bondt and Thaler contend that an investor who bought losers and sold winners short would have beaten the market by about 8 percent on a risk-adjusted basis.

EFFECTS STEMMING FROM CONSERVATISM
3

Analysts who suffer from conservatism due to anchoring-and-adjustment do not adjust their earnings predictions sufficiently in response to the new information contained in earnings announcements. Therefore, they find themselves surprised by subsequent earnings announcements. Unanticipated surprise is the hallmark of overconfidence. However, there is more at work here than plain overconfidence. Conservatism in earnings predictions means that positive surprises tend to be followed by positive surprises and negative surprises tend to be followed by negative surprises.

Does conservatism in analyst earnings predictions cause mispricing? If it does, then we should find that stocks associated with recent positive earnings surprises should experience higher returns than the overall market, while stocks associated with recent negative earnings surprises should earn lower returns than the overall market. Figure 2, taken from an article by the late Victor Bernard and Jacob Thomas (1989), summarizes the evidence.[3] The figure shows the behavior of cumulative returns to portfolios formed based on the size of the most recent earnings surprise. In the sixty days following an earnings announcement, the stocks with the highest earnings surprises outperformed the overall market by about 2 percent, while the stocks with the most negative earnings surprises underperformed the overall market by about 2 percent.

Behavioral finance suggests that heuristic-driven errors cause mispricing. As an example, look at the pricing pattern depicted in Figure 2. Traditional finance holds that this pricing pattern occurs because stocks associated with positive earnings surprises are riskier than the stocks associated with negative earnings surprises.

EFFECTS STEMMING FROM FRAME DEPENDENCE
4

Does frame dependence have an impact on price efficiency? Shlomo Benartzi and Richard Thaler (1995) suggest that the answer is a strong yes. They argue that in the past, loss aversion caused investors to shy away from stocks; therefore, stocks earned very large returns relative to risk-free government securities.

---

[3] I thank Jacob Thomas, coauthor of Bernard and Thomas (1989), for providing me with the data for this figure.

FIGURE 2   Cumulative Abnormal Returns (CAR) to Portfolios Based upon Standardized Unexpected Earnings (SUE)

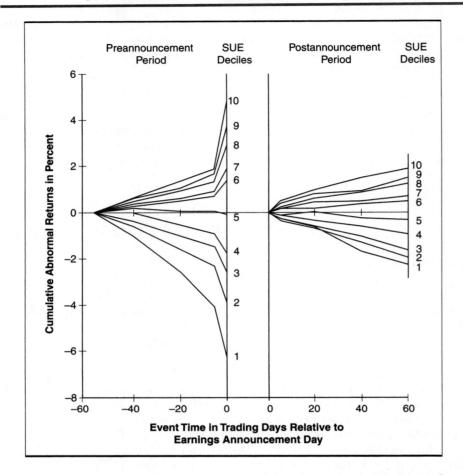

What happens to stock prices after earnings surprises: price momentum is greater for bigger surprises. Cumulative abnormal return pattern is steeper with the magnitude of the surprise (SUE).

Economist Jeremy Siegal documents that over the last two centuries the real return to stocks has been about 7 percent more than risk-free securities. From a theoretical perspective, a premium of 7 percent is enormous, and this differential has come to be called the *equity premium puzzle* (Mehra and Prescott 1985). To understand the character of the puzzle, consider the following question on risk tolerance.

> Suppose that you are the only income earner in your family, and you have a good job guaranteed to give you your current (family) income every year for life. You are given the opportunity to take a new and equally good job, with an even chance it will double your (lifetime family) income and an even chance that it will cut your (lifetime family) income. Indicate exactly what the percentage cut *x* would be that would leave you indifferent between keeping your current job or taking the new job and facing a 50-50 chance of doubling your income or cutting it by *x* percent (Barsky et al. 1997).

When I administer this question to general audiences, the average response comes out at about 23 percent. But the kind of response necessary to justify the historical equity premium is somewhere around 4 percent. The difference between 23 percent and 4 percent is not small. In fact, being willing to tolerate no more than a 4 percent decline seems very extreme, relative to the way people normally respond to the preceding question.

Shmuel Kandel and Robert Stambaugh (1991) suggest that people might be less tolerant of risks whose magnitudes are smaller than those described in the preceding question. However, I find that when the stakes are smaller, people actually become more tolerant of risk, not less tolerant.[4]

Benartzi and Thaler (1995) suggest that individual investors' historical reluctance to hold stocks may have stemmed from their evaluation horizons being too short. They call this reluctance *myopic loss aversion*. Benartzi and Thaler suggest that investors who are prone to myopic loss aversion can increase their comfort with equities by monitoring the performance of their portfolios less frequently, no more than once a year. It appears that investors who hold individual stocks monitor those stocks much more frequently than that. John Pound and Robert Shiller (1989) found that individual investors spent over a half-hour per day following the most recent stock they bought.[5] Nicholas Barberis, Ming Huang, and Tano Santos (1999) use the Thaler-Johnson "house money effect" discussed in the reading on frame dependence to take the argument one step further. They suggest that after a market runup, the house money effect kicks in, raising investors' tolerance for risk, and lowering the equity premium. In a downturn the reverse occurs.

DEPARTURE FROM FUNDAMENTAL VALUE: SHORT-TERM OR LONG-TERM?

5

One of the most striking claims of behavioral finance is that heuristic-driven bias and frame dependence can cause prices to deviate from fundamental values for long periods. Shiller (1979, 1981) argues that there is more volatility in stock markets and bond markets than would be the case if prices were determined by fundamentals alone. His analysis vividly illustrates the length of time stock price and fundamental value can part company.

Shiller computed what the fundamental value of stocks would have been over time for an investor who had perfect foresight about the future value of dividends. He then compared fundamental value and prices.[6] Figure 3 depicts the timelines for two indexes, starting in 1925. The figure is scaled to adjust for the long-term historical growth rate of stock prices. One line depicts the index for fundamental value, while the other shows the index for actual stock prices.

The years 1929 and 1987 were crash years, and, as I discussed in the reading on heuristic-driven bias, 1973 was the beginning of a long bear market. Consider how these events are portrayed in Figure 3. Prior to 1929 and 1973, price lies well above fundamental value. Shortly after those years price falls below fundamental value. The lesson here is that prices move away from fundamental value for long periods, but eventually revert.

---

[4] The questions that I used involved stakes that were near the historical growth rates of real personal consumption expenditures.

[5] In replicating the Shiller–Pound survey in 1998, I obtained a similar result, almost 40 minutes.

[6] I thank Bob Shiller for providing me with this data, updated to 1999.

FIGURE 3   Fundamental Value versus Actual Price, 1925–1999

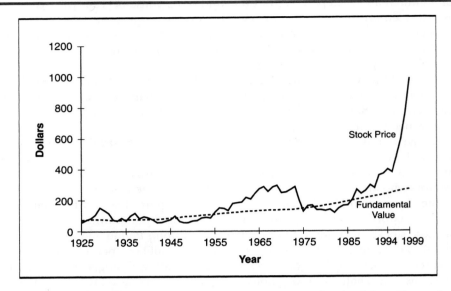

Stock prices tend to stray from fundamental value for long periods of time. The period after 1994 is especially striking.

On December 3, 1996, Shiller, along with John Campbell, expressed his views about the market in joint testimony before the Board of Governors of the Federal Reserve system (Campbell and Shiller 1998). Apparently, their testimony had some influence. Two days later, on December 5, Alan Greenspan, chairman of the Federal Reserve Board, shocked global markets when he used the term "irrational exuberance" to describe the state of the U.S. stock market.[7]

What did Shiller and Campbell tell the Federal Reserve Board? They explained that historically, when the dividend yield (D/P) has been low and the price-to-earnings ratio (P/E) high, the return to holding stocks over the subsequent ten years has tended to be low. This should not be surprising. The earnings yield is E/P, the inverse of P/E. In a rationally priced market, dividend yields and earnings yields form the basis of stock returns.[8] Recall the question in the reading on heuristic-driven bias concerning reinvested dividends and the Dow Jones Industrial Average. One of the lessons from that question is that when it comes to long-run stock returns, compounded dividends swamp stock price.[9] The future course of earnings and dividends would have to be dramatically better than in the past to rationalize high subsequent stock returns in a low D/P and E/P environment.[10]

To place the Campbell–Shiller argument into context, let me point out that the historical mean for the dividend yield is 4.73 percent. But in late 1996, it was an extremely low 1.9 percent. The historical mean for P/E is 14.2. Moreover, for most of the time since 1872, P/E has moved in the range of 8 to 20. Until recently, its peak of 26 dated back to 1929; however, in December 1996, the P/E stood

---

[7]Although he did not shock his audience, most of whom were nodding off at Greenspan's after-dinner speech at the American Enterprise Institute, according to an unnamed source from the Securities and Exchange Commission who was present that evening.

[8]Along with interest rates, inflation, and tolerance for risk.

[9]In the reading on heuristic-driven bias I indicated that the 1998 closing value of the Dow was 9181, but would have been 652,230 if dividends were taken into account.

[10]As can be seen from Figure 3, the low D/P does not stem from low D, but from high P!

at 28. In their joint testimony, Campbell and Shiller predicted that between 1997 and 2006, the stock market would lose about 40 percent of its real value.[11]

Shiller's 1981 work generated considerable controversy and has been the subject of many debates.[12] The central question asks: Do stock prices only change in response to fundamentals? Most of the debate has focused on technical details, which Robert Merton described in his survey of market efficiency.

Merton wrote his survey in 1986 and published it in 1987. Of course, 1987 was a propitious year for debating questions about stock prices and fundamentals, given that the stock market crashed in October. Immediately thereafter, Shiller conducted a major investor survey to identify the information that led stock prices to lose 25 percent of their value in the course of a single day. Shiller (1990) documents that the market crash of 1987 occurred in the *absence* of any major news about changing fundamentals.[13]

With this in mind, I draw your attention to the extreme right of Figure 3. Look at the period 1995 through early 1999, during which price rose well above Shiller's estimate of fundamental value. Note that Figure 3 ends in January 1999, at which time the dividend yield on the S&P 500 had fallen further, to 1.26 percent.[14] The trailing P/E stood at a record 32.7![15]

Like Campbell and Shiller, some Wall Street strategists also placed the market's rise of 1995 and 1996 in historical context. For example, Edward Kerschner, a strategist at PaineWebber, had been bullish during the market's climb in 1995 and 1996 but then turned bearish. In a June 1997 article that appeared in *Barron's* he stated, "In '87 the market went to 135 percent of fair value, and in '73 we got to 155 percent of fair value." Kerschner went on to note that according to his P/E model, the market was 15 percent overvalued, making it the third most expensive market in a quarter of a century.[16]

---

[11] In the reading on heuristic-driven bias, I discussed gambler's fallacy in connection with Robert Farrell's predictions for below-average stock returns. Although Campbell and Shiller consider mean reversion, and predict below-average stock returns over the next ten years, they do not succumb to gambler's fallacy. Their analysis is based on the relationship between valuation measures and subsequent returns. I hasten to emphasize that from a statistical perspective, the confidence associated with the 1996 Campbell–Shiller prediction for the 1997–2006 period is very low. This is because the value of P/E at year-end 1996 was at the extreme end of its historical range, which is where prediction confidence is lowest. It is worth noting that the *Wall Street Journal* reported John Campbell to have been very confident in his analysis. Campbell hedged his entire stock portfolio using futures, as a means of selling his stocks without triggering capital gains. See "The Outlook: Sometimes Stocks Go Nowhere for Years," by David Wessel, January 13, 1997. At the end of 1996, the Dow Jones Industrial Average stood at 6448. It crossed 11,000 on May 3, 1999.

[12] Shiller's work, and that of LeRoy and Porter (1981), which was published at the same time, was based on some controversial technical assumptions. Much of the debate has centered on some of these assumptions. In addition, his measure of fundamental value is based on a time invariant expected real interest rate and the stream of future dividends. Yet, managers appear to smooth dividends over time. See Alan Kleidon (1986) and Robert Merton (1987b).

[13] The *Wall Street Journal* makes the same point in connection with a sharp market drop that took place in August 1998.

[14] What is wrong with this picture? From year-end 1993 through year-end 1998, earnings on the S&P 500 grew at 11.9 percent a year and dividends grew at 4.2 percent a year, but the return on the S&P 500 was 24 percent a year. Earnings in 1997 and 1998 earnings grew at 3 percent and −4 percent at a time when the S&P 500 returned 33.3 percent and 28.4 percent. What dramatic differences are investors expecting in future earnings, dividends, interest rates, or rates of inflation?

[15] The leading P/E ratio was 26.46.

[16] The high P/E environment in the U.S. market, relative to the historical norm, reminds me of the Japanese stock market in the 1980s. In February 1999, the Nikkei stood at 14,232. But it was over three times as high a decade earlier when the P/E on Japanese stocks was over 50. During 1986 and 1987, the Nikkei had risen by more than 28 percent a year. In January, 1988 concerns about the Japanese market being in a bubble started to surface: see Kenneth French and James Poterba (1991). But despite being overvalued the Japanese market rose by a further 64 percent over the next two years. But what about the long-term return? One hundred yen invested in the Nikkei in January 1988 would have been worth 71 yen in March 1999. Yet an investor who pulled out of Japanese stocks in January 1988 would have spent the next two years kicking himself.

In a related vein, Charles Lee, James Myers, and Bhaskaran Swaminathan (1999) have devised an intrinsic measure of the Dow Jones Industrial Average based upon the book-to-market ratio, the long-term return on equity, expected earnings growth, and interest rates. In mid-June of 1997, when Kerschner indicated that the market was 15 percent overvalued, the Lee–Myers–Swaminathan measure indicated that the Dow was 42 percent overvalued.

Kerschner has not been as steadfast in his stated view as some academic scholars have been. Strategists are subject to different pressures than scholars. During strong bull markets, bears become unpopular on Wall Street.[17] In early 1999, as the P/E of the S&P 500 hit a record high 32, the *Wall Street Journal* reported Kerschner's view as "[S]tocks may have gotten a little ahead of themselves . . . but he thinks the fundamentals dictate future stock gains."[18]

6   OVERCONFIDENCE

Take the case of Royal Dutch/Shell. The market values of Royal Dutch and Shell Transport were misaligned relative to fundamental values. Yet, in attempting to exploit the mispricing, hedge fund Long-Term Capital Management (LTCM) managed to lose heavily. There is a moral to that story. Not every instance of mispricing leads to $20 bills on the sidewalk waiting to be picked up, or even to nickels, for that matter.

In fact, there are many behavioral lessons in the saga of LTCM. It does appear that their early success can be attributed to the exploitation of mispricing. At the same time, mispricing does get reduced as investors trade to exploit the associated profit opportunities. And investors do learn, albeit slowly; thus profit opportunities that had existed in 1994 through 1996 in the derivatives markets dried up in 1997. In response, LTCM began to take other kinds of positions, such as bets on the movements of foreign currency movements. Myron Scholes is reported to have been critical of these trades, asking his LTCM colleagues questions like "What informational advantage do we have over other traders?"

Scholes asked an eminently sensible question. Here is an analogy: "How good a driver are you? Relative to the drivers you encounter on the road, are you above average, average, or below average?"

Between 65 and 80 percent of the people who answer the driver question rate themselves above average. Of course, we all want to be above average, but only half of us are! So, most people are overconfident about their driving abilities. I suspect that investors are about as overconfident of their trading abilities as they are about their driving abilities.

There are two main implications of investor overconfidence. The first is that investors take bad bets because they fail to realize that they are at an informational disadvantage. The second is that they trade more frequently than is prudent, which leads to excessive trading volume. See my work with Statman (Shefrin and Statman 1994) and Terrance Odean (1998b).

A *Wall Street Journal* article describing the experience of Long-Term Capital Management quotes Nobel laureate William Sharpe.

---

[17] During the market's strong performance in 1997 and 1998, *Wall $treet Week with Louis Rukeyser* host Louis Rukeyser continually chided panelist Gail Dudack, the most bearish of all the panelists on his program.

[18] E. S. Browning, "Stock Market's New Year's Party Keeps Going," *Wall Street Journal*, 11 January 1999.

"Most of academic finance is teaching that you can't earn 40 percent a year without some risk of losing a lot of money," says Mr. Sharpe, the former Stanford colleague of Mr. Scholes. "In some sense, what happened is nicely consistent with what we teach."[19]

Proponents of behavioral finance, especially those who manage money, recognize that beating the market is no snap, and they try to avoid being overconfident. Russell Fuller and Richard Thaler operate Fuller and Thaler Asset Management. They manage a mutual fund, based on the De Bondt–Thaler effect, called Behavioral Value.[20] It may sound paradoxical, but Fuller believes that markets are, in the main, efficient. He tells me that many of the De Bondt–Thaler losers are, in fact, properly priced, that "most should be losers."[21] What's the lesson? Don't think the streets are paved with gold, or at least Wall Street anyway.

One other thing: Behavioral finance offers refutable hypotheses, but it does not have all the answers. De Bondt and Thaler predicted overreaction based on representativeness. But take another look at Figure 1. It shows that a portfolio of extreme losers does outperform the market. However, a careful inspection of the figure shows that the effect is concentrated in the month of January. I know of nothing that suggests that people rely on representativeness in some months but not others.

---

[19] Browning, "Market's New Year's Party."

[20] As of January 1999, Behavioral Value had been operating for three years, during which time it posted returns of 18.3 percent, net of fees. The Russell 2000 returned 14.4 percent in the same period.

[21] Russ Fuller, interview by author, February 2, 1999. Fuller and Thaler apply a screening procedure to the De Bondt–Thaler losers, in order to select stocks for the Behavioral Value fund. A generic De Bondt–Thaler strategy has an excess return (alpha) of between 3 and 4 percent. Fuller tells me that his screening procedure sifts out the most underpriced 10 percent, with the resulting alpha being 11 percent.

SUMMARY

This reading covered the third theme of behavioral finance, *inefficient markets*, which is connected with the earlier two themes by cause and effect. Heuristic-driven bias and frame dependence cause prices to stray from fundamental values. Three examples are 1) representativeness as a cause of the winner–loser effect; 2) conservatism as a cause of post-earnings-announcement drift; and 3) mental accounting as a cause of a historical equity premium that has been too high, relative to the underlying fundamentals. But as I noted, prices can stray far from fundamental value, and for very long periods.

I conclude the reading with a word of caution. The departure of price from fundamental value does not automatically lead to risk-free profit opportunities. In fact, the "smart money" may avoid some trades, although they have identified mispricing. Why? Because of nonfundamental risk, meaning risk associated with unpredictable sentiment.

PORTFOLIOS, PYRAMIDS, EMOTIONS, AND BIASES

by Hersh Shefrin

LEARNING OUTCOMES

The candidate should be able to:	Mastery
a. discuss the influence of hope and fear on investors' desire for security and investment potential;	☐
b. explain how portfolios can be structured as layered pyramids and how such structures address needs associated with security, potential, and aspiration;	☐
c. evaluate the impact of excessive optimism and overconfidence on investors' decisions regarding portfolio construction.	☐

INTRODUCTION

Harry Markowitz, the pioneer of modern portfolio theory, played it both ways. Markowitz developed the theory of mean-variance portfolios, one of the pillars of standard finance. But he also developed the basic ideas that underlie frame dependence and loss aversion. And when it came time to choose his own retirement portfolio, Harry Markowitz played it the behavioral way (see the reading on frame dependence).

Most investors do the same. Playing it the behavioral way means that they base their portfolio choices not on mean-variance principles but on frame dependence, heuristic-driven bias, and something I call the *emotional time line.* In this reading I describe how these three elements together shape 1) the kinds of portfolios that investors choose, 2) the types of securities investors find attractive, 3) the relationship that investors form with financial advisers, and 4) the biases to which investors are subject.

Beyond Greed and Fear: Understanding Behavioral Finance and the Psychology of Investing, by Hersh Shefrin.
Copyright © 2002 by Oxford University Press. Reprinted with permission of Oxford University Press, Inc.

This reading discusses the following:

▶ the emotional time line—how emotions affect risk tolerance and portfolio choice over time
▶ why the combination of emotion and framing induces many investors to structure their portfolios as "layered pyramids"
▶ how a well-designed security must fit naturally into a layered pyramid
▶ the role of regret in the investor-advisor relationship
▶ how heuristic-driven bias inhibits investors from diversifying fully, and induces them to trade too frequently

1　THE EMOTIONAL TIME LINE

Why is it important to discuss emotion in a reading on portfolio selection? Emotions determine tolerance for risk, and tolerance for risk plays a key role in portfolio selection. Note that investing takes place along a time line. In short, investors experience a variety of emotions as they:

▶ ponder their alternatives;
▶ make decisions about how much risk to bear;
▶ ride the financial roller coaster while watching their decisions play out;
▶ assess whether to keep to the initial strategy or alter it; and
▶ ultimately learn the degree to which they have achieved their financial goals.

Psychologist Lola Lopes (1987) identifies the major emotions along the time line and discusses the way that these emotions influence risk bearing. According to folklore, greed and fear drive financial markets. But this is only partly correct. While fear does play a role, most investors react less to greed and more to *hope*. Fear induces an investor to focus on events that are especially unfavorable, while hope induces him or her to focus on events that are favorable. In addition to hope and fear, that apply *generally*, investors have *specific* goals to which they aspire.

To what kind of goals do investors aspire? Typical goals include purchasing a home, funding children's college education, and having a comfortable retirement.

Think of the emotional time line as a line where time advances from left to right. Investment decisions lie at the left, and goals lie at the right. Investors experience a variety of emotions along the time line as they make decisions at the left, wait in the middle, and learn their fate at the right. Hope and fear are polar opposites, one positive and the other negative. Picture positive emotion above the time line and negative emotion below it. What happens above the time line as time progresses from left to right? Hope becomes anticipation and is then transformed into pride. Below the line, fear becomes anxiety[1] and is then transformed into regret. You may recall from the reading on frame dependence that Harry Markowitz talked about the importance of regret when planning his own retirement, saying "my intention was to minimize my future regret." [*Money* magazine, January 1998, p. 118.]

---

[1] Dread is extreme anxiety.

Hope and fear affect the way that investors evaluate alternatives. Fear causes investors to look at possibilities from the bottom up and ask, How bad can things get? Hope gets investors to look at possibilities from the top down and ask, How good can it get? In Lopes's terminology, the bottom-up perspective emphasizes the desire for security, whereas the top-down perspective emphasizes the need for potential on the upside. Lopes tells us that these two perspectives reside within all of us, as opposite poles. But they tend not to be equally matched: One pole usually predominates.

Barbara O'Neill (1990) has compiled an interesting collection of financial planning cases. The title of her book is *How Real People Handle Their Money*. Here is an example from her casebook, describing the situation of one particular couple, Barbara and Leon Smyth.[2]

> If they lived in a big city, instead of a rural area, you could probably call them "yuppies." Barbara and Leon Smyth, ages 35 and 37, are a two-career couple who earn a combined $45,300.[3] They have a son, aged 14, from Leon's previous marriage. . . . Like many married couples, the Smyths have different attitudes about money. While Barbara is most concerned about safety of principal, Leon's major objective is future growth and he says he's willing to assume some risk to achieve financial gain. [Case study # 21]

The dominant emotion in Barbara is fear, and it leads her to emphasize security. For Leon, the dominant emotion is hope, and it leads him to emphasize potential. One of the great contributions of Lopes is to establish how the interaction of these conflicting emotions determines the tolerance toward risk. If there were one important point to take away from this reading, this would be it!

PORTFOLIOS, GOALS, AND RISK TOLERANCE   2

What about the Smyths' portfolio? Does it reflect the emotional profile of Leon and Barbara with respect to security, potential, and aspiration? The Smyths have two major financial assets: a money market account and a growth mutual fund in a custodial trust that is earmarked to fund their (Leon's) son's college education.

Financial planners often suggest that investors form portfolios using a layered pyramid. Figure 1 offers a representative example from a book by Ginita Wall (1995). The pyramid is structured to address the needs associated with security, potential, and aspiration. At the bottom of the pyramid are securities designed to provide investors with security. These include money market funds and certificates of deposit. Further up the pyramid come bonds. Financial planners often suggest that investors earmark particular investments for specific goals. A common example is to use zero coupon bonds to fund the goal of providing for children's college education. Climbing up one more layer in the pyramid takes us to stocks and real estate. As Wall indicates, these are intended for appreciation, upside potential.

At the pinnacle of the pyramid lie the most speculative investments, such as out-of-the-money call options and lottery tickets, intended for a shot at getting rich. Lopes describes planning as "applied hoping," and she quotes Robin Pope (1983), who discusses the psychological value of such investments. Pope states

---

[2] O'Neill has changed the names to preserve anonymity.

[3] The time period for O'Neill's study was the late 1980s, so the income figure would have to be adjusted up significantly to place it into current dollars.

FIGURE 1   A Portfolio as a Layered Pyramid

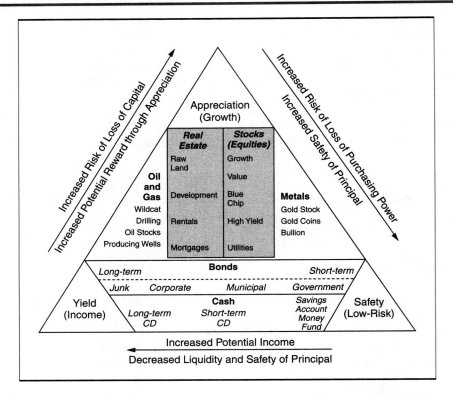

A typical layered pyramid that financial planners use to advise clients about building portfolios. Movements from bottom to top involve moving to riskier assets. Movements from right to left involve higher yield.

Source: *The Way to Save,* Ginita Wall, 1993.

that "after deciding to devote a fraction of the housekeeping funds to a weekly lottery ticket, housekeepers can dream from age nineteen to ninety-nine that they will become millionaires after the next drawing" (p. 156).

Without question, anticipation has value. Economist George Lowenstein (1987) reports an experiment where undergraduate students evaluated how much a kiss from a movie star of their choice was worth to them, depending on when the kiss was received. The students valued a kiss that would come in three days time as being worth more than a kiss received immediately, in three hours, or in one day. Why pay to wait? The opportunity to anticipate the experience.

Jonathan Clements writes a regular column for the *Wall Street Journal* called "Getting Going" that focuses on individual investing. In his column, he frequently quotes financial planners on the issues being discussed in this reading. For example, a December 1997, column contains the following interesting characterization of the pyramid pinnacle: "'With my clients, we set up mad-money accounts,' says Deena Katz, a financial planner in Coral Gables, Fla. 'That's the money they use to buy hot stocks and go to Vegas. You should make a conscious decision about how much you're going to speculate with.'"[4] Clements recommends keeping the speculative portion of a portfolio below 5 percent. But he

---

[4]Jonathan Clements, "Getting Going: If Santa Had This List, He'd Be Wiser, Wealthier and Ready for the New Year," *Wall Street Journal,* 23 December 1997.

clearly recognizes the key emotion driving speculation. In his July 2, 1996, column he lumped lotteries and actively managed stock funds together, choosing as his headline "Hope Springs Eternal." Whereas anticipation is the manifestation of hope along the emotional time line between decision and outcome, anxiety is the manifestation of fear.

In Lopes's framework, the relative strengths of these two emotions, in conjunction with aspiration, determine tolerance for risk. In the context of portfolio selection, risk tolerance determines the allocation between the layers of the pyramid. The relative strengths of hope, fear, and aspiration determine the allocation between stocks and bonds.

Kenneth Fisher and Meir Statman (1997) analyze the nature of the advice that mutual fund companies provide to investors about the appropriate mix of stocks, bonds, and cash in their portfolios. These companies encourage investors who are more tolerant of risk and who have enough time to emphasize stocks in their mix. Financial planners provide similar advice. Of particular interest is the advice they offer when a major goal is financially within reach. In this situation, many planners recommend that investors consider shifting completely out of stocks.

Jonathan Clements discusses the issue of goal horizons in his December 2, 1997, column, in which he makes clear that the issue concerns whether a portfolio without stocks could deliver the returns required to achieve the investor's goal. He states:

> Would you be able to reach your investment goals with those sorts of annual returns? If not, then you really need to have at least some of your money in stocks, which have delivered over 10% a year on average since year-end 1925, according to Ibbotson Associates, the Chicago research firm.
>
> "If you're saving for college or retirement, stocks are really the only way to go," argues Alan Cohn, a financial planner in Bala Cynwyd, Pa. "There's nothing else that will provide you with that high rate of return."
>
> On the other hand, if you don't need high returns, then maybe you shouldn't take the risk of being in stocks.
>
> "We always invest for the lowest level of equity exposure possible," says Harold Evensky, a financial planner in Coral Gables, Fla. "Some of my friends would disagree with that. They would say, if you can live with an all-equity portfolio, you should be all-equity. We say, if all you need is 60% stocks to meet your goals, we should go for 60% stocks."[5]

What is the logic of avoiding equities? This is hardly a mean-variance argument. Mean-variance efficiency prescribes reducing the riskiness of a portfolio by shifting the allocation from stocks and bonds to cash but leaving the relative proportions of stocks and bonds intact. But mean-variance efficiency is ill equipped to deal both with goals and with the attendant psychological factors attached to them.

What about the emotional elements? Well, when a major financial goal is within reach, fear and aspiration combine to favor a conservative strategy. But suppose a conservative strategy virtually guarantees that an investor's aspirations will be unmet. In this case, the desire to increase the probability of reaching her goal will induce an investor to hold equities. There is also a time horizon issue involved. Clements continues:

> How long will you be investing?
>
> Wall Street's conventional wisdom suggests that the older you are, the less you should have in stocks. But in truth, the key factor isn't your age, but how long you will

---

[5] Jonathan Clements, "Getting Going: How Much Should You Invest in Stocks? It All Depends on Goals and Time Frame," *Wall Street Journal,* 11 February 1997.

be investing. If you plan to buy a home next month, for instance, you would be a fool to have your house down payment sitting in stocks, no matter how young you are.

Mr. Evensky offers this rule of thumb: Don't put money into stocks unless you are more than five years from your goal. Suppose your son is nine years from college. Initially, you might put some of junior's tuition money into stocks.

But once college is within five years, lighten up, preferably unloading the shares when the market is booming. "I'm always looking for a five-year window, during which I can decide when to sell," Mr. Evensky says.[6]

What is going on here? Again, the "five-year rule" is hardly a mean-variance strategy. Again, emotional variables drive the behavior. Think about how an investor would feel if he:

1. had sufficient resources to achieve a major goal that was less than five years away by investing in safe fixed income securities; but

2. continued to allocate these resources heavily in equities; and

3. at the end of the horizon for his goal, his equity investments had declined in price, and his goal had moved out of reach.

The dominant emotion in such a case would be regret. Hence moving out of stocks within five years of an attainable goal is a regret-avoidance strategy.

3   FRAME DEPENDENCE: MENTAL ACCOUNTS AND PRIORITIES—IS SAFETY FIRST?

Lopes (1987) discusses a splendid metaphor for portfolio choice: J. Anderson's (1979) description of how subsistence farmers allocate their land between low-risk food crops and high-risk cash crops. Farmers first take care of subsistence needs, and then they plant cash crops. Theirs is a very risky portfolio. Why? It is the only way they have a chance at meeting the goals to which they aspire. Is there an analogy with investors? Here is Clements again, this time from his January 7, 1997, column:

> A lot depends on your financial situation. If you can barely afford to make the house down payment, it would be nice to take greater risks so that you earn higher returns. But if the market turns against you, the consequences could be dire.
>
> On the other hand, if you have more than enough money to make the house down payment, shooting for higher returns is less of a risk, because you could still make the down payment even if you suffered some investment losses. Because you do have plenty of money, however, there's also less incentive to try for higher returns.
>
> Indeed, it's one of the ironies of investing. The rich can afford to take risks, but they don't need to. The poor need to take risks, but they often can't afford to.[7]

To what extent do investors think about their portfolios in layers, with the bottom layer earmarked for security and the top layer earmarked for potential? I ran a small survey asking eighty-one investors a series of questions that bear on this and related points. In the main, I found that investors, like the subsistence farmers described earlier, do think in terms of layers based on security and potential.[8]

---

[6] Ibid.

[7] Jonathan Clements, "Getting Going: Need Cash in Five Years? Dumping Stocks Isn't Always the Best Investment Strategy," *Wall Street Journal*, 7 January 1997.

[8] The investors varied in location, age (mid-twenties to their mid-fifties), income ($30,000 to upwards of $500,000 per year), and wealth. The responses across all three groups were similar.

Less than 20 percent indicated otherwise. Of those that do layer their portfolios, 70 percent concentrate on security first, before investing for potential. Respondents are even stronger in saying that they are willing to take a fair amount of risk on the upside, once they have adequate protection on the downside.[9]

A MEETING OF THE WAYS   **4**

The emotion-based perspective of risk tolerance is very different from the perspective adopted in mean-variance analysis. Yet, the two are beginning to come together, as investors begin to use sophisticated software to make investment decisions. For example, investors can now use the Internet to obtain investment advice about their 401(k) plans. A major Internet provider of 401(k) advice is the firm Financial Engines, cofounded by Nobel laureate William Sharpe. Financial Engines software enables 401(k) investors to access the same mean-variance algorithms that Sharpe developed for institutional money managers.

But do investors think in mean-variance terms? Do they conceptualize their risk tolerance as the maximum increase in return variance that they could accept in return for a 100-basis-point increase in expected return? A June 29, 1998 article in *U.S. News & World Report* describes the performance measurement criterion—and it's neither the mean nor the variance—displayed in the Financial Engines software.

> The most compelling feature is that a user's expected returns are expressed as probabilities—for example, the system might say, "You have a 41 percent chance of reaching your goal of $80,000 per year in retirement."
>
> By adjusting risk, contribution level, and retirement age, a user can see how different combinations affect the chance of succeeding. (Kaye and Ahmad 1998)

Lopes repeatedly stresses that when individuals consider aspiration, they focus on the probability of achieving at least the *aspiration* level. So being told that there is a "41 percent chance of reaching your goal" is precisely what they want to know. Hence, we have a meeting of the ways. Financial Engines software will furnish investors with mean-variance portfolios. But investors will evaluate the risk attached to those portfolios in terms of fear, hope, and aspiration.[10]

SECURITY DESIGN   **5**

British Premium Bonds resemble index-linked certificates of deposit, but with a twist. Holders of these government bonds are assured of receiving their principal. But in lieu of interest, they receive tickets to monthly lotteries that

---

[9] In my survey, I also examined how the choice of securities depended on the time horizon attached to a given goal. I found that when the time horizon is short, such as for a vacation or a home remodel, and investors feel close to being able to fund the goal at the end of their horizon, then the tendency is to invest in low-risk securities such as money market funds. Those investors who indicated that they do not currently have the resources to fund a goal said that they relied on stock options and commodities to provide the necessary funds. This was particularly true for luxury items such as boats and jewelry.

[10] In the interest of disclosure, I should mention that I served as a consultant in the design of the Financial Engines software.

carry prizes between £50 and £250,000. A Premium Bond packages a very safe security with a lottery ticket, and it is very popular. What accounts for the attraction?

Most investors do not choose securities by ascertaining where the risk-return profiles place the securities on the mean-variance frontier. Rather, investors' choices stem from their emotional reaction to the features promised by the securities. Those that promise safety appeal to investors whose primary emotion is fear. Securities that promise potential appeal to investors whose primary emotion is hope. But many investors are driven by both emotions; Lopes calls them "cautiously hopeful." Think about British Premium Bonds in this light: Perhaps the popularity of these bonds stem from the fact that they address both emotional needs.

What types of securities appeal to these investors? Below are two examples, taken from a paper by Statman and me titled "Behavioral Portfolio Theory" (Shefrin and Statman 1999). Dean Witter proposes what they call the Principal Guaranteed Strategy, which they describe as follows:

> "Mr. Stewart" has $50,000 to invest and a time horizon of 10 years. He is looking to add stocks to his portfolio for growth, but is concerned with protecting his principal. Based on his objectives and risk tolerance, "Mr. Stewart's" Dean Witter Account Executive structures the Principal Guaranteed Portfolio below, which includes "buy" rated stocks from Dean Witter's Recommended List.

To "protect" Mr. Stewart's $50,000 investment, the Principal Guaranteed Strategy calls for the purchase, for $24,951, of a zero coupon bond with a face value of $50,000 maturing in ten years. This leaves $25,049 for stocks and brokerage commissions.

The Principal Guaranteed Strategy has a payoff pattern that appeals to both fear and hope. The bond portion ensures that, if held the full ten years, the payoff will not fall below the $50,000 initial purchase price, while the stock portion offers a chance for a gain.

Here is another example. Life USA, an insurance firm, offers Annu-a-Dex. Annu-a-Dex provides a guaranteed return of 45 percent over a seven-year horizon. An additional amount might be paid based on the performance of the stock market. Life USA describes the payoff as follows:

> [Y]our principal will increase by 45% in the next seven years, market correction or not. And if the market does better than that, you get half the action. All without downside risk. You get the ride without the risk.

Annu-a-Dex is appealing to an investor whose aspiration level is 45 percent above current wealth. The payoff distribution has a floor at the aspiration level, and it offers some measure of upward potential beyond that level.[11]

---

[11] There are numerous other examples of securities designed to appeal to cautiously hopeful investors. Merrill Lynch offers S&P 500 Market Index Target-Term Securities (MITTS), which mature in five years and pay the principal but no interest. Instead of interest, they pay 115 percent of the S&P 500 gain, if there is any. Another example involves so-called Click Funds, which offer index-linked investments with specific downside protection. These funds have recently become very popular in the Netherlands. See Smid and Tempelaar (1997). Investors have also been known to simulate securities such as these. John McConnell and Eduardo Schwartz (1992) report that some Merrill Lynch investors held large balances in their money market accounts, and used the interest to buy call options.

REGRET, RESPONSIBILITY, AND FINANCIAL ADVISERS

Regret is a painful experience that has already come up for discussion a couple of times. To help understand its impact on individual investors, consider the following example.

In March and early April 1997, the stock market experienced a substantial decline. At the time, there was a lot of concern expressed in the financial press about whether a crash might be at hand. Suppose that a conversation took place between you and your friends George, John, and Paul.

George had a lot of his portfolio in stocks, and on the basis of his own analysis decided to sell his stocks and buy certificates of deposit (CDs).

John was in the same situation as George, and like him, switched out of stocks and into CDs. However, John based his decision on his financial adviser's recommendation rather than on his own analysis.

Paul has traditionally held CDs. In fact, he follows a CD rollover rule (rolling over the proceeds from a maturing CD into a new one). He had been holding some CDs that had just matured. Paul thought that the market would rebound, and he considered changing his usual practice by purchasing mutual fund shares instead of renewing his CDs. But in the end, he decided to renew his CDs.

Subsequently, the market has appreciated by 15 percent. All three investors held CD portfolios during this period. All would have been better off by buying stocks.

Now consider this: whose self-image do you think suffers the most?

► George, who traded out of stocks and into CDs based on his own analysis

► John, who traded out of stocks and into CDs based on his adviser's recommendation

► Paul, who renewed his CDs

► nobody—self-image plays no role in these situations

When I ask this question to my classes, the typical responses I receive are as follows. About 70 percent choose George, 12 percent choose John, virtually no one chooses Paul, and 18 percent choose "nobody."

The vast majority choose George because he has no one to blame for a decision gone wrong. George must accept one hundred percent of the responsibility. Meir Statman and I discussed this issue in an article we wrote for *Psychology Today* (Shefrin and Statman 1986). Presumably George, John, and Paul all regret their decision to go with CDs: After all, in hindsight all three recognize that they would have been better off had they gone with stocks. But most judge George's pain to be the worst.

John, on the other hand, gets to blame his adviser. I would argue, in fact, that the shifting of responsibility from John to his adviser is one of the main services for which John's adviser gets paid. Hand-holding may be every bit as important as traditional advice, if not more so.

Hardly anyone picks Paul because Paul followed what for him was a *conventional* strategy. Daniel Kahneman and Amos Tversky (1982) argue that people who deviate from what is for them a conventional way of acting become especially vulnerable to the pain of regret if things go badly. Why? Because regret is counterfactual. If Paul were to deviate from his conventional behavior pattern and things were to go wrong, it would be so easy to imagine having done the conventional thing. And the ease of imagining taking the appropriate action is what triggers the emotion of regret.

In this example, both George and John take actions and soon after learn that their action resulted in a situation not to their liking. In short-term situations, regret is mainly associated with the taking of an action. However, when people are asked to think back over their lives, reflect on their regrets, and indicate what caused them the most regret—the things they did, or those they didn't—what do most of them say? Psychologists Thomas Gilovich and Victoria Husted-Medvec (1995) find that people most regret the things they didn't do. When it comes to the long-term, we most regret inaction.

Having a financial adviser enables the investor to carry a psychological call option. If an investment decision turns out well, the investor can take the credit, attributing the favorable outcome to his or her own skill. If the decision turns out badly, the investor can protect his or her ego and lower the regret by blaming the adviser. This phenomenon involves *self-attribution bias*. The investor attributes favorable outcomes to skill, and unfavorable outcomes to either somebody else, or just plain bad luck.

Regret is intertwined with hindsight bias, in which a person regards the events that happened as much more inevitable than they looked before the fact. For example, take Bernard Baruch, the legendary financier from the 1920s and 1930s. Martin Fridson (1998) reports that when Baruch wrote his memoirs in the 1950s he recalls having warned of the impending stock market crash of 1929. But looking back at his 1929 writings, he appears to have been as bullish as anyone was. Memory plays tricks on us. William Goetzmann and Nadav Peles (1994) find that mutual fund owners recollect that their funds performed much better than was in fact the case. Goetzmann and Peles attribute this tendency to *cognitive dissonance*. Not wanting to judge themselves harshly, investors simply remember beating the market.

Regret and hindsight bias come together in the selection of loser stocks for a portfolio. As I discussed in the reading on frame dependence, a portfolio of losers historically outperformed the market by 19 percent on a cumulative three-year basis. But when losers continue to lose, their continued poor performance looks inevitable in hindsight; and it is easy to imagine having avoided them. Indeed, Werner De Bondt and Richard Thaler, who discovered the winner–loser effect, found that people, including themselves, were *fearful* of investing in loser stocks.

7 HEURISTIC-DRIVEN BIAS AND PORTFOLIO SELECTION

Individual investors are especially prone to heuristic-driven bias. Here is some intriguing evidence from a survey of individual investors conducted by De Bondt (1998). A group of forty-five investors were recruited at a conference organized by the National Association of Investment Clubs. Two thirds were men. The average investor in the group was fifty-eight years old, had been trading stocks for the previous eighteen years, and had a financial portfolio (excluding real estate) worth $310,000 that was 72 percent invested in stocks. He or she spent seven hours per week thinking about his or her investments, time that included viewing the television program *Wall $treet Week with Louis Rukeyser*.

Over a period of twenty weeks, De Bondt tracked the group's forecasts for the future performance of both the Dow Jones and their own stocks. Four of his findings are especially fascinating. 1) Investors were excessively optimistic about the future performance of shares they owned, but *not* about the Dow Jones. 2) They were overconfident in that they found themselves surprised by the price changes to their stocks more frequently than they had anticipated. 3) Their stock price forecasts were anchored on past performance: During an uptrend for one of their stocks, investors thought there was little room left for movement on the upside but a lot of room on the downside. The reverse held true for downtrends. 4) They underestimated the degree to which their stocks moved in tandem with the market. In other words, they underestimated beta.

Equally interesting are the *attitudes* that De Bondt's investors expressed. 1) When it comes to picking stocks, they certainly do not believe in throwing darts. 2) Investors stated that they believe a solid understanding of a few firms is a better risk-management tool than diversification. 3) Not only do investors reject the notion that beta measures risk, they reject the fact that risk and return are positively related.

De Bondt's survey informs us that individual investors

▶ display excessive optimism,

▶ are overconfident,

▶ discount diversification, and

▶ reject there being a positive tradeoff between risk and return.

In the next few sections, I take up these issues in detail.

OPTIMISM   8

Let's return to O'Neill's (1990) book of financial planning case studies. Those studies provide a sense of how eclectic, and problematic, the portfolios of individual investors can be. Her examples cover a multitude of sins such as inadequate insurance coverage, the failure to diversify, and excessive risk taking.

Why do so many people appear to have inadequate insurance coverage? Included in her group are the Smyths, whose case we discussed earlier. They lack long-term disability insurance. And the Smyths have plenty of company, especially from people in their twenties. This is one case of insufficient fear. O'Neill points out that the "twentysomethings" are seven times more likely to experience an extended disability than they are to die young. Presumably, they are unduly optimistic.

In fact, excessive optimism is a well-studied phenomenon, especially among people in their teens and early twenties. Psychologist Neil Weinstein (1980) found that people in this age group systematically think that they are less likely to experience bad outcomes, and more likely to experience good outcomes, than their peers. In replicating Weinstein's study, I have found that the same phenomenon holds true for people between the ages of 25 and 45, though to a lesser degree than for the younger cohort.

OVERCONFIDENCE: TOO MUCH TRADING   9

Outside their 401(k) plans, many investors earn mediocre returns because they trade too much. A study by Brad Barber and Terrance Odean (1998b) finds that individual investors tilt their portfolios toward high-beta, small-capitalization value stocks.[12] Barber and Odean examined the trading histories of 60,000 investors over the six-year period ending in 1996. They found that during this time, individuals managed to beat the value-weighted market index by 60 basis points, although that was gross of trading costs. Trading costs ate up 240 basis points of returns. Not surprisingly, the individuals who traded most fared the worst, underperforming the index by 500 basis points.

Why do individual investors trade so much when the net effect is to reduce their returns? Clearly, they believe they can pick winners. But Barber and Odean suggest that investors are overconfident in their abilities. There is good reason to expect that this is the case, since overconfidence is ubiquitous, especially when difficult tasks are involved. Investors may also overrate their abilities. As noted in the reading on inefficient markets, I asked my MBA students to rate themselves as drivers relative to the general population. Only 8 percent rated themselves below average; 65 percent rated themselves above average. The 65 percent figure may actually be low. Kahneman and Mark Riepe (1997) report that the general figure is more like 80 percent.

There is at least one additional explanation for why people trade so much. Lopes (1987) suggests that people are motivated to master their environment, and it is unpleasant to believe that one has no control, especially when chance and skill elements coexist. The trading of stocks fits this bill. Investors who are high in the desire for control and suffer from the illusion of control are prone to trade frequently.

10   THE ONLINE REVOLUTION

Overconfidence, desire for control, and the illusion of control appear to be especially acute when it comes to online trading, Internet stocks, and day trading.

Online trading has made it cheaper and easier for individual investors to trade stocks. Between 1996 and 1998 the average commission charged per trade by the ten largest online trading firms dropped by about 75 percent. The amount of assets managed online went from near zero to about $100 billion in 1997. On June 1, 1999, in a move that may dramatically change the brokerage industry forever, Merrill Lynch broke from its traditional, high-cost, full-service approach and announced its intention to enter the low-cost business of online trading.

In 1998, Internet stocks captured investors' attention, especially those of online traders. On the strength of investors' imagination, and little else, Internet stock prices were propelled into orbit. According to Lipper Analytical Services the best-performing mutual fund in 1998 was the Internet Fund, managed by Kinetics Asset Management. It had a return of 196 percent.

Overconfidence and optimism appear to be particularly severe among day traders, the online traders who have abandoned regular jobs to trade full time from their personal computers. The lure of day trading has soared with the appearance of best-selling books and websites devoted to the subject.

Some things never change. Statman and I (Shefrin and Statman 1993b) discuss the evolution of the 1933 Securities Act and the 1934 Securities Exchange Act as a response to the fate that befell optimistic, overconfident traders in the 1920s.[13] Legislators enacted limits on margin and suitability requirements as a

---

[12] At least, these are the types of stocks they hold.

[13] The broad issues involve the role of financial market regulation as a means of dealing with potential conflicts between fairness and efficiency.

means of mitigating insufficient self-control (gambling addiction) and heuristic-driven bias. On January 27, 1999, Securities and Exchange Commission chair Arthur Levitt warned that online trading was like "a narcotic" to many online traders.[14] The technology may have changed over the last seventy years, but human psychology has not.

Generally speaking, most online investors are between 25 and 45 years old. In 1998, about 75 percent of online traders were men; the most active online cohort was the 30–34 age group. Investors in this age group are especially prone to optimism and overconfidence. A PaineWebber study found that younger investors were more optimistic than older investors were.

As for gender, Barber and Odean (1998a) describe the differences between the trading patterns of men and women. Barber and Odean's data come from a large discount brokerage firm, consist of individual investors' trading records, and cover the period February 1991 through January 1997. During this period, the performance of the stocks picked by men and stocks picked by women were about the same. But men traded 45 percent more than women. And men chose stocks in smaller companies, having higher price-to-book, and higher betas. As a result men earned 1.4 percent less on a risk-adjusted basis. The numbers are even more dramatic for single men and single women. Single men traded 67 percent more but earned 2.3 percent less, on a risk-adjusted basis.

THE FAILURE TO DIVERSIFY   11

The failure to diversify is by now a well-documented phenomenon. One investor who computes mean-variance efficient portfolios for a living confided to me that he had but one stock in his individual retirement account (IRA). Needless to say, I was curious as to which one. The answer? Microsoft. He told me, "I let Bill Gates manage my IRA."

Virtually all academic studies of individual investors' portfolios find that they only contain a few securities. For example, an early study by Blume, Crockett, and Friend (1974) found that 34.1 percent of investors in their sample of 17,056 investors held only one dividend-paying stock, 50 percent held no more than two stocks, and only 10.7 percent held more than ten stocks. A Federal Reserve Board survey on the financial characteristics of consumers showed that the average number of stocks in the portfolio was 3.41 (Blume and Friend 1975). More recently Martha Starr-McCluer (1994), an economist at the Federal Reserve Board in Washington, reports similar findings based upon the Survey of Consumer Finances, sponsored by the Federal Reserve Board.

Lease, Lewellen, and Schlarbaum (1976) surveyed investors who held accounts with a major brokerage company and found that the average number of stocks in a portfolio ranged from 9.4 to 12.1, depending on the demographic group.

While we know that there are only few stocks in the typical portfolio, it is possible that diversification is accomplished through bonds, real estate, and other assets. However, evidence by Mervyn King and Jonathan Leape (1984), as well as most of O'Neill's case studies, indicates that limited diversification is observed even where assets other than stocks are included.

It is abundantly clear that individual investors have a very primitive understanding of what constitutes a well-diversified portfolio. In *The Investment Club*

---

[14] Rebecca Buckman, "These Days, Online Trading Can Become an Addiction," *Wall Street Journal,* 1 February 1999.

Book, John Wasik (1995) indicates that the National Association of Investors Corporations (NAIC), which represents 8,000 stock-picking clubs, advises that portfolios include no fewer than five stocks. The NAIC calls this the *Rule of Five.* The theory is that of the five stocks, one will probably be a loser, three will produce mediocre returns, but the fifth will be a real winner!

Of course, the number of securities in the portfolio is not the sole determinant of the proximity to mean-variance efficiency. Jacob (1974) and others have shown that an investor can reduce unsystematic risk significantly with only a few securities by a judicious selection of securities. However, Blume and Friend (1978) report that the actual degree of diversification for 70 percent of the investors in their study was lower than suggested by the number of securities in the portfolios.

12   NAIVE DIVERSIFICATION

Shlomo Benartzi and Richard Thaler (1998) have written a most intriguing study of the way many investors approach diversification in their 401(k) accounts. They present strong evidence that individuals divide their money evenly across all the choices their 401(k) plan makes available. So, if their plan offers them one bond fund and one stock fund, they will split their contributions fifty-fifty. This is what Harry Markowitz acknowledged doing in his own retirement account (1998).

If there are three choices, a money market fund, a bond fund, and a stock fund, then investors will split their contributions three ways equally. Benartzi and Thaler call this heuristic the $1/n$ rule, and characterize it as *naive diversification.*

The heuristic is important because depending on how the choices are structured, individuals can end up taking too little risk or excessive risk, relative to their risk tolerance. Somebody whose employer offers a plan that has two bond funds and one stock fund will end up with one third of their allocation in equities. However, the reverse will be true for someone who works for a company like TWA that offers a plan with more stock funds than bond funds.

13   HOME BIAS: FAMILIARITY DOES NOT ALWAYS BREED CONTEMPT

Although U.S. stocks only account for 45 percent of global market value of equity, U.S. investors tend to concentrate their holdings in U.S. stocks. This phenomenon is called the *home bias.* Ken French and James Poterba (1993) point out that in 1989 U.S. investors held less than 7 percent of their portfolios in foreign securities. Moreover, Europeans concentrate their portfolios in European stocks, and Japanese concentrate in Japanese stocks. Why?

In a word, familiarity. Remember the aversion to ambiguity discussed in the reading on heuristic-driven bias? In unfamiliar situations, the predominant emotion tends to be fear. Foreign stocks are less familiar than U.S. stocks. Perhaps familiarity also explains why, in their portfolios, people tend to overweight the stocks of companies they work for. Gur Huberman (1997) points out that U.S. investors concentrate their holdings in the Baby Bells—the former Bell operating companies—of their own region. Of course, investors who shun the Baby Bells of other regions, like investors who shun foreign stocks, give up some of the benefits of diversification.

SUMMARY

The major factors driving portfolio selection are much more complex than the mean and variance of future returns. This reading described how frame dependence, heuristic-driven bias, and the emotional time line together shape 1) the kinds of portfolios that investors choose, 2) the types of securities investors find attractive, 3) the relationship that investors form with financial advisers, and 4) the biases to which investors are subject.

The key emotions pertain to fear, hope, and the aspirations attached to investor goals. Heuristic-driven bias stems from a variety of phenomena: naive diversification rules such as the "Rule of Five" and the "$1/n$" heuristic, hindsight bias, excessive optimism, overconfidence, self-attribution bias, and fear of the unfamiliar.

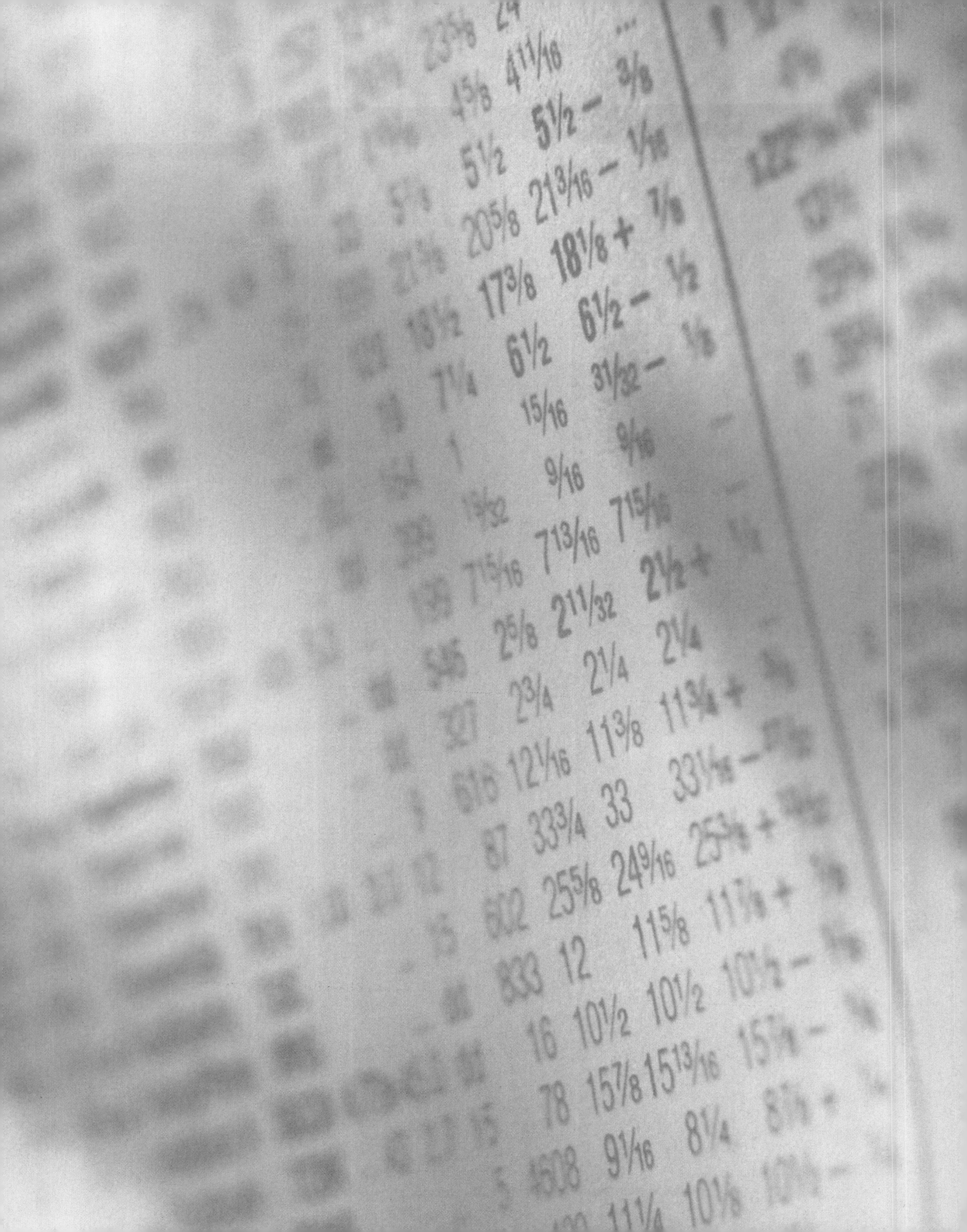

23⅜ 24

4⅝ 4¹¹⁄₁₆ ··· –⅜

5½ 5½ – ⅜

20⅝ 21³⁄₁₆ – ⅛

17⅜ 18⅛ + ⅞

6½ 6½ – ½

7¼ 6½ 31⁄32 – ⅛

15⁄16 9⁄16

9⁄16 7¹³⁄₁₆ 7¹⁵⁄₁₆

7¹⁵⁄₁₆

2⅝ 2¹¹⁄₃₂ 2½ +

2¾ 2¼ 2¼

6⅛ 12¹⁄₁₆ 11⅜ 11¾ +

33¾ 33 33⅛ –

25⅝ 24⁹⁄₁₆ 25⅜ +

12 11⅝ 11⅞ +

16 10½ 10½ 10⅛ –

78 15⅞ 15¹³⁄₁₆ 15⅞ –

9¹⁄₁₆ 8¼ 8⅝ +

11¼ 10⅛

INVESTMENT DECISION MAKING IN DEFINED CONTRIBUTION PENSION PLANS

by Alistair Byrne, CFA

LEARNING OUTCOMES

The candidate should be able to:	Mastery
a. explain how limited participant knowledge and bounds to rationality, self-control, and self-interest may lead defined-contribution (DC) plan participants to construct inefficient investment portfolios;	☐
b. evaluate the impact of status quo bias, myopic loss aversion, $1/n$ diversification, and the endorsement effect on DC plan participants' investment decisions and the risk profile of their investment plans;	☐
c. discuss the factors that may contribute to DC plan participants holding "excess" amounts of their own company's stock in their plan.	☐

INTRODUCTION 1

" **C**onsumers face two challenges: making good decisions and sticking to them. Economists have adopted optimistic assumptions on both counts. The consumers in mainstream economic models are assumed to be both exceptionally good decision makers and to be able to carry out their plans. These economic assumptions are dubious, particularly in regards to saving for retirement."[1]

Most occupational pension plans are either of a defined benefit (DB) or defined contribution (DC) nature. In a DB plan, an employee who qualifies for the

Alistair Byrne is a lecturer at the University of Strathclyde and a consultant to pension funds and pension product providers. Prior to taking up these roles in September 2003, he spent ten years at AEGON Asset Management in a number of positions including Head of Investment Strategy and Head of Equity Research. He has published research in a variety of academic and professional journals.

[1] Laibson, D., Repetto, A. and Tobacman, J. (1998) 'Self-Control and Saving for Retirement', *Brookings Papers on Economic Activity*, 1998:1.

pension will receive an income flow from the employer-sponsored pension scheme from retirement until death. The annual benefit is typically a proportion of the employee's final, or average, salary, with the proportion depending on length of tenure in the pension scheme. In contrast, in a DC scheme contributions are paid into the plan and the employee can usually choose from a range of investment options. The funds, with accumulated investment returns, are then available to provide a retirement income, either directly or by purchasing an annuity.

In recent years there has been a significant shift in retirement income provision in the U.S. from the situation where employers offer these DB promises[2] to individuals, to a self-directed DC basis where the individual bears the risk that the pension contributions—and the investment returns they earn—will be sufficient to fund a comfortable retirement.[3] Surveys by the National Association of Pension Funds (NAPF) show similar trends in place in the U.K.[4]

The growing literature of "behavioral economics"[5] raises interesting questions about whether most individuals are well placed to make the strategic investment decisions this greater responsibility entails. There is evidence individual investors do not always make good decisions. For example, Barber and Odean document a variety of behavioral traits displayed by investors with retail brokerage accounts, including excessive trading and a tendency to sell winning stocks too early, which tend to depress the returns they enjoy.[6] In terms of pensions, a Watson Wyatt study found the returns of pension plans with employee-directed investments lagged professionally managed funds by some 2 percent per year on average.[7] Bodie argues risk is being transferred "to those least able to manage it."[8]

This reading provides a summary of the main U.S. literature on individual investment decision making in DC pension plans, including proposals that have been made for using the insights of behavioral economics to improve pension

---

[2] The extent to which the employee is likely to receive the promised benefits will depend on the funding level of the pension scheme, the solvency of the employer, and the existence of any external guarantees. In the U.S. the Pension Benefit Guarantee Corporation provides support in the case of insolvency and in the U.K. the 2004 Pensions Bill contains provisions for the inception of a similar Pensions Protection Fund.

[3] See for example Friedberg, L. and Owyang, M. (2002) 'Not Your Father's Pension: The Rise of 401(k) and Other Defined Contribution Plans', *Federal Reserve Bank of St Louis Review*, Vol. 84, No. 1, pp. 23–34. U.S. DC pensions are often known as '401(k)' plans after the relevant section of the tax code.

[4] NAPF (2003) 'Pension Scheme Changes—A Snapshot', National Association of Pension Funds, London.

[5] See for example, Mullainathan, S. and Thaler, R. (2000) 'Behavioural Economics', NBER Working Paper 7948, National Bureau of Economic Research, Cambridge MA.

[6] Barber, B. and Odean, T. (1999) 'The Courage of Misguided Convictions', *Financial Analysts Journal*, Vol. 55, No. 6, pp. 41–55.

[7] Watson Wyatt (2001) 'Rethinking the 401(k) Market', *Global Investment Review*, 2001 Issue; Watson Wyatt Worldwide.

[8] Bodie, Z. (2003) 'Thoughts on the Future: Lifecycle Investing in Theory and Practice', *Financial Analysts Journal*, Jan/Feb, pp. 24–29.

plan design. The trend towards DC pensions is also evident in the U.K., but relatively little research has been done looking at the situation here in the light of the U.S. research. This reading also provides a brief overview of the available U.K. evidence against the background of the Department of Work and Pensions' recent proposals for promoting "informed choice" in retirement saving.[9]

PARTICIPANT KNOWLEDGE, CONFIDENCE, AND INVESTMENT CHOICE

2

Saving for retirement is a complex task and the stakes—ensuring an adequate income in retirement—are high. The move from DB to DC pensions puts much more responsibility into the hands of the individual participants, particularly in terms of how much to save and how to invest the resulting funds. This does not appear to be something that comes easily to most people. The 2003 U.S. Retirement Confidence Survey reports only 37 percent of respondents had tried to calculate how much money they should save for retirement.[10] Of those reporting they had tried to calculate their retirement income needs, 36 percent could not provide the results of the calculation and 3 percent stated they had been unable to do it.

The John Hancock insurance company has conducted a regular survey of the attitudes and knowledge of investors in DC pension plans over the past ten years.[11] Only 20 percent of the respondents to the 2002 survey regarded themselves as knowledgeable investors, while a further 38 percent regarded stated they were "somewhat knowledgeable." Forty-two percent said they had little or no investment knowledge. While plan participants on average claimed to be "somewhat familiar" with the main asset types typically available in retirement plans, there is evidence this claim is overstated. For example, 45 percent of respondents correctly identified that money market funds contain short-term investments, but 40 percent thought (or also thought) they contained stocks. Only 8 percent of respondents correctly identified that the funds only contain short-term investments. Less than one participant in five was able to identify the correct relationship between long-term interest rates and bond fund returns.

The survey also asked plan participants for their expectations of future returns. The results—shown in Table 1—look optimistic in the current environment of low inflation and low interest rates.

Survey evidence that many individuals struggle to understand and deal with the choices they face when saving for retirement sits readily with the field of behavioral economics, which suggests that most individuals do not make decisions in the rational, well-informed and unbiased manner assumed by standard economic theory. Mullainathan and Thaler argue the notion that individuals are calculating, unemotional maximizers (*homo economicus*) is incorrect and that more accurate descriptions of actual behavior can yield better predictions of economic systems.[5] They claim there are "bounds" to human rationality, self-control and self-interest.

---

[9] DWP (2004) 'Simplicity, Security and Choice: Informed Choices for Working and Saving' Cm 6111, Department for Work and Pensions, London.

[10] EBRI (2003) '2003 Retirement Confidence Survey Summary of Findings', Employee Benefit Research Institute, Washington DC, September 2003.

[11] Hancock, J. (2003) 'Eighth Defined Contribution Plan Survey', John Hancock Financial Services, Boston MA.

TABLE 1   401(k) Participant Return Expectations

	Five-Year Annual Return %	20-Year Annual Return %
Stocks	10.9	15.8
Bonds	8.1	10.3
Money market	7.7	9.8
Stable value	7.6	9.9

Source: John Hancock 2003.

Simon coined the term "bounded rationality" to describe human problem solving abilities.[12] Limits on intelligence and time mean individuals cannot be expected to solve problems optimally. Experimental evidence suggests most people use rules of thumb (or "heuristics") to cope with the limits of their abilities and these heuristics can—in certain contexts—lead to systematic errors in decision making.[13] Mullainathan and Thaler also argue many individuals have "bounded self control." Standard theory assumes once someone has worked out the optimal choice they will follow through with that course of action. Behavioral economics suggests even when the "right thing to do" is apparent, people may fail to do it for reasons of self-control—most of us at some point have eaten, drank or spent too much, and exercised, saved and worked too little. Finally, most individuals are "boundedly selfish"—and fail to pursue their own self-interest to the extent normally assumed of *homo economicus*.

These behavioral limitations have implications for the study of economic decision making and are relevant to the question of saving for retirement. Mitchell and Utkus note "being good at retirement saving" requires accurate estimates of uncertain quantities such as lifetime earnings, asset returns, tax rates, health status and longevity.[14] Casual inspection of models designed to help with this problem such as those proposed by Blake et al[15] and Hibbert and Mowbray[16] shows the calculations are far from trivial and many of the parameters highly uncertain. As Bodie puts it:

> No one would imagine that you or I could perform surgery to remove our own appendix after reading an explanation in a brochure published by a surgical equipment company. Yet, we seem to expect people to choose an appropriate mix of stocks, bonds and cash after reading a brochure published by an investment company. Some people are likely to make serious mistakes.[8]

---

[12] Simon, H. (1995) 'A Behavioural Model of Rational Choice', *Quarterly Journal of Economics,* Vol. 69, pp. 99–118.

[13] Kahneman, D. and Tversky, A. (1974) 'Judgement Under Uncertainty: Heuristics and Biases', *Science,* Vol. 185, pp. 1124–31.

[14] Mitchell, O. and Utkus, S. (2003) 'Lessons From Behavioural Finance for Retirement Plan Design', Pensions Research Council Working Paper 2003–6, University of Pennsylvania.

[15] Blake, D., Cairns, A. and Dowd, K. (2001) 'Pensionmetrics: Stochastic Pension Plan Design and Value at Risk During the Accumulation Phase', *Insurance, Mathematics and Economics,* Vol. 29, pp. 187–215.

[16] Hibbert, J. and Mowbray, P. (2002) 'Understanding Investment Policy Choices for Individual Pension Plans', *Pensions,* Vol. 8, No. 1, pp. 41–62.

Bernartzi and Thaler cite a 1999 Hewitt survey showing that 401(k) plans on average offer 11 investment choices and question whether this expanded investment choice provides net benefits.[17] Their own research found that when investors were shown the range of likely retirement income consequences of their own portfolio and that of the median investor's portfolio, most expressed a preference for the median portfolio. They argue the results suggest investor autonomy is "not worth much" and that most investors do not have well-defined preferences.

Samuelson and Zeckhauser discuss what they call the "status quo bias" in decision making.[18] They note the standard rational choice model holds that only "preference-relevant" features should affect decisions, but real world choices often have influential labels attached to them, such as the notion of the "status quo"—i.e., the option to do nothing, or to endorse a previous choice. They find that despite an average tenure of 12 years, only 28 percent of participants in the 850,000-member TIAA/CREF retirement scheme had ever changed their asset allocation. An important aspect of these findings is that new entrants to the plan tended to choose a somewhat different asset allocation to similar-aged incumbents who had "grown up" within the scheme. Samuelson and Zeckhauser attribute the status quo bias to a number of well-documented behavioral traits including framing, loss aversion, anchoring, and regret avoidance.

The trend towards DC rather than DB pension provision gives individual employees increased choice in how they save for retirement. The conventional view in economics is that this increased choice is likely to enhance welfare. However, this is arguable if lack of interest or knowledge raises the risk of a significant number of investors making costly mistakes. The following section discusses some of the retirement planning "mistakes" that have been documented in the U.S.

PORTFOLIO DIVERSIFICATION AND INVESTOR PERCEPTIONS OF RISK

There is significant evidence that investors in DC pension plans often display attitudes to risk and portfolio construction that are at odds with accepted investment principles. For example, Bernartzi and Thaler document that DC pension plan investors seem to suffer from "myopic loss aversion," seeking to avoid short-term losses, despite the long time horizon usually involved in planning for retirement.[19] Plan participants shown annual return data for equity and bond funds are found to adopt much more conservative—i.e., low equity—asset allocations than other participants shown 30-year compound returns. The 30-year data appear to draw attention to the low probability of making a loss over that period—a relevant period for retirement planning for many people—while the annual data highlight the prospect of short-term loss, even though short-term volatility should not matter much to these investors.

There is also evidence that the balance of funds on offer unduly influences individuals' choice of asset allocation in DC plans. Bernartzi and Thaler find that where there is a high ratio of equity funds relative to bond funds, plan participants

[17] Bernartzi, S. and Thaler, R. (2002) 'How Much is Investor Autonomy Worth?', *Journal of Finance*, Vol. 57, No. 4, pp. 1593–1616.

[18] Samuelson, W. and Zeckhauser, R. (1988) 'Status Quo Bias in Decision Making', *Journal of Risk and Uncertainty*, Vol. 1, pp. 7–59.

[19] Bernartzi, S. and Thaler, R. (1999) 'Risk Aversion or Myopia? Choices in Repeated Gambles and Retirement Investments', *Management Science*, Vol. 45, No. 3, pp. 364–381.

tend to have higher than average allocations to equities.[20] In an experimental setting they also find support for the existence of a "$1/n$ diversification heuristic" which leads participants to split their contributions equally amongst the n funds on offer, with little regard to the underlying asset composition of the funds.

One possible explanation for the shift in asset allocation as fund choice changes is that employees take the range on offer as implicit guidance from the employer as to the appropriate asset allocation strategy—a so-called "endorsement effect." However, there is little evidence most employers have this outcome in mind when structuring the fund offering. Watson Wyatt argue that in expanding investment choice, many sponsors are reacting to a "vocal minority" demanding the option of investment in "hot" specialist areas, and that these more "speculative" funds have no place in a DC plan's basic investment structure.[7] Iyengar et al provide evidence of another possible cost of offering 401(k) investors "too much choice."[21] They show there is a negative relationship between the level of employee participation in the pension plan and the number of funds on offer, suggesting complexity can dissuade employees from joining.

Perhaps one of the most worrying aspects of the U.S. DC market is the high level of investment in own company stock amongst employees in larger plans. Portfolio theory teaches the benefits of diversification, but a significant number of employees have plans with unduly high concentrations in a single stock—that of their employer. Bernartzi notes about a third of assets in large DC retirement savings plans—and about a quarter of employees' discretionary contributions—are invested in company stock.[22] He describes the strategy as "dubious," particularly because the stock is correlated with the employees' labour income and future employment prospects. The tendency to invest in own company stock is found to be strongest where the past returns on that stock are high, but Bernartzi finds no evidence that the future returns of these "winner" stocks are strong enough to justify the high level of investment.

Employers' enthusiasm for company stock ownership in retirement plans may stem from a more general desire to promote shareholding amongst the workforce, believing this will raise productivity and morale and boost the value of the firm. However, this has to be balanced against potential detriments to the employees and U.S. law gives rather mixed messages on the desirability of "self-investment." The 1974 Employee Retirement Income Security Act (ERISA) sets a limit of 10 percent on the extent to which a plan can invest in the stock of the sponsoring employer. At the time of ERISA's development, however, DB plans were the prominent form of retirement provision and Congress did not extend the provisions of the act to DC plans, allowing company stock allocations in DC plans to continue growing. Subsequent attempts to extend the provisions on company stock to DC plans have run into opposition from employers. Current legislation prevents employers from compelling workers to invest more than 10 percent of their own contributions in company stock, but does not prohibit employees from choosing to do so.[23]

[20] Bernartzi, S. and Thaler, R. (2001) 'Naïve Diversification Strategies in Defined Contribution Saving Plans', *American Economic Review*, Vol. 91, pp. 7–98.

[21] Iyengar, S., Jiang, W. and Huberman, G. (2003) 'How Much Choice is Too Much: Contributions to 401(k) Retirement Plans', Pensions Research Council Working Paper 2003–10, University of Pennsylvania.

[22] Bernartzi, S. (2001) 'Excessive Extrapolation and the Allocation of 401(k) Accounts to Company Stock', *Journal of Finance*, Vol. 56, No. 5, pp. 1747–1764.

[23] Mitchell, O. and Utkus, S. (2002) 'Company Stock and Retirement Plan Diversification', Pensions Research Council Working Paper 2002–4, University of Pennsylvania.

Holden and VanDerhei show the proportion of overall 401(k) assets invested in company stock at the end of 2002 was 16 percent.[24] Some 35 percent of participants in plans that offered company stock had more than 30 percent of their assets invested in that option, and 23 percent had over 50 percent of their assets invested in company stock. VanDerhei[25] notes that the percentages invested in company stock are partly explained by the requirement in some schemes for employer contributions to be invested in company stock, but Bernartzi,[22] Liang and Weisbenner,[26] and Mitchell and Utkus[23] all find significant numbers of employees voluntarily holding high proportions of company stock in their 401(k) accounts.

It appears that employees do not view their employer's stock as risky. The John Hancock survey shows that DC plan participants perceive company stock to be less risky than diversified stock funds.[11] On a risk scale of 1–5, where 5 is "very high risk," company stock was rated 3.1 compared to 3.6 for diversified stock funds. This result has been remarkably consistent through time, based on the evidence of previous surveys. Bernartzi finds that only 16 percent of plan participants realise that company stock is riskier than the overall stock market.[22]

The collapse of Enron provides a high-profile example of the possible pitfalls of investing retirement plan assets in your employer's stock. Almost 58 percent of the employees' 401(k) assets were invested in Enron stock, which subsequently lost almost all of its value as the company was put into bankruptcy. A survey by VanDerhei[25] found 74 percent of respondents thought most employees were aware of what had happened at Enron, but 43 percent did not think the Enron example was relevant to their own situation. Only about a quarter of respondents thought the Enron example had caused employees to review their asset allocation or to question the right of employers to offer company stock as an investment option.

It may be that investors prefer to "invest in the familiar" while ignoring the principles of portfolio theory. Huberman finds that the shareholders of U.S. regional telephone companies tend to live in the area served by the company and argues a similar effect is at play when investors display "home country bias" in their asset allocation and when employees invest large amounts in their employer's stock.[27] Bernartzi argues the observed tendency to invest more employee contributions in company stock where employer contributions must be invested in company stock is consistent with an "endorsement effect" whereby employees take the allocation of the employer's contributions as an implicit form of investment advice.[22]

The studies discussed above provide significant evidence that the investment strategies employed in self-directed retirement plans are often at odds with standard investment theory and suggest much of this can be explained by well-documented behavioral biases. While most of the evidence is based on experimental work, survey data, or relatively small samples, the consistency of the findings provides power in excess of the reliability of any single study. The question of what can be done to mitigate any harmful effects of these biases is discussed below.

---

[24] Holden, S. and VanDerhei, J. (2003) '401(k) Plan Asset Allocation, Account Balances, and Loan Activity in 2002', *EBRI Issue Brief*, Vol. 261, September 2003, Employee Benefit Research Institute, Washington DC.

[25] VanDerhei, J. (2002) 'Company Stock in 401(k) Plans: Results of a Survey of ISCEBS Members', EBRI Special Report, Employee Benefits Research Institute, Washington DC.

[26] Liang, N. and Weisbenner, S. (2002) 'Investor Behaviour and the Purchase of Company Stock in 401(k) Plans—The Importance of Plan Design', Working Paper—University of Illinois.

[27] Huberman, G. (2001) 'Familiarity Breeds Investment', *Review of Financial Studies*, Vol. 14, No. 3, pp. 659–680.

4   PARTICIPANT EDUCATION AND PENSION SCHEME DESIGN

The obvious solution to dealing with significant behavioral barriers to the effective use of DC plans for retirement provision is to offer some form of education to participants. Indeed, this already takes place with the Employee Benefit Research Institute (EBRI) noting that nearly half of U.S. workers with an employment-related pension plan have been provided with educational material or seminars about retirement planning and saving.[10] However, education will only work if it has an impact on behavior, meaning raising issues of self-control need to be considered as well as issues of understanding.

MacFarland et al note that while about half of the U.S. adult population have the attitudinal characteristics to be "planners" and take an active interest in providing for their own retirement, over a third are "avoiders" who are either intimidated by financial matters or simply uninterested.[28] This has important implications for the provision of education on retirement planning, suggesting less attention can be given to the planners who will likely seek out the information they require. In order to have an impact on avoiders, investment education materials need to be short and simple, and emphasise present day benefits—such as employer contributions and tax deductions—rather than long-term goals. Equally, the avoider group is more likely to respond to explicit and direct advice than to conceptual financial education.

However, there are limits to what education can achieve if a significant portion of the population is apathetic to the idea of planning for retirement. Choi et al note that after attending pension seminars many participants say they plan to use the information to make changes to their pension arrangements, but very few actually do.[29] In the cases the authors study, all of the employees who were not already members of the pension plan and who attended education seminars stated they intended to join the plan, but only 14 percent of them actually did so. EBRI data show only 18 percent of those receiving educational material about their pension reported some change in their behavior as a result.[10] These findings suggest scheme design may also need to be used to ensure participants in DC pensions adopt the savings rates and investment strategies most likely to ensure adequate income in retirement.

Thaler and Benartzi argue that employees who fail to join their employer's pension plan, or who contribute at very low levels, appear to be saving less than would be predicted by rational life-cycle theories.[30] They suggest at least some of these low-saving households can be regarded as making a mistake and would benefit from help to increase their saving rate. To the extent these mistakes stem from consistent behavioral biases, it may be possible to use knowledge of these biases to improve the design of pension schemes and mitigate the effects of the biases.

The typical 401(k) plan requires an active decision to enrol and Choi et al report that a move to automatic enrolment tends to increase participation

---

[28] MacFarland, D., Marconi, C. and Utkus, S. (2003) 'Money Attitudes and Retirement Plan Design: One Size Does Not Fit All', Pensions Research Council Working Paper 2003–11, University of Pennsylvania.

[29] Choi, J., Laibson, D., Madrian, B. and Metrick, A. (2002) 'Defined Contribution Pensions: Plan Rules, Participant Decisions, and the Path of Least Resistance', in Poterba, J. (ed) 'Tax Policy and the Economy', Vol. 16, MIT Press, Cambridge MA.

[30] Thaler, R. and Benartzi, S. (2004) 'Save More Tomorrow: Using Behavioural Economics to Increase Employee Saving', *Journal of Political Economy*, Vol. 112, No. 1, pp. 164–186. Save More Tomorrow is a registered trademark.

rates.[31] Very few participants subsequently decide to opt out of the plan, suggesting the employees do not object to saving for retirement, but left to their own devices tend to delay taking action. The potential downside of automatic enrolment is that many of those who are enrolled stick with the low default contribution rate and cautious default asset allocation. Choi et al note that 76 percent of plans with automatic enrolment have a default contribution rate of 2 or 3 percent and 66 percent have a stable value fund as the default investment option.[32] They show that under automatic enrolment 65 to 87 percent of new employees in the companies studied adopt the default fund and the default contribution rate. These percentages decline with tenure, but remain at about 45 percent after three years of employment. The authors question whether the net effect of automatic enrolment makes employees better off, given that earlier participation may be offset by lower contribution rates and more conservative investment choices. Employers may be reluctant to tackle this problem by offering riskier default funds, given the danger of lawsuits if a fund sustains significant losses. Equally, a move to higher default contribution rates may simply cause more employees to opt out of the scheme.

Thaler and Benartzi propose a prescriptive savings plan called "Save More Tomorrow"—or "SMarT"— where employees commit in advance to allocate a portion of future salary rises towards retirement saving.[30] Laibson et al discuss the "hyperbolic discount rates" that can explain why future commitments are more effective than trying to secure immediate change.[1] They note a systematic conflict between long-term and short-term preferences. When rewards are far away in time, most individuals are relatively patient, for example preferring two apples in 101 days to one apple in 100 days. However, moving the reward closer to the present time produces a significant reversal in preferences: one apple today is generally preferred to two apples tomorrow. This structure of discount rates can explain why employees are willing to make future commitments to save more even when they refuse immediate action. Furthermore, the status quo bias identified by Samuelson and Zeckhauser means once the initial commitment is made, few people make the effort to change it.[18]

Thaler and Benartzi's implementation of the SMarT plan at a mid-sized manufacturing firm showed considerable success. The company's employees were offered the chance to see an investment consultant and discuss their retirement provision and most agreed to do so. In many cases the employees were told their current savings rate was inadequate, but only 28 percent were willing to accept the advice and make an immediate increase in contributions. The rest of the participants were offered the chance to join the "SMarT" plan, which would increase their saving rate by 3 percent a year starting from their next pay rise. Of the participants who were unwilling to accept the contribution rate advice of the investment consultant, 78 percent agreed to join SMarT, with 80 percent of these participants remaining in the plan through four pay rises. The average savings rate for these participants rose from 3.5 to 13.6 percent over the course of 40 months.

In addition to evidence that scheme design can affect pension plan participation and contribution rates, the evidence reviewed in Section 3 suggests plan design can have a significant impact on investment choice. Whether investors

---

[31] Choi, J., Laibson, D., Madrian, B. and Metrick, A. (2002) 'Defined Contribution Pensions: Plan Rules, Participant Decisions, and the Path of Least Resistance', in Poterba, J. (ed) 'Tax Policy and the Economy', Vol. 16, MIT Press Cambridge MA. The IRS has only endorsed this 'negative election' approach since 1998 according to EBRI 2003.

[32] Choi, J., Laibson, D., Madrian, B. and Metrick, A. (2003) 'For Better or Worse: Default Effects and 401(k) Savings Behaviour', in Wise, D. (ed) 'Perspectives on the Economics of Aging', University of Chicago Press, Chicago IL.

are using simple $1/n$ heuristics to allocate between funds, or taking implicit guidance from the range of funds on offer, the simple process of the employer choosing the range of funds can significantly influence the asset allocation chosen by many plan participants. Employers with paternalistic instincts may choose to structure their pension plan to maximise the chances of employees choosing what the employer regards as the most appropriate options.[33] The main issues relate to the arrangements for joining the plan (opt-in or opt-out), default contribution rates, default fund options and the range and nature of the fund choice on offer. There are also issues about the nature of the information and advice that is provided to employees.

5   U.K. COMPARISONS

The U.K., like the U.S., is seeing a move from employer provision of DB pensions to a situation where DC is more common. Different types of DC pension are available in the U.K., all of which are relevant to consideration of increased individual responsibility for investment choice.[34] Occupational money purchase (OMP) schemes are the main form of DC scheme where the employer provides sponsorship. Alternatively, an employer may offer a group personal pension (GPP), which is essentially a collection of individual pensions grouped together to provide savings on marketing and administration costs. Finally, a stakeholder pension is a relatively new, low-cost version of a personal pension scheme, governed by detailed rules, including a requirement that total management charges do not exceed 1 percent per annum.[35] It is worth noting that in the case of an OMP scheme, the trustees have responsibility for the investment choice offered within the plan—and are charged with acting in members' best interests—while the choice in a GPP or stakeholder plan will be determined by the product provider (an insurance company) in consultation with the employer.[36]

An NAPF survey[37] shows DC has become the most common form of occupational pension provision in the private sector with 62 percent of employers offering money purchase, 14 percent offering GPP and 24 percent stakeholder. This compares to 46 percent of companies that have DB schemes. The survey shows that 41 percent of companies have closed their DB pension scheme to new members. For new employees, 51 percent of employers offer money purchase schemes, while 18 percent offer stakeholder, and 13 percent GPP. Only 19 percent offer a final salary scheme and 2 percent offer no pension provision. It is worth noting that final salary schemes still tend to be the more common at larger employers, so the split by number of employees rather than number of schemes is less dramatic. The trend towards DC schemes may in part be explained by the proposed implementation of Financial Reporting Standard (FRS) 17 accounting

---

[33] Thaler, R. and Sunstein, C. (2003) 'Libertarian Paternalism', *American Economic Review*, Vol. 93, No. 2, pp. 175–179.

[34] Blake, D. (2003) 'The UK Pension System: Key Issues', *Pensions*, Vol. 8, No. 4, pp. 330–375. Provides a detailed review of the arrangements that apply to the different types of arrangements.

[35] Employers with more than five employees are now required to make available a stakeholder pension to their employees if they do not offer any other form of retirement provision. They are not, however, required to make any contributions to the plan and employees do not need to join. The government has recently announced plans to raise the price cap to 1.5 percent starting from April 2005.

[36] Myners, P. (2001) 'Institutional Investment in the United Kingdom: A Review', HM Treasury, London.

[37] NAPF (2003) 'Pension Scheme Changes—A Snapshot', National Association of Pension Funds, London.

standard—86 percent of respondents to the NAPF 2002 survey thought the standard made offering a DB pension scheme less attractive to employers.[38]

There is little to suggest U.K. employees are much better placed to manage their DC retirement investments than their counterparts in the U.S. The Office of Fair Trading's Inquiry into Pensions[39] commissioned a large-scale survey of consumer attitudes to pensions. The changing landscape for pensions was evident with 72 percent of respondents agreeing or strongly agreeing with the statement, "the responsibility for ensuring that my income in retirement is adequate for the lifestyle I wish to live is mainly mine." However, the challenge of this responsibility is evident in that half of the respondents agreed or strongly agreed that "I have found all the information I have seen, and the advice I have received, on pensions very confusing." Only 44 percent of respondents had sought advice about retirement planning, mostly from financial services firms and most commonly by those who had personal rather than occupational pensions.

More recent research by the Association of British Insurers[40] provides little cause for comfort—44 percent of the population say they understand pensions "very well" or "fairly well," while 56 percent understand them "fairly badly" or "very badly." Some 66 percent have never tried to calculate how much they need to save to fund a comfortable retirement. A total of 61 percent of respondents were either "not particularly" or "not at all" confident that they would have enough money to live comfortably in retirement.

The recent weakness in the stock market—together with limited investment knowledge—appears to have coloured views on the appropriate assets for retirement savings. Sixty-six percent of respondents state that property is the best long-term investment. Only 10 percent favoured equities, less than the 14 percent who thought a savings account was best. It is not clear whether the preference for property reflects use of property as a portfolio asset or whether it reflects an expectation of drawing income from the equity value of the respondents' own homes. A recent report from the Pensions Policy Institute[41] highlights potential problems with the latter approach, including the relatively limited proportion of the accumulated capital that can be accessed through equity release schemes.

While high levels of investment in own company stock are a significant feature of large U.S. DC plans, this issue has little relevance in the context of U.K. pensions. The 1990 Social Security Act placed a 5 percent limit on "self investment" by pension funds and unlike the U.S. these rules apply to DC as well as DB pensions.[42] Investment consultants[43] note they have encountered few examples of companies offering their own stock as an option in U.K. DC plans. It remains to be seen whether U.K. plan participants would be interested in this option if it was available or be prepared to use it to the extent evident in the U.S.

The 2001 NAPF survey[44] gives a good overview of the investment choice available in occupational DC plans in the U.K. showing that 41 percent of

[38] NAPF (2002) 'Twenty-eighth Annual Survey of Occupational Pension Funds 2002', National Association of Pension Funds, London.

[39] Office of Fair Trading (1997) 'Report of the Director General's Inquiry into Pensions', Office of Fair Trading, London.

[40] Association of British Assurers (2003) 'The State of the Nation's Savings', Association of British Insurers, London.

[41] PPI (2004) 'Property or pensions?' Discussion Paper, Pensions Policy Institute, London.

[42] Blake, D. (1995) 'Pension Schemes and Pension Funds in the United Kingdom', Clarendon Press, Oxford.

[43] In private correspondence.

[44] NAPF (2001) 'Twenty-seventh Annual Survey of Occupational Pension Funds 2001', National Association of Pension Funds, London.

schemes offer one to three investment options, while 38 percent offer between four and ten options, and 21 percent offer more than ten options. Some 70 percent of schemes have a default option, of which 50 percent are passively managed and 71 percent are lifestyle-type funds with age dependent asset allocation. While it does not appear the investment choice offered by U.K. DC plans is as wide as that offered in the U.S., many schemes offer enough choice to cause potential difficulties to members lacking in investment knowledge. On the other hand, a Watson Wyatt study cited in the Myners Report[36] shows 23 percent of plans only offer one fund and it is possible to argue this might be restricting choice too much, with the single fund unlikely to meet the needs of different groups of employees.

One of the most significant examinations of pension provision in the U.K. in recent years came in the form of the HM Treasury-sponsored review of institutional investment by Paul Myners.[36] The review dwells mostly on the issues faced by trustees of DB pension schemes, but also identifies issues relevant to the trustees of occupational DC schemes. It notes it is unclear how trustees should decide which and how many investment options to offer to members. If too few choices are offered members could argue that investment choice has been restricted, but more options may make the choice too complex and thus not in the members' best interests. Myners notes the danger trustees will fall back on standard industry practice in terms of the types of funds and defaults offered. In particular, he argues this will mean continued use of balanced managed funds where the asset allocation is set on the basis of an industry consensus which may not be consistent with the strategic asset allocation requirements of any particular group of employees.

Myners outlines a set of principles he thinks the trustees of DC pension schemes should follow. In particular, he argues that trustees should have sufficient investment knowledge for effective decision making and that the funds offered to members should have clear investment objectives and be chosen to take members' strategic asset allocation requirements into account. He also argues there should be a wide enough choice to satisfy the risk/return combinations appropriate for most members.

In a similar vein, Altmann suggests the U.K. could benefit from introducing measures based on U.S. "safe harbor" guidelines, which specify schemes must offer a minimum of three investment choices, that the investment choices must allow for creation of an appropriate, diversified portfolio, that members must be able to change their investment choices, and that they must receive good information upon which to base their decisions.[45]

Richards notes that in most cases literature provided to DC plan members has been supplied by insurance companies, investment firms or actuaries as the trustees are concerned not to breach the restrictions under the Financial Services and Markets Act 2000 on them giving investment advice or issuing investment advertisements.[46] There is obviously a need for good information for members to base their decisions on, but a key group with an interest and potential to provide this—the trustees—is hampered by current financial services legislation.

Overall, it appears the growing use of DC pensions in the U.K. presents many of the same issues as in the U.S., particularly in relation to low levels of investment knowledge and interest. There is probably less of an issue with giving participants

---

[45] Altmann, R. (2001) 'Let's Get DC Right Before It's Too Late', *Journal of Pensions Management*, Vol. 7, No. 1, pp. 38–45.

[46] Richards, K. (2002) 'The Evolving Role of the Pension Fund Trustee', *Pensions*, Vol. 8, No. 1, pp. 17–31.

too much choice—although this may be the case for some schemes—and more risk that some schemes offer too little choice to take account of the differing needs of different sections of the workforce. The U.K. has no problem with inadequate diversification due to excessive investment in own company stock, but potentially faces a similar problem stemming from conviction that residential property provides the most attractive investment prospects. DC pensions in the U.K. have also been criticised for low levels of contributions and high charges, with questions raised about whether participants are aware of the effects of these factors.[34,47] Against this background it is encouraging to note the recently-published Department for Work and Pensions agenda for promoting informed choice in retirement saving.[9] The proposals call for enhanced financial education and the review of regulatory barriers to employers providing advice on retirement saving to their employees and suggest schemes consider automatic enrolment and future commitment devices along the lines of "save more tomorrow" to raise savings rates. This represents an encouraging step towards practical measures based on our knowledge of retirement saving behavior.

CONCLUSION   6

The trend shifting occupational pension provision from a DB to a DC basis looks well entrenched in both the U.S. and the U.K. There is nothing to suggest DC pensions are not an appropriate vehicle for providing employees with retirement income, but there remain significant questions about how to use them effectively. The results of the John Hancock survey[11]—amongst others—challenge the notion that individuals are well placed to manage their own retirement accounts and the limited U.K. evidence we have does not suggest a much better situation here. While any shortfall in retirement income under DC schemes will fall on the individual participants in the first instance, at the extreme it becomes a more general problem for the state, which will have to provide for retirees who lack adequate alternative sources of income.[45]

Improved financial education can benefit many DC plan participants, but intelligent plan design will also be required when many employees show little interest in financial matters and readily accept default options—taking the "path of least resistance." It is clear that employers are well placed to be able to improve both education and scheme design, but could probably receive more regulatory and tax incentives to encourage them to do so.[48]

It is not clear that current plan design in the U.K. and the U.S. reflects the behavioral economics findings discussed in this reading and there is scope for research on this issue. Some of the work that has been done in the U.S. reflects collaboration between academics and plan sponsors and consultants, raising the prospect that the insights from the research will find their way into concrete practical measures. In the U.K., the government's "informed choice" agenda raises a similar prospect. While this is at an early stage, it seems appropriate to end with a positive note acknowledging this movement towards providing employees with better support for their retirement saving decisions.

[47] Blake, D. (2000) 'Does it Matter What Type of Pension Scheme You Have?', *Economic Journal*, Vol. 110, pp. 46–81.

[48] Strattan, D. (2002) 'Designing Pension Solutions in the New Defined Contribution World', *Pensions*, Vol. 8, No. 2, pp. 162–166.

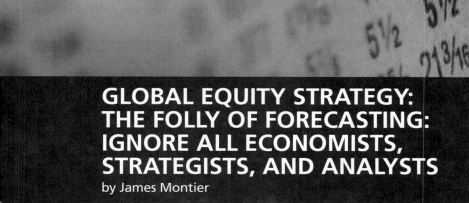

GLOBAL EQUITY STRATEGY: THE FOLLY OF FORECASTING: IGNORE ALL ECONOMISTS, STRATEGISTS, AND ANALYSTS

by James Montier

LEARNING OUTCOMES

The candidate should be able to:	Mastery
a. explain how the illusions of knowledge and control lead expert forecasters to be overconfident in their forecasting skills;	☐
b. explain the ego defense mechanisms that forecasters rely on as justification for inaccurate forecasts;	☐
c. explain why forecasts may continue to be used when previous forecasts have been inaccurate.	☐

INTRODUCTION

Both an enormous amount of evidence and anecdotal experience suggests that people are very bad at forecasting. This is often because we all tend to be massively overconfident. This begs two questions. Firstly, why do we persist in forecasting despite the appalling track record? And, more importantly, why do investors put forecasts at the heart of the investment process?

THE FOLLY OF FORECASTING   1

Those who have endured one of my behavioral finance presentations will have heard me rant and rave over the pointlessness of forecasting. I have finally got around to putting pen to paper on this subject.[1]

The 6th-century BC poet Lao Tzu observed, "Those who have knowledge don't predict. Those who predict don't have knowledge." Despite these age-old

---

[1] I was much inspired to write this after reading Nassim Taleb's recent paper, The Scandal of Prediction (2005). He renewed my vigor for this subject.

63

words of wisdom, our industry seems to eternally persist in basing the investment process around forecasts.

Before exploring the reasons for our dependency upon the irrelevant guess of the unknowable future, I had better buttress my case by showing just how bad the track record of forecasting actually is. The charts below set out the forecasting performance of so-called professionals. For the ease of data accessibility, all series below are taken from the Federal Reserve Bank of Philadelphia Livingston survey or the Survey of professional forecasters. However, the findings are not the result of a strange data set. I have used different data and found similar patterns exist across them all.

Figure 1 shows economists' attempts to forecast the rate of inflation as measured by the GDP deflator. Sadly it reveals a pattern that will become all too common in the next few charts. Economists are really very good at telling you what has just happened! They constantly seem to lag reality. Inflation forecasts appear to be largely a function of past inflation rates.

Our second category are the bond forecasters. Previously, we have analysed their behavior in depth (see *Global Equity Strategy,* 22 February 2005). Much like the economists above, their performance is found to be severely lacking. Not only are bond forecasters bad at guessing the *level* of the yield, they can't get the *direction* of yield changes right either. Figure 2 shows that when yields were forecast to rise, they actually fell 55% of the time!

Just in case you think this is just a case of an equity man picking on debt, Figure 3 shows the feeble forecasting abilities of equity strategists. They too seem to think that the recent past is best extrapolated into the future, and hence end up lagging reality. Acknowledgement of our own limitations is one of the reasons why we don't even attempt to produce index forecasts.

Our last category of truly inept seers are the analysts. Their inability is perhaps the most worrying, as their forecasts are possibly taken far more seriously than the average macro forecast.

The chart overleaf in Figure 4 (indicated by a dotted line) is constructed by removing the linear time trend from both the operating earnings series for the S&P 500 and the analyst forecasts of those same earnings. I have simply plotted

FIGURE 1   U.S. GDP Deflator and Forecasts

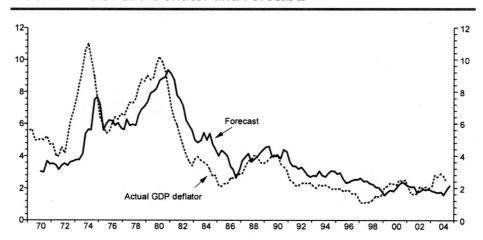

Source: DrKW Macro research.

FIGURE 2 Consensus One Year Ahead Bond Yield Forecasts and Reality (%)

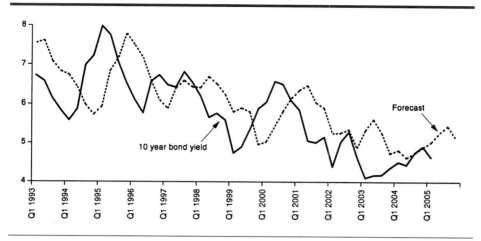

Source: DrKW Macro research.

Predicted vs. Actual Yield Movement (Four Quarters Ahead, 1992–2004)

		% of Occurrences	Actual	
			Up	Down
Predicted	Up		45	55
	Down		22	78

Source: DrKW Macro research.

FIGURE 3 S&P 500 and Forecasts

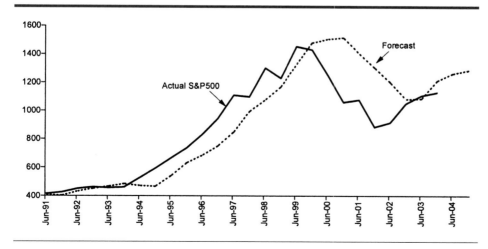

Source: DrKW Macro research.

FIGURE 4   Analysts Lag Reality (Operating Earnings and Forecasts, Deviations from Trend, $/Sh)

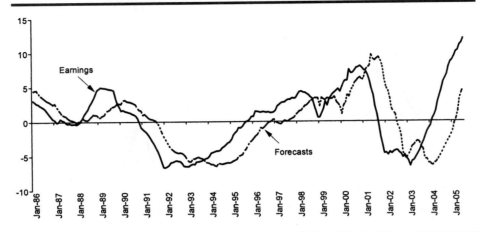

Source: DrKW Macro research.

the deviations from trend in the chart overleaf. It clearly shows that just like the other forecasters examined here, analysts are terribly good at telling us what has just happened but of little use in telling us what is going to happen in the future.

Overconfidence as a Driver of Poor Forecasting

The two most common biases that psychologists have documented are over-optimism and overconfidence. Technically speaking overconfidence refers to a situation where people are surprised more often than they expect to be. Statistically we describe such individuals as "not well calibrated." What we really mean by that is if we ask people for a forecast and then ask them for the 98% confidence intervals, so that the true answer should lie outside of the bounds just 2% of the time, it tends to lie outside of the bounds 30–40% of the time! People are simply far too sure about their ability to predict.

Russo and Schoemaker[2] have devised a simple test. Before you go any further try and answer the questions in Table 1 and see how you do.

The answers can be found at the bottom of this page.[3] If you are properly calibrated only one of the answers to the above questions should lie outside of the limits you wrote down. When I took the test, two of my answers were outside of the bounds so I, like everyone else, am overconfident. However, compared to Russo and Schoemaker's sample of over 1000 participants I didn't do too badly. Less than 1% got nine or more answers correct, with most respondents missing four to seven items!

One key finding in the literature on overconfidence is that experts are even more overconfident than lay people. Experts do know more than lay people, but sadly this extra knowledge seems to trigger even higher levels of overconfidence.

---

[2] Russo and Schoemaker (1989) Decision traps: Ten barriers to brilliant decision making and how to overcome them, Simon & Schuster.

[3] 39 years, 4187 miles, 13 countries, 39 books, 2160 miles, 390,000 pounds, 1756, 645 days, 5959 miles, 36,198 feet.

TABLE 1 Self-Test of Overconfidence	90% Confidence Range	
	Low	**High**
Martin Luther King's age at death		
Length of the Nile River		
Number of countries that are members of OPEC		
Number of books in the Old Testament		
Diameter of the moon in miles		
Weight of an empty Boeing 747 in pounds		
Year in which Wolfgang Amadeus Mozart was born		
Gestation period (in days) of an Asian elephant		
Air distance from London to Tokyo		
Deepest (known) point in the ocean (in feet)		

Source: Russo and Schoemaker.

Overconfidence and Experts

Figure 5 shows the calibration curves for two groups of experts—weathermen and doctors. Each group is given information relative to their own discipline, so weathermen are given weather patterns and asked to predict the weather, doctors are given case notes and asked to diagnose the patient.

We are measuring predicted probability (confidence) against actual probability. So the 45° line is perfect statistical calibration. Weather forecasters actually do remarkably well. In contrast, doctors are a terrifying bunch of people. When they were 90% sure they were correct, they were actually right less than 15% of the time!

FIGURE 5   Calibration of Weathermen and Doctors

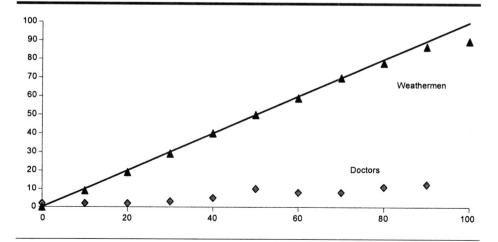

Source: Plous, *The Psychology of Judgement and Decision-Making* (1991).

So why the difference in the performance between these two groups? It largely appears to relate to the illusion of knowledge (defined as a situation where we think we know more than everyone else). Weathermen get rapid undeniable evidence on their abilities as forecasters; all you have to do is look out of the window to see if they managed to get it right or not. Doctors, in contrast, often lack feedback so find it far harder to know when they have been right or wrong.

It might be tempting to think of our industry as akin to weathermen. If we make decisions or forecasts, we should be able to see in the fairly near term if they were correct or not. However, recent evidence suggests that most investors are more akin to doctors than weathermen, at least in terms of the scale of their overconfidence.

Figures 6 and 7 are based on a recent study by Torngren and Montgomery.[4] Participants were asked to select the stock they thought would outperform each month from a pair of stocks. All the stocks were well known blue chip names, and players were given the name, industry and prior 12 months' performance for each stock. Both laypeople (undergrads in psychology) and professional investors (portfolio managers, analysts and brokers) took part in the study.

Overall, the students were around 59% confident in their stock picking abilities. However, the professionals averaged 65% confidence. The bad news is that both groups were worse than sheer luck. That is to say you should have been able to beat both groups just by tossing a coin!

In addition to the overall statistics, at each selection, players were asked to state how confident they were in the outcome predicted. The even worse news was that professionals were really dreadful, underperforming laypeople by a large margin. For instance, when the professionals were 100% sure they were correct, they were actually right less than 15% of the time!

Players were also asked to rank the inputs they used in reaching their decisions. Figure 8 shows the average scores for the inputs. Laypeople were essentially just guessing, but were also influenced by prior price performance. In contrast, the professionals thought they were using their knowledge to pick the winners. It is hard to imagine a better example of the illusion of knowledge driving confidence.

FIGURE 6   Average Accuracy and Confidence on Stock Selection (%)

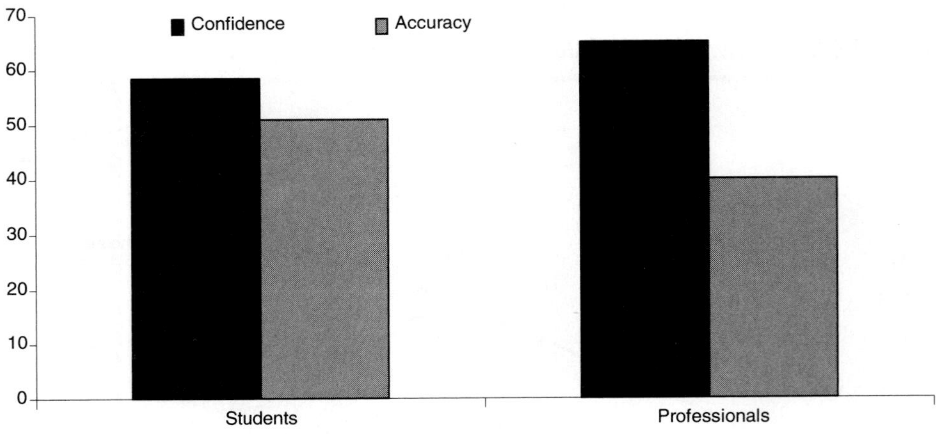

Source: Torngren and Montgomery (2004).

---

[4] Torngren and Montgomery (2004) Worse than chance? Performance and confidence among professionals and laypeople in the stock market, *Journal of Behavioural Finance*, 5.

FIGURE 7   Accuracy and Confidence on Stock Selection

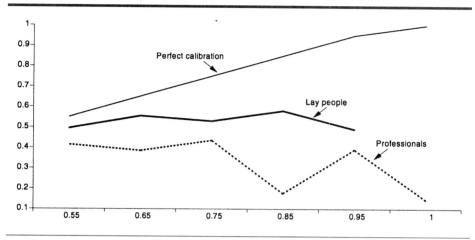

Source: Torngren and Montgomery (2004).

FIGURE 8   Average Rating of Input Importance

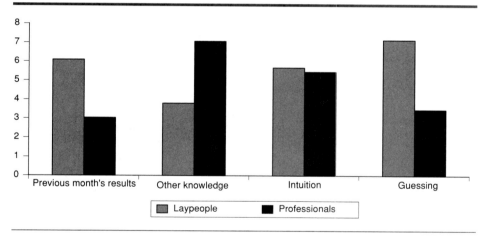

Source: Torngren and Montgomery (2004).

Glaser, Langer and Weber[5] investigate overconfidence in professional investors and laypeople by asking both groups to answer 10 general knowledge questions and 10 finance questions, much like the self-test set out in Table 1. If people are well calibrated, the number of correct answers that fall outside the limits should be about one in ten. Figure 9 shows the actual number of answers that exceeded the confidence limits (the general knowledge and finance questions have been averaged together to give a score out of ten).

The professional investors had a median of nearly 8 questions outside of their confidence intervals; the laypeople (students) had a median 6 questions outside of their confidence ranges. Once again confirming that experts are more overconfident than the rest of us.

---

[5] Glaser, Langer and Weber (2005) Overconfidence of professionals and lay men: Individual difference within and between tasks, University of Mannheim Working Paper.

FIGURE 9   Average Number of Questions Outside of the Confidence Interval

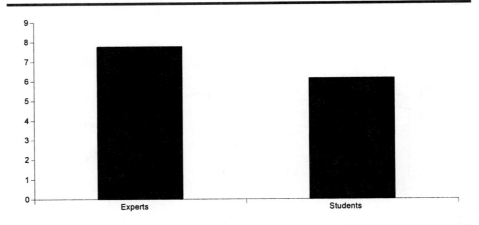

Source: Glaser, Langer and Weber (2005).

A new paper by Stotz and Nitzsch[6] surveyed analysts at major investment banks. They were asked to say how many of their rivals were more accurate and less accurate than they themselves were with respect to both earnings forecasts and target prices. Unsurprisingly, the analysts thought that they were all above average. Indeed the average analyst's overconfidence with regard to earnings was 68.44%, and 61.49% with respect to target prices.

Stotz and Nitzsch also asked the analysts to give reasons for their assessment of their ability. They found that when it came to target prices (where analysts were less overconfident), analysts often argued that "prices sometimes happen by chance," or that they were the result of "irrational investors," or that successful price forecasts had a large element of luck. In contrast, when it came to explain their earnings forecasts (see Figure 10), analysts said "detailed knowl-

FIGURE 10   Average Analysts' Confidence in Their Ability to Forecast Earnings and Prices

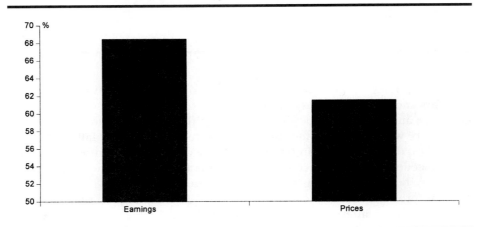

Source: Stotz and Nitzsch (2005).

---

[6] Stotz and Nitzsch (2005) The perception of control and the level of overconfidence: Evidence from analysts earnings estimates and price targets, *The Journal of Behavioural Finance*, Vol 6.

FIGURE 11   Percentage of Fund Managers Who Rate Themselves as Above Average at Their Jobs

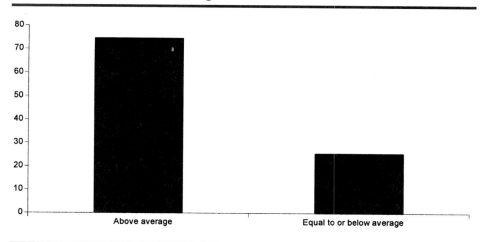

Source: DrKW Macro research.

edge of the company or sector" helped to make good forecasts, as did "experience" and "hard work." This would seem to be further evidence of the illusion of control and the illusion of knowledge driving overconfidence.

I have recently been subjecting participants at my behavioral finance seminars to a questionnaire designed to measure their behavioral biases. I've been collating these results and will soon publish a note on the findings. However, as a sneak preview, one of the questions is: Are you above average at your job? I have around 200 respondents; all of them are professional fund managers.[7] A stunning 75% of those who I have asked think themselves above average at their jobs, as shown in Figure 11. Many have written things like, "I know everyone thinks they are above average, but I am!"

All of this begs at least two questions. Firstly, why do professionals manage to keep forecasting given that the evidence suggests they can't? Secondly, why do we keep using these useless forecasts? So let's examine each of these in turn.

Why Forecast When the Evidence Shows You Can't?

Two areas of psychology help to explain how forecasters keep forecasting in the face of pretty overwhelming evidence that they aren't any good at it. They can perhaps be explained as ignorance (not knowing the overconfidence exists) and arrogance (ego defense mechanism).

Unskilled and Unaware

David Dunning and a variety of co-authors over the years have documented a disturbing pattern of behavior. **Those who are amongst the worst performers actually are the most overconfident.**

---

[7] If anyone is interested in taking the test, please email me (James.Montier@drkw.com), and I will be able to send you the questionnaire and add your response to the sample.

FIGURE 12   Perceived and Actual Scores: Unskilled and Unaware

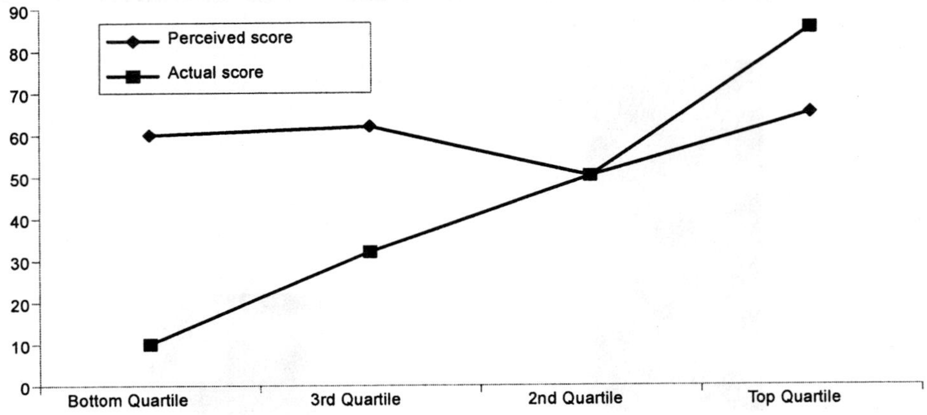

Source: Kruger and Dunning (1999).

For instance, Kruger and Dunning[8] ask people to rate how they have performed on a logic-reasoning test. Figure 12 shows the perceived score and the actual score. Those in the bottom two quartiles by actual score thought they would be in the 60th percentile (i.e., well above average). However, their actual scores put those in the bottom quartile in the tenth percentile. A massive case of overconfidence.

In a follow-up paper, Dunning et al[9] explore some of the mechanisms that prevent people from realizing just how unskilled they actually are. They note "People fail to recognize their own incompetencies because that incompetence carries with it a double curse . . . the skills needed to produce correct responses are virtually identical to those needed to evaluate the accuracy of one's responses. . . . Thus, if people lack the skills to produce correct answers, they are also cursed with an inability to know when their own answers, or anyone else's are right or wrong."

Dunning et al also point out that very often people's estimates of their ability arise from a "top-down" approach. That is to say people start with a preconceived belief about their skills or abilities (along the lines of "I'm good at my job" or "I'm good at forecasting") and use those beliefs to estimate how well they will do at a specific task.

Unfortunately, all the evidence suggests that people's impressions of their skills and abilities are at best moderately correlated and frequently uncorrelated with their actual performance. Indeed this is nicely evidenced by the example above where all groups had a perceived score of between 50 and 60%—bearing no relation to the actual outturn!

Ego Defence Mechanism

A second group of techniques deployed by forecasters could be best described as ego defence mechanisms. Philip Tetlock[10] has investigated the use of "excuses" for forecast failures amongst experts on world politics. Tetlock has been moni-

---

[8] Kruger and Dunning (1999) Unskilled and unaware of it: How difficulties in recognizing one's own incompetence lead to inflated self-assessments, *Journal of Personality and Social Psychology*, Vol. 77.

[9] Dunning, Johnson, Ehrlinger and Kruger (2003) Why people fail to recognize their own incompetence, *Current Directions in Psychological Science*.

[10] Tetlock (2002) Theory-driven reasoning about plausible pasts and probable futures in world politics, in Gilovich, Griffin and Kahneman (2002) Heuristics and Biases: The psychology of intuitive judgement, CUP.

toring experts' views on world politics in real time for more than a decade. He notes, "Almost as many experts as not thought that the Soviet Communist Party would remain firmly in the saddle of power in 1993, that Canada was doomed by 1997, that neo-fascism would prevail in Pretoria by 1994, that EMU would collapse by 1997 . . . that the Persian Gulf Crisis would be resolved peacefully."

He found that across the vast array of predictions with respect to a wide range of political events experts who reported they were 80% or higher confident in their predictions were actually correct only around 45% of the time. Across all predictions, the experts were little better than coin tossers. As Tetlock notes, "Expertise thus may not translate into predictive accuracy but it does translate into the ability to generate explanations for predictions that experts themselves find so compelling that the result is massive overconfidence."

After each of the events passed and the forecasts were shown to be either right or wrong, Tetlock returned to the experts and asked them to reassess how well they thought they understood the underlying process and forces at work. Table 2 shows the experts' belief in their own abilities both before the events and after the events. Look at the judged probabilities both pre and post events for those whose forecasts were incorrect. They are virtually identical. So despite the incontrovertible evidence that they were wrong, the experts showed no sign of cutting their faith in their own understanding of the situation. A true Bayesian would have slashed their assigned probability (last column in the table below). This is prime evidence of the conservatism bias—a tendency to hang on to your views for too long, and only slowly adjust from them.

TABLE 2   Subjective Probabilities Experts Assigned to Their Understanding of the Underlying Forces at the Beginning and End of the Forecast Periods

Predicting the Future of	Status of Forecast	Judged Prior Probability (Before the Outcome Is Known)	Judged Posterior Probability (After the Outcome Is Known)	Bayesian Predicted Posterior Probability
Soviet Union	Inaccurate	0.74	0.7	0.49
	Accurate	0.69	0.83	0.8
South Africa	Inaccurate	0.72	0.69	0.42
	Accurate	0.7	0.77	0.82
EMU	Inaccurate	0.66	0.68	0.45
	Accurate	0.71	0.78	0.85
Canada	Inaccurate	0.65	0.67	0.39
	Accurate	0.68	0.81	0.79

Source: Tetlock (2002).

Tetlock identified five common strategies/defences used to explain the forecast error whilst preserving the faith in the view:

1. The "if only" defence—if only the Federal Reserve had raised rates, then the U.S. stock price bubble would have been avoided. Effectively, the experts claim they would have been correct "if only" their original advice or analysis had been followed. This makes their forecast an historical counterfactual, which is impossible to prove.

2. The "ceteris paribus" defence—Although the experts' advice or analysis was correct, something else occurred, which was covered in the ubiquitous ceteris paribus, that resulted in the forecast being blown off course. So the stock market would have crashed but for the presence of government led manipulation.

3. The "I was almost right" defence—Although the predicted outcome did not occur, it "almost" did. Tetlock gives the examples of so-called close call counterfactuals such as "the hardliners almost overthrew Gorbachev" or "the EU almost disintegrated during the currency crisis of 1992."

4. The "it just hasn't happened yet" defence—although the predicted outcome has not yet occurred, it will eventually come to pass. This is one of my favourites! I know that I regularly use this defense to assert that high valuations will inevitably and eventually lead to low returns for investors, thus maintaining my faith in my view of markets.

5. The "single prediction" defence—Although the conditions of the forecast were met, and the outcome never came close to occurring and now never will, this failure shouldn't be held against the framework/view that inspired it, the "everyone knows (or should know) that forecasting is pointless" view. Thus the analysis is valid, but the act of forecasting was flawed.

These five defence mechanisms are regularly deployed by experts to excuse the dismal failure of their forecasts. Table 3 shows scores (on a nine point scale) of how important these defences are. Unsurprisingly those who gave inaccurate forecasts rely much more heavily upon the mechanisms than those who gave accurate forecasts. In fact, across the five cases used here, those who gave inaccurate forecasts were 1.6 times more likely to reply on one of these defence mechanisms than the accurate forecasters (Figure 13).

Tyszka and Zielonka[11] applied Tetlock's approach to analysts and weathermen. As we have already noted, weathermen are one of those rare groups that

TABLE 3	Average Reactions of Experts to Confirmation and Disconfirmation of Their Conditional Forecasts					
Predicting the Future of	**Status of Forecast**	**If Only**	**Ceteris Paribus**	**I Was Almost Right**	**It Just Hasn't Happened Yet**	**Single Prediction**
Soviet Union	Inaccurate	7	7.1	6.8	6.4	7.3
	Accurate	4.1	3.9	3.6	5	3.1
South Africa	Inaccurate	7.1	7	7.3	7.3	7.1
	Accurate	4.5	3.5	3.3	4	4.8
EMU	Inaccurate	7.2	5.9	6.2	7.8	7
	Accurate	5.1	4.6	4.9	3.8	4.3
Canada	Inaccurate	7.6	6.8	6.5	8	7.2
	Accurate	6.8	3.7	4.2	4.4	4.5

Source: Adapted from Tetlock (2002).

[11] Tyszka and Zielonka (2002) Expert judgements: Financial analysts versus weather forecasters, *The Journal of Psychology and Financial Markets*, Vol. 3.

FIGURE 13   Average Use of Defence Mechanism Across Five Cases

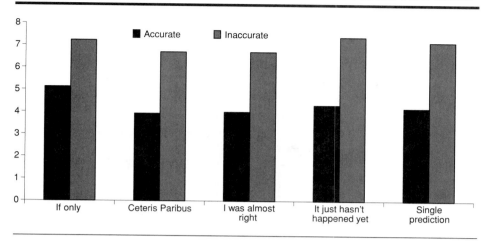

Source: Adapted from Tetlock (2002).

are actually well calibrated. Financial analysts, in contrast, have been found to be very overconfident as documented above.

Tyszka and Zielonka asked financial analysts to predict a stock market level in about a month and a half's time. Weathermen were asked to predict the average temperature in April (again around one and a half months into the future). In both cases, three mutually exclusive and exhaustive outcomes were specified in such a way that each outcome was roughly equally likely (i.e., had a 0.33 chance of happening). For example, the analysts were asked if the index would be below y, between x and y, or above x. They were also asked how confident they were in their predictions.

Figure 14 shows the average scale of overconfidence that was reported. Remember that the three choices were constructed so that each option was roughly equally likely, so a well-calibrated individual would have reported 33% confidence. However, the analysts had an average confidence of just over 58%

FIGURE 14   Average Confidence Probability

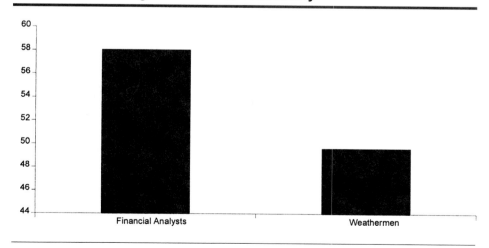

Source: Tyszka and Zielonka (2002).

FIGURE 15   Justifications of the Forecast Failure

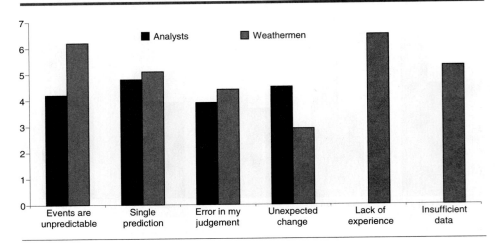

Source: Tyszka and Zielonka (2002).

and the weathermen had an average confidence of just over 50%. So both groups were, as usual, overconfident, but the analysts were more overconfident.

In fact only around one third of the analysts were actually correct, and around two thirds of the weathermen were correct. Those who gave incorrect forecasts were once again contacted and asked to assign importance ratings on an eight-point scale to various reasons for their forecast failure.

It is interesting to note that the less confident weathermen's single biggest justification for their forecast failure was a lack of personal experience, followed by an acknowledgment that the weather is inherently unforecastable (Figure 15). Analysts, on the other hand, argued that they shouldn't be judged on the basis of a single prediction (the single prediction defense), and that something else happened that altered the outcome that would have otherwise been achieved (the "ceteris paribus" defense from above).

So just like Tetlock's political experts, financial analysts seem to be using mental defense mechanisms to protect themselves from the reality of their appallingly bad track record at forecasting.

So Why Use Forecasts?

Given all the evidence that people are generally dreadful at forecasting[12] why do so many investors use forecasts at the very center of their investment processes? In part the obsession with forecasts probably stems from the ingrained love of efficient markets. It might seem odd to talk of efficient markets and active managers in the same sentence, but the behavior of many market participants is actually consistent with market efficiency (EMH). That is, many investors believe they need to know more than everyone else to outperform. This is consistent with

---

[12] Dawes, Faust and Meehl note that there is an important difference between clinical and actuarial forecasts. Clinical forecasts describe those whereby the decision-maker combines or processes information in his head. Actuarial forecasts rely on well-specified models that have been tested. A vast amount of data shows that actuarial forecasts massively outperform clinical forecasts. We will leave a discussion of what this means for investors until another note, but for the time being recognise that our industry is one in which clinical method often hides behind an actuarial façade. See Dawes, Faust and Meehl (1991) Clinical versus Actuarial Judgement, *Science*, 243.

EMH because the only way to beat an efficient market is to know something that isn't in the price (i.e., non public information). One way of knowing more is to be able to forecast the future better than everyone else.

However, one psychological trait above all others helps explain the continued use of forecasts—anchoring. We have discussed anchoring in the context of valuations in a previous note (see *Global Equity Strategy*, 27 August 2004). Anchoring refers to our tendency to grab onto the irrelevant when faced with uncertainty.

The classic example of anchoring comes from Tversky and Kahneman's landmark paper.[13] They asked people to answer general knowledge questions such as "What percentage of the UN is made up of African nations?" A wheel of fortune with the numbers 1 to 100 was spun in front of the participants before they answered. Being psychologists, Tversky and Kahneman had rigged the wheel so it gave either 10 or 65 as the result of a spin. The subjects were then asked if the answer was higher or lower than the number on the wheel, and also asked their actual answer. The median response from the group that saw the wheel spot at 10 was 25%, and the median response from the group that saw 65 was 45%! Effectively, people were grabbing at irrelevant anchors when forming their opinions. (For the record the correct answer was 20%.)

Another well-known example concerns solving 8 factorial (8!). It is presented in two different ways, either i) $1 \times 2 \times 3 \times 4 \times 5 \times 6 \times 7 \times 8$ or ii) $8 \times 7 \times 6 \times 5 \times 4 \times 3 \times 2 \times 1$. The median answer under case i was 512, the median answer under case ii was 2250. So people appear to anchor on the early numbers in forming their expectations. By the way, the actual answer is 40,320.

Anchoring is not just a cheap parlour trick. Englich and Mussweiler[14] take criminal trial judges with an average of more than 15 years of experience as subjects. The judges hear the cases at the end of which the prosecutor asks for either a 36-month sentence, or a 12-month sentence for exactly the same case. Those prosecutors who asked for a 36-month sentence extracted a jail time that was 8 months longer than those who sought a 12-month sentence. Intriguingly, these findings were independent of whether a true prosecutor or a student played the role of the prosecutor!

One of the questions I have asked on my behavioral finance questionnaire is for people to write down the last four digits of their telephone numbers, then say whether the number of doctors in their capital city is higher or lower than the last four digits of their telephone number, and finally to give their best guess as to the number of doctors in their capital city. The results are shown in Figure 16. Those with the last four digits greater than 7000 on average report 6762 doctors, whilst those with telephone numbers below 2000 arrived at an average 2270 doctors! So professional fund managers seem to be as liable as everyone else to suffer from anchoring.

When faced with the unknown, people will grasp onto almost anything. So it is little wonder that investors cling to forecasts, despite their uselessness.

Debasing

So what can be done to avoid these problems? The most obvious solution is to stop relying upon pointless forecasts. This comes as anathema to most investors. But there are plenty of strategies that one can implement without the use of forecasts.

---

[13] Tversky and Kahneman (1974) Judgement under uncertainty, heuristics and biases; *Science*, 185.

[14] Englich and Mussweiler (2001) Sentencing under uncertainty: Anchoring effects in the courtroom, *Journal of Applied Social Psychology*, Vol 31.

FIGURE 16   Anchoring amongst Fund Managers

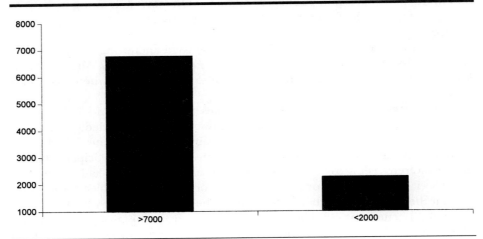

Source: DrKW Macro research.

For example, value-based strategies based on trailing earnings or Graham and Dodd PEs (see *Global Equity Strategy*, 16 March 2005 and 28 June 2005).

Secondly, we should redirect our efforts away from forecasting. Having armies of analysts and economists all forecasting is a complete waste of time. There is a good reason we call analysts analysts not forecasters: they are meant to analyze, not guess, the unknowable future. They would be better utilized in analyzing the present and understanding what that means for the future rather than coming up with spurious anchors for investors to cling to. However, this requires a radical re-think of the investment process and hence is exceptionally unlikely to occur.

SUMMARY

▶ Lao Tzu, a 6th-century BC poet observed, "Those who have knowledge don't predict. Those who predict don't have knowledge." Despite these age-old words of wisdom our industry seems to persist in producing and using forecasts. This is all the more puzzling given the easily available data on the appalling nature of track records in forecasting. Economists, strategists and analysts are all guilty. In general, forecasts seem to be a lagged function of actual outcomes—adaptive expectations dominate forecasts.

▶ The two most common biases are over-optimism and overconfidence. Overconfidence refers to a situation whereby people are surprised more often than they expect to be. Effectively people are generally much too sure about their ability to predict. This tendency is particularly pronounced amongst experts. That is to say, experts are more overconfident than laypeople. This is consistent with the illusion of knowledge driving overconfidence.

▶ Several studies confirm professional investors to be particularly over-confident. For instance, one recent study found that 68% of analysts thought they were above average at forecasting earnings! I've found that 75% of fund managers think they are above average at their jobs.

▶ Why do we persist in forecasting given such appalling track records? There are two avenues to explore—simply put, ignorance and arrogance. Dunning and colleagues have documented that the worst performers are generally the most overconfident. They argue that such individuals suffer a double curse of being unskilled and unaware of it. Dunning et al argue that the skills needed to produce correct responses are virtually identical to those needed to self-evaluate the potential accuracy of responses. Hence the problem.

▶ Tetlock argues that experts regularly deploy five ego defense mechanisms. Experts use various combinations of these defenses to enable them to continue to forecast, despite their poor performance.

▶ Why do we persist in using forecasts in the investment process? The answer probably lies in behavior known as anchoring. That is, in the face of uncertainty we will cling to any irrelevant number as support. So it is little wonder that investors cling to forecasts, despite their uselessness.

▶ So what can be done to avoid these problems? Most obviously we need to stop relying on pointless forecasts. There are plenty of investment strategies that don't need forecasts as inputs, such as value strategies based on trailing earnings or momentum strategies based on past prices. Secondly, we need to redeploy the armies of analysts. They should return to doing as their name suggests: analyzing, rather than trying to guess the unknowable!

4⅝ 4⅛
5½ 5½ − ⅜
5½ 2¹³⁄₁₆ − ⅛
20⅝ 21³⁄₁₆ − ⅛
17⅜ 18⅛ + ⅞
3½ 6½ 6½ − ½
7¼ 6½ 3¹⁄₃₂ − ⅛
15⁄₁₆ 9⁄₁₆
9⁄₁₆ 9⁄₁₆
13⁄₃₂ 7¹³⁄₁₆ 7¹⁵⁄₁₆
7⁵⁄₁₆
2⅝ 2¹¹⁄₃₂ 2½ +
2¾ 2¼ 2¼
6¼ 12¹⁄₁₆ 11⅜ 11¾ +
33¾ 33 33⅛ −
25⅝ 24⁹⁄₁₆ 25⅜ +
12 11⅝ 11⅞ +
16 10½ 10½ 10½ −
78 15⅞ 15¹³⁄₁₆ 15⅞ −
4508 9¹⁄₁₆ 8¼ 8⅜ +
430 11¼ 10⅛ 10⅛

ALPHA HUNTERS AND BETA GRAZERS
by Martin L. Leibowitz

LEARNING OUTCOMES

The candidate should be able to:	Mastery
a. contrast chronic market inefficiencies with acute inefficiencies and describe the behavioral factors (such as convoy behavior, Bayesian rigidity, price-target revisionism, and the ebullience cycle) that may give rise to chronic market inefficiencies;	☐
b. explain the portfolio rebalancing behavior of holders, rebalancers, valuators, and shifters and evaluate the impact these rebalancing behaviors have on market efficiency.	☐

INTRODUCTION

There is a great philosophical divide between passive, efficiency-based "beta grazers" and active "alpha hunters." The explosive growth of hedge funds, of both the traditional and the long-only format, has contributed to this widening chasm between intensely proactive investors and those funds that are indexed or semi-indexed.

This reading presents my personal observations on the general subject of active investing and on the nature, persistence, and discernibility of various market inefficiencies that could give rise to such investment opportunities. Ironically, these behavioral biases can act as frictions as well as opportunities, and this ambiguity may help explain why a few notable investors appear to be almost continuously successful while other active investors fall well short of their alpha targets.

Martin L. Leibowitz is a managing director at Morgan Stanley, New York City.

Financial Analysts Journal, September/October 2005, by Martin L. Leibowitz. Copyright © 2005 by CFA Institute. Reprinted with permission.

At the outset, we should note that there is a middle ground where relatively passive, non-zero-sum forms of alpha return can be found. As described in a series of articles (Leibowitz 2004; Leibowitz and Bova 2005a, 2005c), these "allocation alphas" arise because the volatility risk of typical institutional portfolios is overwhelmingly dominated by their home-market equity exposure. By tilting their strategic allocations toward a more balanced allocation, institutions can often garner enhanced expected returns with only modest increases in marginal volatility. The level of expected benefit obviously depends on the institution's specific return–risk assumptions.

Unlike truly active alphas, *allocation* alphas are broadly accessible through a semipassive process of moving toward an effective strategic allocation. As such, they are akin to the civilized sort of protein-seeking found in shopping at the local supermarket, with the selections determined by personal taste and dietary constraints. These readily available allocation alphas serve a critical and valuable role in moving a fund toward optimal strategic allocation. Allocation alphas are quite distinct, however, from the truly active alphas derived from tracking down— and bagging—the fleeting and elusive opportunities that arise from market inefficiencies. Both forms of alpha offer the potential for enhanced return, and they can sometimes be combined to create exceptional opportunities. They are quite different concepts, however, and are pursued in different ways. Having made this distinction, I focus the remainder of this reading on the truly active-skill-based investments that are intended to add alpha above and beyond the returns passively available in any asset class or strategic portfolio.

1 TRULY ACTIVE ALPHAS

Much of the literature on truly active investing has focused on so-called anomalies—sources of incremental return that appear to have some degree of persistence. In addition, a number of elegant formalizations have been developed for incorporating active return–risk prospects into the investment decision process (Sharpe 1991; Grinold and Kahn 2000; Waring and Siegel 2003; Asness 2004). This discussion should be broadened, however, to include consideration of all frictions and behavioral biases—persistent as well as occasional—that might serve as fundamental sources of inefficiency. Such inefficiencies are not always exploitable: They may take the form of overshoots at certain times and undershoots at other times, their exploitation may be blocked by counterforces or technical restrictions of various sorts, or they may resolve themselves very slowly—or never.

We need to understand, however, that these sources of inefficiency are multifold, broad based, and continually renewing themselves. Most importantly, we need to understand that they really do exist—even if they are not always available, discernible, or directionally consistent. Such pockets of inefficiency at times become reasonably discernible and actionable—to certain active investors. Thus, their very existence becomes one facet of an argument (albeit an admittedly still incomplete argument) for the possibility of successful active investing.

Another argument (also incomplete) is the historical fact that a handful of investors has produced extraordinary performance over a span of many years—often together with equally extraordinary cross-sectional success in their choices of disparate investments. The approaches of these great investors—Warren Buffett, Bill Miller, Leon Levy, Dave Swensen, Jack Meyer—differ in numerous aspects, but as pointed out by Peter Bernstein (2005), the investors share the common feature of not being in the mainstream (i.e., they are all contrarians in one way or another). The great ones share a number of positive characteristics—focus, patience, a clear-cut philosophy, a willingness to go beyond the diversification mantra and accept high concentration risks, an innovation-prone attitude, the organizational sponsorship and personal fortitude to endure significant periods of underperformance, and a disciplined process for pursuing their goals. And in various ways and at various points in time, they have all been willing to stake significant chips on their convictions.

With respect to this latter point, one might well recall Charles Ellis's (1998) wonderful characterization of most investors as playing what in tennis parlance is called "the loser's game." In the loser's game, weekend players, with their readily returnable forehands and backhands, square off against each other and the one who misses the last return loses. The message is to play a consistent game and to avoid miss-hits. It is generally good advice for B players—and beta grazers!

The great ones, however—in tennis and in investing—go one big step beyond. They play a disciplined game until the moment they see what looks like a grand opportunity. At that moment, they move into *carpe diem* mode, gather up their prowess, and take a calculated risk to proactively and aggressively force a win.[1]

Even the great Fischer Black was fascinated by the potential for exploitable inefficiency, although he certainly knew that such opportunities would not be easy, widespread, or available to all. He once famously answered a question about how his view of the investing world had evolved after moving from the Massachusetts Institute of Technology to Goldman Sachs with "the view is much clearer from the banks of the Charles than from the banks of the Hudson." Earlier in his career, he had delivered a wonderful talk at the University of Chicago under the title "Yes, Virginia, There Is Hope," which was later published in the *Financial Analysts Journal* (Black 1973). In that talk, he reported on his study of the Value Line Ranking System, which would have produced superior performance over a long span of years if followed religiously (and with transactional-cost efficiency!).

CHRONIC AND ACUTE INEFFICIENCIES   **2**

Some of my pet sources of inefficiencies are behavioral and organizational distortions that I have observed over the years. I certainly do not mean to imply that they are exploitable anomalies, but they do represent the raw nuclear material out of which discernible opportunities could arise.

In perfectly efficient markets, all information would be immediately embedded in prices. The market would go through a sequence of quantum leaps from one equilibrium value to another. Investors would have no need to trade except

---

[1] Although I argue for the possibility of successful active investing, I do not wish to suggest that everyone can be a winner. Indeed, they cannot. And the narrowness of the list of great investors attests to that dour fact. The great mass of investors should treat the market as being highly efficient and should start with the null hypothesis that all assets are fairly priced.

for liquidity purposes. It would be hard to make a living working in such an idealized world. Fortunately, for those of us in the financial arena, the reality is that the markets are always in transition from one state of inefficiency to . . . maybe equilibrium but, more likely, a new state of inefficiency.

Inefficiencies come in many forms and subforms, but they can be roughly classified as either chronic or acute. *Acute inefficiencies* are the discernible opportunities that can be exploited by accessible arbitrages. With acute inefficiencies, the surrounding uncertainties can be hedged or minimized. Their resolution occurs quickly, well within the relevant time frame of arbitraging participants. *Chronic inefficiencies* tend to be less discernible, more ambiguous, more resistant to rapid resolution from available market forces, and generally longer term in nature. This distinction relates to Jack Treynor's (1976) wonderfully suggestive concept of "fast ideas versus slow ideas."

Obviously, one would prefer to hurl fast ideas at acute inefficiencies, but by their very nature, fast ideas have a short half-life. And that half-life may be condensing with the explosive growth in hedge funds. But even in this era of the hedge fund, only a small minority of market participants spend their days in a high-performance hunt for acute inefficiencies. The vast majority of investors, and certainly the bulk of the assets, swim with the broad currents, while looking for less-fleeting incremental opportunities.

Within this mainstream, one has expanses of apparent efficiency coexisting with pockets of chronic inefficiencies. Chronic inefficiencies arise from structural and behavioral sources, such as trading frictions, organizational barriers, imbalances in capital flows, valuation ambiguities, lack of catalysts for resolution, convoy or herding behavior, artificial peer comparisons, rebalancing inconsistencies, compulsive confirmation seeking, filtering of conflicting data, misreading of market signals, inertia, formulaic action plans, and overly rigid "policy portfolios." These types of chronic inefficiencies can be quite persistent. Few arbitrageurs have mandates that allow them to pursue long-term opportunities, and their absence contributes to the longevity of such inefficiencies. As the well-known saying goes: The market can remain irrational far longer than you can hang onto your position—or your career.

Process versus Outcome

A much-discussed behavioral bias is the tendency to overemphasize recent historical results. As every mutual fund prospectus states, "Past performance should not be taken as a guide to future performance." That warning, although true, is not much help when few other hard facts are available. A more ominous rephrasing would be, "Past performance is not even a good guide to the *quality of the decisions* that went into that past performance." Yet, the ultimate issue is the soundness of the decision process itself: Was all knowable information incorporated? Was the reasoning thorough and sound? Were alternative scenarios considered and contrary views sought? Was a well-planned implementation and monitoring program established—and then followed? Was there a routine postmortem analysis of lessons learned? And are organizational discipline and staff continuity sufficient to achieve consistency in the decision process itself?

Unfortunately, the sort of retrospective analysis that includes these questions occurs more often when the outcomes are bad than when they are good. Participants would be well advised to conduct such postmortems even when the outcomes are happy ones, however, and to ask what *really* led to success. Was the positive result achieved for the reasons thought, or was it simply good fortune in this particular instance?

Even when presented with a regime that has every evidence of success—but only a probabilistic success—few investors are able to bring themselves or their organizations to consistently follow its path. The pressures of benchmarks, peer comparisons, standard accounting, liability and expenditure demands, limited organizational risk tolerance, managerial self-doubt—all can lead to lurching departures from prescribed disciplines, even ones with a high—but probabilistic—success prospect. After all, even a strategy whose success is mathematically provable will generate long runs of underperformance. Indeed, a topic in probability theory deals specifically with the risk of ruin—and the ultimate odds of ruin always favor the infinitely resourced casino.

Convoy Behavior

Traditional modes of investing in the financial markets involve absolute or relative valuations of various market segments or securities—a process in which ambiguities, complexities, and externalities abound. Inefficiencies and opportunities do exist in this area, but they are far from clearly discernible and can only be seen "through a glass darkly."

Many chronic inefficiencies have their roots in the behavioral biases of mainstream participants. For example, consider the herding behavior of institutional funds. Participants in the financial markets find themselves on a sea of ambiguity. They may try to climb up the mast to see what lies ahead, to look for islands of opportunity, but they are always battered by the waves, the weather, and the uncertainties of navigating in uncharted waters. Is there any surprise that one sees so many sailing in convoys?

It is no coincidence that most institutional portfolios are tightly clustered, with total volatilities falling in the 10–11 percent range—regardless of the fund's mission, liability structure, sponsor strength, or funding status (Leibowitz and Bova 2004). When such ambiguity abounds, people naturally assume that their peer groups might just have the right idea. This behavior is not totally irrational where theory is more art than science and where the expertise-to-luck ratio is often tilted in favor of luck. Moreover, a sufficient critical mass of investors with a common belief, even an erroneous one, can forge a pricing consensus that becomes a de facto reality that must be taken seriously.

Another issue is the valuation horizon of the average investor. The true efficient marketeer might argue that the market is continuously efficient over time. It is interesting to speculate, however, whether most investors have some specific span of time—perhaps from six months to three years—on which they focus their investment and valuation decisions. If so, then investors with longer horizons may reap a somewhat larger risk premium than average investors do. In terms of Treynor's fast–slow dichotomy, the advantage might go to investors who are either faster or slower than this hypothetical norm.

Another behavioral bias is the tendency to seek the opinions of other "experts" who can confirm one's own views, which results in what might be called a "compounding consensus." Actually, instead of seeking confirmation, one should actively solicit *contrary* views, hear them out, consider them objectively, and then try to recognize that the financial markets themselves always reflect some balance of conflicting views. In theory, one should always start with the hypothesis that the market is well priced. Then, before acting on any potential opportunity, one should 1) try to ascertain why the market is priced where it is, 2) become convinced that the basis for this current price does not fully reflect the true opportunities, 3) believe that there is some process whereby one's views of the true state of affairs will eventually come to be widely discernible (and in a more compelling fashion than has obviously happened to date), and 4) conclude that this "discernment" will transpire within a relevant time span.

Bayesian Rigidity

The compulsion to seek confirmation also relates to how the unfolding of events is interpreted. The "rigid Bayesians" will relentlessly try to retain their old views in the face of new information. To help counter this all-too-human inclination, one could write down the explicit reasoning behind a projected outcome and then establish the milestones that would have to occur if events took the anticipated path. Such a write-up would be akin to the contingency plans military establishments routinely create for a wide spectrum of geopolitical scenarios.

A French marquis once said:

> He who makes detailed plans about every potential course of action, and then decides—in advance and in great detail—how to respond to the various contingencies that might arise, and then further proceeds to address the subsequent situations that could follow each possible outcome, etc., etc.—this man will make very few mistakes [actually, I'm not sure that this part is true], but he will also do very little [I *am* sure that this part is true].

Yet, although the market's fast pace may limit how much contingency planning makes sense, the investment management profession surely could devote more effort in this direction.

Price-Target Revisionism

Another area of curious behavior has to do with price targets. When a long position is taken and the market moves favorably, the price rise tends to be taken as a confirmation of the wisdom of the purchase decision. To the extent that a price target was established at the outset, the investor may then be tempted to find some rationale for revising the target upward. This revisionism has some rather obvious dangers. A more rational approach would be to assume that as the price moves toward the original target, the prospect for further incremental return decreases while the risk increases. So, as a first cut, one should think in terms of selling off a portion of the position as it moves up. Thus, investors would be well advised to have a plan to reduce the positions as the original target is approached—the burden of proof (or at least the burden of argument) being placed on the investor who wishes to maintain the original position and/or revise the price target upward.

When the market moves against one's position, one might reasonably conclude that the market is giving a clear signal that one is wrong. A more common belief is that the market is wrong and that greater return is to be expected from the lower price. To counter the natural tendency to avoid a frontal look at deteriorating positions, a help, again, might be to have a series of adverse-event milestones that could act as trip wires to signal serious reconsideration. A substantive adverse move should be the basis for asking what the market is trying to reveal and for vigorously seeking those contrary views.

The Ebullience Cycle

Another common behavior is the "unopened envelope" syndrome. Back in the old days when physical envelopes were the primary delivery vehicle for individuals' portfolio statements, a persistently dreary market would lead to these envelopes being redelivered—unopened—into the "circular file." Such a state of denial when the market moves against one is totally human, especially when deciding what to do about it, if anything, is not easy. The unopened envelope reinforces individuals' propensity for inaction in the face of losing positions.

The opposite phenomenon is, of course, that when the markets are moving up, the incoming envelope is eagerly awaited and ripped open with great vigor. High spirits are rampant, and risks are more comfortable. In this ebullient atmosphere, both individual and institutional investors are inclined to hold on firmly to their winning positions, which are shining examples of their brilliance. They may even invest more aggressively, leading to the phenomenon that Jack Bogle (2005) cited of markets providing one return, the mutual funds providing something less, and the investors getting even less (a number that is rarely measured, except by the individuals in pain). This problem of making ever-greater investments as the market rises is a classic cycle that is not likely to abate.

Rebalancing Behavior

Market movements typically elicit different responses from four types of actors: holders, rebalancers, valuators, and shifters (Leibowitz and Hammond 2004).

Holders   As noted, in a deteriorating market, individuals tend to leave their envelopes unopened and positions unchanged. This "holding pattern" effectively reduces their equity allocations.

Rebalancers   Institutions behave very differently from holders. When the market pushes an institutional fund away from its policy portfolio allocation, it usually quickly rebalances back to the original percentage weights. In essence, institutions act as "formulaic rebalancers."

Valuators   Valuators take positions based on the belief that the market is either cheap (or rich) or that it will continue (or reverse) its recent direction. Valuators can obviously play in two directions. As the market moves down, they may, based on the belief that the market has become cheap and will reverse itself, act as contrarians. As momentum players, they may view the market's decline—on either a technical or a fundamental basis—as a harbinger of further downward pressure.

Shifters   This category really represents a transient reaction rather than an ongoing style. Investors in any of the first three categories may find themselves becoming shifters at some point in time. Shifting occurs when a fundamental change in asset allocation is required because of circumstances intrinsic to a fund's or an individual's situation rather than because of their assessment of the market's valuation.[2] That is, shifting is a fundamental move from one strategic stance to another. For example, individuals may increase their short-term fixed-income allocations when suddenly faced with an imminent liquidity need—loss of a job, an upcoming move, a looming major purchase, medical contingencies, and so on.

Institutions are more resistant to shifting behavior. Most institutional funds have a policy portfolio that serves as an anchor for their overall strategy. The

---

[2] In some cases, market movements do ultimately lead to a portfolio shift. For example, a rule of thumb says that many individuals will let their allocations drift until a 15–20 percent decline from some high-water mark forces them to seriously reconsider their risk tolerances. I am drawing a distinction, however, between shifts based on a market-driven change in risk tolerance and those reallocations that are directly valuation motivated.

policy portfolio is intended to be the best possible passive portfolio that encapsulates all relevant information about the nature of the fund, its purpose, and how it interacts with prospective returns and risks in the financial markets. Policy portfolios have great organizational value in forming a baseline for structuring and controlling the investment management process. Following normal market movements, institutions try to rebalance back to their policy portfolios. Significant shifts tend to take place only after a major reallocation study or under extreme organizational duress. A downside to policy portfolios is that they tend to be defined somewhat arbitrarily, to be specified in greater detail than is justified, to be sustained over a longer time than is appropriate, and to form a high barrier for any tactical departure. Bill Jahnke (1999), Rob Arnott (2004), and Bernstein (2004) have written eloquently about the behavioral distortions that can arise from an overly rigid commitment to policy portfolios.

3   MARKET IMPACT

These different responses may either exacerbate or moderate market movements. Obviously, the holders will have little effect on the market; they are out of the game, so to speak. The rebalancers will tend to have a smoothing effect: As the market goes down, they buy more; as the market goes up, they sell. Within the valuator category, the contrarians and "reversionists" will act as moderators whereas those pursuing momentum strategies will have an exacerbating effect. Because shifting tends to become more urgent (and probably more widespread) in adverse conditions, shifters will generally exacerbate market moves.

This four-part categorization also indicates something about how new flows are invested. Holders and rebalancers will usually invest their new funds congruently with their existing allocations. (However, individuals do seem to exhibit somewhat more proactive flexibility in investing their new funds than with their existing allocations. This behavior is rather curious.) Valuators, of course, will make fresh decisions about where to deploy new funds, but this type represents a relatively small part of overall new fund flows. The bulk of flows is concentrated in holders and rebalancers—those with relatively rigid channels who tend to direct new investments largely toward their current allocations.[3]

4   REBALANCING AND MARKET EFFICIENCY

The rebalancing behaviors themselves may become sources of market inefficiency. Consider which of the behaviors really make sense. Suppose a fund starts with a portfolio that mirrors the market as a whole. One could argue that, in a strictly efficient market, price movements would move the fund's portfolio in concert with the evolving equilibrium, and in this case, holding behavior might make eminent sense. Most funds do not, however, have a portfolio that reflects the market as a whole (certainly not on purpose). Moreover, at least in the case of individuals, holding behavior is more likely to be the result of inertia, not sophisticated reasoning.

Some formulaic rebalancers believe they are adhering to an appropriate response in an efficient market. There is some inconsistency, however, in reestab-

---

[3] The large majority of existing dollar assets are also controlled by holders and formulaic rebalancers, which leads to the interesting question of whether the key risk premiums between asset classes are being priced by a relatively minor segment of the investing universe.

lishing the same allocation after an "efficient market" has made a major alteration in global asset weights. After all, a downward move reduces the asset's weight in the market portfolio, which argues for rebalancing back to an allocation somewhat lower than the original policy portfolio weight.

One sometimes hears the rationale for formulaic rebalancing presented in terms of buying cheaper after a decline and selling expensive assets after a rise. But if one really believes that the market has become discernibly cheaper as a result of a decline, shouldn't the right move be to establish an even larger position rather than to rebalance back to the original position? After all, if the policy allocation were done afresh, then (given the newly cheaper valuation) the revised allocation should be even more aggressive than before. Thus, one can reasonably argue that rebalancing should, in general, lead not to a resurrection of the original allocation but, rather, to a higher or lower percentage weighting!

Ideally, rational rebalancing should not be rigidly tethered to a fixed policy portfolio but should respond more fluidly to market signals—to the extent they are interpreted either as an efficient restructuring of the global portfolio or as a *discernible* change in valuation. The problem, of course, is that large investment organizations are not designed to facilitate such judgmental flexibility. And as one astute chief investment officer put it, "Better to have a rigid rebalancing by prior agreement than a portfolio that deteriorates into a holding pattern because the organization lacks the confidence or the will to reestablish the policy portfolio weightings—or to even move back in that direction."

The behavior of valuators is integrally tied into the issue of *discernibility*. To the extent that discernible valuation opportunities truly exist, why not try to take advantage of them? Of course, with valuators, the big question is whether their business models *compel* them to make tactical and timing decisions even when no market opportunities meet this test of "reasonable discernibility."

RISK AS RISK TO THE POLICY PORTFOLIO   5

A fund's strong reluctance to being forced to shift away from its policy portfolio may play an underappreciated role in setting the fund's risk tolerance and in shaping its policy portfolio in the first place. When an institution shifts to a lower-risk allocation, it departs from the policy portfolio that was previously considered to represent an optimal allocation. Institutional funds are understandably reluctant to move away from pre-established policy portfolios. Indeed, their rebalancing behavior is specifically geared toward sustaining this portfolio structure. Most institutional managers view it as most unfortunate if the fund is forced by an extreme market movement—or by the fund's investment committee—to abandon the presumably optimal approach and shift into a lower-risk strategy.

Potential trigger points for such mandated shifts lurk in the background of every investor's mind, however, acting as fence posts that define the outer limits of tolerable risk. These fence posts may also play a feedback role in setting the policy portfolio's overall risk level in the first place. For example, suppose adverse movements of 15–20 percent are considered to be the tolerable outer limit of the risk envelope. Then, a fund might reasonably wish to control the prospect of any such triggering event by reducing its probability to a minimal level (say, 10 percent). This shortfall constraint implies a portfolio volatility (risk) level in the 10–11 percent range, which happens to be exactly where most institutional funds are clustered.

Two further observations on this issue of risk. One is that the standard measure of risk, volatility, is an estimate of the range of returns *at a given horizon*. As pointed out by Mark Kritzman (2000) and by Kritzman and Don Rich (2002), this end-of-horizon distribution is not the same as the distribution of outcomes that could occur at some intermediary time. That distribution is much wider. And logically, this "riskier" intermediary distribution should determine when trigger points might be activated.[4]

6   THE ILLUSION OF GROWTH ETERNAL

Participants in the financial markets are intrinsically oriented toward an optimistic view of a world with a continuously compounding growth of value. Reality reminds us, however, that wealth can also be destroyed—both by "whimpers" and by "bangs." Sidney Homer and I (2004) once posed the following question: If a Roman soldier put just one drachma in a savings account and let it compound at 4 percent throughout the ages, how much money would his descendants have today? The answer turned out to be so many drachmas that, at virtually any exchange rate, it would amount to far more than the total existing wealth in the world. This outcome led to a follow-up question: What happened to it all? The sobering answer is that wealth is destroyed by war, inflation, devaluation, pandemic, political collapse, repudiation, obsolescence, virulent competition, bankruptcy, financial debacle, revolutionary technology, nonproductive investment, and so on. The natural inclination to deny the phantom of such discontinuities may be necessary for moving things forward, but it may also be a chronic source of inefficiency.

7   CONCLUSION

Participants in the financial markets often find themselves sailing on a sea of ambiguity through broad patches of fog, bouts of heavy weather, and occasional balmy periods that may prove only to be the center of passing storms. One can elect the passive approach—fly the beta flag and allow one's portfolio to float on the "index currents." Or one can choose to be an active alpha-seeking investor and try to chip away at the many chronic inefficiencies and behavioral biases that we know exist, even though we can't clearly discern how they are priced and whether they will profitably regress toward equilibrium within a reasonable time. With chronic inefficiencies, by their very definition, discernibility will always be somewhat clouded. (Otherwise, they would become acute—and would be long gone.) So, with these opportunities, one is always acting on imperfect knowledge and playing the odds. But without actively scanning the horizon and being poised to move on reasonably discernible opportunities, investors will surely have no chance of reaping the incremental return inherent in the grand continuous march toward efficiency.

The great investors are like the great sailors: They have the courage to set forth, they know where they want to go, they have a strong gyroscope to keep them on course, they have appropriate respect for the dangers of the sea and its potential for radical shifts in weather and currents, and they are not afraid to be alone for long stretches.

---

[4] An even more severe criterion would be based on the range of declines from a high-water mark (Leibowitz and Bova 2005b).

PRACTICE PROBLEMS FOR READING 13

The following information relates to Questions 1–5 and is based on the readings on Behavioral Finance

Rimfire Investment Management (RIM) is a large mutual fund organization with a tradition of providing individual investors with low-cost mutual fund alternatives. In recent years, RIM funds have experienced relatively poor performance and the result has been a decline in both assets under management and the number of investor accounts.

Donald Tolar, CFA and Maria Bonetti have been charged with the task of recommending changes to the investment research and management functions at RIM. Tolar, Bonetti, and others in RIM management are concerned with deficiencies in three areas; research process and recommendations, asset management, and client education. These concerns have surfaced from conversations with, and surveys of, current, past, and prospective shareholders of RIM mutual funds. Some managers wonder if decision making topics found in behavioral finance readings might be useful for addressing these deficiencies.

Bonetti believes behavioral finance can provide insight. She begins with RIM's chief economist. Two years ago he forecast GDP growth to be strong because the Federal Reserve would keep interest rates low, but instead GDP was marginally positive as the Fed increased rates in order to keep inflation in check. The chief economist blamed his inaccurate forecast on the Fed's decision to raise interest rates.

Tolar mentions that some of RIM's portfolio managers attempt to earn abnormal returns by trading arbitrage situations, but they recognize they are exposed to adverse risk faced by all arbitrageurs. In discussions with Tolar, one portfolio manager states that the specific risks to arbitrage can be managed and provide opportunity for profitable trading. To give an example, the manager first comments that "trading friction is beneficial to arbitrageurs because it provides higher returns," and in a second comment states that "fundamental risk is partially made better by shorting a substitute stock."

At the client level, one recommendation is to improve RIM's services by providing financial planning advice to clients. This service will be accomplished either "in house" with RIM employees acting as financial advisors, or else "out-sourced" to financial planning groups that include the RIM mutual fund family as a component in their asset allocation advice to their clients.

Bonetti notes that an examination of client portfolios shows that many clients with access to defined contribution plans, such as 401(k) and 403(b) plans, have made poor choices. Many portfolios exhibit poor diversification with an excess amount in the employee's own company stock. In addition, some plan participants with long time horizons have excess amounts in stable value funds rather than equity funds that will likely grow in value and provide an inflation hedge.

To increase the amount of funds that clients commit to equities, Tolar will meet with plan sponsors to educate them about the benefits to plan participants of proper diversification. He also will suggest that plan sponsors make available more equity fund choices because such an expansion of choices might result in participants having a higher allocation to equities.

Bonetti remarks "Well, now that we have considered client issues, let's get on with solving the problem of some funds generating poor risk/return performance. One approach to solve the problem is to offer an Alpha fund whose mission is to 'exploit chronic market inefficiencies,' including arbitrage opportunities and other behavioral biases. In order to accomplish that goal the firm has set two guidelines: First, in order to provide a wide selection of opportunities, arbitrage positions will be limited to a one year time horizon. And second, as a price target is approached, the position will be reduced, and any upward price target revision requires justification."

1. The chief economist's response to his forecast error describes an ego defense mechanism *best* identified as the:
   A. "if only" defense.
   B. "ceteris paribus" defense.
   C. "I was almost right" defense.

2. Are the portfolio manager's two comments regarding arbitrage risk correct?
   A. Yes.
   B. No. Only the first comment is correct.
   C. No. Only the second comment is correct.

3. The tendency of some individual investors to have a significant portion of funds allocated to stable value funds is indicative of:
   A. anchoring.
   B. money illusion.
   C. myopic loss aversion.

4. The solution Bonetti proposed to the problem of poor asset allocation choices seeks to exploit:
   A. status quo bias.
   B. myopic loss aversion.
   C. the endorsement effect.

5. Are Alpha fund's guidelines consistent with its mission?
   A. Yes.
   B. No. Only the first guideline is consistent.
   C. No. Only the second guideline is consistent.

SOLUTIONS FOR READING 13

1. A is correct. The economist's forecast assumed the Fed would keep rates low, but instead the Fed raised rates. This argument is the "if only" excuse.

2. C is correct. The first comment is incorrect because trading risk is a chronic inefficiency that can persist and be hard to exploit. The second comment is correct because it exploits an acute inefficiency, mispricing based on fundamentals.

3. C is correct. Myopic loss aversion is behavior associated with investors who focus on short time horizons. They tend to look at one-year returns rather than the longer time horizons appropriate for pension fund investing.

4. C is correct. The endorsement effect refers to the participant inferring the range of fund choices offered as a suggestion (endorsement) of the best way to allocate funds.

5. C is correct. Only the second guideline is consistent with Alpha Fund's mission. Chronic inefficiencies may exist for a number of years. Rigidly adhering to a one-year time horizon may force the manager to sell at a significant loss. The policy of price-target revision is consistent of adhering to a well thought out plan.

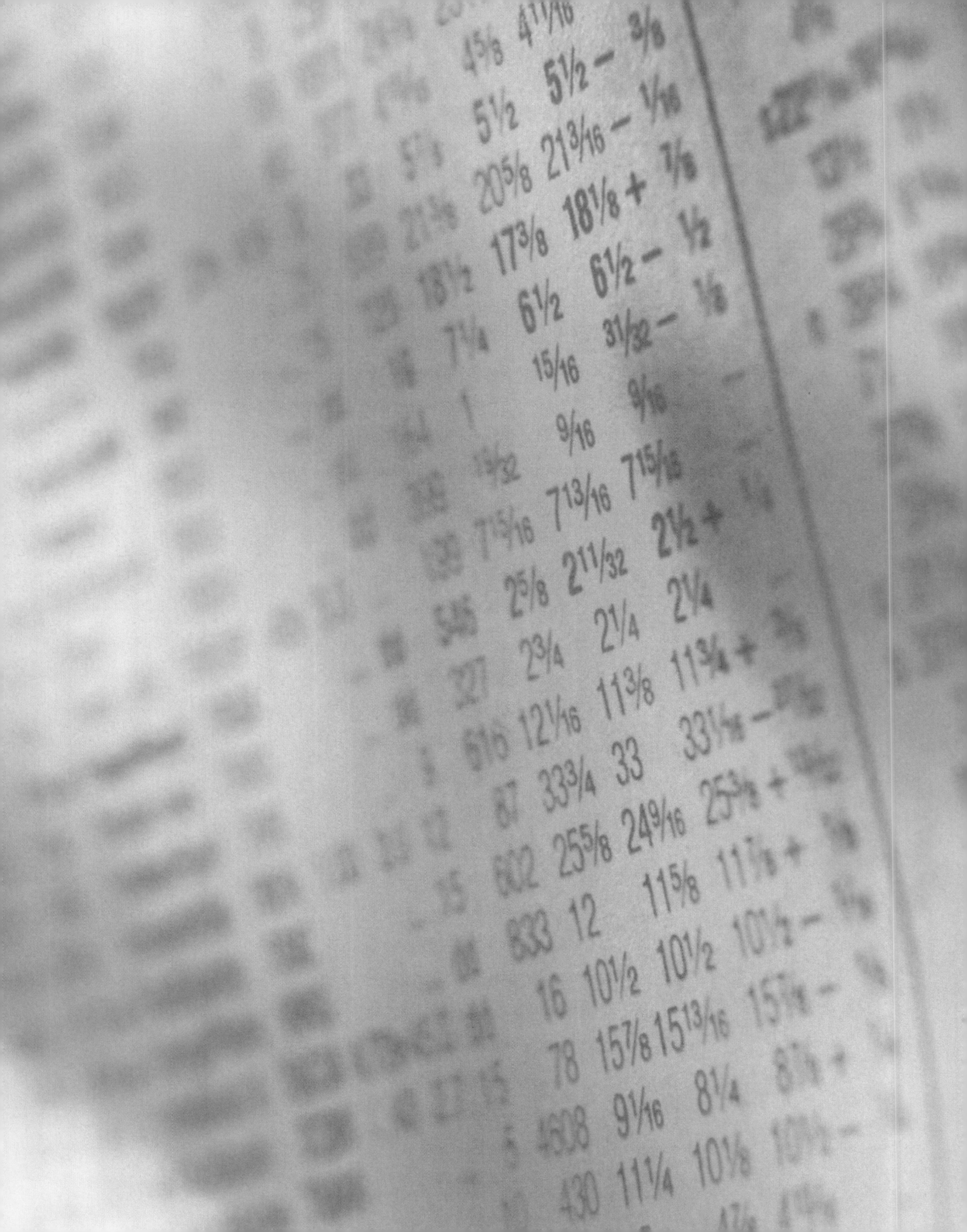

STUDY SESSION 4
PRIVATE WEALTH MANAGEMENT

This study session addresses the process of private wealth management and the construction of an investment policy statement for the individual investor. The investment policy statement is a blueprint for investing client assets—it identifies the needs, goals, and risk tolerance of the investor, as well as constraints under which the investment portfolio must operate, and then formulates an investment strategy to tax-efficiently reconcile these potentially conflicting requirements.

Because taxes and regulations vary from locality to locality, tax-efficient strategies for portfolio construction and wealth transfer are necessarily specific to the locality in which the investor is taxed. The study session focuses on investment strategies applicable across a wide range of localities. Although illustrations of such strategies may be presented from a country-specific perspective, candidates should focus on the underlying investment principles and be able to apply them to other tax settings.

The final reading in this study session examines the dynamic mix of human and financial capital during an investor's lifetime and the challenge of meeting financial goals throughout this uncertain time frame. It specifically addresses mortality and longevity risks by integrating insurance products into the asset allocation solution.

READING ASSIGNMENTS

MANAGING INDIVIDUAL INVESTOR PORTFOLIOS

by James W. Bronson, CFA, Matthew H. Scanlan, CFA, and Jan R. Squires, CFA

LEARNING OUTCOMES

The candidate should be able to:	Mastery
a. discuss how source of wealth, measure of wealth, and stage of life affect an individual investors' risk tolerance;	☐
b. explain the role of situational and psychological profiling in understanding an individual investor;	☐
c. compare and contrast the traditional finance and behavioral finance models of investor decision making;	☐
d. explain the influence of investor psychology on risk tolerance and investment choices;	☐
e. explain the use of a personality typing questionnaire for identifying an investor's personality type;	☐
f. compare and contrast risk attitudes and decision-making styles among distinct investor personality types, including cautious, methodical, spontaneous, and individualistic investors;	☐
g. explain the potential benefits, for both clients and investment advisers, of having a formal investment policy statement;	☐
h. explain the process involved in creating an investment policy statement;	☐
i. distinguish between required return and desired return and explain the impact these have on the individual investor's investment policy;	☐
j. explain how to set risk and return objectives for individual investor portfolios and discuss the impact that ability and willingness to take risk have on risk tolerance;	☐
k. identify and explain each of the major constraint categories included in an individual investor's investment policy statement;	☐
l. formulate and justify an investment policy statement for an individual investor;	☐

Managing Investment Portfolios: A Dynamic Process, Third Edition, John L. Maginn, CFA, Donald L. Tuttle, CFA, Jerald E. Pinto, CFA, and Dennis W. McLeavey, CFA, editors. Copyright © 2007 by CFA Institute. Reprinted with permission.

m. determine the strategic asset allocation that is most appropriate for an individual investor's specific investment objectives and constraints;	☐
n. compare and contrast traditional deterministic versus Monte Carlo approaches to retirement planning and explain the advantages of a Monte Carlo approach.	☐

1 INTRODUCTION

In the context of portfolio management, the terms "private client," "high-net-worth investor," and "individual investor" are used virtually interchangeably to reference the unique challenges of managing personal or family assets. Although a more precise definition of the individual investor is elusive, the basic need to properly manage one's financial affairs is self-evident, and the precedent for seeking professional management is well established. Indeed, Anglo-Saxon law has recognized the role of trustee, responsible for managing assets on behalf of others, as far back as the Middle Ages.

Private asset management has only recently begun to receive greater attention from the academic community and financial press. In contrast to large, tax-exempt institutional portfolios that are typically assumed to operate in perpetuity, the universe of private investors is heterogeneous, burdened by taxes, and less well suited to the simplifying assumptions of modern financial theory. Individual investors have diverse investment objectives, time horizons, and perceptions of risk, all subject to tax schedules that have varying degrees of stability and logic.

The increasing attention to private asset management reflects both a rising demand for financial services and an increased interest in empirical investor behavior. Net wealth in individually managed portfolios increased rapidly in the 1990s and beyond, creating a growth market for personalized financial services. At the same time, increased personal responsibility for investing retirement assets, evidenced by the growth in the self-directed segment of defined contribution pensions and savings plans, as well as the portability of fully vested retirement assets, has further increased the need for professional investment management at the individual level.

With the help of a case study, this reading examines the portfolio management process for individual investors. The Ingers are typical of a successful multigenerational family, with most of their wealth generated by a family business. Now that a cash sale of the business is imminent, they must reassess their financial situation and set appropriate guidelines for their soon-to-be large investment portfolio. The Ingers' goal is to create an investment policy statement (IPS) that recognizes their investment goals and constraints and then establishes consistent parameters for investing portfolio assets. The IPS should serve as the fundamental point of reference for both the Inger family and their investment advisors.

CASE STUDY   2

Victoria Jourdan, CFA, works for an investment firm that manages private client accounts. Both Jourdan and the Inger family reside in a politically stable country whose currency trades at a fixed exchange rate of 1:1 with the Euro. Real GDP growth and inflation both average about 3 percent annually, resulting in nominal annual growth of approximately 6 percent.

The country in which the Ingers reside maintains a flat tax of 25 percent on all personal income and a net capital gains tax (based on the sale of price-appreciated assets) of 15 percent, with no distinction between short- and long-term holding periods. Also incorporated into the tax code is a wealth transfer tax. Any asset transfer between two parties, whether as a gift or family inheritance, is taxed at the flat rate of 50 percent.

The country maintains a national pension plan, but that plan's long-term viability has been called into question because of an unfavorable demographic trend toward older, retirement-age recipients. Public debate has grown about how to assure the financial security of future retirees, and among this debate's chief outcomes has been the creation of self-contributory, tax-advantaged investment accounts for individuals. Taxpayers may annually contribute up to €5,000 of *after-tax* income to a Retirement Saving Account (RSA), which they then control. RSA investment returns are exempt from taxation, and participants may begin making tax-free withdrawals of any amount at age 62.

The Inger Family

Jourdan has been asked to manage the Inger family account, which is a new relationship for her firm. Jourdan observes that the Inger family has no stated investment policy or guidelines, and she arranges for a meeting with Peter and Hilda Inger, who have been married for 37 years, plus their two children, Christa and Hans, aged 25 and 30, respectively. Peter, Hilda, and Hans accept the invitation, but Christa, who currently resides a considerable distance away from her parents, cannot attend.

Peter Inger, 59, is a successful entrepreneur who founded a boat manufacturing business, IngerMarine, when he was 23 years old. He has worked compulsively to build the company into a producer of luxury pleasure boats sold worldwide, but he is now considering a business succession plan and retirement. Peter is eager to "monetize" his equity stake in IngerMarine and believes he will be able to sell his company within the next three months. He is already evaluating three separate bids that indicate probable proceeds, net of taxes on gains, of approximately €55 million to the Inger family in total. The four Inger family members are the sole IngerMarine shareholders, and any sale proceeds will accrue to the four family members in proportion to their percentage ownership in IngerMarine. Peter believes that everyone in his family is financially secure and wishes to preserve that security; he recognizes the family's need for a coherent investment plan.

Hilda Inger, 57, comes from a wealthy family. Since her marriage to Peter, she has been a housewife and mother to Christa and Hans. Hilda is the beneficiary of a trust established by her family. Throughout her lifetime, the trust will distribute to her an inflation-indexed annual payment (currently €75,000), which is taxed as personal income. At her death, payments will stop, and the trust's remaining assets will be transferred to a local charity.

Both Hans and Christa are unmarried. Hans currently works as a senior vice president at IngerMarine and specializes in boat design. Peter has tried to involve Christa in the family business but she has resisted, instead achieving moderate recognition and financial success as an artist. Christa has a 5-year-old son, Jürgen, whom she has chosen to raise alone.

The meeting with Peter, Hilda, and Hans and several telephone discussions with Christa result in the following financial and personal details for the Inger family:

TABLE 1   Inger Family Data

Income (Annual)

Peter salary[a]	€500,000
Hans salary	100,000
Hilda trust payout	75,000
Christa (art sales)	50,000

Peter Personal Assets

Home (fully paid for, held jointly with Hilda)	€1,200,000
IngerMarine company equity[b]	60,000,000
Diversified equity securities	750,000
Fixed income securities	1,000,000
Cash (money market fund)	1,000,000
Gold bullion	500,000
RSA[c]	50,000

Hilda Personal Assets

IngerMarine company equity[b]	€1,200,000

Hans Personal Assets

Home (net of mortgage)	€200,000
IngerMarine company equity[b]	2,400,000
Diversified equity securities	200,000
Cash (money market fund)	100,000

Christa Personal Assets

IngerMarine company equity[b]	€1,200,000
Balanced mutual funds	75,000
Cash (money market fund)	25,000

[a] Peter expects to receive a fixed annual payment of €100,000 (taxable as income) from the IngerMarine pension plan, beginning five years from now.

[b] IngerMarine equity values are pretax market values; the equity has a zero cost basis for purposes of taxation on capital gains. The company stock pays no dividend.

[c] Beginning at age 62, Peter plans to take a fixed annual distribution of approximately €5,000 (tax exempt).

BOX 1 JOURDAN'S FINDINGS AND PERSONAL OBSERVATIONS

Peter

Personality   Peter is a perfectionist and likes to maintain control. Now that he has attained financial success, he seems intent on preserving his wealth. He has consistently been averse to risk, leverage, and change, both in his company and in his personal life. IngerMarine has followed policies of low debt and slow growth, focusing on earnings stability. Like many of his countrymen, Peter holds a portion of his liquid assets in gold bullion. He believes that gold provides a viable hedge against catastrophic economic surprises and plans to maintain his current holding (€500,000) for the foreseeable future. By his own admission, Peter has been slow to adopt a succession plan—he has always believed that he was the best person to run IngerMarine. Although he now wants to sell IngerMarine and retire, in the past he resisted various purchase offers for the company.

Goals   Peter wants to maintain the standard of living that he and Hilda currently enjoy. In fact, he is actively investigating real estate for a second home, and he desires that the new home "make a statement." Hilda hopes the home will ultimately be featured in a magazine and anticipates that it will cost approximately €7 million.

Peter also wants to get to know his grandson better. Since Jürgen's birth, Peter has been estranged from his daughter and he wants to restore the relationship. He would like to provide financial support for Jürgen's health- and education-related expenses, and he plans to begin a gifting program for Jürgen next year; the gifts will be €15,000 per year, increasing with inflation.

Peter has a passion for photography and anticipates purchasing a minority interest (€5 million) in *Exteriors*, a noted photography magazine. The purchase would reflect his desire to support the magazine's high-quality work and might also lead to a post-retirement consulting opportunity. Because the investment is unlikely to produce meaningful current income, Peter does not intend to make any additional investment in *Exteriors*. Finally, Peter also has a strong desire to ensure his family's financial security and feels he will have accumulated enough wealth through the sale of IngerMarine to realize this goal. He does not, however, have a formal estate plan for transferring assets to his children and grandchildren.

Hilda

Personality   Hilda has intentionally removed herself from the family business. She has been a major factor, however, in Peter's decision to retire and have a second home closer to their daughter and grandson. In light of the major changes about to take place, Hilda wants to become more knowledgeable and active in managing the family's wealth.

Goals   Hilda has a strong interest in interior design and two years ago founded a small, sole-proprietorship design company. She is eager to apply her talents to designing and building the Ingers' new home and desires complete freedom in determining the home's interior design. Her company currently operates on a breakeven basis, with revenues approximately matching expenses.

Hans

Personality   Hans appears to be somewhat of a gambler. He has always felt financially secure, and is much more willing than his father Peter to engage in riskier investment opportunities. He sees his father as overly conservative and believes that IngerMarine would be in a more commanding position if Peter had only leveraged the company to expand production and marketing efforts. He drives a very expensive sports car.

> ### BOX 1
>
> **Goals**   Hans does not want to stay in the boat business and would prefer a career that allows him more free time. He has wanted to participate with college friends in various real estate projects, but his father has steadfastly refused to underwrite the investments. Consistent with his attitudes about risk, Hans prefers high-return investments, believing that he has enough time in his life to recover from any occasional losses. Although Hans is in no hurry to marry and have children, he believes he will ultimately do so and has been looking for a new, larger home, in the €500,000 to €700,000 price range. Finally, Hans is considering a minority investment (estimated to be €550,000, with no further investment planned) in a nightclub scheduled to open in his city.
>
> #### Christa
>
> **Personality**   Christa has been estranged from the family for several years. She has resisted pressure to enter the family business, deciding instead to pursue a career in art. She has also elected to raise her son Jürgen without family support, which has created tension within the family. She is very self-reliant but admits to having limited financial expertise. Her relations with the family have recently improved, and she is looking forward to increased contact with her parents.
>
> **Goals**   Christa is hoping to take a more proactive role in her financial affairs. She recognizes the need for a coordinated family financial plan, yet she does not wish to rely solely on the family's wealth to provide for her son's future. She would like to move into a larger apartment that would afford her the opportunity to create a painting studio. Rents are expensive, however, and she needs an assured source of income so that she may focus on her art career.

3   INVESTOR CHARACTERISTICS

A distinguishing characteristic of private asset management is the wide range of personal concerns and preferences that influence the decision-making process. Often unaccounted for in traditional models of "rational investor" behavior, such factors as personality, life experiences, and personal circumstances can play an important role in determining the framework for addressing financial decisions. An investment approach that begins with consideration of the Ingers' biases, preferences, and perceptions of risk paves the way for a meaningful discussion of portfolio objectives and may result in a stronger, more enduring client relationship than if such consideration were not given.

3.1 Situational Profiling

Many useful attempts have been made to categorize individual investors by stage of life or by economic circumstance. Such "situational" profiling runs the risk of oversimplifying complex behavior and should be used with a measure of caution—individual investors are unique and likely to exhibit characteristics that cut across arbitrary lines of categorization. Nonetheless, situational profiling can serve as a useful first step in considering an investor's basic philosophy and preferences, facilitating the discussion of investment risk by anticipating areas of potential concern or special importance to the investor. Examples of situational profiling include approaches based on source of wealth, measure of wealth, and stage of life.

3.1.1 Source of Wealth

Some classification schemes presume that the manner in which an individual investor has acquired wealth offers insight into that investor's probable attitude toward risk. Successful entrepreneurs, such as Peter Inger, who have created their wealth by personally taking business or market risks, are assumed to exhibit a higher level of risk tolerance than those who have been more passive recipients of wealth. "Self-made" investors may have greater familiarity with risk-taking and a higher degree of confidence in their ability to recover from setbacks. Such self-made investors, however, often have a strong sense of personal control over the risks that they assume. Despite their demonstrated willingness to take entrepreneurial risk, they can be very reluctant to cede control to a third party or to accept investment volatility over which they have no influence. Peter's slowness to adopt a succession plan and his largely conservative investment decisions typify such behavior.

In contrast, more-passive recipients of wealth may be associated with reduced willingness to assume risk. Such investors may have inherited their wealth; received a large, one-time payment; or simply accumulated savings during a period of secure employment. Because of the relatively passive nature of their wealth accumulation, these investors are assumed to have less experience with risk-taking, less understanding of what taking risk means, and less confidence that they can rebuild their wealth should it be lost. Christa Inger may be an example of such an investor.

3.1.2 Measure of Wealth

Given the subjective nature of financial well-being, it is difficult to categorize investors based on portfolio size (net worth). A portfolio that one individual considers large and ample to meet future needs may be insufficient in the eyes of another individual. All the same, it is not unreasonable to consider that investors who *perceive* their holdings as small may demonstrate lower tolerance for portfolio volatility than investors who perceive their holdings as large. A portfolio whose returns do not easily support the investor's lifestyle might be considered small. If the investor's ongoing needs are so well covered that succession and estate planning issues have become important, the portfolio might be considered "large."

3.1.3 Stage of Life

In life-stage classifications, investment policy, and particularly risk tolerance, are determined by one's progress on the journey from childhood to youth, adulthood, maturity, retirement, and death. Theoretically, a person's ability to accept risk should begin at a high level and gradually decline through his lifetime, while willingness to assume risk should be driven largely by cash flow considerations (income versus expenses). The human financial condition is driven by additional factors, however, such as life experiences, living conditions, starting point on the scale of wealth, and personal abilities and ambitions. For the sake of illustration, an individual's investment policy can be viewed as passing through four general phases: foundation, accumulation, maintenance, and distribution.

During the *foundation* phase of life, the individual is establishing the base from which wealth will be created. This base might be a marketable skill, the establishment of a business, or the acquisition of educational degrees and certifications. During the foundation phase, the individual is usually young, with a long time horizon, which normally would be associated with an above-average tolerance for risk. Risk tolerance should certainly be above-average in the foundation stage if the individual has inherited wealth. Lacking such wealth, the foundation phase may be the period when an individual's investable assets are at their lowest and financial uncertainty is at its highest. A young entrepreneur may have substantial expenses in establishing a business, resulting in a liquidity need that overrides all other considerations. Marriage and the arrival of children may create a desire for more-rapid wealth accumulation that is not yet matched by either ability or willingness to assume risk.

Ironically, at the point in life when individuals should theoretically be ready to assume risk, many are either unwilling or unable to do so. Christa, because of her desired independence, has many of the financial stresses associated with the foundation phase and may still be building the foundation of her ultimate career as an artist. Her son Jürgen is in the earliest days of this phase as he begins his childhood education.

In the *accumulation* phase, earnings accelerate as returns accrue from the marketable skills and abilities acquired during the foundation period and gradually reach their peak. In the early years of the accumulation phase, income rises and investable assets begin to accumulate. Expenses also rise during this period, through the establishment of family, purchase of homes, and care and education of children. In the middle and later years of wealth accumulation, expenses typically begin to decline as children reach adulthood, educational needs are fulfilled, and home purchases are completed. Income generally continues to rise as the individual reaches peak productivity. If an individual's personal spending habits do not change, the gap between income and expenses may widen throughout the accumulation phase, allowing for an increase in savings.

Some individuals may forgo investing their growing wealth and instead increase spending on luxury items or perhaps make gifts to relatives or charities. For investors, however, the accumulation phase is characterized by increased risk tolerance, driven by their increasing wealth and a still long-term time horizon. Hans is in the early years of this phase and is clearly willing to assume high risk to achieve his wealth and lifestyle goals.

During the *maintenance phase*, the individual has moved into the later years of life and usually has retired from daily employment or the pressures of owning a business. This phase focuses on maintaining the desired lifestyle and financial security. Preserving accumulated wealth begins to increase in importance, while the growth of wealth may begin to decline in importance. Risk tolerance will begin to decline; not only is the individual's time horizon shortening but his confidence in the ability to replace capital or recover from losses is often diminished.

In the maintenance phase, investors will typically reduce exposure to higher-volatility asset classes, such as common stocks, and increase exposure to lower-volatility investments, such as intermediate-term bonds. Because the individual now has less time to recover from poor investment results, portfolio stability becomes increasingly important. In this phase, the challenge is to achieve a desired level of portfolio stability and maintain an exposure to risky assets sufficient to preserve the portfolio's purchasing power. Investors who become too conservative too soon after retirement may reach an elderly age with assets that have suffered significant declines in purchasing power. With the imminent sale of IngerMarine, Peter is about to enter the maintenance phase.

In the *distribution phase*, accumulated wealth is transferred to other persons or entities. For many, this phase begins when the individual is still reaping the benefits of the maintenance phase and retirement. For most, the phase involves a conscious decision to begin transferring wealth. Dealing with tax constraints often becomes an important consideration in investment planning, as investors seek to maximize the after-tax value of assets transferred to others. Although asset distribution may take place in the later stages of life, planning for such transfers can begin much earlier.

For individuals with substantial wealth, the distribution phase should be a well-planned program executed during the course of several years. Efficient wealth transfers take advantage of market conditions, tax laws, and various transfer mechanisms. An individual may consider various transfer strategies: He might establish trusts or foundations for heirs or charities, make outright gifts of cash or assets, modify the legal ownership structure of certain assets, and make advance provisions for care in the event of health problems and to pay wealth transfer taxes.

Although the progression from accumulation to distribution may be linear, it is not necessarily so. Individuals in the accumulation phase may become dissatisfied with a career choice and return to the foundation phase. Some may be forced to make such a move as demand for their skills diminishes. A sudden illness or accident may move an individual unexpectedly to the distribution phase.

In each of the above phases, personal circumstances are a driving force in how an individual responds to each cycle of life. The foundation phase will be different for those who enter life with a base of inherited wealth than it will for those who come from families of modest means. The distribution phase can become increasingly complicated for the very wealthy but remain quite basic for those with little wealth. Because of obligations and lifestyle, some investors never leave the accumulation phase. For others, the stress of an adverse life experience, such as living through an economic calamity or war, may override all phases and never allow them to properly match their willingness and ability to assume risk in a suitable investment program.

Situational assessments allow investment advisors to quickly categorize potential clients and explore investment issues likely to be of greatest importance to them. We must note, however, that investors seldom fall easily into just one category, and clearly a dynamic relationship exists among the above considerations. Peter and Hilda, for example, have a multigenerational planning perspective and a portfolio sufficiently large to maintain a long-term investment time horizon—their risk tolerance is not necessarily diminished because of their age. Although Hans may be moving into the accumulation phase, he clearly retains elements associated with the foundation phase (e.g., above-average risk tolerance). Similarly, Christa's circumstances most directly mirror the accumulation phase, although she has the financial ability to develop a long-term investment plan. Source of wealth considerations play an obvious role in the Inger family situation and are colored by stage-of-life issues. One recipient of inherited wealth (e.g., Hans) in a later life stage may view his or her portfolio as sufficiently large to assume additional risk, but a second recipient in an earlier stage (e.g., Christa), with less experience and lower confidence, may exhibit less willingness to take risk. The value of situational paradigms, therefore, lies more in their general insights into human behavior and less in their ability to fully interpret individual circumstances. Investment advisors should emphasize the *process* of gathering and assessing relevant situational information rather than the specific category in which an individual investor may fall. The advisor who recognizes familiar patterns is better able to anticipate areas of potential concern and to structure a discussion of portfolio policy in terms relevant to the client.

3.2 Psychological Profiling

A determinant of individual investing that has generally received less focus than other, more objective influences is the psychological process by which an individual establishes his or her investment preferences. Clearly, every individual brings to the investment decision-making process an objective set of financial circumstances, goals, and constraints that will strongly influence the set of investment alternatives from which he chooses. Yet underlying behavioral patterns and personality characteristics often also play an important role in setting individual risk tolerance and return objectives. Psychological profiling, sometimes referred to as personality typing, bridges the differences between "traditional finance" (economic analysis of objective financial circumstances) and what has come to be defined as "behavioral finance."

3.2.1 Traditional Finance

Much of the standard history of economic and financial theory rests on the philosophy that financial market participants are rational, information-based investors with dispassionate objectives that maximize the expected utility of wealth.

In models of traditional, or standard, investment decision making, investors are assumed to:

▶ exhibit risk aversion;

▶ hold rational expectations; and

▶ practice asset integration.

Risk aversion implies that investors with otherwise equivalent investment options will prefer the investment with the lowest volatility. They will choose an investment with a certain outcome over an investment with an uncertain outcome that has the same expected value.

Rational expectations assume that investors are coherent, accurate, and unbiased forecasters. Their forecasts will reflect all relevant information, and they will learn from their past mistakes.

Asset integration refers to the process by which investors choose among risky investments. Investors practice asset integration by comparing the portfolio return/risk distributions that result from combining various investment opportunities with their existing holdings. Assets are evaluated in the context of their impact on the aggregate investment portfolio, not as stand-alone investments.

As a consequence of the traditional assumptions about individual economic behavior, traditional models of the portfolio building process have historically relied on the following tenets:

▶ Asset pricing is driven by economic considerations such as production costs and prices of substitutes.

▶ Portfolios are constructed holistically, reflecting covariances between assets and overall objectives and constraints.

3.2.2 Behavioral Finance

A growing body of research points to differences in behavior caused by differences in how individuals approach uncertain situations. In these studies, psychological considerations appear to play an important role in guiding investor behavior, especially during periods of stress. Work done by Daniel Kahneman, Meir Statman, Richard Thaler, Robert Shiller, Amos Tversky, and others has firmly established the field of "behavioral finance," and several investment firms currently incorporate behavioral finance as a cornerstone of their investment philosophy. These decision-making models attempt to incorporate the principles of behavioral finance, in which individual investors are recognized to:

► exhibit loss aversion;

► hold biased expectations; and

► practice asset segregation.

Loss aversion is demonstrated when investors evaluate opportunities in terms of gain or loss rather than in terms of uncertainty with respect to terminal wealth. Faced with the choice between a) a certain loss or b) an uncertain outcome that might produce a smaller loss but whose expected value is a larger loss, investors are likely to exhibit loss aversion by choosing the uncertain alternative. Choosing the uncertain outcome actually demonstrates risk-seeking behavior—traditional finance predicts that investors, being risk averse, should choose the certain loss over an alternative whose expected loss is larger.

In their discussion of "prospect theory," Kahneman and Tversky (1979) found that individuals place different weights on gains and losses. Their studies yielded evidence that most people are more distressed by prospective losses than they are pleased by the prospect of equivalent gains. Further, individuals responded differently to equivalent probabilistic scenarios, depending on whether the outcomes resulted in gains or losses. Kahneman and Tversky found that when subjects were presented with a choice between a sure gain of $500 or a 50/50 chance to either gain $1,000 or receive nothing at all, respondents overwhelmingly chose the "sure gain." Correspondingly, when another group was asked to choose between a sure loss of $500 or a 50/50 chance to lose either $1,000 or nothing at all, a majority gravitated to the uncertain alternative. It appears to be human nature to prefer an uncertain loss to a certain loss but to prefer a certain gain to an uncertain gain.

Biased expectations result from cognitive errors and misplaced confidence in one's ability to assess the future. Examples of cognitive errors include mistaking the skills of the average manager for those of a particular manager; overestimating the significance of low-probability events; and overestimating the representativeness of one asset compared with another asset.

Asset segregation is the evaluation of investment choices individually, rather than in aggregate. Related behavior includes reference dependence, in which economic behavior is shaped by the frame of reference or the context in which choices are presented, and mental accounting (organizing investments into separate psychological accounts depending on purpose or preference).

According to behavioral models of individual decision making, portfolio construction takes place under a more complex set of assumptions than those given previously:

► Asset pricing reflects both economic considerations, such as production costs and prices of substitutes, and subjective individual considerations, such as tastes and fears.

► Portfolios are constructed as "pyramids" of assets, layer by layer, in which each layer reflects certain goals and constraints.

Within this behavioral framework, individuals also have characteristics that either sharpen or blunt the human tendencies for risk avoidance. The process of "personality typing" seeks to identify and categorize these characteristics to facilitate the discussion of risk and risk tolerance. We emphasize, however, that the primary value of any personality typing approach is to provide both the investor and the manager with a framework for thinking about the influence of personality on investment decision-making, not to neatly categorize investors into arbitrarily defined personality types.

3.2.3 Personality Typing

Generally, all investors have unique, complex personality dimensions shaped by socioeconomic background, personal experience, and current wealth status. These diverse factors make it difficult to precisely categorize investors into types. Yet by combining studies of historical behavior with surveys and scenario analysis, we can broadly classify investors into types. Through "personality typing," investment advisors can better understand the behavioral drivers that lead to an individual's goal setting, asset allocation, and risk-taking decisions, and thus advisors can better manage client expectations and behavior.

Personality typing can assist investment advisors in determining an individual investor's propensity for risk taking and his decision-making style in seeking returns. By assigning values to the factors that successfully identify an individual's propensity to assume risk in the investment process, the advisor can obtain very useful information on the client's risk tolerance.

Generally, two approaches to personality classification exist. Often the default option within investment firms is an ad hoc evaluation by the investment advisor, who categorizes the investor based on personal interviews and a review of past investment activity. Although experienced managers may claim proficiency in their ability to profile investor personalities, subjective assessments are difficult to standardize, and their terms often mean different things to different people. Even when the assessment is generally correct, the degree of an individual investor's risk tolerance is difficult to gauge.

Reflecting a discomfort with this ad hoc approach, a growing number of investment firms now employ short client questionnaires to gain insight into the investor's propensity to accept risk and the decision-making style used in pursuing investment returns. These questionnaires address investment topics but may also include self-evaluative statements that have no direct investment context. A hypothetical example of such a questionnaire is presented in Exhibit 1. The classification scheme blends the Bailard, Biehl, and Kaiser approach[1] with the analytical psychology of Carl Jung.[2] The questionnaire is representative but certainly not definitive or exhaustive; it is intended to reflect the process and content typically employed by investment firms and consultants engaged in more or less formal personality typing of clients.

The critical question that must be answered with respect to client questionnaires is whether the results consistently assign respondents to risk-taking and decision-making styles that explain the respondents' actual behavior. In addition, there must be a meaningful link between the survey results and the ultimate personality typing. To obtain the appropriate linkage between investor survey responses and ultimate investment behavior, a stratified sample can be drawn to replicate the overall demographic characteristics of investors. A stratified random sample involves independent sampling from subgroups that, when combined, represent a population's overall characteristics. Results from the sample questions (each question addresses a specific category of investor risk tolerance and decision-making style) are tabulated and used to identify systematic differences in decision-making style and risk tolerance. Continuing with the example from

---

[1] See Bailard, Biehl, and Kaiser (1986).

[2] See, for example, Berens (2000).

EXHIBIT 1	Decision-Making Style and Risk Tolerance Questionnaire

Decision-Making Style Questions	Does Not Apply	Somewhat Applies	Generally Applies	Always Applies
1. I keep all my mail. I never throw anything out.	0	1	2	3
2. My favorite subject in school was mathematics.	0	1	2	3
3. I would rather sit in front of the television than organize one of my closets.	0	1	2	3
4. I would rather work by myself than in groups.	0	1	2	3
5. I consider myself to be independent.	0	1	2	3
6. When asked out to dinner or a movie, I generally organize the event.	0	1	2	3
7. I am bothered by people who don't work hard.	0	1	2	3
8. I never leave anything unfinished.	0	1	2	3
9. I generally drive very fast.	0	1	2	3
10. I enjoy competitive sports.	0	1	2	3
11. I rarely worry about finances.	0	1	2	3
12. I like seeing scary movies.	0	1	2	3
13. I am always eager to meet new people.	0	1	2	3
14. I sometimes become impatient waiting for an elevator.	0	1	2	3
15. People accuse me of having a "quick temper."	0	1	2	3

Risk Tolerance Questions	Does Not Apply	Somewhat Applies	Generally Applies	Always Applies
16. I become nervous when flying.	0	1	2	3
17. I don't like contact sports like football.	0	1	2	3
18. When arguing with friends, I am usually the one who concedes.	0	1	2	3
19. I never had a strong bond with my parents.	0	1	2	3
20. I wish I could be more expressive with my feelings.	0	1	2	3
21. I never raise my voice.	0	1	2	3
22. I don't like to discuss personal items with friends.	0	1	2	3
23. I like art.	0	1	2	3
24. I would classify my political beliefs as liberal.	0	1	2	3
25. I am not easily excitable.	0	1	2	3
26. I don't swim in the ocean.	0	1	2	3
27. I am afraid of public speaking.	0	1	2	3
28. If offered a bigger house, I would pass because I don't like the hassle of moving.	0	1	2	3
29. I have had many relationships with the opposite sex.	0	1	2	3
30. I often wear cutting-edge new fashions.	0	1	2	3
31. I will always take the initiative when others do not.	0	1	2	3

Exhibit 1, raw scores are portrayed across the two dimensions of decision-making style and risk tolerance. Based on these measures, four investment personality types are established. The types are consistent with distinct style/risk tradeoffs and may provide predictive insight into an individual's ultimate investment behavior.

Cautious Investors   Cautious investors are generally averse to potential losses. This aversion may be a consequence of their current financial situation or of various life experiences, but most exhibit a strong need for financial security. Cautious investors usually desire low-volatility investments with little potential for loss of principal. Although these individuals generally do not like making their own decisions, they are not easily persuaded by others and often choose not to seek professional advice. Cautious investors dislike losing even small amounts of money and seldom rush into investments. They often miss opportunities because of overanalysis or fear of taking action. Their investment portfolios generally exhibit low turnover and low volatility.

Methodical Investors   This group relies on "hard facts." Methodical investors may intently follow market analysts or undertake research on trading strategies. Even when their hard work is rewarded, they typically remain on a quest for new and better information. Their reliance on analysis and database histories generally keeps them from developing emotional attachments to investment positions, and their discipline makes them relatively conservative investors.

Spontaneous Investors   Spontaneous investors are constantly readjusting their portfolio allocations and holdings. With every new development in the marketplace, they fear a negative consequence. Although spontaneous investors generally acknowledge that they are not investment experts, they doubt all investment advice and external management decisions. They are over-managers; their portfolio turnover ratios are the highest of any personality type. Although some investors in this group are successful, most experience below-average returns. Their investment profits are often offset by the commission and trading charges generated by second-guessing and frequent adjustment of portfolio positions. Spontaneous investors are quick to make decisions on investment trades and generally are more concerned with missing an investment trend than with their portfolio's level of risk.

Individualist Investors   This group has a self-assured approach to investing. Individualists gain information from a variety of sources and are not averse to devoting the time needed to reconcile conflicting data from their trusted sources. They are also not afraid to exhibit investment independence in taking a course of action. Individualist investors place a great deal of faith in hard work and insight, and have confidence that their long-term investment objectives will be achieved.

An advisor can use questionnaire results to plot an investor's risk/style score, as Exhibit 2 illustrates. Clearly, the more extreme investor personality types will plot farther away from the center of the graph.

As mentioned earlier, a predictive link must exist from the questionnaire responses to the resulting personality typing that is derived, and to the subsequent investment behavior that occurs. If the correlation is high between the

EXHIBIT 2	Personality Types

	Decisions based primarily on thinking	*Decisions based primarily on feeling*
More risk averse	Methodical	Cautious
Less risk averse	Individualist	Spontaneous

personality dimensions outlined in the questionnaire and the individual's ultimate portfolio selections, then the exercise has predictive value. If the results are uncorrelated, then the questionnaire must be revised. In the example above, a stratified sample of clients would complete the questionnaire, and the raw scores would be used to identify subgroups. Each subgroup would then be associated with a specific investment style. A "Methodical" subgroup might be expected to maintain a "value" equity portfolio of very stable stocks, along with a substantial commitment to highly rated fixed income securities.

Correlation analysis can be used to assess a questionnaire's usefulness. By assigning ranks to personality types (1 = Methodical, 2 = Cautious, 3 = Individualistic, 4 = Spontaneous) and to the riskiness of respondents' existing portfolios, standard statistical methods can be used to evaluate whether personality types are correlated with investor behavior, especially risk-taking. If a significant positive correlation exists, the questionnaire may have predictive value and be of practical use to advisors. Note that because questionnaire design and analysis is a specialized area, advisors would be wise to have their classification scheme validated by a psychometrician; the style/risk personality typing example presented here should be viewed as only suggestive of those actually used in practice.

The Inger Family   In trying to classify the Inger family using the above approach, Jourdan asks each family member to complete the investor style/risk survey. Based on their responses, Jourdan classifies the family members as shown in Exhibit 3.

The symbols represent the family member's composite survey score. The position of the symbol relative to the box represents the strength or polarization of the personality type. For example, Hilda scored fairly evenly in all categories with a slight bias toward an "individualist" personality, while Hans' score demonstrates a strong bias toward a "spontaneous" investor.

After reviewing the results of the Inger family's questionnaires, Jourdan notes that their scores are generally consistent with her initial observations. Her only mild surprise is that Christa was positioned as a "cautious" investor, which does not fully coincide with what some would see as a relatively aggressive or

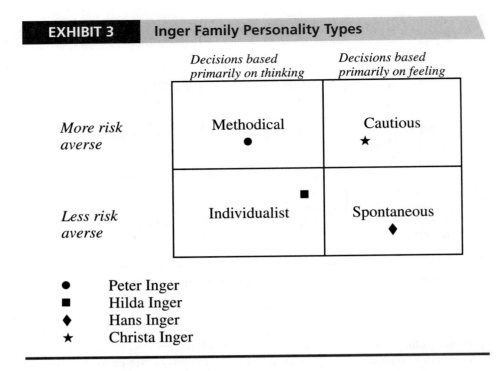

EXHIBIT 3   Inger Family Personality Types

	Decisions based primarily on thinking	Decisions based primarily on feeling
More risk averse	Methodical ●	Cautious ★
Less risk averse	Individualist ■	Spontaneous ◆

●   Peter Inger
■   Hilda Inger
◆   Hans Inger
★   Christa Inger

adventurous decision to ignore the family business and support her child through a career in art.

The survey scores reflect each family member's appetite for risk in his or her individual portfolio, but the challenge remains of integrating these diverse personalities and goals into a coordinated family investment program.

4   INVESTMENT POLICY STATEMENT

The investment policy statement is a client-specific summation of the circumstances, objectives, constraints, and policies that govern the relationship between advisor and investor. A well-constructed IPS presents the investor's financial objectives, the degree of risk he or she is willing to take, and any relevant investment constraints that the advisor must consider. It also sets operational guidelines for constructing a portfolio that can be expected to best meet these objectives while remaining in compliance with any constraints. Finally, the IPS establishes a mutually agreed-upon basis for portfolio monitoring and review.

Constructing an IPS is a dynamic process in which an individual and his investment advisor must identify and then reconcile investment objectives, portfolio constraints, and risk tolerance. The exercise should produce realistic investment goals and, equally important, a common vocabulary for advisor and investor to discuss risk and return.

The process of writing a thorough policy statement ultimately gives the individual investor greater control over her financial destiny. To the extent that drafting the IPS has been an educational process, the investor emerges better able to recognize appropriate investment strategies and no longer needs to blindly trust the investment advisor. Further, an IPS is portable and easily understood by other advisors. If a second opinion is needed, or if a new investment advisor must be introduced, the IPS facilitates a thorough review and ensures investment continuity.

Finally, the IPS serves as a document of understanding that protects both the advisor and the individual investor. If management practices or investor directions are subsequently questioned, both parties can refer to the policy statement for clarification or support. Ideally, the review process set forth in the IPS will identify such issues before they become serious.

4.1 Setting Return and Risk Objectives

Establishing portfolio objectives for return and risk is a systematic process applicable for institutional as well as individual investor portfolios. As one reconciles investment goals with risk tolerance, however, client-specific investment parameters emerge. Both the general process and client-specific results are illustrated as Jourdan continues to work with the Inger family.

4.1.1 Return Objective

The process of identifying an investor's desired and required returns should take place concurrently with the discussion of risk tolerance. In the end, the IPS must present a return objective that is attainable given the portfolio's risk constraints.

It is important at the outset to distinguish between a return requirement and a return desire. The former refers to a return level necessary to achieve the investor's primary or critical long-term financial objectives; the latter denotes a return level associated with the investor's secondary goals. In the case of Peter and Hilda, it appears that their current needs are being met by Peter's salary of €500,000. If IngerMarine is sold, they may *require* a return that replaces Peter's salary (a critical objective) and *desire* a return that will accommodate their major acquisitions and still leave their children financially secure (important but less critical objectives).

Return requirements are generally driven by annual spending and relatively long-term saving goals. Historically, these goals have often been classified as *income* requirements and *growth* requirements, with the presumption that portfolio income (dividends, interest, and rent) is used for current spending, and portfolio gains (from price appreciation) are reinvested for growth. Income needs, therefore, are met with income-producing securities, primarily bonds, and growth objectives are pursued with stocks and other equity-oriented investments.

"Growth" and "income" are intuitively appealing descriptors, and the terms remain in use. The terms are flawed, however, in that they blur the distinction between an investor's return requirements and risk tolerance. Portfolios classified as income-oriented are typically biased toward a lower-risk, heavily fixed-income asset allocation. Conversely, growth-oriented portfolios are biased toward equities, with little direct consideration of risk tolerance.

Return requirements are often first presented in real terms, without adjustment for inflation. When an investor's current spending and long-term savings goals are expressed in terms of purchasing power, however, it becomes clear that even income-oriented portfolios require a considerable element of nominal growth.

As an alternative to "growth" and "income," a "total return" approach to setting return requirements looks first at the individual's investment goals and then identifies the annual after-tax portfolio return necessary to meet those goals. That required return must then be reconciled with the individual's separately determined risk tolerance and investment constraints. With the notable exception of tax considerations, it is typically less important whether the total investment return stems from income or price appreciation.

When an investor's return objectives are inconsistent with his risk tolerance, a resolution must be found. If the investor's return objectives cannot be met without violating the portfolio's parameters for risk tolerance, he may need to modify his low- and intermediate-priority goals. Alternatively, he may have to accept a slightly less comfortable level of risk, assuming that he has the "ability" to take additional risk. An individual, for example, who discovers that his retirement goals are inconsistent with current assets and risk tolerance may have to defer the planned date of

EXHIBIT 4	Peter and Hilda Inger Five-Year Statement of Cash Flows					
	Current	**1**	**2**	**3**	**4**	**5**
	€	€	€	€	€	€
Inflows						
Salary: Peter (taxed as income)	500,000					
Trust payment: Hilda[a] (taxed as income)	75,000	77,250	79,568	81,955	84,413	86,946
Pension: Peter[b] (taxed as income)	–	–	–	–	–	100,000
RSA: Peter[b] (tax-free)	–	–	–	5,000	5,000	5,000
Sale of company (taxed as gain)	–	61,200,000	–	–	–	–
Total inflows	575,000	61,277,250	79,568	86,955	89,413	191,946
Outflows						
Income tax (25%)	(143,750)	(19,313)	(19,892)	(20,489)	(21,103)	(46,737)
Gains tax (15%)		(9,180,000)				
Second home	–	(7,000,000)	–	–	–	–
Investment in magazine	–	(5,000,000)	–	–	–	–
Support for Jürgen[a]	–	(15,000)	(15,450)	(15,914)	(16,391)	(16,883)
Transfer tax on support payment (50%)		(7,500)	(7,725)	(7,957)	(8,196)	(8,442)
Living and miscellaneous expenses[a]	(500,000)	(515,000)	(530,450)	(546,364)	(562,754)	(579,637)
Total expenses	(643,750)	(21,736,813)	(573,517)	(590,724)	(608,444)	(651,699)
Net additions/withdrawals	(68,750)	39,540,437	(493,949)	(503,769)	(519,031)	(459,753)

[a] Assumed to increase with inflation at 3% annually.

[b] Fixed annual payments.

retirement, accept a reduced standard of living in retirement, or increase current savings (a reduction in the current standard of living).

If the investment portfolio is expected to generate a return that exceeds the investor's return objectives, there is the luxury of dealing with a surplus. The investor must decide whether to a) protect that surplus by assuming less risk than she is able and willing to accept or b) to use the surplus as the basis for assuming greater risk than needed to meet the original return goals, with the expectation of achieving a higher return.

To calculate the required return and to fully understand the cumulative effects of anticipated changes in income, living expenses, and various stage-of-life events, an advisor may wish to incorporate a cash flow analysis. The statement of cash flows in Exhibit 4 simplistically highlights a five-year horizon for Peter and Hilda Inger based on information gleaned by Jourdan from interviews and background examination.

Net cash flows for Peter and Hilda conveniently stabilize in Year 2 and decline in Year 5. Consequently, we can estimate their after-tax return objective in Exhibit 5 by dividing projected needs in Year 2 (€493,949) by their net investable assets at the end of Year 1 (€42.3 million). We find that €493,949/€42,300,000 = 1.17 percent. Adding the current annual inflation rate of 3.00 percent to 1.17 percent results in an approximate after-tax nominal return objective of 4.17 percent. [Note: Strictly speaking, the inflation rate should be adjusted upward by the portfolio's average tax rate. For ease of presentation, we have simply added 3 percent inflation.]

EXHIBIT 5	Peter and Hilda Inger Investable Assets, Net Worth, and Required Return	
Investable Assets	**Amount**	**Percent of Net Worth**
Year 1 cash flow	€39,540,437	77
Stock holdings	750,000	1
Fixed-income holdings	1,000,000	2
Cash equivalents	1,000,000	2
RSA account	50,000	0
Total	€42,340,437	83
Real Estate		
First home	€1,200,000	2
Second home	7,000,000	14
Total	€8,200,000	16
Gold	€500,000	1
Net Worth	€51,040,437	100
Return Objective		
Distributions in Year 2	€ 493,949	= 1.17
Divided by investable assets	€42,340,437	
Plus expected inflation	3%	= 4.17

4.1.2 Risk Objective

An individual's risk objective, or overall risk tolerance, is a function of both ability to take risk and willingness to take risk.

Ability to Take Risk   Assessing an individual's ability to take risk is suited to quantitative measurement. It is generally the investment advisor who defines the terms of the analysis and then must explain the results. Although approaches to the analysis will vary, all must address the following questions:

1. What are the investor's financial needs and goals, both long term and short term?

   An investor's ability to take risk is determined by his financial goals relative to resources and the time frame within which these goals must be met. If the investor's financial goals are modest relative to the investment portfolio, clearly he has greater ability, all else equal, to accommodate volatility and negative short-term returns.

   As the investment portfolio grows or as its time horizon lengthens, the ability to recover from intermediate investment shortfalls also increases. All else equal, longer-term objectives allow the investor greater opportunity to consider more-volatile investments, with correspondingly higher expected returns.

   Peter and Hilda Ingers' investment objectives are primarily short to intermediate term in nature:

   ► support for current lifestyle;

   ► construction of second home;

   ► investment in *Exteriors*;

   ► support for Jürgen's education;

   ► expansion of Hilda's design company.

   Longer term, Peter and Hilda wish to preserve the financial security that their family currently enjoys. Preserving purchasing power is apparently more important to them than creating further wealth.

2. How important are these goals? How serious are the consequences if they are not met?

   Critical goals allow lower margin for error and reduce the portfolio's ability to accommodate volatile investments. Financial security and the ability to maintain current lifestyle are generally among the investor's highest priorities; luxury spending, however defined, is least critical.

   Beyond assuring their financial security, the Ingers' investment goals appear *important* but perhaps not *critical*. The second home is important to both Peter and Hilda and will play a major role in defining their future lifestyle. Similarly, Peter's investment in *Exteriors* is not driven by economic need, but it will play an important role in his life after the sale of IngerMarine.

3. How large an investment shortfall can the investor's portfolio bear before jeopardizing its ability to meet major short-term and long-term investment goals?

   The limit of a portfolio's ability to accept risk is reached when the probability of failing to meet a high-priority objective becomes unacceptably high. The investment advisor can provide guidance with probability estimates and identify clearly unrealistic expectations, but the ultimate determination of "acceptable" will also depend on the investor's general willingness to accept risk.

Willingness to Take Risk   In contrast to ability to take risk, investor willingness involves a more subjective assessment. No absolute measure of willingness exists, nor does any assurance that willingness will remain constant through time. Psychological profiling provides estimates of an individual's willingness to take risk, but final determination remains an imprecise science. It may, in fact, be necessary that investors have personal experience with significant losses as well as gains before a productive discussion of risk tolerance with them is possible.

Peter Inger's case illustrates both nuances in his willingness to take risk and a tension between willingness and ability. Peter's risk-taking has clearly centered on the business risk of IngerMarine. He has retained ownership of the company for many years, demonstrating tolerance for business risks that he may feel he controls. In other areas, including company debt policy and expansion plans, Peter has shown less willingness to take risk. His personal debt policy and low-volatility investment portfolio also indicate a conservative approach to finances. When asked what he would consider to be bad portfolio performance, Peter at first answered "any loss greater than 5 percent is unacceptable." After being reminded of his ability to take risk, however, he revised his answer to no loss greater than 10 percent.

4.2 Constraints

The IPS should identify all economic and operational constraints on the investment portfolio. Portfolio constraints generally fall into one of five categories:

▶ liquidity;

▶ time horizon;

▶ taxes;

▶ legal and regulatory environment;

▶ unique circumstances.

4.2.1 Liquidity

Liquidity refers generally to the investment portfolio's ability to efficiently meet an investor's anticipated and unanticipated demands for cash distributions. Two trading characteristics of its holdings determine a portfolio's liquidity:

▶ **Transaction Costs**   Transaction costs may include brokerage fees, bid–ask spread, price impact (resulting, for example, from a large sale in a thinly traded asset), or simply the time and opportunity cost of finding a buyer. As transaction costs increase, assets become less "liquid" and less appropriate as a funding source for cash flows.

▶ **Price Volatility**   An asset that can be bought or sold at fair value with minimal transaction costs is said to trade in a highly liquid market. If the market itself is inherently volatile, however, the asset's contribution to portfolio liquidity (the ability to meet cash flow needs) is limited. Price volatility compromises portfolio liquidity by lowering the certainty with which cash can be realized.

Significant liquidity requirements constrain the investor's ability to bear risk. Liquidity requirements can arise for any number of reasons but generally fall into one of the following categories:

▶ **Ongoing Expenses**   The ongoing costs of daily living create a predictable need for cash and constitute one of the investment portfolio's highest priorities. Because of their high predictability and short time horizon, anticipated expenses must be met using a high degree of liquidity in some portion of the investment portfolio.

▶ **Emergency Reserves** As a precaution against unanticipated events such as sudden unemployment or uninsured losses, keeping an emergency reserve is highly advisable. The reserve's size should be client specific and might cover a range from three months to more than one year of the client's anticipated expenses. Individuals working in a cyclical or litigious environment may require a larger reserve than those in more stable settings. Although the timing of emergencies is by definition uncertain, the need for cash when such events do occur is immediate.

▶ **Negative Liquidity Events** Liquidity events involve discrete future cash flows or major changes in ongoing expenses. Examples might include a significant charitable gift, anticipated home repairs, or a change in cash needs brought on by retirement. As the time horizon to a major liquidity event decreases, the need for portfolio liquidity rises.

For the sake of completeness, positive liquidity events and external support should also be noted in the policy statement. In the case of a multigenerational family plan, positive liquidity events might include anticipated gifts and inheritance; the advisor should note, however, that inheritance planning is a sensitive and potentially divisive topic among family members.

Significant liquidity events facing the Ingers include the sale of IngerMarine and subsequent loss of Peter's salary, the purchase of a second home, and the investment in *Exteriors*. As the potential need for cash distributions increases, so too must the investment portfolio's commitment to assets that can be easily sold at predictable prices. Peter and Hilda have agreed on a normal liquidity reserve equal to two years of Peter's current salary (2 × €500,000) but will maintain an above-average reserve during their transition into retirement.

Illiquid Holdings To ensure that all parties have a complete understanding of portfolio liquidity, the IPS should specifically identify significant holdings of illiquid assets and describe their role in the investment portfolio. Examples might include real estate, limited partnerships, common stock with trading restrictions, and assets burdened by pending litigation.

The home or primary residence, often an individual investor's largest and most illiquid asset, presents difficult diversification and asset allocation issues. Unfortunately, this asset defies easy classification, having investment returns in the form of psychological and lifestyle benefits as well as the economic benefits of shelter and potential price appreciation.

The emotions attached to the primary residence will vary from individual to individual, and investment advisors must be sensitive to their clients' long-term view of the "home." Some investors may view their residence as part of their overall investment portfolio; others may view it as a "homestead" or sanctuary where life is lived, children are raised, and retirements are planned. Whether the primary residence is viewed objectively or with emotional attachment, the fact remains that it generally represents a significant percentage of an individual investor's total net worth. As such, the IPS should address the investment role of the primary residence.

It is not uncommon to exclude the residence from the asset allocation decision, under the premise that the home is a "sunk cost," a "legacy" or "private use" asset that is not actively managed as an investment. A similar approach treats the home as a long-term investment that will be used to meet equally long-term housing needs or estate planning goals. Somewhat analogous to cash-flow matching or bond defeasance, the home and the investment goals that it offsets are removed from consideration in building the actively managed investment portfolio. Parents may, for example, wish to pass on to their children the wealth necessary to purchase a house and meet this goal through their own home ownership. Other investors may view the residence as a source of funding to meet future healthcare and housing costs.

Lifestyle changes often dictate selling a large, primary family residence and moving into a more manageable property or living arrangement (e.g., as an individual or couple matures, or as children move away to start their own lives and families). An increasingly popular option for older individuals in Western Europe and the U.S. is to use the value of the primary residence to fund the costs of living in a managed care facility. Generally, these facilities provide members with progressive levels of healthcare and personal assistance, making it possible to continue living independently.

Alternatively, many individuals plan to retire in their primary residence. The IPS should recognize and discuss financial risks and liquidity issues created by a concentration of net worth in the investor's residence. Although the residence is typically considered to be a long-term, illiquid holding, it can also be the source of significant short-term losses and cash flow problems. Financial engineers continue to develop products and techniques that allow individuals better access to their home equity (current market value, less any debt associated with the home) and better control over their exposure to fluctuations in property values. Some products, such as "reverse mortgages" and other annuity plans, have initially proven to be costly and illiquid. Newer financial vehicles are on the horizon, however, that may efficiently allow homeowners to "lock in" the current equity value of their home. In one such product (Robert Shiller's "macro securities"), hedges are built on the notion of swaps, in which two parties can exchange the returns of home appreciation for a static interest rate return.[3] Any decline in home value would be paid by the counterparty in exchange for the static rate of return.

Factoring the primary residence into a formal retirement plan is an uncertain proposition. Real estate returns vary with location, and the investor's holding period can be difficult to predict. Nonetheless, if the primary residence is treated as part of the investment portfolio, the advisor can use models for forecasting regional real estate inflation rates to approximate future values. Such models can be useful but will not capture the short-term dynamics of real estate markets.

The Inger Family It appears that Peter and Hilda can afford to build their second residence. Nonetheless, they should bear in mind that the two homes will constitute 16 percent of their net worth. Peter and Hilda's primary residence has a current market value of approximately €1,200,000 and could serve in the future as a source of funds.

4.2.2 Time Horizon

The investment time horizon has already been seen to play an important role in setting return objectives and defining liquidity constraints. No universal definition of "long-term" or "short-term" exists, however, and discussion is often left in relative rather than absolute terms. In many planning contexts, time horizons greater than 15 to 20 years can be viewed as relatively long term, and horizons of

---

[3] See Shiller (2003).

less than 3 years as relatively short term. Between 3 years and 15 years, there is a transition from intermediate to long term that different investors may perceive differently.

A second issue relating to the investment time horizon is whether the investor faces a single- or multistage horizon. Certain investor circumstances, such as an elderly investor with limited financial resources, are consistent with a single-stage time horizon. Given the unique nature and complexity of most individual investors' circumstances, however, the time horizon constraint most often takes a multistage form.

"Stage-of-life" classifications, as discussed earlier, often assume that the investment time horizon shortens gradually as investors move through the various stages of life. Although this assumption may often be true, it is not always. Once the primary investors' needs and financial security are secure, the process of setting risk and return objectives may take place in the context of multigenerational estate planning. The advisor's clients may be advanced in years yet be planning for their grandchildren; it may be the grandchildren's personal circumstances that determine the investment portfolio's goals and time horizon.

Peter and Hilda are extremely secure, assuming that the sale of IngerMarine is successful. They have expressed a desire to provide financial security for three generations and clearly have a long-term and probably multistage time horizon.

4.2.3 Taxes

The issue of taxes is perhaps the most universal and complex investment constraint to be found in private portfolio management. Taxation of income or property is a global reality and poses a significant challenge to wealth accumulation and transfer. Although tax codes are necessarily country specific, the following general categories are widely recognized:

▶ **Income Tax**   Income tax is calculated as a percentage of total income, often with different rates applied to various levels of income. Wages, rent, dividends, and interest earned are commonly treated as taxable income.

▶ **Gains Tax**   Capital gains (profits based on price appreciation) resulting from the sale of property, including financial securities, are often distinguished from income and taxed separately. In many countries, the tax rate for capital gains is lower than the corresponding income tax; a minimum holding period between purchase and sale is sometimes required.

▶ **Wealth Transfer Tax**   A wealth transfer tax is assessed as assets are transferred, without sale, from one owner to another. Examples of wealth transfer taxes include "estate" or "inheritance" taxes paid at the investor's death and "gift" taxes paid on transfers made during the investor's lifetime.

▶ **Property Tax**   Property tax most often refers to the taxation of real property (real estate) but may also apply to financial assets. Such taxes are generally assessed annually, as a percentage of reported value. Although straightforward in concept, property taxes present challenges with regard to valuation and compliance.

Taxation varies greatly across regions and continents, but marginal tax rates of 50 percent are not uncommon. With tax burdens of such magnitude, clearly the individual investor must approach investments and financial planning from an after-tax perspective. Exhibit 6 illustrates the degree of variation in top marginal tax rates that can exist internationally at a given point in time.

EXHIBIT 6	Top Marginal Tax Rates		
Country	Income Tax (%)	Gains Tax (%)	Wealth Transfer Tax (%)
Brazil	27.5	15.0	8.0
Canada (Ontario)	46.4	23.2	0.0
Chile	40.0	17.0	25.0
China (PRC)	45.0	20.0	0.0
Egypt	32.0	0.0	0.0
France	48.1	27.0	60.0
Germany	42.0	50.0	50.0
India	30.0	20.0	0.0
Israel	49.0	25.0	0.0
Italy	43.0	12.5	0.0
Japan	37.0	26.0	70.0
Jordan	25.0	0.0	0.0
Korea	35.0	70.0	50.0
Mexico	30.0	30.0	0.0
New Zealand	39.0	0.0	25.0
Pakistan	35.0	35.0	0.0
Philippines	32.0	32.0	20.0
Russian Federation	35.0	30.0	40.0
South Africa	40.0	10.0	20.0
Taiwan	40.0	0.0	50.0
United Kingdom	40.0	40.0	40.0
United States	35.0	35.0	47.0

Note: Rates shown are subject to periodic change and do not fully reflect the complexity of the tax codes from which they were taken; additional regional taxes may also apply. This exhibit should not be used for tax planning purposes.

Source: "The Global Executive," Ernst & Young, 2005.

Taxes affect portfolio performance in two ways. When taxes are paid at the end of a given measurement period, portfolio growth is simply reduced by the amount of tax. When the same tax is assessed periodically throughout the measurement period, growth is further reduced: Funds that would otherwise compound at the portfolio growth rate are no longer available for investment. Exhibit 7 illustrates the effect of taxes on portfolio performance. In Example A, a periodic tax of 25 percent, similar to an annual income tax, is applied against investment returns over five years. In Example B, a tax of 25 percent is applied against the cumulative investment return at the end of a five-year holding period, similar to a capital gains tax. The difference in ending portfolio values demonstrates the benefit of deferring tax payments.

Tax strategies are ultimately unique to the individual investor and the prevailing tax code. Although the details of tax planning often involve complex legal and political considerations, all strategies share some basic principles.

EXHIBIT 7	Effect of Taxes on Portfolio Performance

Example A: *Periodic 25% Tax*

Year	Beginning Value	Returns[a]	Tax (25%)	Ending Value	Cumulative Gain
1	100,000	10,000	(2,500)	107,500	7,500
2	107,500	10,750	(2,688)	115,563	15,563
3	115,563	11,556	(2,889)	124,230	24,230
4	124,230	12,423	(3,106)	133,547	33,547
5	133,547	13,355	(3,339)	143,563	**43,563**

Example B: *Cumulative 25% Tax*

Year	Beginning Value	Returns[a]	Tax	Ending Value	Cumulative Gain
1	100,000	10,000	n/a	110,000	10,000
2	110,000	11,000	n/a	121,000	21,000
3	121,000	12,100	n/a	133,100	33,100
4	133,100	13,310	n/a	146,410	46,410
5	146,410	14,641	n/a	161,051	61,051
		Less 25% Tax	(15,263)	(15,263)	(15,263)
				145,788	**45,788**

[a]Annual return: 10%.

Tax Deferral   For the long-term investor, periodic tax payments severely diminish the benefit of compounding portfolio returns. Many tax strategies, therefore, seek to defer taxes and maximize the time during which investment returns can be reinvested. (Exhibit 7 demonstrated the value of tax deferral in general.) A portfolio strategy focusing on low turnover, for example, extends the average investment holding period and postpones gains taxes.

Loss harvesting, another tax reduction strategy, focuses on realizing capital losses to offset otherwise taxable gains without impairing investment performance. Low turnover and loss harvesting strategies are representative of a general portfolio policy that strives for a low rate of capital gains realization, resulting in deferred tax payments.

Tax Avoidance   The ideal solution is to avoid taxes when legally possible.[4] A number of countries have introduced special purpose savings accounts, such as Peter Inger's RSA account, that may be exempt or deferred from taxation. Tax-exempt bonds may be available as alternative investment vehicles. Estate planning and gifting strategies may allow the investor to reduce future estate taxes by taking advantage of specific tax laws.

---

[4] The term "tax avoidance" is typically used in reference to the legal pursuit of tax efficient investment strategies; the term "tax evasion" typically describes an illegal attempt to circumvent tax liability.

Tax-advantaged investment alternatives typically come at a price, however, paid in some combination of lower returns, reduced liquidity, and diminished control.

▶ Tax-exempt securities typically offer lower returns or involve higher expenses (including higher transaction costs) relative to taxable alternatives, and they are attractive only when the following relationship holds (ignoring differential transaction costs): $R_{\text{Tax-free}} > [R_{\text{Taxable}} \times (1 - \text{Tax rate})]$.

▶ Liquidity is reduced in tax-sheltered savings accounts when a minimum holding period is required or when withdrawals are limited to specific purposes.

▶ The investor must often relinquish or share the direct ownership of assets placed in tax-advantaged partnerships or trusts.

Tax Reduction   If taxes cannot be avoided entirely, opportunities may remain to reduce their impact. When income tax rates exceed the capital gains tax rate, as they do in a number of countries (see Exhibit 6), a portfolio manager may emphasize securities and investment strategies whose investment returns are recognized as gains rather than income (a portfolio "tilt," for example, toward low-dividend-paying stocks). Because the gains tax is assessed only at the time of sale, such strategies may also benefit from tax deferral as well as the lower tax rate. If only *net* gains are taxed, a policy to actively realize offsetting losses ("loss harvesting") will reduce reported gains. To achieve portfolio tax efficiency, a manager may use a variety of additional strategies, an increasing number of which are made possible through the use of derivatives.[5]

Wealth Transfer Taxes   Wealth transfer strategies belong perhaps more to the world of tax- and estate-planning attorneys than to the realm of portfolio management. As a practical matter, however, investment advisors should have a working knowledge of estate planning principles, as it is often the advisor who first recognizes the investor's need for estate planning and makes the necessary recommendation to seek legal counsel.

Multiple variables potentially influence the timing of personal wealth transfers, including the investor's net worth, time horizon, and charitable intentions, as well as the age, maturity, and tax status of the beneficiaries. Generally speaking, strategies for addressing wealth transfers focus on either the timing or the legal structure (partnerships, trusts, etc.) of the transfer. The possible legal structures for a wealth transfer are necessarily country specific. Timing of wealth transfers, however, involves the more universal principles of tax avoidance, tax deferral, and maximized compound returns.

Transfer at Death.   If the investor pursues no other strategy, a wealth transfer tax may be assessed at death (often referred to as an estate tax or death tax). In this scenario, the transfer tax has been deferred for as long as possible, retaining maximum financial flexibility for the individual and maximizing the final value of the investment portfolio. In a multigeneration estate plan, however, this strategy may not minimize transfer taxes.

Early Transfers.   Accelerated wealth transfers and philanthropic gifting may be desirable when the investor wishes to maximize the amount of his or her estate, after taxes, that is passed on to individuals or organizations. Early gifting

[5] See Brunel (2002).

of higher-growth assets into the hands of a younger generation may shelter the subsequent growth of those assets from transfer taxes when the investor ultimately dies. Logically, earlier transfers to younger beneficiaries offer the greatest tax deferral. Because assets transferred to children will quite possibly be taxed again when the children die, it may be advantageous to make gifts directly to grandchildren, effectively skipping a generation of transfer taxes. Note that some tax regimes may differentiate among recipients, taxing gifts made to family members, for example, at lower rates than gifts made to other parties.

The benefit of early wealth transfers is largely determined by tax codes and life expectancies. Additional issues to consider before making a permanent transfer include 1) the amount of retained wealth needed to ensure the financial security of the primary investor; 2) possible unintended consequences of transferring large amounts of wealth to younger, potentially less mature beneficiaries; and 3) the probable stability or volatility of the tax code. Early transfers implicitly assume that the current tax structure will remain relatively constant through time. If an early gift is made and the transfer tax is later abolished, refunds are unlikely.

4.2.4 Legal and Regulatory Environment

In the context of portfolio management for individual investors, legal and regulatory constraints most frequently involve taxation and the transfer of personal property ownership. Legal and regulatory constraints vary greatly from country to country and change frequently. Achieving investment objectives within the constraints of a given jurisdiction frequently requires consultation with local experts, including tax accountants and estate planning attorneys. Whatever a portfolio manager's level of legal and regulatory understanding, she must be careful to avoid giving advice that would constitute the practice of law (the role of a licensed attorney). To the extent that the manager is acting in a fiduciary capacity (e.g., employed as trustee of a trust), prudent investor rules may apply, depending on the legal jurisdiction.

The Personal Trust   The use of trusts to implement investment and estate planning strategies is well established in English and American law, and a basic familiarity with the vocabulary of trusts is often useful in other jurisdictions as well. A trust is a legal entity established to hold and manage assets in accordance with specific instructions.

The term "personal trust" refers to trusts established by an individual, who is called the "grantor." The trust is a recognized owner of assets and can be subject to taxation in much the same manner that individuals are taxed. To form a trust, the creator (grantor) drafts a trust document defining the trust's purpose and naming a trustee who will be responsible for oversight and administration of the trust's assets. The trustee may or may not be the same person as the grantor. Many banks have "trust departments" that provide trustee services, including trust administration, investment management, and custody of assets. "Trust companies" are non-bank providers of trust services that have been granted trust powers by a government or regulatory body; these companies may or may not be owned by a bank.

The trust is funded when the grantor transfers legal ownership of designated assets to the trust. The assets of the trust can include a wide variety of items that the grantor owns, such as investment securities, residential or commercial real estate, farm or timber land, notes, precious metals, oil and gas leases, and collectibles. The valuation, marketability, and restrictions on sale of such assets can present challenges for the trustee trying to prudently manage the trust's holdings.

Personal trusts are not in and of themselves an investment strategy but rather an important tool for implementing certain aspects of an investment strategy (e.g., gifting). The appeal of personal trusts lies in the flexibility and control with which the grantor can specify how trust assets are to be managed and distributed, both before and after the grantor's demise. The two basic types of personal trusts, revocable and irrevocable, differ largely with respect to the issue of control. In a revocable trust, any term of the trust can be revoked or amended by the grantor at any time, including those terms dealing with beneficiaries, trustees, shares or interests, investment provisions, and distribution provisions. Revocable trusts are often used in place of a will or in combination with a will, because of their tax planning efficiency and the generally lower legal expenses associated with transferring ownership of personal property at the time of the grantor's death. Because the grantor retains control over the trust's terms and assets, she also remains responsible for any tax liabilities, such as income and gains taxes, generated by the trust's assets; trust assets remain subject to any wealth transfer tax due after the grantor's demise (often referred to as estate taxes or death taxes). Upon the grantor's death, the trust can typically no longer be amended; in accordance with the terms of the trust, trust assets either continue under management by a trustee or are distributed outright to the trust's beneficiaries.

In an irrevocable trust, the terms of management during the grantor's life and the disposition of assets upon the grantor's death are fixed and cannot be revoked or amended. The creation of an irrevocable trust is generally considered to be an immediate and irreversible transfer of property ownership, and a wealth transfer tax, sometimes called a gift tax, may have to be paid when the trust is funded. U.S. tax treatment of irrevocable trusts is similar to the tax treatment of individuals. The trust, not the grantor, is responsible for tax liabilities generated by trust assets and for filing its own tax return. The grantor retains no control or ownership interest in the trust, and the trust's assets are no longer considered part of the grantor's estate.

The framework for investment decision-making within a trust can vary significantly, but ultimate responsibility for investment oversight resides with the trustee (or co-trustees, if the trust document names multiple trustees). In revocable trusts, the trustee is often the grantor, who may or may not wish to personally manage the investment portfolio. As trustee of a revocable trust, the grantor may 1) appoint an investment manager, who then acts as an "agent" for the trustee; 2) amend the trust document to include a co-trustee with investment responsibility; or 3) manage the investment process directly. In the first two scenarios, the grantor may require that the agent or co-trustee obtain prior approval from the grantor before executing individual transactions. Requiring such prior approval can present difficulties from an investment management perspective, as no party has full authority to act. Upon the death of the grantor/trustee, the trust passes authority on to the successor trustee or co-trustees (named in the trust document), who then have responsibility for managing the assets according to the terms of the trust.

The Family Foundation   Civil law countries, as found in continental Europe, are characterized by the existence of family foundations. Similar to an irrevocable trust, the foundation is an independent entity, often governed by family members. Such foundations can be part of a multigeneration estate plan and often serve as a vehicle for introducing younger family members to the process of managing family assets.

There are many examples of trusts and foundations with customized terms of distribution. It is important to keep in mind, however, that trusts, foundations, and similar structures are only instruments with which to implement an underlying investment, estate-planning, or tax-saving strategy. Following are examples of how the Ingers might use such instruments:

▶ **Gifting to Grandchildren**   Jürgen is currently too young to receive large, direct gifts, but an irrevocable trust might be established for his benefit. The trustee would disburse funds from the trust, in accordance with conditions specified in the trust document by the Ingers. The terms for distribution might limit early access, or allow funding only for specific purposes, such as education expenses. As previously mentioned, generation-skipping gifts may reduce wealth-transfer taxes.

▶ **Gifting to Children**   Although the Ingers are eager to provide for the financial security of their children, they may be reluctant to entrust Hans and Christa with the management of large, unconditional transfers of family wealth. Christa does not seem to have the necessary investment skills or experience, and Hans' appetite for risk-taking may leave his parents uneasy. As an alternative to direct transfers, the Ingers could create a trust or foundation and structure the terms of distribution such that lifetime support is assured. The trust or foundation might be instructed to distribute funds based on reasonable need, as defined by the Ingers, or as the children reach specific ages and stages of life.

▶ **Gifting with Retained Interest**   Various options exist for creating hybrid structures that provide immediate support for one party but ultimately distribute their assets to a second party. The Ingers might consider a trust in which they retain an ownership interest in any income generated by the trust but give up control over the trust's assets. All income would be distributed to Peter and Hilda, making them the income beneficiaries of the trust. When the income beneficiaries die or have no further claim on income, the trust's remaining assets will be distributed to remaindermen, which might be charities, foundations, or other individuals, including the Ingers' children. Such trusts are generally irrevocable and treated as a deferred gift to the remaindermen. Transfer taxes on the gift's present value may have to be paid at the time the trust is created. When the remainder beneficiaries are charities or foundations, such arrangements may be referred to as a "charitable remainder trust."

The conflicting needs and interests of income beneficiaries and remaindermen may present the trustee of an irrevocable trust with portfolio management challenges. Trust beneficiaries will often pressure the trustee to favor either current income or long-term growth, depending on their beneficial interest. Income beneficiaries will typically desire that the trustee seek to maximize current income through the selection of higher income-producing assets. Remainderman beneficiaries will favor investments with long-term growth potential, even if this reduces current income. The trustee has the responsibility to consider the needs of both groups, under guidelines and criteria provided by the trust document. Although many older trust documents commonly define income as "interest, dividends and rents," the trend is to adopt a total return approach, consistent with modern portfolio management, that allows distributions from realized capital gains as well as traditional "income" sources.

Jurisdiction   Individual investors may enjoy a limited degree of flexibility in determining the jurisdiction in which their income and assets will be taxed.

Some countries have both national and regional tax codes. By choosing to live in a region with low tax rates, the investor may be able to reduce his tax liability. Generally speaking, however, all investment returns (including "offshore" investments) are subject to taxation in the investor's country of citizenship or residence. The same is true for trusts, which are taxed in accordance with their "situs" (locality under whose laws the trust operates).

"Offshore" investments and trusts in "tax friendly" countries typically offer some measure of enhanced privacy, asset protection, and estate planning advantages, as well as possible opportunities to reduce tax liabilities. If tax reduction is the investor's only concern, however, an alternative domestic tax strategy may prove more efficient. Again, investors are generally required to declare and pay taxes on returns received from offshore investments, regardless of whether return data are disclosed by the host country.

4.2.5 Unique Circumstances

Not surprisingly, individual investors often present their investment advisors with a wide range of unique circumstances that act to constrain portfolio choices. Such constraints might include guidelines for social or special purpose investing, assets legally restricted from sale, directed brokerage arrangements, and privacy concerns. It is also appropriate to list here any assets held outside the investment portfolio and not otherwise discussed in the IPS.

In the Ingers' case, a unique circumstance exists in the self-imposed limitation on acceptable investments. In the 1960s, Peter and several of his friends lost money in equity investment schemes. Since that time, he has had a bias against putting his money in the stock market. Peter does feel quite comfortable with investments in real estate, however, and mentions that he has always been quite successful and comfortable investing in real estate projects. After several "educational" discussions, Peter still insists that he wants only a limited exposure to common stock investments.

4.2.6 Peter and Hilda Inger's Investment Policy Statement

Using all of the information she has gathered about Peter and Hilda Inger, Jourdan formulates an investment policy statement for them. Exhibit 8 displays the IPS.

EXHIBIT 8	**Investment Policy Statement Prepared for Peter and Hilda Inger**

I. Background

Peter and Hilda Inger own and operate IngerMarine, a producer of luxury pleasure boats sold worldwide. The Ingers are eager to convert their equity stake in IngerMarine to cash and have received bids indicating probable proceeds to Peter and Hilda of €52 million, net of taxes. They consider everyone in their family to be financially secure and wish to preserve that security.

The Ingers' family consists of their son Hans, daughter Christa, and grandson Jürgen. Hans is a senior vice president at IngerMarine, specializing in design. Christa is an artist and a single mother to Jürgen.

(Exhibit continued on next page . . .)

EXHIBIT 8   (continued)

II. Return Objectives

Longer term, the Ingers wish to assure not only their own financial security and standard of living but that of their children as well. The investment portfolio must replace Peter's salary, which currently covers the couple's annual expenses and gifting. It should also provide a return sufficient to offset the effect of inflation (assumed to approximate 3 percent annually) on what will ultimately be their children's inheritance.

Required return[a]	1.17%
Expected inflation	3.00%
Return objective	4.17%

[a]Expected cash flow requirement in Year 2 divided by investable assets (€493,949/€42,340,438).

III. Risk Tolerance

Ability

Following the sale of IngerMarine, the Ingers' investment portfolio will be able to accommodate considerable volatility without endangering its ability to meet their financial objectives. Given Peter and Hilda's cash flow circumstances, their likely wealth position after the IngerMarine sale, and their postretirement objectives, their ability to take risk appears to be "above average."

Willingness

The Ingers are relatively conservative by nature. Personality typing of the Ingers identifies Peter as "methodical" and Hilda as "individualist." Peter seems to have managed IngerMarine with a bias toward low debt and stable earnings rather than rapid expansion. The Ingers have historically held a large portion of their liquid assets in money market accounts. Furthermore, the Ingers do not want a portfolio value decline of more than 10 percent in nominal terms in any given 12-month period. Their willingness to take risk is generally "below average."

To reconcile the portfolio's considerable ability to accommodate risk and the Ingers' apparent preference for lower risk, their overall risk tolerance is described in this policy statement as "moderate" or "average."

IV. Constraints

Liquidity

The Ingers have multiple short- to intermediate-term liquidity constraints:

► Construction of a second home (next one to three years)	€ 7,000,000
► Probable investment in the magazine *Exteriors* (within one year)	€ 5,000,000
► Emergency reserve	€ 1,000,000

(Exhibit continued on next page . . .)

EXHIBIT 8 (continued)

▶ Annual expenses
(estimated to rise with inflation) € 500,000

▶ Annual support for grandson (estimated to
rise with inflation) € 15,000

▶ Illiquid holding: IngerMarine currently represents a disproportionately large and illiquid part of the Ingers' net worth.

▶ Illiquid holding: After the sale of IngerMarine and the construction of their second home, the Ingers will have approximately 16 percent of their net worth committed to personal residences.

Time Horizon

Aside from the liquidity events listed above, the Ingers have a long-term, multi-stage time horizon.

Taxes

The Ingers are subject to their country's tax code and wish to pursue strategies that maximize the wealth passed on to their children.

Legal and Regulatory Environment

Any Retirement Savings Accounts created by the Ingers must be managed in compliance with prevalent fiduciary standards for diversification and prudence.

Unique Circumstances

▶ The critical component of Peter and Hilda's retirement plan is the disposition of IngerMarine stock to a willing buyer. This situation should be continually monitored to ensure that the assumptions made in any plan remain valid.

▶ The Ingers' second home will represent an illiquid portion of their total net worth. They have discussed the possible risks and have decided to not consider the home as part of their actively managed investment portfolio. The second home will not carry a mortgage.

▶ Estate Planning Considerations: 1) *Gifts to children.* The Ingers will consider various means of tax-efficiently securing their children's financial security, including outright gifts and the creation of special purpose trusts or foundations. 2) *Charitable gifts.* In addition to outright gifts, the Ingers will consider special purpose trusts or foundations, naming selected charities as remaindermen and family members as income beneficiaries.

▶ The complex family changes that are about to occur suggest the need for increased flexibility in whatever investment strategy is adopted, to accommodate potentially frequent and abrupt shifts in attitudes and circumstances.

▶ The Ingers want only limited exposure to common stock investments.

▶ The Ingers want to maintain a fixed long-term holding of €500,000 in gold bullion.

5

AN INTRODUCTION TO ASSET ALLOCATION

In establishing a strategic asset allocation policy, the advisor's challenge is to find a set of asset-class weights that produce a portfolio consistent with the individual investor's return objective, risk tolerance, and constraints. This task must be completed from a taxable perspective, taking into consideration 1) after-tax returns, 2) the tax consequences of any shift from current portfolio allocations, 3) the impact of future rebalancing, and 4) asset "location." The issue of asset location results from the individual investor's ownership of both taxable and tax-deferred investment accounts—clearly, nontaxable investments should not be "located" in tax-exempt accounts.

In the balance of the reading, we will illustrate the basic concepts of asset allocation for individual investors with a new case study, followed by a continuation of the Inger case. The reading concludes with a discussion of probabilistic analysis, as applied to individual investor asset allocation and retirement planning.

5.1 Asset Allocation Concepts

This section illustrates how to arrive at an appropriate strategic asset allocation (or set of approximately equivalent allocations) through a process of elimination. Investment objectives and constraints must be formulated prior to addressing asset allocation.

Example 1 introduces a new case study and provides the background information needed to establish asset allocation guidelines for a new private client, Susan Fairfax. The discussion then returns to Peter and Hilda Inger, formulating a strategic asset allocation appropriate to the Ingers' IPS.

EXAMPLE 1

Asset Allocation Concepts (1)

Susan Fairfax is president of Reston Industries, a U.S.-based company whose sales are entirely domestic and whose shares are listed on the New York Stock Exchange. The following additional facts reflect her current situation:

► Fairfax is single and 58 years old. She has no immediate family, no debts, and does not own a residence. She is in excellent health and covered by Reston-paid health insurance that continues after her expected retirement at age 65.

► Her base salary of $500,000 a year, inflation-protected, is sufficient to support her present lifestyle but can no longer generate any excess for savings.

► She has $2,000,000 of savings from prior years held in the form of short-term instruments.

► Reston rewards key employees through a generous stock-bonus incentive plan, but the company provides no pension plan and pays no dividend.

▶ Fairfax's incentive plan participation has resulted in her ownership of Reston stock worth $10 million (current market value). The stock was received tax-free but is subject to tax at a 35 percent rate (on entire proceeds) if sold. She expects to hold the Reston stock at least until her retirement.

▶ Her present level of spending and the current annual inflation rate of 4 percent are expected to continue after her retirement.

▶ Fairfax is taxed at 35 percent on all salary, investment income, and realized capital gains. Her composite tax rate is assumed to continue at this level indefinitely.

Fairfax's orientation is patient, careful, and conservative in all things. She has stated that an annual after-tax real total return of 3 percent would be completely acceptable to her, if it were achieved in a context whereby an investment portfolio created from her accumulated savings was unlikely to decline by more than 10 percent in nominal terms in any given 12-month period.

Working with Fairfax, HH Advisors (HH) created the following draft version of an investment policy statement.

Investment Policy Statement for Susan Fairfax

Overview

Ms. Fairfax is 58 years old and has seven years until her planned retirement. She has a fairly lavish lifestyle but few financial worries: Her salary pays all current expenses, and she has accumulated $2 million in cash equivalents from savings in previous years (the "Savings Portfolio"). Her health is excellent, and her employer-paid health insurance coverage will continue after retirement. She has sought professional advice to begin planning for her investment future, a future that is complicated by ownership of a $10 million block of company stock. The stock is listed on the NYSE, pays no dividends, and has a zero-cost basis for tax purposes. All salary, investment income (except interest on municipal bonds), and realized capital gains are taxed to Ms. Fairfax at a 35 percent rate. This tax rate and a 4 percent annual inflation rate are expected to continue into the future. Ms. Fairfax would accept a 3 percent real, after-tax return from the investment portfolio to be formed from her Savings Portfolio, if that return could be obtained with only modest downside risk (i.e., less than a 10 percent annual decline). She describes herself as being conservative in all things.

Objectives

▶ **Return requirement.** Ms. Fairfax's need for portfolio income begins seven years from now, when her salary stops on the day she retires. The interim return focus for her investment portfolio (to be created from the Savings Portfolio) should be on growing the portfolio's value in a way that provides protection against loss of purchasing power. Her 3 percent real, after-tax return preference implies a gross total return requirement of at least 10.8 percent, assuming her investments are fully taxable (as is the case now) and assuming 4 percent inflation and a 35 percent tax rate. For Ms. Fairfax to maintain her current lifestyle, she must generate $500,000 × $(1.04)^7$, or $658,000, in annual, inflation-adjusted income when she retires. If the market value of

Reston's stock does not change, and if she has been able to earn a 10.8 percent return on the investment portfolio (or 7 percent nominal after-tax return = $2,000,000 \times (1.07)^7 = $3,211,500$), she should accumulate $13,211,500 by retirement age. To generate $658,000, a return on $13,211,500 of approximately 5.0 percent is needed. If she sells her position in Reston Industries leaving $(1 - 0.35)($10,000,000) + $3,211,500 = $9,711,500$ to invest, a return of $658,000/$9,711,500 = 6.8 percent is needed.

▶ **Risk tolerance.** Ms. Fairfax has a below-average *willingness* to take risk, as evidenced by her statement that in any given year, she does not want to experience a decline of more than 10 percent in the value of the investment portfolio. This desire indicates that her portfolio should have below-average risk exposure to minimize its downside volatility. A below-average willingness is also suggested by her generally careful and conservative orientation. Her overall wealth position, however, suggests an above-average *ability* to take risk. Because of her preferences and the nondiversified nature of the total portfolio, an average to below-average risk tolerance objective is appropriate for the portfolio.

It should be noted that truly meaningful statements about the risk of Ms. Fairfax's total portfolio are tied to assumptions about the volatility of Reston's stock (if it is retained) and about when and at what price the Reston stock will be sold. Because the Reston holding constitutes 83 percent of Ms. Fairfax's total portfolio, it will largely determine the large risk she is likely to experience as long as the holding remains intact.

Constraints

▶ **Time horizon.** Ms. Fairfax has a multistage time horizon. The first stage is the intermediate-term period, seven years, until her retirement. The second stage is relatively long term, representing Ms. Fairfax's life expectancy of perhaps 30 years or more. During the first stage, Ms. Fairfax should arrange her financial affairs in preparation for the balance of the second stage, a retirement period of indefinite length. Of the two horizons, the second horizon is the dominant one because it is during this period that her assets must fulfill their primary function of funding her expenses, in an annuity sense, in retirement.

▶ **Liquidity.** With liquidity defined either as income needs or as cash reserves to meet emergency needs, Ms. Fairfax's immediate liquidity requirement is minimal. She has $500,000 of salary available annually, healthcare costs are not a concern, and she has no planned needs for cash from the portfolio.

▶ **Taxes.** Ms. Fairfax's taxable income (salary, taxable investment income, and realized capital gains on securities) is taxed at a 35 percent rate. Careful tax planning and coordination of tax policy with investment planning is required. All else equal, investment strategies should seek to maximize after-tax income and defer the realization of taxable gains. Sale of the Reston stock will have sizeable tax consequences because Ms. Fairfax's cost basis is zero; special planning will be needed for this sale. Ms. Fairfax may want to consider some form of charitable giving, either during her lifetime or at death. She has no immediate family, and no other potential gift or bequest recipients are known.

▶ **Laws and regulations.** Ms. Fairfax should be aware of and abide by all laws and regulations relating to her "insider" status at Reston and her holding of Reston stock. Although no trust instrument is in place, if Ms. Fairfax's future investing is handled by an investment advisor, the responsibilities associated with the Prudent Person Rule will come into play, including the responsibility for investing in a diversified portfolio.

▶ **Unique circumstances and/or preferences.** Clearly, the value of the Reston stock dominates Ms. Fairfax's portfolio value. A well-defined exit strategy must be developed for the stock as soon as is practical and appropriate. If the stock's value increases, or at least does not decline before the holding is liquidated, Ms. Fairfax's present lifestyle can be sustained after retirement. A significant and prolonged setback for Reston Industries, however, could have disastrous consequences for the portfolio. Such circumstances would require a dramatic downscaling of Ms. Fairfax's lifestyle or generation of alternate sources of income to maintain her current lifestyle. A worst-case scenario might be characterized by a 50 percent drop in the market value of Reston's stock and a subsequent sale of the stock, with proceeds subject to a 35 percent tax. The net proceeds from such a sale would be $10,000,000 \times 0.5 \times (1 - 0.35) = \$3,250,000$. When added to the Savings Portfolio, Ms. Fairfax's total portfolio value would be $5,250,000. For this portfolio to generate $658,000 in income, a 12.5 percent return would be required.

Ms. Fairfax will need to seek legal estate planning assistance, especially if she wishes to establish a gifting program.

Synopsis

The policy governing investments in Ms. Fairfax's Savings Portfolio shall emphasize realizing a 3 percent real, after-tax return from a mix of high-quality assets representing, in aggregate, no more than average, and preferably below average, risk. Ongoing attention shall be given to Ms. Fairfax's tax planning and legal needs, her progress toward retirement, and the value of her Reston stock. The Reston stock holding is a unique circumstance of decisive significance; corporate developments should be monitored closely, and protection against the effects of a worst-case scenario should be implemented as soon as possible.

In setting asset allocation guidelines for Ms. Fairfax, one of the constraints that HH Advisors must address is her concern regarding negative portfolio returns. So-called "safety-first" rules[6] provide a means of reasonably approximating and controlling downside risk; HH uses the following safety-first guideline in establishing an asset allocation policy for Ms. Fairfax.

If:
- ▶ the portfolio has an important or dominant equity component,
- ▶ the portfolio does not make significant use of options, and
- ▶ the investment horizon for the shortfall risk concern is not short term;

---

[6]Elton, Gruber, Brown, and Goetzmann (2003) and DeFusco et al. (2004) discuss safety-first rules.

> Then:
>   the normal distribution may reasonably be used as an approximate model of portfolio returns.

Fama (1976) and Campbell, Lo, and MacKinlay (1997), for example, provide evidence about the normal distribution as applied to U.S. common stocks. A 2.5 percent probability of failing to meet a return threshold may be acceptable for many clients. For a normal distribution of returns, the probability of a return that is more than two standard deviations below the mean or expected return is approximately 2.5 percent. If the client is more (less) risk averse, the advisor can choose a larger (smaller) number for standard deviation. Therefore, if we subtract two standard deviations from a portfolio's expected return and the resulting number is above the client's return threshold, the client may find the resulting portfolio acceptable. If the resulting number is below the client's threshold, the portfolio may be unsatisfactory. Of course, the client may have other or different downside risk objectives than the two-standard-deviation approach we have used to illustrate this concept.

Once return and risk objectives and constraints have been established, an advisor sometimes will include a statement of the client's strategic asset allocation as part of the IPS. HH now turns to the task of establishing an appropriate strategic asset allocation for the investment portfolio to be created from Ms. Fairfax's existing savings (the "Savings Portfolio"). An HH analyst has developed the five potential asset allocations presented in Exhibit 9 and Exhibit 10. The analyst has commented that there is more uncertainty in the expectational data for REITs than for small- or large-cap U.S. stocks.

| EXHIBIT 9 | Proposed Asset Allocation Alternatives |

Asset Class	Projected Total Return (%)	Expected Standard Deviation (%)	Allocation				
			A (%)	B (%)	C (%)	D (%)	E (%)
Cash equivalents	4.5	2.5	10	20	25	5	10
Corporate bonds	6.0	11.0	0	25	0	0	0
Municipal bonds	7.2	10.8	40	0	30	0	30
Large-cap U.S. stocks	13.0	17.0	20	15	35	25	5
Small-cap U.S. stocks	15.0	21.0	10	10	0	15	5
International stocks (EAFE)	15.0	21.0	10	10	0	15	10
Real estate investment trusts (REITs)	10.0	15.0	10	10	10	25	35
Venture capital	26.0	64.0	0	10	0	15	5
Total			100	100	100	100	100

Summary Data	Allocation				
	A	B	C	D	E
Expected total return	9.9%	11.0%	8.8%	14.4%	10.3%
Expected after-tax total return	7.4%	7.2%	6.5%	9.4%	7.5%
Expected standard deviation	9.4%	12.4%	8.5%	18.1%	10.1%
Sharpe ratio	0.574	0.524	0.506	0.547	0.574

EXHIBIT 10	Asset Allocation Alternatives: Nominal and Real Expected Returns				

	Allocation				
Return Measure	A (%)	B (%)	C (%)	D (%)	E (%)
Nominal expected return	9.9	11.0	8.8	14.4	10.3
Expected real after-tax return	3.4	3.2	2.5	5.4	3.5

The process of selecting the most satisfactory from among several potential strategic asset allocations, both in the case of Susan Fairfax and for individual investors generally, consists of the following steps:

1. Determine the asset allocations that meet the investor's return requirements. In carrying out this step, the investment advisor should compare expected returns for the different asset allocations on a basis consistent with the IPS. The policy statement might, for example, set return requirements in real, after-tax terms. In that case, the advisor would adjust for the effects of taxes and expected inflation before deciding which allocations meet the investor's return requirement.

2. Eliminate asset allocations that fail to meet quantitative risk objectives or are otherwise inconsistent with the investor's risk tolerance. For example, an investor may have risk objectives related to the expected standard deviation of return, worst-case return, or any of several other downside risk concepts (as is true for Fairfax). On a long-term basis, an individual investor will be unable to apply an asset allocation that violates a risk objective.

3. Eliminate asset allocations that fail to satisfy the investor's stated constraints. For example, an investor may have a liquidity requirement that is appropriately met by holding a certain level of cash equivalents, and allocations must satisfy that constraint. Unique circumstances may also make certain allocations unacceptable to the investor.

4. Evaluate the expected risk-adjusted performance and diversification attributes of the asset allocations that remain after Steps 1 through 3 to select the allocation that is expected to be most rewarding for the investor.

Example 2 applies these four steps to the Fairfax case.

EXAMPLE 2

Asset Allocation Concepts (2)

▶ **Step 1: Return Requirement** Fairfax has stated that she is seeking a 3 percent real, after-tax return. Exhibit 9 provides nominal, pretax figures, which HH must adjust for both taxes and inflation to determine which portfolios meet Fairfax's return guideline. A simple approach is to subtract the municipal bond return component from the stated return, then subject the resulting figure to a 35 percent tax rate and add back tax-exempt municipal bond income. This calculation produces a nominal, after-tax return, from which the expected 4 percent per year inflation rate is subtracted to arrive at the real, after-tax return. For example, Allocation A has an expected real after-tax return of 3.4 percent, calculated by [0.099 − (0.072 × 0.4)] × (1 − 0.35) + (0.072 × 0.4) − 0.04 = 0.034 = 3.4 percent.

Alternately, the return can be calculated by multiplying the taxable returns by their allocations, summing these products, adjusting for the tax rate, adding the result to the product of the nontaxable (municipal bond) return and its allocation, and deducting the inflation rate from this sum. For Allocation A, [(0.045 × 0.10) + (0.13 × 0.2) + (0.15 × 0.1) + (0.15 × 0.1) + (0.1 × 0.1)] × (1 − 0.35) + (0.072 × 0.4) − (0.04) = 0.035 = 3.5 percent.

Exhibit 10 presents the allocations' expected nominal returns—without adjustment for either inflation or taxes—and their expected real after-tax returns calculated by the first of the above approaches. From Exhibit 10, the HH analyst notes that Allocations A, B, D, and E meet Fairfax's real, after-tax return objective of 3 percent a year.

▶ **Step 2: Risk Tolerance** Fairfax has stated that a worst-case nominal return of −10 percent in any 12-month period would be acceptable. As discussed above, the expected return less two times the portfolio risk (expected standard deviation) is a reasonable baseline measure of shortfall risk. If the resulting number is above the client's threshold return level, the criterion is met. Two of the remaining four allocations—A and E—meet the risk tolerance criterion.

	Allocation				
Parameter	A (%)	B (%)	C (%)	D (%)	E (%)
Expected return	9.9	11.0	8.8	14.4	10.3
Exp. standard deviation	9.4	12.4	8.5	18.1	10.1
Worst-case return	−8.9	−13.8	−8.2	−21.8	−9.9

▶ **Step 3: Constraints** Portfolios A and E both meet the stated constraints of Fairfax and neither is eliminated in this step.

▶ **Step 4: Risk-Adjusted Performance and Diversification Evaluation** The recommended allocation is A. The allocations that are expected to meet both the minimum real, after-tax objective and the maximum risk tolerance objective are A and E. Both allocations have similar Sharpe ratios and expected real after-tax returns. Both A and E have large exposures to municipal bonds; Allocation E, however, has a large position in REIT stocks, whereas Allocation A's counterpart large equity allocation is to a diversified portfolio of large- and small-cap domestic stocks. Allocation A provides greater diversification through its large and small stock representation, as opposed to the specialized nature of REIT stocks. Furthermore, because of the great uncertainty in the expectational data for REIT stocks compared with small- and large-cap stocks, we can be more confident in selecting Allocation A that Fairfax's return and risk objectives will be met. Therefore, HH Advisors specifies Allocation A as Fairfax's strategic asset allocation.

The Susan Fairfax case in Examples 1 and 2 presented a process for selecting the strategic asset allocation most appropriate to her objectives and constraints. Example 3 contrasts the asset allocation problem of Peter and Hilda Inger to that of Fairfax.

EXAMPLE 3

Asset Allocation for Peter and Hilda Inger

To recap some important facts presented in the family's IPS, the Ingers have average risk tolerance in general but are relatively averse to common stock investments as a result of Peter's prior negative experience. Peter, however, has always been successful and comfortable investing in real estate projects (even those constituting greater overall risk than corresponding equity investments). Also, the Ingers do not wish to experience a loss greater than 10 percent, in nominal terms, in any given 12-month period. The Ingers' required return was calculated as their estimated disbursements, including taxes, beginning in Year 2, divided by their net worth at the end of Year 1 (€493,949/€42,340,438 = 1.17 percent). Adding expected annual inflation of 3 percent, the Ingers' stated return objective is 4.17 percent.

The critical component of Peter and Hilda's retirement plan is the disposition of IngerMarine stock to a willing buyer. If the sale is not realized, their investment objectives and the associated strategic asset allocation will both require review. We have discussed certain principles of asset allocation for individual investors and illustrated their application in previous examples. In terms of the IPS and asset allocation, what similarities and contrasts would an investment advisor observe in applying the methods used for Fairfax in Examples 1 and 2 to the Ingers? Among the key observations are the following:

▶ **Risk Tolerance and Return Objective** In consultation with the client, the investment advisor needs to develop an IPS prior to embarking on asset allocation. The client's risk tolerance and return objective are important parts of an IPS, and any asset allocation must be appropriate for these objectives. The Ingers want a chosen asset allocation to satisfy a downside risk constraint of −10 percent, just as in the Fairfax case. Yet because the Ingers' objective of a 1.17 percent real, after-tax return is less than one half of Fairfax's in magnitude, all else being equal we would expect a wider variety of asset allocations to satisfy the Ingers' requirements.

▶ **Asset Class Selection** As with Fairfax, the Ingers' investment advisor must establish an appropriate set of asset classes. The asset classes in Exhibit 9 have a U.S. bias. Eurozone equities and fixed-income asset classes for the Ingers would play a similar role to U.S. equities and U.S. fixed income classes for Fairfax, because the Ingers' consumption is in euros. U.S. equities represent a substantial proportion of the market value of world equities, and one might expect them to play a meaningful role in the Ingers' portfolio. The advisor would need to respect Peter's aversion to holding equities, however. On the other hand, because of Peter's prior experience and success with real estate projects, the Ingers might include more than one real estate investment asset type among those permissible for investment. The inclusion of a wide array of asset classes brings diversification benefits, as long as portfolio risk and expected return characteristics remain consistent with the investment policy statement. Emerging Markets, Commodities, and Private Capital Ventures are examples of asset classes that may be strong diversifiers but that also have higher volatility and less liquidity than traditional equity and fixed-income investments. Like Fairfax, the Ingers are taxable investors; if possible in their domestic market, the Ingers should probably also include tax-exempt investments as a permissible asset class.

▶ **Taxation and Asset Allocation Simulation** As in the Fairfax case, the Ingers' advisor should make an asset allocation decision in real, after-tax terms. This observation raises the point that expected after-tax returns for the Ingers will be computed using a tax rate different from Fairfax's, and such returns would incorporate their own expectations concerning future inflation rates.

Taxes present one of the more vexing challenges in asset allocation for private wealth clients, because taxes depend heavily on the regulatory environment and the investor's unique set of financial circumstances. In modeling asset allocation scenarios, the advisor must address the question of whether to use after-tax return assumptions for individual asset classes or to instead use pretax assumptions and apply taxes to the resulting investment outcomes. Running simulations using after-tax return assumptions can be a daunting task—listed below are some of the hurdles in configuring asset allocation scenarios using after-tax estimates.

▶ **Location**   After-tax risk and return assumptions will be influenced by an investment's "location." After-tax returns on common stocks located in a tax-sheltered retirement account, for example, may differ distinctly from the return on common stocks located in an unsheltered account. Consequently, an advisor may need to break down the traditional asset classes into multiple, location-specific subclasses, each with its own risk and return profile.

▶ **Tax Conventions**   Differing tax treatment of investment returns, depending for example on holding period or method of dissolution, may again create multiple risk and return characteristics for a given asset class. Securities held for a required minimum time period may be taxed at different, often more favorable rates. Assets ultimately gifted to charity or family members may be taxed favorably or not at all.

▶ **Investment Instruments**   Investment securities whose tax characteristics are easily recognizable and predictable today may change dramatically over time, through legislative initiative or tax authority interpretations.

5.2 Monte Carlo Simulation in Personal Retirement Planning

Monte Carlo simulation is described in detail in the reading on asset allocation. Here we focus on its applicability to personal retirement planning. With the introduction of Monte Carlo simulation methodologies, the technology of retirement planning for individuals now rivals that of corporate pension planning. Monte Carlo analysis is computer and data intensive, so its availability for personal retirement planning at affordable cost is a direct result of the availability of inexpensive computing power. Such methodologies are now readily available to individual investors and their investment managers, from a variety of vendors.[7]

Monte Carlo simulation is the process by which probability "distributions" are arrayed to create path-dependent scenarios to predict end-stage results.[8] The methodology is useful when trying to forecast future results that depend on multiple variables with various degrees of volatility. Its use in projecting retirement wealth is valuable because the prediction of future wealth depends on multiple factors (e.g., investment returns, inflation, etc.), each with a unique distribution of probable outcomes. Monte Carlo simulation is generally superior to steady-state, or deterministic, forecasting because it incorporates the consequences of variability across long-term assumptions and the resulting path dependency effect on wealth accumulation. Merely using long-term averages for capital market returns or inflation assumptions oversimplifies their variability and leads to the clearly unrealistic implication of linear wealth accumulation. There is also an inherent assumption when using deterministic forecasting that performance in future periods will more or less replicate historical performance. Monte Carlo estimation, in contrast, allows for the input of probability estimates over multi-period time frames and generates a probability distribution of final values rather than a single point estimate. This approach allows the investment advisor to view projections of possible best- and worst-case scenarios and leads to better financial planning over long time frames.

The ultimate objective of probabilistic approaches, such as Monte Carlo simulation, for investment planning is to improve the quality of managers' recommendations and investors' decisions. A brief look at the distinction between traditional deterministic analysis and probabilistic analysis reveals how the latter approach seeks to achieve that objective. In both approaches, the individual supplies a similar set of personal information, including age, desired retirement age, current income, savings, and assets in taxable, tax deferred, and tax-exempt vehicles. In a deterministic analysis, single numbers are specified for interest rates, asset returns, inflation, and similar economic variables. In a Monte Carlo or probabilistic analysis, a probability distribution of possible values is specified for economic variables, reflecting the real-life uncertainty about those variables' future values.

Suppose an individual investor is 25 years away from her desired retirement age. A deterministic retirement analysis produces single number estimates of outcomes for stated objectives, such as retirement assets and retirement income at the end of 25 years. Using the same inputs, a Monte Carlo analysis produces probability distributions for those objective variables by tabulating the outcomes of a large number (often 10,000) of simulation trials, each trial representing a

---

[7] Wei Hu and Robert L. Young, CFA, of Financial Engines Inc. made important contributions to our presentation of Monte Carlo simulation for retirement planning in this section.

[8] Path dependency exists when the outcome in a given period is influenced or constrained by the outcomes of prior events.

possible 25-year experience. Each simulation trial incorporates a potential blend of economic factors (interest rates, inflation, etc.), in which the blending reflects the economic variables' probability distributions.

Consequently, whereas deterministic analysis provides a yes/no answer concerning whether the individual will reach a particular goal for retirement income, or perhaps retirement wealth, mirroring a single set of economic assumptions, a Monte Carlo analysis provides a probability estimate, as well as other detailed information, that allows the investor to better assess risk (for example, percentiles for the distribution of retirement income). Thus Monte Carlo analysis is far more informative about the risk associated with meeting objectives than deterministic analysis. The investor can then respond to such risk information by changing variables under her control. An advisory module may present a range of alternative asset allocations and the associated probabilities for reaching goals and objectives.

A probabilistic approach conveys several advantages to both investors and their investment advisors. First, a probabilistic forecast more accurately portrays the risk–return tradeoff than a deterministic approach. Until recently, advisors nearly exclusively used deterministic projections to inform their recommendations and communicate with their clients. Unfortunately, such projections cannot realistically model how markets actually behave. The probability of observing a scenario in which the market return is constant each year is effectively zero. Fundamentally, deterministic models answer the wrong question. The relevant question is not "How much money will I have if I earn 10 percent a year?" but rather "Given a particular investment strategy, what is the likelihood of achieving 10 percent a year?" By focusing on the wrong question, deterministic models can fail to illustrate the consequences of investment risk, producing, in effect, a misleading "return–return" tradeoff in investors' minds whereby riskier strategies are always expected to produce superior long-term rewards.

In contrast, a probabilistic forecast vividly portrays the actual risk–return tradeoff. For example, an investor considering placing a higher percentage of his portfolio in equities might be told that the average forecast return of the S&P 500 Index is 13 percent. Given an average forecast money market return of 5 percent, it may seem obvious that more equity exposure is desirable. This choice, however, should take into account the risk that the S&P 500 will not achieve its average return every year. Moreover, the median simulation outcome of the S&P 500, using the average return of 13 percent, is likely to be substantially lower because of return volatility. For example, a 20-year forecast of $1,000 invested in the S&P 500, using a riskless average return of 13 percent, yields ending wealth of $11,500. If a simulation is performed assuming normally distributed returns with an annual standard deviation of 20 percent, the median wealth after 20 years is only $8,400. In addition, a simulation-based forecast shows that there is substantial downside risk: The fifth percentile of wealth after 20 years is only approximately $2,000, even before adjusting for inflation.

A second benefit of a probabilistic approach is that a simulation can give information on the possible tradeoff between short-term risk and the risk of not meeting a long-term goal. This tradeoff arises when an investor must choose between lowering short-term volatility on one hand and lowering the portfolio's long-term growth because of lower expected returns on the other hand.

Third, as already discussed, taxes complicate investment planning considerably by creating a sequential problem in which buy and sell decisions during this period affect next-period decisions through the tax implications of portfolio changes. Through its ability to model a nearly limitless range of scenarios, Monte Carlo analysis can capture the variety of portfolio changes that can potentially result from tax effects.

Finally, an expected value of future returns is more complicated than an expected value of concurrent returns, even in the simplest case of independent and normally distributed returns. For concurrent returns, the expected portfolio return is simply the weighted sum of the individual expected returns, and the variance depends on the individual variances and covariances, leading to the benefits of diversification with lower covariances. In this case, the $1 invested is simply divided among several investment alternatives. The future return case, however, involves a multiplicative situation; for example, the expected two-period return is the product of one plus the expected values of the one-period returns, leading to the importance of considering expected geometric return. As Michaud (1981) demonstrates, the expected geometric return depends on the horizon of the investment. The stochastic nature of the problem can be summarized by recognizing that the $1 invested now will then be reinvested in the next period and possibly joined by an additional $1 investment. This scenario clearly differs from the simple one-period case of spreading the dollar among several asset classes. Again, Monte Carlo analysis is well suited to model this stochastic process and its resulting alternative outcomes.

Monte Carlo simulation can be a useful tool for investment analysis but like any investment tool it can be used either appropriately or inappropriately. What should investors and managers know about a particular Monte Carlo product in order to be confident that it provides reliable information? Unfortunately, not all commercially available Monte Carlo products generate equally reliable results, so users should be aware of product differences that affect the quality of results.

First, any user of Monte Carlo should be wary of a simulation tool that relies only on historical data. History provides a view of only one possible path among the many that might occur in the future. As previously mentioned, it is difficult to estimate the expected return on an equity series using historical data, because the volatility of equity returns is large in relation to the mean. For example, suppose we are willing to assume that the expected return of the S&P 500 is equal to the average historical return. Annual data from 1926 through 1994 would yield an average return of 12.16 percent. Adding just five more years of data, however, would produce an average return of 13.28 percent. For a 20-year horizon, this relatively small adjustment in the input data would lead to a difference of more than 20 percent in ending wealth, given returns every year that were equal to the assumed average.

Second, a manager who wants to evaluate the likely performance of a client's portfolio should choose a Monte Carlo simulation that simulates the performance of specific investments, not just asset classes. Although asset class movements can explain a large proportion of, for example, mutual fund returns, individual funds can differ greatly in terms of their performance, fees, fund-specific risk, and tax efficiency. Failing to recognize these factors can yield a forecast that is far too optimistic. As an example of how much fees can affect performance, consider the case of a hypothetical S&P 500 index fund that charges an annual fee of 60 basis points; expected return is 13 percent with annual standard deviation of 20 percent and normally distributed returns, and capital gains are taxed at 20 percent. A Monte Carlo simulation shows that a $1,000 investment will grow to a median after-tax wealth of $6,200 after 20 years, if that fund pays no short-term distributions. In contrast, an investor with access to an institutional fund that charges only 6 basis points will see her after-tax wealth grow to a median of $6,800 after 20 years.

Third, any Monte Carlo simulation used for advising real-world investors must take into account the tax consequences of their investments. Monte Carlo simulation must and can be flexible enough to account for specific factors such

SUMMARY

This reading has presented an overview of portfolio management for individual investors, including the information-gathering process, situational and psychological profiling of clients, formulation of an investment policy statement, strategic asset allocation, and the use of Monte Carlo simulation in personal retirement planning.

► Situational profiling seeks to anticipate individual investors' concerns and risk tolerance by specifying the investor's source of wealth, measure or adequacy of wealth in relationship to needs, and stage of life.

► Psychological profiling addresses human behavioral patterns and personality characteristics and their effect on investment choices. It is particularly important in assessing risk tolerance.

► Underlying behavioral patterns often play an important role in setting individual risk tolerance and return objectives.

► Based on their responses to a questionnaire, individual investors may be classified into descriptive personality types, such as *cautious, methodical, spontaneous*, or *individualist*.

► Using the results of situational and psychological profiling, and the financial information gathered in the interviewing process, an advisor can formulate an investment policy statement.

► A carefully formulated IPS serves as the keystone to the relationship between investor and investment advisor. The process of creating an IPS mirrors the process of portfolio management. The policy statement reconciles investment goals with the realities of risk tolerance and investment constraints, resulting in operational guidelines for portfolio construction and a mutually agreed-upon basis for portfolio monitoring and review. By necessity, the investor and advisor must discuss the construction of an IPS in a linear fashion. In practice, the process is dynamic, similar to solving simultaneously for multiple variables.

► The return objective for an investment portfolio must ultimately be made consistent with the investor's risk tolerance and the portfolio's ability to generate returns. The traditional division of return requirements between "income" and "growth" objectives may seem intuitive, but these terms blur the distinction between return goals and risk tolerance. The "total return" approach seeks to identify a portfolio return that will meet the investor's objectives without exceeding the portfolio's risk tolerance or violating its investment constraints.

► Risk tolerance reflects both an investor's ability and willingness to accept risk. Ability to accept risk is a probabilistic assessment of the investment portfolio's ability to withstand negative investment outcomes and still meet the investor's objectives. Willingness to accept risk is a more subjective assessment of the investor's propensity for risk taking. Because many individuals are unfamiliar with the quantitative terminology of risk tolerance, the investment advisor may use psychological or situational profiling to anticipate client attitudes toward risk.

► Investment constraints include the following:

1. *Liquidity.* Liquidity needs may be categorized as ongoing expenses, emergency reserves, and negative liquidity events. Liquidity is the ease and price certainty with which assets can be converted into cash. Because assets with stable prices and low transaction costs are generally low-risk investments, an increasing need for liquidity will constrain the investment portfolio's ability to accept risk. Significant illiquid holdings and their associated risks should be documented. For many investors, the home or residence represents a large percentage of total net worth and is relatively illiquid. Although the primary residence may be viewed as offsetting long-term needs for care and housing, it should be discussed as a source of investment risk and as a source of funding for future cash flow needs. The investor and advisor should together thoroughly review the risks associated with any concentration of net worth. Large "positive" liquidity events should also be documented, even though they will not act as a constraint.

2. *Time horizon.* The investor's time horizon also constrains his ability to accept risk; shorter investment horizons allow less time to make up portfolio losses. The time horizon constraint may be categorized as short term, intermediate term, or long term and as single stage or multistage. With sufficient assets and multigenerational estate planning, even older investors may retain a long-term investment perspective.

3. *Taxes.* The basic principles of tax deferral, avoidance, and reduction underlie all tax-driven portfolio strategies, but individual solutions are highly country specific and client specific. Taxes relevant to portfolio management generally fall into four major categories: income, gains, wealth transfer, and property.

4. *Legal and regulatory environment.* The investment portfolio's legal and regulatory environment is ultimately country and client specific. A basic knowledge of English and American trust law is often valuable, however, as the terminology is widely recognized and the framework widely applied.

5. *Unique circumstances.* The IPS should capture all unique investment considerations affecting the portfolio. Unique circumstances might include guidelines for social investing, trading restrictions, and privacy concerns.

► As a general rule, only certain asset allocations will be consistent with the client's return objectives, risk tolerance, and investment constraints. The advisor can use a process of elimination to arrive at an appropriate long-term strategic allocation.

► For individual investors, investment decisions, including asset allocation, are made on an after-tax basis. This is a key distinction in contrast to tax-exempt institutions.

► Monte Carlo simulation has certain advantages over deterministic approaches: It more accurately portrays risk–return trade-offs, can illustrate the trade-offs between the attainment of short-term and long-term goals, provides more realistic modeling of taxes, and is better suited to assessing multiperiod effects.

PRACTICE PROBLEMS FOR READING 14

The following information relates to Questions 1–8

Father (Peter), mother (Hilda), son (Hans), and daughter (Christa) and her child (Jürgen). Peter is the founder and majority owner of IngerMarine.

Christa estimates that her revised annual living expenses, including a new studio and apartment, will average €132,500 (excluding Jürgen's educational costs). If necessary, she could combine her apartment and studio to reduce spending by €32,500. She does not want her financial security to be dependent on further gifting from her parents and is pleased that, after the sale of IngerMarine, she will be able to meet her new living expenses with proceeds from art sales (€50,000) and the expected total return of the proposed investment portfolio (€82,500). Because of the uncertainty of art sales, Christa plans to establish an emergency reserve equal to one year's living expenses. Her after-tax proceeds from the sale of IngerMarine are expected to be €1,200,000 × (1 − 0.15) = €1,020,000. She also holds €75,000 in balanced mutual funds and €25,000 in a money market fund. Christa intends to reevaluate her policy statement and asset allocation guidelines every three years.

1. Discuss Christa's liquidity requirements.

2. Determine Christa's return requirement and evaluate whether her portfolio can be expected to satisfy that requirement if inflation averages 3 percent annually and she reduces her annual living expenses to €100,000 by combining her apartment and studio.

3. Explain why an analysis of Christa's investment policy statement might become necessary before the next three-year review.

Hans' increasingly irresponsible lifestyle has become a burden to his parents. Hans was recently arrested for reckless driving—he crashed his car into a restaurant, causing considerable damage and injuring a patron. As a result of Hans' behavior, Peter has placed him on probationary leave of absence from IngerMarine but will allow him to retain his annual salary of €100,000. The restaurant patron is suing Hans for €700,000 in damages, and the restaurant owner estimates that it will take €500,000 to repair damages to his building. Hans' insurance will cover costs to a maximum of only €200,000.

4. Assess the impact of these events on Hans' liquidity and his personal financial statement. What course of action should he pursue?

5. Assess Hans' probable future ability to assume risk, based on information about his background and current living situation.

Peter and Hilda are considering an investment of €1,000,000 in one of the following investment funds. Their tax rates on income and capital gains are 25 percent and 15 percent, respectively.

Practice Problems and Solutions: *Managing Investment Portfolios: A Dynamic Process,* Third Edition, John L. Maginn, CFA, Donald L. Tuttle, CFA, Jerald E. Pinto, CFA, and Dennis W. McLeavey, CFA, editors. Copyright © 2007 by CFA Institute. Reprinted with permission.

Investment	Projected Income (%)	Projected Price Appreciation (%)	Projected Turnover (%)
High-growth stock fund	2.0	12	75
Equity value fund	2.5	10	25
Municipal bond fund	5.0 (tax free)	2	15

6. Evaluate each investment fund based only on its after-tax return.
   Note: Capital gains tax = Price appreciation $\times$ 15% $\times$ Turnover rate.

   IngerMarine has experienced a catastrophic event from which it cannot recover. Damage claims resulting from a design flaw are expected to leave IngerMarine bankrupt and its stock worthless. Peter's pension is also lost.

7. Assess the probable impact on Peter's and Hilda's return requirement.

8. Assess the probable impact on Peter's and Hilda's portfolio constraints.

9. James Stephenson, 55 years old and single, is a surgeon. He has accumulated a $2.0 million investment portfolio with a large concentration in small-capitalization U.S. equities. During the last five years, his portfolio has averaged a 20 percent annual total return on investment. Stephenson's current portfolio of $2.0 million is invested as shown in Exhibit 1.

EXHIBIT 1	Summary of Stephenson's Current Portfolio			
	Value ($)	Percent of Total (%)	Expected Annual Return (%)	Annual Standard Deviation (%)
Short-term bonds	200,000	10	4.6	1.6
Domestic large-cap equities	600,000	30	12.4	19.5
Domestic small-cap equities	1,200,000	60	16.0	29.9
Total portfolio	2,000,000	100	13.8	23.1

His newly hired financial advisor, Caroline Coppa, has compiled the following notes from her meetings with Stephenson:

Stephenson hopes that long term, his investment portfolio will continue to earn 20 percent annually. For the remainder of this year, he would like to earn a return greater than the 5 percent yield to maturity currently available from short-term government notes. When asked about his risk tolerance, he described it as "average." He was surprised when informed that U.S. small-cap portfolios have historically experienced extremely high volatility.

Stephenson does not expect to retire before age 70. His current annual income from his surgical practice is $250,000, which is more than sufficient to meet his current yearly expenses of $150,000. Upon retirement, he plans to sell his surgical practice and use the proceeds to purchase an annuity to cover his post-retirement cash flow needs. He could not state any additional long-term goals or needs.

Stephenson's income and realized capital gains are taxed at a 30 percent rate. No pertinent legal or regulatory issues apply. He has no pension or retirement plan but does have sufficient health insurance for post-retirement needs.

Stephenson soon expects to receive an additional $2.0 million from an inheritance and plans to invest the entire amount in an index fund that best complements the current portfolio. Coppa is evaluating the four index funds shown in Exhibit 2 for their ability to produce a portfolio that will meet the following two criteria relative to the current portfolio:

► maintain or enhance expected return;

► maintain or reduce volatility.

Each fund is invested in an asset class that is not substantially represented in the current portfolio.

EXHIBIT 2	Index Fund Characteristics		
Index Fund	Expected Annual Return (%)	Expected Annual Standard Deviation (%)	Correlation of Returns with Current Portfolio
A	15	25	+0.80
B	11	22	+0.60
C	16	25	+0.90
D	14	22	+0.65

A. Formulate the following elements of Stephenson's investment policy statement and justify your response for each element with two arguments:

   i. Return objective.

   ii. Risk tolerance.

   iii. Liquidity requirements.

   iv. Time horizon.

B. State which fund Coppa should recommend to Stephenson. Justify your choice by describing how your chosen fund best meets both of the criteria set forth by Coppa. (No calculations are required.)

10. Robert Taylor, 50 years old and a U.S. resident, recently retired and received a $500,000 cash payment from his employer as an early retirement incentive. He also obtained $700,000 by exercising his company stock options. Both amounts are net of tax. Taylor is not entitled to a pension; however, his medical expenses are covered by insurance paid for by his former employer. Taylor is in excellent health and has a normal life expectancy.

Taylor's wife died last year after a long illness, which resulted in devastating medical expenses. All their investments, including a home, were liquidated to fully satisfy these medical expenses.

Taylor has no assets other than the $1,200,000 cash referenced above, and he has no debts. He plans to acquire a $300,000 home in three months and insists on paying cash given his recent adverse experience with creditors. When presented with investment options, Taylor consistently selects the most conservative alternative.

After settling into his new home, Taylor's living expenses will be $2,000 per month and will rise with inflation. He does not plan to work again.

Taylor's father and his wife's parents died years ago. His mother, Renee, is 72 years old and in excellent physical health. Her mental health, however, is deteriorating and she has relocated to a long-term care facility. Renee's expenses total $3,500 per month. Her monthly income is $1,500 from pensions. Her income and expenses will rise with inflation. She has no investments or assets of value. Taylor, who has no siblings, must cover Renee's income shortfall.

Taylor has one child, Troy. Troy and a friend need funds immediately for a start-up business with first-year costs estimated at $200,000. The partners have no assets and have been unable to obtain outside financing. The friend's family has offered to invest $100,000 in the business in exchange for a minority equity stake if Taylor agrees to invest the same amount.

Taylor would like to assist Troy; however, he is concerned about the partners' ability to succeed, the potential loss of his funds, and whether his assets are sufficient to support his needs and to support Renee. He plans to make a decision on this investment very soon. If he invests $100,000 in Troy's business, he insists that this investment be excluded from any investment strategy developed for his remaining funds.

With the above information, portfolio manager Sarah Wheeler prepared the investment policy statement for Taylor shown in Exhibit 3.

EXHIBIT 3	Robert Taylor Investment Policy Statement
Return objective	▶ Income requirement is $2,000 monthly.
	▶ Total return requirement is 2.7% annually ($24,000/$900,000).
Risk tolerance	▶ Substantial asset base and low return requirement provide ample resources to support an aggressive, growth-oriented portfolio.
Time horizon	▶ Client is 50 years old, recently retired, and in excellent health.
	▶ Time horizon exceeds 20 years.
Liquidity needs	▶ $300,000 is needed in three months for purchase of home.
	▶ Modest additional cash is needed for normal relocation costs. $100,000 may be needed for possible investment in son's business.
	▶ A normal, ongoing cash reserve level should be established.
Tax concerns	▶ There is little need to defer income.
	▶ Mother's expenses may have an effect.
Legal and regulatory factors	▶ No special considerations exist.
Unique circumstances	▶ Client desires to support mother.
	▶ Client insists that any investment in son's business be excluded from long-term planning.
	▶ Client has strong aversion to debt.

A. Evaluate the appropriateness of Taylor's investment policy statement with regard to the following objectives:

   i. Return requirement.

   ii. Risk tolerance.

   iii. Time horizon.

   iv. Liquidity requirements.

After revising the investment policy statement and confirming it with Taylor, Wheeler is now developing a long-term strategic asset allocation for Taylor. Wheeler will use the following revised information to recommend one of the allocations in Exhibit 4.

▶ Taylor has decided to invest $100,000 in his son's business but still insists that this investment be disregarded in making his allocation decision.

▶ Taylor's total cash flow needs have changed to $4,200 a month.

▶ The available asset base is $800,000.

▶ Wheeler estimates that the inflation rate will be 1 percent next year.

▶ Taylor is determined to maintain the real value of his assets because he plans to set up a charitable foundation in the future.

▶ Taylor insists on taking no more risk than absolutely necessary to achieve his return goals.

▶ The expected annual nominal risk-free rate of return is 3%.

EXHIBIT 4	Potential Long-Term Strategic Asset Allocations			
	Allocation			
	A	**B**	**C**	**D**
Asset Class Weighting				
Stocks	20%	40%	60%	80%
Bonds	75%	55%	35%	15%
Cash	5%	5%	5%	5%
Total	100%	100%	100%	100%
Expected Annual				
Return	6.7%	7.5%	8.2%	9.1%
Standard deviation	9.0%	11.5%	15.3%	19.0%
Potential for Growth				
Asset growth	Very low	Low	Moderate	High
Income growth	Very low	Low	Moderate	High
Current income	High	High	Low	Very low
Stability	Very high	High	Moderate	Low

B. Select the strategic asset allocation that is most appropriate for Taylor and justify your selection with two supporting reasons related to the revised information shown above.

11. Mark and Andrea Mueller, U.S. residents, are reviewing their financial plan. The Muellers, both 53 years old, have one daughter, 18 years old. With their combined after-tax salaries totaling $100,000 a year, they are able to meet their living expenses and save $25,000 after taxes annually. They expect little change in either their incomes or expenses on an inflation-adjusted basis other than the addition of their daughter's college expenses. Their only long-term financial goal is to provide for themselves and for their daughter's education. The Muellers both wish to retire in 10 years.

Their daughter, a talented musician, is now entering an exclusive five-year college program. This program requires a $50,000 contribution, payable now, to the college's endowment fund. Thereafter, her tuition and living expenses, to be paid entirely by the Muellers, are estimated at $40,000 annually.

The Mueller's personal investments total $600,000, and they plan to continue to manage the portfolio themselves. They prefer "conservative growth investments with minimal volatility." One-third of their portfolio is in the stock of Andrea's employer, a publicly traded technology company with a highly uncertain future. The shares have a very low-cost basis for tax purposes. The Muellers, currently taxed at 30 percent on income and 20 percent on net realized capital gains, have accumulated losses from past unsuccessful investments that can be used to fully offset $100,000 of future realized gains.

In 10 years, Mark will receive a distribution from a family trust. His portion is now $1.2 million and is expected to grow prior to distribution. Mark receives no income from the trust and has no influence over, or responsibility for, its management. The Muellers know that these funds will change their financial situation materially but have excluded the trust from their current financial planning.

A. Construct the objectives and constraints portion of an investment policy statement for the Muellers, addressing each of the following:

  i. Return objective.

  ii. Risk tolerance.

  iii. Time horizon.

  iv. Liquidity requirements.

  v. Tax concerns.

  vi. Unique circumstances.

Ten years have passed. The Muellers, now both aged 63, will retire this year. The distribution from Mark's family trust will occur within the next two weeks. The Muellers' current circumstances are summarized below:

Personal Circumstances and Assets

► Pension income will total $100,000 a year and will not increase with inflation.

► Annual expenses will total $180,000 initially and will increase with inflation.

► Inflation is expected to be 2 percent annually.

► Their personal investments now total $1,000,000 (excluding trust distribution).

► The Muellers will rely on this $1,000,000 portfolio to support their lifestyle and do not wish to reduce their level of spending.

► The Muellers have health problems and neither is expected to live more than 10 years. All health care expenses will be covered by employer-paid insurance.

► The Muellers' daughter is now financially independent, and the Muellers' sole investment objective is to meet their spending needs.

► The Muellers are not concerned with growing or maintaining principal. The income deficit may be met with both investment income and by invading principal.

Trust Distribution Assets

► The trust distribution totals $2,000,000 and will occur within the next two weeks. No tax liability is created by the distribution.

► The Muellers will maintain separate accounts for their personal assets and the trust distribution.

► They do not plan to withdraw income or principal.

► Tax liabilities produced by these assets will be paid from this portfolio.

► The Muellers plan to donate these assets to an arts society when the surviving spouse dies. They have made a minimum pledge of $2.6 million toward construction of a new building.

► An after-tax annual return of 5.4 percent is required over five years to meet the minimum pledge.

► The Muellers are concerned only that a minimum gift of $2.6 million is available. The Muellers assume that at least one of them will live at least five years and that neither will live more than 10 years.

Alternative portfolios for the Muellers' consideration appear in Exhibit 5.

EXHIBIT 5

Asset Allocation	Portfolio			
	A (%)	B (%)	C (%)	D (%)
Domestic large-cap stocks	14	30	40	30
Domestic small-cap stocks	3	5	10	25
Foreign stocks	3	5	10	25
Intermediate-term fixed income	70	60	30	20
Cash equivalents	10	0	10	0
Total	100	100	100	100
Expected annual return[a]	4.2	5.8	7.5	8.5
Annual standard deviation	6.0	8.0	13.0	18.0

[a] Nominal after-tax returns.

B. Select and justify with three reasons the most appropriate of the four portfolios from Exhibit 5 as an asset allocation for the Muellers' $1,000,000 in personal assets.

C. Select and justify with three reasons the most appropriate of the four portfolios from Exhibit 5 as an asset allocation for the Muellers' $2,000,000 in trust distribution assets.

12. John Mesa, CFA, is a portfolio manager in the Trust Department of BigBanc. Mesa has been asked to review the investment portfolios of Robert and Mary Smith, a retired couple and potential clients. Previously, the Smiths had been working with another financial advisor, WealthMax Financial Consultants (WFC). To assist Mesa, the Smiths have provided the following background information:

Family   We live alone. Our only daughter and granddaughter are financially secure and independent.

Health   We are both 65 years of age and in good health. Our medical costs are covered by insurance.

Housing   Our house needs major renovation. The work will be completed within the next six months, at an estimated cost of $200,000.

Expenses   Our annual after-tax living costs are expected to be $150,000 for this year and are rising with inflation, which is expected to continue at 3 percent annually.

Income   In addition to income from the Gift Fund and the Family Portfolio (both described below), we receive a fixed annual pension payment of $65,000 (after taxes), which continues for both of our lifetimes.

Financial Goals   Our primary objective is to maintain our financial security and support our current lifestyle. A secondary objective is to leave $1 million to our grandchild and $1 million to our local college. We recently completed the $1 million gift to the college by creating a "Gift Fund." Preserving the remaining assets for our granddaughter is important to us.

Taxes   Our investment income, including bond interest and stock dividends, is taxed at 30 percent. Our investment returns from price appreciation (capital gains) are taxed at 15 percent, at the time of sale. We have no other tax considerations.

General Comments   We needed someone like WFC to develop a comprehensive plan for us to follow. We can follow such a plan once it is prepared for us. We invest only in companies with which we are familiar. We will not sell a security for less than we paid for it. Given our need for income, we invest only in dividend-paying stocks.

Investments   We benefit from two investment accounts:

- ▶ The Gift Fund ($1 million) represents our gift to the college. During our lifetimes, we will receive fixed annual payments of $40,000 (tax free) from the Gift Fund. Except for the annual payments to us, the Gift Fund is managed solely for the benefit of the college—we may not make any other withdrawals of either income or principal. Upon our deaths, all assets remaining in the Gift Fund will be transferred into the college's endowment.

► The Family Portfolio ($1.2 million) represents the remainder of our lifetime savings. The portfolio is invested entirely in very safe securities, consistent with the investment policy statement prepared for us by WFC as shown in Exhibit 6.

| EXHIBIT 6 | WFC Investment Policy Statement for Smith Family Portfolio |

The Smith Family Portfolio's primary focus is the production of current income, with long-term capital appreciation a secondary consideration. The need for a dependable income stream precludes investment vehicles with even modest likelihood of losses. Liquidity needs reinforce the need to emphasize minimum-risk investments. Extensive use of short-term investment-grade investments is entirely justified by the expectation that a low-inflation environment will exist indefinitely into the future. For these reasons, investments will emphasize U.S. Treasury bills and notes, intermediate-term investment-grade corporate debt, and select "blue chip" stocks with assured dividend distributions and minimal price fluctuations.

To assist in a discussion of investment policy, Mesa presents four model portfolios used by BigBanc; Exhibit 7 applies the bank's long-term forecasts for asset class returns to each portfolio.

| EXHIBIT 7 | BigBanc Model Portfolios |

Asset Class	Total Return	Yield	A	B	C	D
U.S. large-cap stocks	13.0%	3.0%	0%	35%	45%	0%
U.S. small-cap stocks	15.0	1.0	0	5	15	0
Non-U.S. stocks	14.0	1.5	0	10	15	10
U.S. corporate bonds (AA)	6.5	6.5	80	20	0	30
U.S. Treasury notes	6.0	6.0	0	10	5	20
Non-U.S. government bonds	6.5	6.5	0	5	5	0
Municipal bonds (AA)[a]	4.0	4.0	0	10	0	10
Venture capital	20.0	0.0	0	0	10	25
U.S. Treasury bills	4.0	4.0	20	5	5	5
Total			100%	100%	100%	100%
After-tax expected return			4.2%	7.5%	13.0%	6.4%
Sharpe ratio			0.35	0.50	0.45	0.45
After-tax yield			4.2%	2.9%	1.9%	3.3%
Expected inflation: 3.0%						

[a] Tax exempt.

A. Prepare and justify an alternative investment policy statement for the Smiths' Family Portfolio.

B. Describe how your IPS addresses three specific deficiencies in the WFC investment policy statement.

C. Recommend a portfolio from Exhibit 7 for the Family Portfolio. Justify your recommendation with specific reference to:

    i. three portfolio characteristics in Exhibit 7 other than expected return or yield; and

    ii. the Smiths' return objectives. Show your calculations.

13. Louise and Christopher Maclin live in London, United Kingdom, and currently rent an apartment in the metropolitan area. Christopher Maclin, aged 40, is a supervisor at Barnett Co. and earns an annual salary of £80,000 before taxes. Louise Maclin, aged 38, stays home to care for their newborn twins. She recently inherited £900,000 (after wealth-transfer taxes) in cash from her father's estate. In addition, the Maclins have accumulated the following assets (current market value):

► £5,000 in cash;

► £160,000 in stocks and bonds;

► £220,000 in Barnett common stock.

The value of their holdings in Barnett stock has appreciated substantially as a result of the company's growth in sales and profits during the past ten years. Christopher Maclin is confident that the company and its stock will continue to perform well.

The Maclins need £30,000 for a down payment on the purchase of a house and plan to make a £20,000 non-tax deductible donation to a local charity in memory of Louise Maclin's father. The Maclins' annual living expenses are £74,000. After-tax salary increases will offset any future increases in their living expenses.

During discussions with their financial advisor, Grant Webb, the Maclins express concern about achieving their educational goals for their children and their own retirement goals. The Maclins tell Webb:

► They want to have sufficient funds to retire in 18 years when their children begin their four years of university education.

► They have been unhappy with the portfolio volatility they have experienced in recent years. They state that they do not want to experience a loss in portfolio value greater than 12 percent in any one year.

► They do not want to invest in alcohol and tobacco stocks.

► They will not have any additional children.

After their discussions, Webb calculates that in 18 years the Maclins will need £2 million to meet their educational and retirement goals. Webb suggests that their portfolio be structured to limit shortfall risk (defined as expected total return minus two standard deviations) to no lower than a negative 12 percent return in any one year. Maclin's salary and all capital gains and investment income are taxed at 40 percent and no tax-sheltering strategies are available. Webb's next step is to formulate an investment policy statement for the Maclins.

A. **i.** Formulate the risk objective of an investment policy statement for the Maclins.

ii. Formulate the return objective of an investment policy statement for the Maclins. Calculate the pre-tax rate of return that is required to achieve this objective. Show your calculations.

B. Formulate the constraints portion of an investment policy statement for the Maclins, addressing *each* of the following:

i. Time horizon.

ii. Liquidity requirements.

iii. Tax concerns.

iv. Unique circumstances.

Note: Your response to Part B should not address legal and regulatory factors.

SOLUTIONS FOR READING 14

1. Need for cash:

Ongoing expenses:	€132,500/year
Emergency reserve:	€132,500
Anticipated income:	€50,000/year art sales
	€82,500/year expected total return on portfolio (subject to risk)
	€1,020,000 after taxes from sale of IngerMarine

The after-tax proceeds from the imminent sale of IngerMarine well exceed Christa's anticipated needs for cash for the coming year (2 × €132,500 = €265,000). Thus her liquidity needs are currently met. Because portfolio returns are risky and her anticipated annual income of €132,500 just covers her annual cash needs, however, Christa may face a challenge in the form of liquidity requirements at some point in the future.

2. After the sale of IngerMarine, Christa's portfolio will have a market value of roughly €1,120,000, taking account of the after-tax proceeds from the sale of IngerMarine (€1,020,000), her balanced mutual funds (€75,000), and her money market fund (€25,000). Her expected portfolio return is €82,500, equal to a 7.4 percent rate of return. Her required real return, if she reduces her spending by combining her apartment and studio, is €50,000 (art sales of €50,000 less €100,000 expenses), or 4.5 percent as a rate of return on her portfolio.

Because the portfolio's expected return of 7.4 percent translates to a real return of approximately 4.4 percent (7.4 percent less 3 percent inflation), the portfolio is *not* expected to meet the return requirement of 4.5 percent.

3. Portfolio guidelines and investment policy should be reviewed whenever a significant change occurs in the underlying assumptions of the policy statement. At Christa's portfolio performance reviews, the need for an interim reevaluation of the policy statement should always be considered. Possible triggers for a policy statement review might include the following:

► A change in personal circumstances affecting risk–return objectives or portfolio constraints. Examples could include an increase in expected income from nonportfolio sources, uninsured health problems, or marriage.

► A change in market conditions affecting long-term risk–return relationships among asset classes. Examples could include a shift in outlook for inflation and global political changes.

► New investment markets or vehicles. Examples could include markets made accessible through commingled investment funds and Retirement Saving Accounts.

► A change in tax laws. An example could be elimination of the capital gains tax.

► A severe performance shortfall, sufficient to jeopardize the portfolio's ability to meet expense needs in excess of income from other sources.

4. Hans' reckless actions will significantly reduce his portfolio. Hopefully this incident will make him aware of his financial vulnerability and the long-term consequences of his actions. The potential costs of the accident have created an immediate need for liquidity. Currently, Hans has a diversified equity portfolio valued at €200,000 and cash of €100,000. If he has not already done so, he should immediately use the cash to retain an attorney for his upcoming legal challenges. He should also make his financial advisor aware of his situation and instruct him or her to establish a high level of portfolio liquidity. Hans may need to convert a portion of his IngerMarine holdings to cash, if he can, and should notify his father of this possibility. Alternatively, Hans may be able to obtain a loan using IngerMarine shares as collateral. If the IngerMarine holdings cannot be monetized, Hans may be able to borrow against the equity in his home.

5. In light of the auto accident, Hans must reassess his investment portfolio. Assuming that the legal challenges against him are successful, he stands to lose €1,000,000 in savings (after insurance). In addition, his legal fees may be large, resulting in a further decline in net worth. His salary has not been reduced, but depending on the outcome of his legal troubles, he may face job termination. His investment personality profile classified Hans as a spontaneous risk-taker, and his propensity to engage in riskier investing will have to be reevaluated. Even though Hans is young, his ability to take risk has been severely curtailed by the recent incident. His net worth may be reduced by as much as half, and he faces the potential loss of his current income. Hans will now need to consider rebuilding his life, engaging in lower-risk investing until his contingent liabilities are settled.

6. Peter and Hilda are subject to a flat tax of 25 percent on all income and a capital gains tax of 15 percent. The analysis below presents comparative after-tax returns. Even though the High Growth Stock Fund maintains high portfolio turnover, its return is high enough to provide superior after-tax performance. Of course, a complete investment evaluation should also address the relative risk of each investment alternative. The High Growth Stock Fund is quite likely to have high portfolio volatility, and this factor must also be considered before a final decision is made.

After-Tax Investment Evaluation

Investment Vehicle	High-Growth Stock Fund (€)	Equity Value Fund (€)	Municipal Bond Fund (€)
Investment	1,000,000	1,000,000	1,000,000
Projected income	20,000	25,000	50,000
Projected price appreciation	120,000	100,000	20,000
Projected income tax liability	(5,000)	(6,250)	0
Projected capital gains tax liability[a]	(13,500)	(3,750)	(450)
Net investment gains	**121,500**	**115,000**	**69,550**

[a] Gains tax liability = Price appreciation × 15% × Turnover rate

7. Remaining investment portfolio:

Stocks	€750,000
Bonds	1,000,000
Cash	1,000,000
Gold	500,000
	€3,250,000

Additional resources:

Hilda's trust distribution	€75,000/year
House	€1,200,000
Peter's RSA	€50,000

The goal of replacing Peter's €500,000 salary has become a "desired" portfolio return that is clearly not realistic. Peter and Hilda must now reconsider the return that they will "require" in order to meet their basic financial goals. The required return must be reconcilable with their new investment constraints and ability to assume risk. Before reaching an achievable return objective, Peter and Hilda will have to address some difficult decisions regarding their future lifestyle and long-term goals. Possible changes might include the following:

▶ postpone retirement;
▶ attempt to rebuild IngerMarine;
▶ return to the workforce as consultants or salaried employees;
▶ sell home;
▶ curtail gifting programs;
▶ cancel plans for second home;
▶ cancel investment in *Exteriors* magazine;
▶ liquidate Hilda's design company.

8. Portfolio Constraints

▶ *Liquidity.* The Ingers' short-term liquidity needs have clearly increased. Because spending commitments are sometimes difficult to curtail, Peter and Hilda may need to withdraw as much as €500,000 in the coming year from their remaining assets, to pay for expenses previously covered by Peter's salary. Fortunately, the Ingers have an emergency reserve of cash and bullion equivalent to approximately three years' salary.

The Ingers must ultimately reconcile their ongoing liquidity needs, as well as targeted liquidity events, with their remaining net worth. Left unchanged, the increased liquidity requirements will require an increasing allocation to investments with lower volatility and lower return. At the same time, withdrawals will begin to outstrip returns, leaving the Ingers' portfolio in a deteriorating situation.

▶ *Time horizon.* Peter and Hilda's investment time horizon has been shortened, as the increased need to secure their own financial future has left them less able to approach portfolio risk from a multigenerational perspective. Their joint life expectancy, however, would reasonably warrant a portfolio time horizon that is still long term (20 to 25 years or more).

▶ *Taxes.* Tax rates remain unchanged for the Ingers, although their tax burden will decline with the loss of Peter's income. Their business loss from IngerMarine may be available to offset future investment gains.

▶ *Regulatory environment.* The regulatory environment is unchanged.

▶ *Unique circumstances.* It would be appropriate to note the bankruptcy of IngerMarine and any consequences it might have for portfolio management, such as the allocation of portfolio assets to build a new family business.

9. A. i. *Return objective.* Stephenson's expressed desire for 20 percent average annual return is unrealistic. Coppa should counsel Stephenson on the level of return he can reasonably expect from the financial markets over long time periods and to define an achievable return objective. Nevertheless, Stephenson's circumstances support an above-average return objective that emphasizes capital appreciation. This formulation is justified by the following:

- ► Because Stephenson has a sizable asset base and ample income to cover his current spending, focus should be on growing the portfolio.
- ► Stephenson's low liquidity needs and long time horizon support a long-term capital appreciation approach.
- ► Stephenson is in the consolidation phase of his life cycle and does not rely on the portfolio to meet living expenses.

Stephenson stated that he wants a return in excess of 5.0 percent for the remainder of the year. This short-term goal needs to be considered to the extent possible but should not be a significant factor in the IPS, which focuses on the client's long-term return objective.

ii. *Risk tolerance.* Stephenson has an above-average risk tolerance.

- ► Although Stephenson describes his risk tolerance as "average," his current investment portfolio indicates an apparent above-average willingness to take risk.
- ► His financial situation (large current asset base, ample income to cover expenses, lack of need for liquidity or cash flow, and long time horizon) indicates an above-average ability to assume risk.

iii. *Liquidity requirements.* Stephenson's liquidity needs are low.

- ► Stephenson has no regular cash flow needs from the portfolio because the income from his medical practice meets all current spending needs.
- ► No large, one-time cash needs are stated. It would be appropriate, however, to keep a small cash reserve for emergencies.

iv. *Time horizon.* Stephenson's time horizon is long term and consists of two stages:

- ► time until retirement, which he expects to be 15 years; and
- ► his lifetime following retirement, which could range from 15 to 20 years.

B. Fund D represents the single best addition to complement Stephenson's current portfolio, given his selection criteria. First, Fund D's expected return (14.0 percent) has the potential to increase the portfolio's return somewhat. Second, Fund D's relatively low correlation coefficient with his current portfolio (+0.65) indicates that it will provide larger diversification benefits than any of the other alternatives except Fund B. The result of adding Fund D should be a portfolio with about the same expected return and somewhat lower volatility compared with the original portfolio.

The three other funds have shortcomings in either expected return enhancement or volatility reduction through diversification benefits:

- ► Fund A offers the potential for increasing the portfolio's return but is too highly correlated to provide substantial volatility reduction benefits through diversification.

▶ Fund B provides substantial volatility reduction through diversification benefits but is expected to generate a return well below the current portfolio's return.

▶ Fund C has the greatest potential to increase the portfolio's return but is too highly correlated to provide substantial volatility reduction benefits through diversification.

10. A. i. The IPS's *return objective* section is inadequate.

▶ Although Wheeler accurately indicates Taylor's personal income requirement, she has not recognized the need to support Renee.

▶ Wheeler does not indicate the need to protect Taylor's purchasing power by increasing income by at least the rate of inflation over time.

▶ Wheeler does not indicate the impact of income taxes on the return requirement.

▶ Wheeler calculates required return based on assets of $900,000, appropriately excluding Taylor's imminent $300,000 liquidity need (house purchase) from investable funds. However, Taylor may invest $100,000 in his son's business. If he does, Taylor insists this asset be excluded from his plan. In that eventuality, Taylor's asset base for purposes of Wheeler's analysis would be $800,000.

▶ Assuming a $900,000 capital base, Wheeler's total return estimate of 2.7 percent is lower than the actual required after-tax real return of 5.3 percent ($48,000/$900,000).

ii. The *risk tolerance* section is inappropriate.

▶ Wheeler fails to consider Taylor's below-average willingness to assume risk as exemplified by his aversion to loss, his consistent preference for conservative investments, his adverse experience with creditors, and his desire not to work again.

▶ Wheeler fails to consider Taylor's below-average ability to assume risk, which is based on his recent life changes, the size of his capital base, high personal expenses versus income, and expenses related to his mother's care.

▶ Wheeler's policy statement implies that Taylor has a greater willingness and ability to accept volatility (higher risk tolerance) than is actually the case. Based on Taylor's need for an after-tax return of 5.3 percent, a balanced approach with both a fixed-income and growth component is more appropriate than an aggressive growth strategy.

iii. The *time horizon* section is partially appropriate.

▶ Wheeler accurately addresses the long-term time horizon based only on Taylor's age and life expectancy.

▶ Wheeler fails to consider that Taylor's investment time horizon is multistage. Stage 1 represents Renee's life expectancy, during which time Taylor will supplement her income. Stage 2 begins at Renee's death, concluding Taylor's need to supplement her income, and ends with Taylor's death.

   iv. The *liquidity* section is partially appropriate.

   ► Wheeler addresses potential liquidity events.

   ► Wheeler fails to specifically consider ongoing expenses ($2,000/month for Taylor's living expenses and $2,000/month to support his mother) relative to expected portfolio returns.

   ► The reference to a "normal, ongoing cash reserve" is vague. The reserve's purpose and size should be specified.

B. Allocation B is most appropriate for Taylor. Taylor's real-return annual return requirement is 6.3 percent, based on his cash flow (income) needs ($50,400 annually), to be generated from a current asset base of $800,000. After adjusting for expected annual inflation of 1.0 percent, the nominal requirement becomes 7.3 percent. To grow to $808,000 ($800,000 × 1.01), the portfolio must generate $58,400 ($50,400 + $8,000) in the first year ($58,400/$800,000 = 7.3%).

   Allocation B meets Taylor's minimum return requirement. Of the possible allocations that provide the required minimum real return, Allocation B also has the lowest standard deviation of returns (i.e., the least volatility risk) and by far the best Sharpe ratio. In addition, Allocation B offers a balance of high current income and stability with moderate growth prospects.

   Allocation A has the lowest standard deviation and best Sharpe ratio but does not meet the minimum return requirement when inflation is included in that requirement. Allocation A also has very low growth prospects.

   Allocation C meets the minimum return requirement and has moderate growth prospects but has a higher risk level (standard deviation) and a lower Sharpe ratio, as well as less potential for stability, than Allocation B.

11. A. The Muellers' investment policy statement should include the following objectives and constraints:

   i. *Return objective.* The Mueller's return objective should reflect a total return approach that combines capital appreciation and capital preservation. After retirement, they will need approximately $75,000 (adjusted for inflation) annually to maintain their current standard of living. Given the Muellers' limited needs and asset base, preserving their financial position on an inflation-adjusted basis may be a sufficient objective. Their long life expectancy and undetermined retirement needs, however, lead to the likely requirement for some asset growth over time, at least to counter any effects of inflation.

   Although the Muellers wish to exclude the future trust distribution from their current planning, that distribution will substantially increase their capital base and dramatically alter the return objective of their future IPS, primarily by reducing their needed return level.

   ii. *Risk tolerance.* The Muellers are in the middle stage of the investor life cycle. Their income (relative to expenses), total financial resources, and long time horizon give them the ability to assume at least an average, if not an above-average, level of investment risk. Their stated preference of "minimal volatility" investments, however, apparently indicates a below-average willingness to assume risk. The large realized losses they incurred in previous investments may contribute to their desire for safety. Also, their need for continuing cash outflow to meet their daughter's college expenses may temporarily and slightly reduce their risk-taking ability. In sum, the Muellers' risk tolerance is average.

Two other issues affect the Muellers' ability to take risk. First, the holding of Andrea's company stock represents a large percentage of the Mueller's total investable assets and thus is an important risk factor for their portfolio. Reducing the size of this holding or otherwise reducing the risk associated with a single large holding should be a priority for the Muellers. Second, the future trust distribution will substantially increase their capital base and thus increase their ability to assume risk.

iii. *Time horizon.* Overall, the Muellers' ages and long life expectancies indicate a long time horizon. They face a multistage horizon, however, because of their changing cash flow and resource circumstances. Their time horizon can be viewed as having three distinct stages: the next five years from now (some assets, negative cash flow because of their daughter's college expenses), the following five years (some assets, positive cash flow), and beyond 10 years (increased assets from a sizable trust distribution, decreased income because they plan to retire).

iv. *Liquidity.* The Muellers need $50,000 now to contribute to the college's endowment fund. Alternatively, they may be able to contribute $50,000 of Andrea's low-cost-basis stock to meet the endowment obligation. In addition, they expect the regular annual college expenses ($40,000) to exceed their normal annual savings ($25,000) by $15,000 for each of the next five years. This relatively low cash flow requirement of 2.7 percent ($15,000/$550,000 asset base after $50,000 contribution) can be substantially met through income generation from their portfolio, further reducing the need for sizable cash reserves. Once their daughter completes college, the Muellers' liquidity needs should be minimal until retirement because their income more than adequately covers their living expenses.

v. *Tax concerns.* The Muellers are subject to a 30 percent marginal tax rate for ordinary income and a 20 percent rate for realized capital gains. The difference in the rates makes investment returns in the form of capital gains preferable to equivalent amounts of taxable dividends and interest.

Although taxes on capital gains would normally be a concern to investors with low-cost-basis stock, this is not a major concern for the Muellers because they have a tax loss carryforward of $100,000. The Muellers can offset up to $100,000 in realized gains with the available tax loss carryforward without experiencing any cash outflow or any reduction in asset base.

vi. *Unique circumstances.* The large holding of the low-basis stock in Andrea's company, a "technology company with a highly uncertain future," is a key factor to be included in the evaluation of the risk level of the Muellers' portfolio and the future management of their assets. In particular, the family should systematically reduce the size of the investment in this single stock. Because of the existence of the tax loss carryforward, the stock position can be reduced by at least 50 percent (perhaps more depending on the exact cost basis of the stock) without reducing the asset base to pay a tax obligation.

In addition, the trust distribution in 10 years presents special circumstances for the Muellers, although they prefer to ignore these future assets in their current planning. The trust will provide significant assets to help meet their long-term return needs and objectives. Any long-term investment policy for the family must consider this circumstance, and any recommended investment strategy must be adjusted before the distribution takes place.

B. *Personal portfolio.* Portfolio A is the most appropriate portfolio for the Muellers. Because their pension income will not cover their annual expenditures, the shortfall will not likely be met by the return on their investments, so the 10 percent cash reserve is appropriate. As the portfolio is depleted over time, it may be prudent to allocate more than 10 percent to cash equivalents. The income deficit will be met each year by a combination of investment return and capital invasion.

Now that their daughter is financially independent, the Muellers' sole objective for their personal portfolio is to provide for their own living expenses. Their willingness and need to accept risk is fairly low. Clearly, there is no need to expose the Muellers to the possibility of a large loss. Also, their health situation has considerably shortened their time horizon. Therefore, a 70 percent allocation to intermediate-term high-grade fixed-income securities is warranted.

The income deficit will rise each year as the Muellers' expenses rise with inflation, but their pension income remains constant. The conservative 20 percent allocation to equities should provide diversification benefits and some protection against unanticipated inflation over the expected maximum 10-year time horizon.

Portfolio B, the second-best portfolio, has no cash reserves, so it could not meet the Muellers' liquidity needs. Also, although it has a higher expected return, Portfolio B's asset allocation results in a somewhat higher standard deviation of returns than Portfolio A.

Portfolios C and D offer higher expected returns but at markedly higher levels of risk and with relatively lower levels of current income. The Muellers' large income requirements and low risk tolerance preclude the use of Portfolios C and D.

C. *Trust distribution portfolio.* Portfolio B is the most appropriate for the trust assets. Portfolio B's expected return of 5.8 percent exceeds the required return of 5.4 percent, and the required return will actually decline if the surviving spouse lives longer than five years. The portfolio's time horizon is relatively short, ranging from a minimum of 5 years to a maximum of 10 years. The Muellers' sole objective for this money is to adequately fund the building addition. The portfolio's growth requirements are modest, and the Muellers have below-average willingness to accept risk. The portfolio would be unlikely to achieve its objective if large, even short-term losses were absorbed during the minimum five-year time horizon. Except for taxes, no principal or income disbursements are expected for at least five years; therefore, only a minimal or even zero cash reserve is required. Accordingly, an allocation of 40 percent to equities to provide some growth and 60 percent to intermediate-term fixed-income to provide stability and capital preservation is appropriate.

There is no second-best portfolio. Portfolio A's cash level is higher than necessary, and the portfolio's expected return is insufficient to achieve the $2,600,000 value within the minimum value in five years. Portfolio C has a sufficient expected return, but it has a higher cash level than is necessary and, more importantly, a standard deviation of return that is too high given the Muellers' below-average risk tolerance. Portfolio D has a sufficient return and an appropriate cash level but a clearly excessive risk (standard deviation) level. Portfolios C and D share the flaw of having excessive equity allocations that fail to recognize the relatively short time horizon and that generate risk levels much higher than necessary or warranted.

12. A.   To prepare an appropriate IPS, a manager should address the Smiths' return objective, risk tolerance, and constraints.

Return objective. To achieve its objectives, the Family Portfolio must provide for after-tax distributions equal to the difference between the Smiths' expenses and their fixed income payments. To maintain its real value, the portfolio must also grow at a rate that offsets inflation's impact on the Smiths' total expenses, including those currently covered by the fixed pension and Gift Fund payments.

A secondary objective is the gifting of $1 million to the Smiths' granddaughter. Because the Family Portfolio will be worth $1 million after the renovation of their house, the Smiths need no further capital growth to reach their nominal goal. To maintain its real value, the portfolio must have growth at least equal to the rate of inflation.

Risk tolerance. The Smiths are in a relatively late stage of the investor life cycle, and their comments suggest a conservative bias or below-average willingness to accept risk. In light of their long-term goals and current financial security, however, the Smiths have the ability to accommodate moderate portfolio volatility.

In the short term, the consequences of an adverse investment outcome are limited; the Smiths could use principal from the Family Portfolio to cover occasional performance shortfalls. They are thus able to accommodate some measure of short-term volatility in return for greater long-term expected returns. In extreme circumstances, the Smiths could modify or forgo their secondary objective of leaving $1 million to their granddaughter.

The consequences of an adverse portfolio outcome in the long term, however, could be serious. Depending on the length of their remaining lifetimes and the growth rate of their expenses, the Smiths could seriously deplete the corpus of the Family Portfolio and jeopardize their financial security.

The Smiths' comments imply that they have spent a lifetime saving and building a "safe" collection of income-oriented investments. Their desire to preserve market value and the WealthMax Financial Consultants (WFC) policy statement's emphasis on secure investments suggest that they may fall, at least partially, into the "cautious" category, a group with below-average risk tolerance.

Time horizon. The Family Portfolio should have an intermediate to slightly longer-term investment horizon.

The Smiths' joint life expectancy, at 65 years of age, is still substantial. Because their objective of financial security is well provided for in the short term (see discussion of risk tolerance), the Smiths can afford to focus more on the long-term aspects of that objective.

To the extent that the Smiths emphasize the objective of leaving $1 million to their granddaughter in their planning, a longer-term time horizon would be warranted.

Liquidity requirements. The Smiths' current annual living costs ($150,000 after taxes) are being met, which allows them to address longer-term growth objectives. The Smiths must plan for the upcoming expense of renovating their home. Their Family Portfolio should anticipate the renovation costs by holding a reserve of at least $200,000 in highly liquid, short-term funds.

Laws and regulations. No special legal or regulatory problems are apparent.

Tax concerns. The Smiths must pay a higher tax on dividends and interest than on capital gains. All else being equal, therefore, they prefer portfolio returns in the form of capital gains rather than equivalent amounts of taxable investment income.

Unique circumstances. Establishment of the Gift Fund had increased the Smiths' dependence on fixed payments. As a consequence of this increased exposure to the eroding effects of inflation, the Smiths' long-term financial security is significantly reduced.

Synopsis. The Smiths may not fully appreciate the impact of inflation and taxes on their financial security. The Family Portfolio can meet their immediate needs, but it is unlikely to grow at the same rate as disbursements. Depending on how long the Smiths live, the secondary objective of giving $1 million to their granddaughter may not be fully attainable, even in nominal terms.

B. Rather than a true policy statement, the WFC statement is a compendium of opinions and assertions that may or may not be supportable by evidence and may or may not be appropriate to the Smiths' specific situation. WFC's statement fails to:

- ► identify specific return requirement;
- ► consider inflation;
- ► consider the Smiths' willingness and ability to accept risk;
- ► consider the Smiths' investment time horizon;
- ► specify the Smiths' liquidity requirements;
- ► address the possibility of legal and regulatory constraints;
- ► consider tax concerns; and
- ► consider possible unique circumstances.

C. **i.** Portfolio B is an appropriate recommendation based on three portfolio characteristics other than expected return and yield: diversification, efficiency (Sharpe ratio), and risk.

- ► Diversification across asset classes contributes to portfolio efficiency and is a desirable portfolio characteristic. Portfolio B appears to be the most broadly diversified.
- ► Efficiency, as measured by return for each unit of risk (Sharpe ratio), is a desirable portfolio characteristic. Portfolio B dominates the other portfolios on this criterion.
- ► Risk is an attribute that must be constrained to fit the Smiths' fiscal and psychological tolerance levels. The 85 percent allocation to equities and venture capital in Portfolio C entails relatively high risk. Portfolio B, which is more balanced between fixed-income and equity markets, is better suited to the Smiths' below-average risk profile.

ii. Meeting the Smiths' return objectives in the first year will require an after-tax total return of 7.5 percent on the $1 million remaining in the Family Portfolio after their house renovation. The Family Portfolio must accommodate a disbursement of $45,000 and grow at a rate that offsets the impact of inflation:

Expenses	($150,000)

Sources of funds		
Pension (after tax)	65,000	
Gift Fund (after tax)	40,000	105,000
Family Portfolio disbursement (after tax)		45,000
		$150,000

Required return	
Disbursement ($45,000)	4.50%
Inflation	3.00%
Total	7.50%

Subsequent distributions from the Family Portfolio will increase at a rate substantially higher than inflation (to offset the lack of growth in $105,000 of fixed pension and Gift Fund payments):

	Year 1	Year 2	Change
Expenses (3% growth)	$150,000	$154,500	3%
Portfolio distribution	$45,000	$49,500	10%

Portfolios B and C both have expected returns that meet the Smiths' projected disbursements in Year 1. Portfolio C's expected return is closer to that necessary to meet their objective over a longer time frame. However, Portfolio C's level of risk is too high given the Smiths' risk tolerance. Although Portfolio C should allow the Smiths to both fund their lifetime real income needs and leave $1 million to their grandchild, the risk in Portfolio C may endanger both their income and the bequest.

The Smiths' advisor should select Portfolio B based on its appropriate risk level and conformity with the Smiths' constraints. As a consequence of Portfolio B's probable inability to meet the Smiths' long-term spending needs, however, principal invasion may be necessary, and the secondary objective of giving $1 million, even in nominal terms, to their granddaughter may be forfeited.

13. A. i. The Maclins' overall risk objective must consider both willingness and ability to take risk:

Willingness. The Maclins have a below-average willingness to take risk, based on their unhappiness with the portfolio volatility they have experienced in recent years and their desire not to experience a loss in portfolio value in excess of 12 percent in any one year.

Ability. The Maclins have an average ability to take risk. Although their fairly large asset base and long time horizon in isolation would suggest an above-average ability to take risk, their living expenses of £74,000 are significantly higher than Christopher's after-tax salary of £80,000(1 − 0.40) = £48,000, causing them to be very dependent on projected portfolio returns to cover the difference and thereby reducing their ability to take risk.

Overall. The Maclins' overall risk tolerance is below average, as their below-average willingness to take risk dominates their average ability to take risk in determining their overall risk tolerance.

ii. The Maclins' return objective is to grow the portfolio to meet their educational and retirement needs as well as to provide for ongoing net expenses. The Maclins will require annual after-tax cash flows of £26,000 (calculated below) to cover ongoing net expenses and will need £2 million in 18 years to fund their children's education and their retirement. To meet this objective, the Maclins' pretax required return is 7.38 percent, which is determined below.

The after-tax return required to accumulate £2 million in 18 years beginning with an investable asset base of £1,235,000 (calculated below) and with annual outflows of £26,000 is 4.427 percent, which when adjusted for the 40 percent tax rate, results in a 7.38 percent pretax return [4.427%/(1 − 0.40) = 7.38%].

Christopher's annual salary	£80,000
Less: Taxes (40%)	−32,000
Living expenses	−74,000
Net annual cash flow	−£26,000
Inheritance	900,000
Barnett Co. common stock	220,000
Stocks and bonds	160,000
Cash	5,000
Subtotal	£1,285,000
Less one-time needs:	
Down payment on house	−30,000
Charitable donation	−20,000
Investable asset base	£1,235,000

Note: No inflation adjustment is required in the return calculation because increases in living expenses will be offset by increases in Christopher's salary.

B. The Maclins' investment policy statement should include the following constraints:

i. *Time horizon.* The Maclins have a two-stage time horizon, because of their changing cash flow and resource needs. The first stage is the next 18 years. The second stage begins with their retirement and the university education years for their children.

ii. *Liquidity requirements.* The Maclins have one-time immediate expenses totaling £50,000 that include the deposit on the house they are purchasing and the charitable donation in honor of Louise's father.

iii. *Tax concerns.* A 40 percent tax rate applies to both ordinary income and capital gains.

iv. *Unique circumstances.* The large holding of the Barnett Co. common stock represents almost 18 percent of the Maclins' investable asset base. The concentrated holding in Barnett Co. stock is a key risk factor of the Maclins' portfolio, and achieving better diversification will be a factor in the future management of the Maclins' assets.

The Maclins' desire not to invest in alcohol and tobacco stocks is another constraint on investment.

TAXES AND PRIVATE WEALTH MANAGEMENT IN A GLOBAL CONTEXT

by Stephen M. Horan, CFA and Thomas R. Robinson, CFA

LEARNING OUTCOMES

The candidate should be able to:	Mastery
a. compare and contrast basic global taxation regimes as they relate to the taxation of dividend income, interest income, realized capital gains, and unrealized capital gains;	☐
b. determine the impact of different types of taxes and tax regimes on future wealth accumulation;	☐
c. calculate accrual equivalent tax rates and after-tax returns;	☐
d. explain how investment return and investment horizon affect the tax impact associated with an investment;	☐
e. discuss the tax profiles of different types of investment accounts and explain their impact on after-tax returns and future accumulations;	☐
f. explain how taxes affect investment risk;	☐
g. discuss the relation between after-tax returns and different types of investor trading behavior;	☐
h. explain the benefits of tax loss harvesting and highest-in/first-out (HIFO) tax lot accounting;	☐
i. demonstrate how taxes and asset location relate to mean–variance optimization.	☐

INTRODUCTION   1

Private wealth managers have the basic goal of maximizing after-tax wealth subject to a client's risk tolerance and portfolio constraints. Portfolio managers can add value in a number of ways, such as buying undervalued securities, selling overpriced securities, and improving asset allocations. This is challenging in highly efficient markets where informational advantages are difficult to exploit as market participants compete with each other in search of abnormal returns. Managing a portfolio efficiently from a tax perspective, however, is a reasonable goal in almost all markets. In most economies around the world, taxes have a significant impact on net performance and affect an adviser's understanding of risk for the taxable investor. Tax rates, particularly those for high-net-worth (HNW) individuals, are non-trivial and typically affect returns more than portfolio management costs.

Despite a long history of high tax rates on investment returns, most modern portfolio theory is grounded in a pretax framework. This phenomenon is understandable because most institutional and pension portfolios are tax-exempt. As more wealth becomes concentrated with individuals, it is important to examine the impact of taxes on risk and return characteristics of a portfolio and wealth accumulation. The purpose of this reading is to outline basic concepts that serve as the foundation for building tax-aware investment models that can be applied in a global environment.

The approach developed here is valuable for several reasons. First, it can be applied in a broad range of circumstances representing different taxing jurisdictions, asset classes, and account types. Second, it can provide a framework with which advisers can better communicate the impact of taxes of portfolio returns to private clients and develop techniques to improve their after-tax performance. Third, tax codes change over time. The models developed here provide the adviser a framework to manage changes should they occur.

2   OVERVIEW OF GLOBAL INCOME TAX STRUCTURES

Tax structures (the specifics of how governments collect taxes) are determined by national, regional, and local jurisdictions in order to meet governmental funding needs. Major sources of government tax revenue include:

► *Taxes on income.* These taxes apply to individuals, corporations, and often other types of legal entities. For individuals, income types can include salaries, interest, dividends, realized capital gains, and unrealized capital gains, among others. Income tax structure refers to how and when different types of income are taxed.

► *Wealth-based taxes.* These include taxes on the holding of certain types of property (e.g., real estate) and taxes on the transfer of wealth (e.g., taxes on inheritance).

► *Taxes on consumption.* These include sales taxes (which are taxes collected in one step from the final consumer on the price of a good or service) and value-added taxes (which are collected in intermediate steps in the course of producing a good or service but borne ultimately by the final consumer).

This reading's focus will be on the taxes that most directly affect tax planning for investments, specifically taxes on investment income to individuals and, secondarily, wealth-based taxes.

In many cases, the tax system is used to encourage or discourage certain activities (for example, investing in domestic companies or encouraging retirement savings). Tax structures vary globally and can change as the needs and objectives of the governmental jurisdiction change. In such a dynamic environment, the investment manager needs to understand the impact of different tax structures on investment returns and wealth. Rather than delineate specific country tax rules, this reading provides a framework for managers to understand and implement investment strategies in a dynamic environment where different tax environments may apply to different clients and tax environments can change over time.

2.1 International Comparisons of Income Taxation

We reviewed the taxation of different types of income, particularly investment income, around the world in order to summarize the major tax regimes.[1] The review was based on data from over 50 countries as reported in the Deloitte Touche Tohmatsu International Business Guides, which were available during the summer of 2007. This summary provided the basis for our discussion of the common elements of individual income taxation around the world and our classification of different countries into general income tax regimes.

2.2 Common Elements

In most tax jurisdictions, a tax rate structure applies to ordinary income (such as earnings from employment). Other tax rates may apply to special categories of income such as investment income (sometimes referred to as capital income for tax purposes). Investment income is often taxed differently based on the nature of the income: interest, dividends, or capital gains and losses. Most of the countries examined in our review have a progressive ordinary tax rate structure. In a progressive rate structure, the tax rate increases as income increases. For example:

Taxable Income (€)		Tax on Column 1	Percentage on Excess Over Column 1
Over	Up to		
0	15,000	—	23
15,000	28,000	3,450	27
28,000	55,000	6,960	38
55,000	75,000	17,220	41
75,000		25,420	43

In such an environment, if an individual has taxable income of €60,000, the first €15,000 is taxed at 23 percent; the next €13,000 (i.e., from €15,000 to €28,000) is taxed at 27 percent; and so on. The amount of tax due on taxable income of €60,000 would be €17,220 + 0.41(€60,000 − €55,000) or €19,270. This would represent an average tax rate of €19,270/€60,000 or 32.12 percent.

---

[1] The guides are available at www.deloitte.com and are updated on a rotational basis. As a result, some data may not be current as of the summer of 2007.

In tax planning for investments, it is useful to think about how much tax would be paid on additional income, known as the marginal tax rate. The marginal rate, or rate on the next €1 of income, would be 41 percent in this example. This taxpayer could have €15,000 more in income before moving into the next tax bracket (a new marginal rate of 43 percent). Some countries do not have a progressive tax system and instead impose a flat tax. In a flat tax structure, all taxable income is taxed at the same rate. For example, at the time of this writing, Russia had a flat tax rate of 13 percent.

Many countries provide special tax provisions for interest income. These special provisions included an exemption for certain types of interest income (for example, Argentina exempted interest income from Argentine banks for residents), a favorable tax rate on interest income (for example, Italy taxed some interest income at 12.5 percent even though the minimum marginal rate is 23 percent), or an exclusion amount where some limited amount of interest income is exempt from tax (for example, Germany provided such an exclusion). Some fixed income instruments are indexed for inflation and this inflation adjustment may not be subject to taxation in some jurisdictions. Unless special provisions exist, interest income, including inflation adjustments, is taxed at the tax rates applicable to ordinary income (ordinary rates).

Similarly, dividend income may have special provisions. In some cases there are exemptions, special tax rates, or exclusions as described above for interest income. In other cases, there may be provisions for mitigating double taxation because dividends are a distribution of company earnings and the company may have already paid tax on the earnings. Tax credits can be used to mitigate the effects of double taxation. For example, the dividend can be taxed at ordinary rates but the individual is entitled to a credit for a portion of the taxes paid by the company (referred to as "franking" in some jurisdictions such as Australia). As with interest income, absent special rules dividend income is taxed at ordinary rates.

Finally, capital gains (losses) may have special provisions or rates. These often vary depending upon how long the underlying investment has been held. Generally, long term gains are treated more favorably than short term gains. Long term is defined differently in different jurisdictions; for example, in the data examined, we observed required holding periods of six months, one year, two years, and five years. Special provisions observed included total exemption of capital gains or long-term capital gains from taxation (for example, Austria exempted long-term gains), exemption of a certain percentage of gains from taxation (for example, Canada exempted 50 percent of gains), a favorable tax rate on capital gains (for example, Brazil provided a flat 15 percent rate for capital gains), or indexing the cost of the investment for inflation (for example, India permitted inflation indexing for some investments). In some cases, countries provided more favorable provisions for domestic companies or companies traded on a local exchange (sometimes applied to both dividend income and capital gains). In most cases, only realized gains were taxed (when the investment was sold). In rare cases, countries impose a tax on unrealized gains (appreciation of the investment prior to sale) either annually, upon exiting the country to relocate domicile, or upon inheritance.[2]

---

[2] In other cases upon inheritance the recipient receives a "step-up in basis" such that for tax purposes the value on the date of death is used to compute any future gain or loss.

EXAMPLE 1

Tax Rates

Vanessa Wong is a new client living in a jurisdiction with a progressive tax rate structure. She expects to have taxable ordinary income of €70,000 this year. The tax rate structure in her jurisdiction is as follows:

Taxable Income (€)		Tax on	Percentage on Excess
Over	Up to	Column 1	Over Column 1
0	30,000	—	20
30,000	60,000	6,000	30
60,000	90,000	15,000	40
90,000		27,000	50

1. Wong's marginal tax rate is *closest* to:
   A. 35%.
   B. 40%.
   C. 50%.
2. Wong's average tax rate is *closest* to:
   A. 27%.
   B. 35%.
   C. 40%.

Solution to 1: B is correct. Wong's marginal tax rate is 40 percent. Because Wong's income is over €60,000 but below €90,000, her next €1 of income would be taxed at 40 percent.

Solution to 2: A is correct. Wong's tax liability would be €15,000 + 0.40 (€70,000 − €60,000) = €19,000. With a tax liability of €19,000 and taxable income of €70,000, her average tax rate would be about 27 percent (€19,000/€70,000).

2.3 General Income Tax Regimes

Each country's income tax structure can be classified as either progressive or flat. Income tax regimes can be further distinguished based on the taxation of investment returns in taxable accounts. Interest income is either taxed at ordinary rates or at favorable rates under special provisions. In this review, interest income is considered to be taxable at ordinary rates unless significant exceptions apply. Similar classifications were used for dividends and capital gains. Seven different tax regimes were observed in the sample of countries examined. Exhibit 1 classifies common elements of tax regimes and is further explained below.

▶ *Common Progressive Regime*: This regime has progressive tax rates for ordinary income, but favorable treatment in all three investment income categories: interest, dividends, and capital gains. This was the most common regime observed. Even though categorized as "common," there is variation within this regime with some countries treating some interest

EXHIBIT 1	Classification of Income Tax Regimes						
Regime	1 – Common Progressive	2 – Heavy Dividend Tax	3 – Heavy Capital Gain Tax	4 – Heavy Interest Tax	5 – Light Capital Gain Tax	6 – Flat and Light	7 – Flat and Heavy
Ordinary Tax Rate Structure	Progressive	Progressive	Progressive	Progressive	Progressive	Flat	Flat
Interest Income	Some interest taxed at favorable rates or exempt	Some interest taxed at favorable rates or exempt	Some interest taxed at favorable rates or exempt	Taxed at ordinary rates	Taxed at ordinary rates	Some interest taxed at favorable rates or exempt	Some interest taxed at favorable rates or exempt
Dividends	Some dividends taxed at favorable rates or exempt	Taxed at ordinary rates	Some dividends taxed at favorable rates or exempt	Some dividends taxed at favorable rates or exempt	Taxed at ordinary rates	Some dividends taxed at favorable rates or exempt	Taxed at ordinary rates
Capital Gains	Some capital gains taxed favorably or exempt	Some capital gains taxed favorably or exempt	Taxed at ordinary rates	Some capital gains taxed favorably or exempt	Some capital gains taxed favorably or exempt	Some capital gains taxed favorably or exempt	Taxed at ordinary rates

(Exhibit continued on next page . . .)

EXHIBIT 1 (continued)

Regime	1 – Common Progressive	2 – Heavy Dividend Tax	3 – Heavy Capital Gain Tax	4 – Heavy Interest Tax	5 – Light Capital Gain Tax	6 – Flat and Light	7 – Flat and Heavy
Example Countries	Austria Brazil China Czech Republic Finland France Greece Hong Kong Hungary Ireland Italy Japan Latvia Malaysia Netherlands Nigeria Philippines Poland Portugal Singapore South Africa Sweden Thailand United Kingdom United States Vietnam	Argentina Indonesia Israel Venezuela	Colombia	Canada Denmark Germany Luxembourg Pakistan	Australia Belgium India Kenya Mexico New Zealand Norway Spain Switzerland Taiwan Turkey	Kazakhstan Russia Saudi Arabia (Zakat)	Ukraine

Sources: Classified based on information provided in International Business Guides from Deloitte Touche Tohmatsu (available at www.deloitte.com) and online database of worldwide taxation provided by PricewaterhouseCoopers (www.taxsummaries.pwc.com).

income as ordinary and other interest income as tax exempt, while other countries provide for exemption or special treatment for all interest.

▶ *Heavy Dividend Tax Regime*: This regime has a progressive tax system for ordinary income and favorable treatment for some interest and capital gains but taxes dividends at ordinary rates.

▶ *Heavy Capital Gain Tax Regime*: This regime has a progressive tax system for ordinary income and favorable treatment for interest and dividends, but taxes capital gains at ordinary rates. Only one such country was observed.

▶ *Heavy Interest Tax Regime*: This regime has a progressive tax system for ordinary income and favorable treatment for dividends and capital gains, but taxes interest income at ordinary rates.

▶ *Light Capital Gain Tax Regime*: This regime has a progressive tax system for ordinary income, interest, and dividends, but favorable treatment of capital gains. This was the second most commonly observed regime.

▶ *Flat and Light Regime*: This regime has a flat tax system and treats interest, dividends, and capital gains favorably.

▶ *Flat and Heavy Regime*: This regime has a flat tax system for ordinary income, dividends, and capital gains. It does not have favorable treatment for dividends and capital gains, but has favorable treatment for interest income.

2.4 Other Considerations

In addition to the different tax regimes in which different types of income are taxed at possibly different rates, there are other important dimensions in tax planning for investments. Some countries permit the use of tax deferred retirement accounts. A tax deferred account

▶ defers taxation on investment returns within the account;

▶ may permit a deduction for contributions;

▶ may occasionally permit tax free distributions.

On the other hand, a few countries impose a wealth tax on accumulations on a periodic basis which reduces after-tax returns and accumulations similar to income taxes.

In the next section we will examine how taxes affect after-tax returns and accumulations. We also examine the impact of tax deferred accounts and wealth taxes. In a later section we will discuss planning opportunities suitable for the various tax regimes.[3]

3   AFTER-TAX ACCUMULATIONS AND RETURNS FOR TAXABLE ACCOUNTS

Taxes on investment returns have a substantial impact on performance and future accumulations. This section develops models to estimate the tax impact on future accumulations in various tax environments. These models enable the

---

[3] Gift, death, or estate taxes are also imposed in some jurisdictions. These are not addressed in this reading.

investment adviser to evaluate potential investments for taxable investors by comparing returns and wealth accumulations for different types of investments subject to different tax rates and methods of taxation (accrued annually or deferred).

3.1 Simple Tax Environments

As the preceding analysis of global tax regimes suggests, investment returns can be taxed in a number of different ways. This section begins with some straightforward methods that illustrate basic concepts and serve as building blocks for more complex environments.

All but four of the countries studied in the tax regime analysis have a progressive income tax system.[4] The discussion in this section assumes uniform marginal tax rates based on the investor's current tax bracket which is effectively flat for some range of income. Models that accommodate multiple tax brackets grow in complexity very quickly. Also, investors are often subject to a single rate on the margin, limiting the usefulness of an analysis based on multiple tax brackets. Finally, much of the intuition and analysis that is derived in a flat tax framework applies in a setting with multiple tax brackets.

3.1.1 Returns-Based Taxes: Accrual Taxes on Interest and Dividends

One of the most straightforward methods to tax investment returns is to tax an investment's annual return at a single tax rate, regardless of its form. Accrual taxes are levied and paid on a periodic basis, usually annually, as opposed to deferred taxes that are postponed until some future date. Most of the countries examined above tax interest income on an accrual basis annually, either at ordinary rates or at favorable rates as the result of special provisions. Germany, Greece, Canada, Columbia, and the United States, for example, tax most interest income at ordinary rates, although some interest income may receive favorable tax treatment. Japan, China, Finland, the Czech Republic, and the United Kingdom tax interest income at a special fixed rate. Dividends, like interest income, are typically taxed in the year they are received, albeit often at different rates.

When returns are subject to accrual taxes, the after-tax return is equal to the pretax return, r, multiplied by $(1 - t_i)$ where t_i represents the tax rate applicable to investment income. For the purposes of this section, we consider an investment with a return that is entirely taxed at a single uniform rate.

The amount of money accumulated for each unit of currency invested after n years, assuming that returns (after taxes at rate t_i are paid) are reinvested at the same rate of return, r, is simply

$$FVIF_i = [1 + r(1 - t_i)]^n \qquad \textbf{(1)}$$

Equation 1 is simply a future value interest factor (FVIF) based on an after-tax return. For example, €100 invested at 6 percent per annum for ten years in an environment in which returns are taxed each year at a rate of 30 percent will accumulate to be €100[1 + 0.06(1 − 0.30)]^{10} = €150.90. Had returns not been taxed, this investment would have grown to €100[1 + 0.06(1 − 0.00)]^{10} = €179.08, a difference of €28.18. Notice that taxes reduce the potential gain on

---

[4] Countries with a flat tax include the Ukraine, Russia, Kazakhstan, and Saudi Arabia. In the case of Saudi Arabia, the system is actually a *zakat*, which is the Islamic concept of tithing, which means donating ten percent of something (such as income) to support a religious organization.

investment by (€179.08 − €150.90)/(€179.08 − €100.00) = €28.18/€79.08 = 35.6 percent, which is more than the ordinary income tax rate. This suggests that the tax drag on capital accumulation compounds over time when taxes are paid each year. (Tax drag refers to the negative effect of taxes on after-tax returns.) By contrast, when taxes on gains are deferred until the end of the investment horizon, the tax rate equals the tax drag on capital accumulation as we shall see in the next section.

Exhibit 2 illustrates the impact of taxes on capital growth for various investment horizons and rates of return and demonstrates several conclusions. First, when investment returns are taxed annually, the effect of taxes on capital growth is greater than the nominal tax rate as noted above. Second, the adverse effects of taxes on capital growth increase over time. That is, the proportional difference between pretax and after-tax gains grows as the investment horizon increases. Third, the tax drag increases as the investment return increases, all else equal. Fourth, return and investment horizon have a multiplicative effect on the tax drag associated with future accumulations. Specifically, the impact of returns on the tax effect is greater for long investment horizons, and the impact of investment horizon is greater for higher returns because figures in the bottom right corner change more rapidly than figures in the upper left corner.

EXHIBIT 2	**Proportion of Potential Investment Growth Consumed by Annual Taxes on Return**						
	Investment Horizon in Years (n)						
r (%)	5	10	15	20	25	30	35	40
2	0.308	0.319	0.330	0.340	0.351	0.362	0.373	0.384
4	0.317	0.338	0.359	0.381	0.403	0.425	0.447	0.469
6	0.325	0.356	0.389	0.421	0.454	0.486	0.518	0.549
8	0.333	0.375	0.418	0.461	0.503	0.545	0.584	0.622
10	0.341	0.393	0.446	0.499	0.550	0.598	0.643	0.684
12	0.348	0.411	0.474	0.535	0.593	0.646	0.694	0.737
14	0.356	0.429	0.501	0.569	0.633	0.689	0.739	0.781
16	0.364	0.446	0.526	0.601	0.669	0.727	0.776	0.818
18	0.371	0.462	0.551	0.631	0.701	0.760	0.808	0.848

Note: The calculations assume a 30 percent annual tax rate on investment returns.

Conceptually, this framework could apply to securities, such as fixed-income instruments or preferred stock, in which most or possibly all of the return is subject to annual taxes. This is an oversimplification, of course, but we will address that concern below.

EXAMPLE 2

Accrual Taxes

Vladimir Kozloski is determining the impact of taxes on his expected investment returns and wealth accumulations. Kozloski lives in a tax jurisdiction with a flat tax rate of 20 percent which applies to all types of income and is taxed annually. Kozloski expects to earn 7 percent per year on his investment over a 20 year time horizon and has an initial portfolio of €100,000.

1. What is Kozloski's expected wealth at the end of 20 years?
2. What proportion of potential investment gains were consumed by taxes?

Solution to 1:

$$FV = €100{,}000 \times FVIF_i = €100{,}000 \times [1 + 0.07$$
$$(1 - 0.20)]^{20} = €297{,}357.$$

Solution to 2: Ignoring taxes, $FV = €100{,}000 [1 + 0.07]^{20} = €386{,}968$. The difference between this and the after tax amount accumulated from above is €89,611. The proportion of potential investment gains consumed by taxes was €89,611/€286,968 = 31.23 percent.

3.1.2 Returns-Based Taxes: Deferred Capital Gains

Another straightforward method of taxing returns is to focus on capital gains, the recognition of which can usually be deferred until realized, instead of interest income and dividends, which are generally taxable each year. A portfolio of non-dividend-paying stocks could fall under this type of framework. The analysis of global tax systems in the previous section indicates that it is very rare for unrealized investment gains to be taxed, so this implicit deferral mechanism has nearly universal application.

If the tax on an investment's return is deferred until the end of its investment horizon, n, and taxed as a capital gain at the rate t_{cg}, then the after-tax future accumulation for each unit of currency can be represented in several ways, including the following:

$$FVIF_{cg} = (1 + r)^n - [(1 + r)^n - 1] t_{cg} \qquad \textbf{(2a)}$$

$$FVIF_{cg} = (1 + r)^n(1 - t_{cg}) + t_{cg} \qquad \textbf{(2b)}$$

The first term of Equation 2a represents the pretax accumulation. The bracketed term is the capital gain (i.e., future accumulation less the original basis), while the entire second term represents the tax obligation on that gain. Viewed differently, the first term of Equation 2b represents the future accumulation if the entire sum (including the original basis) were subject to tax. The second term returns the tax of the untaxed cost (also known as cost basis or basis) associated with the initial investment.

For example, €100 invested at 6 percent for ten years in an environment in which capital gains are taxed at the end of that time at a rate of 30 percent will accumulate to be $€100[(1 + 0.06)^{10}(1 - 0.30) + 0.30] = €155.36$. Notice that this sum is greater than the €150.90 accumulated in the previous example using Equation 1, where returns are taxed annually at the same rate. This comparison illustrates the value of tax deferral.

Notice, as well, that the after-tax investment gain equals the pretax investment gain multiplied by one minus the tax rate. That is, €55.36 = €79.08 × (1 − 0.30). Whereas the tax drag on after-tax accumulations subject to annual accrual taxes compounds over time, the tax drag from deferred capital gains is a fixed percentage regardless of the investment return or time horizon. In other words, when deferral is permitted, the proportion of potential investment growth consumed by taxes is always the same as the tax rate, 30 percent in this case, which is less than that presented in Exhibit 2 when there was annual taxation.

Because the tax drag in Exhibit 2 increases with the investment return and time horizon, the value of a capital gain tax deferral also increases with the investment return and time horizon. One implication of the value of tax deferral is that investments taxed on a deferred capital gain basis can be more tax efficient (i.e., tax advantaged) than investments with returns that are taxed annually, all else equal, even if the marginal tax rate on the two is the same. Moreover, the difference compounds over time. The tax regime analysis from Exhibit 1 reveals that relatively few jurisdictions tax components of equity returns (dividends and capital gains) more heavily than interest income. There are rare exceptions where dividends (but usually not capital gains) are taxed to a greater extent than interest (such as the Heavy Dividend Tax Regime countries in Exhibit 1). Moreover, even if the tax rate on deferred capital gains is greater than the tax rate on interest income, the value of the deferral can more than offset a lower tax rate on annually taxed income, especially over time.

Exhibit 3 illustrates the value of tax deferral and its compounding effects more generally by presenting the ratio of after-tax accumulation in a deferred capital gain regime to after-tax accumulation in a regime in which returns are taxed annually. For example, with a 6 percent annual return, 20-year time horizon and a 30 percent tax rate, the accumulation of €100 in a deferred capital gain environment, is €100[(1 + 0.06)^{20}(1 − 0.30) + 0.30] = €254.50. In an annual taxation environment, it is €100[1 + 0.06(1 − 0.30)]^{20} = €227.70. Therefore, a deferred capital gain environment accumulates €254.50/€227.70 = 1.118 times the amount accumulated in an annual taxation environment. The relative accumulations can be substantially larger when gains are deferred for long time horizons, especially for high returns. It is important to note, however, that the advantages of tax deferral can be offset or even eliminated if securities taxed on an accrual basis have greater risk-adjusted returns.

EXHIBIT 3	Ratio of Future Accumulations: Accumulation in a Deferred Capital Gain Environment to Accumulation in an Annual Taxation Environment

Investment Horizon in Years (n)

r (%)	5	10	15	20	25	30	35	40
2	1.001	1.004	1.008	1.015	1.023	1.033	1.045	1.058
4	1.003	1.014	1.031	1.056	1.086	1.123	1.165	1.213
6	1.007	1.030	1.067	1.118	1.181	1.257	1.346	1.447
8	1.012	1.050	1.113	1.198	1.305	1.432	1.582	1.754
10	1.018	1.075	1.169	1.294	1.453	1.644	1.871	2.136

(Exhibit continued on next page . . .)

| EXHIBIT 3 | (continued) | | | | | | |

Investment Horizon in Years (*n*)

r (%)	5	10	15	20	25	30	35	40
12	1.025	1.104	1.232	1.405	1.624	1.892	2.214	2.598
14	1.033	1.137	1.303	1.529	1.818	2.177	2.616	3.149
16	1.041	1.172	1.380	1.666	2.035	2.500	3.080	3.799
18	1.050	1.210	1.464	1.814	2.273	2.862	3.612	4.561

Note: The calculations assume a 30 percent annual tax rate on investment returns and a 30 percent tax rate on deferred capital gains.

In many countries, the rate applied to capital gains is lower than the rate applied to interest income. In such cases, the investor gets a dual benefit from returns in the form of capital gains: deferral of taxation and a favorable tax rate when gains are realized. The capital gain tax rate may also vary depending on the holding period. Longer holding periods may receive a lower tax rate to encourage long-term rather than short-term investment. Australia, for example, taxes short-term gains (i.e., holding period less than 12 months) at ordinary rates. Only half the gains on assets held for more than 12 months are taxed, however, making the effective long-term capital gain tax rate half of the rate on ordinary income. In such cases the investor gets a dual benefit; deferral of taxation and a favorable rate on realized gains. The holding period can vary. Belgium and the Czech Republic, for example, require a five-year holding period to receive preferential tax treatment on capital gains.

EXAMPLE 3

Deferred Capital Gains

Assume the same facts as in Example 2. Kozloski invests €100,000 at 7 percent. However, the return comes in the form of deferred capital gains that are not taxed until the investment is sold in 20 years hence.

1. What is Kozloski's expected wealth at the end of 20 years?
2. What proportion of potential investment gains were consumed by taxes?

Solution to 1:

$$\text{FV} = €100,000 \times FVIF_{cg} = €100,000 \times [(1 + 0.07)^{20} (1 - t) + t]$$
$$= €100,000 \times [(1 + 0.07)^{20} (1 - 0.20) + 0.20] = €329,575.$$

Solution to 2: Ignoring taxes, FV = €100,000 $[1 + 0.07]^{20}$ = €386,968.

The difference between this and the after-tax amount accumulated from above is €57,393. The proportion of potential investment gains consumed by taxes was €57,393/€286,968 = 20.0 percent. This result compares favorably to the potential investment gains consumed by taxes in Example 2.

3.1.3 Cost Basis

In taxation, cost basis is generally the amount that was paid to acquire an asset. It serves as the foundation for calculating a capital gain, which equals the selling price less the cost basis. The taxable gain increases as the basis decreases. In consequence, capital gain taxes increase as the basis decreases. In some circumstances, this basis may be adjusted under tax regulations or carry over from another taxpayer. The previous capital gains examples assume that cash is newly invested so that the cost basis was equal to the current market value. That is, the tax liability at the end of the investment horizon is based on the difference between the pretax ending value and the current market value today.

In many cases, an investment being evaluated today was purchased some time ago and has a cost basis that is different from the current market value. If a security has risen in value since its initial purchase, the cost basis may be less than its current market value. Cost basis affects an investment's after-tax accumulation because it determines the taxable capital gain. Specifically, the after-tax cash flow from liquidation increases as the cost basis increases, holding all else equal. Put differently, an investment with a low cost basis has a current embedded tax liability because, if it were liquidated today, capital gain tax would be owed even before future capital growth is considered. Newly invested cash has no such current tax liability.

If the cost basis is expressed as a proportion, B, of the current market value of the investment, then the future after-tax accumulation can be expressed by simply subtracting this additional tax liability from the expression in either Equation 2a or 2b. In other words,

$$FVIF_{cgb} = (1 + r)^n(1 - t_{cg}) + t_{cg} - (1 - B)t_{cg} \qquad \textbf{(3a)}$$

Notice that if cost basis is equal to the initial investment, then $B = 1$ and the last term simply reduces to Equation 2b. The lower the cost basis, however, the greater the embedded tax liability and the lower the future accumulation. Distributing and canceling terms produces

$$FVIF_{cgb} = (1 + r)^n(1 - t_{cg}) + t_{cg}B \qquad \textbf{(3b)}$$

This form resembles Equation 2b, and the last term represents the return of basis at the end of the investment horizon. The lower the basis, the lower is the return of basis. For example, suppose an investment has a current market value of €100 and a cost basis of €80. The gain when realized will be subject to a capital gains tax of 30 percent. The cost basis is equal to 80 percent of the current market value of €100. If it grows at 6 percent for 10 years, the future after-tax accumulation is €100 [(1.06)^{10}(1 − 0.30) + (0.30)(0.80)] = €149.36, which is €6 less than the €155.36 accumulation that would result if the basis were equal to €100. The €6 difference represents the tax liability associated with the embedded capital gain.

EXAMPLE 4

Cost Basis

Continuing with the facts in Examples 2 and 3, Kozloski has a current investment with a market value of €100,000 and cost basis of €80,000. The stock price grows at 7 percent per year for 20 years.

1. Express the cost basis as a percent of the current market value.

2. What is Kozloski's expected wealth after 20 years?

Solution to 1:

Cost basis/Current market value = B = €80,000/€100,000 = 0.80.

Solution to 2:

FV = €100,000 × $FVIF_{cgb}$ = €100,000 × $[(1 + 0.07)^{20}(1 - 0.20) + 0.20(0.80)]$ = €325,575.

This amount is €4,000 smaller than Kozloski's expected wealth in Example 3, in which it was assumed that the cost basis equaled the current market value.

3.1.4 Wealth-Based Taxes

Some jurisdictions impose a wealth tax, which is applied annually to a specific capital base. Often the wealth tax is restricted to real estate investments (e.g., Australia, Singapore, Belgium, Germany, and the United Kingdom). In other countries, it is levied on aggregate assets including financial assets above a certain threshold (e.g., Colombia). If limited to real estate holdings, the tax may be levied at the federal level or a municipal level. In any case, the wealth tax rate tends to be much lower than capital gains or interest income rates because it applies to the entire capital base—i.e., principal and return—rather than just the return.

The expression for an after-tax accumulation subject to a wealth tax is therefore different from the previous scenarios in which only incremental gains are taxed. If wealth is taxed annually at a rate of t_w, then after n years each unit of currency accumulates to

$$FVIF_w = [(1 + r)(1 - t_w)]^n \tag{4}$$

For example, if wealth capital is taxed at 2 percent, then €100 invested at 6 percent for ten years will grow to $[(1.06)(1 - 0.02)]^{10}$ = €146.33. Because the form of a wealth tax differs from the form of taxes on either investment returns or deferred capital gains, this figure is not comparable to the previous two examples. This figure is substantially less than the pretax accumulation of €179.08, however. In other words, the two percent wealth tax consumed 41.4 percent of the investment growth that would have accrued over ten years in the absence of a wealth tax (i.e., (€79.08 − €46.33)/€79.08).

Exhibit 4 illustrates the impact of a wealth tax on investment growth for various rates of return and investment horizons. Because wealth taxes apply to the capital base, the absolute magnitude of the liability they generate (measured in units of currency) is less sensitive to investment return than taxes based on returns. Consequently, the proportion of investment growth that it consumes decreases as returns increase. Viewed differently, a wealth tax consumes a greater proportion of investment growth when returns are low. In fact, when returns are flat or negative, a wealth tax effectively reduces principal. Like the previous two types of taxes, however, the wealth tax consumes a greater share of investment growth as the investment horizon increases.

EXHIBIT 4	Proportion of Investment Growth Consumed by Wealth Taxes							
	Investment Horizon in Years (*n*)							
r (%)	5	10	15	20	25	30	35	40
4	0.540	0.564	0.588	0.611	0.635	0.657	0.679	0.700
6	0.380	0.414	0.449	0.483	0.517	0.550	0.583	0.614
8	0.301	0.341	0.382	0.423	0.464	0.505	0.544	0.581
10	0.253	0.298	0.344	0.390	0.437	0.482	0.526	0.567
12	0.222	0.270	0.320	0.371	0.421	0.470	0.517	0.560
14	0.200	0.250	0.304	0.358	0.412	0.464	0.512	0.557
16	0.183	0.237	0.293	0.350	0.406	0.460	0.510	0.556
18	0.171	0.226	0.285	0.345	0.403	0.458	0.508	0.555

Note: The calculations assume a 2 percent annual wealth tax.

EXAMPLE 5

Wealth Tax

Olga Sanford lives in a country that imposes a wealth tax of 1.0 percent on financial assets each year. Her €400,000 portfolio is expected to return 6 percent over the next ten years.

1. What is Sanford's expected wealth at the end of ten years?
2. What proportion of investment gains was consumed by taxes?

Solution to 1: FV = €400,000[(1.06)(1 − 0.01)]^{10} = €647,844.

Solution to 2: Had the wealth tax not existed, FV = €400,000(1.06)^{10} = €716,339. This sum represents a €316,339 investment gain compared to a €247,844 gain in the presence of the wealth tax. Therefore, the one percent wealth tax consumed 21.65 percent of the investment gain (i.e., (€316,339 − €247,844)/€316,339).

3.2 Blended Taxing Environments

The discussion in the previous section is an oversimplification because each model assumes that investment gains were taxed according to only one of a number of possible taxes. In reality, portfolios are subject to a variety of different taxes depending on the types of securities they hold, how frequently they are traded, and the direction of returns. The different taxing schemes mentioned above can be integrated into a single framework in which a portion of a portfolio's investment return is received in the form of dividends (p_d) and taxed at a rate of t_d; another portion is received in the form of interest income (p_i) and taxed as such at a rate of t_i; and another portion is taxed as realized capital gain (p_{cg}) at t_{cg}. The remainder of an investment's return is unrealized capital gain, the tax on which is deferred until ultimately recognized at the end of the investment horizon.[5] These return proportions can be computed by simply dividing each income component by the total dollar return.

EXAMPLE 6

Blended Tax Environment

Zahid Kharullah has a balanced portfolio of stocks and bonds. At the beginning of the year, his portfolio has a market value of €100,000. By the end of the year, the portfolio was worth €108,000 before any annual taxes had been paid, and there were no contributions or withdrawals. Interest of €400 and dividends of €2,000 were reinvested into the portfolio. During the year, Kharullah had €3,600 of realized capital gains. These proceeds were again reinvested into the portfolio.

1. What percentage of Kharullah's return is in the form of interest?
2. What percentage of Kharullah's return is in the form of dividends?
3. What percentage of Kharullah's return is in the form of realized capital gain?
4. What percentage of Kharullah's return is in the form of deferred capital gain?

Solution to 1: p_i = €400/€8,000 = 0.05 or 5 percent.

Solution to 2: p_d = €2,000/€8,000 = 0.25 or 25 percent.

Solution to 3: p_{cg} = €3,600/€8,000 = 0.45 or 45 percent.

Solution to 4: Unrealized gain = €8,000 − €400 − €2,000 − €3,600 = €2,000. Expressed as a percentage of return, €2,000/€8,000 = 0.25, or 25 percent. The unrealized gain is the portion of investment appreciation that was not taxed as either interest, dividends, or realized capital gain.

---

[5] Capital gains are almost always taxed when recognized. Some countries, such as Denmark and Australia, however, impose an exit tax on some unrealized gains for residents who become non-residents. In Canada, capital gains are taxed at death as if realized unless the property is transferred to a surviving spouse.

In this setting, the annual return after realized taxes can be expressed as

$$r^* = r(1 - p_i t_i - p_d t_d - p_{cg} t_{cg})$$

In this case, r represents the pre-tax overall return on the portfolio. From the preceding example, note that the pre-tax return was 8 percent [(€108,000/€100,000) − 1], however there would be taxes due on the interest, dividends and realized capital gains. The effective annual after-tax return, r^*, reflects the tax erosion caused by a portion of the return being taxed as ordinary income and other portions being taxed as realized capital gain and dividends. It does not capture tax effects of deferred unrealized capital gains. One can view this expression as being analogous to the simple expression in which after-tax return equals the pretax return times one minus the tax rate. The aggregate tax rate has several components in this case, but the intuition is the same.[6]

EXAMPLE 7

Blended Tax Environment: After Tax Return

Continuing with the facts in Example 6, assume that dividends and realized capital gains are taxed at 15 percent annually while interest is taxed at 35 percent annually.

1. What is the annual return after realized taxes?
2. Assuming taxes are paid out of the investment account, what is the balance in the account at the end of the first year?

Solution to 1:

$$\begin{aligned} r^* &= r(1 - p_i t_i - p_d t_d - p_{cg} t_{cg}) \\ &= 8\%[1 - (0.05 \times 0.35) - (0.25 \times 0.15) - (0.45 \times 0.15)] \\ &= 7.02\% \end{aligned}$$

Solution to 2: Using the income data from above,

Income Type	Income Amount (€)	Tax Rate (%)	Tax Due (€)
Interest	400	35	140
Dividends	2,000	15	300
Realized capital gains	3,600	15	540
Total tax due			980

After paying taxes there would be €107,020 in the account (€108,000 − €980). Note that this is consistent with the 7.02 percent return computed for the first question.

---

[6] This expression could be expanded to incorporate any number of different taxable components, such as a different rate for short term capital gains or special treatment of certain types of taxable income. The general principle is that a portfolio can generate return in different forms, each of which may be taxed differently.

A portion of the investment return has avoided annual taxation, and tax on that portion would then be deferred until the end of the investment horizon. Holding the tax rate on capital gains constant, the impact of deferred capital gain taxes will be diminished as more of the return is taxed annually in some way as described above. Conversely, as less of the return is taxed annually, more of the return will be subject to deferred capital gains. One can express the impact of deferred capital gain taxes using an effective capital gain tax rate that adjusts the capital gains tax rate gain t_{cg} to reflect previously taxed dividends, income, or realized capital gains. The effective capital gains tax rate can be expressed as[7]

$$T^* = t_{cg}(1 - p_i - p_d - p_{cg})/(1 - p_i t_i - p_d t_d - p_{cg} t_{cg})$$

The adjustment to the capital gains tax rate takes account of the fact that some of the investment return had previously been taxed as interest income, dividends, or realized capital gain before the end of the investment horizon and will not be taxed again as a capital gain.

The future after-tax accumulation for each unit of currency in a taxable portfolio can then be represented by

$$FVIF_{Taxable} = (1 + r^*)^n(1 - T^*) + T^* - (1 - B)t_{cg} \qquad \textbf{(5)}$$

Although this formulation appears unwieldy, $(1 + r^*)^n(1 - T^*) + T^*$ is analogous to the after-tax accumulation for an investment taxed entirely as a deferred capital gain in Equation 3. The only difference is that r^* is substituted for r, and T^* is substituted for t_{cg} in most places.[8]

Different assets and asset classes generate different amounts of return as interest income, dividends, or capital gain, and will thus have different values for p_i, p_d, and p_{cg}. Moreover, Equation 5 can replace the equations introduced in the previous sections.[9] For example, the return on a hypothetical taxable bond with no capital appreciation or depreciation over the course of a tax year might be taxed entirely at ordinary rates so that $p_i = 1$, $p_d = 0$, and $p_{cg} = 0$. If the cost basis is equal to market value (i.e., $B = 1$), the expression for the after-tax future value simply reduces to $[1 + r(1 - t_i)]^n$.

On the other hand, the return for a passive investor with a growth portfolio of non-dividend paying stocks and no portfolio turnover may be entirely tax-deferred such that $p_d = 0$, $p_i = 0$ and $p_{cg} = 0$, and the future value reduces to $(1 + r)^n(1 - t_{cg}) + t_{cg}$. The return for an active investor with a similar growth portfolio might be composed entirely of realized long-term capital gains and taxed annually at t_{cg} in which case $p_d = p_i = 0$ and $p_{cg} = 1$, and the after-tax future value is $[1 + r(1 - t_{cg})]^n$.

Most accounts conform to none of these extremes, but can be accommodated by simply specifying the proper distribution rates for interest income, dividends, and capital gain. It is useful then to have an understanding of how investment style affects the tax-related parameters (e.g., p_i, p_d, and p_{cg}).

---

[7] Horan and Peterson (2001) and Horan (2002) provide more thorough developments of these expressions.

[8] Although Equation 5 ignores the wealth tax, it could be modified to incorporate it.

[9] Equation 5 does not replace the equation for the wealth tax. It can be modified, however, to do so.

EXAMPLE 8

Blended Tax Environment: Future Long Term Accumulation

Continuing with the facts in the previous example, assume there is a five-year investment horizon for the account. Annual accrual taxes will be paid out of the account each year with the deferred tax on previously unrealized capital gains paid at the end of the five-year horizon. The account is rebalanced annually. Consider a €100,000 portfolio with the return and tax profile listed in Panel A of Exhibit 5. What is the expected after-tax accumulation in five years?

EXHIBIT 5	Hypothetical Tax Profile

Panel A: Tax Profile

	Annual Distribution Rate (p)	Tax Rate (T)
Ordinary Income (i)	5%	35%
Dividends (d)	25%	15%
Capital Gain (cg)	45%	15%
Investment Horizon (n)		5 years
Average Return (r)		8%
Cost Basis		€100,000

Panel B: Intermediate Accumulation Calculations

Annual after-tax return ($r*$)	7.02%
Effective capital gains tax rate ($T*$)	4.27%

In this case, 25 percent of the return is composed of dividends; 5 percent is composed of realized short-term capital gains; and 45 percent is composed of realized long-term gains. These figures imply that the remaining 25 percent (i.e., $1 - 0.05 - 0.25 - 0.45$) of portfolio returns are deferred capital gains and not taxed until the end of the investment horizon.

The annual return after realized taxes, $r*$, is $0.08[1 - (0.05)(0.35) - (0.25)(0.15) - (0.45)(0.15)] = 7.02$ percent as computed previously. This figure reflects the annual return after having accounted for the tax drag imposed by annually levied taxes on the portion of return composed of elements like dividends, interest, and realized capital gains. It does not take into account, however, tax obligations from gains not yet realized; that effect is considered in the effective capital gains tax rate, $T*$, which equals $0.15[(1 - 0.05 - 0.25 - 0.45)/(1 - 0.05 \times 0.35 - 0.25 \times 0.15 - 0.45 \times 0.15)] = 0.15(0.25/0.8775) = 4.27$ percent. The figure is relatively low in this example because a relatively small proportion of return, 25 percent, is subject to deferred capital gains tax.

> Because the cost basis and the current market value portfolio are both €100,000, the cost basis expressed as a percent of current market value is 1.00. Substituting these intermediate results into Equation 5, the expected future accumulation of the portfolio in 5 years equals €100,000$[(1 + r^*)^n(1 - T^*) + T^* - (1 - B)t_{cg}]$ = €100,000$[(1.0702)^5$ $(1 - 0.0427) + 0.0427 - (1 - 1.00)0.15]$ = €138,662.

3.3 Accrual Equivalent Returns and Tax Rates

Because returns can come in various forms and be taxed in various ways, an overall understanding of the impact of taxes on return can be obscure. A useful way to summarize the impact of taxes on portfolio returns is to calculate an accrual equivalent after-tax return. Conceptually, an accrual equivalent after-tax return is the tax-free return that, if accrued annually, produces the same after-tax accumulation as the taxable portfolio.[10] For example, in the previous example Kharullah's €100,000 portfolio earned an 8 percent return before taxes and will grow to €138,662 over a 5 year period after accrued and deferred taxes are considered. The tax-free return that will accumulate €138,662 over 5 years is the accrual equivalent return. The difference between the accrual equivalent return and the taxable return of 8 percent is a measure of the tax drag imposed on the portfolio.

An analogous way to measure tax drag is with the accrual equivalent tax rate. An accrual equivalent tax rate finds the annual accrual tax rate (of the simple form described in Section 3.1.1) that would produce the same after-tax accumulation as a tax system based in whole or in part on deferred realized gains (such as those described in Sections 3.1.2 or 3.2). Both these concepts recognize that deferring taxes through unrealized gains does not eliminate the tax liability but moves its payment through time.

3.3.1 Calculating Accrual Equivalent Returns

Calculating accrual equivalent returns is straightforward. In the previous example, the €100,000 portfolio has an after-tax accumulation 5 years hence of €138,662. The accrual equivalent return is found by solving for the return that equates the standard future value formula to the after-tax accumulation and solving for the return. In this example, we solve the following equation for R_{AE}:

$$€100,000(1 + R_{AE})^5 = €138,662$$

The accrual equivalent return, R_{AE}, is 6.756 percent. Notice that this rate is less than the annual return after realized taxes, r^*, of 7.02 percent because the accrual equivalent return incorporates the impact of deferred taxes on realized gains as well as taxes that accrue annually. The accrual equivalent return is always less than the taxable return, r. It approaches the pretax return, however, as the time horizon increases. This phenomenon demonstrates the value of tax deferral. The value of deferral in this example is relatively modest, however, because only 25 percent of the tax obligation associated with the return is assumed to be deferred. If more of the return is in the form of deferred gains, the value of the deferral increases.

---

[10] This term is coined by Poterba (2000).

3.3.2 Calculating Accrual Equivalent Tax Rates

The accrual equivalent tax rate is derived from the accrual equivalent return. It is the hypothetical tax rate, T_{AE}, that produces an after-tax return equivalent to the accrual equivalent return. In our example, it is found by solving for T_{AE} in the following expression:

$$r(1 - T_{AE}) = R_{AE} \tag{6}$$

In the blended tax regime example, $0.08(1 - T_{AE}) = 0.06756$. Solving for T_{AE}, the accrual equivalent tax rate is therefore, 0.1555 or 15.55 percent. This rate is much lower than the marginal tax rate on ordinary income and only slightly higher than the favorable rate on dividends and capital gains in this example because a relatively small portion (i.e., 5 percent) of the portfolio's return is generated from highly taxed income. Most of the return receives preferential tax treatment in either the form of a reduced rate for dividends or a reduced rate on realized capital gains combined with valuable deferral for unrealized gains. As a result, investments with this tax profile are relatively tax efficient. The accrual equivalent tax rate would increase if either the return had a larger component taxed at ordinary rates, or if dividends and capital gains received less favorable treatment. In either case, R_{AE} would be smaller, implying a higher value of T_{AE} for a given level of pretax return r in Equation 6.

    The accrual equivalent tax rate can be used in several ways. First, it can be used to measure the tax efficiency of different asset classes or portfolio management styles. Second, it illustrates to clients the tax impact of lengthening the average holding periods of stocks they own. Third, it can be used to assess the impact of future tax law changes. If the client's tax rate is likely to change in the future, the manager can determine the impact of the expected change on the accrual equivalent tax rate. The future tax rate could change for several reasons such as tax law changes, changes in client circumstances, or the client taking advantage of tax rules designed to encourage certain behaviors such as charitable contributions which may be deductible in some tax regimes.

EXAMPLE 9

Accrual Equivalent Return

We extend Example 3 with the same facts repeated here: Vladimir Kozloski is determining the impact of taxes on his expected investment returns and wealth accumulations. Kozloski lives in a tax jurisdiction with a flat tax rate of 20 percent, which applies to all types of income and is taxed annually. He expects to earn 7 percent per year on his investment over a 20-year time horizon and has an initial portfolio of €100,000. The 7 percent return is expected to come from deferred capital gains, which are not taxed until sold in 20 years. Kozloski's expected wealth at the end of 20 years is:

$$FV = €100,000 \times FVIF_{cg} = €100,000 \times [(1 + 0.07)^{20}(1 - 0.2) + 0.2] = €329,575$$

1. What is the accrual equivalent return?
2. What is the accrual equivalent tax rate?

Solution to 1:

$$€100,000 \, (1 + R_{AE})^{20} = €329,575$$
$$R_{AE} = 6.1446 \text{ percent}$$

Kozloski would be just as well off if he could find a tax-free investment earning 6.1446 percent.

Solution to 2:

$$0.07 \, (1 - T_{AE}) = 0.061446$$
$$T_{AE} = 12.22 \text{ percent}$$

This rate is lower than the stated tax rate on dividends because there is an advantage from the deferral of taxes.

TYPES OF INVESTMENT ACCOUNTS   4

The previous section examined models for taxable accounts in which the tax profile was determined by the asset class and/or the portfolio management style. The impact of taxes on future accumulations often depends heavily on the type of account in which assets are held. Many countries have account structures with different tax profiles designed to provide some relief to the taxable investor. These structures are often intended to encourage retirement savings, but may also accommodate savings for health care and education. Most industrialized and developing countries have tax incentives to encourage retirement savings. An international survey of 24 industrialized and developing countries commissioned by the American Council for Capital Formation (ACCF) indicates that tax-advantaged savings accounts are offered to taxpayers by two-thirds of the countries surveyed, including Australia, Canada, Germany, Italy, the Netherlands, and the United Kingdom.[11]

Most types of investment accounts can be classified into three categories. The first type is taxable accounts. Investments to these accounts are made on an after-tax basis and returns can be taxed in a variety of ways as discussed in the previous section. A second class of accounts can be called tax-deferred accounts, or TDAs. Contributions to these accounts may be made on a pretax basis (i.e., tax-deductible), and the investment returns accumulate on a tax-deferred basis until funds are withdrawn at which time they are taxed at ordinary rates. As such, these accounts are sometimes said to have front-end loaded tax benefits. All but one of the countries in the ACCF study have some kind of retirement account that permits tax deductible contributions. In Canada they are called Registered Retirement Savings Plans (RRSPs), and in the United States some are called Individual Retirement Accounts (IRAs). In some countries, like Australia and Chile, individuals are mandated to contribute a fixed proportion of their income to these accounts. Many types of defined contribution pension plans, whether sponsored by the state or an employer, fall into this category. Argentina, for example, offers citizens the option to make contributions to a public pension fund company.

---

[11] American Council for Capital Formation, "An International Comparison of Incentives for Retirement Saving and Insurance" (June 1999).

A third class of accounts has back-end loaded tax benefits. These accounts can be called tax-exempt (at least on a forward-looking basis) because although contributions are not deductible, earnings accumulate free of taxation even as funds are withdrawn, typically subject to some conditions. An example is the Roth IRA in the United States.

4.1 Tax-Deferred Accounts

Assets held in a TDA accumulate on a tax deferred basis. Tax is owed when funds are withdrawn at the end of an investment horizon at which time withdrawals are taxed at ordinary rates or another rate, T_n, prevailing at the end of the investment horizon. The future after-tax accumulation of a contribution to a TDA is therefore equal to

$$FVIF_{TDA} = (1 + r)^n(1 - T_n) \qquad\qquad \textbf{(7)}$$

The form of Equation 7 is similar to the future value interest factor when tax is based entirely on capital gains that are recognized at the end of the investment horizon with a cost basis equal to zero (see Equation 3).

4.2 Tax-Exempt Accounts

Tax-exempt accounts have no future tax liabilities. Earnings accumulate without tax consequence and withdrawals create no taxable event. Therefore, the future accumulation of a tax-exempt account is simply

$$FVIF_{TaxEx} = (1 + r)^n \qquad\qquad \textbf{(8)}$$

Potential insights are available in comparing Equations 7 and 8. First, we notice that $FVIF_{TDA} = FVIF_{TaxEx}(1 - T_n)$, which means that future after-tax accumulation of assets held in a tax deferred account are less than the after-tax accumulation of the same assets when held in a tax-exempt account regardless of the type of asset (assuming equivalent returns). Put simply, assets in a TDA have a built-in tax liability whereas assets in a tax-exempt account do not. It can be shown that the value of an asset held in a TDA measured on an after-tax basis is therefore equal to $(1 - T_n)$ times the value of the same asset held in a tax-exempt account. The taxing authority essentially owns T_n of the principal value of a TDA, regardless of the type of asset held in it, leaving the investor effectively owning only $(1 - T_n)$ of the principal.

EXAMPLE 10

Comparing Accumulations of Account Types

Extending Examples 2 and 3, recall that Vladimir Kozloski lives in a tax jurisdiction with a flat tax rate of 20 percent which applies to all types of income. Kozloski expects to earn 7 percent per year on his investment over a 20 year time horizon and has an initial portfolio of €100,000. Assume that Kozloski has the following current investments:

1. €100,000 invested in a taxable account earning 7 percent taxed annually

2. €100,000 invested in a taxable account earning 7 percent deferred capital gains (cost basis = €100,000)

3. €100,000 invested in a tax deferred account earning 7 percent

4. €100,000 invested in a tax exempt account earning 7 percent

Compute the after-tax wealth for each account at the end of 20 years assuming all assets are sold and accounts liquidated at the end of 20 years and assuming a tax rate of 20 percent.

Solution to 1: $FVIF = €100,000 [1 + 0.07(1 - 0.20)]^{20} = €297,357$

Solution to 2: $FVIF = €100,000 [(1 + 0.07)^{20}(1 - 0.20) + 0.20]$
$$= €329,575$$

Solution to 3: $FVIF = €100,000 [(1 + 0.07)^{20}(1 - 0.20)] = €309,575$

Solution to 4: $FVIF = €100,000 [(1 + 0.07)^{20}] = €386,968$

4.3 After-Tax Asset Allocation

The notion that a TDA is worth $(1 - T_n)$ times an otherwise equivalent tax-exempt account has implications for after-tax asset allocation, which is the distribution of asset classes in a portfolio measured on an after-tax basis. Consider, for example, an investor with €1,500,000 worth of stock held in a TDA and €500,000 of bonds held in a tax-exempt account as displayed in Exhibit 6. Withdrawals from the TDA account will be taxed at 40 percent. A traditional view of asset allocation based on pretax values would suggest the investor has €2,000,000 of assets, 75 percent of which are allocated in stocks and 25 percent of which are allocated in bonds. In after-tax terms, however, the total portfolio is worth only €1,400,000 because the TDA has a built-in tax liability of €600,000, money the investor cannot spend. Moreover, because the investor is holding stock in the TDA, her after-tax equity exposure is less than a pretax analysis would suggest. Specifically, the after-tax equity allocation is only 64.3 percent rather than 75 percent.[12]

EXHIBIT 6	Simple Example of After-Tax Asset Allocation				
Account Type	Asset Class	Pretax Market Value (€)	Pretax Weights (%)	After-Tax Market Value (€)	After-Tax Weights (%)
TDA	Stock	1,500,000	75	900,000	64.3
Tax-Exempt	Bonds	500,000	25	500,000	35.7
Total Portfolio		2,000,000	100	1,400,000	100

Note: Withdrawals at the end of the investment horizon are assumed to be taxed at a rate of 40 percent.

---

[12] Reichenstein (1998, 2001, 2006, 2007) and Horan (2007a and 2007b) develop the concept of after-tax asset allocation in more detail.

This simple example excludes taxable accounts and does not depend on an investor's time horizon. However, the after-tax value of taxable accounts may depend on an investor's time horizon, which can be difficult to estimate and may change over time. Therefore, estimating an investor's time horizon presents a potential impediment to incorporating after-tax asset allocation in portfolio management. Another challenge is improving client awareness, understanding, and comfort with asset allocation from an after-tax perspective. Suppose an adviser increases pretax equity exposure to achieve a target after-tax asset allocation. Her client may have difficulty accepting the notion of after-tax asset allocation, especially in a bear market when the extra equity exposure would hinder performance.

4.4 Choosing Among Account Types

A euro invested in a tax-exempt account always has a higher after-tax future value than a euro invested in a TDA, all else equal. Based on this, one may infer that it is always better to save in a tax-exempt account instead of a TDA. That conclusion would be premature, however, because the comparison overlooks the fact that contributions to TDAs are often tax-deductible whereas contributions to the tax-exempt accounts considered here generally are not.

Let's compare after-tax future values of contributions of a *pretax* euro to a tax-exempt account and a TDA. Because contributions to a tax-exempt account are taxable, a pretax investment is reduced by taxes such that the after-tax investment is $(1 - T_0)$, where T_0 is the tax rate applicable to the initial pretax contribution. The future value of a pretax dollar invested in a tax-exempt account is therefore $(1 - T_0)(1 + r)^n$. This expression reflects that taxes reduce the initial investment. The future value of a pretax dollar invested in a TDA is $(1 + r)^n(1 - T_n)$ because withdrawals are taxed at T_n. The only difference between the equations is the beginning and ending tax rates. The tax-exempt account is taxed at today's rate, T_0, while the TDA is eventually taxed at the tax rate in the withdrawal year, T_n. Therefore, comparing the attractiveness of the two types of accounts reduces to comparing the tax rate today to the expected tax rate when funds are withdrawn. If the prevailing tax rate when funds are withdrawn is less than the tax rate when they are invested, the TDA will accumulate more after-tax wealth than the tax-exempt account, and vice versa.

For example, consider an investor currently in the 40 percent tax bracket who is willing to forego €1,200 of spending this year. He could invest €2,000 pretax dollars in a TDA or €1,200 after taxes in a tax-exempt account. Both investments will reduce this year's spending by €1,200 because the €2,000 TDA contribution would reduce this year's taxes by €800. He invests in an asset that earns a 5 percent annual return for ten years. Assuming his tax rate is unchanged, in ten years, the TDA will be worth $€2,000(1.05)^{10}(1 - 0.40) = €1,955$ after taxes. The tax-exempt account will be worth $€1,200(1.05)^{10} = €1,955$, the same as the TDA.

In this example, he could invest $2,000 in the TDA or $1,200 in the tax-exempt account; a contribution limit did not affect his choice of account type. However, annual contribution limits are usually expressed as a set amount whether the contribution is made with pretax or after-tax funds. A $2,000 contribution of after-tax funds to a tax-exempt account is effectively a larger contribution than a $2,000 contribution of pretax funds to a TDA. As a result, the tax-exempt account allows the investor to put more after-tax funds in a tax-sheltered account than a TDA, all else equal. Horan (2003, 2005) developed a more general approach that incorporates contribution limits in the balance of considerations.

Suppose, however, that the investor's tax rate upon withdrawal will be 20 percent, which is lower than his current tax rate. The future value of the €1,200 contribution to tax-exempt accumulation is unchanged at €1,955, but the TDA accumulation increases to €2,606 or $2,000(1.05)^{10}(1 - 0.20)$ making the TDA the better choice. The decision would be reversed if the tax rate at withdrawal exceeds the current tax rate.

EXAMPLE 11

Choosing Among Account Types

Bettye Mims would like to invest for retirement and is willing to reduce this year's spending by €3,000. She will invest €3,000 *after taxes* this year and is in a 25 percent tax bracket, which is the top marginal tax rate in her jurisdiction. Mims is considering three types of accounts but would invest in the same portfolio which is expected to have a pre-tax return of 6 percent annually. If invested in a taxable account the income would be taxed each year at the same 25 percent rate.

Assuming Mims will make a single contribution today and withdraw all funds—paying any necessary taxes in 30 years—which of the following accounts will result in the largest after-tax accumulation?

► *Account A.* A taxable account with an initial investment of €3,000.

► *Account B.* A tax deferred account, where Mims can make a €4,000 tax deductible contribution (a €3,000 after tax cost to Mims).

► *Account C.* A tax exempt account, where a €3,000 contribution is not deductible.

Solution: The taxable account would accumulate €11,236 after taxes:

For A, $FVIF = €3,000 [1 + 0.06 (1 - 0.25)]^{30} = €11,236$

The tax deferred account would accumulate €17,230 after taxes:

For B, $FVIF = €4,000 [(1 + 0.06)^{30} (1 - 0.25)] = €17,230$

The tax exempt account would also accumulate €17,230 after taxes:

For C, $FVIF = €3,000 [(1 + 0.06)^{30}] = €17,230$

Both B and C achieve the same after-tax accumulation assuming her tax rates in the contribution year and withdrawal year are the same.

TAXES AND INVESTMENT RISK   5

It is fairly obvious that taxes reduce returns. Less obvious is the impact of taxes on investment risk. A fundamental premise regarding taxes and risk is that, by taxing investment returns, a government shares risk as well as return with the investor. Because the returns on assets held in TDAs and tax-exempt accounts are not currently taxed, investors bear all of the risk associated with returns in these accounts. Even in the case of TDAs in which the government effectively owns T_n of the principal, the variability of an investor's return in relation to the current after-tax principal value is unaffected by the tax on withdrawals.[13]

Because the returns on assets held in taxable accounts are typically taxed annually in some way, investors bear only a fraction of the risk associated with these assets. Suppose asset returns are taxed entirely as ordinary income at a rate of t_i. If the standard deviation of pretax returns is σ, returns are fully taxed at ordinary rates (and all investment losses can be recognized for tax purposes in the year they are incurred), then the standard deviation of after-tax returns for a taxable account is $\sigma(1 - t_i)$. That is, an investor bears only $(1 - t_i)$ of the pretax risk.

This concept is best demonstrated by way of example. Consider a €100,000 investment with an expected return of 10 percent, which is taxed annually at 40 percent. A three-state probability distribution of equally likely outcomes is presented in Exhibit 7. The standard deviation of pretax returns is 15 percent. The after-tax accumulations one year hence and the after-tax returns are presented in the last two columns.[14]

The standard deviation of after-tax returns equals 9 percent, which also equals $0.15(1 - 0.40)$. In other words, taxes absorbed $(1 - t_{oi})$ of the pretax volatility. As a result, the taxes not only reduce an investor's returns, but also absorb some investment risk. This concept has implications for portfolio optimization discussed below.

EXHIBIT 7		Simple Example of Investment Risk and Taxes			
Outcome	Prob.	Pretax Accumulation (€)	Pretax Return (%)	After-Tax Accumulation (€)	After-Tax Returns (%)
Good	1/3	125,000	25	115,000	15
Average	1/3	110,000	10	106,000	6
Bad	1/3	95,000	−5	97,000	−3
Exp. Value		110,000	10	106,000	6
Std. Dev. (σ)			15		9

Note: Investment returns are assumed to be taxed at a rate of 40 percent in the year they are earned.

To see how taxes affect after-tax risk in a portfolio context, consider an investor with 50 percent of her wealth invested in equities and 50 percent invested in fixed income, both held in taxable accounts. The equity has a pretax standard deviation of 20 percent and is relatively tax-efficient such that all

[13] For example, the after-tax accumulation of €1 in a TDA that earns a pretax return of r for n years is $(1 + r)^n(1 - T_n)$. The euro can be conceptually separated into $(1 - T_n)$ of the investor's funds plus T_n, the taxing authority's portion of the current principal. The investor's portion grows tax exempt from $(1 - T_n)$ today to $(1 + r)^n(1 - T_n)$ at withdrawal.

[14] Readers will recognize that this analysis assumes symmetry in the tax system. That is, the €5,000 pretax loss in the bad state is partially offset by a €2,000 tax deduction in the same way a pretax gain is partially offset by a tax liability. Some jurisdictions do not build this symmetry into the tax code or may at least place restrictions on the amount of losses that can be used to reduce taxes. These complexities are not considered here.

returns are taxed each year at a 20 percent tax rate. The fixed income is also taxed annually but at a 40 percent rate with pretax volatility of 5 percent. If the two asset classes are perfectly correlated, the pretax portfolio volatility is $0.50(0.20) + 0.50(0.05) = 0.125 = 12.5$ percent. On an after-tax basis, however, portfolio volatility is $0.50(0.20)(1 - 0.20) + 0.50(0.05)(1 - 0.40) = 0.095 = 9.5$ percent. This example illustrates that annually paid taxes reduce portfolio volatility.[15]

Alternatively, suppose that the equity is held in a taxable account and the fixed income is held in a tax-exempt account like those described in the previous section. In this case, the investor absorbs all of the bond volatility in the tax-exempt account, and the new portfolio volatility is $0.50(0.20)(1 - 0.20) + 0.50(0.05) = 0.105 = 10.5$ percent. After-tax volatility increased from the previous measure of after-tax volatility of 9.5 percent because one of the assets (bonds) became tax sheltered. The government therefore absorbed less investment risk through taxes, and the investor is left bearing more investment risk.

IMPLICATIONS FOR WEALTH MANAGEMENT 6

The concepts introduced above have several important implications for financial analysts and portfolio managers. The value created by using investment techniques that effectively manage tax liabilities is sometimes called tax alpha. This section briefly discusses some opportunities for considering taxation in the management of individual's portfolios and tax-planning opportunities to maximize the after-tax accumulation of wealth.

6.1 Asset Location

In most tax regimes, a security's asset class determines its tax profile when held in taxable accounts. Interest income on fixed income securities are often taxed differently from capital gains on stocks, for example. We have also seen how the account structure (e.g., TDAs or tax-exempt accounts) can override this tax treatment. Further, investments in TDAs and tax-exempt accounts are limited such that investors may not place all of their investments in these types of accounts. Investors, therefore, often have multiple types of accounts (e.g., taxable, TDAs, and tax-exempt) when tax advantaged accounts are permitted. An interaction exists between deciding what assets to own and in which accounts they should be held. The choice of where to place specific assets is called the asset location decision. It is distinct from the asset allocation decision. A well designed portfolio not only prescribes a proper asset allocation but simultaneously tells the portfolio manager the proper location for those assets. This section presents some valuable intuition and general guidance derived from the literature.

Much of the intuition is based on an arbitrage argument developed for corporate pension fund policy by Black (1981) and Tepper (1980). Suppose contributions to a pension plan are tax-deductible and the returns on pension assets are exempt from tax, much like a TDA for an individual investor. The basic idea behind the arbitrage argument is that a company should place assets that would

---

[15] The arithmetic is somewhat more complicated when the two assets are not perfectly correlated in which case one would use the standard expression for the volatility of a two security portfolio, $\sigma_p = (w_a^2\sigma_a^2 + w_b^2\sigma_b^2 + 2\ w_aw_b\rho\sigma_a\sigma_b)^{1/2}$. The general point that taxes reduce portfolio volatility remains unaffected.

otherwise be heavily taxed assets within the tax shelter of the pension fund, and locate more lightly taxed securities outside the pension fund. If this strategy causes the allocation of the heavily taxed asset held in the pension fund to be too high, an offsetting short position in the heavily taxed asset outside the pension fund can offset the excessive exposure in the pension fund.

For example, suppose bonds are more heavily taxed than equity. Moreover, suppose filling a company's pension fund with bonds causes an excessive allocation to bonds. The company can borrow (i.e., short bonds) outside the pension fund and invest the proceeds in equities. In this way, lending (i.e., investing in bonds) in the pension fund offsets borrowing outside the pension fund, allowing the company to achieve the desired overall asset allocation. The exact amount of borrowing required to offset the fixed-income investment in the pension fund depends on the tax rate and how assets are taxed, but the concept remains the same.

This same logic applies to individual investors. That is, investors would place in TDAs and tax-exempt accounts those securities that would otherwise be heavily taxed if held in taxable accounts (e.g., securities subject to high tax rates and/or annual taxation). The taxable account would hold lightly taxed assets (e.g., securities subject to low rates and/or tax deferral). For example, suppose an investor has €100,000 in tax-deferred accounts and €25,000 in taxable accounts as in Exhibit 8. As suggested, the €100,000 of bonds is placed in the TDA, and €25,000 of stock is placed in the taxable account, creating a pretax bond allocation of 80 percent. Suppose that the target pretax allocation is 60 percent bonds and 40 percent stocks. The investor would borrow €25,000 and purchase additional stock in the taxable account for a total of €50,000 stock. The overall asset allocation is €75,000 bonds and €50,000 stock, which attains the target allocation of 60 percent bonds and 40 percent stock.[16]

EXHIBIT 8		Simple Example of Asset Location				
Account Type	Asset Class	Existing Pretax Market Value (€)	Existing Pretax Allocation (%)	Asset Class	Target Pretax Market Value (€)	Target Pretax Allocation (%)
TDA	Bond	100,000	80	Bond	100,000	80
Taxable	Stock	25,000	20	Stock	50,000	40
				Short Bond	(25,000)	(20)
Total		125,000	100		125,000	100

There are limitations to this basic arbitrage argument. Investors may face restrictions on the amount and form of borrowing. For instance, the tax arbitrage argument assumes that investors can borrow and lend at the same rate in whatever amounts they wish. In reality, this is not the case. Investors are

---

[16] In this example, asset allocation is expressed in pretax terms. Technically, the asset location question should be solved jointly with asset allocation because changing locations changes asset allocation in after-tax terms. We abstract from that complexity in this example and the following examples for illustrative ease.

undoubtedly subject to borrowing costs that are greater than the yield on a bond of similar risk. At least a portion of the tax gains from the arbitrage are therefore consumed by this rate differential. Moreover, behavioral constraints can limit implementation because some investors are apprehensive about borrowing money (i.e., shorting bonds) to manage their retirement portfolio.

In addition, investors may face liquidity constraints (e.g., margin requirements or withdrawal penalties from TDAs and tax-exempt accounts) that would make the arbitrage strategy costly. For example, margin rules may preclude investors from borrowing as much as the arbitrage strategy would suggest or force them to borrow at rates in excess of the bond returns in the TDA. In some jurisdictions investors face penalties for withdrawing assets held in a TDA or tax-exempt account prior to a particular date. If the equity in a taxable account suffers a substantial decline in value, an investor may be forced to liquidate assets in the tax-deferred account to finance consumption, which may trigger an early withdrawal penalty for some investors. These constraints may make strictly executing the arbitrage strategy costly or impossible.

In these cases, asset location is still important. If there are constraints to borrowing in the taxable account then the investor may hold €25,000 in stocks in the taxable account. In the TDA, she could hold €75,000 in bonds and €25,000 in stocks in the TDA. This would achieve the target allocation, while following the location preference in the absence of borrowing.

Separately, suppose she has borrowing constraints and needs €5,000 as a cash reserve in her taxable account. She could hold €20,000 in stocks and €5,000 in cash in the taxable account. In the TDA, she could hold €70,000 in bonds and €30,000 in stocks, which would achieve her target asset allocation. In each example, she follows the asset location preference to the extent possible, while satisfying her other constraints and target asset allocation.

Some jurisdictions exempt municipal bond interest or other types of interest from taxes. In this case, it could conceivably make sense to place tax-free municipal bonds in a taxable account and more heavily taxed stock in the TDA. The yield on tax-free bonds, however, is generally much lower than those on taxable bonds so that in a well functioning market their after-tax returns are approximately equal. This yield concession is a significant disadvantage to placing low yielding tax-free bonds in a taxable account and equity in a TDA. In most instances the yield concession more than offsets the value of sheltering equity returns from taxes. As a result, it is generally better to follow the general strategy of locating bonds in TDAs and equity in taxable accounts.[17]

The tax regime governing the investor determines the relative importance of asset location. In a regime where all income is taxed annually (including unrealized capital gains) and at the same rates, asset location would not matter. As noted earlier, however, these regimes are rare. In most regimes the individual tax structure should be examined to determine which assets are taxed annually and highly versus those that are tax deferred or taxed lightly. Additionally, investment style impacts how an asset or asset class is taxed. For example, active management (discussed further below) or a covered call strategy for an equity portfolio may eliminate the ability to defer taxes.

Of course, taxes are only one of many factors that go into the asset location decision. Others include behavioral constraints, access to credit facilities, age, time horizon, and investment availability. Another factor is planned holding period. If the investor has two accounts—a tax deferred account and a taxable account—that contain funds intended for retirement, then they would both

---

[17] See Dammon, Spatt, and Zhang (2004).

have long term objectives and locating assets based on their taxation makes sense. However, if the tax deferred account contains retirement funds and the taxable account contains funds held for short term needs, it may not be appropriate to locate assets based strictly on their taxation. The asset allocation should be appropriate to the client's time horizon for each account.

6.2 Trading Behavior

The tax burden for many asset classes, such as equities when held in taxable accounts, depends on an investor's trading behavior or that of the mutual fund held by an investor. Consider four types of equity investors. The first type is a *trader* who trades frequently and recognizes all portfolio returns in the form of annually taxed short term gains. This equity management style may subject investment returns to tax burdens similar to those applied to interest income thereby eroding possible tax efficiencies associated with equities. An *active investor*, who trades less frequently so that gains are longer term in nature, may receive more favorable tax treatment.[18] The *passive investor* passively buys and holds stock. The *exempt investor* not only buys and holds stocks, but he never pays capital gains tax.[19] Optimal asset allocation and asset location for each of these investors is likely to differ.

For example, suppose these four individuals invest €1,000 in non-dividend paying stocks that earn 8 percent annually for 20 years. They live in a country that taxes capital gains realized within a year at 40 percent and gains realized after at least one year at 20 percent. The after-tax accumulations and accrual equivalent tax rates are listed in Exhibit 9.

EXHIBIT 9	Future Accumulations for Different Types of Investors			
Investor Type	**Future Accumulation (€)**	**Expression (€)**	**Accrual Equivalent Return (%)**	**Accrual Equivalent Tax Rate (%)**
Trader	2,554	$1,000[1 + 0.08(1 - 0.4)]^{20}$	4.8	40.0
Active Investor	3,458	$1,000[1 + 0.08(1 - 0.2)]^{20}$	6.4	20.0
Passive Investor	3,929	$1,000[(1.08)^{20}(1 - 0.2) + 0.2]$	7.1	11.5
Exempt Investor	4,661	$1,000(1.08)^{20}$	8.0	0.0

Holding all else constant, the trader accumulates the least amount of wealth, and the tax exempt investor accumulates the most. The active and passive investors fall in between. This comparison illustrates that trading behavior affects the tax burden on stocks (and other assets that provide capital gain appreciation) when held in taxable accounts.

Research suggests that active managers must earn greater pretax alphas than passive managers to offset the tax drag of active trading.[20] Other research sug-

---

[18] Examples include Australia, Belgium, Denmark, Germany, Japan, Latvia, Luxemburg, the United Kingdom, and the United States.

[19] Some jurisdictions permit capital gains tax to be avoided by making charitable contributions or passing assets to an estate upon death.

[20] See, for example, Jeffrey and Arnott (1993).

gests that mutual fund rankings change significantly depending on whether performance is measured on a pretax or after-tax basis.[21] Therefore, it is important for the taxable investor to consider the impact of taxes on after-tax returns. Generally, for assets held in taxable accounts, portfolio turnover generates taxable gains that might otherwise be deferred. Because a number of countries have lower long-term capital gains tax rates for investment held beyond a particular holding period, higher portfolio turnover also foregoes preferential tax treatment associated with longer holding periods and lower turnover.

It is important to note that although locating highly taxed assets in tax sheltered accounts can add value for investors, a proper investment management strategy remains more important than the proper asset location strategy. That is, optimally locating assets in TDAs and taxable accounts cannot overcome the negative impact of a poor investment strategy that either produces a negative pretax alpha or is highly tax inefficient.[22]

6.3 Tax Loss Harvesting

Although the previous section indicates that active management can create a tax drag, not all trading is necessarily tax inefficient. While jurisdictions allow realized capital losses to offset realized capital gains, limitations are often placed on the amount of net losses that can be recognized or the type of income it can offset (e.g., short-term capital gains, long-term capital gains, or ordinary income). Canada, for example, only allows tax deductible losses up to the level of realized taxable gains. Realized losses in excess of realized gains may be used to offset gains realized within the last three years. Realized losses beyond that point can be carried forward and applied against gain realized at some future date.

Regardless of the specific tax rules the opportunity to recognize a loss that offsets some kind of taxable gain in a given tax year can create value. The practice of realizing a loss to offset a gain or income—and thereby reducing the current year's tax obligation—is called tax loss harvesting.

EXAMPLE 12

Tax Loss Harvesting: Current Tax Savings

Eduardo Cappellino has a €1,000,000 portfolio held in a taxable account. The end of the 2008 tax year is approaching and Cappellino has recognized €100,000 worth of capital gains. His portfolio has securities that have experienced €60,000 of losses. These securities have not yet been sold and their losses are therefore unrecognized. Cappellino could sell these securities and replace them with similar securities expected to earn identical returns.[23] The federal government taxes capital gains at 20 percent.

1. Without making any further transactions, how much tax does Cappellino owe this year?

---

[21] See, for example, Dickson and Shoven (1993).

[22] See Reichenstein (2001).

[23] Realizing losses by selling and buying similar securities may be subject to certain restrictions by the government or taxing authority.

> **2.** How much tax will Cappellino owe this year if he sells the securities with the €60,000 loss?
>
> **3.** How much tax will Cappellino save this year if he sells the securities with the €60,000 loss?
>
> **Solution to 1:** Capital gain tax = 0.20 × €100,000 = €20,000.
>
> **Solution to 2:** If Cappellino realizes €60,000 of losses, the net gain will be reduced to €40,000. New capital gain tax = 0.20 × (€100,000 − €60,000) = €8,000.
>
> **Solution to 3:** Tax Savings = €20,000 − €8,000 = €12,000.

It is important to understand that the tax savings realized in a given tax year from tax loss harvesting overstates the true gain. Selling a security at a loss and reinvesting the proceeds in a similar security effectively resets the cost basis to the lower market value, potentially increasing future tax liabilities. In other words, taxes saved now may be simply postponed. The value of tax loss harvesting is largely in deferring the payment of tax liabilities.[24]

EXAMPLE 13

Tax Loss Harvesting: Tax Deferral

In the previous example, the securities with an unrealized loss have a current market value of €110,000 and cost basis of €170,000 (an unrealized loss of €60,000). Cappellino could:

Option A.   Hold the securities with the unrealized loss, or

Option B.   Sell the securities in 2008 and replace them with securities offering the same return.

Next tax year (2009), the securities increase in value to €200,000 and the securities are sold regardless of which option Cappellino chooses.

1. Calculate Cappellino's 2009 tax liability if he holds the securities until year end 2009.

2. Calculate Cappellino's 2009 tax liability if he recognizes the loss today in 2008, replaces them with securities offering the same return, and realizes the capital gain at year end 2009.

3. Compare the total two-year tax liability under both options using the 2008 tax liability computed in Example 12, in which the 2008 tax liability was €20,000 if the loss was not realized and €8,000 if the loss was realized.

---

[24] In cases where securities receive a step up in basis upon inheritance or are gifted to charity, the government will never recapture the current year tax savings, greatly increasing the harvesting value to the investor. Furthermore, in the United States the value of a built-in capital loss is lost at death. For example, someone could realize a $1,000 loss before death and save taxes. But the asset sold immediately after his death would not benefit from this tax loss.

Solution to 1: Capital gain tax $= 0.20(€200{,}000 - €170{,}000) = €6{,}000.$

Solution to 2: If Cappellino recognizes the loss in 2008 and replaces the securities, the basis will be reset to €110,000 from €170,000.

Capital gain tax in 2009 $= 0.20(€200{,}000 - €110{,}000) = €18{,}000.$

Solution to 3: The two-year tax liability for both options is the same:

	2008 (€)	2009 (€)	Total (€)
Option A	20,000	6,000	26,000
Option B	8,000	18,000	26,000

Although the two-year tax liability does not change, an advantage of tax loss harvesting is pushing a portion of the tax liability into subsequent years.

A subtle benefit of tax loss harvesting is that recognizing an already incurred loss for tax purposes increases the amount of net-of-tax money available for investment. Realizing a loss saves taxes in the current year, and this tax savings can be reinvested. This technique increases the amount of capital the investor can put to use.

EXAMPLE 14

Tax Loss Harvesting: Adding Net-of-Tax Principal

In the previous example, suppose Cappellino reinvests the 2008 tax savings if he sells the securities with an unrealized loss of €60,000. His two options are therefore:

Option A. Hold the securities, or

Option B. Sell the securities, and reinvest the proceeds and the tax savings in nearly identical securities.

In 2009, the securities experience an 81.81 percent increase regardless of which option Cappellino chooses.

1. Calculate the securities' pretax value next year if he holds the securities.

2. Calculate the securities' pretax value next year if he recognizes the loss, and reinvests the proceeds and the tax savings in nearly identical securities.

3. What will the after-tax value be under both options if the securities are sold the next year?

Solution to 1: FV $= €110{,}000(1.8181) = €200{,}000$ (approximately).

Solution to 2: If Cappellino replaces the securities and invests the tax savings of €12,000, the invested capital will become €110,000 + €12,000) = €122,000.

FV $= €122{,}000(1.8181) = €221{,}808.$

Solution to 3: The new capital gain tax for Option B at the end of the next tax year is $0.20(€221,808 - €122,000) = €19,962$.

	Pretax (€)	Tax (€)	After-Tax (€)
Option A	200,000	6,000	194,000
Option B	221,808	19,962	201,846

Another advantage of tax loss harvesting is increasing the net-of-tax capital invested in the portfolio.

A concept related to tax loss harvesting is using highest-in, first-out (HIFO) tax lot accounting to sell a portion of a position. When positions are accumulated over time, lots are often purchased at different prices. Depending on the tax system, investors may be allowed to sell the highest cost basis lots first, which defers realizing the tax liability associated with lots having a lower cost basis.

Opportunities to create value through tax loss harvesting and HIFO are greater in jurisdictions with high tax rates on capital gains. Studies have shown that a tax loss harvesting program can yield substantial benefits. Although cumulative tax alphas from tax loss harvesting increase over time, the annual tax alpha is largest in the early years and decreases through time as deferred gains are ultimately realized.[25] The complementary strategies of tax loss harvesting and HIFO tax lot accounting have more potential value when securities have relatively high volatility, which creates larger gains and losses with which to work.

The previous section suggests that active trading creates a tax drag on portfolio performance. A certain amount of trading activity is required, however, to harvest tax losses if a portfolio contains unrealized losses. That is, tax-efficient management of stocks in taxable accounts does not require passive management. It requires passively allowing gains to grow unharvested, but actively realizing losses.

Harvesting losses is not always an optimal strategy. For example, in cases where an investor is currently in a relatively low tax rate environment and will face higher tax rates on gains in a subsequent period (either because her tax bracket will increase or because tax rates generally are increasing) the best strategy may be to defer harvesting losses. Doing so would offset gains that will be taxed relatively lightly compared to subsequent gains if tax rates will increase.[26] Likewise, one might want to liquidate low basis stock (lowest in, first out or LIFO) if the current tax rate is temporarily low.

6.4 Holding Period Management

The tax regime analysis earlier in the reading indicated that many jurisdictions encourage long-term investing (or equivalently discourage short-term trading) by reducing tax rates on long-term gains. The required holding period varies, of course. Depending on the magnitude of gain from waiting, short-term trading can

---

[25] See, for example, Berkin, Ye, and Arnott (2001), Stein (2004b), and Berkin and Ye (2003).

[26] See Stein (2004a) for further discussion.

be difficult to justify on an after-tax basis. If short-term gains are taxed at 40 percent and long-term gains are taxed at 20 percent, then 20 percent (i.e., 40 percent less 20 percent) of an investor's gains are dictated by the holding period.

Exhibit 10 shows the relative benefit of gains subject to a lower tax rate. Using a twelve-month holding period requirement for a long-term capital gain tax of 20 percent versus a short-term capital gain tax of 40 percent, the table assumes that the entire return is taxed each year. For example, consider an 8 percent return over ten years. If returns are completely taxed each year as long term gains at 20 percent, €100 will grow to €100$[1 + 0.08(1 - 0.20)]^{10}$ = €185.96. If returns are completely taxed as short-term gains at 40 percent, the accumulation is €100$[1 + 0.08(1 - 0.40)]^{10}$ = €159.81. The ratio between the two figures is €185.96/€159.81 = 1.164. The benefit of realizing long-term gains in lieu of short-term gains is substantial, especially for long investment horizons and higher returns.

The penalty associated with realizing short-term gains in this environment can be viewed from a different perspective. An investment earning a 10 percent pretax return subject to a long term rate yields 8 percent after-tax [i.e., 0.10 × (1 − 0.20)]. A 13.33 percent pretax return taxed as a short-term gain is necessary to produce the same result [e.g., 0.08/(1 − 0.40)]. In other words, the pretax return must be one-third greater to produce the same after-tax result. It can be quite difficult to generate enough pretax alpha to overcome the effect of taxes on short capital gains in these types of tax environments.

Another aspect of holding period management is more tactical in terms of which tax year the tax is due. If a taxpayer subject to taxation on a calendar year basis is contemplating an asset sale in December, it may be wise to defer the sale until January if there is a built-in capital gain or sell the asset in December if there is a built-in loss. Of course the timing of taxation is not the only consideration. The attractiveness of this investment relative to alternative investments must be considered.

EXHIBIT 10	Ratio of Future Accumulations: Accumulation Using Long-Term Capital Gains Tax Rate to Accumulation Using Short-Term Capital Gains Tax Rate

Investment Horizon in Years (n)

r (%)	5	10	15	20	25	30	35	40
2	1.020	1.040	1.061	1.082	1.104	1.126	1.148	1.171
4	1.040	1.081	1.124	1.168	1.215	1.263	1.313	1.365
6	1.059	1.122	1.189	1.259	1.334	1.413	1.496	1.585
8	1.079	1.164	1.255	1.354	1.461	1.575	1.699	1.833
10	1.098	1.206	1.324	1.453	1.596	1.752	1.924	2.112
12	1.117	1.248	1.394	1.557	1.739	1.943	2.170	2.425
14	1.136	1.290	1.466	1.665	1.892	2.149	2.441	2.773
16	1.155	1.333	1.540	1.778	2.053	2.371	2.738	3.162
18	1.173	1.377	1.615	1.896	2.224	2.610	3.062	3.593

Note: Capital gains are assumed to be taxed each year. Short-term gains are taxed at a rate of 40 percent. Long-term gains are taxed at 20 percent.

EXAMPLE 15

Long-Term Gain

Gretel Hazburger is considering two different portfolio strategies. The first is a hyper-active market-timing trading strategy that is expected to yield a pretax return of 12 percent. All gains will be recognized each year and taxed at the short term capital gain rate of 50 percent. Alternatively, a less active tactical asset allocation trading strategy is expected to yield a pretax return of 10 percent. All gains will be recognized each year but classified as long term and taxed at 30 percent.

1. Which strategy is likely to produce a better after tax return?
2. What pretax return is required on the market timing strategy to produce the same after-tax return as the tactical asset allocation strategy?

Solution to 1: After-tax return to market timing = $0.12(1 - 0.50) = 0.06 = 6$ percent.
   After-tax return to tactical asset allocation = $0.10 (1 - 0.30) = 0.07 = 7$ percent.
   The tactical asset allocation strategy produces a better return.

Solution to 2: Required return for market timing = $0.07/(1 - 0.50) = 0.14 = 14$ percent.

6.5 After-Tax Mean–Variance Optimization

We have seen how basic principles of measuring asset allocation in a pretax environment do not necessarily apply in a more economically relevant after-tax environment. The same is true for portfolio optimization techniques. That is, pretax efficient frontiers may not be reasonable proxies for after-tax efficient frontiers. It is beyond the scope of this reading to develop specific after-tax mean–variance optimization (MVO) methods. However, an important concept supporting those methods is that the same asset held in different types of accounts is essentially a distinct after-tax asset because it will produce different after-tax accumulations. In other words, an investor optimizing between two different asset classes (e.g., stocks and bonds) across two types of accounts (e.g., taxable and tax deferred accounts) has four different after-tax assets to allocate—stocks or bonds in each of the two accounts.

After recognizing that important insight, an important element in developing an after-tax MVO model is to substitute accrual equivalent returns, like those introduced above, for pretax returns in developing return expectations. Similarly, a portfolio manager would substitute the asset's after-tax standard deviation of returns for pretax standard deviations in the optimization algorithm.

The optimization process must include some constraints. For example, an optimization algorithm cannot allocate more to a tax deferred account than the funds that are available in that account. Specific investment options may also be constrained in some types of accounts. For example, privatized retirement accounts in certain countries may limit investors' options to certain types of securities. In sum, however, standard portfolio optimization practices can be adapted to consider the impact of taxes on investment returns and risk.

SUMMARY

Taxes can have a significant impact on investment returns and wealth accumulation, and managing taxes in an investment portfolio is one way advisers can add value. Taxes come in various forms and each country has its own tax code. Nonetheless, many jurisdictions share some common salient features, and many of those common elements can be identified. This allows one to define regimes that include countries with similar rules of taxation and to build models that capture the salient features of these regimes. That is the approach taken here and the resulting analysis suggests the following:

▶ Taxes on investments can take at least three primary forms as discussed here. They can be based on:

  ▶ returns—accrued and paid annually;

  ▶ returns—deferred until capital gains are recognized;

  ▶ wealth—accrued and paid annually.

▶ The impact of taxes on wealth accumulation compounds over time.

▶ Deferred taxes on capital gains have less impact on wealth accumulation than annual tax obligations for the same tax rate.

▶ An investment with a cost basis below its current market value has an embedded tax liability that may reduce future after-tax accumulations.

▶ Wealth taxes apply to principal rather than returns and in consequence wealth tax rates tend to be much lower than returns-based tax rates.

▶ Investments are typically subject to multiple forms of taxation. The specific exposure depends on the asset class, portfolio management style, and type of account in which it is held.

▶ An accrual equivalent after-tax return is the tax-free return that, if accrued annually, produces a given after-tax accumulation.

▶ An accrual equivalent tax rate is the annually accrued tax rate that, when applied to the pretax return, produces a given after-tax accumulation.

▶ Sometimes the type of investment account overrides the tax treatment of an investment based on its asset class.

▶ Tax-deferred accounts allow tax-deductible contributions and/or tax-deferred accumulation of returns, but funds are taxed when withdrawn.

▶ Tax-exempt accounts do not allow tax-deductible contributions, but allow tax-exempt accumulation of returns even when funds are withdrawn.

▶ By taxing investment returns, a taxing authority shares investment risk with the taxpayer. As a result, taxes can reduce investment risk.

▶ The practice of optimally placing particular asset classes in particular types of accounts is called asset location.

▶ Tax loss harvesting defers tax liabilities from current to subsequent periods and permits more after-tax capital to be invested in current periods.

▶ When short-term gains are taxed more heavily than long-term gains, it can be difficult for a short-term trading strategy to generate enough alpha to offset the higher taxes associated with short term trading.

▶ Traditional mean–variance optimization can be modified to accommodate after-tax returns and after-tax risk.

▶ Otherwise identical assets held in different types of investment accounts should be evaluated as distinct after-tax assets.

▶ An after-tax portfolio optimization model that optimizes asset allocation also optimizes asset location.

PRACTICE PROBLEMS FOR READING 15

The following information relates to Questions 1–7

Alan Jackson has a new client, Aldo Motelli, who expects taxable ordinary income (excluding investments) of €200,000 this tax year. Motelli currently has €250,000 in a taxable investment account for which his main objective is retirement in 15 years. He is considering making the maximum investment of €10,000 in a new type of tax deferred account permitted in his country of residence. The contribution would be deductible and distributions are expected to be taxed at a 20 percent rate when withdrawn. The income tax structure of his country is:

Taxes on Ordinary Income

| Taxable Income (€) | | Tax on | Percentage on Excess |
Over	Up to	Column 1 (€)	Over Column 1
0	20,000	—	10
20,000	40,000	2,000	15
40,000	60,000	5,000	20
60,000	80,000	9,000	25
80,000	100,000	14,000	30
100,000		20,000	35

Taxes on Investment Income

Interest	10% flat rate
Dividends	10% flat rate
Realized capital gains	10% flat rate

1. What is Motelli's average tax rate on ordinary income?
   A. 22.5%.
   B. 27.5%.
   C. 35.0%.

2. If Motelli's current investment account of €250,000 is invested in an asset which is expected to earn annual interest of 6.5 percent and no capital gains, what is his expected after tax accumulation in 15 years?
   A. €578,664.
   B. €586,547.
   C. €642,960.

3. What is the accrual equivalent return assuming the facts in Question 2?
   A. 5.85%.
   B. 6.50%.
   C. 7.22%.

4. If Motelli's current investment account of €250,000 is invested in an investment which is expected to earn a return of 7.5 percent, all of which are deferred capital gains, what is his expected after-tax accumulation in 15 years? The account's market value is equal to its cost basis.

   A. €640,747.

   B. €665,747.

   C. €690,747.

5. If Motelli's current investment account of €250,000, has a cost basis of €175,000, and is invested in an investment which is expected to earn a return of 7.5 percent, all of which are deferred capital gains, what is his expected after tax accumulation in 15 years?

   A. €673,247.

   B. €683,247.

   C. €690,747.

6. How much after-tax wealth would Motelli accumulate assuming the same facts as in Question 4 except that 50 percent of all capital gains are recognized each year?

   A. €640,747.

   B. €665,747.

   C. €678,158.

7. Assuming an annual return of 7.5 percent, what would be the after-tax wealth accumulated in 15 years for a single current contribution to the TDA? Assume the contribution would be deductible but taxed at the end of 15 years at a 20 percent tax rate.

   A. €23,671.

   B. €23,965.

   C. €29,589.

---

8. Sam Nakusi is managing a balanced portfolio of fixed income and equity securities worth £1,000,000. The portfolio's pretax expected return is 6.0 percent. The percentage of return composed of interest, dividends and realized capital gain as well as the associated tax rates are listed below. Assume the portfolio's cost basis equals market value.

Hypothetical Tax Profile and Example

Tax Profile	Annual Distribution Rate (*p*)	Tax Rate (*T*)
Interest (*i*)	20%	35%
Dividends (*d*)	30%	15%
Capital gain (*cg*)	40%	25%

What is the expected future accumulation in 15 years assuming these parameters hold for that time period?

   A. £1,930,929.

   B. £1,962,776.

   C. £1,994,447.

9. In the previous question, recalculate the expected accumulation assuming the portfolio's costs basis is equal to £700,000.

   A. £1,373,943.

   B. £1,962,776.

   C. £1,887,776.

10. Gloria Vander is pursuing a buy-and-hold equity strategy on non-dividend paying stocks. She expects her €400,000 portfolio to experience no turnover over the next 10 years but expects to liquidate it at that time. The cost basis is currently equal to market value. If Vander expects an 8 percent pretax return and capital gains are taxed at 20 percent, what is her accrual equivalent return over that time period?

    A. 6.40%.

    B. 6.78%.

    C. 4.60%.

11. What is the accrual equivalent tax rate in the previous question?

    A. 15.25%.

    B. 20.00%.

    C. 84.75%.

12. Peter Cavuto lives in a country that imposes a wealth tax of 0.5 percent on financial assets each year. His €500,000 portfolio is expected to return 5 percent per year over the next twenty years. Assuming no other taxes, what is Cavuto's expected wealth at the end of twenty years?

    A. €1,200,100.

    B. €1,205,857.

    C. €1,326,649.

13. A client has funds in a tax deferred account and a taxable account. Which of the following assets would be *most appropriate* in a taxable account in a Flat and Heavy Tax Regime, in which dividends and capital gains are taxed at ordinary rates and interest income is tax exempt? Assume that all assets are held in a client's overall portfolio.

    A. Bonds.

    B. Actively traded stocks.

    C. High dividend paying stocks.

14. John Kaplan and Anna Forest both have €100,000 each split evenly between a tax deferred account and a taxable account. Kaplan chooses to put stock with an expected return of 7 percent in the tax-deferred account and bonds yielding 4 percent in the taxable account. Forest chooses the reverse, putting stock in the taxable account and bonds in the tax deferred account. When held in taxable account, equity returns will be taxed entirely as deferred capital gains at a 20 percent rate, while interest income is taxed annually at 40 percent. The tax rate applicable to withdrawals from the tax deferred account will be 40 percent. Cost basis is equal to market value on asset held in taxable account.

Kaplan's and Forest's Asset Location

Tax Profile	Kaplan (€)	Forest (€)
Taxable Account	50,000 bonds	50,000 stock
Tax deferred Account	50,000 stock	50,000 bonds
Total (Before-tax)	100,000	100,000

What is Kaplan's after-tax accumulation after 20 years?

A. €196,438.

B. €220,521.

C. €230,521.

15. In the previous question, what is Forest's after-tax accumulation after 20 years?

A. €196,438.

B. €220,521.

C. €230,521.

16. What is the after-tax asset allocation for the following portfolio if withdrawals from the TDA will be taxed at 40 percent?

Account	Pretax Market Value (€)	Asset Class
TDA	200,000	Bonds
Tax-exempt	80,000	Stock
Total	280,000	

A. 71.4% bonds; 28.6% stock.

B. 50% bonds; 50% stock.

C. 60% bonds; 40% stock.

17. Lorraine Newman is evaluating whether to save for retirement using a TDA or a tax-exempt account. The TDA permits tax-deductible contributions but withdrawals will be taxed at 30 percent. The tax-exempt account permits tax-free accumulation and withdrawals but contributions are taxable at a 40 percent tax rate. Assuming contribution limits do not affect Newman's choice of accounts, which account should she choose?

   A. TDA.

   B. Tax-exempt.

   C. The choices are the same.

18. Which of the following assets would be most appropriate to locate in a tax deferred account in a Heavy Interest Tax Regime assuming all assets are held in a client's overall portfolio?

   A. Low dividend paying stock.

   B. Tax exempt bonds.

   C. Taxable bonds.

19. Consider a portfolio that is generally appreciating in value. Active trading is most likely to be *least* attractive in a:

   A. taxable account.

   B. tax deferred account.

   C. tax exempt account.

20. Jose DiCenzo has some securities worth €50,000 that have a cost basis of €75,000. If he sells those securities and can use the realized losses to offset other realized gains, how much can DiCenzo reduce his taxes in the *current* tax year assuming capital gains are taxed at 30 percent?

   A. €7,500.

   B. €15,000.

   C. €17,500.

21. In the previous question, suppose DiCenzo sells the securities in the current tax year and replaces them with securities having the same returns. He will then sell the new securities in the next tax year. What is the total tax savings assuming DiCenzo does *not* reinvest the tax savings?

   A. €0.

   B. €7,500.

   C. €15,000.

22. Tax loss harvesting is most effective when:

   A. there are few similar investment opportunities for the security with the loss.

   B. the taxpayer is currently in a relatively high tax environment.

   C. the taxpayer is currently in a relatively low tax environment.

SOLUTIONS FOR READING 15

1. B is correct. Motelli's tax liability on ordinary income is €20,000 (on the first €100,000, third column of table, last row) + (€200,000 − €100,000) × 0.35, or €55,000. The average tax rate on ordinary income is €55,000/€200,000, or 27.5 percent.

2. B is correct. The after tax wealth accumulation for annually taxable income is

$$FVIF_i = [1 + r(1 - t_i)]^n$$
$$FV = €250,000 \times FVIF_i = €250,000 \times [1 + 0.065\,(1 - 0.10)]^{15}$$
$$= €586,547$$

3. A is correct. The accrual equivalent return is found by the following equation:

$$€250,000\,(1 + R_{AE})^{15} = €586,547$$
$$R_{AE} = 5.85\%$$

4. C is correct. The after tax wealth accumulation for deferred capital gains is

$$FVIF_{cg} = (1 + r)^n(1 - t_{cg}) + t_{cg}$$
$$FVIF_{cg} = €250,000 \times [(1 + 0.075)^{15}\,(1 - 0.1) + 0.1] = €690,747$$

5. B is correct. The after tax wealth accumulation for deferred capital gains is

$$FVIF_{cg} = (1 + r)^n(1 - t_{cg}) + t_{cg} - (1 - B)\,t_{cg}$$
$$FVIF_{cg} = €250,000 \times [(1 + 0.075)^{15}\,(1 - 0.1) + 0.1$$
$$- (1 - 0.70)(0.10)] = €683,247$$

6. C is correct.

$$
\begin{aligned}
r^* \quad &= r\,(1 - p_{cg}t_{cg}) \\
&= 0.075(1 - (0.5)(0.10)) = 0.075(1 - 0.05) = 0.07125 \\
T^* \quad &= t_{cg}(1 - p_{cg})/(1 - p_{cg}t_{cg}) \\
&= 0.10[(1 - 0.5)/(1 - 0.5 \times 0.10)] = 0.052632 \\
FVIF_{Taxable} &= (1 + r^*)^n(1 - T^*) + T^* - (1 - B)\,t_{cg},\ B = 1 \\
FV \quad &= €250,000 \times [(1 + 0.07125)^{15}(1 - 0.052632) + 0.052632] \\
&= €678,158
\end{aligned}
$$

7. A is correct.

$$FVIF_{TDA} = (1 + r)^n(1 - T_n)$$
$$FVIF = €10,000\,[(1 + 0.075)^{15}\,(1 - 0.20)] = €23,671$$

8. B is correct.

$$
\begin{aligned}
r^* &= r(1 - p_d t_d - p_i t_i - p_{cg} t_{cg}) \\
&= 0.06^*[1 - (0.30)(0.15) - (0.20)(0.35) - (0.40)(0.25)] \\
&= 0.0471 \text{ or } 4.71 \text{ percent} \\
T^* &= t_{cg}(1 - p_d - p_i - p_{cg})/(1 - p_d t_d - p_i t_i - p_{cg} t_{cg}) \\
&= t_{cg}(1 - 0.30 - 0.20 - 0.40)/[1 - (0.30)(0.15) \\
&\quad - (0.20)(0.35) - (0.40)(0.25)] \\
&= 0.0318 \\
FVIF_{Taxable} &= £1{,}000{,}000[(1 + r^*)^n(1 - T^*) + T^*] \\
&= £1{,}000{,}000[(1 + 0.0471)^{15}(1 - 0.0318) + 0.0318] \\
&= £1{,}962{,}776
\end{aligned}
$$

9. C is correct.

$$
\begin{aligned}
B &= £700{,}000/£1{,}000{,}000 = 0.70 \\
FV_{Taxable} &= £1{,}000{,}000[(1 + r^*)^n(1 - T^*) + T^* - (0.25)(1 - 0.70)] \\
&= £1{,}000{,}000[(1 + 0.0471)^{15}(1 - 0.0318) + 0.0318 - 0.075] \\
&= £1{,}887{,}776
\end{aligned}
$$

10. B is correct.

$$
\begin{aligned}
FV_{cg} &= €400{,}000[(1 + r)^n(1 - t_{cg}) + t_{cg}] \\
&= €400{,}000[(1 + 0.08)^{10}(1 - 0.20) + 0.20] \\
&= €770{,}856
\end{aligned}
$$

Solving for the rate set equates €770,856 with its present value of €400,000

$$
\begin{aligned}
€770{,}856 &= €400{,}000(1 + R_{AE})^{10} \\
R_{AE} &= 0.0678 \text{ or } 6.78 \text{ percent}
\end{aligned}
$$

11. A is correct.

$$
\begin{aligned}
r(1 - T_{AE}) &= R_{AE} \\
0.08(1 - T_{AE}) &= 0.0678 \\
T_{AE} &= 0.1525 \text{ or } 15.25 \text{ percent}
\end{aligned}
$$

12. A is correct.

$$
\begin{aligned}
FVIF_w &= [(1 + r)(1 - t_w)]^n \\
FV &= €500{,}000[(1.05)(1 - 0.005)]^{20} = €1{,}200{,}100
\end{aligned}
$$

13. A is correct. Tax-exempt assets are not appropriate for tax deferred accounts. In a Flat and Heavy Tax Regime, dividends and capital gains are taxed at ordinary rates and are not the best choices for taxable accounts.

14. A is correct. The taxable account will accumulate to

$$
\begin{aligned}
FV_i &= €50{,}000[(1 + r(1 - t_i)]^n \\
&= €50{,}000[1 + 0.04(1 - 0.4)]^{20} \\
&= €80{,}347
\end{aligned}
$$

The tax deferred account will accumulate

$$FV_{TDA} = €50,000(1 + r)^n(1 - T_n)$$
$$= €50,000(1.07)^{20}(1 - 0.40)$$
$$= €116,091$$
$$\text{Total} = €196,438$$

15. C is correct. The taxable account will accumulate to

$$FV_{cg} = €50,000[(1 + r)^n(1 - t_{cg}) + t_{cg}]$$
$$= €50,000[(1.07)^{20}(1 - 0.20) + 0.20]$$
$$= €164,787$$

The tax deferred account will accumulate

$$FV_{TDA} = €50,000(1 + r)^n(1 - T_n)$$
$$= €50,000(1.04)^{20}(1 - 0.40)$$
$$= €65,734$$
$$\text{Total} = €230,521$$

16. C is correct. The after-tax value of the TDA account is $€200,000(1 - 0.40) = €120,000$. The after-tax value of the tax-exempt account is €80,000. The total after-tax value of the portfolio is €200,000. Stock represents $€80,000/€200,000 = 40$ percent of the total, whereas bonds represent $€120,000/€200,000 = 60$ percent of the total.

17. A is correct. The future accumulation of the TDA is $(1 - 0.30)(1 + r)^n$, whereas the future accumulation of the tax-exempt account is $(1 + r)^n(1 - 0.40)$. Therefore, the TDA will accumulate more wealth.

18. C is correct. In this regime, interest would be taxed heavily and is most appropriate for a tax deferred account.

19. A is correct. Active trading would generate annually taxed income and is most appropriate for a tax-exempt account, all else equal. If a portfolio contains unrealized losses, however, a certain amount of trading activity is required to harvest tax losses. That is, tax-efficient management of stocks in taxable accounts does not require passive management. It requires passively allowing gains to grow unharvested, but actively realizing losses.

20. A is correct. DiCenzo has a $€75,000 − €50,000 = €25,000$ unrealized loss. Assuming that realizing this loss will decrease his taxable gains by the same amount, his tax bill in the current year will be reduced by $0.30 × €25,000 = €7,500$.

21. A is correct. Assuming DiCenzo does not reinvest the tax savings, tax loss harvesting does not reduce the total tax paid over time. It only defers taxes because recognizing the loss resets the cost basis to a lower figure which will ultimately increase the gain realized late by the same amount. Tax loss harvest can augment return by postponing tax liabilities. Reinvesting the current year's tax savings increases the after-tax principal investment, which can augment the value of tax loss harvesting further.

22. B is correct. Tax loss harvesting is best used when tax rates are relatively high.

ESTATE PLANNING IN A GLOBAL CONTEXT

by Stephen M. Horan, CFA and Thomas R. Robinson, CFA

LEARNING OUTCOMES

The candidate should be able to:	Mastery
a. discuss the purpose of estate planning and explain the basic concepts of domestic estate planning, including estates, wills, and probate;	☐
b. explain the two principal forms of wealth transfer taxes and discuss the impact of important non-tax issues, such as legal system, forced heirship, and marital property regime;	☐
c. determine a family's core capital and excess capital, based on mortality probabilities and Monte Carlo analysis;	☐
d. evaluate the relative after-tax value of lifetime gifts and testamentary bequests;	☐
e. explain the estate planning benefit of making lifetime gifts when gift taxes are paid by the donor, rather than the recipient;	☐
f. evaluate the after-tax benefits of basic estate planning strategies, including generation skipping, spousal exemptions, valuation discounts, and charitable gifts;	☐
g. explain the basic structure of a trust and discuss the differences between revocable and irrevocable trusts;	☐
h. explain how life insurance can be a tax-efficient means of wealth transfer;	☐
i. discuss the two principal systems (source jurisdiction and residence jurisdiction) for establishing a country's tax jurisdiction;	☐
j. discuss the possible income and estate tax consequences of foreign situated assets and foreign-sourced income;	☐
k. evaluate a client's tax liability under each of three basic methods (credit, exemption, and deduction) that a country may use to provide relief from double taxation;	☐
l. describe the impact of increasing international transparency and information exchange on international estate planning.	☐

217

1

INTRODUCTION

Estate planning is a critical component of wealth management for private clients. Translating the goals of an individual or family into effective legal and tax-efficient solutions can be a challenging task, which requires an intimate knowledge of, among other things, the tax and inheritance laws in a particular jurisdiction. The challenge is often magnified when a client has family members, assets, or income in multiple jurisdictions. Increasingly, high-net-worth individuals (HNWI) and families have these types of international interests.

Identifying the real needs of HNWI is crucial for the portfolio management and estate planning process. The issues are broad and differentiated. For example, non-taxable concerns for HNWI include succession and inheritance planning, business succession, charitable intentions, asset gathering and identification, asset protection and preservation, managing risks of divorce, "living" wills, privacy, second families, special assets like art, "toys," and more. Depending on the home country, forced heirship, political risk, kidnapping and security, and confidentiality could also be elements to consider in estate planning.

The wealth manager can add value to the advisor–client relationship by understanding salient tax and inheritance planning issues in a client's home country as well as those in other jurisdictions affecting the client's welfare. Professional tax and legal assistance is typically required to conceive, draft, and execute an estate plan or a particular solution within that plan because the field of estate planning falls largely outside the purview of the wealth manager. As such, this reading should not be considered legal advice or interpreted as a substitute for it. It is important, however, for the wealth manager to understand fundamental estate planning principles to identify issues that deserve attention and to integrate the solutions into an overall estate plan. This reading provides a framework for understanding generic tax and non-tax estate planning considerations in both a domestic and cross-border context. It also explores various approaches that different jurisdictions use to structure rules of wealth transfer.

On one hand, the complexity is daunting. On the other hand, a basic understanding of the landscape creates opportunities to develop valuable solutions to common problems. The approach developed here is valuable for several reasons. First, it can be applied in a variety of jurisdictions. The terminology used is intended to be generic and have international interpretation, but the local lexicon may vary from one jurisdiction to the next. Second, it provides an international perspective that advisors can use to counsel clients with a multi-jurisdictional footprint. Third, it provides a framework advisors can use to communicate tax and succession planning considerations to private clients and develop techniques to address the needs and objectives of such clients. Finally, inheritance laws and tax codes in many jurisdictions are fluid. They change over time as governments use them to affect social and economic objectives. The framework developed in this reading will help the advisor manage those changes and understand their impact should they occur.

DOMESTIC ESTATE PLANNING: SOME BASIC CONCEPTS

2.1 Estates, Wills, and Probate

An **estate**[1] is all of the property a person owns or controls. The property in one's estate may consist of financial assets (e.g., bank accounts, stocks, bonds, or business interests), tangible personal assets (e.g., artwork, collectibles, or vehicles), immovable property (e.g., residential real estate or timber rights), and intellectual property (e.g., royalties).

An estate might exclude, however, assets that a settlor transferred to an irrevocable trust during his or her lifetime as a gift, which would be considered an example of a lifetime gratuitous transfer, also known as an *inter vivos* gift. This is discussed in more detail below. It is important to note that the elements of an estate can differ for legal and tax purposes. For example, assets transferred to a trust may no longer be considered to be legally owned by the trust settlor, or the person giving the assets to the trust, whereby the trustee of the trust becomes the legal owner of the trust assets. The assets may be considered the settlor's assets for tax purposes, however, depending on applicable tax law and the trust structure.

Estate planning is the process of preparing for the disposition of one's estate (e.g., the transfer of property) upon death and during one's lifetime. It may involve making arrangements for other personal matters, as well, such as burial arrangements and end-of-life medical instructions should one become incapacitated. It can require the counsel of a variety of professionals including financial, legal, and taxation.

The core document most closely associated with an estate plan is a will or testament. A **will** (or testament) outlines the rights others will have over one's property after death. A testator is the person who authored the will and whose property is disposed of according to the will. **Probate** is the legal process to confirm the validity of the will so that executors, heirs, and other interested parties can rely on its authenticity. A decedent without a valid will or with a will that does not dispose of their property is considered to have died **intestate**. In that case, a court will often decide on the disposition of assets under applicable intestacy laws during the probate process.

Some individuals may wish to avoid probate. Court fees may be sizable, and the process can cause a delay in the transfer of assets to intended beneficiaries. A

---

[1] Terminology will vary from jurisdiction to jurisdiction depending upon the legal structure of the jurisdiction. The term "estate" comes from common law. Legal structures such as common law are described further.

will can be challenged, and its contents are often a matter of public record, which may concern some wealthy families as it can cause embarrassment or divulge sensitive financial information. Moreover, many problems can arise in probate when multiple jurisdictions are involved. In some instances, probate can be avoided or its impact limited by holding assets in other forms of ownership, such as joint ownership (e.g., joint tenancy with right of survivorship), living trusts, or retirement plans. Through these structures, ownership of property is transferred to beneficiaries without the need for a will and hence the probate process can be avoided or substantially reduced.

Property in an estate can be held in a variety of ways including sole ownership, joint ownership, partnership, trust, or through life insurance. Assets held in **sole ownership** are typically considered part of a decedent's estate. The transfer of their ownership is dictated by the decedent's will (or, in the absence of their disposition under the decedent's will, applicable intestacy law) through the probate process. In some jurisdictions, assets held in **joint ownership with right of survivorship** automatically transfer to the surviving joint owner or owners, as the case may be, outside the probate process. The transfer of assets held in trust and the payout of death benefit proceeds under a life insurance policy depends on the terms of the trust deed and the provisions of the life insurance contract, respectively. Trusts, life insurance, and other similar planning techniques can, therefore, transfer assets outside the probate process and can be important estate planning tools.

2.2 Legal Systems, Forced Heirship, and Marital Property Regimes

A country's legal system can affect the disposition of a will. For example, common law jurisdictions, such as the United Kingdom and the United States, generally allow a **testator** (i.e., a person who makes a will) testamentary freedom of disposition by will; that is, the right to use their own judgment regarding the rights others will have over their property after death. Most civil law countries place restrictions on such disposition.

Civil law, which is derived from Roman law, is the world's predominant legal system. In civil law states, judges apply general, abstract rules or concepts to particular cases. **Common law** systems, which usually trace their heritage to Britain, draw abstract rules from specific cases. The distinction is arguably analogous to the distinction between deductive and inductive reasoning. Put differently, in civil systems law is developed primarily through legislative statutes or executive action. In common law systems, law is developed primarily through decisions of the courts.

Countries following **Shari'a**, the law of Islam, have substantial variation, but are more like civil law systems especially in regard to estate planning. In addition to the law of the land, Muslims may wish to consider guidance on inheritance provided by Shari'a or Islamic law. Because Shari'a is often not the law of the land in most countries, including many countries where a majority of the population is Muslim, those who wish to follow Islamic guidance on inheritance are usually able to do so through the making of a will, as long as the contents of the will are not in conflict with the concerned law of the land.

Appendix A presents a comparison of non-tax issues related to estate planning for 37 jurisdictions including the legal system of each.[2] Compiled by LawIn-

---

[2] None of the referenced appendixes are included or assigned as part of the curriculum. For those interested in further study, all three appendixes have been made available online under the heading "Supplemental Materials" at www.cfainstitute.org/cfaprog/resources.

Context, Appendix A shows that 22 of the 37 jurisdictions have civil law regimes, which are common in Europe, South America, and some larger Asian countries.

The legal concept of a trust is unique to the common law. A trust is a vehicle through which an individual (called a settlor) entrusts certain assets to a trustee (or trustees) who manages the assets. Civil law countries may not recognize foreign trusts. In fact, twelve of the 22 civil law jurisdictions, including France and Germany, do not recognize trusts at all.

Ownership, like other legal principles in civil law, is a precise concept tempered by statutes that place certain limitations on the free disposition of one's assets. Under **forced heirship rules**, for example, children have the right to a fixed share of a parent's estate. This right may exist whether or not the child is estranged or conceived outside of marriage. Wealthy individuals may attempt to move assets into an offshore trust governed by a different domicile to circumvent forced heirship rules. They may alternatively attempt to reduce a forced heirship claim by gifting or donating assets to others during their lifetime to reduce the value of the final estate upon death. In a number of jurisdictions, however, "clawback" provisions bring such lifetime gifts back into the estate to calculate the child's share. If the assets remaining in the estate are not sufficient to cover the claim, the child may be able to recover his or her forced share from the donees who received the lifetime gifts.[3] Twenty-five of the 37 jurisdictions in Appendix A have forced heirship rules of some variety, creating a common estate planning consideration.

Spouses typically have similar guaranteed inheritance rights under civil law forced heirship regimes. In addition, spouses have marital property rights, which depend on the marital property regime that applies to their marriage. For example, under **community property** regimes, each spouse has an indivisible one-half interest in income earned during marriage. Gifts and inheritances received before and after marriage may still be retained as separate property. Upon death of a spouse, the property is divided with ownership of one-half of the community property automatically passing to the surviving spouse. Ownership of the other half is transferred by the will through the probate process.

In **separate property regimes**, prevalent in civil law countries, each spouse is able to own and control property as an individual, which enables each to dispose of property as they wish, subject to a spouse's other rights. Italian forced heirship rules, for example, apply to the decedent's community and separate property. It is noteworthy that, in many civil law countries, couples can elect the marital property regime that will apply to their property. The marital property regimes of each of the 37 jurisdictions are summarized in Appendix A.

EXAMPLE 1

Community Property and Forced Heirship

Philippe and Helena Berelli live in a community property regime with their two children. The community property regime entitles a surviving spouse to receive one-half of the community property after the first spouse's death. There are also forced heirship laws in their country that entitle a spouse to one-third of the total estate and the children are entitled to split one-third of the total estate. After their marriage, Philippe received an inheritance that was retained as separate property and is

---

[3] See Hayton (2003).

worth €200,000 today. The remainder of the estate is considered community property. Suppose Philippe passes away today with a total estate of €800,000 and wishes to bequeath €300,000 to his surviving mother.

1. What is the minimum that Helena should receive?
2. What is the minimum amount the children should receive under forced heirship rules?
3. May Philippe bequeath €300,000 to his mother?

Solution to 1: Helena is entitled to the greater of her share under community property or forced heirship rules. Under community property, she is entitled to receive one-half of the community property, or 0.50(€800,000 − €200,000) = €300,000. Under forced heirship rules she is entitled to one-third of the total estate, or (1/3)(€800,000) = €266,667. Therefore, Helena is entitled to €300,000.

Solution to 2: The children are collectively entitled to receive one-third of the total estate equal to €266,667, or €133,333 for each child.

Solution to 3: Philippe is able to freely dispose of the remainder, which is €800,000 − €300,000 − €266,667 = €233,333. Therefore, Philippe is unable to bequeath €300,000 to his mother, but may bequeath the remainder of €233,333.

2.3 Income, Wealth, and Wealth Transfer Taxes

An important part of estate planning is an understanding of how (or whether) assets are taxed when their ownership is transferred at or before death. In general, taxes are levied in one of four general ways:[4]

1. Tax on income
2. Tax on spending
3. Tax on wealth
4. Tax on wealth transfers

Taxes on income can be levied at different rates for a variety of income categories such as compensatory income, investment income, etc. Appendix B provides a brief description of income taxes (excluding separate capital gains tax regimes, if any), as well as wealth and gratuitous transfer taxes in 37 different jurisdictions.[5] Almost all jurisdictions in Appendix B, with the exception of the Bahamas, Cayman Islands, and the United Arab Emirates, impose income taxes.

Investment income is typically taxed in several possible ways. It can be taxed annually on either an accrual or cash basis as income or gains are received. Alternatively, tax can be deferred until the gain on an asset is ultimately recognized upon the sale or disposition of the asset. Horan and Robinson (2008) review the

---

[4] This categorization is based primarily on Wilcox, Horvitz, and diBartolomeo (2006) and Horvitz (2008), and corresponds closely with Bronson, Scanlan, and Squires (2007).

[5] See Horan and Robinson (2008) for further details on global income tax regimes including capital gains taxes.

investment tax regimes of over 50 developed economies and discuss their investment implications in detail.

Taxes on spending normally take the form of sales taxes where a tax is applied to certain types of purchases. These can be applied at the time of purchase or periodically through some computation of consumption.

Wealth-based taxes can come in several forms. A jurisdiction may levy taxes annually on the principal value of real estate, financial assets, tangible assets, etc. Tax based on one's comprehensive wealth is often referred to as **net worth tax** or **net wealth tax**. According to Appendix B, only seven of the 37 jurisdictions covered in the appendix impose such wealth taxes. The economic implications of wealth-based taxes are different from taxes on investment returns because the asset's entire capital base (less liabilities associated with the relevant asset), rather than only incremental gains, is subject to tax. These implications are discussed in greater detail elsewhere.[6]

Taxes on wealth transfers are the purview of estate planning and will be a focus of this reading.[7] The two primary forms of taxes on wealth transfers correspond to the primary ways of transferring assets: gifting assets during one's lifetime, and bequeathing assets upon one's death through a will or via some other structure.

In an estate planning context, lifetime gifts are sometimes referred to as **lifetime gratuitous transfers**, or *inter vivos* transfers, and are made during the lifetime of the donor. The term "gratuitous" refers to a transfer made with purely donative intent, that is, without expectation of anything in exchange. Gifts may or may not be taxed depending on the jurisdiction. Where gift tax applies, taxation may also depend on other factors such as the residency or domicile of the donor, the residency or domicile of the recipient, the tax status of the recipient (e.g., nonprofits), the type of asset (moveable versus immovable), and the location of the asset (domestic or foreign).

Bequeathing assets or transferring them in some other way upon one's death is referred to as a **testamentary gratuitous transfer**. The term "testamentary" refers to a transfer made after death. From a recipient's perspective, it is called an inheritance. Similar to lifetime gifts, the taxation of testamentary transfers (transfers at death) may depend upon the residency or domicile of the donor, the residency or domicile of the recipient, the type of asset (moveable versus immovable), and the location of the asset (domestic or foreign).

Taxes on wealth transfer may be applied to the transferor or the recipient. For example, in the case of testamentary gratuitous transfers, some jurisdictions impose an estate tax that is generally on the liability of the transferor (or more precisely, the estate of the transferor). Other jurisdictions impose liability for wealth transfer taxes on the recipient, often referred to as an inheritance tax.[8] These taxes may be applied at a flat rate or based on a progressive tax rate schedule, where the tax rate increases as the amount of wealth transferred increases. Often the tax is applied after the deduction of a statutory allowance. The tax rate may also depend on the relationship between transferor and recipient. Transfers to spouses, for instance, are often tax exempt.

---

[6] See, for example, Wilcox, Horvitz, and diBartolomeo (2006), Horan and Robinson (2008), Horvitz (2008).

[7] Wilcox, Horvitz, and diBartolomeo (2006) categorize estate or inheritance taxes as a wealth-based tax, but we and others (including Horvitz 2008) categorize it as a transfer tax because the ownership of inherited assets is transferred to heirs and it is this transaction that is taxed. In addition, an inheritance tax is typically levied once rather than repeatedly as is the case for most wealth-based taxes.

[8] As noted earlier, terminology differs from jurisdiction to jurisdiction, and the terms *estate tax* and *inheritance tax* are sometimes used interchangeably.

EXAMPLE 2

U.K. Inheritance Tax Example

Paul Dasani, an unmarried individual, passed away in November 2008. Dasani was a resident of London at the time of his death and had a total estate valued at £600,000. His children are the beneficiaries of the estate. The United Kingdom imposes an inheritance tax threshold on estates valued above £312,000 in 2008. The tax is payable by the trustee of the estate out of estate assets at a rate of 40 percent on the amount over the statutory allowance of £312,000.

What is the amount of inheritance tax payable?

Solution: The inheritance tax is computed as:

Estate value	£600,000
Less threshold	(£312,000)
Excess	£288,000
Rate on excess	40%
Inheritance tax	£115,200

EXAMPLE 3

Progressive Estate Tax Example

Ya-wen Chao passed away in a jurisdiction with progressive estate tax rates as provided in the table below. After all applicable exemptions, Chao had a taxable estate of €2,000,000. What is Chao's estate tax?

Taxable Estate (€)	Tax Rate (%)
Up to 600,000	2
600,001–1,500,000	4
1,500,001–3,000,000	7
3,000,001–4,500,000	11
4,500,001–6,000,000	15
6,000,001–10,000,000	20
10,000,001–15,000,000	26
15,000,001–40,000,000	33
40,000,001–100,000,000	41
Over 100,000,000	50

Solution: The estate tax is computed as:

Tax on first 600,000 (2%) =	€12,000
Tax on next 900,000 (4%) =	36,000
Tax on remaining 500,000 (7%) =	35,000
Total estate tax	€83,000

CORE CAPITAL AND EXCESS CAPITAL   3

Developing an estate plan that will sustain a family and their descendants over multiple generations is a challenging task. A mathematical reality is that the sheer number of family members has a tendency to grow exponentially from one generation to the next as members of subsequent generations propagate, often doubling from one generation to the next.

To put the problem into perspective, consider the case of a 60-year-old couple with no bequest motive; that is, no specific desire to transfer wealth to their children or beyond. One of their likely concerns is how much they can spend from their portfolio without depleting their resources before the end of their lifetimes, which probably means sustaining wealth for at least another 30 years. Estimates vary, but researchers place the sustainable spending rate between 3.5 percent and 6 percent of the initial portfolio value, assuming that spending increases by the inflation rate in subsequent years.[9] To many, these values are surprisingly modest and illustrate how easily a family can adopt a spending rate that is unsustainable, especially over a time horizon that extends beyond one generation. This challenge of sustaining wealth over multiple generations is magnified as the number of family members grows. Exacerbating the problem further is the potential erosion caused by taxes each time assets are transferred from one generation to the next.

Difficulties also arise when managing the conflicting interests within and across generations. The first generation's wealth transfer goals are often informed by the character, maturity, and circumstances of the individuals involved. In any case, the starting point in developing an estate plan is deciding how much wealth to transfer and whether to transfer wealth to future generations, philanthropic causes, or elsewhere. The answer to this question begins with an understanding of the spending needs of the first generation.

Wilcox, Horvitz, and diBartolomeo (2006) developed the notion of a life balance sheet, which is a comprehensive accounting of an investor's assets and liabilities, both explicit and implied. Explicit assets consist of financial assets (e.g., stocks and bonds), real estate, and other property that can be readily liquidated. A notable implied asset for many is the present value of one's employment capital, often referred to as **human capital** or **net employment capital**. Expected pension benefits are another implied asset that, although non-tradable, provide specific value to the investor.[10]

On the right-hand side of the life balance sheet are an investor's liabilities. Explicit liabilities, such as mortgages or margin loans, are fairly obvious entries. Less obvious are implied liabilities that represent the capitalized value of the investor's desired spending goals. These goals may include providing for a secure retirement, funding children's education, providing a safety reserve for emergencies, or earmarking seed capital for business ventures. The amount of capital required to fund spending to maintain a given lifestyle, fund these goals, and provide adequate reserves for unexpected commitments is called **core capital**.

An investor with more assets than liabilities on the life balance sheet has more capital than is necessary to fund their lifestyle and reserves and therefore has **excess capital** that can be safely transferred to others without jeopardizing the investor's lifestyle.[11] Exhibit 1 presents a hypothetical life balance sheet with

---

[9] See, for example, Bengen (1994, 1996, 1997), Guyton (2004), Milevsky and Robinson (2005), Spitzer and Singh (2006), Spitzer, Strieter, and Singh (2007), Stout and Mitchell (2007).

[10] Wilcox, Horvitz, and diBartolomeo (2006) and Ibbotson, Milevsky, Chen, and Zhu (2006) discuss human capital and its relation to life cycle planning in more detail.

[11] Wilcox, Horvitz, and diBartolomeo (2006) refer to this excess capital as "discretionary wealth."

assets listed on the left-hand side. Notice that the capitalized value of the investor's college funding obligations, retirement spending, and safety reserve, is represented by the implied liabilities on the right-hand side of the hypothetical balance sheet.

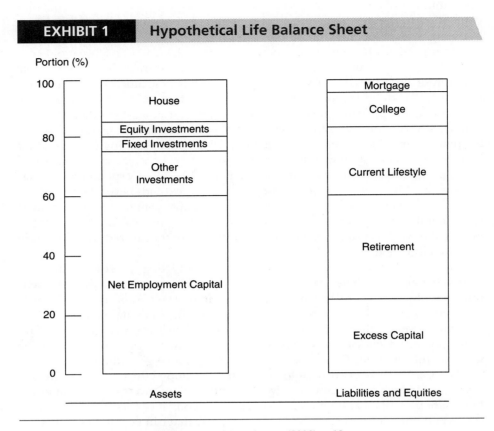

EXHIBIT 1   **Hypothetical Life Balance Sheet**

Source: Adapted from Wilcox, Horvitz, and diBartolomeo (2006), p.18.

3.1 Estimating Core Capital with Mortality Tables

The amount of core capital needed to maintain an investor's lifestyle in a proba-bilistic sense can be estimated in a number of ways. First, it is important to incor-porate the effects of inflation, particularly over long time horizons. One can either forecast nominal spending needs discounting them to the present values using nominal discount rates, or forecast real spending needs discounting them using real discount rates. The two approaches are indistinguishable.

The most straightforward way of calculating core capital is to calculate the present value of anticipated spending over one's remaining life expectancy. One problem with this approach is that, by definition, an investor has a significant probability of living past their remaining life expectancy because life expectancy is an average that has substantial variation. Estimates of core capital based on life expectancy will fall short of what is actually required in a great many cases.[12]

---

[12] See Wilcox (2008) for a more thorough discussion.

Another approach is to calculate expected future cash flows by multiplying each future cash flow needed by the probability that such cash flow will be needed, or **survival probability**. When more than one person is relying on core capital (e.g., two spouses), the probability of survival in a given year is a joint probability that either the husband or the wife survives. Specifically, the probability that either the husband or the wife survives equals:

$$p(\text{Survival}) = p(\text{Husband survives}) + p(\text{Wife survives}) \\ - p(\text{Husband survives}) \times p(\text{Wife survives}) \tag{1}$$

assuming their chances of survival are independent of each other. The present value of the spending need is then equal to:

$$PV(\text{Spending need}) = \sum_{j=1}^{N} \frac{p(\text{Survival}_j) \times \text{Spending}_j}{(1 + r)^j} \tag{2}$$

The numerator is the expected cash flow in year j, that is, the probability of surviving until that year times the spending in that year should the person survive.

For example, consider Ernest and Beatrice Webster, ages 79 and 68, respectively. Their individual probabilities of survival are shown in Columns 3 and 5 of Exhibit 2. Over the next year, Ernest has approximately a 93.6 percent chance of survival, while the younger Beatrice has a 98.3 percent chance of survival.[13] The chance of either one of them surviving, however, is greater than either of their individual probabilities of survival. Specifically, the combined probability that either or both survive for the first year is $0.9989 = 0.9355 + 0.9831 - 0.9355 \times 0.9831$. This figure is represented in Column 6.

The Websters' inflation adjusted annual spending needs are calculated based on their current spending of €500,000 per year and are increased annually using a 3 percent real growth rate (that is, 3 percent annual spending growth after inflation). The Websters' *expected* spending need each year is presented in the column labeled *Expected Spending* (Column 8). It is calculated as the product of their joint survival probability and their required spending for that year (*Annual Spending*, Column 7). Each year's expected spending is discounted back to the present, using in this case a real risk-free discount rate of 2.0 percent. The sum of each year's present value of expected spending represents the investor's core capital. In this case, Ernest and Beatrice Webster have core capital spending needs of about €9,176,955.[14]

This approach can be modified by conditioning each year's spending based on each spouse's expected survival. For example, if Ernest were to pass away, Beatrice's independent spending needs may be lower than what would have been required if Ernest were also alive. Alternatively, her spending need could be higher. Estimates vary and would certainly be affected by individual circumstances, but some economists estimate that two people can maintain the same living standard for 1.6 times the cost of one. Using this estimate, Beatrice could

---

[13] It is worth noting that survival probabilities change each year. They are conditioned on one surviving until a particular age. For example, Ernest is currently 79 years old and has an 87.02% chance of surviving two more years until age 81. Moving forward one year, if Ernest survives until age 80, his chances of surviving until age 81 increase because he has already made some progress in that direction. Therefore, the probabilities change from one year to the next and will warrant updating.

[14] A more conservative approach is assuming that both Ernest and Beatrice survive throughout the forecast horizon provided, rather than assigning probabilities to their combined survival each year.

EXHIBIT 2					Example of Core Capital Calculation for Ernest and Beatrice Webster			
	Ernest		Beatrice		Combined	Annual	Expected	Discounted
Year (1)	Age (2)	p(Survival) (3)	Age (4)	p(Survival) (5)	p(Survival) (6)	Spending (7)	Spending (8)	Value (9)
1	80	0.9355	69	0.9831	0.9989	500,000	499,457	489,664
2	81	0.8702	70	0.9649	0.9954	515,000	512,654	492,747
3	82	0.8038	71	0.9457	0.9893	530,450	524,800	494,531
4	83	0.7339	72	0.9249	0.9800	546,364	535,443	494,666
5	84	0.6686	73	0.9025	0.9677	562,754	544,581	493,244
6	85	0.6001	74	0.8785	0.9514	579,637	551,476	489,695
7	86	0.5327	75	0.8526	0.9311	597,026	555,893	483,938
8	87	0.4674	76	0.8252	0.9069	614,937	557,682	475,976
9	88	0.4048	77	0.7958	0.8785	633,385	556,412	465,580
10	89	0.3459	78	0.7646	0.8460	652,387	551,947	452,789
11	90	0.2912	79	0.7311	0.8094	671,958	543,909	437,446
12	91	0.2414	80	0.6952	0.7688	692,117	532,095	419,553
13	92	0.1968	81	0.6582	0.7254	712,880	517,156	399,778
14	93	0.1576	82	0.6173	0.6776	734,267	497,573	377,098
15	94	0.1239	83	0.5775	0.6298	756,295	476,345	353,931
16	95	0.0955	84	0.5340	0.5785	778,984	450,638	328,265
17	96	0.0720	85	0.4894	0.5262	802,353	422,165	301,494
18	97	0.0532	86	0.4441	0.4736	826,424	391,431	274,064
19	98	0.0373	87	0.3987	0.4211	851,217	358,456	246,055
20	99	0.0262	88	0.3538	0.3707	876,753	325,053	218,751
21	100	0.0180	89	0.3100	0.3224	903,056	291,161	192,101
22	101	0.0000	90	0.2679	0.2679	930,147	249,204	161,195
23	102	0.0000	91	0.2281	0.2281	958,052	218,569	138,607
24	103	0.0000	92	0.1912	0.1912	986,793	188,652	117,289
25	104	0.0000	93	0.1575	0.1575	1,016,397	160,043	97,551
26	105	0.0000	94	0.1273	0.1273	1,046,889	133,275	79,643
27	106	0.0000	95	0.1009	0.1009	1,078,296	108,795	63,739
28	107	0.0000	96	0.0783	0.0783	1,110,645	86,937	49,935
29	108	0.0000	97	0.0594	0.0594	1,143,964	67,905	38,238
30	109	0.0000	98	0.0439	0.0439	1,178,283	51,764	28,578
31	110	0.0000	99	0.0317	0.0317	1,213,631	38,452	20,812
32	111	0.0000	100	0.0000	0.0000	1,250,040	—	—
							Total	9,176,955

maintain the same lifestyle with $1/1.6$ (or 62.5%) of the amount of spending if Ernest passed away.

In this approach, spending needs are discounted using the real risk-free rate to match the risk of the cash flows. To be sure, the cash flows are not without risk but their uncertainty is most likely unrelated to market risk factors that would be priced in a normal asset pricing model, making their beta equal to zero. One may argue that, although mortality risk in this context is non-systematic, it is also non-diversifiable. However, mortality risk can be hedged with traditional life insurance allowing the individual to eliminate the non-systematic risk even if it is non-diversifiable. Therefore, discounting spending needs with the risk-free rate is appropriate.

It is tempting to discount spending needs using the expected return of the assets used to fund them. This would be problematic because the risk of the Websters' spending needs is fundamentally unrelated to the risk of the portfolio used to fund those needs. Merton (2007) draws this distinction in the context of a defined-benefit pension plan. He points out that using the expected return of pension fund assets to discount the liabilities they are intended to fund systematically under-prices those liabilities, and has contributed to the decline of defined-benefit pension plans. Another approach using Monte Carlo simulation with expected returns and volatility is discussed below.

3.1.1 Safety Reserve

This approach does not, however, fully account for the risk inherent in capital markets. For example, there is no guarantee that capital markets will produce returns greater than the risk-free rate even over long periods of time. Therefore, the present value of the Websters' spending needs underestimates their true core capital needs. One way to adjust for this underestimation is to augment core capital with a safety reserve designed to incorporate flexibility into the estate plan.[15] Incorporating flexibility in this way can be important for at least two reasons. First, it provides a capital cushion if capital markets produce a sequence of unusually poor returns that jeopardize the sustainability of the planned spending program. Second, it allows the first generation to increase their spending beyond that explicitly articulated in the spending program. In this way, the safety reserve addresses not only the uncertainty of capital markets, but the uncertainty associated with a family's future commitments.

The size of the safety reserve can be based on a subjective assessment of the circumstances. For example, Evensky (1997) advocates a safety reserve equal to two years of spending. His reasons are behavioral as well as practical. The reserve

---

EXAMPLE 4

Core Capital with Mortality Probabilities

Kenroy and Alicia Trudeau live in South Africa and are 64 and 61 years old, respectively. Their survival probabilities based on their current ages are listed in the table below. They would like to maintain annual spending of ZAR 1,000,000 on an inflation-adjusted basis. Inflation is expected to be 3 percent, and the nominal risk-free rate is 5 percent.

---

[15] Wilcox (2008) proposes a more complex solution that accounts for the joint distribution of uncertain life spans and asset returns and that produces even more conservative estimates of core capital.

	Kenroy		Alicia	
Year	Age	p(Survival)	Age	p(Survival)
1	65	0.991	62	0.996
2	66	0.981	63	0.986
3	67	0.971	64	0.976

1. What is the probability that either Kenroy or Alicia will survive in each of the next three years?

2. What is the capitalized value of their core capital spending needs over the next three years?

Solution to 1: The probability that either Kenroy or Alicia will survive is equal to the sum of their individual probabilities less the product of their individual probabilities.

$$p(\text{Joint survival}) = p(\text{Kenroy survives}) + p(\text{Alicia survives})$$
$$- p(\text{Kenroy survives})\,p(\text{Alicia survives})$$

For the next three years, the joint probability of survival is:

Year	Joint p(Survival)
1	0.9999
2	0.9997
3	0.9993

Solution to 2: The capitalized value of their core capital spending needs equals the product of the joint probability of survival and the real spending need for each year discounted using the real risk-free rate. Alternatively, one may discount the nominal expected cash flow at the nominal risk-free rate. Using the first approach, the real cash flows will remain constant and be discounted at 2 percent (or 5 percent less 3 percent).[16]

Year	Annual Spending	Expected Spending	Discounted Value
1	1,000,000	999,960	980,360
2	1,000,000	999,730	960,910
3	1,000,000	999,300	941,670
			2,882,940

---

[16] Two percent is an approximation. A more precise calculation is: $(1.05/1.03) - 1 = 1.94\%$.

provides a psychological buffer between an investor and the volatility of capital markets. The investor perceives that their spending needs are unaffected by short-term capital market volatility and is better able to adhere to a particular investment strategy during turbulent markets.

3.2 Estimating Core Capital with Monte Carlo Analysis

Another approach to estimating core capital uses Monte Carlo analysis, a computer-based simulation technique that allows the analyst to forecast a range of possible outcomes based on, say, 10,000 simulated trials.[17] Rather than discounting future expenses, this approach estimates the size of a portfolio needed to generate sufficient withdrawals to meet expenses, which are assumed to increase with inflation. This approach more fully captures the risk inherent in capital markets than the mortality table approach described above. For example, one could forecast a particular path of portfolio values based on a hypothetical sequence of returns that conforms to the statistical properties associated with the portfolio's expected return. That particular path is one of an infinite set of possible outcomes. The analyst can then forecast another path based on the same set of statistical properties, which will lead to a different outcome. Repeating this procedure thousands of times provides a range of possible outcomes and an understanding of the risk of the portfolio.

One can incorporate recurring spending needs, irregular liquidity needs, taxes, inflation, and other factors into the analysis. In the context of calculating core capital, the wealth manager might estimate the amount of capital required to sustain a pattern of spending over a particular time horizon with, for example, a 95 percent level of confidence. That is, the analyst determines the core capital that sustains spending in at least 95 percent of the simulated trials. A higher level of confidence leads to larger estimates of core capital, and vice versa. The safety reserve may also be added to accommodate flexibility in the first generation's spending patterns. It need not be quite as large as that used in the mortality table method, however, because Monte Carlo analysis already captures the risk of producing a sequence of anomalously poor returns. In contrast to the mortality table method in which cash flows are discounted at the risk-free rate of return, the expected returns used in Monte Carlo analysis are derived from the market expectations of the assets comprising the portfolio.

Milevsky and Robinson (2005) developed a method to calculate sustainable spending rates that approximate those produced from a Monte Carlo simulation but without the need for simulation. Their analysis incorporates life-span uncertainty as well as financial market risk. Exhibit 3 presents an example of ruin probabilities (i.e., the probability of depleting one's financial assets before death) based on their analysis. For example, consider Mr. Harper, a single 65-year-old with the same €500,000 annual spending need as the Websters. He is willing to accept a nine percent chance that his spending pattern may exhaust his portfolio before the end of his life (e.g., 91 percent level of confidence). This represents the probability of ruin, or the probability that his spending is unsustainable.

---

[17] See Sharpe, Chen, Pinto, and McLeavey (2007) for a more detailed discussion of its applications within the context of a retirement portfolio. In addition, Bernstein (2008) presents Monte Carlo analysis in the larger context of estate planning.

EXHIBIT 3   Ruin Probability for Balanced Portfolio of 50 Percent Equity and 50 Percent Bonds

Retirement Age	Median Age at Death	Hazard Rate, λ (%)	Real Annual Spending per $100 of Initial Nest Egg									
			$2.00 (%)	$3.00 (%)	$4.00 (%)	$5.00 (%)	$6.00 (%)	$7.00 (%)	$8.00 (%)	$9.00 (%)	$10.00 (%)
Endowment	Infinity	0.00	6.7	24.9	49.0	70.0	84.3	92.5	96.6	98.6	99.4
50	78.1	2.47	1.8	6.4	14.0	24.0	35.2	46.3	56.8	66.0	73.8
55	83.0	2.48	1.8	6.3	14.0	24.0	35.1	46.2	56.7	65.9	73.7
60	83.4	2.96	1.5	5.2	11.6	20.1	29.9	40.1	50.0	59.1	67.2
65	83.9	3.67	1.1	4.0	9.0	15.8	24.0	32.8	41.8	50.5	58.5
70	84.6	4.75	0.8	2.8	6.3	11.4	17.6	24.7	32.2	39.8	47.2
75	85.7	6.48	0.5	1.7	3.9	7.2	11.4	16.3	21.9	27.8	33.9
80	87.4	9.37	0.3	0.9	2.0	3.8	6.2	9.1	12.5	16.3	20.5

Note: Mean arithmetic portfolio return = 5 percent; standard deviation of return = 12 percent; mean geometric portfolio return = 4.28 percent.

Source: Milevsky and Robinson (2005).

This analysis assumes the balanced portfolio has a mean arithmetic return of 5 percent and volatility of 12 percent. It also assumes that the spending rate is determined by the initial portfolio value and increased by the rate of inflation annually thereafter. Under these conditions, Mr. Harper can spend €4.00 for each €100 of core capital, or 4 percent of capital. The core capital required for Mr. Harper to spend €500,000 per year is therefore €12,500,000 = €500,000/0.04. If he is willing to accept a higher probability of failure, Mr. Harper will need less capital. For example, a 15.8 percent chance of Mr. Harper's spending outlasting his portfolio allows him to spend €5.00 for every €100, which requires only €10,000,000, or €500,000/0.05, of core capital.

Asset allocation affects the expected return and volatility of the portfolio, which in turn affects the sustainability of a given spending rate. Obviously, higher return improves sustainability and would require less core capital to generate the same level of spending. Volatility must also be considered, however, because it decreases the sustainability of a spending program for at least two reasons. First, even in the absence of a spending rule, volatility decreases future accumulations. This concept can be illustrated by noting that future accumulations per unit of currency are equal to the product of one plus the geometric average return, or:

$$\text{FV} = (1 + R_G)^N = \prod_{n=1}^{N} (1 + R_n)$$
$$= (1 + R_1)(1 + R_2)(1 + R_3)...(1 + R_N) \qquad \textbf{(3)}$$

where R_G is the geometric average return over period N. It is commonly referred to as the compounded return. The geometric average return is related to the arithmetic average return and its volatility in the following way:

$$R_G \cong r - \frac{1}{2}\sigma, \qquad \textbf{(4)}$$

where r is the arithmetic average return and σ is the volatility of the arithmetic return. According to Equation 4, higher volatility decreases the geometric average return and hence future accumulations, which in turn decreases sustainability. Another way to illustrate this point is to consider a €100 portfolio that experiences sequential returns of +50 percent followed by –50 percent. Although the arithmetic average of those returns is zero, the portfolio's value after two years is only €75. The €25 decline in value is due to the volatility of returns represented by the second term in Equation 4.

The second reason volatility decreases sustainability relates to the interaction of periodic withdrawals and return sequences. Equation 3 shows that future accumulations do not depend on the sequence of returns in the absence of periodic spending withdrawals. That is, the future value calculation is unchanged regardless of whether R_1 and R_2 (or any other two periodic returns) are reversed. Put differently, in the example of +50 percent and –50 percent returns, the ending value after two years is the same regardless of whether the portfolio returns are sequenced with the positive return first or last.

This independence disappears when withdrawals are introduced. Specifically, the sustainability of a portfolio is severely compromised when the initial returns are poor because a portion of the portfolio is being liquidated at relatively depressed values, making less capital available for compounding at potentially higher subsequent returns. If the portfolio in our example were to experience a €10 withdrawal at the end of each year, the portfolio would be worth €60 at the end of two years if the positive return occurs first but only €50 if the negative return occurs first. A fixed withdrawal program can be thought of as the opposite of dollar-cost averaging in which volatility has a positive effect on future accumulations, holding the expected return constant.

Several authors have examined the return-volatility trade-off on portfolio sustainability in the context of asset allocation. Diversification is particularly useful in this context because it reduces volatility without necessarily decreasing return. Not surprisingly, recommendations vary; but equity allocations between 30 percent and 75 percent of total portfolio value seem to maximize portfolio sustainability.

EXAMPLE 5

Core Capital with Monte Carlo Analysis

Sophie Zang is a recent widow, 55-years old, living in Singapore. Upon his passing, her husband's estate and life insurance proceeds provided a total of SGD 2,000,000 to maintain her lifestyle. With no children, Zang has no bequest motives but she has established a charitable remainder trust (CRT) upon which she will rely to maintain her lifestyle in real terms for the rest of her life, with the balance going to her favorite charity upon her death. Assume the trust's asset allocation conforms to the capital market expectations from Exhibit 3.

1. How much can Zang withdraw from the CRT if she wants to be at least 98 percent certain that the portfolio will last for the remainder of her life?

2. How much can Zang withdraw from the CRT if she is willing to be only 94 percent certain that the portfolio will last for the remainder of her life?

Solution to 1: The 55-year old retirement age row in Exhibit 3 indicates that Zang's median age at death is approximately 83 years old, or 28 years away. However, she is as likely to live longer than age 83 as she is to die prior to age 83. To be at least 98 percent certain that she does not run out of money, Zang's maximum probability of exhausting her assets should not exceed 2 percent. A spending rate of $2 per $100 of assets has a ruin probability of 1.8 percent. So Zang can withdraw approximately $0.02 \times$ SGD 2,000,000 = SGD 40,000 with 98% certainty that the portfolio will last for the remainder of her life.

Solution to 2: If Zang can tolerate a 6 percent failure rate, then she can withdraw almost three percent from the CRT annually on an inflation-adjusted basis, or $0.03 \times$ SGD 2,000,000 = SGD 60,000, according to Exhibit 3. A spending rate of SGD 3 per SDG 100 of assets has a ruin probability of 6.3 percent, which is very close to the stated failure rate of 6 percent.

TRANSFERRING EXCESS CAPITAL

The first generation's core capital implicitly determines their discretionary wealth, or excess capital, which equals their assets less their core capital. For example, if the Websters have €20,000,000 of capital to meet their spending and discretionary needs and their core capital is €9,200,000, then excess capital is €10,800,000. The challenge then becomes developing a plan to transfer this wealth that matches the Websters' goals (e.g., family, philanthropy), accounts for the tax implications, and provides the desired amount of control and flexibility. As Bronson, Scanlan, and Squires (2007) point out, "The possible legal structures for a wealth transfer are necessarily country specific. Timing of wealth transfers, however, involves the more universal principles of tax avoidance, tax deferral, and maximized compound return."

4.1 Lifetime Gifts and Testamentary Bequests

An obvious method of transferring discretionary wealth is to donate it immediately or during one's lifetime through a series of gratuitous transfers. In jurisdictions having an estate or inheritance tax, gifting has the advantage of lowering the value of the taxable estate, thereby lowering estate or inheritance taxes (except where under applicable law the value of the gift is added back to the estate for estate or inheritance tax purposes). To mitigate this tax minimization strategy, jurisdictions that impose estate or inheritance tax typically also impose gift or donation taxes.

4.1.1 Tax-Free Gifts

Some gifts can escape transfer tax by falling below periodic or lifetime allowances. South Africa, for example, allows taxpayers to make tax-free gifts of up to ZAR 100,000 per tax year. During their lifetime, U.K. taxpayers may make gifts up to £312,000 that escape inheritance tax. Germany has gift allowances for gifts to close family members. Each parent may make a €205,000 gift to a child (€410,000 total from both parents) every 10 years, allowing a substantial amount of wealth to be transferred over time.

Other exclusions or relief may apply, as well. In France, for instance, a 50 percent relief applies to gifts from donors less than 70 years old, and a 30 percent relief applies if the donor is between 70 and 80 years old.[18] It is therefore common to be able to transfer some assets by gift in a tax-efficient manner.

Even in jurisdictions with relatively small annual exclusions, a gifting program that is started early and implemented over long periods of time can transfer substantial wealth in a tax efficient manner. In the United States, for example, a donor's annual gift exclusions are currently limited to US$13,000 per year (for 2009), per donee (e.g., a parent may annually transfer US$13,000 to each child or US$26,000 from both parents). Exhibit 4 shows that an annual gifting program of transferring US$13,000 per year tax free implemented over a 30-year period transfers over US$640,000 inflation-adjusted dollars at an eight percent nominal return that is taxed at 25 percent annually with a 2.5 percent inflation rate (i.e., five and a half percent real rate of return).[19] The dashed line

---

[18] LawInContext Private Banking Helpdesk.

[19] Five and a half percent is an approximation. A more precise calculation is $1.08/1.025 - 1 = 5.36\%$.

in Exhibit 4 represents the accumulated value of the gifts themselves, excluding investment returns. After 30 years, gifts total US$390,000 = US$13,000 × 30. If the donor had kept this amount, any future appreciation would have increased the value in his estate and hence the estate tax liability. Assuming an eight percent nominal pretax return that is subject to a 25 percent annual tax would add an additional US$305,000 of real appreciation (after adjusting for inflation), for a total value of US$695,000. A tax-efficient investment strategy that defers the 25 percent tax until the end of the investment horizon increases the accumulated sum to almost US$843,000. Because these figures are based on real inflation-adjusted returns, this sum represents the amount of capital that can be transferred in today's dollars, and can therefore be a sizable proportion of many estates. Obviously, the amount of real wealth that can be transferred without tax increases with the rate of real return and the time horizon.

The benefit of this strategy is that appreciation on gifted assets is effectively transferred to the donee without gift or estate tax. Importantly, appreciation on the gifted asset is likely still subject to tax on investment returns (e.g., dividends and capital gains) whether it remains in the donor's estate or is transferred to a donee. But if the tax-free gift had not been made and had remained in the estate, the appreciation on it would have been subject to estate or inheritance tax.

In general, the relative after-tax value of a tax-free gift made during one's lifetime compared to a bequest that is transferred as part of a taxable estate is

$$RV_{TaxFreeGift} = \frac{FV_{Gift}}{FV_{Bequest}} = \frac{[1 + r_g(1 - t_{ig})]^n}{[1 + r_e(1 - t_{ie})]^n(1 - T_e)} \tag{5}$$

EXHIBIT 4   Inflation-Adjusted Wealth Transferred

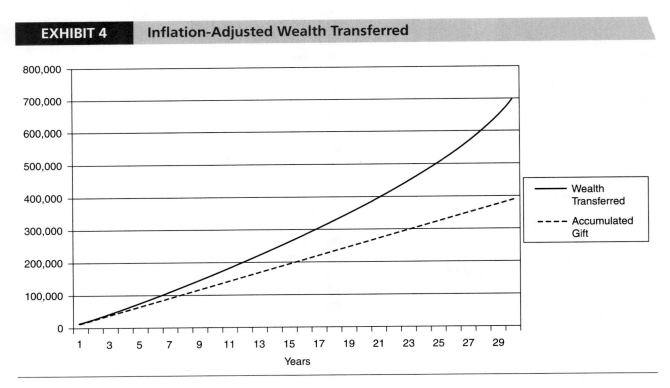

Note: Assumes a constant 5 percent real return.

where T_e is the estate tax if the asset is bequeathed at death; r_g and r_e are pretax returns to the gift recipient and the estate making the gift; t_{ig} and t_{ie} are the effective tax rates on investment returns on both the gift recipient and the estate making the gift; and n is the expected time until the donor's death at which point the asset would transfer and be subject to estate tax if it had not been gifted. The numerator is the future after-tax value of the tax-free gift. The denominator is the future after-tax value of a taxable transfer by bequest. The ratio is the relative value of making the tax-free gift compared to the bequest.

If the pretax return and effective tax rates are equal for both the recipient and donor, the relative value of the tax-free gift in Equation 5 simply reduces to $1/(1 - T_e)$. For example, consider the value of a €10,000 bequest in today's value subject to a 40 percent inheritance tax, netting €6,000 after tax. If the wealth is instead transferred as a tax-free gift without having to pay the 40 percent inheritance tax, the relative value of the tax-free gift is 1.67 times [i.e., $1/(1 - 0.40)$] as great as the taxable bequest, or €10,000 versus €6,000.

In the case of annual exclusions or allowances, individuals have the opportunity to transfer wealth without taxes each year. If these allowances or exclusions expire at the end of a tax year and do not accumulate over time, tax-free gifts not made in a particular tax year are lost opportunities to capture this value. It is, therefore, often beneficial for a family with wealth transfer goals to commence an early gifting program, which takes advantage of annual exclusions, where applicable.

4.1.2 Taxable Gifts

Opportunities to add value may even exist when a lifetime gift is taxable. In general, the value of making taxable gifts rather than leaving them in the estate to be taxed as a bequest, can be expressed as ratio of the after-tax future value of the gift and the bequest, or:

$$RV_{TaxableGift} = \frac{FV_{Gift}}{FV_{Bequest}} = \frac{[1 + r_g(1 - t_{ig})]^n(1 - T_g)}{[1 + r_e(1 - t_{ie})]^n(1 - T_e)} \tag{6}$$

where T_g is the tax rate applicable to gifts. It is important to note that this model assumes that the gift tax is paid by the recipient rather than the donor. We consider the alternative below.

If the after-tax returns associated with the gift and the asset to be bequeathed are identical, then the value of a taxable gift reduces to $(1 - T_g)/(1 - T_e)$. If the gift tax rate is less than the estate rate, gifting can still be tax efficient. For example, according to Appendix B, lifetime gratuitous transfers over £312,000 in the United Kingdom are taxed at 20 percent, while testamentary gratuitous transfers over £312,000 are taxed at 40 percent. The relative value of each pound of lifetime gift compared to each pound of bequest is therefore $1.33 = (1 - 0.20)/(1 - 0.40)$. Australia is another example in which the tax consequence of lifetime gifts can be less than the tax consequence of a testamentary bequest.

Opportunities to create value may even exist when the gift and estate tax rates are equal. As an illustration, in the Netherlands lifetime gifts and bequests are subject to the same progressive tax rate schedule, with tax rates ranging from 5 percent for smaller gifts to 68 percent for larger gifts (see Appendix B). Transferring wealth in smaller portions during one's lifetime, rather than transferring wealth in one large transaction when the owner dies, subjects each small transfer to a lower tax rate than one large transfer. Note that some jurisdictions, such as the United States, require a cumulative lifetime gift and estate tax computation that eliminates this benefit.

It is commonly believed that currently gifting assets that are expected to appreciate rather than bequeathing them later is more tax efficient because the future tax liability will be greater at death. If the donee pays the gratuitous transfer tax, however, the present value of the future inheritance tax obligation equals the gift tax. This balance of consideration changes if the donor pays tax, which is discussed in the next section. Similarly, many believe that transferring highly appreciating assets during one's lifetime and bequeathing lower return assets reduces transfer taxes. A valid comparison of the gift versus the bequest, however, requires the risk (and hence return) of the two to be held constant unless the high return asset is somehow valued below its intrinsic value, such as a valuation discount discussed later.

Alternatively, if a wealth manager is able to manage a family portfolio in the aggregate, and considers a family's overall asset allocation without being limited by constraints that dictate which types of assets must be held by which generation, then he or she may be able to place assets tax efficiently. If the return on the transferred assets will be taxed at a lower rate than if the assets were retained in the estate, the aggregate family portfolio can benefit because the numerator in Equation 6 will be greater than the denominator.

For example, consider a Japanese family contemplating a JPY 30 million lifetime gratuitous transfer in 2009. According to Appendix B, JPY 18 million can be transferred free of tax, but the remaining JPY 12 million transfer is subject to a 50 percent tax rate. The same 50 percent rate applies if the gift is delayed and transferred as a bequest, so no tax advantage related to transfer tax rates exists. However, if the recipient of the JPY 12 million gift had a lower marginal tax rate on investment returns (perhaps due to a progressive income tax schedule) of, say, 20 percent compared to the estate's marginal tax rate of, say, 50 percent, the gift can still create a tax advantage. Over a ten year horizon, the advantage for locating an asset with an eight percent pretax return with the donee rather than the donor would be equal to:

$$RV_{TaxableGift} = \frac{FV_{Gift}}{FV_{Bequest}} = \frac{[1 + 0.08(1 - 0.20)]^{10}(1 - 0.50)}{[1 + 0.08(1 - 0.50)]^{10}(1 - 0.50)} = \frac{0.9298}{0.7401} = 1.256$$

That is, the lower 20 percent tax rate associated with the gift recipient will create 25.6 percent more wealth in 10 years than if the asset had remained in the estate and been taxed at 50 percent annually for 10 years.

Another common strategy for wealth managers managing an aggregate family portfolio is to gift assets with higher expected returns to the second generation or, in general, position assets with higher expected returns in the portfolios of the second generation, leaving the first generation to hold assets with lower expected returns. The additional expected growth of their assets escapes estate tax when the older generation passes on. Of course, assets with higher expected returns generally have higher return volatility, as well, so there is no guarantee that the second generation's portfolio will necessarily experience greater growth. But the strategy may nonetheless produce a better after-tax result on average.

Conceptually, the family portfolio can be balanced whether higher return/risk assets are held in second generation or first generation accounts. The wealth manager may need to make an adjustment, however, to ensure the after-tax risk is comparable between the two options. For example, consider a family with €4,000,000. €3,000,000 is held by the first generation (which is subject to a 40% estate tax) and €1,000,000 is held by the second generation (which will escape estate tax). Suppose further that the second generation holds bonds and the first generation holds equity as illustrated in Panel A of Exhibit 5.

EXHIBIT 5	Simple Example of After-Tax Asset Allocation					
Account Type	Estate Tax Rate (%)	Asset Class	Pretax Market Value	Pretax Weights (%)	After-Tax Market Value	After-Tax Weights (%)
Panel A: Bonds with Second Generation						
First Generation	40	Equity	€3,000,000	75	€1,800,000	64.3
Second Generation	0	Bonds	1,000,000	25	1,000,000	35.7
Total Portfolio			€4,000,000	100	€2,800,000	100
Panel B: Bonds with First Generation						
First Generation	40	Bonds	€1,000,000	25	€600,000	21.4
First Generation	40	Equity	2,000,000	50	1,200,000	42.9
Second Generation	0	Equity	1,000,000	25	1,000,000	35.7
Total Portfolio			€4,000,000	100	€2,800,000	100
Panel C: Bonds with First Generation and Asset Allocation Adjustment						
First Generation	40	Bonds	€1,666,667	41.7	€1,000,000	35.7
First Generation	40	Equity	1,333,333	33.3	800,000	28.6
Second Generation	0	Equity	1,000,000	25	1,000,000	35.7
Total Portfolio			€4,000,000	100	€2,800,000	100

A traditional view of asset allocation based on pretax values suggests the family has €4,000,000 of assets, 75 percent of which are allocated in stocks and 25 percent of which are allocated in bonds. In after-tax terms, however, the first generation's portfolio has a built-in tax liability of €1,200,000 because it will ultimately be subject to 40 percent tax. Therefore, the family portfolio is really only worth €2,800,000 after estate taxes. Moreover, the after-tax equity allocation is only 64.3 percent rather than 75 percent.[20]

Suppose the adviser were to locate equity with a higher expected return in the second generation portfolio so that its greater expected future growth escapes estate tax. The asset allocation may be unaffected based on pretax market values, but the after-tax asset allocation changes. For example, consider placing the €1,000,000 of bonds in the first generation portfolio as in Panel B of Exhibit 5. The pretax asset allocation is still 75 percent equity and 25 percent bonds. However, the after-tax asset equity allocation has increased from 64.3 percent to 78.6 percent because the estate tax decreases the bonds' after-tax value.

To hold the after-tax asset allocation constant, the wealth manager would increase the bond exposure until the after-tax asset allocation returns to its previous level. In this case, the family requires an additional €400,000/(1 − 0.40) = €666,667 of pretax bond exposure.

Long-term after-tax asset allocation is difficult to apply in countries such as France and Germany that regularly modify tax rates, rules, and entities.

---

[20] Horan and Robinson (2008), Reichenstein (1998, 2001, 2006, 2007), and Horan (2007a,b) develop the concept of after-tax asset allocation in more detail.

4.1.3 Location of the Gift Tax Liability

The preceding discussion implicitly assumes that the tax liability associated with the lifetime gratuitous transfer in the numerator of Equation 6 is borne by the recipient. According to Appendix B, examples of jurisdictions that impose gift tax on the recipient include Colombia, Cyprus, Czech Republic, France, Germany, Italy, Japan, Netherlands, Russia, and Spain.

Other jurisdictions, such as Brazil, South Africa, and Switzerland, impose the tax liability on the donor. The distinction can be important for several reasons. First, a cross-border gift could result in both the donor and the recipient being taxed in their respective home countries. Second, if the tax liability is imposed on the donor's taxable estate rather than on the recipient, the tax benefit of the lifetime gift versus the bequest increases. Paying the tax liability from the donor's taxable estate decreases the size of the taxable estate and hence the ultimate estate tax (assuming the recipient's estate will either not be taxed or taxed at a lower rate). Gifting therefore becomes more attractive from a tax perspective when the gift tax is paid by the donor. The relative after-tax value of the gift when the donor pays gift tax and when the recipient's estate will not be taxable (assuming $r_g = r_e$ and $t_{ig} = t_{ie}$) is:

$$RV_{TaxableGift} = \frac{FV_{Gift}}{FV_{Bequest}} = \frac{[1 + r_g(1 - t_{ig})]^n(1 - T_g + T_gT_e)}{[1 + r_e(1 - t_{ie})]^n(1 - T_e)} \qquad (7)$$

The last term in the second set of parentheses in the numerator, T_gT_e, represents the tax benefit from reducing the value of the taxable estate by the amount of the gift tax. In this way, allowing the transfer tax to be deducted from the taxable estate can be viewed as a partial gift tax credit.[21]

The size of the partial gift credit equals the size of the gift times T_gT_e. For example, consider Akio and Haruko Tochigi—a couple wishing to transfer JPY 100 million to their child. They have a JPY 500 million estate, most of which is taxable. Exhibit 6 illustrates the after-tax outcomes of a JPY 100 million gift made just prior to death or a JPY 100 million bequest made just after death, both of which would be subject to a 45 percent transfer tax. The gift reduces the size of the taxable estate to JPY 400 million, but the JPY 45 million gift tax further

EXHIBIT 6	Illustration of Gift versus Bequest When Donor Pays Transfer Tax	
	Gift	**Bequest**
Gift	100	0
Gift Tax	45	0
Net After-Tax Amount	55	0
Taxable Estate	355	500
Estate Tax	160	225
Net After-Tax Amount	195	275
After-Tax Estate plus Gift	295	275

Note: All amounts are in millions of JPY and rounded to the nearest million.

---

[21] Horvitz and Wilcox (2003) demonstrate this in the context of U.S. estate tax law.

reduces the size of the taxable estate from JPY 400 million to JPY 355 million. Under the gifting strategy, the sum of the after-tax estate and gift is approximately JPY 295 million compared to only JPY 275 million for the bequest. As a result, the gift strategy saves JPY 100 million × 0.45 × 0.45 ≈ JPY 20 million in taxes. The economic impact of this difference grows as the time difference between the gift and bequest grows because of the compounding effect.

In some situations, the primary liability for the transfer tax may lie with the donor, but a secondary liability may rest on the recipient if the donor is unable to pay. The United Kingdom, for example, imposes gratuitous transfer tax liability on anyone with a vested interest in the gift. In addition to tax considerations, the location of the tax liability has potential implications for a recipient. For example, a recipient may receive an illiquid asset as a gift or bequest. If the recipient is responsible for the tax liability and has limited access to other liquid assets to pay that liability, then the recipient may face unintended liquidity constraints. In extreme cases, taxing authorities may take possession of the asset if the recipient is unable to pay.

EXAMPLE 6

Gift and Estate Taxes

Philippe Zachary is 50 years old and resides in France. He is working with his wealth manager, Pierre Robé, to develop an estate planning strategy to transfer wealth to his second cousin, Etienne. Annual exclusions allow Zachary to make tax-free gifts of €20,000 per year, and gratuitous transfer tax liabilities are the responsibility of the recipient. Zachary notes that the relevant tax rate for bequests from the estate is likely to be as high as 60 percent (see Appendix A). He notes further, however, that gifts (in excess of the €20,000 exception mentioned above) made prior to age 70 enjoy 50 percent relief of the normal estate tax of 60 percent, for an effective tax rate of 30 percent. In addition, Etienne enjoys a low tax rate of 20 percent on investment income because he has relatively low income. Zachary, on the other hand, is subject to a 48 percent tax rate on investment income. Zachary is considering gifting assets that are expected to earn a 6 percent real return annually over the next 20 years.

1. Considering the first year's tax-free gift associated with the annual exclusion, how much of his estate will Zachary have transferred on an inflation-adjusted basis in 20 years without paying estate tax?

2. What is the relative value of the tax-free gift compared to the value of a bequest in 20 years?

3. Suppose Zachary wishes to make an additional gift that would be subject to gift tax. What would be the relative after-tax value of that taxable gift compared to a bequest 20 years later?

4. What would be the relative value of the gift if Zachary were responsible for paying the gift tax rather than Etienne?

Solution to 1: In 20 years, the future value (measured in real terms) equals €20,000 × $[1 + 0.06(1 - 0.20)]^{20}$ = €51,080.56. Note that although the gift was not subject to a wealth transfer tax, its subsequent investment returns are nonetheless taxable at 20 percent.

Solution to 2: The relative value of the tax-free gift compared to the bequest is

$$RV_{TaxFreeGift} = \frac{FV_{Gift}}{FV_{Bequest}} = \frac{[1 + 0.06(1 - 0.20)]^{20}}{[1 + 0.06(1 - 0.48)]^{20}(1 - 0.60)}$$

$$= \frac{2.5540}{0.7347} = 3.47$$

The gift is substantially more tax efficient in this case for three reasons. First, the gift is tax free and the bequest is heavily taxed. Second, if Etienne receives the gift, subsequent investment returns will be taxed at a much lower rate than if it is kept inside the estate. Third, the difference has time to compound over a relatively long period of time since the time horizon is twenty years.

Solution to 3: In this case, the recipient is responsible for paying the gift tax at 30 percent, or half of the 60 percent estate tax. The relative value of the tax-free gift compared to a bequest subject to inheritance tax is:

$$RV_{TaxableGift} = \frac{FV_{Gift}}{FV_{Bequest}} = \frac{[1 + 0.06(1 - 0.20)]^{20}(1 - 0.30)}{[1 + 0.06(1 - 0.48)]^{20}(1 - 0.60)}$$

$$= \frac{1.7878}{0.7395} = 2.42$$

Although the gift is taxed, the after-tax value of the gift relative to the bequest is still quite large because the gift tax rate is low and because the gift is located in a lightly taxed place (i.e., with Etienne) for a long period of time.

Solution to 4: An additional benefit may accrue if Zachary is responsible for paying gift tax because the tax payment decreases the size of his taxable estate upon death. Assuming Etienne's estate will not be taxable, the relative value of the gift is:

$$V_{TaxableGift} = \frac{FV_{Gift}}{FV_{Bequest}}$$

$$= \frac{[1 + 0.06(1 - 0.20)]^{20}(1 - 0.30 + 0.30 \times 0.60)}{[1 + 0.06(1 - 0.48)]^{20}(1 - 0.60)}$$

$$= \frac{2.2475}{0.7395} = 3.04$$

4.2 Generation Skipping

Often, high-net-worth individuals have wealth transfer goals that extend beyond the second generation (i.e., their children). In these cases, transferring assets directly to the third generation (i.e., grandchildren) or beyond may reduce transfer taxes where permitted. In jurisdictions that tax gifts or bequests, transfers from the first generation to the second will be taxed. The same capital may be taxed again if it is transferred from the second to the third generation, and the second generation's estate is taxable. Transferring capital in excess of the second generation's needs for spending, safety, and flexibility, directly to the third generation can avoid a layer of this double taxation.

For example, consider Kenichi and Fumiko Kawaguchi, who have JPY 1,000,000,000 of first generation excess capital they would like to transfer to fulfill their goals of securing a sound financial future for their children and grandchildren. Suppose that core capital for their children amounts to JPY 800,000,000, leaving JPY 200,000,000 of excess capital for the second generation that can be transferred to the third generation. According to Appendix B, Japan imposes tax rates up to 50 percent on the recipient of a gift or inheritance. Suppose the second generation excess capital of JPY 200,000,000 is transferred twice—once from the first generation to the second in 10 years, and again from the second to the third generation 25 years beyond that. Its future value at a five percent real rate of return (e.g., eight percent nominal return with three percent inflation) will be equal to:

$$\text{JPY } 200{,}000{,}000 \times [(1.05)^{10}(1-0.50)(1.05)^{25}(1-0.50)] = \text{JPY } 275{,}800{,}768$$

If the Kawaguchis instead transfer this sum directly to their grandchildren, the transfer is taxed only once and the future value is

$$\text{JPY } 200{,}000{,}000 \times [(1.05)^{35}(1-0.50)] = \text{JPY } 551{,}601{,}537$$

or twice as much as when the capital is taxed twice. In general, the relative value of skipping generations to transfer capital that is excess for both the first and second generations is $1/(1-T_1)$ where T_1 is the tax rate of capital transferred from the first to the second generation.

In at least one jurisdiction (e.g., U.S.), the taxing authorities discourage this strategy by imposing a special generation skipping transfer tax. This tax, in addition to the usual transfer tax, is imposed on transfers to, among others, grandchildren or subsequent generations and is intended to produce the same overall tax effect had the assets passed sequentially through two generations.

4.3 Spousal Exemptions

Most jurisdictions with estate or inheritance taxes (such as South Africa, the United Kingdom, and the United States) allow decedents to make bequests and gifts to their spouses without transfer tax liability. In these jurisdictions, gratuitous transfer tax exclusions also apply to smaller estates. In the case of the United Kingdom, estates less than £312,000 can pass without inheritance tax (see Appendix B). In these situations, it is worthwhile to note that a couple actually has two exclusions available—one for each spouse. As a result, it is often advisable to take advantage of the first exclusion when the first spouse dies by transferring the exclusion amount to someone other than the spouse.

For instance, consider Will and Samantha Quackenbush who have a £700,000 estate. If Will is the first to die and leaves the entire estate tax-free to his wife, Samantha, they have lost an opportunity to transfer £312,000 out of the taxable estate upon Will's death. If the £312,000 was excess capital that would likely be transferred to the next generation anyway, then transferring the £312,000 to the second generation upon Will's death will not trigger additional inheritance tax due to the exclusion and will reduce the taxable value of Samantha's estate to £388,000. In sum, even when assets can be transferred to a surviving spouse without tax consequences, it may be valuable to take advantage of any estate tax exclusions upon the death of the first spouse. Otherwise, the opportunity to use the exclusion to transfer wealth without tax consequences will be lost.

4.4 Valuation Discounts

Gift and estate taxes might also be mitigated by transferring assets that qualify for valuation discounts (or, in appropriate cases, structuring assets to qualify for such discounts). Typically, tax is levied on the fair market value of the asset being transferred, which is a straightforward determination in the case of cash or marketable securities. If shares in a privately held family business are being transferred, establishing fair market value is not obvious and requires a valuation according to some pricing model or models, which, in turn, requires assumptions. In addition to the inputs that must be estimated or forecasted to determine the intrinsic value of an otherwise similar publicly traded company, the valuation of privately held companies is often discounted at a higher cost of capital to reflect the lack of liquidity associated with their shares. Estimates of the average discount for lack of liquidity range from 20 percent to 25 percent of the value of an otherwise identical publicly traded company. The size of the discount tends to be inversely related to the size of the company and its profit margin.[22]

If the shares being transferred represent a minority interest in the privately held company, an additional discount is taken for lack of control associated with a minority interest. This valuation is distinct from, but not independent of, an illiquidity discount because positions of control are more marketable than minority positions that lack control. Minority interest discounts can be very large, ranging between 25 percent and 40 percent, but their interaction with illiquidity discounts is not additive. For example, if a stake in a privately held business warrants a 10 percent illiquidity discount and 15 percent lack of control discount, the combined discount may be a lower figure, such as 18 percent, rather than 25 percent.[23]

Transferring assets subject to valuation discount reduces the basis on which transfer tax is calculated, and hence the transfer tax. For this reason, HNWIs in some jurisdictions may intentionally create illiquidity and lack of control by placing assets in a family limited partnership (FLP). Rather than gift or bequeath the underlying assets, the first generation transfers minority interests in the FLP, which also is illiquid, to separate individuals. The lack of liquidity and control of an FLP structure may make it eligible for valuation discounts in some jurisdictions. In general, FLPs comprising cash and marketable securities will receive less of a discount than a privately held operating company.

FLPs may have non-tax benefits as well. By pooling the assets of multiple family members together, the family can gain access to certain asset classes requiring minimum investments (e.g., hedge funds, private equity, venture capital), which would be prohibitively large for the individual family members to invest in alone. An FLP also allows participating family members to share in a pro-rata fashion in the gains and losses of family investments. This equitable distribution of gains and losses can be an important consideration in some family dynamics.

---

[22] See, for example, Block (2007).
[23] See Horvitz (2008).

4.5 Deemed Dispositions

Rather than impose an estate or inheritance tax on the amount of capital bequeathed at death, some countries treat bequests as **deemed dispositions**, that is, as if the property were sold. The deemed disposition triggers the realization of any previously unrecognized capital gains and liability for associated capital gains tax. The tax is therefore levied not on the principal value of the transfer, but only on the value of unrecognized gains, if any. According to Appendix B, Australia, Canada, and Colombia are examples of jurisdictions with deemed disposition regimes. Australia and Canada impose no gift taxes, making it potentially advantageous to gift highly appreciated assets that are not likely to be liquidated during one's lifetime anyway. In this way, one can extend the capital gain deferral that might otherwise be cut short by the donor's death.

4.6 Charitable Gratuitous Transfers

Most jurisdictions provide two forms of tax relief for wealth transfers to not-for-profit or charitable organizations. First, most charitable donations are not subject to a gift transfer tax. Of the jurisdictions listed in Appendix B, only Belgium and South Africa impose a transfer tax on charitable gratuitous transfers. Second, most jurisdictions permit income tax deductions for charitable donations. Only four jurisdictions with income taxes listed in Appendix B do not offer income tax deductions for charitable donations. Therefore, families with philanthropic aspirations can transfer wealth very tax efficiently.

Charitable organizations may also be exempt from paying tax on investment returns, as well. Therefore, the early structuring of assets into a charitable organization allows investment returns to compound tax free, which has a significant impact on wealth accumulation especially over long time horizons. Therefore, the relative after-tax future value over n years of a charitable gift is compared to a taxable bequest as shown in Equation 8 below:

$$RV_{CharitableGift} = \frac{FV_{CharitableGift}}{FV_{Bequest}}$$

$$= \frac{(1 + r_g)^n + T_{oi}[1 + r_e(1 - t_{ie})]^n(1 - T_e)}{[1 + r_e(1 - t_{ie})]^n(1 - T_e)} \qquad (8)$$

The first term in the numerator has no deduction for either gift tax or taxes on investment returns. The second term of the numerator represents the additional value created in the estate associated with the income tax deduction. T_{oi} is the tax rate on ordinary income and represents the current income tax benefit associated with a charitable transfer. The tax advantages of charitable giving allows the donor to either increase the charitable benefit associated with a given transfer of excess capital from the estate, or to use less excess capital to achieve a given charitable benefit.

EXAMPLE 7

Charitable Gifts

Continue with the example of Philippe Zachary in Example 6. France imposes an estate tax at rates of up to 60 percent, but qualifying charitable donations are not subject to inheritance tax. In addition, donations are eligible for income tax deductions at the same income tax rate of 48 percent, which also applies to investment income. What is the relative after-tax value of a charitable donation as compared to a taxable bequest?

Solution:

$$RV_{TaxableGift} = \frac{FV_{Gift}}{FV_{Bequest}}$$
$$= \frac{(1.06)^{20} + 0.48[1 + 0.06(1 - 0.48)]^{20}(1 - 0.60)}{[1 + 0.06(1 - 0.48)]^{20}(1 - 0.60)}$$
$$= \frac{3.5621}{0.7395} = 4.82$$

The relative value of the charitable gift is so large because the gift a) escapes estate tax, b) accrues investment returns free of taxes inside the tax-exempt organization, and c) provides Zachary with an income tax deduction.

5   ESTATE PLANNING TOOLS

The gratuitous transfers described above are often implemented through structures that either maximize tax benefit, produce a non-tax benefit, or both. Common estate planning tools include, among others, trusts (a common law concept), foundations (a civil law concept), life insurance, and companies. As noted earlier, partnerships may also be used in some circumstances. The structure of each has implications for how assets are controlled, whether they are protected from potential claims of future creditors, and how they are taxed. The availability of each of these tools and the tax and tax reporting ramifications to their use depends upon the jurisdiction or jurisdictions of relevance in the given case. Note that while foundations may have originated in civil law jurisdictions, they are also available in some common law jurisdictions. Similarly, trusts are recognized by some civil law jurisdictions.

5.1 Trusts

A trust is an arrangement created by a **settlor** (or **grantor**) who transfers assets to a trustee. The trust is not a legal entity. Rather, it is a relationship in which the trustee holds and manages the assets for the benefit of the beneficiaries. As a result, the trustee is considered to be the legal owner of the trust assets and the beneficiaries are considered to be the beneficial owners of the trust assets. The terms of the trust relationship and the principles used by the trustee to manage the assets and distributions to the beneficiaries are outlined in the trust document. It is possible for the settlor of a trust to also be one of the beneficiaries.

Trusts can be categorized in many ways, but two dimensions are particularly important in understanding their character. First, a trust can be either revocable or irrevocable. In a **revocable trust** arrangement, the settlor (who originally transfers assets to fund the trust) retains the right to rescind the trust relationship and regain title to the trust assets. Under these circumstances, the settlor is generally considered to be the owner of the assets for tax purposes in many jurisdictions. As a result, the settlor is responsible for tax payments and reporting on the trust's investment returns. Additionally, the settlor's revocation power makes the trust assets vulnerable to the reach of creditors having claims against the settlor.

Alternatively, where the settlor has no ability to revoke the trust relationship, the trust is characterized as an **irrevocable trust**. In an irrevocable trust structure, the trustee may be responsible for tax payments and reporting in his or her capacity as owner of the trust assets for tax purposes. An irrevocable trust structure generally provides greater asset protection from claims against a settlor than a revocable trust.[24] In any event, both a revocable and an irrevocable trust structure can result in the transfer of assets to the beneficiaries without the time, expense, potential challenges, and publicity associated with probate because the settlor transfers legal ownership of the assets to the trustee and the transfer of those assets is dictated by the terms of the trust and not the settlor's will.

Second, trusts can be structured to be either fixed or discretionary. Distributions to beneficiaries of a **fixed trust** are prescribed in the trust document to occur at certain times or in certain amounts. For example, Maria Valez, a first generation wealth owner, may wish to make a large *inter vivos* transfer to her son, Conner, who is too young to manage the assets himself. Valez could fund a trust that directs the trustee to hold the assets until Conner's 21st birthday and begin making annual distributions of a specific amount over 10 years, at which time any remaining assets will be distributed to Conner. The trust is said to be fixed because the terms of the distributions are pre-determined in the trust documentation.

In contrast, if the trust document enabled the trustee to determine whether and how much to distribute based on Conner's general welfare and in the sole and uncontrolled discretion of the trustee, the trust would be called **discretionary**. The settlor can make her wishes known to the trustee through language in the trust document and/or through a non-binding letter of wishes.

The legal concept of a trust is unique to the common law. Civil law countries may not recognize foreign trusts because it is a legal relationship, not a legal person. In fact, twelve of the 22 civil law jurisdictions in Appendix A do not recognize trusts.

5.1.1 Control

A common motivation for using a trust structure is to make resources available to a beneficiary without yielding complete control of those resources to them. For example, spendthrift trusts can be used to provide resources to beneficiaries who may be unable or unwilling to manage the assets themselves, perhaps because they are young, immature, or disabled. Or perhaps the settlor wishes assets to be used for particular purposes. In any case, the trust relationship can permit a settlor to transfer assets without the expense or publicity associated with probate, yet still retain control of those assets.

5.1.2 Asset Protection

In general, creditors are unable to reach assets that an individual does not own. Just as an irrevocable trust can protect assets from claims against the settlor, as outlined above, discretionary trusts can protect assets from claims against the beneficiaries. Under a discretionary trust, the beneficiaries have no legal right to

---

[24] This is true provided the settlor was neither insolvent nor rendered insolvent when he settled the trust, and any such creditor claims arose after the trust settlement date.

income generated by the trust or to the assets in the trust itself. Therefore, the creditors of the beneficiaries cannot reach the trust assets.

In the example on the previous page, suppose Maria Valez is concerned that Conner's new wife may divorce him and lay a claim on his trust assets in a divorce settlement. If the trust to which Conner is a beneficiary is discretionary, then his wife would be unable to lay claim to them because it is within the trustee's power to avoid making distributions to Conner. It is important to note that these structures must generally be established in advance of a claim, or even a pending claim, to effectively protect assets.

Trusts may also be used in circumstances where forced heirship laws permit the use of lifetime gifts and trusts to avoid the strict application of forced heirship rule. In fact, many countries specifically prohibit the application of forced heirship rules to trusts, making trusts an especially useful tool in this regard.

5.1.3 Tax Reduction

Trusts can be used to reduce taxes for either the settlor or the beneficiaries. Continuing the illustration above, suppose Valez creates an irrevocable trust such that she is no longer considered the owner of the assets held in the trust for tax purposes. The income generated by the trust assets may be taxed at a lower rate inside the trust than if they were owned by Valez for several possible reasons. In many countries, income is commonly taxed according to a progressive tax schedule (see Horan and Robinson 2008). A progressive tax rate schedule applied to trust income or beneficiary distributions may allow either the trust or beneficiary to apply taxable income to lower tax brackets unavailable to Valez whose income may be taxed at relative high rates.[25] Moreover, if an irrevocable trust is structured as discretionary, a trustee can consider a beneficiary's tax situation to decide whether or not to make a distribution in a particular tax period to the beneficiary. Alternatively, a settlor may create a trust in a jurisdiction with a low tax rate or even no taxes. As is the case with any trust planning technique, this strategy requires a consideration of the tax systems governing the settlor and beneficiary in their home country, which is discussed in more detail in Section 6.2.

The tax laws of some jurisdictions allow tax planning with the use of a trust in which assets are successfully transferred for estate tax purposes, but not for income tax purposes. That is, the assets are no longer part of the settlor's estate, but the income generated from the assets remains taxable to the settlor. In this way, assets can be successfully transferred from a settlor to a beneficiary under a gifting strategy and avoid estate tax. However, the income generated by the assets would nonetheless be taxable to the settlor, thereby further reducing the size of the settlor's taxable estate over time.[26] Section 4.1.3 discusses the value of locating the tax liability with the donor. A similar concept applies to the location of the income tax liability on trust asset returns.

5.2 Foundations

A foundation is a legal entity available in some jurisdictions. Foundations are typically set up to hold assets for a particular purpose—such as to promote education or for philanthropy. When set up and funded by an individual or family and

---

[25] In some jurisdictions, however, the progressive rate schedule applicable to trusts may be more compressed than that which applies to individuals. It is therefore important to determine and compare the rate structure that applies to individuals and trusts in the individual case.

[26] See Brunel (2002) for a more thorough discussion of these structures.

managed by its own directors, it is called a private foundation. Similar to trusts, foundations survive the settlor, allow the settlor's wishes to be followed after the settlor's death, and can accomplish the same types of objectives as a trust (control, avoidance of probate, asset protection, and tax minimization). A foundation is based on civil law and, unlike a trust, is a legal person. Often, the choice of a trust or foundation depends on a client's residence or nationality.

5.3 Life Insurance

In creating a trust, a settlor divests himself of assets by transferring them to a trustee for the benefit of beneficiaries, creating potential advantages regarding how the assets are controlled, protected, and taxed. Life insurance is another planning tool in which the policy holder transfers assets (called a **premium**) to an insurer who, in turn, has a contractual obligation to pay death benefit proceeds to the beneficiary named in the policy. As is the case with trusts, insurance can produce tax and estate planning benefits. It can be a useful alternative to a trust in circumstances where the trust relationship is not recognized under applicable law or its legal and tax consequences are uncertain, such as some civil law countries common in Europe and South America that do not recognize trusts.

From a tax perspective, life insurance is afforded beneficial tax treatment in many jurisdictions. Death benefit proceeds paid to life insurance beneficiaries are tax exempt in many jurisdictions and, in some cases, no tax reporting consequences arise. In addition, premiums paid by the policy holder are typically neither part of the policy holder's taxable estate at the time of his or her death, nor subject to a gratuitous transfer tax.[27] Therefore, it may be possible to transfer money or other assets through life insurance without tax consequence. Life insurance can also offer income tax advantages in jurisdictions that allow any cash value in the policy to build tax deferred. A life insurance contract can also include provisions that allow a surrender or withdrawal (or partial surrender or withdrawal) of policy value during the policy term, as well as a loan facility, which, in some jurisdictions, can be made with advantageous tax consequences to the policy holder.

Tax authorities in many countries recognize these advantages and typically require that life insurance be properly structured to avoid abuse. For example, most jurisdictions require a certain minimum level of risk before a life insurance policy will be treated as such. Other laws mandate that the policy holder must typically have an insurable interest in the life assured to be a valid life insurance contract.

In addition to possible tax benefits, life insurance effectively allows assets to transfer to the policy holder's beneficiaries without the time, expense, potential challenges, and publicity associated with probate. Premiums paid by the policy holder are no longer part of the policy holder's estate at the time of death, and death benefit proceeds under a life insurance contract pass directly to policy beneficiaries outside the probate process. While this is also true of trusts, insurance is recognized in almost every country and generally regarded with less suspicion by tax authorities.

Many wealth owners also use life insurance to help heirs pay inheritance tax triggered by the wealth owner's death. In other words, life insurance is a liquidity planning technique in that it can generate liquidity to pay gratuitous transfer tax. It is, therefore, especially valuable if an inheritance of illiquid assets creates

---

[27] In some jurisdictions the value of the policy may attract gratuitous transfer tax exposure to the policy holder, insured, or beneficiaries; it is therefore important in the individual case to determine the tax consequences of life insurance to the parties.

a liquidity crisis for the heir as discussed in Section 4.1.3. In addition, life insurance policies can be used to transfer assets outside forced heirship rules, which normally do not apply to life insurance proceeds.

Life insurance policies can also offer asset protection in their own right or in combination with a trust. Premiums paid for life insurance are generally outside the reach of creditors' claims against the policy holder. Additionally, an insurance policy can assign a discretionary trust as the policy beneficiary. In this way, the use of life insurance in combination with a trust may be useful if the ultimate beneficiaries (i.e., beneficiaries of the trust) are unable to manage the assets themselves (e.g., in the case of minors, disabilities, or spendthrifts).

5.4 Companies and Controlled Foreign Corporations

Companies may also be a useful tool in which to place assets. For example, a **controlled foreign corporation** (CFC) is a company located outside a taxpayer's home country and in which the taxpayer has a controlling interest as defined under the home country law. A possible benefit of placing income generating assets in a CFC is that tax on earnings of the company may be deferred until either the earnings are actually distributed to shareholders or the company is sold or shares otherwise disposed. In addition, a CFC may be established in a jurisdiction that does not tax the company or its shareholders.

Many countries have CFC rules designed to prevent taxpayers from avoiding the taxation of current income by holding assets in a CFC. CFC rules can be triggered if a taxpayer owns more than, say, 50 percent of the foreign company's shares although the ownership threshold will vary from one jurisdiction to the next. CFC rules may also look beyond direct ownership of CFC shares and consider beneficial ownership in a trust, for example, or even ownership attributed to related parties, such as a taxpayer's family members. Therefore, CFC rules may tax shareholders of a CFC on the company's earnings as if the earnings were distributed to shareholders even though no distribution has been made. This treatment of earnings is called a **deemed distribution**.

6   CROSS-BORDER ESTATE PLANNING

Individuals and families with business and personal interests in more than one country face special estate planning challenges. A family with assets located in multiple jurisdictions may have difficulty passing ownership of those assets upon the wealth owner's death. For example, income generated by assets located outside an investor's home country may be taxed in both the country where the income originates and the home country of the wealth owner. Passing ownership of overseas assets upon death may also be difficult and may trigger multiple tax liabilities from both the home country and country in which the asset is located.

Even when assets are located within a single jurisdiction, passing their ownership to heirs located outside the country through a will, gifting technique, or other strategy can be legally complex and may pose certain tax considerations. This section discusses some of these cross-border estate planning issues.

6.1 The Hague Conference

A legal document created in one country may not necessarily enjoy legal recognition in another country. The **Hague Conference** on Private International Law is an intergovernmental organization that works toward the convergence of pri-

EXHIBIT 7	Members of the Hague Conference

Albania	The European	The former	Serbia
Argentina	Community	Yugoslav	Slovakia
Australia	Finland	Republic of	Slovenia
Austria	France	Macedonia	South Africa
Belarus	Georgia	Malaysia	Spain
Belgium	Germany	Malta	Sri Lanka
Bosnia and	Greece	Mexico	Suriname
Herzegovina	Hungary	Monaco	Sweden
Brazil	Iceland	Montenegro	Switzerland
Bulgaria	India	Morocco	Turkey
Canada	Ireland	Netherlands	Ukraine
Chile	Israel	New Zealand	United Kingdom
China	Italy	Norway	of Great
Croatia	Japan	Panama	Britain and
Cyprus	Jordan	Paraguay	Northern
Czech Republic	Republic of	Peru	Ireland
Denmark	Korea	Poland	United States
Ecuador	Latvia	Portugal	of America
Egypt	Lithuania	Romania	Uruguay
Estonia	Luxembourg	Russian	Venezuela
		Federation	

Source: Hague Conference on International Private Law (www.hcch.net).

vate international law.[28] Its 69 members consist of countries and regional economic integration organizations, like the European Community (see Exhibit 7). The Conference has developed a series of conventions, or multilateral treaties, that have addressed a variety of international issues, including those related to cross-border transactions. The purpose is to simplify or standardize processes and facilitate international trade. Members of the Conference may or may not ratify a particular convention. Ratification by a country implies a legal obligation to apply the convention within its borders. Non-member countries may participate, as well, by electing to accede to be bound by the treaty, a process that sometimes requires acceptance by states already a party to the convention.

Because the typical form of a will can vary substantially from one state to the next, their recognition from one jurisdiction to the next can be especially troublesome. The Hague Convention of the Conflict of Laws Relating to the Form of Testamentary Dispositions addresses this particular issue and has been ratified by 39 countries, including most developed nations, but notably excluding the United States. Under this convention, a will is valid in the participating jurisdictions if it is consistent with the internal law associated with:

► the place the will was made;

► the nationality, domicile, or habitual residence of the testator; or

► the location of immovable assets covered under the will.

---

[28] More detailed information is available at www.hcch.net.

Some participating countries have exceptions, however. Therefore, separate wills for different jurisdictions may be required, especially in relation to real estate.

An important area in which the Hague Conference affects wealth management is in relation to trusts. Common law jurisdictions recognize trusts, but civil law jurisdictions may not. The Hague Convention of the Law Applicable to Trusts and on Their Recognition is designed to harmonize the recognition of the trust relationship. By ratifying or acceding to this convention, a participating country recognizes the existence and validity of trusts with a written trust instrument as long as they have the following characteristics (outlined in Article 2 of the convention):

A. The assets constitute a separate fund and are not a part of the trustee's own estate.

B. Title to the trust assets stands in the name of the trustee or in the name of another person on behalf of the trustee.

C. The trustee has the power and the duty, in respect of which he is accountable, to manage, employ, or dispose of the assets in accordance with the terms of the trust and the special duties imposed upon him by law.

Twelve countries participate in this convention. Nonetheless, a participating country may view ownership and beneficial interests related to trust relationships in various ways, which may limit some of their advantages. It is important for a wealth manager to know whether a trust will be recognized in the way it is intended by authorities in the countries of relevance to the trust relationship.

6.2 Tax System

Taxable claims for a particular country are based on its jurisdiction claim, that is, the conceptual framework that determines the basis for taxing income or transfers. A country that taxes income as a source within its borders is said to impose **source jurisdiction**, also referred to as a **territorial tax system**.[29] This jurisdiction is derived from the relationship between the country and the source of the income. Countries imposing income tax exercise source jurisdiction.

Countries may also impose tax based on residency, called **residence jurisdiction**, whereby all income (domestic and foreign sourced) is subject to taxation. In this case, the jurisdiction is derived from the relationship between the country and the person receiving the income. Most countries use a residential tax system.

According to Appendix B, only three of the 37 jurisdictions surveyed with income taxes have territorial-based systems (Hong Kong, Singapore, and Taiwan).

6.2.1 Taxation of Income

Although our primary concern will relate to gratuitous transfer taxes either on or before death for estate planning purposes, the basic concepts relate to income taxes equally well. Persons subject to residence jurisdiction are taxed on their worldwide income. Most countries impose residence jurisdiction on non-citizen residents, but not citizens who are non-resident in the jurisdiction. The United States is a notable exception given that both citizens (regardless of where

---

[29] Arnold and McIntyre (2002), p. 21. Much of the discussion in this and the following section is based on this reading.

resident) and residents are subject to U.S. taxation on their worldwide income and estates.

There is no international standardized residency test that applies to individuals. Therefore, residency tests differ between countries. In determining residency, tax authorities may consider subjective standards, such as the extent of an individual's social, familial, and economic ties to the jurisdiction; e.g., whether the individual maintains a dwelling in the country, whether the individual has income producing activities in the country, etc. The tax authorities may also consider objective standards to determine residency, such as the number of days of physical presence the individual has within the country during the relevant tax period. High-net-worth individuals may want to acquire or avoid residency in a particular country, depending on the country's tax burden. It is critical to understand the tax residency rules in the relevant countries to achieve the objectives of such individuals.

For example, U.K. residents are considered non-domiciled in the United Kingdom if they do not form an intention to permanently remain in the United Kingdom. These resident, non-domiciliaries (RNDs) are taxed only on income sourced in the United Kingdom. Non-U.K. income is only subject to U.K. tax when it is remitted (or deemed remitted) to the United Kingdom. The U.K. RND tax regime is considered to be a very attractive regime for HNW RNDs when compared to tax regimes imposing tax based on residence. RNDs in the United Kingdom may therefore choose to locate assets outside the United Kingdom in countries having advantageous tax regimes, such as Singapore or Hong Kong, and avoid remittances (or deemed remittances) to the United Kingdom.

6.2.2 Taxation of Wealth and Wealth Transfers

Like income, wealth and wealth transfers may be subject to tax based on source or residence principles. The source principle taxes wealth economically sourced in a specific country, such as real estate. Eight of the 37 jurisdictions in Appendix B impose a wealth tax beyond that often imposed on real property (Colombia, France, Hungary, India, Mexico, Netherlands, Spain, and Switzerland). The residence principle, should it apply, would tax worldwide wealth with some exceptions, such as real estate situated abroad.

Gifts and bequests may be subject to different tax treatments depending on the tax regime of the donor's country, recipient's country, and the location of the asset being transferred. For example, the source principle would tax assets that are economically sourced or transferred within a particular country, whereas the residence principle would impose transfer tax on all assets transferred by a donor.

Again, the United States is unique in this regard. Not only does the United States impose estate tax on the worldwide assets of its citizens (regardless of where resident) and residents, it also imposes estate tax on non-U.S. individuals holding assets situated in the United States, including U.S. real estate, movable property located in the United States, and security holdings (public or private) of U.S. companies. This may cause some asset transfers to be taxed twice by two different jurisdictions, but many estate tax treaties (discussed below) and, where available, foreign estate tax credits, can eliminate or mitigate this conflict.[30] This illustrates, however, that individuals need to be aware of the wealth transfer tax rules of the countries tied to the assets they hold.

---

[30] See Marcovici (2007).

6.2.3 Exit Taxation

In an effort to mitigate their income, wealth, and estate taxes, HNWIs may sometimes choose to renounce their citizenship in one country and expatriate to another country. To offset the lost tax revenue from such repatriation, some countries impose a so-called "exit tax" on individuals giving up their citizenship or residency. Seven of the 37 jurisdictions listed in Appendix B impose an exit tax (Australia, Canada, Germany, Israel, Netherlands, Sweden, and the United States). Exit taxation is generally not applicable for capital moving between EU countries, but could apply to capital moving outside the EU. In most cases, the exit tax amounts to a tax on unrealized gains accrued on assets leaving the taxing jurisdiction. This approach is called a deemed disposition. The exit tax may also include an income tax on income earned over a fixed period after expatriation, called a "shadow period."

6.3 Double Taxation

The interaction of country tax systems can result in tax conflicts in which two countries claim to have taxing authority over the same income or assets. This conflict can relate to either income tax or estate/inheritance tax and arise in a number of ways. For example, two countries may claim residence of the same individual, subjecting the individual's worldwide income to taxation by both countries. This situation represents a **residence–residence conflict.**

Alternatively, two countries may claim source jurisdiction of the same asset (i.e., **source–source conflict**). This conflict can arise, for example, on income from a company situated in Country A but managed from Country B. Both countries may claim that the company income is derived from their jurisdiction.

In other situations, an individual in Country A may be subject to residence jurisdiction and, therefore, taxation on worldwide income. Some of the individual's assets may be located in Country B, which exercises source jurisdiction on those assets, creating a **residence–source conflict.** For example, a U.S. citizen owning Singapore situated real estate would be subject to U.S. income tax and Singapore income tax on rental income from the property. Residence–source conflicts are the most common source of double taxation and the most difficult to avoid through tax planning without a separate mechanism for relief that can mitigate or eliminate double taxation through either foreign tax credit provisions or double taxation treaties. Because a source country is commonly viewed to have primary jurisdiction to tax income within its borders, the residence country is typically expected to provide double taxation relief if any is provided.

6.3.1 Foreign Tax Credit Provisions

A residence country may choose to unilaterally provide its taxpayers relief from residence–source conflicts within its own tax code using one or more of the following methods: credit method, exemption method, or deduction method.

In the **credit method**, the residence country reduces its taxpayers' domestic tax liability for taxes paid to a foreign country exercising source jurisdiction. The credit is limited to the amount of taxes the taxpayer would pay domestically, which completely eliminates double taxation. Under this method the tax liability equals the greater of the tax liability due in either the residence or source country.

$$T_{CreditMethod} = Max[T_{Residence}, T_{Source}] \tag{9}$$

For example, suppose a residence country imposes a 50 percent tax on world-wide income but offers a relief for tax paid on foreign-sourced income via the credit method. If the foreign government taxes the foreign-sourced income at 40 percent, the taxpayer will pay a 50 percent tax rate (e.g., Max[50 percent, 40 percent]). Of the total, 40 percent is paid to foreign authorities and 10 percent is paid to the domestic authorities.

In the **exemption method**, the residence country imposes no tax on foreign-source income by providing taxpayers with an exemption, which, in effect, eliminates the residence–source conflict by having only one jurisdiction impose tax. The tax liability under the exemption method is simply the tax imposed at the foreign source, or:

$$T_{ExemptionMethod} = T_{Source} \tag{10}$$

In the previous example, the tax liability would be 40 percent, all of which is collected by the foreign taxing authority. Only the few jurisdictions using territorial-based tax systems (Hong Kong, Singapore, Taiwan, and Thailand) have adopted the exemption method.

Under the **deduction method**, the residence country allows taxpayers to reduce their taxable income by the amount of taxes paid to foreign governments in respect of foreign-source income (i.e., provides a tax deduction rather than a credit or exemption). The taxpayer is still responsible for both taxes, but the aggregate liability is less than the sum of the two with the residence country reducing the size of its percentage claim by the product of the two tax rates. The tax rate under the deduction method is therefore equal to:

$$\begin{aligned} T_{DeductionMethod} &= T_{Residence} + T_{Source}(1 - T_{Residence}) \\ &= T_{Residence} + T_{Source} - T_{Residence}T_{Source} \end{aligned} \tag{11}$$

It is clear from this equation that the deduction method results in a higher tax liability than either the credit or exemption method. Using rates from the previous example, the total tax liability equals 70 percent = 0.50 + 0.40 − (0.50 × 0.40). In this case, the source country receives 40 percent and the residence country receives 30 percent [i.e., 0.50 − (0.50 × 0.40)]. The residence country makes a partial concession recognizing the primacy of source jurisdiction.

The diagonal of double taxation matrix in Appendix C lists jurisdictions that have foreign tax credit relief provisions in their domestic tax code. The small case letters indicate whether the provisions apply to income (*i*), gift (*g*), or estate (*e*) taxes. The United States, for example, provides domestic relief for income and estate taxes, but not gift taxes. Therefore, by way of example, a U.S. resident may choose to delay an *inter vivos* wealth transfer of an asset situated in another country with a gift tax (which would not receive double taxation relief under a double taxation treaty) until the death of the donor at which time it would receive estate tax relief under the United States foreign estate tax credit. France provides foreign tax credit provisions for gift and estate taxes but not for income taxes, whereas Spain provides provisions for all three types of taxes.

It is important to note that the term "foreign tax credit provision" in this context does not imply that the country applies the credit method in providing its relief. It could apply the exemption, deduction method, or some other method. Very few countries, however, have credit provisions based purely on the exemption or credit method.

6.3.2 Double Taxation Treaties

Relief from double taxation may be provided through a double taxation treaty (DTT) rather than domestic tax laws (i.e., foreign tax credit, deduction or exclusion provisions). Tax treaties, of which there are over 2,000 in effect, are intended to facilitate international trade and investment by eliminating double taxation. By limiting source jurisdiction, DTTs resolve residence–source conflicts that are the most frequent cause of double taxation. Virtually all modern tax treaties are based on the OECD (Organisation for Economic Co-operation and Development) Model Treaty.[31] The OECD Model Treaty sanctions the exemption and credit method to resolve residence–source conflicts.

With regard to investment income, the OECD Model Treaty endorses the notion that interest income and dividend income have their source in the country of the entity paying the interest or dividend. This type of investment income is taxed through a withholding from the source country. The OECD Model Treaty strongly endorses that withholding tax rates paid to the source country for dividends (paid to other persons) and interest, be limited to 15 percent and 10 percent, respectively; but higher withholding rates are common. Additional tax may be owed to the residence country if the credit or deduction method is used. These relatively low rates are intended to allow tax revenue sharing between the source and residence country.

By contrast, capital gains are taxed in the seller's country of residence. Gains on immovable property, however, are typically taxed in the source country where the property is located.

In addition to residence–source conflicts, DTTs resolve residence–residence conflicts. A resident is taxable in a particular country "by reason of his domicile, residence, place of management or any other criterion of similar nature."[32] Should these criteria give rise to a "dual resident taxpayer," the OECD model outlines tie-breakers in the following order based on the location of an individual's:

1. permanent home

2. center of vital interests

3. habitual dwelling

4. citizenship[33]

DTTs typically do not resolve source–source conflicts.

A detailed OECD Commentary aids the interpretation of the OECD Model Treaty. The legal status of OECD Commentary and Model Treaty regarding the interpretation of tax treaties is ambiguous. The Vienna Convention on the Law Treaties, which governs the interpretation of all treaties (not just tax treaties), states that supplemental means of interpretation can only confirm meaning that is inferred from the treaty itself and other agreements between the parties unless these agreements produce an absurd result. In this regard, the OECD commentary provides guidance regarding the interpretation of double tax treaties, but is not binding.

As is the case with double taxation relief under domestic provisions, the nature of the relief under a DTT can be either through the credit, exemption, or deduction method, although the OECD model endorses the credit and exemp-

---

[31] See www.oecd.org/dataoecd/52/34/1914467.pdf.

[32] Article 4(1) of the OECD Model Treaty.

[33] Article 4(2) of the OECD Model Treaty.

tion methods. Switzerland, for example, usually applies the exemption method in its treaties. It applies the credit method, however, for foreign-source taxes in countries with which it does not have a DTT. Appendix C summarizes the DTTs in existence between 37 jurisdictions as of September 2008. The upper-case letters *I*, *G*, and *E*, refer to treaties for income taxes, gift taxes, and estate taxes, respectively, between the entity listed in the row and the entity listed in the column. For example, France has a DTT covering income, gift, and estate taxes with Sweden. The French treaty with Spain covers only income taxes, but because both countries provide foreign tax credit provisions in their domestic tax codes for gift and estate tax (see the small letters down the diagonal), individuals may nonetheless be able to avoid or mitigate double taxation. Most DTTs relate to income taxes partly because many jurisdictions (15 of 37 in this sample) do not have estate taxes, eliminating the need for an estate DTT. In any case, a taxpayer must qualify as a resident under the terms of the treaty to be eligible for its benefits.

EXAMPLE 8

Double Taxation Credit Provisions

Boris Yankevich is a citizen and resident of Country A and has investments in Country B. The tax rates on investment income and bequests for both countries are listed below. Country A has a residence-based tax system and Country B has a source jurisdiction on income generated within its borders. Country A and Country B have a double tax treaty (DTT) to address this residence–source conflict.

	Country A (%)	Country B (%)
Investment Income Tax	25	40
Estate Tax	50	30

1. What is Yankevich's tax rate on investment income under the DTT if it provides for the credit method? How much is remitted to Country A and how much is remitted to Country B?
2. What is Yankevich's tax rate on bequests under the DTT if it provides for the exemption method?
3. What is Yankevich's tax rate on bequests under the DTT if it provides for the deduction method?

Solution to 1: Under the credit method, $T_{CreditMethod} = \text{Max}[T_{Residence}, T_{Source}]$. Therefore, $T_{CreditMethod} = \text{Max}[0.25, 0.40] = 40$ percent. In this case, 40 percent is remitted to Country B. Nothing is remitted to Country A because it provides Yankevich with a credit for his entire domestic tax liability.

Solution to 2: Under the exemption method, the resident country relinquishes the tax jurisdiction, so that the tax rate on bequests would be only 30 percent, all of which is remitted to Country B.

Solution to 3: Under the deduction method, Yankevich receives a home country tax deduction (rather than a credit) for estate taxes paid to Country B. In this case:

$$T_{DeductionMethod} = T_{Residence} + T_{Source} - T_{Residence}T_{Source}$$
$$= 0.50 + 0.30 - (0.50 \times 0.30) = 0.65$$

Country A receives 35 percent, and Country B receives 30 percent.

6.4 Transparency and Offshore Banking

A wealth management advisor can often create value for a client or family by developing an estate plan that minimizes taxes. In that regard, it must be emphasized that a distinction exists between tax avoidance (sometimes referred to as "tax minimization") and tax evasion. **Tax avoidance** is developing strategies that conform to both the spirit and the letter of the tax codes of jurisdictions with taxing authority. **Tax evasion**, on the other hand, is the practice of circumventing tax obligations by illegal means such as misreporting or not reporting relevant information to tax authorities.

International wealth management is occasionally characterized as the practice of placing assets in jurisdictions with bank secrecy laws to avoid detection by taxing authorities in an individual's home country. Income on these "undeclared funds" would therefore escape taxation by the home country that might otherwise impose a tax obligation if the income were reported. Recent private banking scandals have highlighted this practice. Although such behavior is not appropriate, banking secrecy may provide legitimate benefits in the form of security, privacy, intra-family dynamics, and politics. Moreover, offshore banking centers (such as those in London, New York, Paris, Zurich, Luxembourg, Singapore, and Hong Kong) can be an efficient way to provide financial services to clients residing in other countries. So, offshore banking should not be equated with tax evasion.

Information exchange between tax authorities, however, is becoming increasingly fluid and increasingly exposing tax evasion strategies predicated on bank secrecy.[34] Marcovici (2007) outlines regulatory and other trends that contribute to this growing trend toward transparency. For example, in an effort to enforce the taxation of worldwide income on its residents and citizens, the United States demanded that banks around the globe provide the names of beneficial owners of all U.S. securities whether the owners were U.S. or non-U.S. citizens. Fearing that the United States could share this ownership information with authorities in the home country of their non-U.S. customers, most banks agreed to become Qualified Intermediaries (QIs). In exchange for not being required to categorically supply the names of beneficial owners of U.S. securities, QIs agree to document this information for all their customers and provide information about U.S. customers upon request. In this way, QIs are able to preserve the confidentiality of their non-U.S. customers but are still required to gather information that could be shared with the U.S. authorities.

Similarly, the European Union Savings Directive (EUSD) is a system to collect tax on interest payments made in one EU country for the benefit of an indi-

---

[34] See Marcovici (2007) for a more thorough discussion of the regulatory climate on which this section is largely based.

vidual in another EU country. Under the EUSD system, EU members agree to automatically exchange information with each other with the exception of Austria, Belgium, and Luxembourg. These countries apply a tax at the source and transfer the respective proportion of the pooled tax revenues to the EU country of residency of the concerned EU national.

Other trends are also contributing to the increasing rate of information exchange between jurisdictions. In some cases authorities collect information from credit card companies about individuals who use credit cards in their country, whether or not they are citizens of that country. This information can then be shared with the individual's home country. Tax treaties not only provide relief from double taxation, but may also provide for far-reaching exchange of information between countries.

In sum, estate planning strategies designed around an understanding of the economics of taxation and law are likely to provide lasting benefit for wealthy individuals and families. Families that build wealth management plans on a foundation of bank secrecy and of "hiding the money" impose archaic and potentially costly structures on subsequent generations, who will likely be operating in a more transparent and compliant legal and tax environment. Moreover, these structures pass on values that may not match subsequent generations' attitudes toward integrity, compliance, and transparency.

SUMMARY

Estate planning is a multidisciplinary endeavor that involves the intersection of tax, law, and finance. An understanding of the primary legal, tax, and financial issues affecting clients can help wealth managers effectively and strategically create tax-efficient wealth transfer strategies that meet clients' needs and objectives. The major points of this reading include:

▶ Assets in an estate can have ownership transferred by virtue of the type of ownership (e.g., sole versus joint), a will, or a trust.

▶ Probate is the process by which a will is validated and can be relied on by interested parties.

▶ A country's legal system can limit the freedom of a testator to dispose of assets as he or she sees fit (e.g., forced heirship, community property rules, etc.).

▶ The two primary ways of transferring ownership of assets are lifetime gratuitous transfers (i.e., gifts) and testamentary gratuitous transfers (i.e., bequests).

▶ A wealth transfer strategy involves estimating an individual's or a family's core capital and excess capital.

▶ Core capital is the amount of capital required to maintain a given lifestyle and provide adequate reserves for unexpected commitments and can be estimated using mortality tables or Monte Carlo analysis.

▶ Excess capital represents assets above and beyond core capital that can be safely transferred without jeopardizing the first generation's lifestyle.

▶ Tax-free gifts that fall below periodic or lifetime allowances can be an effective means of minimizing estate tax, especially if a gifting program is developed early.

▶ Opportunities for tax-efficient gifting programs also exist when lifetime gifts are taxed, especially when the gift tax is paid by the donor rather than by the recipient.

▶ Transferring capital in excess of a second generation's need for spending, safety, and flexibility directly to the third generation or beyond (i.e., generation skipping) can help to minimize taxes where permitted.

▶ Taxpayers in jurisdictions with both spousal exemptions and exclusions for smaller estates in effect have two estate exclusions available—one for each spouse.

▶ Tax efficiencies are possible using valuation discounts and charitable gratuitous transfer strategies.

▶ Common estate planning tools include trusts, foundations, insurance, and companies, each of which can provide benefits related to asset control, protection from creditors, and taxation.

▶ The control and protection trusts offer, whether structured as revocable or irrevocable, can provide flexibility as well as legal validity.

▶ Families with an international footprint face special issues relating to the drafting and recognition of legal documents, such as wills and trusts.

▶ The taxing authority of a country is determined by its tax system (e.g., source versus residence) and may conflict with the tax authority of another country.

► Jurisdictional claims based on source or residency can conflict with source jurisdictions typically given primacy.

► Double taxation conflicts can be resolved through either foreign tax credit provisions of the home country or double taxation treaties with other countries.

► The ability of locating undeclared funds in offshore savings accounts and other offshore structures to avoid detection by home country tax authorities is being eroded by trends toward an increase in information exchange and transparency across countries; compliant, tailored, tax-efficient strategies are key to meet the needs and objectives of clients and of their successor generations.

PRACTICE PROBLEMS FOR READING 16

1. The drawing up of a will is an area of estate planning that requires an individual to have a clear understanding of the tax and succession (or inheritance) laws of any jurisdiction of relevance to the testator. Although an individual may elect to draw up a will, the validity of the will could be subject to various challenges in the probate process. In addition, probate may create sizeable court fees as well as unwelcome publicity and a delay in the distribution of assets. Describe how an individual can attempt to reduce or even avoid the impact of:

   A. probate.

   B. forced heirship.

2. After a lengthy career as a metallurgical engineer, Greg Pearsall recently retired at age 70 and is looking forward to spending retirement with his wife Christine, who is 75 years old. Although both Greg and Christine are now retired, they would prefer to maintain their present lifestyle which currently requires annual spending of $75,000 in real terms. Inflation is expected to be 6 percent, and the nominal risk-free rate is 10 percent. The Pearsalls' survival probabilities for the next five years based on their current age are listed in the table below.

	Greg		Christine	
Year	Age	p(Survival)	Age	p(Survival)
1	71	0.9660	76	0.8235
2	72	0.9371	77	0.7996
3	73	0.9152	78	0.7727
4	74	0.8883	79	0.7208
5	75	0.8544	80	0.6919

   A. What is the probability that either Greg or Christine will survive over each of the next five years?

   B. Is it appropriate to use the expected return of the assets used to fund their spending needs when calculating the capitalized value of the Pearsalls' core capital spending needs? Why or why not?

   C. What is the capitalized value of the Pearsalls' core capital spending needs over the next five years?

3. Tony and Eleanor Hall currently own a $2.5 million portfolio of equities and bonds that has an average annual pretax return of 10 percent. The Halls' after-tax return on the portfolio is 7 percent (the tax rate is 30%). Due to the rapid deterioration in their health, the Halls are considering transferring the $2.5 million portfolio to their eldest grandchild, Joe, during the current financial year. By transferring their investment portfolio directly to their grandson, the Halls are attempting to reduce the transfer taxation effect of their inheritance. Although $1.5 million can be transferred tax free, local jurisdiction requires that the remaining $1 million transfer be subject to a 30 percent tax rate, which is Joe's responsibility as donee. The Halls have consulted with their financial planner as they are uncertain whether the 30 percent tax rate would also apply if their gift to their grandson is delayed and transferred as a bequest five years from today. Their grandson currently pays a marginal tax rate of 25 percent.

   A. Discuss the effectiveness of the Halls' generation skipping strategy.

   B. Calculate the relative after-tax value of the Hall's $1 million gift (above and beyond the $1.5 million exclusion) to their grandson. Assume the $1 million transfer is subject to 30 percent tax whether it takes place today or is delayed and transferred as a bequest in five years.

   C. Given that the $1 million transfer is subject to 30 percent tax whether it takes place today or is delayed and transferred as a bequest in five years, is there any advantage in delaying payment of the gift by five years?

   D. How would the analysis change if the gratuitous transfer tax were paid by the Halls and reduced the value of their taxable estate?

4. After five decades of living in Country A, a wealthy entrepreneur, Andrew Lloyd, has recently retired and taken up residency in Country B. Although he now lives in Country B, Lloyd has retained a number of investment properties in Country A. The investment income tax rate is 45 percent and 30 percent in Country A and Country B, respectively.

   A. Define source and residence tax as two possible primary tax systems of Country A and Country B.

   B. Discuss three potential double taxation conflicts that could arise due to Lloyd's new residency in Country B.

   C. Calculate Lloyd's tax rate liability under the following three methods providing for double taxation relief, assuming scenarios where either country claims source or residence jurisdiction:

   i. Credit method.

   ii. Exemption method.

   iii. Deduction method.

SOLUTIONS FOR READING 16

1. A. There is often a desire to avoid probate as court fees may be sizable, and the process can cause a delay in the transfer of assets to intended beneficiaries. A will can be challenged, and its contents are often a matter of public record, which may concern some wealthy families as it may cause embarrassment or divulge sensitive financial information. Moreover, many problems can arise in probate when multiple jurisdictions are involved. In some instances, probate can be avoided or its impact limited by holding assets in joint ownership (e.g., joint tenancy with right of survivorship), living trusts, retirement plans, or life insurance strategies. Through these structures, ownership transfers without the need for a will, and hence the probate process can be avoided.

B. Under civil law, ownership is a precise concept that is tempered by statutes that place certain limitations on the free disposition of one's assets. Under forced heirship rules, for example, children have the right to a fixed share of a parent's estate. This right may exist whether or not the child is estranged or conceived outside of marriage. Forced heirship in civil law countries may reduce or eliminate the need for a will. Wealthy individuals may attempt to move assets into an offshore trust governed by a different domicile to circumvent forced heirship rules. Spouses typically have similar guaranteed inheritance rights under civil law forced heirship regimes. In addition, spouses have marital property rights, which depend on the marital property regime that applies to their marriage. Individuals can attempt to reduce or avoid forced heirship by:

- ▶ moving assets into an offshore trust governed by a different jurisdiction;

- ▶ gifting or donating assets to others during their lifetime to reduce the value of the final estate upon death; or

- ▶ purchasing life insurance, which can move assets outside of realm of forced heirship provisions.

Such strategies, however, may be subject to "clawback" provisions that provide a basis for heirs to challenge these solutions in court.

2. A. Greg and Christine Pearsall's joint survival probabilities are equal to the sum of their individual probabilities less the product of their individual probabilities, calculated as follows:

$$p(\text{Joint survival}) = p(\text{Greg survives}) + p(\text{Christine survives}) \\ - p(\text{Greg survives})p(\text{Christine survives})$$

For each of the next five years, their joint probability of survival is:

Year	Joint p(Survival)
1	0.9940
2	0.9874
3	0.9807
4	0.9688
5	0.9551

B. It is not appropriate to use the expected return of the assets used to fund spending needs to calculate the capitalized value of their core capital needs, because the risk of the Pearsalls' spending needs is unrelated to the risk of the investment portfolio used to fund those needs. Although the annual spending cash flows are not riskless, a risk-free rate should be used to calculate the present value of the cash flows as their uncertainty is unrelated to market risk factors that would be priced in a normal asset pricing model, making their beta equal to zero.

C. The capitalized value of their core capital needs equals the product of the joint probability of survival and the real spending need for each year discounted using the real risk-free rate. The real risk-free rate is calculated as follows:

Real risk-free rate = [(1 + Nominal risk-free rate) ÷ (1 + Inflation rate) − 1]
$$3.7736\% = [(1 + 0.10) \div (1 + 0.06) - 1]$$

Year	Annual Spending	Expected Spending	Discounted Value
1	75,000	74,550	71,839
2	75,000	74,055	68,767
3	75,000	73,553	65,817
4	75,000	72,660	62,654
5	75,000	71,633	59,522
			$328,599

$$\text{Discounted value} = \frac{\text{Real spending} \times \text{Joint probability}}{(1 + \text{Real risk-free rate})^t}$$

Alternatively, annual spending can be adjusted for inflation and these nominal expected cash flows can be discounted at the nominal risk-free rate.

Year	Annual Spending	Expected Spending	Discounted Value
1	79,500	79,023	71,839
2	84,270	83,208	68,767
3	89,326	87,602	65,817
4	94,686	91,731	62,654
5	100,367	95,861	59,522
			$328,599

$$\text{Discounted value} = \frac{\text{Real spending} \times (1 + \text{Inflation})^t \times \text{Joint probability}}{(1 + \text{Risk-free rate})^t}$$

Greg and Christine Pearsall have core capital spending needs of $328,599 for the next five years.

3. A. Transferring their investment portfolio assets directly to the third generation (grandson), the Halls may reduce transfer tax liabilities. In jurisdictions that tax gifts or bequests, transfers from the first generation to the second will be taxed. The same capital may be taxed again if it is transferred from the second to third generation and the second generation's estate is taxable. Transferring capital in excess of the second generation's needs for spending, safety, and flexibility directly to the third generation can avoid a layer of this double taxation. However, in the United States, taxing authorities discourage this strategy by imposing a special generation skipping tax. This tax, in addition to the usual transfer tax, is imposed on transfers to grandchildren or subsequent generations and is intended to produce the same overall tax effect had the assets passed sequentially through two generations.

B. $$RV_{TaxableGift} = \frac{FV_{Gift}}{FV_{Bequest}}$$

$$= \frac{[1 + 0.10(1 - 0.25)]^5(1 - 0.30)}{[1 + 0.10(1 - 0.30)]^5(1 - 0.30)} = \frac{1.0049}{0.9818} = 1.02$$

C. There is no advantage in delaying payment of the gift because their grandson has a lower marginal tax rate on investment returns compared to the estate's marginal tax rate; the gift still creates a tax advantage if donated today. As their grandson is subject to a lower tax rate of 25 percent, subsequent investment returns will be taxed at a lower rate than if it is kept inside the estate. As the calculation in Solution B indicates, 2 percent more wealth will be created in five years than if the portfolio had remained in the estate and been taxed at 30 percent annually. This analysis assumes that the gratuitous transfer tax is paid by the grandson rather than by the Halls.

D. If the Halls were responsible for paying the gratuitous transfer tax, the relative value of the gift compared to the bequest is:

$$RV_{TaxableGift} = \frac{FV_{Gift}}{FV_{Bequest}}$$

$$= \frac{[1 + 0.10(1 - 0.25)]^5(1 - 0.30 + 0.30 \times 0.30)}{[1 + 0.10(1 - 0.30)]^5(1 - 0.30)}$$

$$= \frac{1.1341}{0.9818} = 1.16$$

The gift receives a partial tax credit because it reduces the size of the Halls' taxable estate. This would make the gratuitous transfer (*inter vivos* gift) even more valuable because 16 percent more wealth would be created in five years than if it had remained in the estate and been taxed at 30 percent annually.

4. A. *Source tax system:* A jurisdiction that imposes tax on an individual's income that is sourced in the jurisdiction.

Residence tax system: A jurisdiction that imposes a tax on an individual's income based on residency whereby all income (domestic and foreign sourced) is subject to taxation.

B. The interaction of countries' taxation jurisdictions can create tax conflicts in which Country A and B can claim to have authority to tax the same investment properties. This conflict can arise in three ways:

► *Residence–residence conflict:* If he were a resident of both countries, Country A and B would both claim residence of Mr. Lloyd, subjecting his worldwide income to taxation by both countries.

► *Source–source conflict:* Both Country A and B may claim source jurisdiction of the same investment properties as income from the investments that are in Country A, but managed from Country B.

► *Residence–source conflict:* Because Lloyd lives in Country B, but has investment properties in Country A, he may be subject to a combination of two taxation jurisdictions. As a resident of Country B he could be taxed on worldwide income; and if Country A exercises source jurisdiction on his assets, he will be taxed on these as well. In this case, the source country (Country A) is commonly viewed to have primary jurisdiction to tax income within its borders and the residence country (Country B) is expected to provide double taxation relief.

C. i. In the credit method, the residence country reduces its taxpayers' domestic tax liability for taxes paid to a foreign country exercising source jurisdiction. The credit is limited to the amount of taxes the taxpayer would pay domestically, which completely eliminates double taxation. Under this method the tax liability equals the greater of the tax liability due in either the residence or source country.

If Country A claims source jurisdiction and Country B residence jurisdiction:

$$T_{CreditMethod} = \text{Max}[T_{Residence}, T_{Source}]$$
$$T_{CreditMethod} = \text{Max}[0.30, 0.45] = 45\%$$

In this case, Lloyd remits the entire 45 percent to Country A, which has the source claim.

If Country A were to exercise residence jurisdiction and Country B source jurisdiction, the effective tax rate is the same:

$$T_{CreditMethod} = \text{Max}[T_{Residence}, T_{Source}]$$
$$T_{CreditMethod} = \text{Max}[0.45, 0.30] = 45\%$$

However, Lloyd would remit 30% to Country B and apply that remittance toward Country A's 45% tax liability, effectively paying Country A 15%.

ii. Under the exemption method, the residence country imposes no tax on foreign-source income by providing taxpayers with an exemption, which, in effect, eliminates the residence–source conflict by having only one jurisdiction impose tax. The tax liability under the exemption method is simply the tax imposed at the foreign source, so the source tax rate prevails:

If Country A is the source country, Lloyd's tax rate is 45 percent.
If Country B's is the source country, Lloyd's tax rate is 30 percent.

iii. Under the deduction method, the residence country allows taxpayers to reduce their taxable income by the amount of taxes paid to foreign governments in respect of foreign-source income (i.e., provides a tax deduction rather than a credit or exemption). The taxpayer is still responsible for both taxes, but the aggregate liability is less than the sum of the two taxes individually with the residence country reducing the size of its percentage claim by the product of the two tax rates.

$$T_{DeductionMethod} = T_{Residence} + T_{Source} - (T_{Residence}T_{Source})$$

Country A: Residence jurisdiction and Country B: Source jurisdiction
= 0.45 + 0.30 − (0.45 × 0.30) = 0.6150
Country A receives 31.50% and Country B receives 30%

Country A: Source jurisdiction and Country B: Residence jurisdiction
= 0.30 + 0.45 − (0.30 × 0.45) = 0.6150
Country A receives 45%, and Country B receives 16.50%

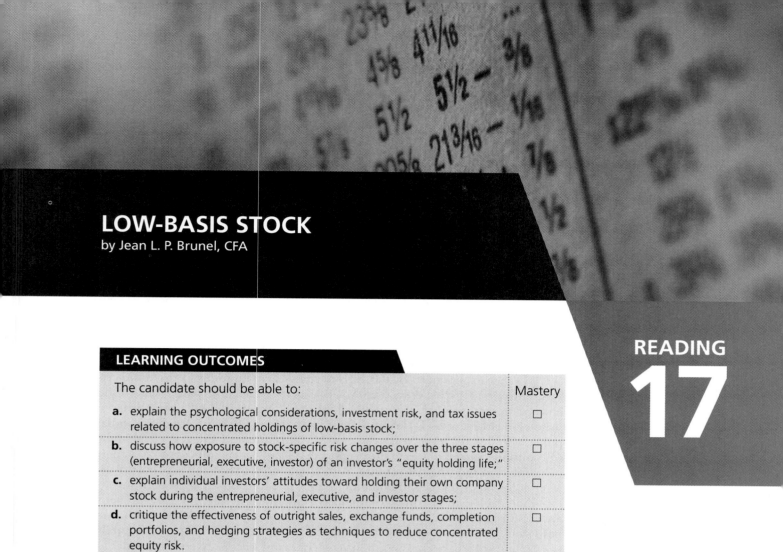

LOW-BASIS STOCK
by Jean L. P. Brunel, CFA

LEARNING OUTCOMES

The candidate should be able to:	Mastery
a. explain the psychological considerations, investment risk, and tax issues related to concentrated holdings of low-basis stock;	☐
b. discuss how exposure to stock-specific risk changes over the three stages (entrepreneurial, executive, investor) of an investor's "equity holding life;"	☐
c. explain individual investors' attitudes toward holding their own company stock during the entrepreneurial, executive, and investor stages;	☐
d. critique the effectiveness of outright sales, exchange funds, completion portfolios, and hedging strategies as techniques to reduce concentrated equity risk.	☐

INTRODUCTION

For many individual investors, the question of what to do about low-basis holdings is very significant. In this context, "low-basis" simply means that the stock or stocks that they hold now have a much higher market value than their tax cost.

DEFINING THE PROBLEM   1

What "Basis" Means

Basis is a term, used principally for tax purposes, referring to the price that serves as the basis for the computation of capital gains. Though, under U.S. tax rules, the basis of an investment is not always the price at which it was purchased, net of any applicable commission or related transaction cost, it is often the case that tax cost is very often close to an accounting book value concept.

However, depending upon the actual means through which the investment was acquired, the basis might be different from its initial cost. The simplest illustration would be the case of a transmission through an estate, in which case the basis is "stepped up" to the value of the investment at the time the estate matured. Also, there are instances where the basis of an investment may be adjusted, upwards or downwards. The simplest example would be when there is a wash sale, in which case the basis of the remaining investment may be its cost adjusted for the capital loss incurred in the sale of the investment that generated the cash needed to buy it.

How Low-Basis Stock Is Acquired

The mode through which low-basis stock is accumulated is important. We will see later that it can have a significant influence on the way the investor looks at these investments and, consequently, on his or her willingness to sell the security at some future point in time. Low-basis holdings in individual portfolios arise through a number of circumstances, but three principal events typically lead to the situation: entrepreneurial success, executive success, or investment success.

Whether experienced by the current senior generation or by distant ancestors, entrepreneurial success usually will lead to the total or partial sale of the entrepreneurial venture. A partial sale of the company will take place when a privately held business is "taken public," with shares offered through an initial public offering, for instance. In this case, the entrepreneur and his or her family will continue to own shares in the original company, with a tax cost equal to their investment in the original venture. A total sale of the company will take place when it is sold or merged into another entity, in a transaction potentially involving some exchange of equity. In the case of an outright sale, the entrepreneur and his or her family will hold cash, and thus not have any problem with low-basis stock. In the case of a sale for stock, the entrepreneur and his or her family will be left with shares in the purchasing company, with a tax cost still equal to their investment in the original venture.

A variant on the entrepreneurial theme can be found in the case of senior executives whose compensation includes a substantial equity component. Whether made up of restricted stock or options, this equity compensation leads the executive to have accumulated substantial shareholdings in the company over time. The value of these holdings may have risen substantially above the cost at which the stock was vested or the exercise price of the options.

Although usually not leading to a single low-basis stock holding, but rather to a portfolio comprising several substantially appreciated securities, investment success can also create problems. This can occur in a variety of circumstances. The most frequent instance is the case of family wealth transferred across generations through trust vehicles. Specifically, a portfolio may own stocks that were purchased many years or decades ago, at prices substantially below currently prevailing levels. Yet it can occur in other ways, for instance in the case of passive venture capitalists who happen to invest in a particularly successful company, or in the case of the purchase in a portfolio of one or two brilliant investments that appreciate substantially over a generation or less.

Dealing with Low-Basis Holdings

Deciding on a strategy to deal with such low-basis holdings is one of the most daunting challenges faced by individuals. This challenge has several facets, but two dominate.

Psychological issues are very important as, often, there is some history to the investment. It may be that an ancestor founded the company; it may still bear the family's name. The investment may have been acquired by a loved and revered relative. The investment may be the source of the family's fortune, and there is therefore some feeling of loyalty attached to it.

Investment issues are no less important, and they typically fall into at least two baskets. The first relates to the question of risk and return, the essence of the traditional investment problem. Am I going to be rewarded for the risk I am taking? Is there any other investment capable of providing the kind of returns I expect from this one? The second basket incorporates the inevitable question of taxes. How much will I need to pay just to sell some, or all, of this holding? How sure am I of getting the benefits that I hope to get, in exchange for the certainty associated with the initial tax-based transaction cost?

UNDERSTANDING STOCK RISK   **2**

Before delving into the emotional and tax aspects of concentrated holdings, let us step back from the problem, in order to put it in the appropriate perspective. Investment theory teaches that the risk of any individual investment can be broken down into two components:

▶ *market (or systematic) risk,* which affects all securities in the same class, for instance all U.S. equities; and

▶ *specific risk,* which relates to each security in particular.

Visualizing the difference between market and specific risks is helped by a quotation (kindly provided to me by John W. Mitchell, U.S. Bancorp's Western Chief Economist) from a paper by Steven McNees and Geoffrey Tortell,[1] which says it all, though it applies to economic performance rather than investment risk: "A region's economy floats on a national sea, while being buffeted by local tides and winds." It would not be inaccurate to view specific risk through an analogous assertion: an individual stock floats on the broader market, while being buffeted by its own corporate tides and winds.

Diversification theory tells us that, if we own a sufficient number of sufficiently different individual securities, specific risk can be diversified. It is important here to place some emphasis on the term "sufficiently different." Indeed, it is worth remembering that a portfolio comprising 20 bank stocks, for instance, is a well diversified bank portfolio, but not necessarily a well diversified equity portfolio.

What is left after any level of specific risk diversification has taken place is known as *residual risk.*[2] Residual risk can include counterparty or regulatory risks. *Counterparty risk* exists for as long as you are still dependent upon a counterparty to complete a transaction, for example a broker, when receiving the proceeds of a sale, or a bank, in relation to the value of a hedging strategy. Regulatory risk exists for as long as the tax authorities can still query any transaction and reject the tax treatment that you have chosen. We will not be discussing residual risks in much detail in this reading, but they should not be forgotten.

---

[1] McNees, Steven and Geoffrey Tortell, *New England Economic Review,* July–August, 1991.

[2] For a discussion of this topic, see Jacobs, Bruce I., and Kenneth N. Levy, 'Residual Risks: How Much is Too Much?,' *The Journal of Portfolio Management,* Spring 1996, pp. 10–16.

EXHIBIT 1	The Four Stages of Specific Stock Risk

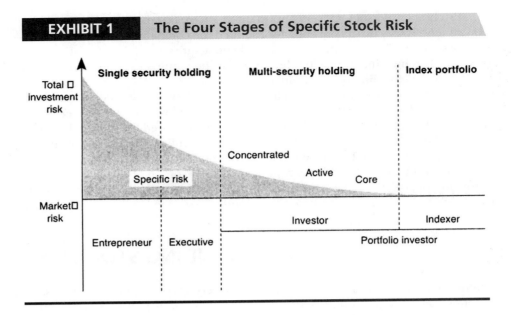

Visualizing Equity Portfolio Risk

Exhibit 1 depicts the various levels of risk that an investor may choose to retain in an equity portfolio. It comprises two lines. The first reflects market risk, which, in this instance, is kept constant. The assumption is, therefore, that the investor has made no effort to diversify it, in the context of a balanced, or diversified portfolio, by combining several asset classes in the hypothetical portfolio, for instance by combining domestic and international stocks, or equities and bonds, or nondi-rectional hedge funds. The second line depicts total risk, which comprises both market and specific risk. The zone between the two lines represents specific risk.

Note that specific risk and, thus, total risk both decline substantially as we move from left to right. As the portfolio is increasingly diversified, the specific risk incurred by the investor tails off, at first rapidly, then more gradually. At the extreme right-hand side of the graph, the portfolio replicates the index, is fully diversified, and is therefore no longer exposed to specific risk. Note, however, that it is still fully exposed to the market risk.

Diversification and the "Equity Holding Lives" of Individual Investors

Exhibit 1 illustrates the idea that there are three essential stages to the "equity holding life" of an individual. They recall and, in fact, mirror the way in which we described the acquisition of low-basis holdings.

We start with the *entrepreneurial stage*. At the extreme left-hand end of the graph, specific risk is very high, as we are dealing both with a single security and with a company that is somewhat immature. The entrepreneur works with a new idea, develops it into a business, grows the business and, eventually and poten-tially, takes it public.

Once the business is public, we are dealing with the *executive stage*, where the specific risk of the company is still high, yet somewhat lower, as the business is arguably more mature than a brand new venture. The high specific risk reflects the fact that the equity holding is not diversified. Indeed, we are thinking here of an executive who still has the bulk of his or her financial wealth in that one security. Note that the executive stage encompasses both individuals who are still responsible for the management of the firm and individuals whose compensation incorporates restricted stock or options, but who do not occupy the highest positions in the company.

The next phase, the *investor stage,* moves us away from a single stock to a multisecurity portfolio. There can be no question then that each investment is held as a part of a portfolio, rather than as a means of owning a piece of a business. We saw earlier that the focus during the investor stage should shift from creating significant wealth to protecting and growing wealth.

There are two variants to the generic investor stage. The *diversified investor stage* involves a multistock portfolio that can be concentrated, actively managed or highly diversified through a core strategy. An important element of the investment strategy is to diversify specific risk, down to some acceptable level of tracking error, which is defined as the volatility of the performance of the portfolio relative to the relevant index.

The ultimate variation on this theme is the *indexing stage,* where the investor aims to replicate the risk of the relevant index and thus holds a portfolio that has virtually eliminated specific risk.

Exhibit 1 can help the advisor or the wealthy individual identify the appropriate equity portfolio strategy for the particular circumstances. It says, for instance, that it is perfectly normal for an entrepreneur to have the bulk of his or her wealth in that single venture. The purpose of the venture is for the entrepreneur to create wealth, and the risks associated with it are well understood. At the other end of the spectrum, it also tells us that investors should hold diversified portfolios, in the process eschewing the advice, often attributed to Warren Buffet, that individuals should own a few stocks in a few businesses that they understand well and that are managed by top-class executives.[3]

APPLYING THE MODEL TO INDIVIDUAL CIRCUMSTANCES

3

The conceptual framework illustrated in Exhibit 1 is most useful when it comes to helping individuals with concentrated low-basis stock positions. We know that we will need to deal with both emotional and investment issues, and one of the important first steps must therefore be to try and get to some agreed base from which to move forward. This goal can be achieved by helping the individual, or the family, explore this stock diversification spectrum and ask themselves what kind of risk they should be taking. Let us look at each of the diversification stages in turn.

The Entrepreneurial Stage

As we saw earlier, no diversification is desired during the entrepreneurial stage. In fact, the investor will usually only diversify if and when selling stock in his or her company is necessary to generate the capital needed to grow the business. Venture capitalists tend to value the fact that entrepreneurs have most of their eggs in the

---

[3] For a comment on the relationship between investment performance and management quality, see Granatelli, Andy, and John D. Martin, 'Management Quality and Investment Performance,' *Financial Analysts Journal,* Vol. 40, No. 6, November/December 1984, pp. 72–74.

one basket, just as many wealth managers value the fact that investment managers have substantial stakes in the strategies that they execute on behalf of their clients. The corollary of the desire by venture capitalists to see entrepreneurs financially committed is that they are usually particularly cautious when they hear that an insider is selling stock in a secondary offering. This worries them, unless there is a very good reason, because they question the entrepreneur's commitment or perceptions as to the future of the business. Meir Statman[4] explains that perception in the context of any generic transaction. He says that a transaction, when looked at in isolation, must involve a winner and a loser. Either the price of the stock goes up and the seller has experienced some opportunity loss, or it goes down and the buyer has experienced a real loss. Statman therefore suggests that prudence requires the buyer to make sure that the seller does not know something he or she (the buyer) does not know.

Entrepreneurs are not expected to want to diversify their exposure to their original great idea. Rather, they should seek maximum profit from it and would only reluctantly share in it when the alternative reduces the profit potential of the business. Entrepreneurs rarely ask themselves questions about wealth management or portfolio diversification, but when they do they should always seek advice relating to structuring the ownership of the asset. They should be looking for ways to minimize the likely transfer costs that will eventually arise as they pass their wealth onto their heirs.

The Executive Stage

During the executive stage, the extent to which the individual requires diversification is linked to the degree of control that he or she has over the fortunes of the company. Clearly, diversification is also dependent upon the feasibility of any sale of corporate equity, as certain executives have "handcuffs," or the equity they own may only vest over time and substantially into the future.

In practice, the higher the individual is in the corporate hierarchy, the greater the appetite seems to be for specific risk. This is logical, as one can argue that there is some entrepreneurial bent still at work in the most senior executive positions. It follows that the tendency should be to seek greater diversification as one descends the management hierarchy. Ultimately, the individual would view equity ownership as only one element of compensation and not as an entrepreneurial endeavor, as proposed by Heidi Schneider and John Geer.[5] Yet, in the end, whether mostly undiversified or somewhat diversified, the ownership model remains influenced by the fact that we are still dealing with relatively concentrated positions, with higher levels of specific risk.

The Investor Stage

The greatest diversification challenge concerns individuals who are no longer in either the entrepreneurial or the executive stages. The fact that they no longer exercise significant control over the fortunes of the underlying company

---

[4] Meir Statman, Glenn Klimek Professor of Finance at the Leavey School of Business, Santa Clara University, made the comment referenced here at the 8th Annual Family Office Forum, hosted on June 25 and 26, 2001 by the Institute for Investment Research in Chicago.

[5] See Schneider, Heidi L., and John Geer, 'Stock-based Compensation: New Opportunities, New Risks For Senior Executives,' *The Journal of Wealth Management*, Summer 2001, pp. 55–57. Both these authors are senior executives of money manager Neuberger Berman.

requires them to start to think in terms of that investment being essentially a financial holding.

C. Nicholas Potter, the former head of J.P. Morgan's Asset Management Group (and the individual most often credited for having turned it around in the early 1980s), once told me that he believed that "one of the most important contributions of modern portfolio theory was to change a stock from being the same thing as a company, to becoming a set of investment characteristics."[6] This insight is invaluable, as it recognizes that, once you no longer are in the position to direct the fortunes of a company or to access this or that asset, you are only buying the right to a dividend flow and to sell the stock to someone else at some future date.

Let me illustrate this point with an example. Recently, I was discussing this issue with a family on a day when an article in the *Wall Street Journal* mentioned a stock as being apparently cheap, as you were paying less than "cash per share" to buy it. I did not believe the article made sense, for at least two reasons. First, singling out a significant cash reserve does not make much sense, as it is possible that the company is in fact running a negative cash flow. Thus, it may be using that cash in the next several months, without my being able, in any way, to affect it. It turns out this was a very important piece of the puzzle, as the company was a dot-com and was indeed in need of further funding a few months later. Second, and more broadly, individual shareholders do not have access to single entry on the balance sheet, and thus must look at the total package, unless they have the power to remove senior management and appoint either themselves or someone who will do their bidding. It is indeed always worth remembering the legal admonition according to which you own a proportional share of the stockholders' equity of a company, and a proportional share of each asset and liability in a trust.

Focusing on the fundamentals of a company, as a proxy for it being a valuable investment, therefore makes sense only if the present value of the expected dividend flow and the likely terminal value (at which I will sell the stock) is greater than today's price. This is the essence of security analysis. Any other extrapolation effectively relies on the "greater fool" theory, which holds that there is a greater fool (than I) who will be prepared to buy the stock from me and at a higher price, based on my current reading of the corporate fundamentals. Though arguably in keeping with the behavioral finance principles of optimism and over-confidence, this approach is fraught with danger.

I have found that getting an individual to understand the difference between an operating investment and a financial investment is a critical element of the process through which he or she eventually accepts the need to diversify a low-basis holding. At the same time, dealing with low-basis holdings requires advisors to make special efforts to understand the psychology of the individual investor.

Two cases come to mind. I have seen individuals who, though no longer in control in the underlying company, were still afforded special status. This could involve some residual honorific role or just some special recognition at annual meetings. It is important to appreciate that these will extend the direct link between the individual and the company, and require that diversification be handled in a sensitive fashion. Similarly, a public company may still bear the name of the founder, though the founder's family no longer exercises any management control. The loyalty link to one's ancestors requires sensitivity on the part of the advisor when discussing diversification.

---

[6] For a discussion of "company-ness" versus "stock-ness," see Clayman, Michelle, 'Excellence Revisited,' *Financial Analysts Journal*, Vol. 49, No. 3, May/June 1993, pp. 61–65.

4   REDUCING A CONCENTRATED EXPOSURE

Once the investor has dealt with emotional issues and accepted the need to diversify some or all of the concentrated position, several options are available. Scott Welch proposes five most commonly used approaches to diversify concentrated equity positions.[7] He distinguishes between two fundamentally different sets of tools: financial strategies and charitable strategies. Charitable strategies allow an individual to diversify out of an appreciated asset through gifting. We will not discuss these here, as we already looked into gifting strategies when we reviewed multiple asset locations. Financial strategies, however, deserve a more detailed analysis: specifically, outright sales, exchange funds, completion portfolios, and hedging strategies. Outright sales are the simplest, but most investors recoil at the idea of paying the tax bill associated with them and opt for one of the more complex financial strategies.

Outright Sale

The simplest and often most expensive strategy involves an outright sale of the security. Though the move will trigger the realization of an unrealized capital gain and the associated payment of capital gains tax, it is the preferred option of individuals who want to have maximum flexibility. Once the sale has been settled and the cash proceeds have been received, all residual risks (as discussed above) are eliminated, and the investor has total freedom to dispose of the proceeds of the sale as he or she wishes. Note, however, that there will typically be a lower amount of money to reinvest. If the investor is a U.S. tax resident, the net proceeds available for reinvestment would be 80% of the original amount, assuming that the tax basis in the security was zero, that it had been held for at least one year, and that the investor is subject only to federal taxes.

Exchange Funds

The classic exchange fund is created when an advisor brings together a number of individuals, each having a different concentrated position, and invites them to pool their assets. Imagine that you are an investment advisor and that you know of 50 investors, each having a position in one stock that they would like to diversify. Imagine that these 50 stocks are sufficiently different from one another that a portfolio comprising all of them would have a risk profile substantially lower than each individual stock and could, if the portfolio is constructed in the appropriate manner, be more or less similar to that of some broad market index. Note that the portfolio may hold each of these stocks in equal proportions, or may be constructed in a more complex manner, with different weightings for different companies, so that it may more closely mimic the performance of the index.

Public Exchange Funds

In a traditional, public exchange fund under U.S. tax law, the investors enter into a partnership for a minimum of seven years. Their portfolio will further need to comprise, at the outset, a 20% exposure to other illiquid investments, to satisfy U.S. tax requirements. Thus, they will have achieved their diversification

---

[7] See Welch, Scott D., 'Diversifying Concentrated Holdings,' AIMR Conference Proceedings: *Investment Counseling for Private Clients III*, March 27–28, 2001, pp. 30–35 and 42–44. Scott Welch is the Director of Equity Risk Management at CMS Financial Services.

goal, immediately and in the future, without needing to realize a capital gain at the outset. Indeed, for the first seven years the portfolio's behavior will reflect the combined performance of the original stocks, together with the returns on the illiquid investments. Depending upon the diversification within these original names and the way in which the portfolio is constructed, it may in fact mimic the return on some relevant index. At the end of the seven years, each partner may receive a proportional distribution of his or her share of the fund, that distribution now comprising that partner's proportional share of all the components of the portfolio—that is, the stocks currently in the portfolio plus the illiquid investments—rather than his or her original stock.

Note that each investor has only deferred and not eliminated the liability for capital gains tax associated with the original stock holding. Indeed, no capital gains tax has been paid as a result of entering into the partnership. However, the tax basis for the "diversified" portfolio received upon the partnership being wound up will be the same as the tax basis of the original single stock. Diversification taxes have been deferred, but not eliminated. Yet, because the investor is now exposed to the risk of a broader basket of stocks, the specific downside risk associated with his or her low-basis holding has been effectively eliminated.

The shortcomings of exchange funds include management costs, lack of control, and inflexibility. Public exchange funds are typically costly, as the manager of the fund charges an initial fee for bringing the investors together, selecting the stocks, and deciding on their relative proportions. He or she also charges for the selection and purchase of the illiquid investment, as well as for the ongoing management of the fund.

Public exchange funds are also somewhat inflexible. Investors must accept both the fact that the fund will hold 20% of its assets in illiquid investments and the list of stocks comprising the fund. Though potential investors are shown the list of the other investments likely to be held in the fund, and are free to accept or reject the partnership, they cannot control the composition of the portfolio. They may only accept or reject the offer to join.

Public exchange funds are typically passively managed. The ongoing management of the fund principally boils down to the reinvestment of dividends. Therein lies a third, admittedly less important, shortcoming: there is usually little scope for the manager to eliminate a holding whose fundamentals have substantially deteriorated, or to buy into an interesting new opportunity.

A Private Exchange Fund Alternative

As this is being written, private exchange funds are being discussed and introduced to selected investors. However, they have yet to be tested in the broad market place and their ability to stand up to the scrutiny of the tax authorities is still unknown.

Private exchange funds are designed to address the shortcomings of public exchange funds. They usually involve a single security. The investor or investors holding that single security join forces with an external party, who purchases the same stock at current market prices and partners with the original investor or investors. Having at least one "unrelated investor" entering into a partnership "with a valid business purpose other than that of hedging the security" is generally thought to qualify the proposed venture as a bona fide private exchange fund.

The partnership then enters into a series of partial hedging, borrowing and reinvesting transactions. These transactions are designed to provide the owners of the low-basis stock with the diversification that they seek. Hedging the low-basis stock in a way that does not trigger constructive sale rules will have two benefits. First, it will create the opportunity to borrow against that stock at more advantageous terms than would be the case if it were not hedged, and without creating the additional risks associated with leverage. Second, it also helps soften the psychological blow at times associated with the sale of a low-basis stock, as the transaction is typically designed to allow the owner of the stock to retain some exposure to potential upside price movements in that stock.

Interestingly, this diversification is achieved without the constraints associated with a public exchange fund. There is no need to have a fixed exposure to illiquid investments. Further, the partners in a private exchange fund have the ability to choose, and vary over time, the investments bought with the proceeds of the borrowing. Provided the partners do not break the partnership for at least the same seven years as is the case with a public exchange fund, it is possible that the investor will have achieved his or her diversification goals in a more effective fashion.

However, the structure contains a number of residual risks, principally of a regulatory nature, as the U.S. Internal Revenue Service has not ruled on all the aspects of the transaction.

Completion Portfolios

Single Asset Class Completion Portfolios

Completion portfolios can be of interest to individuals who have access to other liquid assets besides their single concentrated low-basis position. These liquid funds can come from a variety of sources, such as other financial assets that may be sold without an undue tax penalty. The concept of a completion portfolio is to allow the investor to create a portfolio that behaves like some desired index or basket, by combining the low-basis position with some or all of his or her additional liquid assets. The investor "completes" the single security by purchasing a basket of other securities that, together with the initial stock, help reduce the overall risk of the single position and may in fact bring it closer to a reference index.

The simplest incarnation of such a strategy would be the case of an individual who has both an appreciated stock and an equal amount of cash. Let us imagine that the stock is a large bank, J.P. Morgan Chase, for instance. Let us assume finally that the investor's goal is to replicate the risk profile of the S&P 500 Index, which tracks the performance of the large-capitalization universe within the U.S. equity market. The investor could use his or her available cash to purchase a portfolio, which on its own will appear somewhat skewed. For instance, it will most certainly not include any additional exposure to other money center banks. It may in fact further eschew exposure to companies whose business is closely or even more remotely tied to interest rate movements, as it would be assumed that they have more than enough interest rate risk in their bank holding. Conceivably, they might also avoid investments in multinational companies, as the global nature of the bank's business might be deemed to provide the needed risk exposure. By contrast, they might seem to own disproportionate exposures to technology and basic industries to which the bank is not directly exposed.

The portfolio may actually be constructed and managed in at least two different ways. The simplest approach involves managing the completion portfolio through the systematic reinvestment of the dividends paid out by all stocks, thus including those paid out by the low-basis stock, in order to purchase further diversification. A more sophisticated approach involves the use of the *passive structured strategy*. The manager would go beyond using dividends to generate diversification over time, and use all available opportunities to harvest the inevitable losses experienced by one or several of the stocks in the completion portfolio. These losses would be used to chip away at the concentrated holding, sheltering the capital gain realized each time any of that low-basis stock is sold.

Multi-Asset Class Completion Portfolios

Completion portfolios do not have to be constrained to the asset class to which the low-basis holding belongs, but may reach across asset or sub-asset classes. An example, appropriately modified to disguise the actual circumstances, will illustrate this point.

EXAMPLE 1

In the late 1980s, a large and very well known U.S. family had a substantially concentrated holding in a few health care companies that members of the family had helped build over the years. The family sought diversification, but could not accept the costs associated with unrealized capital gains. The family hired an advisor to construct and manage a portfolio of small stocks, indexed to the Russell 2000, an index produced by The Frank Russell Company that tracks the 2,000 smallest stocks in the firm's broad universe of 3,000 stocks. The manager was charged with the systematic harvesting of any loss that could be realized within the portfolio. These losses would then be used, over time, to shelter the unrealized gains in the family's low-basis legacy stocks. The portfolio was not tilted away from the drug industry.

The rationale for this strategy was that small-capitalization stocks would produce higher returns than large-capitalization equities over the long term, and would have more individual volatility. The family and its advisor thus implicitly "credited" this outperformance against the higher cost of managing the portfolio. These higher expenses referred principally to transaction costs. The family had considered investing in large-capitalization international stocks, or even emerging market equities, but rejected these solutions for cost and risk reasons.

Knowing what we know today, and with the greater availability of selected derivative instruments, it might make sense to consider multi-asset completion portfolios. This is because they incorporate more diversified sources of risk, and thus of volatility. As we have seen earlier, the more uncorrelated volatility we can find, the greater the potential to manage the assets in a tax-efficient manner.

The major shortcomings of this strategy are twofold. First, *the strategy is ill-suited to investors who do not have a substantial pool of other financial assets alongside the low-basis holding*. In the absence of such a pool, the investor must sell some of the appreciated stock to raise the funds initially needed to diversify. An alternative would be to raise cash by leveraging the portfolio. Yet this effectively raises the portfolio's systematic risk in a fashion that may negate the diversification of the specific risk associated with the low-basis position. Some form of hedging within the scope of "constructive sale rules" could alleviate the concern. Note that there may be some tax efficiency dimension, depending on the ability of the investor to use the interest on the debt. Having to sell some of the appreciated holding to construct a completion portfolio would usually not be viewed as tax-efficient, as taxes will be due upon the sale, in relation to the capital gains thus realized.

Second, *the diversification process typically takes time unless the low-basis position was quite a small part of the investor's wealth at the outset*. Indeed, the initial scope for diversifying the low-basis holding is directly proportional to the availability of cash to make the completion portfolio as broad as possible. Unless the investor has a substantial cash pool available, this means that, at the outset and for some time, there is little or no protection against the downside risk of the low-basis holding.

Hedging Strategies

Hedging strategies have become the technique of choice for low-basis diversification. They typically comprise two distinct steps. First, the risk in the original low-basis holding is diversified, at least in the U.S. context, within the constraints of the Taxpayer Relief Act of 1997, which defined and prohibited "constructive sales." Mark Anson[8] suggests that a taxpayer makes a constructive sale of an appreciated financial position if the taxpayer enters into:

▶ a short sale of the same or substantially identical property;

▶ an offsetting notional principal contract with respect to the same or substantially identical property; or

▶ a futures or forward contract to deliver the same or substantially identical property.

Second, the investor borrows against the value of his or her portfolio, in a transaction often called "monetization," in that the individual effectively monetizes an otherwise illiquid position. The proceeds from this borrowing are then appropriately reinvested.

Before going any further, it is worth citing the advice of Robert Gordon,[9] who says that the most important initial decision is for the investor to choose between two fundamentally different alternatives:

▶ Does he or she want to protect his or her gains and let profits run? or

▶ Does he or she want to get the money out of a position without triggering a taxable event?

Gordon's advice is that in the first case the investor should hedge, while in the second he or she should monetize. This is indeed an important distinction, as the typical solution offered to investors involves a bit of both.

A pure hedging strategy involves finding a way to eliminate or reduce the downside risk associated with the stock's downward price movements, in a transaction that in many ways is akin to purchasing insurance. (Note that "insurance" in this context is understood in a looser sense than that to which we are most accustomed. Insurance here means that the investor still accepts structural and/or counterparty risks. "Portfolio insurance," for example, came to grief in October 1987, because the critical assumption underpinning the strategy, the continuous pricing of physical and derivative securities, did not materialize. Similarly, in the Russian bond debacle of 1998, many investors thought they had bought a hedge, but did not expect the counterparty that had sold it to default on its obligations.) However, because most hedges appear expensive, investors often choose to accept some limit to the upside potential of their current investment.

A pure monetization strategy involves borrowing against a position and reinvesting the proceeds in the way you want. However, because most lenders will demand some security against the borrowing, and because many investors are wary about excessive portfolio leverage, many monetization strategies involve a partial hedging of the low-basis position.

---

[8] See Anson, Mark J. P., 'The Impact of the Taxpayer Relief Act of 1997 on Derivatives Transactions,' *Journal of Derivatives,* Summer 1998, pp. 62–72.

[9] See Gordon, Robert M., 'Hedging Low Cost Basis Stock,' AIMR Conference Proceedings, *Investment Counseling for Private Clients III,* March 27–28, 2001. Robert Gordon is the President of Twenty First Securities.

Equity Collars

An equity collar can be a pure hedging strategy. Using this strategy, the investor selects a combination of put and call options. (A call option is the right, but not the obligation, to purchase a security at some pre-agreed price, known as the "strike price." European-style contracts usually allow the purchase to take place at some precise future date; American-style options allow the purchase to take place at any time until the option matures. A put option is the right, but not the obligation, to sell a security at some pre-agreed price.) The selected combination is to provide protection at or very close to the current market price, and allow some participation in a defined amount of the upside price potential for the stock. Usually, the investor will purchase a put option, which provides the downside protection. Purchasing the put will require the payment of a "premium," which can be viewed as the price paid for that insurance policy. Depending upon whether the investor wishes to offset some of, all of, or even more than the price of the put, he or she will then sell a call option.

The collar can thus have one of three characteristics. First, it can *cost some money,* if the proceeds from the sale of the call option fall short of the cost of the put option. Second, it can be a *cashless collar,* if the proceeds from the sale of the call equal the cost of the put. Third, it can be an *income-producing collar,* if the proceeds from the sale of the call exceed the cost of the put.

The principal requirement of an equity collar is that the transaction does not run afoul of the constructive sale rule (as it is known in the U.S., but there are similar rules elsewhere). Broadly, the rule mandates that the investor must retain some ability to make or lose money. Robert Gordon believes that a 15% or more risk exposure is likely to suffice, given the fact that the example published by the Internal Revenue Service at the time the rule was introduced involved a 15% remaining risk exposure.

Monetization of the Position

The investor may, however, elect to monetize the equity position on which the equity collar has been created. The collar sets a minimum value for the underlying equity position and thus may increase the collateral value of that equity from the point of view of a lender. Depending upon how the investor intends to deploy the proceeds from these borrowings, he or she may be able to borrow as much as 90% of the strike price of the put option, or as little as 50%. Usually, under U.S. tax rules, for the investor to be able to borrow more than 50%, the loan must be considered a nonpurpose loan and be intended for investments in anything other than equities. In fact, the investor may still reinvest in equities and borrow more than 50%, as he or she may be able to "margin" the securities purchased with the loan, in effect borrowing against both the original low-basis position and against the new portfolio.

Variable Pre-Paid Forwards

Scott Welch[10] has provided the best definition of a variable pre-paid forward: "it is essentially a forward sale of a contingent number of shares of an underlying stock, with an agreed future delivery date, in exchange for a cash advance today."

---

[10] See Welch, Scott, 'Was Going "Short Against The Box" Really a Perfect Hedge?,' *The Journal of Private Portfolio Management,* Winter 1999, pp. 41–50.

Under such an arrangement, the investor enters into a contract to deliver some or all of the underlying shares at a future date, in exchange for payment received today in cash. Welch takes this further: "properly constructed and documented, a variable pre-paid forward does not constitute a constructive sale and is not subject to margin lending restrictions." A variable forward contract can be viewed as an "unbalanced collar," a collar where the investor does not have the same number of calls and puts.

An example will help illustrate what this means. In 1998, I analyzed a variable forward contract, the TRACES on Estee Lauder stock, which was brought to the market and listed on the New York Stock Exchange by Goldman Sachs and Co. I found that the variable forward contract could be analyzed as a combination of three steps. First, the stock was sold forward, with an agreed delivery several years hence. Second, a number of calls at US$60.875, equal to the number of shares sold, were purchased. Third, calls with a 15% higher strike price were written (the functional equivalent of a sale) on a number of shares equal to 86.7% of the underlying shares sold (note that $86.7\% \times 1.15 = 1$).

The investor was protected against the price of the Estee Lauder stock falling below US$60.875. He or she would participate one for one in any appreciation of the stock above US$60.875 until US$70.01, and would receive only 15% of the appreciation of the stock should it rise beyond US$70.01.

Relative Attractiveness of Hedging Transactions

The relative attractiveness of a monetized collar or a variable pre-paid forward relates to the deductibility of the interest paid on the borrowings associated with the collar.

There is little debate on the fact that the borrowing costs built into a variable pre-paid forward are capitalized. The investor will effectively be able to offset only a part of these costs, as they will help reduce the capital gain taxes due at maturity. However, with the capital gain tax rate less than 100%, a portion of that capitalized interest will indeed be paid by the investor.

By contrast, there is a debate as to the tax status of the interest paid on the borrowings associated with the equity collar. The "straddle" rules, which apply to stocks bought after 1984, seem to mandate that the cost be capitalized, but certain advisors have come to believe that the interest expense can be offset against the income earned on the portfolio purchased with the borrowings. In such an instance, raising as it would the tax efficiency of the portfolio, an equity collar would seem the better alternative, though there is still considerable fiscal risk in this interpretation.

5 SUMMARY AND IMPLICATIONS

Having looked at both the emotional and investment dimensions of the sale of low-basis stock, the conclusion still seems to be that the decision is anything but obvious or easy. Helping the investor process through the ownership risks that he or she wishes to take, and the corresponding returns that can be expected, has the potential to clarify some of the murkiness. Nevertheless, as a member of the board of a family office whose name is still directly associated with a highly prominent company traded on the New York Stock Exchange, I can testify to the fact that the decision to diversify or not to diversify is still quite a challenging one.

Though I have seen many of the possible variations on the theme, I still cannot find a simple way to predict how individuals will respond to the challenge of diversifying low-basis holdings. I do not mean that individual investors behave in a totally irrational fashion: far from it.

This is an area where the way in which Meir Statman defines behavioral finance best illustrates the issue. He says that: "standard finance assumes that investors are rational, while behavioral finance only assumes that they are normal."

Three Case Studies

Three examples illustrate the different ways in which different individuals behave. Note that, in all three cases, there are sincere and logical reasons behind each of the different behaviors.

EXAMPLE 2

1. The co-founder of a high-technology company made the seemingly heroic decision first to step down from the company's management and then to sell out all of his shares near the stock's top market valuation. There was no personal acrimony between the two founders, but rather a fair strategic disagreement. In this instance, it seemed pretty clear that the individual had first voted with his feet and then naturally did not feel much subsequent attachment to the investment. Thus, he found it relatively easy to sell, though he did hesitate at one point when the price started to fall sharply. The main lesson, however, is that he had a systematic and orderly sale program in place, and mostly stuck with it.

2. The widow of a successful investor found herself holding nearly 50% of her financial portfolio in one stock in the early 1990s. She could not accept the idea of diversifying the portfolio by selling that holding. It was the last investment her late husband had made and her recollection of her husband's investment prowess was that he had never made a bad investment. In this instance, it was clear that she insisted on keeping the high concentration in his memory, and that time would probably help her deal with the inherent risk. Indeed, even if her late husband was an exceptional investor, he was certainly more familiar with the company and its industry than she was. Yet she needed time to learn that she could take only those risks that she and her advisors understood well.

3. The children of a highly successful entrepreneur were unwilling to sell the stock inherited from their father. In their view, the company was still exceptional and would continue to do as well as it had in the past. They had an instinctive trust in the remaining management, although, when questioned, they accepted that they really did not have any privileged access to information (which would have made them insiders and could have prevented them from disposing of the security if they wanted to do so). As the stock started to go down, they would look back and, in an attitude predicted by Meir Statman, they would "view the stock's most recent high as its fair value." In the end, the decision not to sell caused them to end up with a small fortune, having started with a much larger one.

The Need for a Dispassionate Decision-Making Process

Experience suggests that the more the individual can be taken through a dispassionate and logical process, focused on why they need to hold on to a stock, and how much of it they should sell, the more they are able to start and stay on the right track. The focus is twofold. First, one must try to understand what motivates the investor and help him or her appreciate it. Second, one must be able to differentiate between making the decision to diversify and executing that decision.

Though one certainly does not want to lead the investor on an endless cycle of "trigger points," which rise and fall with the daily fluctuations of the market, it is worth remembering the earlier advice: individual investors need the best strategy with which they can live, not the best strategy in absolute terms. Getting an individual started on the right path is certainly more effective, in the end, than holding out for the absolute best theoretical decision, which the individual will never implement anyway.

The real and understandable difficulty that many investors have in dealing with the immediate, often psychological, pain associated with diversification makes strategies geared to reducing that pain particularly attractive. Hedging strategies that provide the potential to defer the realization of taxable capital gains and preserve some upside, should the price of the stock keep rising, seem to make the decision that much easier.

Making Diversification More Palatable

A final point is worth highlighting. Diversification is rarely palatable, when considered solely in a "negative" sense. Unless the individual is clearly motivated by fear, for instance the fear of losing their wealth, the notion that a single stock is a riskier investment than a diversified portfolio is not a strongly persuasive rationale. Rather, it may be useful for individual investors or their advisors to think in terms of diversification allowing them to take advantage of opportunities that might otherwise not be available. Let me illustrate this with four simple examples.

EXAMPLE 3

1. Recently, a family had, after a long internal debate, decided to diversify some of its legacy holdings. It executed the move through a strategy that allowed it to participate in private equity investments. It had hitherto had minimal exposure to private equities, and had come to believe that venture capital and buyout investments offered important opportunities that it was not able to consider. Diversification away from the legacy stock became a means to a desirable end, rather than a negative experience.

2. Another family agreed to diversify one of its two legacy stocks to participate in nondirectional hedge funds, which it could not otherwise purchase, given its lack of cash. Again, the issue that the family confronted was no longer whether the risk in its portfolio would decline if it had a smaller proportion of its wealth in those legacy holdings. Rather, it was the question of how to finance a desired purchase. Should the family raise cash by leveraging its legacy holdings, or sell some of these holdings?

---

3. A third family is diversifying to start executing a broad philanthropic strategy. Note that the philanthropic nature of the move makes the diversification process easier, because it eliminates, or at least substantially reduces, adverse tax consequences. Yet the psychological issues are the same as for the other families, and they are addressed through the use of a positive motivation.

4. Finally, a fourth family is diversifying away from the stock of a company that has acquired the family business, in order to be able to buy some income-producing assets that will allow it to meet the income needs of selected individual members of the family. Here, the psychological issues are somewhat easier to address, as the stock being sold is not the original venture, but the equity of the group that acquired the family company. Yet I have seen families hesitate to carry out this step, when viewing solely as a diversification step, as there can be some residual loyalty to the firm that allowed them to realize the value of their wealth. The positive motivation associated with the production of income made diversification considerably more palatable.

In summary, diversifying a low-basis holding is a complex exercise, with investment, tax and estate planning, and psychological dimensions. The challenge set before the wealthy individual or the advisor is to appreciate the full extent of the problem and to work to address all dimensions as simultaneously as possible. Understanding the complex interactions between these different variables will allow progress to be made, though one should be prepared for an ultimate outcome that does not necessarily reflect the principles assumed to be optimal in investment theory. They will, however, be optimal if the solution is one with which the family can live and upon which it builds over time.

$4\frac{5}{8}$ $4\frac{7}{8}$ ... $\frac{3}{8}$

$5\frac{1}{2}$ $5\frac{1}{2}$ $-$ $\frac{3}{8}$

$5\frac{1}{2}$ $21\frac{3}{16}$ $-$ $\frac{1}{16}$

$20\frac{5}{8}$ $21\frac{3}{16}$ $-$ $\frac{1}{16}$

$17\frac{3}{8}$ $18\frac{1}{8}$ $+$ $\frac{7}{8}$

$18\frac{1}{2}$ $6\frac{1}{2}$ $-$ $\frac{1}{2}$

$6\frac{1}{2}$ $6\frac{1}{2}$ $-$ $\frac{1}{2}$

$7\frac{1}{4}$ $31\frac{1}{32}$ $-$ $\frac{1}{8}$

$15\frac{1}{16}$

1 $9\frac{9}{16}$

$9\frac{9}{16}$

$1\frac{1}{32}$ $7\frac{13}{16}$ $7\frac{15}{16}$

$7\frac{5}{16}$ $7\frac{13}{16}$ $7\frac{15}{16}$

$2\frac{5}{8}$ $2\frac{11}{32}$ $2\frac{1}{2}$ $+$

$2\frac{3}{4}$ $2\frac{1}{4}$ $2\frac{1}{4}$

127 $2\frac{3}{4}$ $2\frac{1}{4}$ $2\frac{1}{4}$

$6\frac{1}{8}$ $12\frac{1}{16}$ $11\frac{3}{8}$ $11\frac{5}{8}$ $+$

87 $33\frac{3}{4}$ 33 $33\frac{1}{8}$ $-$

652 $25\frac{5}{8}$ $24\frac{9}{16}$ $25\frac{3}{8}$ $+$

833 12 $11\frac{5}{8}$ $11\frac{7}{8}$ $+$

16 $10\frac{1}{2}$ $10\frac{1}{2}$ $10\frac{1}{2}$ $-$

78 $15\frac{7}{8}$ $15\frac{13}{16}$ $15\frac{7}{8}$ $-$

4808 $9\frac{1}{16}$ $8\frac{1}{4}$ $8\frac{1}{2}$ $+$

430 $11\frac{1}{4}$ $10\frac{1}{8}$ $10\frac{1}{2}$

GOALS-BASED INVESTING: INTEGRATING TRADITIONAL AND BEHAVIORAL FINANCE

by Daniel Nevins, CFA

LEARNING OUTCOMES

The candidate should be able to:	Mastery
a. explain the benefits of defining portfolio efficiency in terms of client goals rather than traditional measures of risk and return;	☐
b. explain the limitations of traditional risk measurement and risk profiling in setting investment policy for individual investors;	☐
c. justify the use of absolute performance and cash flow matching objectives to meet the goal of lifestyle protection;	☐
d. compare lifestyle protection strategies with fixed horizon strategies and explain when the use of each approach is appropriate.	☐

We have now begun the important job of trying to document and understand how investors, both amateurs and professionals, make their portfolio choices.
　　　　　　　　　—Nicholas Barberis and Richard Thaler [2003]

INTRODUCTION

Since Harry Markowitz wrote his groundbreaking paper, "Portfolio Selection," in 1952, investment professionals have been schooled in a well-known approach to portfolio management. The goal is to build efficient portfolios, those that maximize return for a given level of risk. Efficient portfolios are combined to create an efficient frontier of return opportunities. Investors then select from the frontier, choosing a portfolio that matches their risk tolerance.

Daniel Nevins is managing director of Investment Strategy Research at SEI Investments in Oaks, PA.

287

The Markowitz approach to portfolio selection led to the development of modern portfolio theory and influences most investment processes used today. It was subjected to a severe test during the recent bear market. As U.S. equity prices fell by 49% from the peak in March 2000 to the trough in October 2002,[1] the strengths and weaknesses of traditional investment methods were exposed.

The bear market reinforced the benefits of diversification, which is the key to portfolio efficiency and underpins Markowitz's work. The principle of diversification is as simple as it is powerful. By spreading a portfolio among a variety of investments, investments that are performing poorly are balanced by those that are performing well, resulting in a more consistent pattern of returns. Many investors found that diversification mitigated the effects of falling stock prices. Consider Tiger Woods, better known for his golf game, who gave this confident response to a reporter's questions about volatility in the midst of the bear market: "That's one of the reasons why you diversify yourself." Other investors failed to diversify and fared poorly as a result, such as those who were concentrated in technology stocks.

In most cases, however, even well-diversified investors were unprepared for the full extent of the bear market. Many had implemented strategies in rising markets with neither clear objectives nor a clear understanding of the risks. As they were forced to rethink their strategies, investment practices have come under greater scrutiny. Areas where traditional methods have been disappointing, including goal setting and risk assessment, have received particular attention. More broadly, the investment community is seeking new approaches that are less reliant on traditional investment theory.

1   THE ROLE OF BEHAVIORAL FINANCE

The search for new ideas gained support in October 2002, when the Nobel Prize for Economics was awarded to Professor Daniel Kahneman of Princeton University. Kahneman's work is often at odds with traditional investment theory. He is among a group of behavioral finance theorists who have challenged the investment community to better reflect the way that investors think and behave. Although most investment processes used today are effective by the standards of Harry Markowitz's theory of portfolio selection, they are less impressive when evaluated in the context of behavioral finance.

Behavioral theorists have disproved many of the assumptions underlying modern portfolio theory, or standard finance as it is now sometimes called. These assumptions have been shown to be inconsistent with individual investor behavior. For example, the rational investor assumption—that investors have perfect information about economic and market events and utilize that information to make rational decisions—is a stretch at best. Among the implications is that investors choose portfolios with either too much or too little risk. In the 1990s investors seemed to have forgotten that markets can fall and they

---

[1] According to the S&P 500 Index.

implemented aggressive portfolios with disastrous consequences. Today, many of the same investors have been frightened by market events and selected portfolios that are overly conservative.

Behavioral theorists Nicholas Barberis and Richard Thaler [2003] have described the direction of behavioral research as follows:

> We have now begun the important job of trying to document and understand how investors, both amateurs and professionals, make their portfolio choices. Until recently such research was notably absent from the repertoire of financial economists, perhaps because of the mistaken belief that asset pricing can be modeled without knowing anything about the behavior of the agents in the economy.

As the theorists rethink the principles of financial economics, it is incumbent upon the investment community to consider the practical implications of their work. In some respects this has already occurred. For example, savvy traders and money managers have long sought to exploit investors' behavioral tendencies for profit. In other areas progress has been slower, such as helping those same investors to manage wealth and achieve goals.

In this reading, we suggest that behavioral finance should play a critical role in wealth management, one that reinforces the benefits of standard finance. Too often, standard and behavioral finance are seen as competing philosophies with investment professionals expected to choose one side or the other. We believe there is value in both disciplines and recommend an approach to wealth management that blends traditional investment theory with the observations of behavioral theorists.

A GOALS-BASED APPROACH TO WEALTH MANAGEMENT

2

With our approach, investment principles are redefined from the viewpoint of the investor rather than the practitioner. We define portfolio efficiency in terms of client goals instead of relying on traditional measures of return and standard deviation. Risk management is also based on client goals, using measures to capture the risk of failing to achieve those goals. Based on our custom measures of portfolio efficiency and risk, we then create investment solutions by matching each goal with an appropriate strategy rather than creating a single overall portfolio. The investment solution is reevaluated over time, maintaining consistency with new circumstances and changing goals.

While this approach is certainly more complex than traditional methods of wealth management, it offers valuable benefits. Investors should have more confidence in strategies that are explicitly aligned with their own objectives. They should also have a clearer understanding of their risk exposure, which is expressed in terms that relate more directly to the achievement of goals. Greater confidence and clarity will not prevent disappointment when markets fall; however, the investor should be better prepared for bear markets and more likely to maintain perspective and discipline. In addition, and probably most tangibly, this approach should increase the likelihood of achieving goals.

The main body of our reading is divided into two sections. In the first section, we examine the shortcomings of traditional investment methods, considering the reasons why investors often fail to achieve their goals. We focus on processes for risk measurement, risk profiling, and managing behavioral biases. Several suggestions are provided for improving upon traditional methods, drawing on the lessons of behavioral finance. In the second section, we outline an approach for implementing our findings. We describe a goals-based investing process that links investment strategy selection to client goals. Investment strategy examples are provided for two common goals: meeting current lifestyle expenses and investing for a fixed planning horizon.

3   MEETING INVESTOR GOALS

Investor goals are best stated in terms of the lifestyle needs, wealth transfers, and charitable gifts to which investment capital will ultimately be applied. Lifestyle needs describe the capital that is required to achieve a desired standard of living. Wealth transfers refer to funds that are transferred to one's children or other family members. Charitable gifts represent support for one's community, defined broadly to include any cause to which the investor wishes to contribute. Wealth management requires planning for each of these three uses of capital.

Despite the efforts of investment professionals to understand their clients' goals for their lifestyle, family, and community, these goals are often unfulfilled. Weak markets commonly receive the blame. However, while it is difficult to build strategies that meet goals in all types of markets, effective investment planning should do exactly that. Lee Munder, founder of the Lee Munder Capital Group, delivered this harsh commentary on the investment industry in February 2003:

> We have to prove our worth. We are not delivering performance. Clients want competitive rates of return. . . . And we have to be able to produce investment results in all kinds of markets.

In this section of our reading, we critique the effectiveness of traditional investment methods in meeting this challenge. Particular attention is given to the tension between the assumptions of standard finance, which require statistical measures such as expected returns, standard deviations, and Sharpe ratios, and the viewpoint of the individual investor, which is based on goals and human psychology. We seek opportunities to improve upon traditional investment practices, raising the likelihood of achieving goals in both strong and weak markets. Opportunities are identified in the areas of measuring risk, risk profiling, and managing behavioral biases.

Risk Measurement

It is not so much that people hate uncertainty—but rather, they hate losing.
—Amos Tversky [2001]

Risk measurement traditionally relies on portfolio statistics like standard deviation and tracking error, which have convenient properties that make them easy to calculate and manipulate. The development of standard finance would not have been possible without these statistics. However, they have weaknesses related to both their ability to capture market behavior and their relevance from the individual investor's perspective.

While standard deviations fully explain the uncertainty that investors face when we assume that return distributions are normal and unchanged from one period to the next, it is easy to show that markets exhibit non-normalities and that risk changes through time. In the language of the risk manager, there is ample evidence of skew, kurtosis, and heteroskedasticity. Skew is the degree of asymmetry in the probability distribution and is especially relevant when it is negative, suggesting more downside risk than would be expected using only the standard deviation. Kurtosis describes the degree to which the tail ends of the distribution are more concentrated, or "fatter," than predicted by a normal distribution, implying that extreme results are more likely. Heteroskedasticity indicates that risk changes through time, such that the standard deviation measured over a historical period may not reflect risks going forward. Each of these properties suggests that risks could be overlooked if one were to rely on standard deviation alone, and should be considered within the risk management process.

Linking Risk Measurement to Investor Goals

In addition to the complex statistical properties that we observe, perhaps more damaging to the challenge of meeting investor goals is inconsistency between traditional risk measures and the way that individual investors experience risk. We argue below that these measures can be hard to interpret, fail to capture the risk of losing money, and relate to time intervals rather than events.

Consider, for example, an investment in the S&P 500 between 2000 and 2002. The standard deviation of the S&P 500 over this period was 19%. The total portfolio loss over the same period was 38%. Few individual investors are able to connect the standard deviation of 19% with the possibility that they could lose over one-third of their wealth. Fewer still can connect the 19% standard deviation with the implications for their capacity to fund their goals. Investors can struggle to find meaning in a measure that doesn't describe risk in terms of clear outcomes. A standard deviation of 19% could coincide with a loss of much more than 19%, a gain of much more than 19%, or anything in between.

Leslie Kiefer [2000] summarizes the challenges of integrating the risk perspectives of the practitioner and the individual investor as follows:

> Investment managers talk about risk as volatility, a tendency that leads them to frame the discussion of risk in terms of the kinds of volatility that can be diversified away. Individual clients, however, are usually much less focused on volatility. Their perceptions of risk are often driven by emotions and, therefore, are easily misunderstood or ignored by managers who take a strictly rational approach to risk. In order to be successful, managers must identify how clients actually perceive risk.

Loss Aversion

Among the emotions that determine the individual investor's perceptions of risk is an aversion to losses. The idea that investors are not risk-averse but loss-averse is one of the main tenets of behavioral finance.[2] While the distinction may seem

---

[2] Kahneman and Tversky [1979] considered the implications of loss aversion in a landmark paper in which they questioned the validity of the utility function of standard finance. In its place, they introduced a model of investor preferences called a value function. Their value function accommodates the observation that investors are not risk-averse but loss-averse. More broadly, their approach, which they called prospect theory, measures value using reference points rather than total wealth outcomes and, therefore, is more consistent with the behaviors that researchers have observed.

trivial, studies have shown that investors will increase their risk, defined in terms of uncertainty, to avoid even the smallest probability of loss. Thus, the assumption that investors are always risk-averse, which underpins modern portfolio theory, is incorrect. According to behavioral theorist Amos Tversky [2001], "It is not so much that people hate uncertainty—but rather, they hate losing."

Loss aversion suggests that risk measurement should explicitly consider the risk of loss. Measures of the risk of loss can capture the likelihood that a loss will occur, the severity of loss, or both. Examples include the probability of loss, which considers likelihood but not severity, and the downside deviation, which captures both the likelihood and severity of loss by adjusting the standard deviation formula to isolate return outcomes below a certain threshold (Nawrocki [1999]). In the second section of our study we describe another measure, the potential portfolio loss, which considers loss severity only. We also provide examples of investment strategies that directly manage the risk of loss. By using measures of the risk of loss to guide strategy development, we can align investment choices more closely with the investor preferences that behavioral theorists have observed.

Measuring the Risk of Events

Another limitation of traditional risk measures is that they are specified in terms of time intervals. Standard deviations tend to be annualized, describing the dispersion of returns over a one-year period. Value-at-risk is also calibrated to a specific time interval, usually considering periods shorter than a year. Because they are calibrated to a single time period, these measures do not capture the risks that investors face when their portfolios fall for several periods in succession. They also do not consider risks that come and go prior to the end of the period.

When risk measures cover periods of a year or shorter, the failure to convey risks extending beyond a single period is the primary concern. In the example used above, investors who know only the annualized standard deviation for the S&P 500 may not have an accurate view of the amount that they could lose over multiple periods. Conversely, when the time period is significantly longer than a year, a particular concern is the failure to consider the path that the portfolio follows between the beginning and end of the period. Annualized risk figures are often extended to 5 or 10 years or longer by projecting forward the distribution of returns. Because this method balances bad years with good years, it can lead investors to lower their view of the risks that they face. Its drawback is that it does not consider the troughs that the portfolio can reach prior to the end date (Kritzman and Rich [2002]). After the recent market cycle, investors do not need to be reminded that these troughs can affect their well-being as much as the end result.

An alternative to using period-specific measures is to measure the risk of events without specifying a time interval. Although the term event risk is commonly used to refer to extreme economic and market developments (see, for example, Powers [2003]), for our purposes events are defined as violations of investor preferences or goals. We seek to measure the risk that a strategy will fail rather than defining risk in terms of time periods and regardless of whether or not extreme circumstances are present. For example, to capture loss aversion, risk measures might consider the potential portfolio loss that could occur between any two points in time. The event in this example is a portfolio loss of a certain amount. Alternatively, risk measures might estimate the probability that an investment strategy fails to achieve a particular goal at any time in the future. In this case, the event is the breach of a goal. Event risk measures such as potential portfolio loss and probability of failing to achieve a goal are discussed further in the second section of our study, where we demonstrate how they can be used for strategy development.

Our premise is that investors should be more concerned about specific events, whenever they may occur, than performance outcomes for a single time period. Therefore, we should aim to define risk according to events rather than defaulting to traditional measures. Event risks are more difficult to calculate than statistical measures such as standard deviations, often requiring Monte Carlo simulations, but better aligned with the way that the individual investor experiences risk.

Risk Profiling

In the old days, many people kept their money for rent, furniture, groceries, and so on, in separate jars. Today, we have the same mental accounting approach to our various pools of assets.

—Meir Statman [2002]

Risk profiling is used to establish the client's risk tolerance, which is often the primary link between the client and the investment recommendation. Like risk measurement, it is an important part of investment planning but one that is sometimes poorly executed. We consider below two of the difficulties involved in building an effective risk profiling process. First, the information that people provide about their attitudes towards risk can be misleading and hard to interpret. Second, it is not easy to integrate risk tolerance estimates with other factors affecting strategy selection, notably client goals.

Proper risk profiling requires some type of questioning, either verbal or in questionnaire form, with most advisors using both. The drawbacks of relying solely on verbal questioning are described by researchers Victor Callan and Malcolm Johnson [2002]:

> It is often difficult for clients to describe in their own words their attitudes about risk. The initial meetings with financial advisers can be quite difficult for some clients because of the lack of understanding that they might have about their "financial selves," and the investment risks that they might be willing to accept.

Callan and Johnson also note that "most forms of communication between people, even between people who know each other very well, involves a fair degree of miscommunication," and suggest that risk profiling requires a scientifically developed measure of risk tolerance, obtained using a questionnaire.

While many advisors accept the views of Callan and Johnson and other proponents of questionnaires, the effectiveness of questionnaires is open to debate. In a study by Ken Yook and Robert Everett [2003], six different questionnaires were evaluated by administering them to MBA students, with the conclusion that some provide accurate risk tolerance estimates while others do not. The correlations among the six questionnaires were relatively low, indicating that all of them could not be correct. Furthermore, the relationship between the subjects' responses and their investment decisions was found to be weak.

Decision Framing

The challenges involved in risk profiling are perhaps best understood in the context of decision framing, an area of behavioral research that has been led by Kahneman and Tversky. Decision framing research indicates that slight differences in the way that questions are posed lead to very different answers about people's preferences.[3] Roszkowski [2002] provides the following example:

> Consider research in which one group of people is informed that there is a 50 percent chance of success in a particular venture. Another group is told that this same venture has a 50 percent chance of failure. Logically, the same proportion of people in each group should be willing to take this risk. Yet this was not the case. When the risk was described (framed) in terms of the probability of success, more people were willing to take it than when this same risk was described in terms of the chances of failure.

The implication is that questions for risk profiling should be worded carefully to isolate the investor's attitudes without introducing biases. Even accurate risk tolerance estimates, however, can lead to a poor strategy choice. If, for example, the client is by nature a risk taker, a risk tolerance estimate might suggest a risky strategy in situations in which a conservative portfolio is sufficient to meet the stated goals. In other situations, a naturally cautious person might opt for a conservative strategy despite goals that are more likely to be met with an aggressive approach.

Mental Accounting

More fundamentally, the notion of an overall risk tolerance for each investor is flawed. Behavioral theorists have shown that investors have not just one but multiple attitudes about risk. For some goals and investment accounts, risk tolerance may be low, while other goals and accounts may be associated with a high risk tolerance. For instance, most investors are unwilling to risk capital that has been allocated to their children's education costs. However, they may have other accounts, sometimes described as fun money, that are not needed for lifestyle expenses and are invested adventurously, seeking the highest return opportunities.

Investors who manage risk on a goal-by-goal basis exhibit mental accounting, referring to the practice of maintaining separate investment accounts, either mentally or in practice, and making decisions differently depending on the nature of the account.[4] Behavioral finance professor Meir Statman [2002] observes that:

> We tend to compartmentalize the assets we use for downside protection from the assets we use for upside potential. In the old days, many people kept their money for rent, furniture, groceries, and so on, in separate jars. Today, we have the same mental accounting approach to our various pools of assets.

---

[3] The study of decision framing is related to prospect theory (Kahneman and Tversky [1979]). See, for example, Thaler [1980], Kahneman and Tversky [1984], and Tversky and Kahneman [1986].

[4] The study of mental accounting also emerged from prospect theory (Kahneman and Tversky [1979]) and the observation that value functions are defined relative to a reference point rather than in absolute terms. Multiple reference points imply multiple and separate mental accounts. Mental accounting has been used to explain many investor behaviors, including the tendency to manage investment accounts differently depending on the purpose of the account (Thaler [1985, 1999], Shefrin and Thaler [1988], Shefrin and Statman [2000]).

Behavioral theorists have argued that mental accounting, and the multiple goals on which it is based, is incompatible with traditional investment theory. Traditional theory suggests that an allocation should be established for an investor's total portfolio. Risk is also managed at the total portfolio level, using an estimate for the investor's overall risk tolerance. It is difficult to reconcile this single portfolio framework with separate mental accounts linked to multiple goals.

An alternative to the traditional investment approach is to allow more than one strategy, as discussed by Shefrin and Statman [2000] and Brunel [2003]. Each strategy is linked to a goal and managed according to the risk measures and risk tolerance that are most appropriate for that goal. This approach, which we call goals-based investing, is compatible with mental accounting. Another advantage is that it manages the risk of not achieving goals rather than relying on traditional risk measures. Further benefits are considered in the next sub-section, where we discuss behavioral biases.

Managing Behavioral Biases

Follow the pattern of the physician: Ask, listen, diagnose, educate, and treat.
—Meir Statman [2002]

Thanks to the work of Kahneman, Tversky, Statman, and others in their field, we are learning more about investor behaviors such as loss aversion and mental accounting. These behaviors are characterized as preferences and should be reflected in the investment process. For example, practitioners should accommodate loss aversion by developing strategies that seek to manage losses. Similarly, they should accommodate mental accounting by developing strategies that can be aligned with investors' separate goals and accounts. Practitioners who fail to accommodate investor preferences are ignoring the criteria by which their performance will be judged.

Other behaviors that theorists have studied are characterized as biases rather than preferences. Biases can lead to failed investment strategies and should be controlled rather than accommodated. Below we consider several examples of potentially damaging biases, including overconfidence, hindsight bias, overreaction, belief perseverance, and regret avoidance. In each case, research indicates that these are common behavioral traits.

Overconfidence

Overconfidence suggests that investors overestimate their ability to predict market events. Because of overconfidence, investors often take risks without receiving commensurate returns. Another effect of overconfidence is overtrading, which can lead to poor investment decisions and excessive transactions costs. Behavioral theorists Brad Barber and Terrance Odean have reinforced the dangers of overconfidence with a series of studies showing that portfolio performance is inversely related to the amount of trading in the portfolio. In one study [2000], they divided 78,000 investors with a large brokerage firm into five groups according to the frequency of trading, and showed that the annual return for the group that traded most frequently was about 6% less, after transactions costs, than the return for the group that traded the least. While there could be a variety of behavioral traits that help to explain the 6% difference, those investors who trade most often while performing poorly would appear to be overconfident of their investment skills.

Hindsight Bias

Hindsight bias refers to evidence that people often believe they had predicted an event when in fact they had not. Kahneman and Mark Riepe [1998] write that most people "are honestly deceived when they exaggerate their earlier estimate of the probability that the event would occur." Hindsight is a trait that reinforces tendencies towards overconfidence. As advisors are well aware, it can also lead to difficult customers who demand explanations for why their advisors did not anticipate events that were obvious in hindsight.

Overreaction

Overreaction suggests that people are overly influenced by random occurrences. Kahneman and Riepe [1998] note that "the human mind is a pattern-seeking device, and it is strongly biased to adopt the hypothesis that a causal factor is at work behind any notable sequence of events." As a result, investors tend to over-interpret patterns that are coincidental and unlikely to persist. They react to recent history and their own experiences, without paying enough attention to events that were not directly experienced or retained in memory. When we see investors squandering their wealth by buying high and selling low, overreaction is frequently the cause.

Belief Perseverance

Belief perseverance indicates that people are unlikely to change their opinions even when new information becomes available (Lord, Ross, and Lepper [1979]). According to Barberis and Thaler [2002]:

> At least two effects appear to be at work. First, people are reluctant to search for evidence that contradicts their beliefs. Second, even if they find such evidence, they treat it with excessive skepticism.

Belief perseverance can cause investors to stick with the wrong approach for longer than they otherwise would if they were taking a more balanced view.

Regret Avoidance

Regret avoidance is the tendency to avoid actions that could create discomfort over prior decisions, even though those actions may be in the individual's best interest. Among other effects, it can help to explain why investors commonly retain their losing investments longer than they hold on to winning investments, a behavioral characteristic that Shefrin and Statman [1985] have termed the disposition effect. Researchers have argued that one of the reasons that investors are reluctant to sell losing positions is because to do so is to admit a bad decision. This reluctance can be linked to both regret avoidance and belief perseverance. To avoid the stress associated with admitting a mistake, the investor holds onto the losing position and hopes for a recovery. Odean [1998] demonstrated the pitfalls of the disposition effect in a study showing that investors would achieve higher returns if they sold winners and losers with equal regularity.

Biases such as those described above were certainly understood before the emergence of behavioral finance, if not proven through behavioral research. In fact, practitioners typically find that the assertions of behavioral theorists are not unlike their own observations. Despite this, the investment community's track record for managing investor behavior is open to question. Traditional processes are simply not well matched to the psychology of the individual investor.

Statman [2002] argues that financial advisors should think of themselves as financial physicians. He urges them to:

Follow the pattern of the physician: Ask, listen, diagnose, educate, and treat. Financial advisors who act as financial physicians combine the science of finance and securities with the ability to empathize with and guide clients—thinking not about risk and return but about investors' fears, aspirations, and the errors they are likely to make. Financial advisors promote wealth and well-being just as physicians promote health and well-being.

While Statman's advice may have been considered unconventional 10 years ago, today the ideas of behavioral theorists are entering the mainstream. Practitioners recognize that investor biases are difficult to manage without considering the behavioral side of investing. It is our contention that a goals-based investing process can capture the lessons of both standard and behavioral finance, avoiding many of the pitfalls that behavioral researchers have identified. As discussed earlier, client goals should determine the way that risk is defined, the method for estimating risk tolerance, and the choice of investment strategy.

A goals-based approach works by reducing the friction between the practitioner's perspective, which is based on traditional investment principles, and the investor's perspective, which is determined by goals and psychological makeup. When these perspectives are not well integrated, strategy selection becomes arbitrary. Investors have greater flexibility to use their portfolio as a testing ground, trying different approaches and changing strategies based on their outlook and emotions. They are then exposed to many of the biases that behavioral researchers have identified. If, however, strategy selection is closely linked to the investor's goals, then it becomes more difficult for damaging behaviors to take hold.

We recommend a disciplined process that is customized to each investor. Goals and preferences should be defined as clearly as possible and supported through risk management, using measures such as the probability of breaching a goal and potential loss. Progress towards goals should be monitored, with performance evaluated in this context. Strategy adjustments should be based on changes in circumstances or goals rather than behavioral factors. This approach heeds the lessons of behavioral finance by seeking consistency with the investor's aspirations and preferences while suppressing the biases that can lead to failed strategies.

IMPLEMENTING A GOALS-BASED APPROACH 4

The goals-based investing process is illustrated in Exhibit 1. As the exhibit shows, the process links client goals to risk management objectives and investment strategies. Client goals are based on the investment portfolio's eventual use, such as current or future lifestyle needs. Risk management objectives are stated in terms of risk measures that are best matched to the particular goal. Investment strategies are designed to be efficient in the context of their corresponding goals and risk management objectives. Each combination of goal, risk management objective, and investment strategy may comprise a separate subportfolio, which we call an asset pool. Asset pools are combined to create a full investment solution.

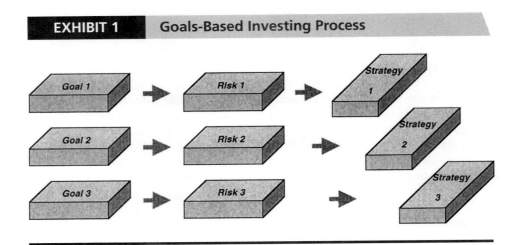

EXHIBIT 1   Goals-Based Investing Process

Exhibit 2 compares a goals-based investment solution to a traditional investment solution. With a traditional investment process, efficient portfolios are created using standard investment theory. The investor's overall risk tolerance is established through risk profiling. The risk tolerance estimate is then mapped to one of the efficient portfolios. Goals-based investing seeks to improve upon traditional methods by aligning investment strategies with the goals of the individual investor. This approach may not be appropriate for all investors, particularly those without precise goals, but when goals are clearly identified it has valuable benefits. As noted in the previous section, it improves upon traditional methods in risk measurement, risk profiling, and managing behavioral biases.

The idea that investors may require multiple strategies for multiple goals is not new, but has gained legitimacy as practitioners have explored the implications of behavioral theory and questioned the single portfolio framework of traditional finance. Recent articles proposing multi-strategy approaches include Shefrin and Statman [2000] and Brunel [2003]. Shefrin and Statman [2000] consider separate investor goals within their specification of behavioral portfolio theory, describing multi-strategy portfolios as "layered pyramids where investors divide their current wealth between a bottom layer, designed to avoid poverty, and a top layer, designed for a shot at riches." Brunel [2003] further develops the recommendations of Shefrin and Statman, conducting a complete asset

EXHIBIT 2   Goals-Based Investing versus Traditional Investing

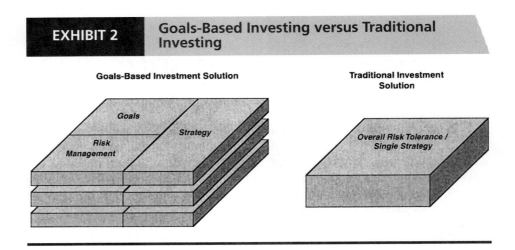

allocation analysis derived from investor goals. He suggests a framework in which investment strategies are matched to "buckets" assigned to four fundamental goals: liquidity, income, capital preservation, and growth. He compares the "bucket analysis" based on goals to a traditional approach, stating that:

> . . . as individuals go through the asset allocation process looking at the same "buckets" through which they do look at their wealth in their everyday circumstances, the allocations they eventually choose will feel both more comfortable and more reasonable, and thus should be more easily sustainable over time. They will not feel they are "boxed into" a fixed long-term allocation, with which they find it difficult to associate.

Brunel also notes that the approach still relies on sophisticated analytical tools and, therefore, can be applied to investors seeking detailed analyses.

The principal drawback to a goals-based investing process is its complexity, which makes it challenging to implement. Among the issues to be resolved for successful implementation are the appropriate level of customization and the process for investment strategy development. While goals-based investing in its purest form implies customized strategies for each investor, when costs are considered, full customization is rarely feasible. A more sensible and equally effective approach is to build a suite of investment products that can be matched to common investor goals. We then create customized solutions by selecting from the suite of products on a goal-by-goal basis.

With this approach, products are developed according to performance or risk management objectives. For example, consider a strategy managed to limit the risk of a decline in portfolio value of 10% or more. This strategy is characterized by its risk management objective. It might be matched to an asset pool for short-term lifestyle expenses, which needs a high degree of principal stability. A second strategy, with very different objectives, could be managed to limit risk at a particular time in the future without regard to principal stability. In other words, the second strategy allows volatility as long as it does not affect the outcome at the horizon date. It might be used for an asset pool with a clearly defined investment horizon, perhaps coinciding with a retirement date. For both strategies, the risk management objective is aligned with investor goals for the particular asset pool.

Many strategies widely used today work well with a goals-based approach. For instance, laddered bond portfolios can be matched to asset pools for current lifestyle expenses. Other strategies are less compatible with goals-based investing but still have a role to play. Consider model portfolios that are characterized by an asset allocation mix, or asset allocation models. Asset allocation models appeal to investors without precise goals who are seeking well-diversified portfolios.

More importantly, additional strategies that are not commonly used today can provide investors with both closer matches for common goals and more choices. In the remainder of this section of our reading, we discuss two common goals that warrant further strategy development: investing to meet current lifestyle needs and investing for a fixed planning horizon. We also propose investment strategies that can be applied to these goals.

Investing to Meet Current Lifestyle Needs

There are a variety of strategies that can be applied towards current lifestyle needs, including absolute return strategies, cash flow matching, and income strategies. Strategy selection depends on the way that the decision is framed. For instance, does the investor set precise cash flow targets for each period, suggesting that a cash flow match might be appropriate? Is the investor encouraged to meet lifestyle needs through coupons and dividends without drawing down principal? In this sub-section, we modify the Markowitz or traditional investment framework to frame the decision in a way that investors can easily see the connection to their goals. Investor goals are then translated into performance criteria that can be used to construct a portfolio.

According to traditional investment theory, investors should manage the trade-off between expected portfolio return and portfolio risk. A higher expected return is the reward for bearing more risk. Risk is measured in traditional theory as the standard deviation of return. When a portfolio is being used to fund lifestyle expenses, we can create a different framework that is more meaningful to the investor by redefining reward and risk. With new measures of reward and risk, portfolio efficiency takes on a different meaning. We can create an efficient frontier that is comparable to the traditional Markowitz frontier but more consistent with the investor's goals.

In Exhibit 3, we show a frontier of reward and risk opportunities using measures that are based on lifestyle goals. We constructed portfolios of two asset classes, U.S. stocks and U.S. bonds, and used data from 1926 to 2002 to calculate the return distribution for each portfolio. Return distributions are then rolled forward using Monte Carlo simulations to project wealth and spending for a hypothetical investor. The investor is assumed to be drawing from an asset pool of $1 million, which is fully exhausted after covering lifestyle expenses for the next 10 years.

Reward is defined in Exhibit 3 as maximizing the amount of spending that the portfolio is expected to fund. The measure that we use is an expected value, or average of all potential outcomes. The risk to the goal of maximizing spending is that spending falls below the expected level. Different methods for measuring this risk can lead to very different conclusions. For this reason, the approach to risk measurement merits particular attention.

EXHIBIT 3   Frontier of Reward and Risk Opportunities for Current Lifestyle Expenses

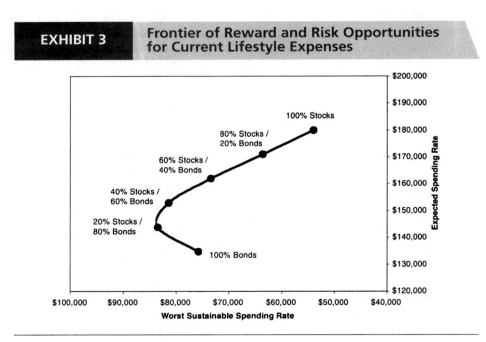

Source: Ibbotson Associates, SEI Investments.

Measuring the Risk to Current Lifestyle Goals

Practitioners who use cash flow modeling often define risk according to the end result after an investment period of 10 or 20 years or more. They may focus on the worst possible result for the amount of spending that the portfolio can accommodate, on average over the investment horizon. Strategies may be chosen to ensure that the average spending rate exceeds a certain threshold. This approach has the benefit of linking the risk measure to the investor's lifestyle goals. Its drawback is that it does not consider risks that come and go prior to the horizon date. For average cash flow or other results measured at the end of a long horizon, there are always scenarios in which a desired outcome is achieved only after appearing unlikely at some point along the way. At the point at which the outcome is uncertain, the investor is forced to reconsider his or her situation. Lifestyle goals may be pared back and plans changed. The original investment strategy may be altered, either decreasing aggressiveness to avoid further damage or increasing aggressiveness in an attempt to reverse past losses. The implication is that the individual's well-being depends on performance throughout the investment period, not just on the average or final outcome. When people lose confidence that they will reach their goals, even if that confidence is eventually restored, that is rarely a satisfactory result.

In Exhibit 3, we use a risk measure that considers the path that the investor experiences between the present and the horizon date. We estimate the worst sustainable spending rate that could occur prior to the horizon. The sustainable spending rate is defined as the amount of spending that the investor can be confident of maintaining without running out of capital.[5] The worst sustainable spending rate considers the lowest level that the sustainable spending rate might reach at any time prior to the horizon. It is defined using a 99% confidence interval, allowing a 1% probability that the sustainable spending rate will fall as far as or below the worst level, according to our assumptions for the distribution of portfolio returns. This is an event-specific rather than period-specific measure. It considers the risk that sustainable spending could fall to a certain level, which is the event, *regardless of the time at which the event might occur.* Although they are more difficult to calculate than period-specific measures, event-specific measures are better correlated with the individual investor's perceptions about the success or failure of his or her investment strategy.

Ideally, communications between advisors and investors should be based on reward and risk measures such as those in Exhibit 3. Investors are better equipped to select investments when decisions are framed in terms of their goals. Institutional investors have long recognized the importance of translating performance measures into terms that are more meaningful to them. For example, pension plan sponsors use asset-liability models to understand the implications of their investment decisions for pension expense and plan contributions, the financial measures most critical to policy success or failure. Endowments use similar models to assess the effects of different investment strategies on their spending policies. Compared to institutions, individual investors are often less familiar with investment theory and with the statistics traditionally used to measure performance and risk. Therefore, they have perhaps an even greater need to restate portfolio characteristics in non-investment terms.

---

[5] For Exhibit 3, investors are considered to be confident when there is a 95% probability that the spending rate can be maintained without running out of capital, based on estimates for the distribution of portfolio returns.

Implementing the New Measures of Reward and Risk

The practitioner, however, cannot rely entirely on the reward and risk measures that are most meaningful to the client. From the practitioner's perspective, it can be difficult to build portfolios based on characteristics such as those measured in Exhibit 3. Two observations can help to resolve this conflict. The first observation is that the expected spending rate is determined largely by the expected portfolio return. The higher the expected portfolio return, the more the investor can expect to spend in each period without running out of capital. The second observation is that the worst sustainable spending rate is closely related to the portfolio's downside risk, measured as the potential loss. The greater the potential loss, the more severe is the potential drop in sustainable spending.[6] Like the worst sustainable spending rate, the potential loss is an event-specific risk measure that is estimated using Monte Carlo simulations and confidence intervals. It considers the amount that the investor could lose between any two points in time, from peak to trough.

In Exhibit 4, we demonstrate the relationship between potential loss and the worst sustainable spending rate. We consider portfolios with potential losses of 10%, 20%, and 30%. In each case, we assume an expected portfolio return of 6%. We then measure the worst sustainable spending rate over horizons of 10, 20, and 30 years for an asset pool of $2 million. The worst sustainable spending rate falls as the horizon lengthens because the spending rate has to be maintained for a longer period. As discussed above, it also falls as the potential loss increases.

EXHIBIT 4	Relationship between Potential Loss and Worst Sustainable Spending Rate

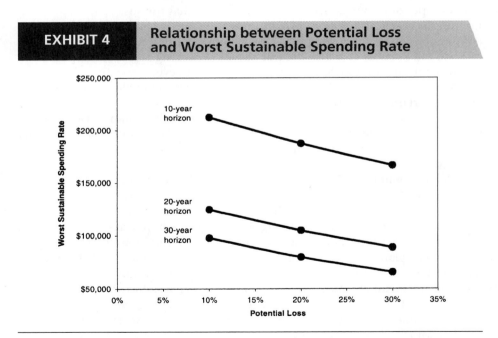

Source: SEI Investments.

---

[6] Consider that the sustainable spending rate at any point in time is a function of the size of the portfolio. Risk to the size of the portfolio is determined primarily by the potential portfolio loss.

Lifestyle Protection Strategies

Investors and their advisors can use the relationship between sustainable spending and potential loss to choose an investment portfolio. The investor determines the minimum sustainable spending rate based on lifestyle needs. The minimum sustainable spending rate is translated into a target for potential loss according to the relationship shown in Exhibit 4. The investor and advisor can then consider alternative portfolios with a potential loss equal to or below the target and choose the portfolio with the highest expected return.

This process implies different portfolio construction methods than those most commonly used today. Portfolios would be built to manage the trade-off between expected returns and potential loss rather than managing risk versus an index. Put differently, performance objectives are stated in absolute rather than relative terms. Strategies for managing absolute performance are prevalent in the hedge fund arena, where they are often called absolute return strategies. Absolute performance objectives can be extended to other asset classes as well by eliminating the tracking error constraint that often guides security selection. Asset classes can then be combined to create a diversified strategy with desired characteristics for expected return and potential loss. For the purposes of our study, we will call these lifestyle protection strategies.

Lifestyle protection strategies have the benefit of aligning the investment process with spending goals. Another benefit is that investors can choose a lifestyle protection strategy according to its performance characteristics. Strategies are described by reward and risk measures, and investors make a selection based on their preferred balance between these two characteristics. For example, the expected spending rate can be increased if the investor is willing to accept a lower sustainable spending rate in a worst-case scenario. This differs from a traditional approach of differentiating portfolios by the mix of asset classes. When characteristics are provided for a traditional strategy, they are usually stated in investment terms using single period measures, without a clear relationship to the investor's goals.

The principal disadvantage to lifestyle protection strategies is their performance in bull markets. To manage potential losses, these strategies are constructed with a beta of less than one to the broad market. Therefore, they are likely to lag broad market indices in bull markets while outperforming those indices in bear markets. This performance profile is appealing for many investors, particularly those with the spending goals that we have discussed. Investors with different goals should consider whether another type of strategy is more appropriate.

Cash Flow Matching

Thus far, our analysis has considered the goal of maximizing expected spending while managing worst-case results for sustainable spending. In some instances, current lifestyle goals can be stated more precisely, using targets for the amount of cash required in each period. When goals are expressed using precise cash flow targets, cash flow matching may be the best investment approach. Laddered bond portfolios can be built to match an investor's expenses with the cash flows generated by the portfolio. The risk management objective in this case is to ensure a high degree of certainty that cash flow targets are met.

A number of questions can be asked to test whether cash flow matching is the best fit in a particular situation. First, are the spending targets likely to change? With changes to the objectives of the cash flow match, a bond ladder may need to be unwound prior to maturity at unfavorable market prices. Therefore, if required cash flows for the bond ladder cannot be forecast accurately, then cash flow matching is probably not the best approach. Second, is the investor satisfied with the yield available on the cash flow matched portfolio? Investors seeking high returns may find a better fit with strategies that are invested more aggressively than a bond ladder. Third, is the investor comfortable focusing on cash flows without worrying about the market value of the portfolio? While their cash flows are fixed when held to maturity, bonds included in a ladder can exhibit significant price volatility. For investors who are uncomfortable with volatility, a better approach may be to manage volatility directly rather than managing cash flows as the principal objective.

If the answers to any of these questions suggest that cash flow matching is not the best approach, then lifestyle protection strategies may be a better fit. However, if the right conditions are present, then cash flow matching has notable benefits. A cash flow match provides a high degree of comfort that the investor's stated goals will be met. The investor may also be in a better position to pursue other goals once the cash flow match is established. After allocating capital to current lifestyle needs, the investor knows precisely how much capital is available for other goals and can identify strategies to meet those goals.

Investing for a Fixed Planning Horizon

For portfolios used for growth rather than current expenses, there are once again a variety of strategies that could be suitable with strategy selection depending on the way the decision is framed. In this sub-section, we consider a decision framework characterized by a fixed planning horizon. The planning horizon could coincide with a life event such as a retirement date or college enrollment date. Or, it could simply represent a time period used for planning purposes. For example, an investor who has created an asset pool to cover the next 10 years of living expenses may have a second asset pool with a 10-year planning horizon to be applied to future expenses once the first pool is exhausted. Whether it is based on a life event or a planning period, the investor's goals and risk management objectives are determined by the fixed horizon.

Like the process that we applied to current expense asset pools, we redefine portfolio efficiency to be consistent with investor goals by identifying appropriate measures of reward and risk. Reward can be measured as the expected portfolio value at the horizon date or, equivalently, expected asset growth. Growth is the reason we invest—to have a larger portfolio in the future than we have today. While growth is universal, risk can be measured differently depending on the psychology of the investor. Below we consider two risk measurement approaches and the implications for strategy selection.

One approach is to consider the amount of capital that could be lost, recognizing that losses are the opposite of growth. Defining risk in this way is consistent with the observations of behavioral theorists (and practitioners) that investors are loss-averse, and suggests a role for the lifestyle protection strategies described in the previous sub-section. However, a drawback to this approach is that the investment process for managing the trade-off between growth and loss is unlikely to be the best process for managing the portfolio value at the horizon date. Rather than constraining the risk of loss, it may be more consistent with investor goals to use measures that are directly linked to the planning horizon.

The second approach is to measure the worst portfolio value at the horizon date. It is defined using a 99% confidence interval, indicating a 1% probability that the portfolio value will be equal to or less than the worst outcome. This is a period-specific risk measure; it does not consider the path that the portfolio takes between the present and the horizon. For this reason, it may be inappropriate for investors who are uncomfortable with a long-term view. However, unlike many period-specific measures, the worst portfolio value is tailored to the investor's planning horizon. Investors may value an approach that manages the distribution of portfolio values at their horizon date. Strategies can be designed to provide a high degree of certainty that the portfolio value will exceed a minimum level.

In Exhibit 5, we show a frontier of reward and risk opportunities for a hypothetical investor, constructed using data from 1926 to 2002. The reward measure is the expected portfolio value, or average of all possible outcomes. The risk measure is the worst portfolio value as described above. The investor is assumed to be investing $500,000 for a retirement date 10 years in the future and choosing from portfolios of U.S. stocks and bonds. The chart provides a framework that the investor can use to select a portfolio for a fixed planning horizon.

Fixed Horizon Strategies

In practice, efficient portfolios would be diversified among more asset classes than shown in Exhibit 5. To construct diversified portfolios that are efficient in the context of a fixed planning horizon, practitioners should identify the risk-free investment. This is different from the risk-free investment for either relative return or absolute return strategies. For relative return strategies, the risk-free investment is one that replicates the index against which returns are compared. For absolute return strategies, the risk-free investment is cash. For strategies linked to a fixed planning horizon, the risk-free investment is a high-quality zero-coupon bond that matures near the horizon date. A zero-coupon bond delivers only one cash flow, the principal payment. Both the amount and the timing of the principal payment are known with certainty.

| EXHIBIT 5 | Frontier of Reward and Risk Opportunities for Fixed Investment Horizon |

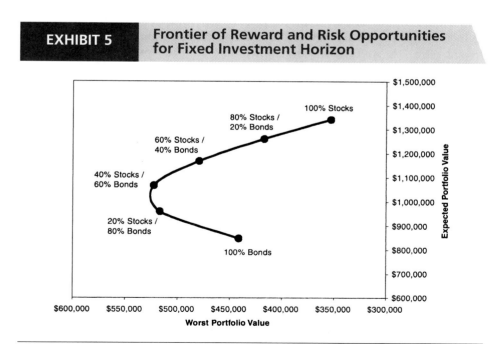

Source: Ibbotson Associates, SEI Investments.

With a zero coupon bond identified as the risk-free investment, portfolio construction depends on finding the right balance between the zero and other more aggressive assets. The other assets can be combined in a separate sub-portfolio. Because the zero is used to control risk, the separate sub-portfolio can be managed aggressively to maximize return. We refer to the combination of the zero and the aggressive sub-portfolio as a fixed horizon strategy.

Relative allocations between the zero and the aggressive sub-portfolio are set according to the investor's risk tolerance, which can be captured using confidence intervals for the worst portfolio value as in Exhibit 5. This is similar to the process for selecting a lifestyle protection strategy. The investor sets a target for the worst portfolio value. The investor and advisor then consider portfolios with a worst portfolio value equal to or above the target, and choose the portfolio with the highest expected return.

Alternatively, the investor's risk tolerance can be established without using confidence intervals. It can be based on a minimum portfolio value that is certain to hold, barring a government debt default. This process is illustrated in Exhibit 6. As shown in the exhibit, if the desired minimum portfolio value at the horizon date is equal to the portfolio value today, then the investor purchases a zero coupon Treasury bond with a principal amount equal to the portfolio value today. Because the price of the bond is lower than the principal amount, the investor does not need to apply the full value of the current portfolio to purchase it. The difference between the current portfolio and the amount needed to purchase the zero can be invested in the aggressive sub-portfolio to increase the expected growth rate.

The strategy demonstrated in Exhibit 6 is highly conservative, ensuring that the portfolio at the horizon is larger than the portfolio today. The zero coupon bond delivers a known principal payment, returning the full amount of the investor's initial capital, while the aggressive sub-portfolio provides additional asset growth. Even if the aggressive sub-portfolio declines in value, the total strategy will have a positive return. In practice, investors may not need to lock in a positive return. If the desired minimum portfolio value at the horizon date can be set below the portfolio value today, then the allocation to the zero can be reduced, implying a lower level of protection while allowing a higher allocation to aggressive assets. As above, the appropriate level for the minimum portfolio value and, therefore, the allocation to zero coupon bonds, depends on the investor's risk tolerance.

EXHIBIT 6   Achieving a Minimum Portfolio Value

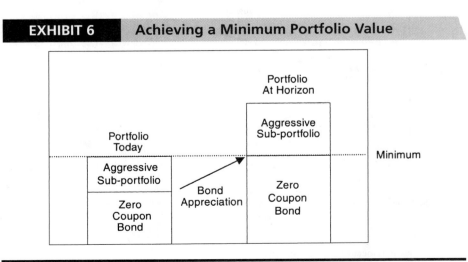

To test the suitability of a fixed horizon strategy, we consider again the approach used for cash flow matching. There are three questions that are especially relevant and these are similar to the questions posed in the previous subsection. First, is the investment horizon likely to change? If the horizon changes, then zero coupon bonds may need to be sold at unfavorable prices and the minimum portfolio value no longer holds. Second, is the investor satisfied with the return on the zero coupon bond? If not, he or she might consider a larger allocation to the aggressive sub-portfolio or explore other strategies. Third, can the investor tolerate the volatility of the zero coupon bond, knowing that the principal payment does not change even as market prices fluctuate? If volatility is a particular concern, then alternative approaches such as the lifestyle protection strategies discussed earlier may be a better fit.

CONCLUSIONS   5

We have met the enemy and he is us.
—Pogo

Despite the efforts of investment professionals to understand their clients' goals, actual results commonly fall short of those goals. Friction between the practitioner's approach and the individual investor's perspective is often to blame. In particular, traditional investment methods favored by practitioners do not always capture the way that investors think and behave.

In this reading, we suggest an approach to wealth management that draws from both traditional investment theory and behavioral theory, closing the gap between the practitioner and the investor. We propose that portfolio construction and risk management should be closely aligned with client goals, and provide several examples, comparing strategies for meeting current lifestyle expenses with strategies for a fixed investment horizon. Unlike the single portfolio framework of traditional finance, with our approach investment solutions might consist of multiple strategies linked to multiple goals.

Goals-based investing improves upon traditional approaches in the areas of measuring risk, risk profiling, and managing behavioral biases. Furthermore, it should help to restore investor confidence after the events of the last market cycle. At a time when failed strategies have forced investors to rethink plans for their lifestyle, family, and community, the investment industry needs to create better solutions. By combining the older ideas of traditional finance with the newer thinking of behavioral finance, we believe we can meet this challenge.

I would like to thank my colleagues at SEI Investments who helped to contribute to the ideas in this article, including Lori Heinel, Chris Hylen, Jerry Lezynski, Greg McIntire, Kevin Robins, Phil Wagner, Denise Williams, and Ken Zimmer. I would also like to thank Christine Galati, Lori Heinel, Nancy Kimelman, and Frank Mercurio for reading earlier drafts and providing many helpful comments and suggestions.

4⅝ 4¹¹/₁₆ ⅜
5½ 5½ — ⅜
5½ 2¹³/₁₆ — ¹/₁₆
20⅝ 21³/₁₆ — ¹/₁₆
17⅜ 18⅛ + ⅞
6½ 6½ — ½
7¼ 3¹/₃₂ — ⅛
15/₁₆
9/₁₆ ⁹/₁₆
1¹/₃₂ 7¹³/₁₆ 7¹⁵/₁₆
7⁵/₁₆
2⅝ 2¹¹/₃₂ 2½ +
2¾ 2¼ 2¼
12¹/₁₆ 11⅜ 11¾ +
87 33¾ 33 33¼ —
602 25⅝ 24⁹/₁₆ 25⅜ +
833 12 11⅝ 11⅜ +
16 10½ 10½ 10½ —
78 15⅞ 15¹³/₁₆ 15⅝ —
4608 9¹/₁₆ 8¼ 8⅝ +
430 11¼ 10⅛
4⅞

LIFETIME FINANCIAL ADVICE: HUMAN CAPITAL, ASSET ALLOCATION, AND INSURANCE

by Roger G. Ibbotson, Moshe A. Milevsky, Peng Chen, CFA, and Kevin X. Zhu

LEARNING OUTCOMES

The candidate should be able to:	Mastery
a. explain the concept and discuss the characteristics of "human capital" as a component of an investor's total wealth;	☐
b. discuss the earnings risk, mortality risk, and longevity risk associated with human capital and explain how these risks can be reduced by appropriate portfolio diversification, life insurance, and annuity products;	☐
c. illustrate how asset allocation policy is influenced by the risk characteristics of human capital and the relative relationships of human capital, financial capital, and total wealth;	☐
d. discuss and illustrate how asset allocation and the appropriate level of life insurance are influenced by the joint consideration of human capital, financial capital, bequest preferences, risk tolerance, and financial wealth;	☐
e. discuss the financial market risk, longevity risk, and savings risk faced by investors in retirement and explain how these risks can be reduced by appropriate portfolio diversification, insurance products, and savings discipline;	☐
f. discuss the relative advantages of fixed and variable annuities as hedges against longevity risk;	☐
g. recommend basic strategies for asset allocation and risk reduction when given an investor profile of key inputs, including human capital, financial capital, stage of life cycle, bequest preferences, risk tolerance, and financial wealth.	☐

Note:
Candidates should focus on the framework, concepts, and conclusions of this reading, rather than the specific formulas used to optimize investor utility.

INTRODUCTION

We can generally categorize a person's life into three financial stages. The first stage is the growing up and getting educated stage. The second stage is the working part of a person's life, and the final stage is retirement. This reading focuses on the working and the retirement stages of a person's life because these are the two stages when an individual is part of the economy and an investor.

Even though this reading is not really about the growing up and getting educated stage, this is a critical stage for everyone. The education and skills that we build over this first stage of our lives not only determine who we are but also provide us with a capacity to earn income or wages for the remainder of our lives. This earning power we call "human capital," and we define it as the present value of the anticipated earnings over one's remaining lifetime. The evidence is strong that the amount of education one receives is highly correlated with the present value of earning power. Education can be thought of as an investment in human capital.

One focus of this reading is on how human capital interacts with financial capital. Understanding this interaction helps us to create, manage, protect, bequest, and especially, appropriately consume our financial resources over our lifetimes. In particular, we propose ways to optimally manage our stock, bond, and so on, asset allocations with various types of insurance products. Along the way, we provide models that potentially enable individuals to customize their financial decision making to their own special circumstances.

On the one hand, as we enter the earning stage of our lives, our human capital is often at its highest point. On the other hand, our financial wealth is usually at a low point. This is the time when we began to convert our human capital into financial capital by earning wages and saving some of these wages. Thus, we call this stage of our lives the "accumulation stage." As our lives progress, we gradually use up the earning power of our human capital, but ideally, we are continually saving some of these earnings and investing them in the financial markets. As our savings continue and we earn returns on our financial investments, our financial capital grows and becomes the dominant part of our total wealth.

As we enter the retirement stage of our lives, our human capital may be almost depleted. It may not be totally gone because we still may have Social Security and defined-benefit pension plans that provide yearly income for the rest of our lives, but our wage-earning power is now very small and does not usually represent the major part of our wealth. Most of us will have little human capital as we enter retirement but substantial financial capital. Over the course of our retirement, we will primarily consume from this financial capital, often bequeathing the remainder to our heirs.

Thus, our total wealth is made up of two parts: our human capital and our financial capital. Recognizing this simple dichotomy dramatically broadens how we analyze financial activities. We desire to create a diversified overall portfolio at the appropriate level of risk. Because human capital is usually relatively low risk (compared with common stocks), we generally want to have a substantial amount of equities in our financial portfolio early in our careers because financial wealth makes up so little of our total wealth (human capital plus financial capital).

Over our lifetimes, our mix of human capital and financial capital changes. In particular, financial capital becomes more dominant as we age so that the lower-risk human capital represents a smaller and smaller piece of the total. As this happens, we will want to be more conservative with our financial capital because it will represent most of our wealth.

Recognizing that human capital is important means that we also want to protect it to the extent we can. Although it is not easy to protect the overall level of our earnings powers, we can financially protect against death, which is the worst-case scenario. Most of us will want to invest in life insurance, which protects us against this mortality risk. Thus, our financial portfolio during the accumulation stage of our lives will typically consist of stocks, bonds, and life insurance.

We face another kind of risk after we retire. During the retirement stage of our lives, we are usually consuming more than our income (i.e., some of our financial capital). Because we cannot perfectly predict how long our retirement will last, there is a danger that we will consume all our financial wealth. The risk of living too long (from a financial point of view) is called "longevity risk." But there is a way to insure against longevity risk, which is to purchase annuity products that pay yearly income as long as one lives. Providing that a person or a couple has sufficient resources to purchase sufficient annuities, they can insure that they will not outlive their wealth.

This reading is about managing our financial wealth in the context of having both human and financial capital. The portfolio that works best tends to hold stocks and bonds as well as insurance products. We are attempting to put these decisions together in a single framework. Thus, we are trying to provide a theoretical foundation—a framework—and practical solutions for developing investment advice for individual investors throughout their lives.

In this reading, we review the traditional investment advice model for individual investors, briefly introduce three additional factors that investors need to consider when making investment decisions, and propose a framework for developing lifetime investment advice for individual investors that expands the traditional advice model to include the additional factors that we discuss in the reading.

The Changing Retirement Landscape

According to the "Survey of Consumer Finances" conducted by the U.S. Federal Reserve Board (2004), the number one reason for individual investors to save and invest is to fund spending in retirement. In other words, funding a comfortable retirement is the primary financial goal for individual investors.

Significant changes in how individual investors finance their retirement spending have occurred in the past 20 years. One major change is the increasing popularity of investment retirement accounts (IRAs) and defined-contribution (DC) plans. Based on data from the Investment Company Institute, retirement assets reached $14.5 trillion in 2005. IRAs and DC plans total roughly half of that amount—which is a tremendous increase from 25 years ago. Today, IRAs and DC plans are replacing traditional defined-benefit (DB) plans as the primary accounts in which to accumulate retirement assets.

Social Security payments and DB pension plans have traditionally provided the bulk of retirement income in the United States. For example, the U.S. Social Security Administration reports that 44 percent of income for people 65 and older came from Social Security income in 2001 and 25 percent came from DB pensions. As Figure 1 shows, according to Employee Benefit Research Institute reports, current retirees (see Panel B) receive almost 70 percent of their retirement income from Social Security and traditional company pension plans whereas today's workers (see Panel A) can expect to have only about one-third of their retirement income funded by these sources (see GAO 2003; EBRI 2000). Increasingly, workers are relying on their DC retirement portfolios and other personal savings as the primary resources for retirement income.

The shift of retirement funding from professionally managed DB plans to personal savings vehicles implies that investors need to make their own decisions about how to allocate retirement savings and what products should be used to generate income in retirement. This shift naturally creates a huge demand for professional investment advice throughout the investor's life cycle (in both the accumulation stage and the retirement stage).

This financial advice must obviously focus on more than simply traditional security selection. Financial advisers will have to familiarize themselves with longevity insurance products and other instruments that provide lifetime income.

In addition, individual investors today face more retirement risk factors than did investors from previous generations. First, the Social Security system and many DB pension plans are at risk, so investors must increasingly rely on their own savings for retirement spending. Second, people today are living longer and could face much higher health-care costs in retirement than members of previous generations. Individual investors increasingly seek professional advice also in dealing with these risk factors.

Traditional Advice Model for Individual Investors

The Markowitz (1952) mean–variance framework is widely accepted in academic and practitioner finance as the primary tool for developing asset allocations for individual as well as institutional investors. According to modern portfolio theory, asset allocation is determined by constructing mean–variance-efficient portfolios for various risk levels.[1] Then, based on the investor's risk tolerance, one of these efficient portfolios is selected. Investors follow the asset allocation output to invest their financial assets.

---

[1] In addition to Markowitz (1952), see Merton (1969, 1971).

FIGURE 1 How Will You Pay for Retirement?

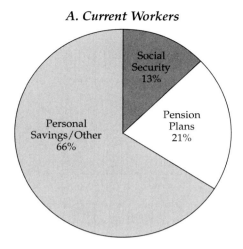

A. Current Workers

Social Security 13%

Pension Plans 21%

Personal Savings/Other 66%

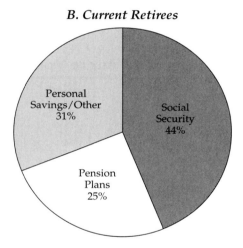

B. Current Retirees

Personal Savings/Other 31%

Social Security 44%

Pension Plans 25%

Source: Based on data from EBRI (2001).

The result of mean–variance analysis is shown in a classic mean–variance diagram. Efficient portfolios are plotted graphically on the *efficient frontier*. Each portfolio on the frontier represents the portfolio with the smallest risk for its level of expected return. The portfolio with the smallest variance is called the "minimum variance" portfolio, and it can be located at the left side of the efficient frontier. These concepts are illustrated in Figure 2, which uses standard deviation (the square root of variance) for the *x*-axis because the units of standard deviation are easy to interpret.

This mean–variance framework emphasizes the importance of taking advantage of the diversification benefits available over time by holding a variety of financial investments or asset classes. When the framework is used to develop investment advice for individual investors, questionnaires are often used to measure the investor's tolerance for risk.

Unfortunately, the framework in Figure 3 considers only the risk–return trade-off in financial assets. It does not consider many other risks that individual investors face throughout their lives.

FIGURE 2   Mean–Variance-Efficient Frontier

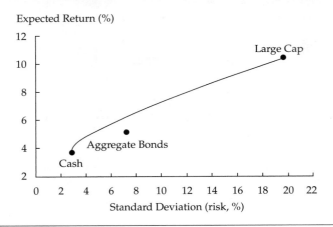

Note: "Large Cap" refers to large-capitalization stocks.

FIGURE 3   Traditional Investment Advice Model

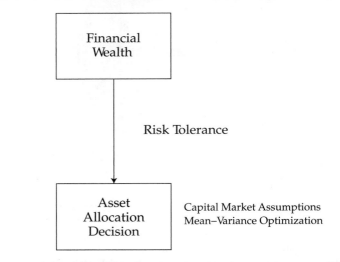

Three Risk Factors and Hedges

We briefly introduce three of the risk factors associated with human capital that investors need to manage—wage earnings risk, mortality risk, and longevity risk—and three types of products that should be considered hedges of those risks. Note that these risk factors, or issues, are often neglected in traditional portfolio analysis. Indeed, one of the main arguments in this monograph is that comprehensive cradle-to-grave financial advice cannot ignore the impact and role of insurance products.

Human Capital, Earnings Risk, and Financial Capital

The traditional mean–variance framework's concentration on diversifying financial assets is a reasonable goal for many institutional investors, but it is not a realistic framework for individual investors who are working and saving for retirement. In fact, this factor is one of the main observations made by Markowitz (1990). From a broad perspective, an investor's total wealth consists of two parts. One is readily tradable financial assets; the other is human capital.

Human capital is defined as the present value of an investor's future labor income. From the economic perspective, labor income can be viewed as a dividend on the investor's human capital. Although human capital is not readily tradable, it is often the single largest asset an investor has. Typically, younger investors have far more human capital than financial capital because young investors have a longer time to work and have had little time to save and accumulate financial wealth. Conversely, older investors tend to have more financial capital than human capital because they have less time to work but have accumulated financial capital over a long career.

One way to reduce wage earnings risk is to save more. This saving converts human capital to financial capital at a higher rate. It also enables the financial capital to have a longer time to grow until retirement. The value of compounding returns in financial capital over time can be very substantial.

And one way to reduce human capital risk is to diversify it with appropriate types of financial capital. Portfolio allocation recommendations that are made without consideration of human capital are not appropriate for many individual investors. To reduce risk, financial assets should be diversified while taking into account human capital assets. For example, the employees of Enron Corporation and WorldCom suffered from extremely poor overall diversification. Their labor income and their financial investments were both in their own companies' stock. When their companies collapsed, both their human capital and their financial capital were heavily affected.

There is growing recognition among academics and practitioners that the risk and return characteristics of human capital—such as wage and salary profiles—should be taken into account when building portfolios for individual investors. Well-known financial scholars and commentators have pointed out the importance of including the magnitude of human capital, its volatility, and its correlation with other assets into a personal risk management perspective.[2] Yet, Benartzi (2001) showed that many investors invest heavily in the stock of the company they work for. He found for 1993 that roughly a third of plan assets were invested in company stock. Benartzi argued that such investment is not efficient because company stock is not only an undiversified risky investment; it is also highly correlated with the person's human capital.[3]

Appropriate investment advice for individual investors is to invest financial wealth in an asset that is not highly correlated with their human capital in order to maximize diversification benefits over the entire portfolio. For people with "safe" human capital, it may be appropriate to invest their financial assets aggressively.

---

[2] For example, Bodie, Merton, and Samuelson (1992); Campbell and Viceira (2002); Merton (2003).

[3] Meulbroek (2002) estimated that a large position in company stock held over a long period is effectively, after accounting for the costs of inadequate diversification, worth less than 50 cents on the dollar.

Mortality Risk and Life Insurance

Because human capital is often the biggest asset an investor has, protecting human capital from potential risks should also be part of overall investment advice. A unique risk aspect of an investor's human capital is mortality risk—the loss of human capital to the household in the unfortunate event of premature death of the worker. This loss of human capital can have a devastating impact on the financial well-being of a family.

Life insurance has long been used to hedge against mortality risk. Typically, the greater the value of human capital, the more life insurance the family demands. Intuitively, human capital affects not only optimal life insurance demand but also optimal asset allocation. But these two important financial decisions—the demand for life insurance and optimal asset allocation—have, however, consistently been analyzed *separately* in theory and practice. We have found few references in either the risk/insurance literature or the investment/finance literature to the importance of considering these decisions jointly within the context of a life-cycle model of consumption and investment. Popular investment and financial planning advice regarding how much life insurance one should carry is seldom framed in terms of the riskiness of one's human capital. And optimal asset allocation is only lately being framed in terms of the risk characteristics of human capital, and rarely is it integrated with life insurance decisions.

Fortunately, in the event of death, life insurance can be a perfect hedge for human capital. That is, term life insurance and human capital have a negative 100 percent correlation with each other in the "living" versus "dead" states; if one pays off at the end of the year, the other does not, and vice versa. Thus, the combination of the two provides diversification to an investor's total portfolio. The many reasons for considering these decisions and products jointly become even more powerful once investors approach and enter their retirement years.

Longevity Risk and the Lifetime-Payout Annuity

The shift in retirement funding from professionally managed DB plans to DC personal savings vehicles implies that investors need to make their own decisions not only about how to allocate retirement savings but also about what products should be used to generate income throughout retirement. Investors must consider two important risk factors when making these decisions. One is financial market risk (i.e., volatility in the capital markets that causes portfolio values to fluctuate). If the market drops or corrections occur early during retirement, the portfolio may not be able to weather the added stress of systematic consumption withdrawals. The portfolio may then be unable to provide the necessary income for the person's desired lifestyle. The second important risk factor is longevity risk—that is, the risk of outliving the portfolio. Life expectancies have been increasing, and retirees should be aware of their substantial chance of a long retirement and plan accordingly. This risk is faced by every investor but especially those taking advantage of early retirement offers or those who have a family history of longevity.

Increasingly, all retirees will need to balance income and expenditures over a longer period of time than in the past. One factor that is increasing the average length of time spent in retirement is a long-term trend toward early retirement. For example, in the United States, nearly half of all men now leave the workforce by age 62 and almost half of all women are out of the workforce by age 60. A second factor is that this decline in the average retirement age has occurred in an environment of rising life expectancies for retirees. Since 1940, falling mortality rates have added almost 4 years to the expected life span of a 65-year-old male and more than 5 years to the life expectancy of a 65-year-old female.

FIGURE 4   Probability of Living to 100

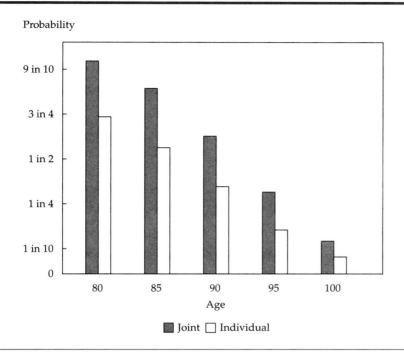

Source: Society of Actuaries, 1996 U.S. Annuity 2000 table.

Figure 4 illustrates the survival probability of a 65-year-old. The first bar of each pair shows the probability of at least one person from a married couple surviving to various ages, and the second bar shows the probability of an individual surviving to various ages. For married couples, in more than 80 percent of the cases, at least one spouse will probably still be alive at age 85.

Longevity is increasing not simply in the United States but also around the world. Longevity risk, like mortality risk, is independent of financial market risk. Unlike mortality risk, longevity risk is borne by the investor directly. Also unlike mortality risk, longevity risk is related to income needs and so, logically, should be directly related to asset allocation.

A number of recent articles—for example, Ameriks, Veres, and Warshawsky (2001); Bengen (2001); Milevsky and Robinson (2005); Milevsky, Moore, and Young (2006)—have focused financial professionals' as well as academics' attention on longevity risk in retirement. A growing body of literature is trying to use traditional portfolio management and investment technology to model personal insurance and pension decisions. But simple retirement planning approaches ignore longevity risk by assuming that an investor need only plan to age 85. It is true that 85 is roughly the life expectancy for a 65-year-old individual, but life *expectancy* is only a measure of central tendency or a halfway point estimate. Almost by definition, half of all investors will exceed their life expectancy. And for a married couple, the odds are more than 80 percent that at least one spouse will live beyond this milestone. If investors use an 85-year life expectancy to plan their retirement income needs, many of them will use up their retirement resources (other than government and corporate pensions) long before actual mortality. This longevity risk—the risk of outliving one's resources—is substantial and is the reason that lifetime annuities (payout annuities) should also be an integral part of many retirement plans.

A lifetime-payout annuity is an insurance product that converts an accumulated investment into income that the insurance company pays out over the life of the investor.[4] Payout annuities are the opposite of life insurance. Consumers buy life insurance because they are afraid of dying too soon and leaving family and loved ones in financial need. They buy payout annuities because they are concerned about living too long and running out of assets during their lifetime.

Insurance companies can afford to provide this lifelong benefit by 1) spreading the longevity risk over a large group of annuitants and 2) making careful and conservative assumptions about the rate of return they will earn on their assets. Spreading or pooling the longevity risk means that individuals who do not reach their life expectancy, as calculated by actuarial mortality tables, subsidize those who exceed it. Investors who buy lifetime-payout annuities pool their portfolios together and collectively ensure that everybody will receive payments as long as each lives. Because of the unique longevity insurance features embedded in lifetime-payout annuities, they can play a significant role in many investors' retirement portfolios.

An Integrated Framework

This reading was inspired by the need to expand the traditional investment advice framework shown in Figure 3 to integrate the special risk factors of individual investors into their investment decisions. The main objective of our study was to review the existing literature and develop original solutions—specifically:

1. To analyze the asset allocation decisions of individual investors while taking into consideration human capital characteristics—namely, the size of human capital, its volatility, and its correlation with other assets.

2. To analyze jointly the decision as to how much life insurance a family unit should have to protect against the loss of its breadwinner and how the family should allocate its financial resources between risk-free (bondlike) and risky (stocklike) assets within the dynamics of labor income and human capital.[5]

3. To analyze the transition from the accumulation (saving) phase to the distribution (spending) phase of retirement planning within the context of a lifecycle model that emphasizes the role of payout annuities and longevity insurance because of the continuing erosion of traditional DB pensions.

To summarize, the purpose here is to parsimoniously merge the factors of human capital, investment allocation, life insurance, and longevity insurance into a conventional framework of portfolio choice and asset allocation. We plan to establish a unified framework to study the total asset allocation decision in accumulation

---

[4] In this reading, we use various terms synonymously to represent *lifetime-payout annuity*—lifetime annuity, payout annuity, and immediate annuity.

[5] How much an investor should consume or save is another important decision that is frequently tied to the concept of human capital. In this reading, we focus on only the asset allocation and life insurance decisions; therefore, our model has been simplified by the assumption that the investor has already decided how much to consume or save. Our numerical cases assume that the investor saves a constant 10 percent of salary each year.

and retirement, which includes both financial market risk as well as other risk factors. We will try to achieve this goal with a minimal amount of technical modeling and, instead, emphasize intuition and examples, perhaps at the expense of some rigor. In some cases, we will provide the reader with references to more advanced material or material that delves into the mathematics of an idea.

We are specifically interested in the interaction between the demand for life insurance, payout annuities, and asset allocation when the correlation between the investor's labor income process and financial market returns is not zero. This project significantly expands our earlier works on similar topics.[6] First, we analyze portfolio choice decisions at both the preretirement stage and in retirement, thus presenting a complete life-cycle picture. Second, instead of focusing on traditional utility models, we explore lifetime objective functions and various computational techniques when solving the problem. Third, we include a comprehensive literature review that provides the reader with background information on previous contributions to the field.

The rest of the reading is organized into two general segments. This first segment investigates the advice framework in the accumulation stage. Then we analyze the impact of human capital on the asset allocation decision. Next, we present the combined framework that includes both the asset allocation decision and the life insurance decision. We present a number of case studies to illustrate the interaction between the two decisions and the effects of various factors.

The second segment investigates the retirement stage. We analyze the risk factors that investors face in retirement. We focus our discussion on longevity risk and the potential role that lifetime-payout annuities can play in managing longevity risk.

OPTIONAL SEGMENT
ENDS

HUMAN CAPITAL AND ASSET ALLOCATION ADVICE

1

In determinations of the appropriate asset allocation for individual investors, the level of risk a person can afford or tolerate depends not only on the individual's psychological attitude toward risk but also on his or her total financial situation (including the types and sources of income). Earning ability outside of investments is important in determining capacity for risk. People with high earning ability are able to take more risk because they can easily recoup financial losses.[7] In his well-known *A Random Walk Down Wall Street,* Malkiel (2004) stated, "The risks you can afford to take depend on your total financial situation, including the types and sources of your income exclusive of investment income" (p. 342). A person's financial situation and earning ability can often be captured by taking the person's human capital into consideration.

A fundamental element in financial planning advice is that younger investors (or investors with longer investment horizons) should invest aggressively. This advice is a direct application of the human capital concept. The

---

[6] For example, Chen and Milevsky (2003); Huang, Milevsky, and Wang (2005); Chen, Ibbotson, Milevsky, and Zhu (2006).

[7] Educational attainments and work experience are the two most significant factors determining a person's earning ability.

impact of human capital on an investor's optimal asset allocation has been studied by many academic researchers. And many financial planners, following the principles of the human capital concept, automatically adjust the risk levels of an individual investor's portfolio over the investor's life stages. In this reading, we discuss why incorporating human capital into an investor's asset allocation decision is important. We first introduce the concept of human capital; then, we describe the importance of human capital in determining asset allocation. Finally, we use case studies to illustrate this role of human capital.

What Is Human Capital?

An investor's total wealth consists of two parts. One is readily tradable financial assets, such as the assets in a 401(k) plan, individual retirement account, or mutual fund; the other is human capital. Human capital is defined as the economic present value of an investor's future labor income. Economic theory predicts that investors make asset allocation decisions to maximize their lifetime utilities through consumption. These decisions are closely linked to human capital.

Although human capital is not readily tradable, it is often the single largest asset an investor has. Typically, younger investors have far more human capital than financial capital because they have many years to work and they have had few years to save and accumulate financial wealth. Conversely, older investors tend to have more financial capital than human capital because they have fewer years ahead to work but have accumulated financial capital. *Human capital should be treated like any other asset class;* it has its own risk and return properties and its own correlations with other financial asset classes.

Role of Human Capital in Asset Allocation

In investing for long-term goals, the allocation of asset categories in the portfolio is one of the most crucial decisions (Ibbotson and Kaplan 2000). However, many asset allocation advisers focus on only the risk–return characteristics of readily tradable financial assets. These advisers ignore human capital, which is often the single largest asset an investor has in his or her personal balance sheet. If asset allocation is indeed a critical determinant of investment and financial success, then given the large magnitude of human capital, one must include it.

Intuitive Examples of Portfolio Diversification Involving Human Capital

Investors should make sure that their total (i.e., human capital plus financial capital) portfolios are properly diversified. In simple words, investment advisers need to incorporate assets in such a way that when one type of capital zigs, the other zags. Therefore, in the early stages of the life cycle, financial and investment capital should be used to hedge and diversify human capital rather than used naively to build wealth. Think of financial investable assets as a defense and protection against adverse shocks to human capital (i.e., salaries and wages), not an isolated pot of money to be blindly allocated for the long run.

For example, for a tenured university professor of finance, human capital—and the subsequent pension to which the professor is entitled—has the properties of a fixed-income bond fund that entitles the professor to monthly coupons. The professor's human capital is similar to an inflation-adjusted, real-return bond. In light of the risk and return characteristics of this human capital, therefore, the professor has little need for fixed-income bonds, money market funds, or even Treasury Inflation-Protected Securities (real-return bonds) in his financial portfolio. By placing the investment money elsewhere, the total portfolio of human and financial capital will be well balanced despite the fact that if each is viewed in isolation, the financial capital and human capital are not diversified.

In contrast to this professor, many *students* of finance might expect to earn a lot more than their university professor during their lifetimes, but their relative incomes and bonuses will fluctuate from year to year in relation to the performance of the stock market, the industry they work in, and the unpredictable vagaries of their labor market. Their human capital will be almost entirely invested in equity, so early in their working careers, their financial capital should be tilted slightly more toward bonds and other fixed-income products. Of course, when they are young and can tolerate the ups and downs in the market, they should have some exposure to equities. But all else being equal, two individuals who are exactly 35 years old and have exactly the same projected annual income and retirement horizon should not have the same equity portfolio structure if their human capital differs in risk characteristics. Certainly, simplistic rules like "100 minus age should be invested in equities" have no room in a sophisticated, holistic framework of wealth management.

It may seem odd to advise future practitioners in the equity industry *not* to "put their money where their mouths are" (i.e., not to invest more aggressively in the stock market), but in fact, hedging human capital risks is prudent risk management. Indeed, perhaps with some tongue in cheek, we might disagree with famed investor and stock market guru Peter Lynch and argue that you should *not* invest in things you are familiar with but, rather, in industries and companies you know nothing or little about. Those investments will have little correlation with your human capital. Remember the engineers, technicians, and computer scientists who thought they knew the high-technology industry and whose human capital was invested in the same industry; they learned the importance of the human capital concept the hard way.

Portfolio allocation recommendations that do not consider the individual's human capital are not appropriate for many individual investors who are working and saving for retirement.

Academic Literature

In the late 1960s, economists developed models that implied that individuals should optimally maintain constant portfolio weights throughout their lives (Samuelson 1969, Merton 1969). An important assumption of these models was that investors have no labor income (or human capital). This assumption is not realistic, however, as we have discussed, because most investors do have labor income. If labor income is included in the portfolio choice model, individuals will optimally change their allocations of financial assets in a pattern related to the life cycle. In other words, the optimal asset allocation depends on the risk–return characteristics of their labor income and the flexibility of their labor income (such as how much or how long the investor works).

Bodie, Merton, and Samuelson (1992) studied the impact of labor income flexibility on investment strategy. They found that investors with a high degree of labor flexibility should take more risk in their investment portfolios. For example, younger investors may invest more of their financial assets in risky assets than older investors because the young have more flexibility in their working lives.

Hanna and Chen (1997) explored optimal asset allocation by using a simulation method that considered human capital and various investment horizons. Assuming human capital is a risk-free asset, they found that for most investors with long horizons, an all-equity portfolio is optimal.

In our modeling framework, which we will present in a moment, investors adjust their financial portfolios to compensate for their risk exposure to nontradable human capital.[8] The key theoretical implications are as follows: 1) younger investors invest more in stocks than older investors; 2) investors with safe labor income (thus safe human capital) invest more of their financial portfolio in stocks; 3) investors with labor income that is highly correlated with the stock markets invest their financial assets in less risky assets; and 4) the ability to adjust labor supply (i.e., higher flexibility) increases an investor's allocation to stocks.

Empirical studies show, however, that most investors do not efficiently diversify their financial portfolios in light of the risk of their human capital. Benartzi (2001) and Benartzi and Thaler (2001) showed that many investors use primitive methods to determine their asset allocations and many of them invest heavily in the stock of the company for which they work.[9] Davis and Willen (2000) estimated the correlation between labor income and equity market returns by using the U.S. Department of Labor's "Current Occupation Survey." They found that human capital has a low correlation (−0.2 to 0.1) with aggregate equity markets. The implication is that the typical investor need not worry about his or her human capital being highly correlated with the stock market when making asset allocation decisions; thus, most investors can invest the majority of their financial wealth in risky assets.[10]

Empirical studies have also found that for the majority of U.S. households, human capital is the dominant asset. Using the U.S. Federal Reserve Board's 1992 "Survey of Consumer Finances," Lee and Hanna (1995) estimated that the ratio of financial assets to total wealth (including human capital) was 1.3 percent for the median household. Thus, for half of the households, financial assets represented less than 1.3 percent of total wealth. The 75th percentile of this ratio was 5.7 percent. The 90th percentile was 17.4 percent. In short, financial assets represented a high percentage of total wealth for only a small proportion of U.S. households. The small magnitude of these numbers places a significant burden on financial advisers to learn more about their clients' human capital, which is such a valuable component of personal balance sheets.

FIGURE 5   Human Capital and Asset Allocation

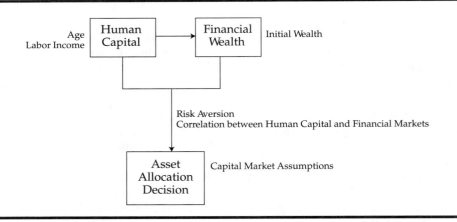

---

[8] See Merton (1971); Bodie, Merton, and Samuelson (1992); Heaton and Lucas (1997); Jagannathan and Kocherlakota (1996); Campbell and Viceira (2002).

[9] Heaton and Lucas (2000) showed that wealthy households with high and variable business income invest less in the stock market than similarly wealthy households without that sort of business income, which is consistent with the theoretical prediction.

[10] Although this might be true in aggregate, it can vary widely among individuals.

Figure 5 shows the relationships among financial capital, human capital, other factors (such as savings and the investor's aversion to risk), and the asset allocation of financial capital.

Human Capital and Asset Allocation Modeling

This section provides a general overview of how to determine optimal asset allocation while considering human capital. Human capital can be calculated from the following equation:

$$HC(x) = \sum_{t=x+1}^{n} \frac{E[h_t]}{(1 + r + v)^{t-x}}, \tag{1}$$

where

x	= current age
$HC(x)$	= human capital at age x
h_t	= earnings for year t adjusted for inflation before retirement and after retirement, adjusted for Social Security and pension payments
n	= life expectancy
r	= inflation-adjusted risk-free rate
v	= discount rate[11]

In the model, we assume there are two asset classes.[12] The investor can allocate financial wealth between a risk-free asset and a risky asset (i.e., bonds and stocks). We assume the investor has financial capital W_t at the beginning of period t. The investor chooses the optimal allocation involving the risk-free asset and the risky asset that will maximize expected utility of total wealth, which is the sum of financial capital and human capital, $W_{t+1} + H_{t+1}$. We assume the investor follows the constant relative risk aversion (CRRA) utility function. In our case, it is

$$U = \frac{(W_{t+1} + H_{t+1})^{1-\gamma}}{1 - \gamma} \tag{2}$$

for $\gamma \neq 1$ and

$$U = \ln(W_{t+1} + H_{t+1}) \tag{3}$$

for $\gamma = 1$. In Equations 2 and 3, γ is the coefficient of relative risk aversion and is greater than zero.

In the model, labor income and the return of risky assets are correlated.

---

[11] The discount rate should be adjusted to the risk level of the person's labor income.

[12] The model was inspired by an early model by Campbell (1980) that seeks to maximize the total wealth of an investor in a one-period framework. The total wealth consists of the investor's financial wealth and human capital. In this reading, we focus on the asset allocation decision for investors' financial capital instead of the life insurance decision in Campbell's paper.

The investor's human capital can be viewed as a "stock" if both the correlation with a given financial market index and the volatility of labor income are high. It can be viewed as a "bond" if both correlation and volatility are low. In between these two extremes, human capital is a diversified portfolio of stocks and bonds, plus idiosyncratic risk.[13] We are quite cognizant of the difficulties involved in calibrating these variables that were pointed out by Davis and Willen (2000), and we rely on some of their parameters for our numerical examples in the following case studies.

Case Studies

In the cases, we look at some specific parameters and the resulting optimal portfolios. In the first case, we treat future labor income as certain (i.e., there is no uncertainty in the labor income). The model indicates that human capital in this case is a risk-free asset (as in the case of our professor). Then, we add uncertainty into consideration. Specifically, we treat human capital as a risky asset.

For example, let us assume that we have a male U.S. investor whose annual income is expected to grow with inflation and there is no uncertainty about his annual income—which is $50,000. He saves 10 percent of his income each year. He expects to receive Social Security payments of $10,000 each year (in today's dollars) when he retires at age 65. His current financial wealth is $50,000, of which 40 percent is invested in a risk-free asset and 60 percent is invested in a risky asset. Finally, he rebalances his financial portfolio annually back to the initial portfolio allocation. Human capital was estimated by using Equation 1.

Financial capital for the examples, in contrast to human capital, can be easily parameterized on the basis of the evolution of returns over time. Table 1 provides the capital market assumptions that are used in this computation for this and other cases in this reading.

TABLE 1   Capital Market Return Assumptions

Asset	Compounded Annual Return (%)	Risk (Standard Deviation) (%)
Risk free (bonds)	5	—
Risky (stocks)	9	20
Inflation	3	—

Note: These capital market assumptions are comparable to the historical performance of U.S. stocks and bonds from 1926 to 2006, after adjusting for investment expenses the investor would have to pay. According to Ibbotson Associates (2006), the compounded annual return for that period was 10.36 percent for the S&P 500 Index (with a standard deviation of 20.2 percent), 5.47 percent for U.S. government bonds, and 3.04 percent for inflation.

---

[13] Note that when we make statements such as "this person's human capital is 40 percent long-term bonds, 30 percent financial services, and 30 percent utilities," we mean that the unpredictable shocks to future wages have a given correlation structure with the named subindices. Thus, as in our previous example, the tenured university professor could be considered to be a 100 percent real-return (inflation-indexed) bond because no shocks to his wages would be linked to any financial subindex.

Figures 6 and 7 illustrate the relationships of financial capital, human capital, and total wealth (defined as the sum of financial capital and human capital) that investors might expect over their working (preretirement) years from age 25 to age 65. For example, under our assumptions and calculation of human capital, for a male investor who is 25 years old, Figure 6 shows that his human capital is estimated to be about $800,000; Figure 7 shows that it represents 94 percent of his total wealth and far outweighs his financial capital at that age. His financial capital is only $50,000. As the investor gets older and continues to make savings

FIGURE 6   Expected Financial Capital, Human Capital, and Total Wealth over Life Cycle with Optimal Asset Allocation

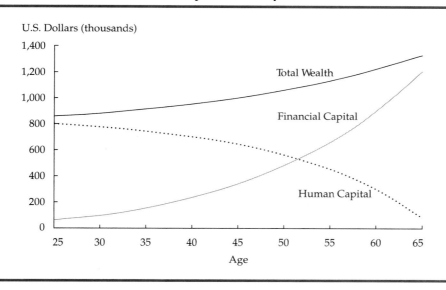

FIGURE 7   Financial Capital and Human Capital as Share of Total Wealth over Life Cycle

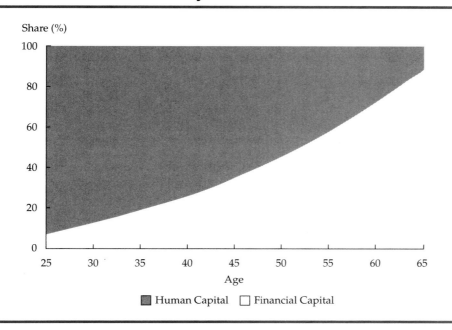

contributions, these monies plus the return from the existing portfolio increase the proportion of financial capital. At age 65, Figure 6 shows the human capital decreasing to $128,000 (to come from future Social Security payments) and the financial portfolio peaking just above $1.2 million.

Case #1. Human Capital as a Risk-Free Asset

In this case, we assume that there is no uncertainty about the investor's annual income, so his human capital is a risk-free asset because it is the present value of future income. He is age 25 with annual income of $50,000 and current financial wealth of $50,000. The coefficient of relative risk aversion for this investor is assumed to be 5.5 (i.e., $\gamma = 5.5$).

Figure 8 shows the optimal asset allocation of this investor's financial capital from age 25 to 65. As can be seen, the allocation of financial wealth to risk-free assets increases over time. In other words, the investor increases allocations to the risk-free asset in order to maintain a desired risk exposure in the total wealth portfolio. Households will tend to hold proportionately less of the risk-free financial asset when young (when the value of human capital is large) and tend to increase the proportion of financial wealth held in the risk-free financial asset as they age (as the amount of human capital declines).

Now, let's analyze the risk exposure of the investor's total portfolio at different ages in this case. When considering human capital, to keep the desired risk exposure of his total portfolio at the level indicated by $\gamma = 5.5$, the investor will choose a 100 percent stock asset allocation because he already has 94 percent of his total wealth (represented by his human capital) invested in bonds. Investing 100 percent in stocks is the closest we can get his total portfolio to the target desired risk exposure level without borrowing. When the investor is 45, his total wealth consists of about 40 percent financial assets and 60 percent human capital; the asset allocation for his financial assets is about 60 percent stocks and

FIGURE 8   Case #1: Optimal Asset Allocation to the Risk-Free Asset over Life Cycle

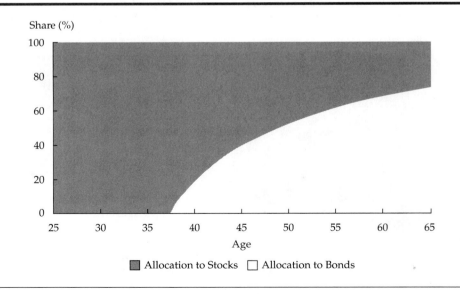

Note: Risk tolerance level at 5.5.

40 percent bonds. At age 65, he ends up with a financial portfolio of 27 percent stock and 73 percent bonds.

This simple example illustrates that when an investor's human capital is riskless, the investor should invest more in stocks than an investor closer to retirement, and when an investor gets older, his or her human capital will decrease and financial capital will increase. Thus, the investor should gradually scale back the amount invested in stocks.

Unfortunately, although investors are almost always given the discretion to change their allocations to various assets and account managers usually even maintain a website for this purpose, empirical studies (e.g., Ameriks and Zeldes 2001) suggest that only a small minority of investors actually make any adjustments.

Case #2. Human Capital as a Risky Asset

In Case #1, we assumed that human capital was 100 percent risk free. But only a small portion of investors would have this kind of "safe" human capital. Labor income is uncertain for most investors for a number of reasons, including the possibilities of losing one's job or being laid off. The uncertainty in labor income makes human capital a risky asset.

But the riskiness varies by individual; for example, a business owner, a stock portfolio manager, a stockbroker, and a schoolteacher have different risk profiles in their human capital. To incorporate human capital in total wealth, we need to consider the unique risk and return characteristics of each individual's human capital.

There are two basic types of risk for an investor's human capital. The first type can be treated as risk related to other risky assets (such as stocks). The second type is risk uncorrelated with the stock market. Let's look at the two types and how they affect optimal asset allocation.

To analyze the impact of the two types of human capital risk on the investor's allocation of financial capital, we constructed the following two scenarios. In Scenario 1, human capital is risky and highly correlated with the stock market ($\alpha_h = 0.2$, where α_h is the volatility of the shocks to the labor income, and $\rho_{hs} = 0.5$, where ρ_{hs} is the correlation between shocks to labor income and shocks to the risky asset's returns). In Scenario 2, human capital is risky but it is uncorrelated with the stock market ($\alpha_h = 0.2$ and $\rho_{hs} = 0$).

Figure 9 shows the optimal asset allocations of financial capital in the two scenarios. The assumptions used in Case #1 prevail except for the assumption about volatility and correlation between human capital and the stock market.

Let's start by analyzing the first type of risk (Scenario 1), in which the human capital risk is highly correlated with the risk of other risky financial assets. A simple example of this scenario would be the perfect correlation of labor income with the payoffs from holding the aggregate stock market—for example, a stockbroker or a stock portfolio manager. In this situation, our hypothetical investor will use his financial assets to balance his human capital risk. The stockbroker's human capital is far more sensitive to the stock market than a schoolteacher's. If a stockbroker and a schoolteacher have the same total wealth and similar risk tolerances, human capital theory recommends that the stockbroker invest a smaller portion of his financial assets in the stock market than the schoolteacher because the stockbroker has implicitly invested his human capital in the stock market. For young investors with equitylike human capital, the financial assets should be invested predominantly in fixed-income assets. Because the value of one's human capital declines with age, the share of risk-free assets in the stockbroker's portfolio will also decline and the share of risky assets in the portfolio of financial assets will rise until retirement.

FIGURE 9   Case #2: Proportion of Risk-Free Asset in Scenarios 1 and 2

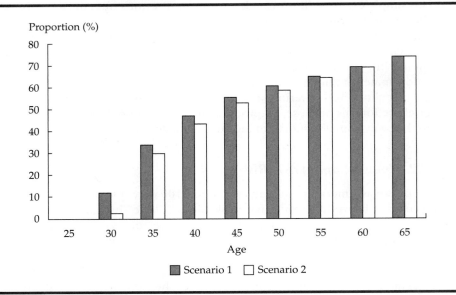

Now, let's consider Scenario 2, in which the investor's labor income is risky but not correlated with the payoffs of the risky assets (i.e., is independent of financial market risk). In this case, the investor's optimal financial asset allocation follows, by and large, the same pattern as the case in which the investor's human capital is risk free—especially when the risk of human capital is small (variance in the income over time is small). The reason is that, similar to the risk-free asset, human capital is uncorrelated with financial market risk. When the risk of human capital increases, however, the investor should reduce overall risk in the financial portfolio. In other words, if your occupational income (and future prospects for income) is uncertain, you should refrain from taking too much risk with your financial capital.

Case #3. Impact of Initial Financial Wealth

The purpose of this case is to show the impact of different amounts of current financial wealth on optimal asset allocation. Assume that we hold the investor's age at 45 and set risk preference at a moderate level (a CRRA risk-aversion coefficient of 4). The correlation between shocks to labor income and risky-asset returns is 0.2, and the volatility of shocks to labor income is 5 percent. The optimal allocations to the risk-free asset for various levels of initial financial wealth are presented in Figure 10.

Figure 10 shows that the optimal allocation to the risk-free asset increases with initial wealth. This situation may seem to be inconsistent with the CRRA utility function because the CRRA utility function implies that the optimal asset allocation will not change with the amount of wealth the investor has. Note, however, that "wealth" here includes both financial wealth and human capital. In fact, this situation is a classic example of the impact of human capital on optimal asset allocation. An increase in initial financial wealth not only increases total wealth but also reduces the percentage of total wealth represented by human capital. In this

FIGURE 10   Case #3: Optimal Asset Allocation to the Risk-Free Asset at Various Financial Wealth Levels

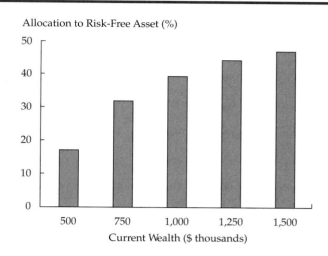

case, human capital is less risky than the risky asset.[14] When initial wealth is low, human capital dominates total wealth and asset allocation. As a result, to achieve the target asset allocation of a moderate investor—say, an allocation of 60 percent to the risk-free asset and 40 percent to the risky asset—the closest allocation is to invest 100 percent of financial wealth in the risky asset because human capital is illiquid. As initial wealth rises, the asset allocation gradually approaches the target asset allocation that a moderately risk-averse investor desires.

In summary, for a typical investor whose human capital is less risky than the stock market, the optimal asset allocation is more conservative the more financial assets the investor has.

Case #4. Correlation between Wage Growth Rate and Stock Returns

In this case, we examine the impact of the correlation between shocks to labor income and shocks to the risky asset's returns. In particular, we want to evaluate asset allocation decisions for investors with human capital that is highly correlated with stocks. Examples are an investor's income that is closely linked to the stock performance of her employer's company or an investor's compensation that is highly influenced by the financial markets (e.g., the investor works in the financial industry).

Again, the investor's age is 45 and the coefficient of relative risk aversion is 4. The amount of financial capital is $500,000. The optimal asset allocations to the risk-free asset for various correlations are presented in Figure 11.

As Figure 11 shows, the optimal allocation becomes more conservative (i.e., more assets are allocated to the risk-free asset), with increasing correlation between income and stock market returns. One way to look at this outcome is that a higher correlation between human capital and the stock market results in less

---

[14] In this case, income has a real growth rate of 0 percent and a standard deviation of 5 percent, yet the expected real return on stocks is 8 percent and the standard deviation for stock returns is 20 percent.

FIGURE 11   Case #4: Optimal Asset Allocation to the Risk-Free Asset at Various Correlation Levels

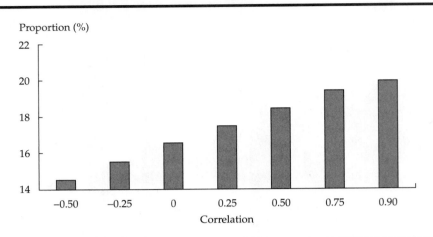

diversification and thus higher risk for the total portfolio (human capital plus financial capital). To reduce this risk, an investor must invest more financial wealth in the risk-free asset. Another way to look at this result is in terms of *certainty equivalents* (or utility equivalents) of wealth. The higher the uncertainty (or volatility), all else being equal, the lower the certainty-equivalent value. In utility terms, with increasing correlation and rising volatility, this investor is actually poorer!

Implications for Advisers

A financial adviser or consultant should be aware of the following issues when developing a long-term asset allocation plan for typical individual investors:

1. Investors should invest financial assets in such a way as to diversify and balance out their human capital.

2. A young investor with relatively safe human capital assets and greater flexibility of labor supply should invest more financial assets in risky assets, such as stocks, than an older investor should, perhaps even with leverage and debt. The portion of financial assets allocated to stocks should be reduced as the investor gets older. Also, if the stock market performs well, the investor's financial capital will grow, and again, the implication is to reduce the portion of financial assets invested in stocks.

3. An investor with human capital that has a high correlation with stock market risk should also reduce the allocation to risky assets in the financial portfolio and increase the allocation to assets that are less correlated with the stock market.[15]

In short, the risk characteristics of human capital have a significant impact on optimal financial portfolio allocation. Therefore, to effectively incorporate human capital into making the asset allocation decision, financial advisers and consultants need to determine 1) whether the investor's human capital is risk free or risky and 2) whether the risk is highly correlated with financial market risk.

---

[15] For example, all else being equal, alternative assets with low correlations with the stock market (e.g., commodities, certain hedge funds) can be attractive for these investors.

Summary

Human capital is defined as the present value of future labor income. Human capital—not financial assets—is usually the dominant asset for young and middle-aged people.

Many academic researchers have advocated considering human capital when developing portfolio allocations of an investor's financial assets. That is, investors should invest their financial assets in such a way as to diversify and balance their human capital.

In addition to the size of the investor's human capital, its risk–return characteristics, its relationship to other financial assets, and the flexibility of the investor's labor supply also have significant effects on how an investor should allocate financial assets. In general, a typical young investor would be well advised to hold an all-stock investment portfolio (perhaps even with leverage) because the investor can easily offset any disastrous returns in the short run by adjusting his or her future investment strategy, labor supply, consumption, and/or savings. As the investor becomes older, the proportion of human capital in total wealth becomes smaller; therefore, the financial portfolio should become less aggressive.

Although the typical U.S. investor's income is unlikely to be highly correlated with the aggregate stock market (based on results reported by Davis and Willen 2000), many investors' incomes may be highly correlated with a specific company's market experience. Company executives, stockbrokers, and stock portfolio managers (whose labor income and human capital are highly correlated with risky assets) should have financial portfolios invested in assets that are little correlated with the stock market (e.g., bonds).

HUMAN CAPITAL, LIFE INSURANCE, AND ASSET ALLOCATION

2

In the first part of this reading, we discussed how human capital plays an important role in developing the appropriate investment recommendations for individual investors. In addition, recognition is growing among academics and practitioners that the risk and return characteristics of human capital (wage and salary profiles) should be taken into account when building portfolios for the individual investor. Therefore, we expanded the traditional investment advice framework to include not only an investor's financial capital but also human capital. To illustrate the effect of human capital in the expanded framework, we used case studies in which the human capital characteristics were quite different.

In this section, we study another (perhaps even more important) risk aspect of human capital—*mortality risk*.[16] And we further expand the framework developed previously to include the life insurance decision. We first explain the rationale for examining the life insurance decision together with the asset allocation decision. We develop a unified model to provide practical guidelines on developing optimal asset allocation and life insurance allocation for individual investors in their preretirement years (accumulation stage). We also provide a number of case studies in which we illustrate model allocations that depend on income, age, and tolerance for financial risk.

---

[16] This discussion is partly based on material in Chen, Ibbotson, Milevsky, and Zhu (2006).

Life Insurance and Asset Allocation Decisions

A unique aspect of an investor's human capital is mortality risk—the family's loss of human capital in the unfortunate event of the investor's premature death. This risk is huge for many individual investors because human capital is their dominant asset.

Life insurance has long been used to hedge against mortality risk. Typically, the greater the value of the human capital, the more life insurance the family demands. Intuitively, human capital affects not only optimal asset allocation but also optimal life insurance demand. These two important financial decisions have consistently been analyzed separately, however, in theory and practice. We found few references in the literature to the need to consider these decisions jointly and within the context of a life-cycle model of consumption and investment. Popular investment and financial planning advice regarding how much life insurance one should acquire is never framed in terms of the riskiness of one's human capital. And the optimal asset allocation decision has only lately come to be framed in terms of the risk characteristics of human capital. Rarely is the asset allocation decision integrated with life insurance decisions.

Motivated by the need to integrate these two decisions in light of the risk and return characteristics of human capital, we have analyzed these traditionally distinct lines of thought together in one framework. These two decisions must be determined jointly because they serve as risk substitutes when viewed from an individual investor's portfolio perspective.

Life insurance is a perfect hedge for human capital in the event of death. Term life insurance and human capital have a negative 100 percent correlation with each other. If one pays off at the end of the year, then the other does not, and vice versa. Thus, the combination of the two provides great diversification to an investor's total portfolio. Figure 12 "updates" Figure 5 to illustrate the types of decisions the investor faces when jointly considering human capital, asset allocation, and life insurance decisions together with the variables that affect the decisions.

FIGURE 12   Relationships among Human Capital, Asset Allocation, and Life Insurance

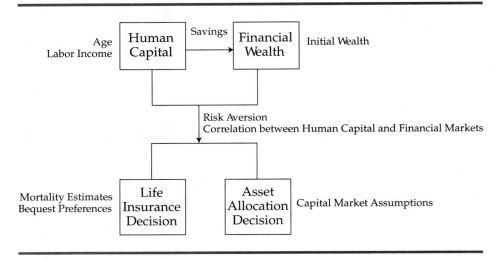

Human Capital, Life Insurance, and Asset Allocation

We have discussed the literature on human capital and asset allocation extensively to this point, so now we concentrate on the link between life insurance and human capital. A number of researchers have pointed out that the lifetime consumption and portfolio decision models need to be expanded to take into account lifetime uncertainty (or mortality risk). Yaari's 1965 paper is considered the first classical work on this topic. Yaari pointed out ways of using life insurance and life annuities to insure against lifetime uncertainty. He also derived conditions under which consumers would fully insure against lifetime uncertainty (see also Samuelson 1969; Merton 1969). Like Yaari, Fischer (1973) pointed out that earlier models either dealt with an infinite horizon or took the date of death to be known with certainty.

Theoretical studies show a clear link between the demand for life insurance and the uncertainty of human capital. Campbell (1980) argued that for most households, the uncertainty of labor income dominates uncertainty as to financial capital income. He also developed solutions based on human capital uncertainty to the optimal amount of insurance a household should purchase.[17] Buser and Smith (1983) used mean–variance analysis to model life insurance demand in a portfolio context. In deriving the optimal insurance demand and the optimal allocation between risky and risk-free assets, they found that the optimal amount of insurance depends on two components: the expected value of human capital and the risk–return characteristics of the insurance contract. Ostaszewski (2003) stated that life insurance—by addressing the uncertainties and inadequacies of an individual's human capital—is the business of human capital "securitization."

Empirical studies of life insurance adequacy have shown that underinsurance, however, is prevalent (see Auerbach and Kotlikoff 1991). Gokhale and Kotlikoff (2002) argued that questionable financial advice, inertia, and the unpleasantness of thinking about one's death are the likely causes.

Zietz (2003) has provided another excellent review of the literature on insurance.

Description of the Model

To merge considerations of asset allocation, human capital, and optimal demand for life insurance, we need a solid understanding of the actuarial factors that affect the pricing of a life insurance contract. Note that, although numerous life insurance product variations exist—such as term life, whole life, and universal life, each of which is worthy of its own financial analysis—we focus exclusively on the most fundamental type of life insurance policy—namely, the *one-year, renewable term policy*.[18]

On a basic economic level, the premium for a one-year, renewable term policy is paid at the beginning of the year—or on the individual's birthday—and protects the human capital of the insured for the duration of the year.[19] (If the insured person dies within that year, the insurance company pays the face value

---

[17] Economides (1982) argued in a corrected model that Campbell's approach underestimated the optimal amount of insurance coverage. Our model takes this correction into consideration.

[18] One-year, renewable term life insurance is used throughout this reading. Although an analysis is beyond the scope of this reading, we believe that all other types of life insurance policies are financial combinations of term life insurance with investment accounts, added tax benefits, and embedded options.

[19] In this description, we are obviously abstracting somewhat from the realities of insurance pricing, but to a first-order approximation, the descriptions capture the essence of actuarial cost.

to the beneficiaries soon after the death or prior to the end of the year.) Next year, because the policy is renewable, the contract is guaranteed to start anew with new premium payments to be made and protection received.

In this section, we provide a general approach to thinking about the joint determination of the optimal asset allocation and prudent life insurance holdings.

We assume there are two asset classes. The investor can allocate financial wealth between a risk-free asset and a risky asset (i.e., bonds and stocks). Also, the investor can purchase a term life insurance contract that is renewable each period. The investor's objective is to maximize overall utility, which includes utility in the investor's "live" state and in the investor's "dead" state, by choosing life insurance (the face value of a term life insurance policy) and making an asset allocation between the risk-free and risky assets.[20] The optimization problem can be expressed as follows:

$$
\max_{(\theta_x, \alpha_x)} E\big[(1 - D)(1 - \bar{q}_x)\, U_{alive}(W_{x+1} + H_{x+1})
$$
$$
+ D(\bar{q}_x)\, U_{dead}(W_{x+1} + \theta_x) \big], \tag{4}
$$

where

θ_x	= amount of life insurance
α_x	= allocation to the risky asset
D	= relative strength of the utility of bequest
$\bar{q}_x$	= subjective probabilities of death at the end of the year $x+1$ conditional on being alive at age x
$1 - \bar{q}_x$	= subjective probability of survival
W_{x+1}	= wealth level at age $x + 1$
H_{x+t}	= human capital

and $U_{alive}(\cdot)$ and $U_{dead}(\cdot)$ are the utility functions associated with the alive and dead states.

We extend the framework of Campbell (1980) and Buser and Smith (1983) in a number of important directions. First, we link the asset allocation decision to the decision to purchase life insurance in one framework by incorporating human capital. Second, we specifically take into consideration the effect of the bequest motive (attitude toward the importance of leaving a bequest) on asset allocation and life insurance.[21] Third, we explicitly model the volatility of labor income and its correlation with the financial market. Fourth, we also model the investor's subjective survival probability.

Human capital is the central component that links both decisions. Recall that an investor's human capital can be viewed as a stock if both the correlation with a given financial market subindex and the volatility of the labor income are high. Human capital can be viewed as a bond if both the correlation and the volatility are low. In between those two extremes, human capital is a diversified portfolio of stocks and bonds, plus idiosyncratic risk. Again, we rely on some of

---

[20] We assume that the investor makes asset allocation and insurance purchase decisions at the start of each period. Labor income is also received at the beginning of the period.

[21] Bernheim (1991) and Zietz (2003) showed that the bequest motive has a significant effect on life insurance demand.

the Davis–Willen (2000) parameters for our numerical case examples. It is important to distinguish between, on the one hand, correlations and dependence when considering human capital and aggregate stock market returns (such as return of the S&P 500 Index) and, on the other hand, correlations of human capital with individual securities and industries. Intuitively, a middle manager working for Dow Corning, for example, has human capital returns that are highly correlated with the performance of Dow Corning stock. A bad year or quarter for the stock is likely to have a negative effect on financial compensation.

The model has several important implications. First, as expressed in Equation 4, it clearly shows that both asset allocation and life insurance decisions affect an investor's overall utility; therefore, the decisions should be made jointly.[22] The model also shows that human capital is the central factor. The impact of human capital on asset allocation and life insurance decisions is generally consistent with the existing literature (e.g., Campbell and Viceira 2002; Campbell 1980). One of our major enhancements, however, is the explicit modeling of correlation between the shocks to labor income and financial market returns. The correlation between income and risky-asset returns plays an important role in both decisions. All else being equal, as the correlation between shocks to income and risky assets increases, the optimal allocation to risky assets declines, as does the optimal quantity of life insurance. Although the decline in allocation to risky assets with increasing correlation may be intuitive from a portfolio theory perspective, we provide precise analytic guidance on how it should be implemented. Furthermore, and contrary to intuition, we show that a higher correlation with any given subindex brings about the second result—that is, reduces the demand for life insurance. The reason is that the higher the correlation, the higher the discount rate used to estimate human capital from future income. A higher discount rate implies a lower amount of human capital—thus, less insurance demand.

Second, the asset allocation decision affects well-being in both the live (consumption) state and the dead (bequest) state whereas the life insurance decision affects primarily the bequest state. Bequest preference is arguably the most important factor, other than human capital, in evaluating life insurance demand.[23] Investors who weight bequest as more important (who have a higher D) are likely to purchase more life insurance.

Another unique aspect of our model is the consideration of subjective survival probability, $1 - \bar{q}_x$. The reader can see intuitively that investors with low subjective survival probability (i.e., those who believe they have a high mortality rate) will tend to buy more life insurance. This "adverse selection" problem is well documented in the insurance literature.[24]

Other implications are consistent with the existing literature. For example, our model implies that the more financial wealth one has—all else being equal— the less life insurance one demands. More financial wealth also indicates more conservative portfolios when human capital is "bondlike." When human capital is "stocklike," more financial wealth calls for more aggressive portfolios. Naturally, risk tolerance also has a strong influence on the asset allocation decision.

---

[22] The only scenarios in which the asset allocation and life insurance decisions are not linked are when the investor derives his or her utility 100 percent from consumption or 100 percent from bequest. Both are extreme—especially the 100 percent from bequest.

[23] A well-designed questionnaire can help elicit individuals' attitudes toward bequest, even though a precise estimate may be hard to obtain.

[24] The actuarial mortality tables can be taken as a starting point. Life insurance is already priced to take into account adverse selection.

Investors with less risk tolerance will invest conservatively and buy more life insurance. These implications will be illustrated in the case studies.

We emphasize at this point that our analysis completely ignores the nonhuman-capital aspects of insurance purchases. For example, a wide variety of estate planning, business succession, and tax minimization strategies might increase demand for insurance much more than the level we have derived in our models. These aspects are beyond the scope of our analysis.

Case Studies

To illustrate the predictions of the model, we analyze the optimal asset allocation decision and the optimal life insurance coverage for five different cases. We solve the problem via simulation.

For all five cases, we assumed the investor can invest in two asset classes. We used the capital market assumptions given in Table 1, which can be summarized as follows: compound annual geometric mean returns for bonds of 5 percent and for stocks of 9 percent, standard deviation of stock returns of 20 percent, and an inflation rate of 3 percent.

In these case studies, the investor is female. Her preference toward bequest is one-fourth of her preference toward consumption in the live state.[25] She has no special information about her relative health status (i.e., her subjective survival probability is equal to the objective actuarial survival probability). Her income is expected to grow with inflation, and the volatility of the growth rate is 5 percent.[26] Her real annual income is $50,000, and she saves 10 percent each year. She expects to receive a Social Security payment of $10,000 each year (in today's dollars) when she retires at age 65. Her current financial wealth is $50,000. She is assumed to follow constant relative risk aversion (CRRA) utility with a risk-aversion coefficient of γ. Finally, we assume that her financial portfolio is rebalanced and the term life insurance contract renewed annually.[27] These assumptions remain the same for all cases. Other parameters, such as initial wealth, will be specified in each case.

Case #1. Human Capital, Financial Asset Allocation, and Life Insurance Demand over the Lifetime

In this case, we assumed that the investor has a CRRA, γ, of 4. Also, the correlation between the investor's income and the market return of the risky asset is 0.20.[28] For a given age, the amount of insurance this investor should purchase can be determined by her consumption/bequest preference, risk tolerance, and financial wealth. Her expected financial wealth, human capital, and the derived optimal insurance demand over the investor's life from age 25 to age 65 are presented in Figure 13.

Several results of modeling this investor's situation are worth noting. First, human capital gradually decreases as the investor gets older and her remaining

---

[25] That is, we set D equal to 0.2 in the model.

[26] The salary growth rate and the volatility were chosen mainly to show the implications of the model. They are not necessarily representative.

[27] The mortality and insurance loading is assumed to be 12.5 percent.

[28] Davis and Willen (2000) estimated the correlation between labor income and equity market returns by using the U.S. Department of Labor's "Current Occupation Survey." They found that the correlation between equity returns and labor income typically lies in the interval from –0.10 to 0.20.

FIGURE 13   Case #1: Human Capital, Financial Asset Allocation, and Insurance Demand over Lifetime

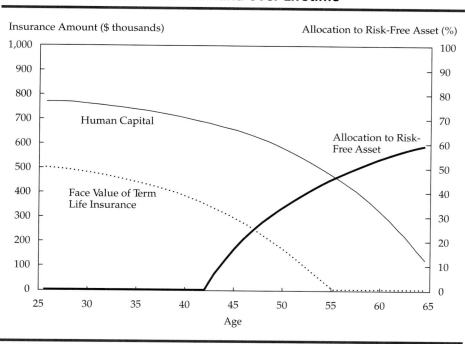

number of working years becomes smaller. Second, the amount of her financial capital increases as she ages as a result of growth of her existing financial wealth and the additional savings she makes each year. The allocation to risky assets decreases as the investor ages because of the dynamic between human capital and financial wealth over time. Finally, the investor's demand for insurance decreases as she ages. This result is not surprising because the primary driver of insurance demand is human capital, so the decrease in human capital reduces insurance demand.

These results appear to be consistent with conventional financial planning advice to reduce insurance holdings later in life, even though mortality risk itself has increased. In fact, one of the widespread misunderstandings about insurance, especially among young students of finance, is that a person needs large amounts of life insurance only when facing the greatest chance of death (i.e., only for older people). To the contrary, the magnitude of loss of human capital at younger ages is far more important than the higher probability of death at older ages.

Case #2. Strength of the Bequest Motive

This case shows the impact of the bequest motive on the optimal decisions about asset allocation and insurance. In this case, we assume that the investor is age 45 and has an accumulated financial wealth of $500,000. The investor has a CRRA coefficient of 4. The optimal allocations to the risk-free asset and insurance for various bequest preferences are presented in Figure 14.

In this case, insurance demand increases as the bequest motive strengthens (i.e., as D gets larger). This result is expected because an investor with a strong bequest motive is highly concerned about her heirs and has an incentive to purchase a large amount of insurance to hedge the loss of human capital. In

FIGURE 14   Case #2: Optimal Insurance Demand and Allocation to the Risk-Free Asset by Strength of Bequest Preference

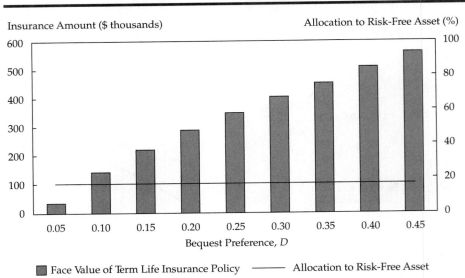

contrast, Figure 14 shows almost no change in the proportional allocation to the risk-free asset at different strengths of bequest motive. This result indicates that asset allocation is primarily determined by risk tolerance, returns on the risk-free and risky assets, and human capital. This case shows that the bequest motive has a strong effect on insurance demand but little effect on optimal asset allocation.[29]

Case #3. The Impact of Risk Tolerance

In this case, we again assume that the investor is age 45 and has accumulated financial wealth of $500,000. The investor has a moderate bequest preference level (i.e., $D = 0.2$). The optimal allocations to the risk-free asset and the optimal insurance demands for this investor for various risk-aversion levels are presented in Figure 15.

As expected, allocation to the risk-free asset increases with the investor's risk-aversion level—the classic result in financial economics. Actually, the optimal portfolio is 100 percent in stocks for risk-aversion levels less than 2.5. The optimal amount of life insurance follows a similar pattern: Optimal insurance demand increases with risk aversion. For this investor with moderate risk aversion (a CRRA coefficient of 4) and the human and financial assumptions that we have made, optimal insurance demand is about $290,000, which is roughly six times her current income of $50,000.[30] Therefore, conservative investors should invest more in risk-free assets and buy more life insurance than aggressive investors should.

---

[29] In this model, subjective survival probability and the bequest motive have similar impacts on the optimal insurance need and asset allocation. When subjective survival probability is high, the investor will buy less insurance.

[30] This result is close to the typical recommendation made by financial planners (i.e., purchase a term life insurance policy that has a face value four to seven times one's current annual income). See, for example, Todd (2004).

FIGURE 15   Case #3: Optimal Insurance Demand and Allocation to the Risk-Free Asset by Risk-Aversion Level

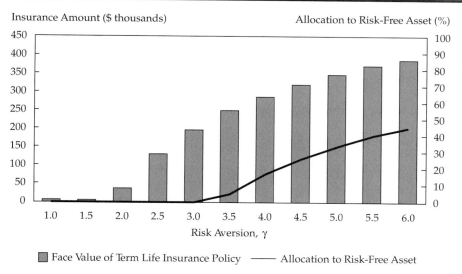

FIGURE 16   Case #4: Optimal Insurance Demand and Allocation to the Risk-Free Asset by Level of Financial Wealth

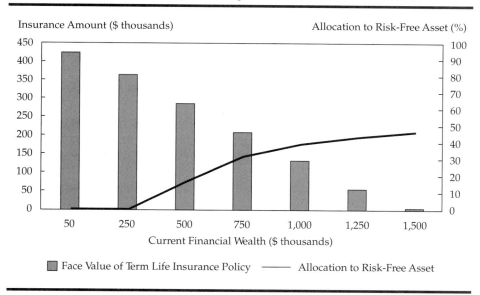

Case #4. Financial Wealth

For this case, we hold the investor's age at 45 and her risk preference and bequest preference at moderate levels (a CRRA coefficient of 4 and bequest level of 0.2). The optimal asset allocation to the risk-free asset and the optimal insurance demands for various levels of financial wealth are presented in Figure 16.

First, Figure 16 shows that the optimal allocation to the risk-free asset increases with initial wealth, which we discussed extensively earlier.

Second, optimal insurance demand decreases with financial wealth. This result can be intuitively explained through the substitution effects of financial wealth and life insurance. In other words, with a large amount of wealth in hand, one has less demand for insurance because the loss of human capital will have much less impact on the well-being of one's heirs. In Figure 16, the optimal amount of life insurance decreases from more than $400,000 when the investor has little financial wealth to almost zero when the investor has $1.5 million in financial assets.

In summary, for an investor whose human capital is less risky than the stock market, the more substantial the investor's financial assets are, the more conservative optimal asset allocation is and the smaller life insurance demand is.

Case #5. Correlation between Wage Growth Rate and Stock Returns

In this case, we want to evaluate the life insurance and asset allocation decisions for investors with a high correlation between the risky asset and the investors' income. This kind of correlation can happen when an investor's income is closely linked to the stock performance of the company where the investor works or when the investor's compensation is highly influenced by the financial market (e.g., the investor works in the financial industry).

Again, the investor's age is 45 and she has a moderate risk preference and bequest preference. Optimal asset allocation to the risk-free asset and insurance demand for various levels of correlations in this situation are presented in Figure 17.

The optimal allocation becomes more conservative (i.e., more allocation is made to the risk-free asset) as income and stock market return become more correlated, which is similar to the results described earlier in this reading. The optimal insurance demand decreases as the correlation increases. Life insurance is purchased to protect human capital for the family and loved ones. As the correlation between the risky asset and the income flow increases, the *ex ante* value of human capital to the surviving family decreases. This lower valuation on human capital induces a lower demand for insurance. Also, less money spent on life insurance indirectly increases the amount of financial wealth the investor

**FIGURE 17   Case #5: Optimal Insurance Demand and Allocation
to the Risk-Free Asset by Correlation Level**

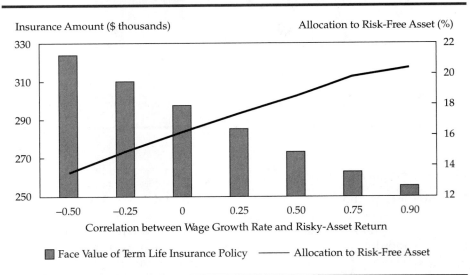

can invest, so the investor can invest more in risk-free assets to reduce the risk associated with her total wealth.[31]

Another way to think about these results is to consider the certainty (or utility) equivalent of risky human capital, which can be thought of as the economic present value of a cash flow stream. The higher the correlation with other financial assets and the higher the volatility of the cash flow stream, the lower the certainty equivalent value and, therefore, the lower the demand for insurance.

In summary, as wage income and stock market returns become more correlated, optimal asset allocation becomes more conservative and the demand for life insurance falls.

Summary

We have expanded on the basic idea that human capital is a "shadow" asset class that is worth much more than financial capital early in life and that it also has unique risk and return characteristics. Human capital—even though it is not traded and is highly illiquid—should be treated as part of a person's endowed wealth that must be protected, diversified, and hedged.

We demonstrated that the correlation between human capital and financial capital (i.e., whether the investor resembles more closely a bond or a stock) has a noticeable and immediate effect on the investor's demand for life insurance—in addition to the usual portfolio considerations. Our main argument is that the two decisions—quantity of life insurance and asset allocation—cannot be solved in isolation. Rather, they are aspects of the same problem.

We developed a unified human capital-based framework to help individual investors with both decisions. The model provided several key results:

▶ Investors need to make asset allocation decisions and life insurance decisions jointly.

▶ The magnitude of human capital, its volatility, and its correlation with other assets significantly affect the two decisions over the life cycle.

▶ Bequest preferences and a person's subjective survival probability have significant effects on the person's demand for insurance but little influence on the person's optimal asset allocation.

▶ Conservative investors should invest relatively more in risk-free assets and buy more life insurance.

We presented five case studies to demonstrate the optimal decisions in different scenarios.

RETIREMENT PORTFOLIO AND LONGEVITY RISK

3

Thus far, we have studied human capital and its impact on asset allocation and life insurance decisions for investors in the accumulation stage (i.e., when people are generally saving money prior to retirement). Now we shift our attention to the retirement stage.

In this section, we investigate the risk factors that investors face when making decisions about saving for and investing their retirement portfolios. We illustrate

---

[31] See Case #3 for a detailed discussion of the wealth impact.

the common mistakes that investors experience when making their asset allocation and spending decisions in retirement. Through the use of Monte Carlo simulation techniques, we illustrate the longevity risk that investors face and the potential benefits of including lifetime-payout annuities in retirement portfolios.

Three Risk Factors in Retirement

A typical investor has two goals in retirement. The primary goal is to ensure a comfortable life style during retirement. In other words, investors would like to enjoy roughly the same life style in retirement that they had before (or a better one). Second, they would like to leave some money behind as a bequest. Three important risks confront individuals when they are making saving and investment decisions for their retirement portfolios: 1) financial market risk, 2) longevity risk, and 3) the risk of not saving enough (spending too much). Part of the third risk is the risk of inflation.

Financial Market Risk

Financial market risk, or volatility in the capital markets, causes portfolio values to fluctuate in the short run even though they may appreciate in the long run. If the market drops or corrections occur early during retirement, the individual's portfolio may not be able to weather the stress of subsequent systematic withdrawals. Then, the portfolio may be unable to generate the income necessary for the individual's desired life style or may simply run out of money before the individual dies.

Investors often ignore financial market risk by assuming a constant rate of return from their retirement portfolio (i.e., no market volatility). As a result, they make inappropriate asset allocations and product selections. For an illustration of the impact of the constant-return assumption, consider the following case. Assume that a 65-year-old investor has $1 million invested in a 60 percent stock/40 percent bond portfolio (hereafter, 60/40).[32] He would like to have $75,000 a year worth of income in retirement. Social Security and his defined-benefit (DB) pension plan will provide about $25,000 of this annual retirement income. Thus, he needs his investment portfolio to generate $50,000 each year from age 65 for the remainder of his life. Assuming that the compounded annual nominal returns for stocks and bonds are, respectively, 9 percent and 5 percent, the estimated average compounded annual nominal return on the portfolio is 7.4 percent. We assume inflation to be 3.0 percent.

Figure 18 shows the wealth and income levels projected for the constant returns in this case.[33] If we assume that the future return is constant, each year the portfolio will generate a 6.14 percent compounded return after expenses and fees, or roughly 3.14 percent after inflation. The $1 million portfolio will be able to sustain a withdrawal of more than $50,000 a year in real terms for the investor's life expectancy and beyond. In other words, with constant returns, the investor will meet his income needs and not run out of money.

Market return, however, is not the same every year. In some periods, the portfolio returns will be much lower than 6.14 percent and may even be negative—as occurred in 2000, 2001, and 2002. So, although 6.14 percent may

---

[32] All dollar amounts presented in this section are in real dollars (i.e., inflation-adjusted amounts).

[33] All illustrations in this study are net of fees and expenses. Fee amounts were obtained from Morningstar Principia as of March 2006. They are 1.26 percent for mutual funds and 2.40 percent for variable annuities.

FIGURE 18   Projected Wealth

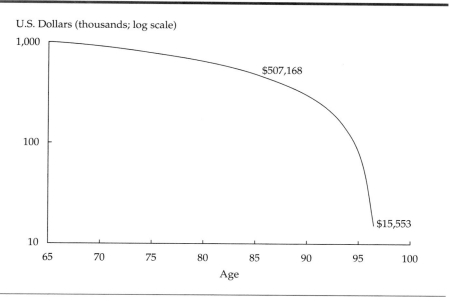

U.S. Dollars (thousands; log scale)

$507,168

$15,553

Age

Note: 65-year-old male investor; $1 million; 60/40 portfolio.

be a reasonable average assumption, it is unrealistic for the investor to make decisions based purely on the average return. Doing so underestimates the risk, and investors are generally risk averse by nature.

To show the impact of the entire return spectrum, we used a Monte Carlo simulation. Monte Carlo simulation is a technique to evaluate the outcome of portfolios over time by using a large number of simulated possible future return paths. In this case, the returns were randomly generated from a normal distribution with a 6.14 percent compounded average return and a 13 percent standard deviation.[34]

Panel A of Figure 19 presents the Monte Carlo analysis results for the same case used in Figure 18. This analysis shows a 10 percent chance that this portfolio will be depleted by age 82, a 25 percent chance it will be depleted by age 88, and a 50 percent chance it will be depleted by age 95. When considered in light of the uncertain life spans of investors, this result reveals a much larger risk than many investors would accept. Panel B of Figure 19 shows the wealth produced by a nonannuitized 60/40 portfolio plus Social Security and DB plan payments of $25,000 a year.

Longevity Risk

Longevity risk is the risk of living longer than planned for and outliving one's assets. With life expectancies continuing to increase, retirees—especially those who retire early or have a family history of long lives—must be aware of the possibility of a long lifetime and adjust their plans accordingly.

Americans are living longer, on average, than ever before. The probability that an individual retiring at age 65 will reach age 80 is greater than 70 percent

---

[34] In this study, we generated 2,000 return paths. Each path contained 35 years (from age 65 to age 100).

FIGURE 19   Nonannuitized Portfolio

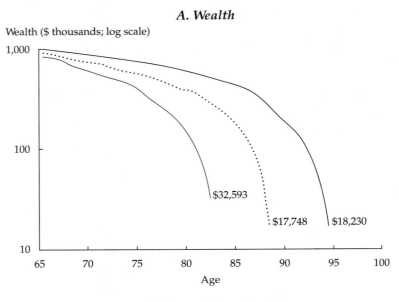

A. Wealth

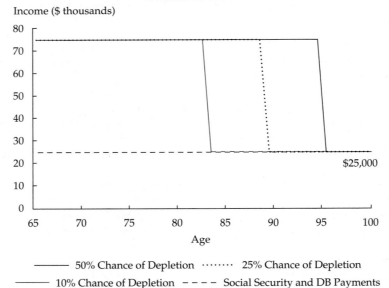

B. Annual Income

———— 50% Chance of Depletion   ········ 25% Chance of Depletion
———— 10% Chance of Depletion   – – – – Social Security and DB Payments

for females and greater than 62 percent for males. For a married couple, the odds reach nearly 90 percent that at least one spouse will live to age 70. As Figure 4 illustrated, in more than 80 percent of cases, at least one spouse will still be alive at age 85.

Simple retirement planning approaches ignore longevity risk by assuming the investor needs to plan only to age 85. It is true that 85 years is roughly the life expectancy for an individual who is 65 years old, but life expectancy is only the average estimate. Roughly half of investors will live longer than life expectancy. Therefore, investors who have used an 85-year life expectancy to plan their retirement income needs may find they have used up their retirement resources (other than government and corporate pensions) long before actual mortality. This longevity risk is substantial.

Risk of Spending Uncertainty

Investors may not save enough to adequately fund their retirement portfolios. Retirees are increasingly relying on investment income from their own portfolios, such as defined-contribution (DC) plans and individual retirement accounts, to fund their retirements. The ambiguity in this situation is that investors cannot determine exactly what they will earn between now and retirement. Moreover, they may not have the discipline to save adequately.

The evidence is that most investors do not save enough (Benartzi and Thaler 2001). A large proportion of investors do not even fund their 401(k) plans enough to use the match that their employers provide. If an employer provides a 50 percent match, then for each dollar an investor puts into her or his 401(k) plan, the employer puts in 50 cents. This immediate 50 percent "return" should not be given up by any rational employee, but it often is.

Although most savings can generate only normal capital market returns, savings are critical to meet retirement needs. To expect investment returns to compensate for a savings shortfall is not reasonable. To the contrary, investment returns allow the savings to multiply several times over the course of a retirement.

Controlling the Three Risks

Financial risk can be mitigated by using modern portfolio theory, which provides methods to reduce portfolio risk by capturing the long-term diversification benefits among investments. Insurance products can hedge away longevity risk. The risk of inadequate savings is primarily a behavioral issue.

For financial market risk, investors can turn to the rich literature and models of modern portfolio theory. Although financial market risk cannot be completely eliminated, investors can take advantage of the benefits of diversifying among various investments by following long-term asset allocation policies. The Markowitz mean–variance model is widely accepted as the gold standard for asset allocation.

Mean–variance optimization is a first step, but it considers only the risk and return trade-off in the financial market. It does not consider the longevity risk that people face during retirement.

DB pension plans provide longevity insurance by supplying their plan participants with income that cannot be outlived. In many cases, this income is also adjusted for inflation, which provides a further hedge against unexpected shocks to inflation. Fewer and fewer U.S. workers, however, are being covered by DB plans.

Because living a long life means needing more resources to fund longer-term income needs, rational investors will have to turn to sources other than DB plans. One approach is to take on more financial risk, if the investor can tolerate the risk, in the hopes of gaining more return. This plan can be accomplished by selecting an aggressive asset allocation policy (typically by using more stocks than the usual 60 percent and/or by adding higher-risk assets, such as hedge funds).

Rational investors will also want to hedge away the financial aspect of longevity risk because this type of risk exposure offers no potential reward.[35] In

---

[35] Living a long life is desirable, of course, from many aspects; we are focusing here only on the financial aspect of longevity.

other words, investors should be willing to pay an insurance premium to hedge away the longevity risk. This approach is similar to the concept of homeowner insurance, which protects against hazard to one's home. Lifetime annuities (payout annuities) provide investors with this type of longevity insurance. And lifetime annuities should be an integral part of many retirement plans precisely because of the real and substantial longevity risk—which should be treated just as seriously as the risks of disability, critical illness, and premature death.

Recently, behavioral economists have developed some innovative ways to help investors overcome the myopic behavior of spending today instead of saving for retirement. For example, Thaler and Benartzi (2004) pioneered the "Save More Tomorrow" (SMarT) program. SMarT takes advantage of the behavioral theory that people heavily weight current consumption over future (retirement) consumption. The program encourages workers to save some portion of their future *raises,* not their current income, in their 401(k) plans. In this plan, when they receive their raises, their savings rates go up but they still get to take home part of the extra compensation for immediate consumption. The plan is palatable because raises are in the future and people are less averse to trading future consumption for savings than to trading current consumption in order to save.

Longevity Risk and Sources of Retirement Income

Social security, DB pension plans, and personal savings (including DC savings) are the main sources of retirement income for Americans. In this section, we look closely at the effectiveness of various sources in managing longevity risk.

Social Security and DB Pension Plans

Traditionally, Social Security and DB pension plans have provided the bulk of retirement income. For example, the U.S. Social Security Administration has reported that 39 percent of the income of persons 65 and older came from Social Security income in 2001 and 18 percent came from DB pensions (see GAO 2003). According to Employee Benefit Research Institute reports, current retirees receive about 60 percent of their retirement income from Social Security and traditional company pension plans, whereas today's workers can expect to have only about one-third of their retirement income funded by these sources (EBRI 2000).

Longevity insurance is embedded in U.S. government-funded Social Security and DB pension benefits because the benefits are paid out for as long as the beneficiary (and, typically, the beneficiary's spouse) lives. In DB pension plans, the employer (as plan sponsor) agrees to make future payments during retirement and is responsible for investing and managing the pension plan assets, thus bearing the investment and longevity risks. Because a DB pension plan typically covers a large number of employees, the overall longevity risk of the plan is significantly mitigated for the employer.

In the past two decades, a shift has been going on from DB plans to DC plans.[36] Over the past 20 years, the percentage of private-sector workers who par-

---

[36] The U.S. Department of Labor has reported that private-sector employers sponsored only approximately 56,000 tax-qualified DB plans in 1998, down from more than 139,000 in 1979. The number of tax-qualified DC plans sponsored by private employers more than doubled over the same period—from approximately 331,000 to approximately 674,000 (see GAO 2003).

ticipate in a DB plan has decreased and the percentage of such workers who participate in a DC plan has consistently increased. Today, the majority of active retirement plan participants are in DC plans, whereas most plan participants were in DB plans 20–30 years ago.

DC Plans and Other Personal Savings

Because workers increasingly must rely on their DC retirement portfolios and other personal savings as their primary sources of retirement income, workers must now bear longevity risk. DC plans contain no promise by an employer or the government that money will be available during retirement.

In addition to being exposed to longevity risk as never before, today's workers who are saving for retirement through DC plans have to manage this risk themselves. Personal savings are used to fund retirement income in two ways. First, a retiree may receive a lump sum directly from the plan as a cash settlement and then invest and withdraw from the portfolio during retirement. This plan is typically referred to as a "systematic withdrawal strategy." Second, a retiree may receive a lump sum and preserve the assets by purchasing a lifetime annuity with some or all of the proceeds to provide a stream of income throughout retirement. This plan is typically referred to as "annuitization."

Annuitization and systematic withdrawals (from an invested portfolio) have different advantages and risks for retirees. A life annuity, whether received from an employer-sponsored pension plan or purchased directly through an insurance company, ensures that a retiree will not run out of income no matter how long he or she lives. If a retiree dies soon after purchasing an annuity, however, he or she will have received considerably less than the lump sum a systematic withdrawal strategy would provide. With payout annuities, the investor will also be unable to leave that asset as a bequest, and the income from the annuity may not be adequate to pay for unexpected large expenses.

Retiring participants who systematically withdraw lump sums have the flexibility of preserving or drawing down those assets as they wish, but they risk running out of assets if they live longer than expected, if assets are withdrawn too rapidly, or if the portfolio suffers poor investment returns. Payout annuities offer a means to mitigate much of the financial uncertainty that accompanies living to a very old age but may not necessarily be the best approach for all retirees. For example, an individual with a life-shortening illness might not be concerned about the financial needs that accompany living to a very old age.

Longevity Risk and Payout Annuities

Because mean–variance optimization addresses only the risk and return trade-offs in the financial markets, we focus our attention on the importance of longevity insurance. We touch on the difference between fixed- and variable-payout annuities and then move on to address the proper allocation of retiree income between conventional financial assets and payout annuity products that help to manage longevity risk.

Living a long life means more resources are needed to fund longer-term income needs. On the one hand, rational investors may decide to take on more financial risk in hopes of gaining more return. On the other hand, rational investors would also want to hedge away the financial aspect of longevity risk because there is no potential financial reward for this type of risk exposure. In other words, investors should be willing to pay an insurance premium to hedge away longevity risk. Lifetime-payout annuities provide investors with this type of longevity insurance.

A lifetime-payout annuity is an insurance product that converts an accumulated investment into income that the insurance company pays out over the life of the investor. Payout annuities are the opposite of life insurance. Investors buy life insurance because they are afraid of dying too soon and leaving family and loved ones in financial need. They buy payout annuities because they are concerned about living too long and running out of assets during their lifetime. Insurance companies can provide this lifelong benefit by spreading the longevity risk over a large group of annuitants and making careful and conservative assumptions about the rate of return to be earned on their assets.

Spreading or pooling the longevity risk means that individuals who do not reach their life expectancy (as calculated by actuarial mortality tables) subsidize those who exceed it. Investors who buy lifetime-payout annuities pool their portfolios and collectively ensure that everybody will receive payments as long as they live. Because of the unique longevity insurance features embedded in lifetime-payout annuities, they can play a significant role in many investors' retirement portfolios.

The two basic types of payout annuities are fixed and variable. A fixed-payout annuity pays a fixed nominal dollar amount each period. A variable annuity's payments fluctuate in accord with the performance of the fortunes of the underlying investments chosen by the buyer of the annuity. Payments from a lifetime-payout annuity are contingent on the life span of the investor. Other payout options are available, however, that might guarantee that payments will be made for a specified period of time or might offer refund guarantees.

If an investor buys a life annuity from an insurance company, the investor is transferring the longevity risk to the insurance company, which is in a far better position than an individual to hedge and manage those risks. But of course, the investor pays a price. Should an investor self-insure against longevity risk?

Fixed-Payout Annuity

Figure 20 illustrates the payment stream from an immediate fixed annuity. With an initial premium or purchase amount of $1 million, the annual income payments for our 65-year-old male would be $6,910 a month, or $82,920 a year.[37] The straight line represents the annual payments before inflation. People who enjoy the security of a steady and predictable stream of income may find a fixed annuity appealing. The drawback of a fixed annuity, however, becomes evident over time. Because the payments are the same year after year, purchasing power is eroded by inflation as the annuitant grows older. The curved line in Figure 20 represents the same payment stream after taking into account a hypothetical 3 percent inflation rate.[38] Although the annuitant receives the same payment amount, that payment no longer purchases as much as it used to.

Despite the benefits of longevity insurance and fixed nominal payout amounts, a portfolio that consists solely of fixed lifetime annuities has several drawbacks. First, as noted, is decline in the value of the payments over time because of inflation. Second, one cannot trade out of the fixed-payout annuity

---

[37] This rate is the quote obtained in July 2006 for a 65-year-old male living in Illinois with $1 million to spend. The quote was obtained from www.immediateannuities.com.

[38] The average inflation rate in the United States from 1926 to 2006 was 3.04 percent.

FIGURE 20   Income from Fixed Annuity

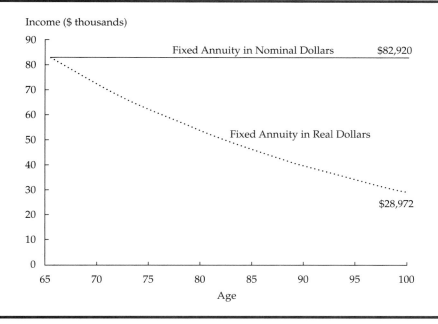

once it has been purchased.[39] This aspect may be a problem for investors who need or prefer liquidity. Finally, when an investor buys a fixed annuity, the investor locks in payments based on the current interest rate environment. Payout rates from today's fixed-payout annuities are near historical lows because of current low interest rates. Our 65-year-old male might have received as much as $11,500 a month in the early 1980s in exchange for a $1 million initial premium. In 2003, that same $1 million bought only $6,689 a month. These drawbacks do not mean that fixed annuities are a poor investment choice. On the contrary, as we will show, fixed annuities can be a crucial part of a well-diversified retirement income portfolio.

Variable-Payout Annuities

A variable-payout annuity is an insurance product that exchanges accumulated investment value for annuity units that the insurance company pays out over the lifetime of the investor. The annuity payments fluctuate in value depending on the investments held; therefore, disbursements also fluctuate. To understand variable-payout annuities, think of a mutual fund whose current net asset value (NAV) is $1 per unit. The unit fluctuates each day. On any given day in any given week, month, or year, the price may increase or decrease relative to the previous period. With a variable annuity, instead of receiving fixed annuity payments, the investor receives a fixed number of fund units. Each month, the insurance company converts the fund units into dollars based on the NAV at the end of the month to determine how much to pay the investor. Therefore, the cash flow from the variable-payout annuity fluctuates with the performance of the funds the investor chooses.

---

[39] Payout annuities are available that do allow the investor to withdraw money from them, but the investor typically has to pay a surrender charge or market value adjustment charge. Furthermore, this flexibility applies only during the period of the annuity when payments are guaranteed regardless of life status.

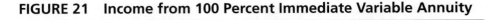

FIGURE 21   Income from 100 Percent Immediate Variable Annuity

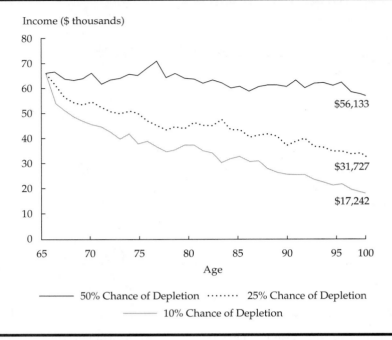

Figure 21 illustrates the annuity payment stream, in real terms, from a 60/40 portfolio and a life-only payment option in an immediate variable annuity. We conducted a Monte Carlo simulation to illustrate the various payment scenarios. The simulation was generated for the case of the same investor discussed earlier from historical return statistics for stocks, bonds, and inflation for 1926–2006; a $1 million initial portfolio; and a 3 percent assumed investment return (AIR).[40] The initial payment at age 65 is estimated to be $66,153 a year.[41] The three lines in the chart show the 10th, 25th, and 50th percentiles. As Figure 21 demonstrates, there is a 10 percent chance that annual inflation-adjusted annuity payments will fall below $17,300 if the investor reaches 100, a 25 percent chance that they will be around $32,000 or lower, and a 50 percent chance that they will fall below $57,000.

Asset Allocation, Payout Annuities, and Disciplined Savings

Figure 22 shows the probability of success for two retirement income strategies—one using 100 percent systematic withdrawal from a 60/40 portfolio without any lifetime annuity (as depicted in Figure 18) and a second strategy using a payout annuity (25 percent fixed annuitization, 25 percent variable annuitization) and 50 percent systematic withdrawal from the same 60/40 portfolio. The systematic withdrawal strategy with no annuity has a higher risk of causing the portfolio to

---

[40] The AIR is an initial interest rate assumption that is used to compute the amount of an initial variable annuity payment. Subsequent payments will either increase or decrease depending on the relationship of the AIR to the actual investment return.

[41] All initial payments for immediate payout annuities were obtained from www.immediateannuity.com on 12 June 2005 for an assumed 65-year-old female living in Illinois and a $100,000 premium.

FIGURE 22   Probability of Meeting Income Goal: Payout Annuities vs. Systematic Withdrawal

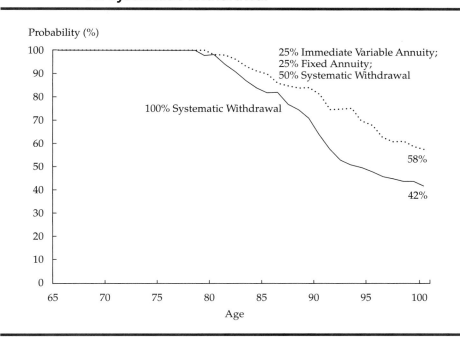

fall short of funding the required income need. The probability of success begins to drop before age 80 and falls to a low of 42 percent by age 100. The combination strategy is a far better strategy for increasing the odds of meeting income goals over this investor's lifetime. Although the probability of not being able to meet the income goal 100 percent of the time remains, the shortfall comes at a later stage in life and the success rate remains the highest.

For retirees, such a combination of types of annuitization and systematic withdrawal could help manage the financial risks and the income needs they face during retirement.

Summary

In this section, we presented the three risk factors that investors face when making retirement portfolio decisions: financial market risk, longevity risk, and the risk of spending too much (which includes inflation risk). We focused on the role that lifetime-payout annuities should play in a retirement portfolio to alleviate both financial market and longevity risks. First, we demonstrated that traditional wealth-forecasting techniques that use a constant-return assumption can lead investors to believe they face little or no risk in funding retirement income needs. We then used a Monte Carlo simulation to illustrate more realistically the market risks in systematic withdrawal from a mutual fund portfolio, and we compared the results of withdrawal strategies with the benefits of payout annuities. Our analysis made clear that combining immediate fixed and variable life annuities with conventional investment instruments, such as mutual funds, is the optimal solution to providing retirement income.

This section demonstrated that an immediate payout annuity is an effective way to manage longevity risk in retirement. Buying a lifetime-payout annuitization is not, however, an all-or-nothing decision; the investor can choose how much to allocate between mutual fund accounts and annuitization. Combining nonannuitized assets with annuitized assets can help investors manage financial market risk, longevity risk, and bequest desires.

STUDY SESSION 5
PORTFOLIO MANAGEMENT FOR INSTITUTIONAL INVESTORS

Broadly defined, institutional investors include defined-benefit pension plans, defined-contribution plans, foundations, endowments, insurance companies, banks, and investment intermediaries. Each group faces a unique set of portfolio management investment objectives and constraints that must be addressed to effectively manage their investment portfolios.

The study session begins with an introduction of the concepts and practices important to determining the investment policy statement for an institutional investment management client. The next two readings then examine the specific issue of asset/liability management in the context of defined-benefit pension plans. The implications for asset allocation and risk management are relevant, however, for a wide range of institutions that manage assets to fund anticipated liabilities.

READING ASSIGNMENTS

Reading 20   Managing Institutional Investor Portfolios
Managing Investment Portfolios: A Dynamic Process, Third Edition, John L. Maginn, CFA, Donald L. Tuttle, CFA, Jerald E. Pinto, CFA, and Dennis W. McLeavey, CFA, editors

Reading 21   Linking Pension Liabilities to Assets
by Aaron Meder and Renato Staub

Reading 22   Allocating Shareholder Capital to Pension Plans
Journal of Applied Corporate Finance

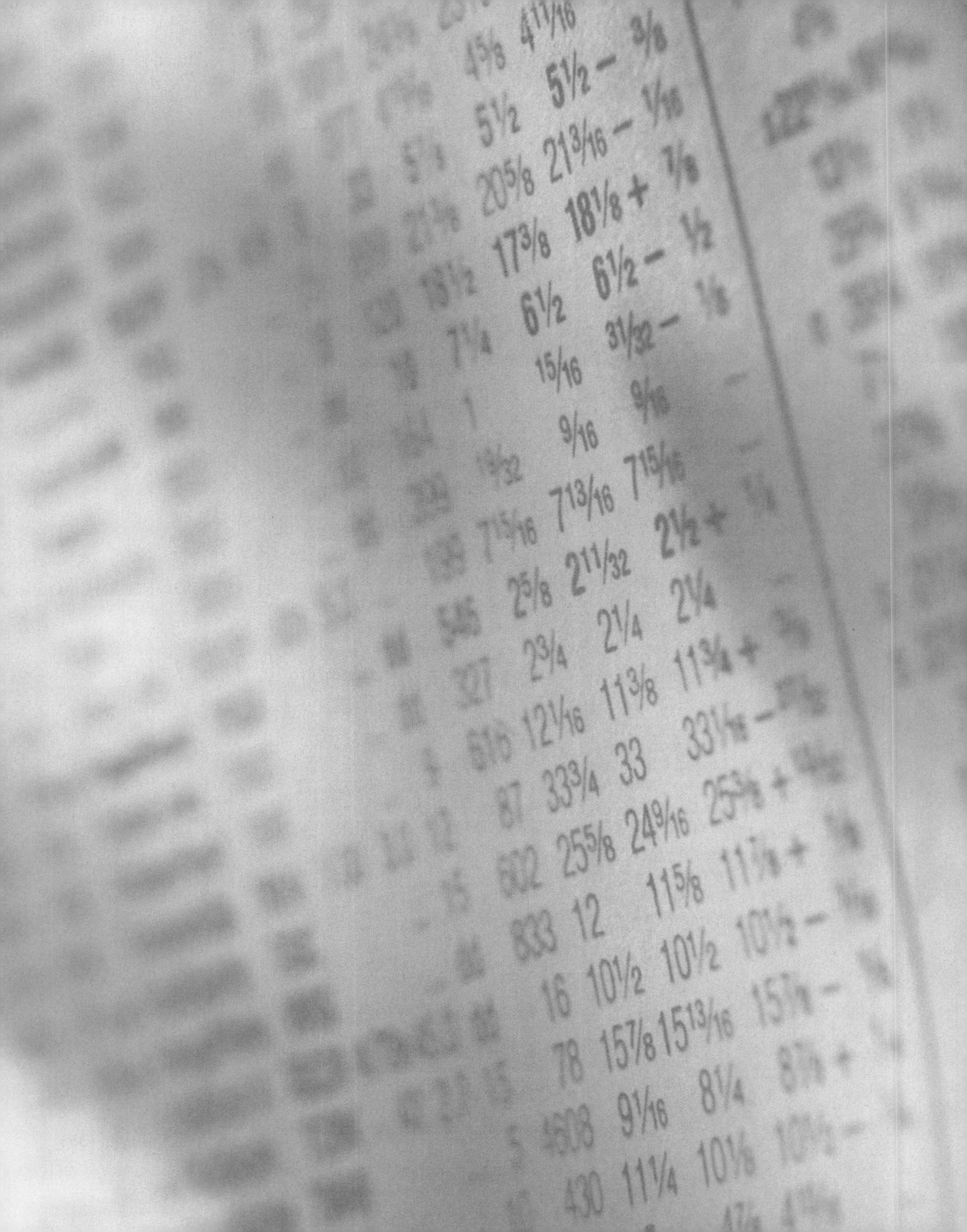

4⅝ 4 11/16
45/8 411/16 – 3/8
5½ 5½ – 3/8
5½ 20⅝ 21 3/16 – 3/16
173/8 18⅛ + 7/8
13½ 17⅜
6½ 6½ –
7¼ 6½ 3 1/32 – ½
15/16 – 1/8
9/16 9/16
1 1/32 7 13/16 7 15/16
25/8 2 11/32 2½ +
2¾ 2¼ 2¼
6⅛ 12 1/16 11⅜ 11¾ +
87 33¾ 33 33⅛ –
602 25⅝ 24 9/16 25⅝ +
833 12 11⅝ 11⅞ +
16 10½ 10½ 10⅛ –
78 15⅞ 15 13/16 15⅞ –
4508 9 1/16 8¼ 8⅛ +
430 11¼ 10⅛

MANAGING INSTITUTIONAL INVESTOR PORTFOLIOS

by R. Charles Tschampion, CFA, Laurence B. Siegel, Dean J. Takahashi, and John L. Maginn, CFA

LEARNING OUTCOMES

The candidate should be able to:	Mastery
a. contrast a defined-benefit plan to a defined-contribution plan, from the perspective of the employee and employer and discuss the advantages and disadvantages of each;	☐
b. discuss investment objectives and constraints for defined-benefit plans;	☐
c. evaluate pension fund risk tolerance when risk is considered from the perspective of the 1) plan surplus, 2) sponsor financial status and profitability, 3) sponsor and pension fund common risk exposures, 4) plan features, and 5) workforce characteristics;	☐
d. formulate an investment policy statement for a defined-benefit plan;	☐
e. evaluate the risk management considerations in investing pension plan assets;	☐
f. formulate an investment policy statement for a defined-contribution plan;	☐
g. discuss hybrid pension plans (e.g., cash balance plans) and employee stock ownership plans;	☐
h. distinguish among various types of foundations, with respect to their description, purpose, source of funds, and annual spending requirements;	☐
i. compare and contrast the investment objectives and constraints of foundations, endowments, insurance companies, and banks;	☐
j. formulate an investment policy statement for a foundation, an endowment, an insurance company, and a bank;	☐
k. contrast investment companies, commodity pools, and hedge funds to other types of institutional investors;	☐
l. discuss the factors that determine investment policy for pension funds, foundations, endowments, life and nonlife insurance companies, and banks;	☐
m. compare and contrast the asset/liability management needs of pension funds, foundations, endowments, insurance companies, and banks;	☐
n. compare and contrast the investment objectives and constraints of institutional investors given relevant data, such as descriptions of their financial circumstances and attitudes toward risk.	☐

1   INTRODUCTION

The two broad classes of investors active in capital markets internationally are individual and institutional investors. **Institutional investors** are corporations or other legal entities that ultimately serve as financial intermediaries between individuals and investment markets. Frequently representing large pools of money, institutional investors have attained great importance—in many cases dominance—in financial markets worldwide. Institutional investors have also made important contributions to the advancement of investment knowledge and techniques, spurred by the challenges of effectively managing large amounts of money.

Today, advances in portfolio theory, performance pressures, and an ever-increasing array of new investment instruments surround the institutional portfolio manager and both test and enhance the manager's skills. As the manager meets these challenges and pressures, he or she should reflect that behind all investment portfolios lie "flesh and blood" individuals whose financial wellbeing is affected by the manager's actions. News reports remind us that ethical lapses occur with serious consequences for both clients and errant portfolio managers. The client's interests must come first. Ethical conduct is the fundamental requirement for managing an institutional or any other type of portfolio.

This reading presents the portfolio management process from the perspective of five different groups of institutional investors: pension funds, foundations, endowments, insurance companies, and banks. These five classes cover a wide spectrum of investment policy considerations and are well suited to illustrating the challenges and complexity of the institutional portfolio manager's tasks.

We have organized this reading as follows. In Section 2 we present the background and investment setting of pension funds, which fall into two main types: defined benefit and defined contribution. For each of these types of pensions, we discuss the elements of formulating an investment policy statement (IPS)—the governing document for all investment decision-making. We follow the same pattern of presentation for foundations and endowments in Section 3, insurance companies in Section 4, and banks in Section 5. The final section summarizes the reading.

2   PENSION FUNDS

Pension funds contain assets that are set aside to support a promise of retirement income. Generally, that promise is made by some enterprise or organization—such as a business, labor union, municipal or state government, or not-for-profit organization—that sets up the pension plan. This organization is referred to as the **plan sponsor**.

Pension plans divide principally into one of two broad types, based on the nature of the promise that was made. They are either defined-benefit (DB) plans or defined-contribution (DC) plans. A **defined-benefit plan** is a pension plan that specifies the plan sponsor's obligations in terms of the benefit to plan participants. In contrast, a **defined-contribution plan** specifies the sponsor's obligations in terms of contributions to the pension fund rather than benefits to plan participants. There are also some hybrid types of plans (or *schemes*, as they often are called outside of North America), such as cash balance plans, that have characteristics of both DB and DC plans. A **cash balance plan** is a defined-benefit plan whose benefits are displayed in individual recordkeeping accounts. These accounts show the participant the current value of his or her accrued benefit and facilitate portability to a new plan.

It is useful to understand the distinctions between DB and DC plans in greater detail. A DB plan sponsor promises the organization's employees or members a retirement income benefit based on certain defined criteria. For example, a worker may be promised that for every year employed by the company, he or she will receive a certain fixed money benefit each month. Alternatively, a plan sponsor might promise to pay a certain percentage of some factor related to the employee's pay (e.g., final year, average of final five years, average of top 5 of last 10 years, etc.). The sponsor might also promise to adjust benefit payments for those already retired in order to reflect price inflation. Additionally, the plan may have a whole list of other plan provisions dealing with early retirement supplements, surviving spouse benefits, and so forth.

All DB plans share one common characteristic: They are promises made by a plan sponsor that generate a future financial obligation or "pension liability." The nature and behavior of this liability is uncertain and often complex; consequently, setting investment policy for DB plans presents unique challenges.

The sponsor's promise for DB plans is made for the retirement stage—what the employee will be able to withdraw. In contrast, the promise for DC plans is made for the current stage—what the plan sponsor will contribute on behalf of the employee. This contribution promise at its most basic might be a fixed percentage of pay that is put into the plan by the employer. Alternatively, it could be a contribution based on a formula tied to the profitability of the sponsor. It could also be a promise to match a certain portion of a participant's own contributions into the plan.

DC plans encompass arrangements that are 1) pension plans, in which the contribution is promised and not the benefit, and 2) **profit-sharing plans**, in which contributions are based, at least in part, on the plan sponsor's profits. We can also classify as DC plans the miscellaneous individual, private business, and governmental tax-advantaged savings plans in which the benefit is not promised and in which participants typically make contributions to the plans (for example, Individual Retirement Accounts, or IRAs). The common elements of all these plans are 1) a contribution is made into an account for each individual participant, 2) those funds are invested over time, 3) the plans are tax-deferred, and 4) upon withdrawal from the plan or reaching retirement, the participants receive the value of the account in either a lump sum or a series of payments.

The key differences between DC and DB plans are as follows:

► For DC plans, because the benefit is not promised, the plan sponsor recognizes no financial liability, in contrast to DB plans.

► DC plan participants bear the risk of investing (i.e., the potential for poor investment results). In contrast, in DB plans the plan sponsor bears this risk (at least in part) because of the sponsor's obligation to pay specified future pension benefits. DB plan participants bear early termination risk: the risk that the DB plan is terminated by the plan sponsor.

▶ Because DC plan contributions are made for individual participants' benefit, the paid-in contributions and the investment returns they generate legally belong to the DC plan participant.

▶ Because the records are kept on an individual-account basis, DC plan participants' retirement assets are more readily **portable**—that is, subject to certain rules, vesting schedules, and possible tax penalties and payments, a participant can move his or her share of plan assets to a new plan.[1]

From an investment standpoint, DC plans fall into two types:

▶ Sponsor directed, whereby much like a DB plan, the sponsor organization chooses the investments. For example, some profit-sharing plans (retirement plans in which contributions are made solely by the employer) are sponsor directed.

▶ Participant directed, whereby the sponsor provides a menu of diversified investment options and the participants determine their own personalized investment policy. Most DC plans are participant directed.

For a participant-directed DC plan, there is very little the institutional sponsor can do in the context of establishing a single investment policy allocation for the plans. Even for sponsor-directed DC plans, the investment policy is substantially less complex than for DB plans. We thus address DB plans first.

2.1 Defined-Benefit Plans: Background and Investment Setting

Defined-benefit plans have existed for a long time, with the first such corporate arrangement established in the United States by American Express in 1928. Today the incidence of DB plans varies internationally, although in recent years the overall use of DC plans has been increasing. In the United States, defined-benefit plan assets stood at almost $2.5 trillion as of the end of 2000. Judging by both the number of plan participants and the aggregate amount of plan assets, however, in the United States DC plans predominate. The increasing dominance of DC plans in the United States has been fueled chiefly by the growth of 401(k) plans in the corporate sector. In the United Kingdom, the DB model has traditionally dominated, accounting for approximately four-fifths of all private sector schemes (plans) as of 2001; however, the percentage of companies operating defined-benefit plans that are open to new members fell to 38 percent in 2004 from 56% in 2002.[2] Elsewhere in Europe, DB plans continue to follow the basic pension model as well, although DC plans are increasingly accepted. Japanese private pensions are overwhelmingly defined-benefit, although Japanese companies now offer cash balance and DC plans as well.

Pension assets fund the payment of pension benefits (liabilities). Thus a pension plan's investment performance should be judged relative to the adequacy of its assets with respect to funding pension liabilities, even if it is also judged on an absolute basis. Understanding pension liabilities is important for knowledgeably setting investment policy.

---

[1] Transfer of assets from a DB plan may be feasible; if so, it requires an actuary's calculations. For example, in Canada a terminated employee can request that the dollar value of his vested benefits in a DB plan (as determined by an actuary) be transferred to an individual registered retirement plan. In this context, **vested** means owned by the plan participant.

[2] Sarah Veysey referencing a Mercer Human Resource Consulting study in her article, "Attraction Fading: Fewer U.K. Companies Keep DB Plans for New Members," *Pensions and Investments*, 20 September 2004, p. 40.

The sponsor's plan actuary is a mathematician who has the task of estimating the pension liabilities. In addition to the specifics of defining benefits, the estimation of liabilities also involves projecting future workforce changes, determining wage and salary growth levels, estimating probabilities of early retirement elections, applying mortality tables, and other factors. The plan actuary's work provides the following key information to the plan sponsor.

First, an actuary will determine the liability's size and how its present value relates to the portfolio's existing asset size. The relationship between the value of a plan's assets and the present value of its liabilities is known as the plan's **funded status**. In a **fully funded plan**, the ratio of plan assets to plan liabilities is 100 percent or greater (a funded status of 100 percent or greater). The **pension surplus** equals pension plan assets at market value minus the present value of pension plan liabilities. In an **underfunded plan**, the ratio of plan assets to plan liabilities is less than 100 percent.

Three basic liability concepts exist for pension plans:

▶ **Accumulated benefit obligation (ABO)**. The ABO is effectively the present value of pension benefits, assuming the plan terminated immediately such that it had to provide retirement income to all beneficiaries for their years of service up to that date (**accumulated service**). The ABO excludes the impact of expected future wage and salary increases.

▶ **Projected benefit obligation (PBO)**. The PBO stops the accumulated service in the same manner as the ABO but projects future compensation increases if the benefits are defined as being tied to a quantity such as final average pay. The PBO thus includes the impact of expected compensation increases and is a reasonable measure of the pension liability for a going concern that does not anticipate terminating its DB plan. Funding status is usually computed with respect to the PBO.

▶ **Total future liability**. This is the most comprehensive, but most uncertain, measure of pension plan liability. Total future liability can be defined as the present value of accumulated *and* projected future service benefits, including the effects of projected future compensation increases. This financial concept can be executed internally as a basis for setting investment policy.

An actuary's work will also determine the split of the plan liability between retired and active **lives** (employees). This distinction will indicate two important factors:

▶ Because retirees are currently receiving benefits, the greater the number of retired lives, the greater the cash flows out of the fund each month, and thus the higher the pension fund's liquidity requirement. The portion of a pension fund's liabilities associated with retired workers is the **retired-lives** part; that associated with active workers is the **active-lives** part.

▶ Because the same mortality table is being applied to both active and retired plan beneficiaries, a plan with a greater percentage of retirees generally has a shorter average life or duration of future pension liabilities.

We now turn to developing the investment policy statement elements for a DB plan.

2.1.1 Risk Objectives

In setting a risk objective, plan sponsors must consider plan status, sponsor financial status and profitability, sponsor and pension fund common risk exposures,

EXHIBIT 1	Factors Affecting Risk Tolerance and Risk Objectives of DB Plans	
Category	**Variable**	**Explanation**
Plan status	Plan funded status (surplus or deficit)	Higher pension surplus or higher funded status implies greater risk tolerance.
Sponsor financial status and profitability	Debt to total assets Current and expected profitability	Lower debt ratios and higher current and expected profitability imply greater risk tolerance.
Sponsor and pension fund common risk exposures	Correlation of sponsor operating results with pension asset returns	The lower the correlation, the greater risk tolerance, all else equal.
Plan features	Provision for early retirement Provision for lump-sum distributions	Such options tend to reduce the duration of plan liabilities, implying lower risk tolerance, all else equal.
Workforce characteristics	Age of workforce Active lives relative to retired lives	The younger the workforce and the greater the proportion of active lives, the greater the duration of plan liabilities and the greater the risk tolerance.

plan features, and workforce characteristics, as shown in Exhibit 1. (Risk tolerance, to review, is the willingness and ability to bear risk.)

The points in Exhibit 1 deserve comment. In principle, an overfunded pension plan can experience some level of negative returns without jeopardizing the coverage of plan liabilities by plan assets because the plan surplus acts as a cushion. Thus the sponsor's ability to assume investment risk in the plan increases with funded status, even though it may have no need to do so. An underfunded plan may increase the plan sponsor's willingness to take risk in an attempt to make the plan fully funded; however, all else equal, an underfunded plan has less ability to take risk because a funding shortfall already exists. Consequently, an underfunded plan must de-emphasize its willingness to take risk.

If a plan is not fully funded, the plan sponsor has an obligation to make contributions to the plan. The sponsor's financial strength and profitability can affect the sponsor's ability and willingness to make such contributions when needed. When the sponsor is financially weak, it has a reduced ability to fund shortfalls that might occur from unfavorable investment experience.[3] Further, when the spon-

---

[3] Historically, in some countries such as Germany and the United Kingdom, DB pensions are not set up as separate entities and pension liabilities are set up as book reserves on a company's own balance sheet. In such cases, pension benefits are direct liabilities of the company. However, the European Union prescription that International Accounting Standards be adopted by 2005 (or 2007 in some cases) by companies listed within the EU is one of several forces at work reducing national differences.

sor's operating results are highly correlated with pension asset returns, the size of pension contributions may increase when the sponsor's operating results are weak.

Certain plan provisions may give participants options to speed up the disbursement of benefits, decreasing risk tolerance, all else equal. Older workforces mean shorter duration liabilities and higher liquidity requirements, implying lower risk tolerance in general. Also, for a plan with an older workforce, if the plan becomes underfunded, the company will have less time to generate and make contributions to the plan.

Example 1 illustrates some of these concepts.

EXAMPLE 1

Apex Sports Equipment Corporation (1)

George Fletcher, CFA, is chief financial officer of Apex Sports Equipment Corporation (ASEC), a leading producer of winter and water sports gear. ASEC is a small company, and all of its revenues come from the United States. Product demand has been strong in the past few years, although it is highly cyclical. The company has rising earnings and a strong (low debt) balance sheet. ASEC is a relatively young company, and as such its defined-benefit pension plan has no retired employees. This essentially active-lives plan has $100 million in assets and an $8 million surplus in relation to the projected benefit obligation. Several facts concerning the plan follow:

▶ The duration of the plan's liabilities (which are all U.S. based) is 20 years.

▶ The discount rate applied to these liabilities is 6 percent.

▶ The average age of ASEC's workforce is 39 years.

Based on the information given, discuss ASEC's risk tolerance.

Solution: ASEC appears to have above average risk tolerance, for the following reasons:

1. The plan has a small surplus (8 percent of plan assets); that is, the plan is overfunded by $8 million.
2. The company's balance sheet is strong (low use of debt).
3. The company is profitable despite operating in a cyclical industry.
4. The average age of its workforce is low.

The primary purpose of DB pension fund assets is to fund the payment of pension liabilities. DB plans share this characteristic with insurance companies and banks, as we shall later see. For all these investors, risk relative to liabilities is important and the asset/liability management (ALM) perspective on risk and on investing more generally is a primary concern. **Asset/liability management** is a subset of a company's overall risk management practice that typically focuses on financial risks created by the interaction of assets and liabilities; for given financial liabilities, asset/liability management involves managing the investment of assets to control relative asset/liability values. For a DB plan, one key ALM concept is the pension surplus, defined as pension assets at market value minus the present value of pension liabilities. DB plans may state a risk objective relative to the level of pension surplus volatility (i.e., standard deviation). Another kind of ALM risk objective relates to shortfall risk with respect to plan liabilities. (**Shortfall risk** is the risk that portfolio value will fall below some minimum acceptable level over some time horizon; it can be stated as a probability.) Shortfall risk may relate to achieving:

▶ a funded status of 100 percent (or some other level) with respect to the ABO, PBO, or total future liability;

▶ a funded status above some level that will avoid reporting a pension liability on the balance sheet under accounting rules; and

▶ a funded status above some regulatory threshold level. Examples (in the United States) include:

  ▶ levels under the Employee Retirement Income Security Act (ERISA) that would trigger additional contribution requirements; and

  ▶ levels under which the Pension Benefit Guaranty Corporation (PBGC) would require additional premium payments.[4]

Other goals that may influence risk objectives include two that address future pension contributions:

▶ Minimize the year-to-year volatility of future contribution payments.

▶ Minimize the probability of making future contributions, if the sponsor is currently not making any contributions because the plan is overfunded.

The risk considerations given above interact with each other extensively. For example, for a plan to maintain its funded status, the plan sponsor may need to increase contributions. Prioritizing risk factors is an integral part of establishing the sponsor's risk objectives. In addition to risk objectives relative to liabilities and contributions (which are characteristic of DB investment planning), sponsors may state absolute risk objectives, as with any other type of investing.

EXAMPLE 2

Apex Sports Equipment Corporation (2)

George Fletcher now turns to setting risk objectives for the ASEC pension plan. Because of excellent recent investment results, ASEC has not needed to make a contribution to the pension fund in the two most recent years. Fletcher considers it very important to maintain a plan surplus in relation to PBO. Because an $8 million surplus will be an increasingly small buffer as plan liabilities increase, Fletcher decides that maintaining plan funded status, stated as a ratio of plan assets to PBO at 100 percent or greater, is his top priority.

Based on the above information, state an appropriate type of risk objective for ASEC.

---

[4] The PBGC is a U.S. government agency that insures the vested DB pension benefits of beneficiaries of terminated DB plans. The premium rates charged by PBGC increase with the insured DB plan's level of unfunded vested benefits.

> **Solution:** An appropriate risk objective for ASEC relates to shortfall risk with respect to the plan's funded status falling below 100 percent. For example, ASEC may want to minimize the probability that funded status falls below 100 percent, or it may want the probability that funded status falls below 100 percent to be less than or equal to 10 percent. Another relevant type of risk objective would be to minimize the probability that ASEC will need to make future contributions.

In summary, plan funded status, sponsor financial status, plan features, and workforce characteristics influence risk tolerance and the setting of risk objectives. The plan sponsor may formulate a specific risk objective in terms of shortfall risk, risk related to contributions, as well as absolute risk.

2.1.2 Return Objectives

A DB pension plan's broad return objective is to achieve returns that adequately fund its pension liabilities on an inflation-adjusted basis. In setting return objectives, the pension sponsor may also specify numerical return objectives. A pension plan must meet its obligations. For a DB pension plan, the *return requirement* (in the sense of the return the plan needs to achieve on average) depends on a number of factors, including the current funded status of the plan and pension contributions in relation to the accrual of pension benefits. If pension assets equal the present value of pension liabilities and if the rate of return earned on the assets equals the discount rate used to calculate the present value of the liabilities, then pension assets should be exactly sufficient to pay for the liabilities as they mature. Therefore, for a fully funded pension plan, the portfolio manager should determine the return requirement beginning with the discount rate used to calculate the present value of plan liabilities.[5] That discount rate may be a long-term government bond yield, for example. The pension fund's stated return desire may be higher than its return requirement, in some cases reflecting concerns about future pension contributions or pension income:

▶ **Return objectives relating to future pension contributions.** The natural ambitious or "stretch target" of any DB plan sponsor is to make future pension contributions equal zero. A more realistic objective for most is to minimize the amount of future pension contributions, expressed either on an undiscounted or discounted basis.

▶ **Return objectives related to pension income.** Both U.S. Generally Accepted Accounting Principles (GAAP) and International Accounting Standards (IAS) incorporate accounting rules that address the recognition of pension expense in the corporate plan sponsor's income statement. The rules are symmetrical—that is, a well-funded plan can be in a position of generating negative pension expense, i.e. pension income. In periods of strong financial market performance, a substantial number of corporations will have pension income that is a measurable

---

[5] See Scanlon and Lyons (2006) for a detailed discussion of current issues related to return requirements.

portion of total net income reported on the corporate plan sponsor's income statement. A sponsor in this position may have an objective of maintaining or increasing pension income.[6]

Just as risk tolerance increases with the duration of plan liabilities, in general, so may the stated return desire—within realistic limits. For example, if the plan has a young and growing workforce, the sponsor may set a more aggressive return objective than it would for a plan that is currently closed to new participants and facing heavy liquidity requirements.

It is worth noting that pension plan sponsors may manage investments for the active-lives portion of pension liabilities according to risk and return objectives that are distinct from those they specify for the retired-lives portion. Retired-lives benefits may be fixed in nominal terms—for example, based on a worker's final wages. For assets associated with such liabilities, return and risk objectives may be more conservative than for assets associated with liabilities for active lives, because active-lives liabilities will grow with inflation.

EXAMPLE 3

Apex Sports Equipment Corporation (3)

George Fletcher now addresses setting return objectives for ASEC. Because the plan is fully funded, Fletcher is proposing a return objective of 7.5 percent for the plan. Referring to the information in Examples 1 and 2, as well as to the above facts, answer the following questions.

1. State ASEC's return requirement.

2. State one purpose Fletcher might have in proposing a desired return of 7.5 percent.

3. Create and justify the return objective element of an investment policy statement for the ASEC pension plan.

Solution to 1: The discount rate applied to finding the present value of plan liabilities is 6 percent. This discount rate is ASEC's return requirement.

Solution to 2: Besides meeting pension obligations, Fletcher may have one of the following objectives in mind:

▶ To minimize ASEC's future pension contributions.

▶ To generate pension income (negative pension expense).

Solution to 3: A statement such as the following is appropriate:
Return objectives. The primary return objective for the ASEC pension plan is to achieve a total return sufficient to fund its liabilities on an inflation-adjusted basis. The ASEC pension plan has a long-term growth orientation, with a total return objective of 7.5 percent per year.

---

[6] In considering whether to adopt this as an objective, however, a plan sponsor must recognize that pension income is based on the *expected* future return on pension assets. Many analysts exclude pension income from measures of core or underlying earnings.

Justification. In formulating a return objective for this essentially active-lives fund, considerations include:

▶ The return requirement is 6 percent. The objectives are consistent with achieving at least this level of return and with meeting pension liabilities.

▶ Because the plan has a long duration, little need for immediate liquidity, and a fully funded status, and because the sponsor's financial strength and profitability are strong, ASEC has above-average risk tolerance and can adopt an aggressive return objective. Thus a long-term growth orientation with a focus on capital appreciation, as well as a specific objective of 7.5 percent, appears to be appropriate.

In the next sections, we address the five broad categories of constraints.

2.1.3 Liquidity Requirement

A DB pension fund receives pension contributions from its sponsor and disburses benefits to retirees. The net cash outflow (benefit payments minus pension contributions) constitutes the pension's plan liquidity requirement. For example, a pension fund paying $100 million per month in benefits on an asset base of $15 billion, and receiving no sponsor pension contribution, would have an annual liquidity requirement of 8 percent of plan assets. During the year, the asset base would need to grow to $16.2 billion in order to meet the payout requirement without eroding the capital base. The following issues affect DB plans' liquidity requirement:

▶ The greater the number of retired lives, the greater the liquidity requirement, all else equal. As one example, a company operating in a declining industry may have a growing retired-lives portion placing increasing liquidity requirements on the plan.

▶ The smaller the corporate contributions in relation to benefit disbursements, the greater the liquidity requirement. The need to make contributions depends on the funded status of the plan. For plan sponsors that need to make regular contributions, young, growing workforces generally mean smaller liquidity requirements than older, declining workforces.

▶ Plan features such as the option to take early retirement and/or the option of retirees to take lump-sum payments create potentially higher liquidity needs.

EXAMPLE 4

Apex Sports Equipment Corporation (4)

Recall the following information from Example 1. ASEC is a relatively young company, and as such its defined-benefit pension plan has no retired employees. This essentially active-lives plan has $100 million in assets and an $8 million surplus in relation to the PBO. Several facts concerning the plan follow:

▶ The duration of the plan's liabilities (which are all U.S.-based) is 20 years;

▶ The discount rate applied to these liabilities is 6 percent; and

▶ The average age of the workforce is 39 years.

Because of excellent recent investment results, ASEC has not needed to make a contribution to the pension fund in the most recent two years.

Based on the above information, characterize ASEC's current liquidity requirement.

Solution: ASEC currently has no retired employees and is not making pension contributions into the fund, but it has no disbursements to cover. Thus, ASEC has had no liquidity requirements recently. Given that the average age of ASEC's workforce is 39 years, liquidity needs appear to be small for the near term as well.

When a pension fund has substantial liquidity requirements, it may hold a buffer of cash or money market instruments to meet such needs. A pension fund with a cash balance can gain equity market exposure by holding stock index futures contracts, or bond market exposure by holding bond futures, if it desires.

2.1.4 Time Horizon

The investment time horizon for a DB plan depends on the following factors:

▶ whether the plan is a going concern or plan termination is expected; and

▶ the age of the workforce and the proportion of active lives. When the workforce is young and active lives predominate, and when the DB plan is open to new entrants, the plan's time horizon is longer.

The overall time horizon for many going-concern DB plans is long. However, the horizon can also be multistage: for the active-lives portion the time horizon is the average time to the normal retirement age, while for the retired-lives portion, it is a function of the average life expectancy of retired plan beneficiaries.

EXAMPLE 5

Apex Sports Equipment Corporation (5)

Based on the information from Example 4, characterize the time horizon for ASEC's pension plan.

Solution: On average, the plan participants are 39 years old and the duration of plan liabilities is 20 years. The "time to maturity" of the corporate workforce is a key strategic element for any DB pension plan.

Having a younger workforce often means that the plan has a longer investment horizon and more time available for wealth compounding to occur. These factors justify ASEC adopting a relatively long time horizon for as long as ASEC remains a viable going concern.

2.1.5 Tax Concerns

Investment income and realized capital gains within private defined-benefit pension plans are usually exempt from taxation. Thus investment planning decisions at the level of the plan itself can generally be made without regard to taxes. Although corporate contribution planning involves tax issues, as do plan terminations and the form of distributions to beneficiaries, defined-benefit pension fund investment planning usually does not. However, Example 6 illustrates a case in which tax considerations do arise.

EXAMPLE 6

Taxation and Return Objectives

In 1997, the U.K. government abolished a rule that had allowed pension funds to receive dividends gross of tax (that is, tax free). Discuss the probable impact of the change on the prior return objectives of pension funds, given that pension schemes often invest in dividend-paying ordinary shares.

Solution: Total return on ordinary shares is the sum of capital appreciation and dividend yield. After the rule change, the after-tax total return became less than pretax total return for dividend-paying shares, so a given prior (pretax) return target became less effective at the margin in funding liabilities.

2.1.6 Legal and Regulatory Factors

All retirement plans are governed by laws and regulations that affect investment policy. Virtually every country that allows or provides for separate portfolio funding of pension schemes imposes some sort of regulatory framework on the fund or plan structure. In the United States, corporate plans and multi-employer plans are governed by the Employee Retirement Income Security Act of 1974 (ERISA), although state and local government plans as well as union plans are not. State and local government plans are subject to state law and regulations that can differ from each other and also from ERISA. In the United States, union plans are subject to regulation under the Taft–Hartley Labor Act. An important attribute of ERISA is that it preempts state and local law, so that those plans that are subject to it must deal with only a single body of regulation. Both ERISA and state law and regulations generally specify standards of care that pension plan sponsors must meet in making investment decisions.

A pension plan trustee is an example of a **fiduciary**, a person standing in a special relation of trust and responsibility with respect to other parties (from the Latin word *fiducia*, meaning trust). A trustee is legally responsible for ensuring that assets are managed solely in the interests of beneficiaries (for a pension, the pension plan participants). Depending on legal jurisdiction, fiduciaries are subject to various legal standards of care as they execute their responsibilities. Beneficiaries may attempt to recover their losses from fiduciaries that fail to meet appropriate standards of care.

In Canada, pension funds are regulated at the provincial level, but the Ontario Pension Commission has arguably set the standard with an ERISA-like body of regulation. In the United Kingdom, recent years have seen the work of blue ribbon panels such as the Free Commission and the Myner Commission become standards for guiding investment policy. European countries such as the Netherlands; Asia-Pacific nations including Australia, Japan, and Singapore; and Latin American countries such as Brazil, Chile, and Mexico are examples of countries having regulatory frameworks for employee pension and savings plans.

Historically in some major developed markets, the pension plan structure does not involve having to deal with investment policy issues. For example, France has a state-run scheme requiring plan sponsor organizations to contribute. But apart from the countries where funded plans are not used, it is important for the institutional practitioner to understand and apply the law and regulations of the entity having jurisdiction when developing investment policy.

2.1.7 Unique Circumstances

Although we cannot make general statements about unique circumstances, one constraint that smaller pension plans sometimes face relates to the human and financial resources available to the plan sponsor. In particular, investment in alternative investments (for example, private equity, hedge funds, and natural resources) often requires complex due diligence. (**Due diligence** refers to investigation and analysis in support of an investment action or recommendation; failure to exercise due diligence may sometimes result in liability according to various laws.)

Another unique circumstance for a plan might be a self-imposed constraint against investing in certain industries viewed as having negative ethical or welfare connotations, or in shares of companies operating in countries with regimes against which some ethical objection has been raised. Such ethical investment considerations have played a role in the investment policy of many public employee pension plans and some private company and union pension plans. Australian and several European regulators require that pension funds disclose whether they include ethical criteria in their decision-making processes. In the United Kingdom, such legislation (imposed in 1999) contributed significantly to the growth of socially responsible investing in pension plans.

To conclude, Example 7 shows how Apex Sports Equipment might formulate an investment policy statement that incorporates the analysis in Examples 1 through 5.

EXAMPLE 7

Apex Sports Equipment Corporation Defined-Benefit Plan Investment Policy Statement

Apex Sports Equipment Corporation (the "Company") operates in the recreation industry. The Company sponsors the Apex Sports Equipment Corporation Pension Plan (the "Plan"), the purpose of which is

---

to accumulate assets in order to fund the obligations of the Plan. The Plan fiduciary is the Apex Sports Equipment Corporation Plan Investment Committee (the "Committee"). The Plan is an employer contributory defined-benefit pension plan covering substantially all full-time Company employees.

Purpose

The purpose of the Investment Policy Statement (the "Policy") is to provide clear guidelines for the management of plan assets. This Policy establishes policies and guidelines for the investment practices of the Plan. The Committee has reviewed and, on 21 April 2002, adopted this Policy. The Policy outlines objectives, goals, restrictions, and responsibilities in order that:

▶ the Committee, staff, investment managers, and custodians clearly understand the objectives and policies of the Plan;

▶ the investment managers are given guidance and limitations concerning the investment of the Plan's assets; and

▶ the Committee has a meaningful basis for evaluating the investment performance of individual investment managers, as well as evaluating overall success in meeting its investment objectives.

The Plan shall at all times be managed in accordance with all state and federal laws, rules, and regulations including, but not limited to, the Employee Retirement Income Security Act of 1974 (ERISA).

Identification of Duties and Investment Responsibilities

The Committee relies on staff and outside service providers (including investment managers and bank custodians) in executing its functions. Each entity's role as fiduciary must be clearly identified to ensure clear lines of communication, operational efficiency, and accountability in all aspects of operation.

Investment committee. The Committee is responsible for managing the investment process. The Committee, with the assistance of staff, monitors the performance of investments; ensures funds are invested in accordance with Company policies; studies, recommends, and implements policy and operational procedures that will enhance the investment program of the Plan; and ensures that proper internal controls are developed to safeguard the assets of the Plan.

Investment managers. Investment managers will construct and manage investment portfolios consistent with the investment philosophy and disciplines for which they were retained. They will buy and sell securities and modify the asset mix within their stated guidelines. The Committee believes that investment decisions are best made when not restricted by excessive limitations. Therefore, full discretion is delegated to investment managers to carry out investment policy within their stated guidelines. However, investment managers shall respect and observe the specific limitations, guidelines, attitudes, and philosophies stated herein and within any implementation guidelines, or as expressed in any written amendments. Investment managers are expected to communicate, in writing, any developments that may affect the Plan's portfolio to the Committee within five business days of occurrence. Examples of such events include, but are not limited to, the following:

▶ a significant change in investment philosophy;

▶ a change in the ownership structure of the firm;

▶ a loss of one or more key management personnel; and

▶ any occurrence that might potentially affect the management, professionalism, integrity, or financial position of the firm.

Bank custodian. The bank trustee/custodian(s) will hold all cash and securities (except for those held in commingled funds and mutual funds) and will regularly summarize these holdings for the Committee's review. In addition, a bank or trust depository arrangement will be used to accept and hold cash prior to allocating it to the investment manager and to invest such cash in liquid, interest-bearing instruments.

Investment Goals and Objectives

The Plan's overall investment objective is to fund benefits to Plan beneficiaries through a carefully planned and well-executed investment program.

Return objectives. The overall return objective is to achieve a return sufficient to achieve funding adequacy on an inflation-adjusted basis. Funding adequacy is achieved when the market value of assets is at least equal to the Plan's projected benefit obligation as defined in Statement of Financial Accounting Standards No. 87, as calculated by the Plan's actuary. The Plan has a total return objective of 7.5 percent per year. In addition, the Plan has the following broad objectives:

▶ The assets of the Plan shall be invested to maximize returns for the level of risk taken.

▶ The Plan shall strive to achieve a return that exceeds the return of benchmarks composed of various established indexes for each category of investment, in which the weights of the indexes represent the expected allocation of the Plan's investments over a three- to five-year time horizon.

Risk objectives.

▶ The assets of the Plan shall be diversified to minimize the risk of large losses within any one asset class, investment type, industry or sector distributions, maturity date, or geographic location, which could seriously impair the Plan's ability to achieve its funding and long-term investment objectives.

▶ The Plan's assets shall be invested such that the risk that the market value of assets falls below 105 percent of the Plan's projected benefit obligation in a given year is 10 percent or less.

Constraints.

▶ The assets of the Plan shall maintain adequate liquidity to meet required benefit payments to the Plan's beneficiaries. The Plan currently and for the foreseeable future has minimal liquidity requirements.

▶ The Plan's assets shall be invested consistent with the Plan's long-term investment horizon.

▶ As a tax-exempt investor, the Plan shall invest its assets with a focus on total return without distinction made between returns generated from income and returns generated from capital gains.

Review Schedule

The Committee will review investment performance on a quarterly basis. This investment policy statement will be reviewed annually or more frequently as required by significant changes in laws or regulations, in the funded status of the Plan, or in capital market conditions.

Asset Allocation

The Committee believes that the level of risk assumed by the Plan is largely determined by the Plan's strategic asset allocation. The Committee has summarized the factors that should be considered in determining its long-term asset allocation as follows:

▶ the Plan's time horizon;

▶ the funded status of the Plan; and

▶ the Company's financial strength.

In establishing the long-run asset allocation for the Plan, the Committee will consider conservative long-run capital market expectations for expected return, volatility, and asset class correlations. The Plan's strategic asset allocation will be set out by the Committee in a separate strategic asset allocation document.

Rebalancing

The Committee is responsible for the Plan's asset allocation decisions and will meet to review target allocations as required based on market conditions, but at least every three years. Until such time as the Committee changes target allocations, the portfolio must periodically be rebalanced as a result of market value fluctuations. The Committee has delegated to staff the duty of implementing such rebalancing. After the Plan has reached its target equity allocation, the equity allocation shall be rebalanced to its equity target on a quarterly basis using index-based vehicles. Specific investment manager allocations will be rebalanced back to target on an annual basis. Staff will report rebalancing activity to the Committee.

2.1.8 Corporate Risk Management and the Investment of DB Pension Assets

A DB pension plan can potentially so significantly affect the sponsoring corporation's financial performance that the study of DB pension asset investment in relation to pension and corporate objectives has developed into a wide-ranging literature. Practically, we can make several observations. From a risk management perspective, the two important concerns are[7]:

► managing pension investments in relation to operating investments; and

► coordinating pension investments with pension liabilities.

To explain the first concern, in Exhibit 1 we identified the correlation between sponsor operating results and pension asset returns as one variable to monitor in assessing risk tolerance. We explained that the lower the correlation, the greater the risk tolerance, all else equal. Assuming that business and pension portfolio risks are positively correlated, a high degree of operating risk would tend to limit the amount of risk that a pension portfolio could assume, and vice versa. Although we are concerned with the IPS, our view will be more rounded if we look at the different perspective of building the pension portfolio. One question to address in that regard is whether the pension portfolio diversifies risk relative to the sponsor's operating activities. All else equal, a portfolio that diversifies sponsor operational risk increases the chance that, if the sponsor needs to increase contributions to support the payment of plan pension benefits, the sponsor will be in a position to do so. Consider a portfolio with actively managed equity holdings that overweight the telecommunications sector. Such a portfolio would be less risky for a plan sponsor operating in the consumer staples sector, which has a relatively low correlation to telecom, than for one operating in a telecom-related technology sector (e.g., a supplier of DSL equipment to telephone companies).

With respect to the second concern, coordination, the plan manager's objective is to increase the probability that pension plan assets will be sufficient to fund pension plan benefits with the minimal requirement for additional contributions by the corporate plan sponsor. For a fully funded pension plan, the goal is to maintain the plan's funded status (pension surplus) relative to plan liabilities. Although both stated concerns are consistent from a comprehensive risk management perspective, asset/liability management approaches to portfolio construction emphasize managing investments relative to liabilities. From an ALM perspective, the characterization of risk in the IPS needs to be stated in *relative* terms. The emphasis shifts from the expected volatility of pension *assets* to the expected volatility of pension *surplus* and to probabilities concerning expected levels of funded status over appropriate time frames. In practice, we can use tools such as simulation to explore whether specific portfolios can be expected to satisfy such relative risk objectives. The volatility of surplus is lower if changes in the value of plan assets are positively correlated with changes in the value of plan liabilities. Because pension plan liabilities are interest rate sensitive, pension plan sponsors emphasizing an ALM approach tend to make more intensive use of interest-rate-sensitive securities (in particular, bonds) than would otherwise be the case.

2.2 Defined-Contribution Plans: Background and Investment Setting

Two broad types of defined-contribution plans are those where the investment of the assets is directed by the plan sponsor and those where the investment is participant-directed. Because setting investment policy for sponsor-directed

---

[7] See Haugen (1990). Coordinating pension liabilities with corporate liabilities has also been suggested as a risk management focus.

plans is a simpler subset of the process for DB plans, here we will focus on participant-directed plans.

The principal investment issues for DC plans are as follows:

▶ **Diversification.** The sponsor must offer a menu of investment options that allows participants to construct suitable portfolios. For example, in the United States, Section 404(c) of ERISA establishes a safe harbor for DC plan sponsors against claims of insufficient or imprudent investment choice if the plan has 1) at least three investment choices diversified versus each other and 2) provision for the participant to move freely among the options. Sponsors of participant-directed DC plans frequently make available to participants sophisticated retirement planning tools such as Monte Carlo simulation to aid in decision-making.

▶ **Company Stock.** Holdings of sponsor-company stock should be limited to allow participants' wealth to be adequately diversified.

Even for participant-directed DC plans, the plan sponsor must have a written investment policy statement. The IPS documents the manner in which the plan sponsor is meeting the fiduciary responsibility to have an adequate process for selecting the investment options offered to plan participants as well as for periodically evaluating those options; furthermore, the establishment of an IPS may be legally mandated. DC plans, however, call for quite different IPSs than do DB plans. A DC investment policy statement establishes procedures to ensure that a myriad of individual investor objectives and constraints can be properly addressed. This can best be seen in a sample statement, an example of which follows.

2.2.1 The Objectives and Constraints Framework

In the DC setting, the plan sponsor does not establish objectives and constraints; rather, the plan participants set their own risk and return objectives and constraints. The plan sponsor provides educational resources, but the participant is responsible for choosing a risk and return objective reflecting his or her own personal financial circumstances, goals, and attitudes toward risk.

EXAMPLE 8

Participant Wanting to Make Up for Lost Time

A middle-aged man joined the participant-directed DC plan of BMSR five years ago. He had no previous retirement plan or asset base aside from home equity, and he states that he needs to take more risk than most people so that he can catch up. In fact, the participant's asset base, current income, and desired spending rate for retirement at age 65 all indicate that the participant needs a very high annual rate of return to deliver his desired retirement income.

1. Does the participant have a higher than average risk tolerance?

2. If the participant's risk objectives are not appropriate, would BMSR counsel him to change them?

Solution to 1: No. This participant's ability to take risk is less than his willingness because of his small asset base and the limited time left until he needs to draw on his retirement assets; his risk tolerance is not above average.

Solution to 2: BMSR would not counsel the participant because the plan is participant-directed. The employee needs to educate himself about the objectives and constraints framework as applied to individual investors.

EXAMPLE 9

Participant Early in Career

A 25-year-old plan participant joined BMSR recently. She is single and in good health. She has always been conservative and does not feel confident in her ability to choose funds for her retirement plan. She thinks that perhaps she should just put half in the money market fund and half in the large-capitalization value common stock fund. How do this participant's plan choices match her situation?

Solution: Given her investment time horizon, she may benefit by increasing her willingness to take risk to match her ability to take risk. She could adopt a more aggressive risk stance while increasing diversification by moving money from the money market fund to a bond fund and/or another equity fund (for example, a growth-oriented fund). If her company offers an investor education program, this participant should attend so that she can explore the elements of assessing risk tolerance.

As mentioned, participants in DC plans bear the risk of investment results. As a consequence, an investment policy statement for a DC plan fulfills a much different role than an investment policy statement for a DB plan. For example, an IPS for a participant-directed DC plan is the governing document that describes the investment strategies and alternatives available to the group of plan participants characterized by diverse objectives and constraints. Such an IPS necessarily becomes an overall set of governing principles rather than an IPS for a specific plan participant. Example 10 provides sample excerpts from an investment policy statement for a participant-directed DC plan.

EXAMPLE 10

Investment Policy Statement for BMSR Company Defined-Contribution Plan

Purpose

The purpose of this Investment Policy Statement is to assist the members of the Retirement Policy Committee (RPC) in effectively establishing, monitoring, evaluating, and revising the investment program established for the defined-contribution plan (the Plan) sponsored by the BMSR-Company (BMSR). The authority for establishing this responsibility is by action of the BMSR Board of Directors at its 26 March 2002 meeting. The primary focuses of this Investment Policy Statement are as follows:

▶ Clearly distinguish among the responsibilities of the RPC, the Plan participants, the fund managers, and Plan trustee/recordkeeper selected by the RPC.

▶ Provide descriptions of the investment alternatives available to Plan participants.

▶ Provide criteria for monitoring and evaluating the performance of investment managers and investment vehicles (funds) relative to appropriate investment benchmarks.

▶ Provide criteria for manager/fund selection, termination and replacement.

▶ Establish effective communication procedures for the fund managers, the trustee/recordkeeper, the RPC, and the Plan participants.

RPC Roles and Responsibilities

The RPC's responsibilities, in carrying out this Investment Policy Statement, include:

▶ monitoring the fund objectives and selecting specific funds to be offered to the Plan participants to provide sufficient diversification possibilities;

▶ monitoring the investment performance, including fees, of funds made available to Plan participants and terminating and replacing funds when judicious and appropriate;

▶ assuring ongoing communications with, and appropriate educational resources for, the Plan participants;

▶ selecting, monitoring and, if necessary, recommending the replacement of the Trustee/Recordkeeper of the Plan; and

▶ assuring that the interest rate for Plan loans is in accordance with the provisions of the Plan.

Plan Participant Roles and Responsibilities

The responsibilities of plan participants include the allocation of Plan contributions and accumulations among the various fund choices made available and the obligation to educate themselves sufficiently in order to make appropriate allocations over their career or life span. A participant's appropriate asset allocation is a function of multiple factors, including age, income, length of time before retirement, tolerance for risk, accumulation objectives, retirement income replacement objectives, and other assets. To permit participants to establish savings and investment strategies to suit their individual needs, the Plan offers a number of investment alternatives with varying return and risk characteristics.

The participant is best positioned to make the individual decision on how to allocate assets among the investment alternatives. As such, the investment direction of employees' elective deferrals and contributions made by BMSR will be each individual participant's responsibility. It is also each individual participant's responsibility to reallocate assets among funds as personal circumstances change.

To help address the factors mentioned above, BMSR will provide information to participants regarding the investment alternatives and basic principles of investing. However, the dissemination of information and the provision of investment alternatives by BMSR do not constitute advice to participants.

The return/risk concept is basic to investments. Over time, investment alternatives offering higher expected returns will exhibit higher risk (e.g., volatility of returns or of principal values). The Plan offers a variety of investment choices in order to provide participants the opportunity to select return/risk strategies that meet their savings and investment objectives and to adequately diversify.

ERISA 404(c) Compliance

BMSR intends to comply with ERISA Section 404(c) regulations by, among other things, offering a broad, diversified range of investment choices; allowing transfers of funds between investment choices at least once every 90 days; and providing sufficient investment information to participants on a regular basis.

Selection of Investment Alternatives

The RPC's role is to provide participants with an array of investment choices with various investment objectives that should enable participants to invest according to their varying investment needs. The investment choices offered should represent asset classes with different risk and return characteristics and with sufficient diversification properties. The following asset classes have the investment characteristics currently desired:

- ► money market instruments;
- ► intermediate-term fixed-income instruments;
- ► intermediate-term Treasury Inflation-Indexed Securities;
- ► equity
  - ► large-cap growth
  - ► large-cap blend/core
  - ► large-cap value
  - ► mid-cap blend/core
  - ► small-cap blend/core
  - ► international;
- ► life-cycle mutual funds (funds customized for various retirement dates).

The criteria for selection and for replacement of funds include the following:

- ► The array of investment options should be chosen with the goal of permitting participants to diversify their investments and to align the risk of their investments to their risk tolerance.

- ▶ The funds must have reasonable fees, including advisor fees, 12(b)-1 fees, and other fees.
- ▶ Every fund must have a clearly articulated and explained investment strategy, accompanied by evidence that the strategy is followed over time.
- ▶ The funds' time-weighted returns and volatility of returns over at least the three (and preferably five) prior years must compare favorably with the performance of a passively-managed index with the same style (e.g., large-cap growth). This is the primary performance criterion.
- ▶ Funds selected must:
  - ▶ be managed by a bank, insurance company, investment management company, or investment advisor (as defined by the Registered Investment Advisers Act of 1940) that has had significant assets under management for at least 10 years and has exhibited financial stability throughout that period;
  - ▶ provide historical quarterly performance calculated on a time-weighted basis and reported net and gross of fees;
  - ▶ provide performance evaluation reports that illustrate the risk–return profile of the manager relative to passive indexes and other managers of like investment style; and
  - ▶ clearly articulate the investment strategy to be followed and document that the strategy has been successfully executed over time.
- ▶ Transfers among investment funds are permitted on at least a quarterly basis, thus fulfilling an ERISA 404(c) requirement.

Monitoring Investment Performance

The RPC will monitor each fund's return and risk performance on a quarterly basis relative to appropriate investment benchmarks. In the event a fund over a five-year time frame:

- ▶ underperforms a passively managed (index) fund with similar objectives (i.e., same style) or, alternatively,
- ▶ ranks worse than the 50th percentile in terms of investment performance relative to funds with similar investment objectives,

the RPC will review the fund to determine whether its performance has resulted from the fund manager, the style of management, or market volatility, and decide whether the fund should be eliminated from the menu of possible investment choices. The RPC will also consider the fund's performance over periods of more than five years, if available, before making a decision.

As noted above, the RPC will evaluate each fund's performance using a five-year time horizon. The RPC realizes that most investments go through cycles; therefore, at any given time a fund may encounter a time period in which the investment objectives are not met or when a fund fails to meet its expected performance target. The fund's performance should be reported in terms of an annualized time-weighted rate of return. As noted above, the returns should be compared to appropriate market indexes and to peer group universes for the most recent five-year (or longer) period.

> In light of the evaluation of each fund's performance, the RPC has the authority to recommend the replacement or elimination of an investment objective or fund if, in the opinion of the RPC, the investment objective or fund does not, or is not expected to, meet the specified performance criteria; is no longer suited to the needs of the Plan participants; or if, in the sole opinion of the RPC, a more appropriate investment choice exists.

EXAMPLE 11

BMSR Committee Decision

A member of the RPC committee for BMSR is concerned about the small-cap growth fund. During the last two years, this fund has ranked in the top half of small-cap growth funds and has outperformed a passively managed small-cap growth benchmark. However, the fund has dropped in value far more than the overall market. The concerned member suggests that the RPC replace the fund. Do the IPS criteria support this suggestion?

Solution: According to IPS guidelines, investment performance must be evaluated over time horizons longer than two years. The IPS also specifies a comparison to a passively managed benchmark with the same style rather than to the overall market. For these reasons, the IPS cannot support the suggestion that the fund be eliminated.

2.3 Hybrid and Other Plans

During the 1990s, many employers concluded that neither the traditional DB nor DC plan structure exactly met their pension plan objectives. Hybrid plans began to emerge that combined the features of DB and DC plans.[8] Examples of hybrid plans include cash balance plans, pension equity plans, target benefit plans, and floor plans. These plans sought to combine some of the most highly valued features of a DC plan (such as portability, administrative ease, and understandability by participants) with the highly valued features of a DB plan (such as benefit guarantees, years of service rewards, and the ability to link retirement pay to a percentage of salary). In this section, we discuss cash balance plans as one example of a hybrid plan as well as another important type of plan, the employee stock ownership plan (ESOP).

A cash balance plan is a DB plan, in that the employer bears the investment risk. To employees, however, it looks like a DC plan because they are provided a personalized statement showing their account balance, an annual contribution credit, and an earnings credit. The contribution credit is a percentage of pay based on age, while the earnings credit is a percentage increase in the account balance that is typically tied to long-term interest rates. In reality, the account

---

[8] In 1985 only 1 percent of Fortune 100 companies offered a hybrid plan; by 2002 that fraction had grown to 33 percent. See Scanlan and Lyons (2006, p. 38).

balance is hypothetical because unlike in a DC plan, the employee does not have a separate account. Some plans allow investment choices among fixed-income and equity-based options, which introduces investment risk for the employee.

Cash balance plans usually are not start-up plans but rather are traditional DB plans that have been converted in order to gain some of the features of a DC plan. Some of these plans have come under criticism as being unfair to older workers with many years of service, who may have accrued higher retirement benefits under the DB plan than the cash balance plan offers. In response to this criticism, some companies have offered a "grandfather" clause to older workers, allowing them to choose between joining a new cash balance plan or continuing with an existing traditional DB plan.

Finally, most developed countries allow for retirement or other savings plans that encourage employees to become stockholders of their employer. These plans may be complex qualified plans that purchase stock in a DC pension plan with pretax money, or they may be simple savings plans that allow employees to buy stock personally with their after-tax pay. The acronym ESOP refers to an employee *stock* ownership plan (in the United States) or employee *share* ownership plan (United Kingdom). These are DC plans that invest all or the majority of plan assets in employer stock. ESOPs are DC plans because the contribution is set as a percentage of employee pay. The final value of the plan for the employee will depend on the vesting schedule, the level of contributions, and the change in the per-share value of the stock.

Although ESOPs all share the common goal of increasing employee ownership in a company, they vary widely from country to country in terms of regulation. Some ESOPs may sell stock to employees at a discount from market prices, while others may not. Some require employee contribution; others prohibit such. Some ESOP trusts may borrow to purchase large amounts of employer stock, while others must rely solely on contributions.

In addition to encouraging ownership of one's employer, ESOPs have been used by companies to liquidate a large block of company stock held by an individual or small group of people, avoid a public offering of stock, or discourage an unfriendly takeover by placing a large holding of stock in the hands of employees via the ESOP trust. Apart from his or her investment in the ESOP, a plan participant may have a major investment of human capital in the company by virtue of working for that company. Should the company fail, the participant might see the value of the ESOP investment plummet at the same time that he or she becomes unemployed. An important concern for ESOP participants is that their overall investments (both financial and **human capital**) reflect adequate diversification.[9]

FOUNDATIONS AND ENDOWMENTS   3

Foundations and endowments provide vital support for much of today's philanthropic and charitable activities. **Foundations** are typically grant-making institutions funded by gifts and investment assets. **Endowments**, on the other hand, are long-term funds generally owned by operating non-profit institutions such as universities and colleges, museums, hospitals, and other organizations involved in charitable activities.

---

[9] Many 401(k) plans, especially large ones, have company stock as an investment option. For participants in such plans, similar issues arise.

Although both are created by donations, foundations and endowments usually develop differently over time. Private foundations typically are created and funded by a single donor to fund philanthropic goals. The investment portfolio provides the dominant source of revenue, and the purchasing power of its corpus is either maintained or eventually given away. In the United States, tax law essentially mandates minimum levels of annual spending for some types of foundations. By donating cash and securities, many of the world's great industrialists and financiers have created foundations that bear their name (e.g., the Ford, Rockefeller, and Gates foundations). Endowments, by contrast, are often built up over time by many individual gifts to the endowed institution. Spending distributions are determined by the beneficiary institution, supplementing other revenue sources such as tuition, grants, fees, or gifts for current use. Prominent endowments, such as those of Harvard, Yale, and Princeton universities, have grown along with their institutions over centuries.

In Sections 3.1 and 3.2, we discuss the investment objectives and constraints of foundations and endowments, respectively.

3.1 Foundations: Background and Investment Setting

Foundations provide essential support of charitable activity. In broad terms, four types of foundations exist: independent, company sponsored, operating, and community.[10] Exhibit 2 briefly describes the principal types of foundations in the United States, as distinguished by their purpose, sources of funds, and annual spending requirements.[11] Independent foundations, also referred to as private or family foundations, are grant-making organizations funded by an individual donor and generally required to pay out a minimum of 5 percent of assets annually. Company-sponsored foundations tend to have a short-term investment focus to facilitate philanthropic funding from the corporation to grantees. Operating foundations, much like endowments, provide income to support specific programs. Community foundations draw upon broad support for donations to fund a variety of grants. Most of the following discussion relates to independent (private and family) foundations, which represent the majority of investment assets in the foundation sector.

The most noteworthy aspect of foundations is that they can vary widely in their investment goals and time horizons. For example, a foundation may be the primary or even sole source of funding for a charitable program. In such a case, a stable, reliable flow of funds is extremely important because the program has few alternative sources of funding to make up the shortfall. On the other hand, many foundations give funding for numerous independent projects or programs for only a few years at most. Because such foundations are generally not those projects' primary means of support, the funded programs can handle drops in spending by the foundation relatively easily because funding reductions are less likely to critically disrupt their operations. Often, a foundation's mission may address a problem with a limited time horizon or an urgent need (e.g., a need resulting from a natural disaster or an environmental emergency).

Another distinctive characteristic of the foundation sector, as contrasted to endowments, is that most private and family foundations must generate their entire grant-making and operating budget from their investment portfolio for

---

[10] Community foundations are a prominent type of public charity (meeting tax code tests for public support) in the United States and are used to represent public charities as a group.

[11] The international links at the Association of Charitable Foundations (www.acf.org.uk/linksinter.htm) are good starting points for researching the diversity of foundations worldwide.

EXHIBIT 2	Types of Foundations in the United States			
Foundation Type	**Description**	**Source of Funds**	**Decision-Making Authority**	**Annual Spending Requirement**
Independent foundation (private or family)	Independent grant-making organization established to aid social, educational, charitable, or religious activities.	Generally an individual, family, or group of individuals.	Donor, members of donor's family, or independent trustees.	At least 5% of 12-month average asset value, plus expenses associated with generating investment return.
Company-sponsored foundation	A legally independent grant-making organization with close ties to the corporation providing funds.	Endowment and/or annual contributions from a profit-making corporation.	Board of trustees, usually controlled by the sponsoring corporation's executives.	Same as independent foundation.
Operating foundation	Organization that uses its resources to conduct research or provide a direct service (e.g., operate a museum).	Largely the same as independent foundation.	Independent board of directors.	Must use 85% of interest and dividend income for active conduct of the institution's own programs. Some are also subject to annual spending requirement equal to 3.33% of assets.
Community foundation	A publicly supported organization that makes grants for social, educational, charitable, or religious purposes. A type of public charity.	Multiple donors; the public.	Board of directors.	No spending requirement.

the following reasons: These institutions generally do not engage in fund-raising campaigns; they may not receive any new contributions from the donor; and they do not receive any public support. These unique conditions help to guide the investment approach taken by foundations. In addition, as mentioned earlier, private and family foundations are subject to a payout requirement that mandates a minimum level of spending, while university endowments and many other nonprofit institutions face no such requirement.

3.1.1 Risk Objectives

Because foundations' goals differ somewhat from those of traditional defined-benefit pension funds and other asset pools, foundations can have a higher risk tolerance. Pension funds have a contractually defined liability stream (the pension payments expected to be made to retirees); in contrast, foundations have no such defined liability. The desire to keep spending whole in real terms, or to grow the institution, is simply that: a desire. Foundation investment policy can thus be more fluid or creative, and arguably more aggressive, than pension fund policy.

It is also acceptable, if risky, for foundations to try to earn a higher rate of return than is needed to maintain the purchasing power of assets—in essence, seeking to make as much money as possible. Such behavior makes it possible for the institution to increase its grant-making over time because the funding needs of organizations supported by foundations are essentially unbounded.

3.1.2 Return Objectives

Foundations differ in their purposes, and so vary in their return objectives. Some foundations are meant to be short lived; others are intended to operate in perpetuity. For those foundations with an indefinitely long horizon, the long-term return objective is to preserve the real (inflation-adjusted) value of the investment assets while allowing spending at an appropriate (either statutory or decided-upon) rate. Such a policy, if successful, keeps spending constant in real terms, on average over time, achieving what is sometimes called intergenerational equity or neutrality: an equitable balance between the interests of current and future beneficiaries of the foundation's support.[12]

If we look at the 5 percent annual spending minimum for foundations as a benchmark and add 0.3 percent as a low-end estimate of investment management expenses (i.e., the cost of generating investment returns), we thus have calculated that the fund must generate a return of 5.3 percent, plus the inflation rate, to stay even in real terms. We can use 5.3 percent plus the expected inflation rate as a starting point for setting the return objective of a foundation. If the expected inflation rate is 2 percent, the minimum return requirement will be 7.3 percent. This additive formulation of the return objective is intuitive but approximate. The most precise formulation is multiplicative, which accounts for the effect of compounding in a multiperiod setting and results in a higher requirement. For our example, the multiplicative calculation is $(1.05)(1.003)(1.02) - 1.0 = 0.0742$, or 7.42 percent.

3.1.3 Liquidity Requirements

A foundation's liquidity requirements are anticipated or unanticipated needs for cash in excess of contributions made to the foundation. Anticipated needs are captured in the periodic distributions prescribed by a foundation's spending rate. In the United States, the spending policy of private foundations is dictated, at least as concerns the 5 percent annual minimum, by the Tax Reform Act of 1969 and subsequent amendments. Expenses associated with management of the foundation's investments do not count toward the payout requirement, so one must add this cost (conservatively, 0.3 percent annually) to the minimum that the foundation is required to spend. "Overhead" associated with grant

---

[12] Think of a school that spends so much on scholarships in the current time frame that the endowment becomes depleted. A generation hence, the school will be in a poor financial position to give scholarships or otherwise compete for good students and professors. Under such a policy, intergenerational neutrality is clearly defeated. The underlying philosophy is that a long-lived foundation, or endowment, should not favor one particular generation of would-be recipients over another. A similar tension exists in certain types of trusts that must balance the interests of life-income beneficiaries and remaindermen (who receive the trust corpus after the death of the income beneficiaries).

making—for example, the salaries of program officers and other executives—does count toward the payout requirement.

To avoid erosion in the portfolio's real value over time, many foundations try to spend only the minimum or else set a maximum that only slightly exceeds the minimum. In addition, to avoid large fluctuations in their operating budget, foundations may use a smoothing rule. A **smoothing rule** averages asset values over a period of time in order to dampen the spending rate's response to asset value fluctuation.

The U.S. Internal Revenue Service (IRS) allows carry-forwards and carry-backs, within limits, so that a foundation may avoid being penalized for under-spending by spending more than 5 percent of assets in a subsequent year. Conversely, as a result of overspending in prior years, a foundation may be allowed to underspend in a subsequent year. Carry-forwards and carry-backs not only make smoothing rules workable but also allow a foundation to make a large grant in a single year without compromising the long-run soundness of its invest-ment program.

The 5 percent payout requirement for private and family foundations, com-bined with the desire to maintain the portfolio's value in real terms, can be daunting. Foundation executives may disagree about whether the 5 percent spending requirement motivates an aggressive investment policy or a conserva-tive one. Clearly, motivation refers to willingness to bear risk, but ability to bear risk must also be considered in determining a foundation's risk tolerance.

It is prudent for any organization to keep some assets in cash as a reserve for contingencies, but private and family foundations need a cash reserve for a spe-cial reason: They are subject to the unusual requirement that spending in a given fiscal year be 5 percent or more of the 12-month average of asset values *in that year*. One cannot, of course, know what this amount will be in advance, so one cannot budget for it. Instead, a well-managed foundation places some (say 10 percent or 20 percent) of its annual grant-making and spending budget in a reserve. This reserve may simply be in the form of not spending budgeted money until the year is mostly over and the 12-month average of asset values is known with greater certainty. In an "up" year for markets, this method may cause a rush of grants to be paid by the foundation at the end of the year, to avoid spending less than the minimum required amount. A year-end rush should be more acceptable to the foundation than the alternative that would occur without a reserve—overspending in flat or "down" market years.

3.1.4 Time Horizon

The majority of foundation wealth resides in private and other foundations established or managed with the intent of lasting into perpetuity. Our discussion has thus focused on strategies for preserving capital in real terms after spending. Some institutions, however, are created to be "spent down" over a predefined period of time; therefore, they pursue a different strategy, exhibiting an increas-ing level of conservatism as time passes. All else equal, investors often assume that a longer time horizon implies a greater ability to bear risk because a longer horizon affords them more time to recoup losses.

3.1.5 Tax Concerns

In the United States, income that is not substantially related to a foundation's charitable purposes may be classified as **unrelated business income** and be sub-ject to regular corporate tax rates. For instance, a museum gift shop that sells artwork has business income related to its purposes; if it sells motorcycles, it has unrelated business income. Income from real estate is taxable as unrelated business income if the property is debt financed, but only in proportion to the fraction of the property's cost financed with debt.

In the United States, a private foundation must estimate and pay quarterly in advance a tax (currently set at 2 percent) on its net investment income. "Net investment income" includes dividends, interest, and capital gains, less the foundation's expenses related directly to the production of such income. The excise tax may be reduced to 1 percent if the charitable distributions for the year equal or exceed both 5 percent and the average of the previous five years' payout plus 1 percent of the net investment income. In creating this requirement, Congress hoped that foundations would translate their tax savings into increased charitable activities.

3.1.6 Legal and Regulatory Factors

Foundations may be subject to a variety of legal and regulatory constraints, which vary by country and sometimes by type of foundation. As one example, in the United States, the Internal Revenue Code (Section 4944) addresses private foundations, imposing a graduated series of excise taxes if a private foundation invests in a manner that jeopardizes the carrying out of its tax-exempt purposes. In the United States, many states have adopted the Uniform Management of Institutional Funds Act (UMIFA) as the primary legislation governing any entity organized and operated exclusively for educational, religious, or charitable purposes. We will present some of the details of UMIFA that concern investing activities when we address endowments.

3.1.7 Unique Circumstances

A special challenge faces foundations that are endowed with the stock of one particular company and that are then restricted by the donor from diversifying. The asset value of such an institution is obviously subject to the large market fluctuations attendant to any one-stock position.

With the permission of the donor, some institutions have entered into swap agreements or other derivative transactions to achieve the payoffs of a more diversified portfolio. Such a strategy achieves the donor's goal of retaining voting rights in the stock, while providing the foundation with a more stable asset value. Other institutions simply tolerate the fluctuations associated with a single-stock position.

Against the background of investment objectives and constraints for foundations, Example 12 illustrates how all these elements come together in an investment policy statement.

EXAMPLE 12

The Fund for Electoral Integrity

A group of major foundations has endowed a new organization, the Fund for Electoral Integrity, to supervise elections and political campaigns in countries undergoing a transition to democracy. The fund is headquartered in a developing country. It has received initial grants of $20 million, with $40 million expected to be received in further grants over the next three years. The fund's charter expressly decrees that the fund should spend itself out of existence within 10 years of its founding rather than trying to become a permanent institution. Determine and justify appropriate investment policy objectives and constraints for the Fund for Electoral Integrity.

Solution:

Risk Objective

Although the fund has a 10-year life, it is receiving donations over a period of years and it is also constantly spending money on programs. Thus, it can be assumed to have a five-year investment horizon on average and should *initially* adopt a conservative or below-average risk profile (a standard deviation of annual returns in the range of 5 percent to 7 percent).[13] Over the life of the fund, the risk objective should gradually migrate to an even more conservative profile (standard deviation of 3 percent to 5 percent). The relatively short time horizon calls for a below-average risk tolerance. Both the risks inherent in markets and the fund's risk tolerance may change, so it is important to periodically review the investment policy and the portfolio from a risk management perspective. In making their investment recommendations, the board and investment committee should take the following into account:

▶ market risk (fluctuation in asset values);

▶ liquidity risk;

▶ political, regulatory, and legal risks;

▶ operations and control risks;

▶ any other risks that the board and investment committee deem relevant.

Return Objective

The fund's broad return objective is to earn the highest inflation-adjusted return consistent with the risk objective. At inception, the fund's return objective is to equal or better the total return of an average five-year maturity U.S. Treasury note portfolio over a rolling four-year period.

Constraints

Liquidity. The fund must pay out roughly $6 million annually for 10 years.
Time horizon. The fund has a 10-year time horizon.
Tax concerns. The fund is a tax-exempt organization in the country in which it is organized.
Regulatory factors. No special legal or regulatory factors impinge on the organization's ability to invest as it chooses.
Unique circumstances. The fund has no constraints in the sense of prohibited investments.

---

[13] The standard deviation of annual returns on intermediate-term bonds typically falls in this range.

3.2 Endowments: Background and Investment Setting

Endowments play a critical role in the vitality and success of today's charitable activity. As the long-term investment portfolios of nonprofit operating institutions, endowments provide a significant amount of budgetary support for universities, colleges, private schools, hospitals, museums, and religious organizations.

The term "endowment" has taken on two related but distinct meanings. As commonly understood, an endowment is simply the long-term investment portfolio of a charitable organization. Legally and formally, however, the term "endowment" refers to a permanent fund established by a donor with the condition that the fund principal be maintained over time. In contrast to private foundations, endowments are not subject to a specific legally required spending level.

Donors establish true endowments by making gifts with the stipulation that periodic spending distributions from the fund be used to pay for programs and that the principal value of the gift be preserved in perpetuity. Thus, true endowments are funds permanently restricted in terms of spending. Many schools and nonprofit organizations will supplement true endowments with voluntary savings in the form of quasi-endowments, sometimes referred to as funds functioning as endowment (FFE). Although designated as long-term financial capital, quasi-endowments have no spending restrictions; the institution may spend such funds completely. Because endowments are owned by nonprofit organizations, they generally are exempt from taxation on investment income derived from interest, dividends, capital gains, rents, and royalties.

Typically, the large investment pools commonly referred to as endowments consist of a variety of individual funds, including true endowments and FFEs. Each endowment fund is established with a specific indenture detailing the conditions and intended uses of the gifts. Although many endowment funds are unrestricted, meaning that endowment spending can be used for the general purposes of the beneficiary institution, others are restricted so that monies can be spent only for specified purposes. For instance, one restricted fund might support a professorship, while another fund might support student financial aid. Spending from these funds must be kept distinct and support only the specified use—money from a professorship endowment, for example, cannot be used to provide student aid.

Endowments are a vital source of funding for many charitable programs, and spending distributions should be substantial to support such programs' needs. Large fluctuations in year-to-year spending can disrupt the endowed institution's operating budget, finances and staffing. Therefore, spending distributions should be stable and reliable. Because donors establish endowment funds with the intention of funding an activity in perpetuity, recipient institutions generally operate with the fiduciary intent of preserving the fund's purchasing power. The nonprofit should not count on new gifts to supplement endowment funds whose value has been eroded by spending beyond investment returns. In summary, endowments should provide substantial, stable, and sustainable spending distributions.

Historically, prior to the 1970s, income provided the basis for determining an endowment's spending distributions. Institutions invested their endowments primarily in stocks, bonds and cash, and they spent the dividend and interest income. Unfortunately, in following such policies, endowment spending was not tied to the investment portfolio's total return after inflation. Institutions skewed portfolios toward high-yielding fixed-income instruments at the expense of equities in order to increase current endowment spending. Although high-quality bonds typically make their promised nominal payments, unanticipated inflation reduces those payments' real values below anticipated levels. Furthermore, shifts toward higher-yielding assets allowed increased portfolio spending but decreased an endowment's ability to generate adequate inflation-adjusted long-term returns.

Educated and encouraged by a seminal Ford Foundation report published in 1969, many endowed institutions adopted a new approach to determining spending based on the concept of total return.[14] As codified by UMIFA in 1972, income and capital gains (realized and unrealized) are now included in determining total return in the United States. Freed from the strictures of yield, institutions could determine endowment-spending levels as a percentage of an endowment's market value.

Today, most endowed institutions determine spending through policies based on total return as reflected in market values. A spending rule, by defining the amount of the distribution from the endowment available for spending, helps instill discipline into the budgeting and financial management process. A balanced budget is not a meaningful achievement if it results from pulling from the endowment whatever is needed to cover a deficit.

Spending is typically calculated as a percentage, usually between 4 percent and 6 percent of endowment market value (endowments are not subject to minimum spending rates as are private foundations in the United States).[15] In calculating spending, endowments frequently use an average of trailing market values rather than the current market value to provide greater stability in the amount of money distributed annually. In computing such an average, the endowment manager may adjust historical market values to reflect inflation. A common, simple rule might call for spending 5 percent of the average of the past three years' ending market values of the endowment. One problem with this rule is that it places as much significance on market values three years ago as it does on more recent outcomes. Even if endowment values were relatively stable for the last two years, an extraordinary return three years ago could force a dramatic change in spending this year. A more refined rule might use a geometrically declining average of trailing endowment values adjusted for inflation, placing more emphasis on recent market values and less on past values. Examples of spending rules include the following:

▶ **Simple spending rule.** Spending equals the spending rate multiplied by the market value of the endowment at the beginning of the fiscal year.

$$\text{Spending}_t = \text{Spending rate} \times \text{Ending market value}_{t-1}$$

▶ **Rolling three-year average spending rule.** Spending equals the spending rate multiplied by the average market value of the last three fiscal year-ends.

$$\text{Spending}_t = \text{Spending rate} \times (1/3)\,[\text{Ending market value}_{t-1} + \text{Ending market value}_{t-2} + \text{Ending market value}_{t-3}]$$

▶ **Geometric smoothing rule.** Spending equals the weighted average of the prior year's spending adjusted for inflation and the product of the spending rate times the market value of the endowment at the beginning

---

[14] See Cary and Bright (1969) for more information.

[15] According to Swensen (2000), 90 percent of endowments spend between 4 percent and 6 percent of endowment market value annually.

of the prior fiscal year. The smoothing rate is typically between 60 and 80 percent.

$$\text{Spending}_t = \text{Smoothing rate} \times [\text{Spending}_{t-1} \times (1 + \text{Inflation}_{t-1})]$$
$$+ (1 - \text{Smoothing rate}) \times (\text{Spending rate} \times \text{Beginning market value}_{t-1})$$

Because most endowed institutions complete their budget planning process well before the endowment market value at the beginning of a fiscal year becomes known, it may be advisable to calculate spending from an endowment value based on a date in advance of the final budget process. The geometric smoothing rule description reflects this approach and uses the prior year's beginning, rather than ending, endowment market value.

3.2.1 Risk Objectives

An endowment's investment risk should be considered in conjunction with its spending policy and in the context of its long-term objective of providing a significant, stable, and sustainable stream of spending distributions. Spending policies with smoothing or averaging rules can dampen the transmission of portfolio volatility to spending distributions, allowing the institution to accept short-term portfolio volatility while striving for high long-term investment returns necessary to fund programs and maintain purchasing power. Endowments that do not use a smoothing rule may have less tolerance for short-term portfolio risk. Investment portfolios with very low volatility, or investment risk, usually provide low expected returns, which increases the risk of failing to achieve the endowment's goals of significant, stable, and sustainable spending. Low investment risk does not equate to low risk for meeting endowment objectives.

An institution's risk tolerance depends on the endowment's role in the operating budget and the institution's ability to adapt to drops in spending. If endowment income represents only a small portion of the budget, poor investment returns may have little impact on the bottom line. On the other hand, modest drops in endowment value may have serious consequences if endowment income contributes a large part of overall revenues. If the same market forces affect both its donor base and its endowment, an institution that relies heavily on donations for current income may see donations drop at the same time as endowment income. Large fixed expenditures such as debt service can aggravate damage inflicted by drops in endowment income.

On a short-term basis, an endowment's risk tolerance can be greater if the endowment has experienced strong recent returns and the smoothed spending rate is below the long-term average or target rate. In such a case, the endowment value could drop and spending might still increase the following year. On the other hand, endowment funds with poor recent returns and a smoothed spending rate above the long-term average run the risk of a severe loss in purchasing power. High spending rates can aggravate the erosion of the endowment's corpus at the same time that institution comes under pressure to cut operating expenses.

Because of the assumed positive relation between risk and return, a high required return objective and a willingness to meet relatively high spending needs often imply a high willingness to accept risk. On the other hand, short-term performance pressures will indicate a low willingness to accept risk. Despite their long-term investment mandate, endowment managers often come under pressure to perform well over relatively short-term time horizons for several reasons. Poor investment results may lead to reductions in the level of endowment spending. In addition, investment staff and trustees with oversight responsibility are evaluated formally or informally on relatively short time frames—often yearly. Many large endowments are highly visible; supporters and peers closely scrutinize their annual performance. Endowed institutions thus need to objectively assess and, if necessary, enhance their actual tolerance for short-term volatility before pursuing investment strategies that really are consistent with only a very long-term investment horizon.

3.2.2 Return Objectives

Endowments have high return objectives, reflecting the goal of providing a significant, stable and sustainable flow of income to operations. Endowments typically provide vital support of ongoing operations and programs, and distributions from endowment to operations should be as large as practical. An endowment manager must thus balance this objective of providing substantial resources to programs with the need to provide a stable flow. Erratic and volatile endowment distributions are unsuitable for programs with permanent staff or recurring expenses. Furthermore, an endowment must balance significant and stable spending objectives with the imperative to provide sustainable support—in other words, endowment funds should maintain their long-term purchasing power after inflation.

Endowments often need to generate relatively high long-term rates of return in order to provide a substantial flow of spending to institutions affected by rates of inflation above those of the general economy. The growth of higher education expenses in the United States is a case in point. Inflation for U.S. higher education expenses has been generally above that for the broad economy such as the gross domestic product (GDP) deflator or for consumers as measured by the U.S. Consumer Price Index (CPI). Since 1960, annual inflation for colleges and universities, as measured by the Higher Education Price Index (HEPI), averaged approximately 1 percentage point more than the CPI or the GDP deflator.[16] A major factor for this higher inflation rate is the difficulty of increasing faculty productivity without impairing the quality of education. For instance, colleges and universities cannot simply improve efficiency by increasing class size or student-to-faculty ratios. Because faculty compensation typically constitutes a majority portion of higher education operating budgets, many of the costs associated with increasing salaries cannot be offset by efficiency gains. In order to maintain long-term support of an academic program, therefore, a higher education institution must increase spending over time to adjust for inflation that is higher than the CPI or the GDP deflator.

The objective of providing a significant, stable, and sustainable flow of funds to support operating programs provides a useful framework for evaluating investment and spending policies. We may ask questions such as: How do the trade-offs of expected risk and returns relate to meeting endowment objectives? What spending policy makes sense for the institution? What long-term rate of spending can the portfolio support without unduly risking impairment of purchasing power? Conventional mean–variance analysis can help to suggest appropriate asset allocations. Computer simulations using Monte Carlo techniques can be extremely helpful in comparing and assessing investment and spending policies and their ability to meet endowment objectives. Monte Carlo techniques use random numbers to develop multiple, simulated time-series of annual returns given a portfolio's risk and return characteristics. Applying the

---

[16] According to Research Associates of Washington.

spending rule to each time series, we can evaluate the interaction of investment choices and spending policy.

Monte Carlo simulations illustrate the effect of investment and spending policies on the likelihood that an endowment will provide a stable and sustainable flow of operating funds for an institution. How do various portfolios and spending rules affect the risk that the endowment will need to severely cut back on spending in the short term? How should the endowment's board set spending policies so as to support the objective of preserving the real purchasing power of the endowment? To answer these questions, an endowment must quantify risk measures. A severe drop in support for the operating budget might be defined as a real reduction of 10 percent from year to year. The risk of a dramatic decline in endowment purchasing power might be defined as the probability of more than a 50 percent real decline over a 50-year horizon. The specific pain threshold or downside risk tolerance would depend on the endowment's role with respect to operations and the endowed institution's ability to adapt to endowment spending declines.

Simulations can demonstrate several key aspects of the interaction of investment and spending policies on managing endowment risk. First, the endowment's spending rate must be lower than its expected rate of return in order to preserve purchasing power long term. For example, if an endowment has a 6 percent simple spending rate and 6 percent expected real returns with 12 percent annual standard deviation of returns, the probability that its purchasing power will fall by more than 50 percent over a 50-year period is 41 percent, according to Monte Carlo simulation. With the same portfolio return of 6 percent and a 5 percent simple spending rate, the long-term risk of such purchasing power impairment falls to 19 percent.

If returns had no volatility, an endowment could set spending at a rate that equated to the real return—that is, the nominal return net of inflation. Returns above spending would be reinvested to compensate for inflation, and the endowment would retain its purchasing power. With the introduction of volatility, however, the endowment's long-term purchasing power would be impaired more than 40 percent of the time according to the simulations. In order to achieve its objective of maintaining purchasing power, an endowment must keep its long-term average spending rate below its long-term expected real return.

From simulations, we can also observe that the risk of short-term disruptive spending may be reduced with a smoothing rule. For instance, there is a 17 percent risk of a 10 percent real drop in spending in any year with a simple 5 percent spending rule for an endowment with a 6 percent expected real return and 12 percent annual standard deviation of returns. With the same portfolio, a 70/30 smoothing rule (70 percent of last year's spending and 30 percent of 5% of last year's endowment market value) would reduce the risk of a short-term spending drop from 17 percent with a simple 5 percent rule to less than 3 percent.

Finally, a low-volatility, low-return portfolio increases the risk of an endowment failing to meet its objectives. For example, an endowment with a 5 percent spending target, a 70/30 smoothing rule, and a portfolio with a 5 percent real return and a 9 percent annual standard deviation of returns would lose half its purchasing power 34 percent of the time at the end of 50 years. Low investment risk does not equate to low risk of purchasing power impairment.

In summary, an endowment must coordinate its investment and spending policies. An endowment's returns need to exceed the spending rate to protect against a long-term loss of purchasing power. Calculating the return objective as the sum of the spending rate, the expected inflation rate, and the cost of generating investment returns can serve as a starting point for determining an endowment's appropriate return objective (analogous to the approach previously discussed for foundations). As is clear from Monte Carlo analysis in a multi-period setting, however, an endowment may need to set its return objective higher than the above starting point in order to preserve its purchasing power. In addition, an endowed institution should adopt a spending policy that appropriately controls the risk of long-term purchasing power impairment and dampens short-term volatility in spending distributions. Unlike foundations, endowments are not subject to specific payout requirements. The endowment can set a long-term spending rate consistent with its investment approach. Furthermore, spending policies can include a smoothing rule, which gradually adjusts to changes in endowment market values, to dampen the effects of portfolio volatility on spending distributions.

3.2.3 Liquidity Requirements

The perpetual nature and measured spending of true endowments limit their need for liquidity. They must, however, have cash to make spending distributions, to meet capital commitments, and to facilitate portfolio-rebalancing transactions. In addition to gifts, an endowment's investment yield, the normal sale of securities, and maturation of bonds meet much of its need for cash. Although the typical endowment maintains more liquidity than required, managers of quasi-endowments should monitor the potential for major capital projects, such as a planned capital outlay for the construction of a building.

In general, endowments are well suited to invest in illiquid, non-marketable securities given their limited need for liquidity. Care and discipline should be exercised in valuing non-marketable investments because endowments must use accurate market values estimates to determine spending, calculate performance, and establish unit values for funds entering and exiting pooled endowment portfolios.

3.2.4 Time Horizon

In principle, endowment time horizons are extremely long term because of the objective of maintaining purchasing power in perpetuity. Annual draws for spending, however, may present important short-term considerations, because endowments often use yearly market values to determine spending, and each annual withdrawal of capital has its specific time horizon. Such considerations, as well as planned decapitalizations (reductions in capital, e.g., to fund large projects) for quasi-endowments, may suggest a multistage time horizon, in certain cases.

3.2.5 Tax Concerns

Although taxation may vary by domicile internationally, taxes are not a major consideration for endowments, in general. In the United States, for example, endowments owned by non-profit organizations are exempt from taxation on investment income derived from interest, dividends, capital gains, rents, and royalties. Under certain circumstances, unrelated business taxable income (UBTI) from operating businesses or from assets with acquisition indebtedness may be subject to tax. In addition, a portion of dividends from non-U.S. securities may be subject to withholding taxes that cannot be reclaimed or credited against U.S. taxes.

3.2.6 Legal and Regulatory Factors

In the United States, few laws and regulations exist regarding the management and conduct of endowment funds. Most states have adopted UMIFA as the primary governing legislation for endowments. First promulgated in 1972, UMIFA authorizes a broad range of investments for endowments. It also allows for the delegation of investment responsibility to external advisors and managers, as well as for wide discretion in setting the compensation for such services.

An endowed institution's governing board must "exercise ordinary business care and prudence" in dealing with investments. UMIFA explicitly authorizes institutions to spend endowment investment gain as well as income. Endowment spending must, however, respect any use restriction imposed by the donor, and it should not include principal when an endowment fund's market value falls below its historical book value. In other words, only income may be spent when an endowment's market value is less than its original gift value.[17] This requirement can lead to disruptive spending patterns, particularly for new funds or funds with market value at or near book value. To maintain normal spending patterns, institutions may consider an accounting reclassification or transfer of unrestricted FFE to fulfill balance sheet requirements that the market value of an endowment fund not fall below its historical book value.

At the federal level, U.S. endowed institutions must comply with tax and securities laws and reporting requirements. To achieve and maintain tax-exempt status under Section 501(c)(3) of the U.S. Internal Revenue Code, an institution must ensure that no part of its net earnings inure or accrue to the benefit of any private individual. The code provides for intermediate sanctions in the form of excise taxes against individuals in a position to exercise substantial authority who engage in "excess benefit transactions" whereby they receive unreasonably high compensation or inappropriately derive private benefit from the tax-exempt organization. With little governmental oversight, endowed institutions must develop, maintain, and enforce clear guidelines and policies to prohibit improper behavior and manage conflicts of interest.

3.2.7 Unique Circumstances

Endowments vary widely in their size, governance, and staff resources, and thus in the investment strategies that they can intelligently and practically pursue. Endowments range from the very small, providing financial aid for a day care center, to the very large, supporting a major university. The responsibility of managing the endowment might fall to an unsophisticated board or to a collection of individuals knowledgeable about investments. Likewise, the investment staff responsible for managing and administering the endowment may be nonexistent or consist of many highly paid and experienced professionals. This wide variety in expertise and resources suggests that an endowment's specific circumstances may constrain the types of investments its board should consider.

Many large endowments have been leaders in adopting investments in alternative investments, such as private equities, real estate, natural resources, and absolute return strategies. These investments often require significant staff time and expertise to find, evaluate, select, and monitor. Because the **active management** component of returns in these alternative, less-efficient markets is extremely important to long-term success, endowments should have significant resources and expertise before investing in nontraditional asset classes.

---

[17] A few states supplement UMIFA with this fiduciary standard of preserving the purchasing power of endowment values.

Often, alternative investment funds in the United States will seek exemption from registration under the Investment Company Act of 1940 and accept capital commitments only from investors who are Qualified Purchasers. Generally, endowments must have at least $25 million of investments to qualify. In some instances, investments are placed privately without SEC registration and are limited to accredited investors with assets in excess of $5 million. Thus the resources and size of an endowment or foundation can dictate its universe of potential investments.

Some endowed institutions develop ethical investment policies that become constraints to help ensure that portfolio investment activity is consistent with the organization's goals and mores. These policies can guide portfolio managers in voting shareholder proxies on issues of social or political significance. In certain circumstances, such as apartheid in South Africa, ethical investment policies have been used in an attempt to foster change through shareholder resolutions and divestment. Other examples of socially responsible investing include the application of exclusion criteria related to child labor, gambling, tobacco, firearms, and violation of human rights. In Example 13, we show how investment objectives and constraints come together in the formulation of an investment policy statement for an endowment.

EXAMPLE 13

The City Arts School

The City Arts School (CAS) is an independent private school educating 500 children from 9th through 12th grade. Founded in 1920, it is located in a modest-sized city in the northeastern United States with a diverse socioeconomic and racial population. CAS has an outstanding reputation and draws students from the city and surrounding suburban communities. The school has an excellent program in the performing and visual arts; in addition, it offers a broad and innovative curriculum with small class sizes.

CAS has an annual operating budget of approximately $10 million, more than 90 percent of which goes to salaries and benefits for teachers and a small administrative staff. With conservative fiscal management, the school has built and maintained a fine campus over the years without the use of debt. Due to the limited availability of adjacent land or other space, the school is unlikely to expand in the foreseeable future. CAS's inflation rate has averaged 1 percent above that of the economy in general.

CAS has an endowment of $30 million, composed of $10 million for general unrestricted support, $10 million for financial aid, $5 million of small funds with various donor-specified use restrictions, and $5 million of unrestricted funds functioning as endowment.

The CAS board consists of 15 elected directors, each serving three-year terms. In addition, the head of the school serves on the board *ex officio*. The board delegates responsibility for investing the endowment to an investment committee that includes at least three board members as well as other members of the CAS community who can offer investment expertise and guidance. Investments are monitored and implemented by the school's business and operations manager.

Proposed Statement of Endowment Goals

The goal of the CAS Endowment (and funds that the board has designated as endowment) is to provide significant, stable, and sustainable funding to support the school's annual operating budget and specific donor-designated programs. Endowment funds will be invested with the objective of earning high, long-term returns after inflation without undue risk of permanently impairing the long-term purchasing power of assets or incurring volatile short-term declines in asset values or annual spending flows.

Spending Policy for Endowment

The goal of the CAS Endowment spending policy is to provide a sustainable, stable annual source of income from the endowment to the operating budget of CAS. The spending policy helps provide financial discipline to the school by providing a clear, unequivocal amount of annual funding from the endowment consistent with sustainable long-term operations.

Spending from the endowment (and funds designated as endowment by the board) shall be determined by a spending rule that smoothes the volatility of spending from year to year using a weighted-average formula. The formula takes into account spending from the prior year as well as the endowment's current market value. Spending for a fiscal year shall be calculated by adding 70 percent of the prior year's spending amount to 30 percent of the endowment market value at the beginning of the prior fiscal year times the policy spending rate of 4.5 percent.

$$
\begin{aligned}
\text{Spending for fiscal year } t = {} & 70\% \times [\text{Spending for fiscal year} \\
& (t-1)] + 30\% \times [4.5\% \\
& \times \text{Endowment market value at} \\
& \text{beginning of fiscal year } (t-1)]
\end{aligned}
$$

Adjustments will be made to incorporate the effects of new gifts, additions, or fund decapitalizations. Spending from new gifts or additions to the endowment in their first year shall be at the same rate as other endowment funds adjusted pro rata to reflect the partial year of inclusion in the endowment.

Given these goals for the endowment, specify appropriate objectives and constraints.

Solution:

Return Objectives

The goal of the CAS Endowment is to provide a significant annual distribution to support the school's programs while maintaining the fund's long-term purchasing power. In general, inflation for the school runs about 1 percent above that of the economy. Therefore, in order to maintain the fund's purchasing power with a 4.5 percent spending rate, net of investment management expenses the portfolio must generate a long-term return greater than 5.5 percent above a broad measure of inflation such as the U.S. CPI.

Risk Objectives

CAS must address two primary risks in investing its endowment. As discussed above, CAS must protect the endowment's long-term purchasing power by generating real returns above spending. In the short term, the CAS Endowment should produce a reliable and somewhat stable flow of funding for programs. This short-term risk is tempered by CAS's spending rule, which smoothes distributions with a geometric moving average spending rate. In addition, endowment spending is not a very large part of the school's annual budget (less than 14 percent of revenues). Endowment spending could fall by as much as 20 percent and the impact on the budget would be less than 3 percent of revenues. CAS is debt free and has an above-average risk tolerance.

Constraints

Liquidity. Only a small percentage of the fund, approximately 4 or 5 percent, is spent each year, and the fund's historical gift value should remain invested and not spent. A portion of the CAS Endowment pool, however, is composed of funds functioning as endowment. The board, in extraordinary circumstances, may decide to spend the FFE because the monies are not permanently restricted.

Time horizon. Endowment funds have an extremely long time horizon because they are expected to support activities in perpetuity.

Tax concerns. CAS is a tax-exempt organization, and returns on its investments are not taxed in most circumstances. The school should carefully consider any investment or gift that generates UBTI, because such an item could dramatically increase tax reporting requirements.

Legal and regulatory factors. CAS's investments have very few legal and regulatory constraints. The school should, however, take precautions to avoid conflicts of interest, or the perception of conflicts, involving committee or board members. In addition to being poor and wasteful management, inappropriate transactions with individuals in a supervisory role may lead to sanctions and penalties under IRS regulations. In general, the school's financial and investment activities are under the purview of the state attorney general. Trustees are expected to act prudently, consistent with standards of sound business practice.

Unique circumstances. CAS is a small school with limited administrative and investment resources. Its endowment portfolio, although meaningful to the school and its operations, is not of sufficient scale to support dedicated internal investment staffing. All investments should be managed externally. CAS should view skeptically any investment that requires extensive monitoring, a close long-term relationship with external investment managers, or a high degree of sophisticated expertise to manage properly. Similarly, CAS should be wary of investments that require a high degree of active management skill to generate satisfactory returns. The school does not have the resources to identify, evaluate, and monitor the top managers in specialized investment areas. Furthermore, the size of its portfolio will not support a diversified investment program in nontraditional alternatives such as private equity. Even an aggressive allocation of 20 percent would amount to only $6 million, barely enough to make a single commitment to a top-tier private equity investment fund.

The investment committee has a relatively high turnover, with members serving only three-year terms. CAS runs the risk that new committee members renounce some long-term investments and act hastily to liquidate or pull support from worthy but underperforming investments. This risk is greatest with volatile, unconventional investments that may require patience, fortitude, and a contrarian mindset to endure difficult market environments.

4   THE INSURANCE INDUSTRY

The economic significance of the insurance industry lies in its unique role as an absorber of personal and business risks. By providing financial protection, the industry plays a key role in a country's economic growth and development. Because of the risk aspects of the business and the contractual obligations to policyholders, the insurance industry's traditional investment practices have been characterized as conservative. As we will discuss later, however, insurers have shown increasing risk tolerance in recent years.

The insurance industry is complex but can be divided into three broad product categories: life insurance, health insurance, and property and liability insurance. For purposes of considering investment policy, it is sufficient to narrow the categories to life and non-life (casualty) insurance companies. This division is consistent with the major classifications established by the insurance regulatory bodies and some, if not most, taxing authorities in the world's industrialized countries.

Insurance companies, whether life or casualty, are established either as **stock companies** (companies that have issued common equity shares) or as **mutuals** (companies with no stock that are owned by their policyholders). Mutuals traditionally have played a major role in certain segments of the insurance industry, but stockholder-owned companies are now the primary form of entry into the industry. Many of the major mutual insurance companies in the United States, Canada, the United Kingdom, and continental Europe have completed or are in the process of **demutualizing** (converting to stock companies). Although the investment operations of mutual and stock companies differ only slightly, the differences between life and non-life insurers are substantial, as we illustrate in the following sections.

4.1 Life Insurance Companies: Background and Investment Setting

Exposure to interest-rate-related risk is one major characteristic of life insurers' investment setting. Besides fixed-income portfolio gains and losses related to interest rate changes, many life insurance company liabilities such as annuity contracts are interest rate sensitive. In addition, insurers also face the risk of disintermediation, which often becomes acute when interest rates are high.[18]

One type of disintermediation occurs when policyholders borrow against the accumulated cash value in insurance products such as ordinary life insurance.[19] U.S. life insurance companies experienced unprecedented disintermediation in the early 1980s. As interest rates reached record high levels (in the mid to high teens) during that period, policyholders took advantage of the option to borrow some or all of the accumulated cash value in their policies at the below-market policy loan rates (generally 5 to 9 percent) that were contractually defined in

---

[18] **Disintermediation** occurs when individuals withdraw funds from financial intermediaries for deposit or investment in other financial intermediaries or investments offering a higher return (yield).

[19] **Ordinary life insurance** (also called **whole life insurance**) is a type of policy that typically provides level death benefits for the whole of the insured's life. The premium is typically a level amount determined by such factors as the insured's sex and age at the time the policy is issued, and the cash value is based on the insurer's estimate of the expected return on the investments that fund policy reserves. In contrast, **term life insurance** provides death benefits for a specified length of time and accumulates little or no cash values.

their insurance policies. The policy loan feature has long been considered an important life insurance policy provision. In the 1980s, the true cost of this option became clear to the industry, as cash available for investment at the then prevailing double-digit interest rates was siphoned off in part to fund policy loans. When interest rates are high, insurers also face another type of disintermediation: the risk that policyholders will surrender their cash value life insurance policies for their accumulated cash values, in order to reinvest the proceeds at a higher interest rate. As a result of these forces, insurers face marketplace pressures to offer competitive cash value accumulation rates or **credited rates** (rates of interest credited to a policyholder's reserve account).

These developments have made the liabilities of life insurers more interest rate sensitive than before and have tended to shorten the duration of liabilities. Policyholders are now more prone to exercise their option to surrender a life insurance policy or annuity contract as they seek the most competitive credited rates and/or policy benefits. Surrender rates triggered by interest rate changes are more difficult to predict than mortality rates and thus are the more critical variable for many interest-sensitive life insurance products. Shorter liability durations have necessitated the shortening of the duration of life insurance company portfolios, or at least those segments designed to fund these interest-rate-sensitive product liabilities.

Universal life, variable life, and variable universal life represent the insurance industry's response to disintermediation.[20] Companies developed these products to offset the competitive appeal of buying term insurance and investing the difference between term insurance premiums and the often higher premiums of ordinary life insurance policies. These new products provide life insurance buyers with a viable means of purchasing varying amounts of insurance protection along with an opportunity to save or invest at rates that vary with capital market and competitive conditions.

Exhibit 3 illustrates the growth of new individual life insurance forms in the United States, based on data provided by the American Council of Life Insurers. As the increase in term life insurance purchases demonstrates, there is a trend toward unbundling insurance risk management and investment management. To attract customers, each of the new policy forms must offer competitive rates of return.

4.1.1 Risk Objectives

An insurance company's primary investment objective is to fund future policyholder benefits and claims. Because of the economic importance of the insurance industry, the investment portfolio of an insurer (life or non-life) is looked upon from a public policy viewpoint as a quasi-trust fund. Accordingly, conservative fiduciary principles limit the risk tolerance of an insurance company investment portfolio. Confidence in an insurance company's ability to pay benefits as they come due is a crucial element in the economy's financial foundation. Therefore, insurance companies are sensitive to the risk of any significant chance of principal loss or any significant interruption of investment income.

---

[20] **Universal life** provides premium flexibility, an adjustable face amount of death benefits, and current market interest rates on the savings element. The universal life policyholder pays a specified amount for the insurance protection desired and can deposit funds in a savings account, for a fee. **Variable life insurance** (**unit-linked life insurance**) is a type of ordinary life insurance for which death benefits and cash values are linked to the investment performance of a policyholder-selected pool of investments held in a so-called separate account. **Variable universal life** (**flexible-premium variable life**) combines the flexibility of universal life with the investment choice flexibility of variable life.

EXHIBIT 3	Analysis of Life Insurance Purchases in the United States: Selected Years, 1978–2002			
	Percentage of Dollar Amount of Life Insurance Purchases			
Policy Type	1978 (%)	1988 (%)	1999 (%)	2002 (%)
Term life	52	40	57	69
Whole life	45	30	13	10
Universal life	na	20	11	9
Variable life	na	9	19	12
Other	3	1	0	0
Total	100	100	100	100

na = not applicable.

Source: *Life Insurance Fact Book* (1979, 1989, 2000) and *ACLI Survey* (2003).

To absorb some modest loss of principal, U.S. life insurance companies are required to maintain an asset valuation reserve, a reserve established by the National Association of Insurance Commissioners (NAIC). Companies use specific NAIC-developed "quality tests" for each class of invested assets to determine the annual contributions to, and maximum amounts of, the reserve. The maximum reserve rates establish a substantial margin for absorbing investment losses. With a growing portfolio, however, a life company's asset valuation reserves may be inadequate. Surplus is thus vulnerable to write-downs if significant losses occur.[21]

Insurance regulators worldwide have been moving toward risk-based capital (RBC) requirements to assure that companies maintain adequate surplus to cover their risk exposures relating to both assets and liabilities. In the United States, RBC calculations are somewhat complex and attempt to allocate surplus in proportion to the asset and liability risk exposures of each insurance company. By subtracting the risk-based capital required from each company's total surplus, the regulators can estimate whether the company's surplus is sufficient. In addition, applying GAAP to both mutual and stock insurance companies requires the use of market valuation for most classes of assets and thus has increased balance sheet volatility. Absent a requirement that life insurance liabilities be marked to market, however, accounting statement implications may affect a company's risk tolerance in ways that are inconsistent with a market-based-valuation perspective of the company's risk exposure.

Asset/liability risk considerations figure prominently in life insurers' risk objectives, not only because of the need to fund insurance benefits but also because of the importance of interest-rate-sensitive liabilities. Examples of such liabilities are annuities and deposit-type contracts, such as GICs and funding agreements (stable-value instruments similar to GICs).

---

[21] The excess of losses on assets over the assets' valuation reserve is a direct reduction in surplus. A **valuation reserve** is an allowance, created by a charge against earnings, to provide for losses in the value of the assets. **Surplus** is the net difference between the total assets and total liabilities of an insurance company; it is equivalent to policyholders' surplus for a mutual insurance company and stockholders' equity for a stock company.

The two aspects of interest rate risk are valuation concerns and reinvestment risk:

▶ **Valuation concerns.** In a period of changing interest rates, a mismatch between the duration of an insurance company's assets and that of its liabilities can lead to erosion of surplus. Life insurance companies are particularly sensitive to the losses that can result during periods of rising interest rates from holding assets with an average duration that exceeds the average duration of liabilities. (Adding to insurers' concerns is the fact that the risk of disintermediation is greatest in such interest rate environments.) In these situations, the existence of valuation reserves alone may be insufficient to prevent a write-down of surplus, possibly creating a capital adequacy problem. Consequently, valuation concerns tend to limit insurers' risk tolerance.

▶ **Reinvestment risk.** For many life insurance companies, especially those competing for annuity business, yet another risk factor can be significant—reinvestment risk. **Reinvestment risk** is defined as the risk of reinvesting coupon income or principal at a rate less than the original coupon or purchase rate. For annuity contracts on which no interest is paid until maturity (the terminal date) of the contract, the guarantee rate typically includes the insurance company's best estimate of the rate(s) at which interest payments will be reinvested. If a company does not carefully manage its asset and liability durations, an unexpected decline in interest rates can jeopardize the profitability of these contracts. Thus, controlling reinvestment risk is also an important risk objective.

Asset/liability management is the foundation for controlling both interest rate risk and liquidity for a life insurance company. Risk objectives addressing the mismatch of the duration of assets and liabilities are common.

Credit risk is also important in meeting insurance promises:

▶ **Credit risk. Credit risk** represents another potential source of income loss for insurance companies, although credit analysis has long been considered one of the industry's strengths. Insurers seek to control this risk through broad diversification and seek adequate compensation for taking risk in terms of the expected return or interest rate spread when investing in various asset classes. Risk objectives may relate to losses caused by credit risk.[22]

Another risk consideration relates to uncertainty in the timing of receipt of cash flows:

▶ **Cash flow volatility.** Loss of income or delays in collecting and reinvesting cash flow from investments is another key aspect of risk for which life insurance companies have low tolerance. Compounding (interest on

---

[22] Recent changes in GAAP have further complicated the management of credit risk by U.S. insurance companies. The Financial Accounting Standard 115 and subsequent interpretative documents require a permanent write-down of the value of securities that have experienced an "Other Than Temporary Impairment" (OTTI). This type of impairment in value is defined as an unrealized loss that results from the decline in the market value of a security below its cost for an extended period of time. This Standard has been controversial and most likely will undergo additional modification because it does not allow for any subsequent write-up in value if the credit quality of the issuer improves and is so recognized in the market value. Also, declines in market value below cost that are caused by an increase in interest rates may require a permanent write-down under the current interpretation of FAS 115.

interest) is an integral part of the reserve funding formula and a source of surplus growth. Actuaries assume that investment income will be available for reinvestment at a rate at least equal to an assumed (minimum return) rate. Controlling cash flow volatility is thus a risk objective.

Despite the above four risk-related considerations, competition has modified the traditional conservatism of life insurance companies, motivating them to accept and manage varying degrees of risk in pursuit of more competitive investment returns.

4.1.2 *Return Objectives*

Historically, a life insurance company's return requirements have been specified primarily by the rates that actuaries use to determine policyholder reserves, i.e., accumulation rates for the funds held by the company for future disbursement.[23] In effect, the rate either continues as initially specified for the life of the contract or may change to reflect the company's actual investment experience, according to the contract terms. Interest is then credited to the reserve account at the specified rate; this rate can thus be defined as the minimum return requirement. If the insurer fails to earn the minimum return, its liabilities will increase by an accrual of interest that is greater than the increase in assets. The shortfall is reflected in a decrease in surplus or surplus reserves, assuming the simplest case. The insurer, in short, desires to earn a positive net interest spread, and return objectives may include a desired net interest spread. (The **net interest spread** is the difference between interest earned and interest credited to policyholders.) Reserve funding adequacy is monitored carefully by management, regulatory commissions, and insurance rating agencies such as A.M. Best, as well as through the claims paying rating services initiated by Moody's Investors Service, Standard & Poor's Corporation, and Fitch Ratings.

In the mid to late 1980s, Japanese life insurance companies issued policies that guaranteed what proved to be unsustainable reserve crediting rates—and guaranteed those rates for as long as 10 years. With the sharp decline in interest rates, stock prices, and real estate values during the 1990s in Japan, these companies sustained unprecedented losses and consequent erosion of the surplus of the Japanese life insurance industry. These events provided an important lesson regarding the setting of return objectives, crediting rates, and guarantee periods in a volatile investment environment.

In the United States, with whole-life insurance policies, the minimum statutory accumulation rate for most life insurance contracts ranges between 3 and 5.5 percent. Thus, in the higher interest rate environment of the 1970s and 1980s, the spread between life insurance companies' return on new investments and even the return on their entire portfolio exceeded the minimum returns by a widening margin. But as growing investor sophistication and competition in insurance markets led to higher credited rates, and as interest rates declined in the 1990s and early 2000s, the net interest spread narrowed quickly and dramatically. As a result, U.S. regulators have permitted minimum statutory accumulation rates to be reduced.

Consistently above-average investment returns should and do provide an insurance company with some competitive advantage in setting premiums. Life

---

[23] **Policyholder reserves** are a balance sheet liability for an insurance company; they represent the estimated payments to policyholders, as determined by actuaries, based on the types and terms of the various insurance policies issued by the company.

EXHIBIT 4	Portfolio Yields of U.S. Life Insurance Companies: Selected Years, 1975–2004			
		Major Life Insurance Companies		
	Industry Rate (%)	**Prudential (%)**	**Lincoln National (%)**	**AXA Equitable-NY (%)**
1975	6.44	6.47	6.98	6.22
1985	9.87	9.07	8.49	8.72
1995	7.90	7.47	7.87	6.88
2000	7.40	6.41	6.93	6.70
2004	5.93	5.55	5.82	6.23

Note: Portfolio yield equals the ratio of net investment income (after expenses and before income taxes) to mean cash and invested assets.

Sources: *Life Insurance Fact Book* (2001); *Best's Insurance Reports* (2005).

insurance companies have found that an improvement as small as 10 basis points (0.10 percent) in the total portfolio yield improves their competitive position and profitability significantly. Portfolio yields for most life portfolios, however, are more similar than different, as Exhibit 4 shows. To a large extent, this similarity reflects the role regulation plays in constraining the asset mix and quality characteristics of every life insurance company portfolio and the historical evolution of portfolio asset allocation in that regulatory environment.

Some companies have experimented with using total return rather than interest rate spread to measure their investment portfolios' performance and their products' profitability. When only the asset side of a balance sheet reflects market volatility, it is difficult to use total return measures. To the extent that comprehensive fair market value accounting standards are developed in the future, they will greatly enhance asset/liability management and performance and profitability measurement on a total return basis.

For companies selling annuity and guaranteed investment contracts, competitive investment returns have become necessary and spread margins are narrow. The annuity segment of the life insurance business has accounted for approximately two-thirds of total industry reserves for more than a decade (see Exhibit 5).

EXHIBIT 5	Reserves for Annuities and Guaranteed Investment Contracts for the U.S. Life Insurance Industry: Selected Years, 1970–2002
	Percentage of Total Reserves
1970	26.6%
1980	45.4
1990	66.7
2002	64.6

Source: *Life Insurance Fact Book* (2003).

For these lines of business, competition comes from outside as well as from within the industry. These competitive pressures create a dilemma for insurance companies. While insurance companies are required to control risk, many companies feel compelled to mismatch asset/liability durations or downgrade the credit quality of their investments in an attempt to achieve higher returns for competitive reasons.

Segmentation of insurance company portfolios has promoted the establishment of sub-portfolio return objectives to promote competitive crediting rates for groups of contracts. The major life insurance companies find themselves specifying return requirements by major line of business, the result being that a single company's investment policy may incorporate multiple return objectives.

Another dimension of return objectives for life insurance companies relates to the need to grow surplus to support expanding business volume. Common stocks, equity investments in real estate, and private equity have been the investment alternatives most widely used to achieve surplus growth. Life companies establish return objectives for each of these classes of equity investments to reflect historical and expected returns. Many life insurance companies are evaluating a variety of capital appreciation strategies, as well as financial leverage, to supplement the narrowing contribution to surplus from the newer product lines that are more competitive and have lower profit margins.

4.1.3 Liquidity Requirements

Traditionally, life insurance companies have been characterized as needing minimal liquidity. Except during the depression of the 1930s and the disintermediation of the early 1980s, annual cash inflow has far exceeded cash outflow. Thus, the need to liquidate assets has been negligible, reflecting the growing volume of business, the longer-term nature of liabilities, and the rollover in portfolio assets from maturing securities and other forms of principal payments. However, volatile interest rate environments and the ever-increasing importance of annuity products require that life companies pay close attention to their liquidity requirements. Otherwise, insurers may be forced to sell bonds at a loss to meet surrenders of insurance policies in periods of sharply rising interest rates. In assessing their liquidity needs, insurers must address disintermediation and asset marketability risk.

▶ **Disintermediation.** In the United States, on four different occasions in the past 40 years (1966, 1970, 1974, and 1979–1981), inflation and high interest rates have forced life insurance companies to take measures to accommodate extraordinary net cash outflows. Initially, policy loan drains in conjunction with heavy forward commitment positions forced some remedial but temporary changes in investment strategies. Likewise, the trend of policy surrenders caused 1) actuaries to reevaluate and reduce their estimates of the duration of liabilities and 2) portfolio managers to reduce the average duration of the portfolio and in some cases add to liquidity reserves.

In a period of rising interest rates, a mismatch between the duration of an insurance company's assets and its liabilities can create a net loss if the assets' duration exceeds that of the liabilities. If disintermediation occurs concurrently, the insurer may need to sell assets at a realized loss to meet liquidity needs. Thus, an asset/liability mismatch can exacerbate the effects of disintermediation.

▶ **Asset marketability risk.** The marketability of investments is important to insure ample liquidity. Life insurance companies have traditionally invested some portion of their portfolios in less liquid investments, such as private placement bonds, commercial mortgage loans, equity real estate, and venture capital. Increasingly, liquidity considerations are constraining the percentage invested in these asset classes. Also, forward commitment activity has been slowed by liquidity considerations. Such commitments represent agreements by life insurance companies to purchase private placement bonds or mortgages, with part or all of the settlement typically delayed from 6 to 18 months. The traditional stability and growth of cash flow fostered this practice in the 1960s and 1970s, but volatile interest rates and disintermediation have undermined the predictability of life companies' cash flow. Forward committing has thus waned in importance in recent years.

The growth and development of the derivatives market has broadened the life insurance industry's ability to manage interest rate risk and reduced companies' need to hold significant liquidity reserves. Many companies also maintain lines of credit with banks for added liquidity.

4.1.4 Time Horizon

Life insurance companies have long been considered the classic long-term investor. Traditionally, portfolio return objectives have been evaluated within the context of holding periods as long as 20 to 40 years. Most life insurance companies have traditionally sought long-term maturities for bond and mortgage investments. In addition, life companies have found equity investments (real estate, common stocks, convertible securities, and venture capital) attractive because of their capital appreciation potential and inflation (purchasing power) risk protection.

One reason that life insurance companies have traditionally segmented their portfolios is the recognition that particular product lines or lines of business have unique time horizons and return objectives. For example, group annuities are generally written with maturities of 2 to 10 years. Therefore, many, if not most, of the assets funding those products have comparable maturities (or, more accurately, durations).

Asset/liability management practices have tended to shorten the overall investment time horizon of the typical life insurance company. Today, portfolio segments have differing time horizons, reflected in each segment's investment policies.

4.1.5 Tax Concerns

Unlike pension funds and endowments, insurance companies are tax-paying rather than wholly or partially tax-exempt investors. As commercial enterprises, they are subject to income, capital gains, and other types of taxes in the countries where they operate. The types and application of taxes differ by country, but in all cases, taxes mean that insurance companies must focus on after-tax returns in their investment activities.

In a very simplified context, life insurance companies' investment income can be divided into two parts for tax purposes: the policyholders' share (that portion relating to the actuarially assumed rate necessary to fund reserves) and the corporate share (the balance that is transferred to surplus). Under present U.S. law, only the latter portion is taxed.

One very important tax consideration being watched carefully by the U.S. life insurance industry relates to the tax treatment of the so-called inside buildup of cash values under a life insurance policy or annuity. The deferral of taxes on the accumulation of cash values within a life insurance contract has been a longstanding characteristic of such products. In the United States, Congress periodically reassesses the tax deferral of such inside buildup for life and annuity products. Tax law changes that would reduce or eliminate the tax deferral granted to the inside buildup would create significant competitive issues for the life insurance industry.

4.1.6 Legal and Regulatory Factors

Insurance is a heavily regulated industry. In the United States, state rather than federal regulation prevails. The lack of uniformity of state regulation and the cost of meeting the unique requirements imposed by 50 different states impose costs on insurers. Currently, state regulation pervades all aspects of an insurance company's operations—permitted lines of business, product and policy forms, authorized investments, and the like. The NAIC, whose membership includes regulators from all 50 states, promulgates insurance industry accounting rules and financial statement forms. In 1999, the U.S. Congress passed the Financial Modernization Act, which essentially removed barriers to entry for banks, insurance companies, and investment brokerage firms that dated back to the Great Depression of the 1930s. Regulation of financial institutions in the United States is now more closely aligned with prevailing regulation in many other parts of the world. In Canada, regulation is federal, except for those companies doing business only within a specific province. At either level—federal or provincial—Canadian regulation is as pervasive as U.S. regulation. In Japan, the Ministry of Finance regulates insurance companies, while in the United Kingdom, the Department of Trade is the responsible governmental authority.

The relevant insurance department or ministry audit procedures ensure compliance with the regulations of the state or country where the company is domiciled. In most cases, these regulations are the primary constraint affecting investment policy. Important concepts related to regulatory and legal considerations include eligible investments, the prudent investor rule, and valuation methods.[24]

> ► **Eligible investments.** Insurance laws determine the classes of assets eligible for investment and may specify the quality standards for each asset class. In the United States, for example, many states' insurance laws require that for a bond issue to be eligible for investment, its interest coverage ratio (earnings plus interest divided by interest) must meet minimum standards over a specified time period (e.g., 1.5 times coverage over each of the past five years) or minimum credit ratings. Generally, regulations specify the percentage of an insurance company's assets that may be invested in a specific class of eligible assets. For example, in the United States, most states limit the value (at cost) of life companies' common stock holdings to no more than 20 percent of total admitted assets. Non-U.S. investments are also limited to some extent as a percentage of admitted assets in most states.

> ► **Prudent investor rule.** Although the scope of regulation is extensive, it is important to note that the prudent investor concept has been adopted in some U.S. states. Replacing traditional "laundry lists" of approved

---

[24] The scope of regulation is not limited to these areas. Many life insurance and annuity products have investment features. In the United States and the European Union, life insurance companies are subject to anti-money-laundering regulation to prevent the use of such products for illegal purposes.

investments with prudent investor logic simplifies the regulatory process and allows life insurance companies much needed flexibility to keep up with the ever-changing array of investment alternatives. New York's leadership in this area is important because, traditionally, regulations of this state have been the model for insurance regulation in the United States. Despite a major effort in the mid-1990s, however, no model law or universal investment standards have been adopted by all U.S. states.

▶ **Valuation methods.** In the European Union, International Accounting Standards specify a set of valuation procedures. In the United States, uniform valuation methods are established and administered by the NAIC. In fact, the NAIC's *Security Valuation Book*, published at the end of each year, compiles the values or valuation bases to be used by insurance companies for portfolio securities. This book is the source of the valuation data listed in Schedule D of the annual statement that each company files with the insurance departments of the states in which it operates. Schedule D is an inventory of all bond and stock holdings at year-end and a recap of the year's transactions.

In summary, regulation has a profound effect on both the risk and return aspects of a life insurance company portfolio, primarily because it constrains two critical aspects of portfolio management—asset allocation and the universe of eligible investments.

4.1.7 Unique Circumstances

Each insurance company, whether life or non-life, may have unique circumstances attributable to factors other than the insurance products it provides. These idiosyncrasies may further modify portfolio policies. The company's size and the sufficiency of its surplus position are among the considerations influencing portfolio policy.

To conclude, we provide a sample investment policy statement. Although the format and content of investment policy statements are unique to each insurance company, Example 14 represents a typical IPS for a stock life insurance company.[25]

EXAMPLE 14

Investment Policy Statement for a Stock Life Insurer

ABC Life Insurance Company ("the Company") underwrites and markets life insurance and annuity products. The Company is licensed to do business in all 50 U.S. states. In recent years, the Company has expanded its operations outside the United States and now is licensed and doing business in one Asian and two European countries. The Company's total assets exceed $15 billion; the Company has surplus of more than $1 billion. Competition in its markets is increasing both from traditional insurance company competitors and more recently, from other financial institutions, such as banks and mutual funds. In response to this increased competition, the Company must take more risk and establish higher return objectives for its investment portfolio so as to

---

[25] A stock life insurance company is organized as a corporation owned by stockholders.

maintain an adequate margin (spread) between its investment portfolio return and the weighted-average rates of return being credited to its interest-rate-sensitive life insurance policies and annuity contracts. The Company's investment objectives may be defined in terms of its return and risk objectives for each of the portfolio segments (for example, its real estate portfolio). The statement below reflects a common set of objectives that applies in whole or in part to each of the respective portfolio segments. Policy statements exist for each segment that contain details on segment-specific risk and return specifications. Capital market and insurance market conditions shape the achievement of these policy objectives.

Investment Philosophy

The assets of the Company should be invested to provide for the payment of all contractual obligations to policyholders and to contribute to the growth of surplus over the long-term. Therefore, the investment strategy will be based on prudent investment principles within the context of applicable insurance regulations. The strategy will seek to achieve the appropriate balance between: providing investment income to enhance profitability; maintaining liquidity and generating cash flow to meet all obligations; funding policyholder reserves within pricing strategies; and growing the value of surplus over time, thereby contributing to the Company's future growth.

Investment Goals, Objectives and Constraints

The Company's investment goals and objectives will be stated in terms of return expectations and requirements and risk tolerance. The constraints under which the investment portfolio will be managed include liquidity considerations, time horizon, regulatory restrictions, tax considerations and unique requirements.

Return Objectives

The return objectives of the Company are twofold: a) earn a sufficient return to fund all policyholder liabilities and match or exceed the expected returns factored into the pricing of the Company's various products, and b) contribute to the growth of surplus through capital appreciation. The return objectives will be stated in terms of meeting or exceeding projected needs related to investment income, product pricing spreads, and total return. The return requirements may vary by portfolio segments that have been established for certain product lines or groupings of product lines.

Risk Tolerance

The risk tolerance of the Company is based on the competitive requirements of various product lines, asset/liability management factors, risk-based capital considerations, rating agency parameters and the responsibility to fulfill all short-term and long-term obligations to policyholders. Interest rate risk and credit (default) risk need to be monitored and managed to support the competitive position of the Company while providing for its long-term viability. The risk parameters may vary by segment.

Investment Constraints

The Company's investment constraints are defined in terms of the following factors, all or some of which may apply to specific portfolio segments.

Liquidity. The portfolio will be managed to meet the liquidity requirements so as to pay all benefits and expenses in a timely manner. Investment cash flows will be a primary source of liquidity, so as to minimize the need to hold lower yielding cash reserves. In addition, publicly traded securities will provide an additional source of liquidity.

Time Horizon. The Company is a long-term investor and will establish duration targets for the portfolio and any product segments based on appropriate asset/liability management specifications.

Tax. Income tax considerations determine the mix of investments that provides the most favorable after-tax returns. From time to time, operating conditions or corporate tax planning requirements may mandate the realization or postponement of capital gains.

Regulatory. All investments must qualify under the insurance code of the state in which the Company is domiciled and the nondomestic insurance companies' regulations in the countries in which the Company operates.

Unique Circumstance. The Company may invest in less liquid private placement bonds, commercial mortgage loans, real estate and private equity to enhance returns so long as liquidity requirements are not compromised.

Review Schedule

This policy statement will be reviewed at least annually by the Board of Directors and is subject to modification based on significant changes in insurance or tax regulations as well as significant changes in the Company's financial position and/or capital- or insurance-market conditions.

Asset Allocation

The Company's strategic allocation is designed to identify and authorize the strategies for achieving the objectives specified by the investment policy statement. The strategic asset allocation also recognizes the constraints (both regulatory and self-imposed) specified in the investment policy statement. The selection of authorized asset classes and their allocation percentages are recognized as key determinants of the success of the Company's investment activities. The strategic asset allocation will be set out in a separate document.

Rebalancing

Changes in market values and market conditions require periodic portfolio rebalancing on at least a quarterly (and in some cases a more frequent) basis. Cash flow, insofar as it is available, will be used to rebalance. It should be recognized that some asset classes, such as private placement bonds, private equity, commercial mortgage loans, and real estate, are less liquid than publicly traded securities. Therefore, under most conditions, these asset classes should not be allowed to exceed the target allocations specified in the strategic asset allocation.

Investment Responsibilities

The Board of Directors is responsible for overseeing the invested assets and the investment process of the Company. The Board will rely on both Company employees and/or external investment service providers for the ongoing management of the investment portfolio. Because of the number of parties involved, each entity's role must be identified to ensure operational efficiency, clear lines of communication and accountability in all aspects of the management of the investment portfolio of the Company.

Board of Directors. The Board of Directors approves the investment policy statement and asset allocation at least annually. At least quarterly, the Board will review the performance of the investment portfolio and review and approve all transactions for that quarter.

Investment Management Committee. The Investment Management Committee will be composed of investment and financial officers of the Company. They will have ongoing responsibility for the management of the investment portfolio. On a quarterly basis, the Investment Management Committee will review investment performance and cash flow requirements with the Board of Directors. On an annual basis, or when either the Company's financial condition or capital market conditions change, the Investment Management Committee will review the investment policy statement and asset allocation and recommend changes to the Board.

External Investment Advisors. With the approval of the Board of Directors, the Investment Management Committee may retain external investment consultants and advisors to assist in the management of the investment portfolio or subparts thereof. All external investment advisors will be expected to manage all or any part of the portfolio in conformity with the investment policy statement and asset allocation.

Custodian. The Investment Management Committee is authorized to retain the services of a regulated bank or trust company to safeguard the cash and invested assets of the Company. The custodian will also be responsible for the payment and collection of all investment funds.

4.2 Non-Life Insurance Companies: Background and Investment Setting

The second broad insurance category is the non-life (casualty) sector, which includes but is not limited to health, property, liability, marine, surety, and workers' compensation insurance. For purposes of considering investment policy, these non-life companies are really quite similar even though the products they sell are rather diverse. The investment policies of a non-life company differ significantly from those of a life insurance company, however, because the liabilities, risk factors, and tax considerations for non-life companies are distinctly different from those for life companies. For example:

▶ non-life liability durations tend to be shorter, and claim processing and payments periods are longer, than for life companies;

▶ some (but not all) non-life liabilities are exposed to inflation risk, although liabilities are not directly exposed to interest rate risk as those of life insurance companies; and

▶ in general, a life insurance company's liabilities are relatively certain in value but uncertain in timing, while a non-life insurance company's liabilities are relatively uncertain in both value and timing, with the result that non-life insurance companies are exposed to more volatility in their operating results.

As detailed in this section, the investment policies and practices of non-life insurance companies in the United States are evolving, with changes brought on by both operating considerations and new tax laws. In fact, tax planning has dominated the investment policy of non-life companies for decades, reflecting the cyclical characteristics of this segment of the insurance industry. For reasons described in the following pages, asset/liability management is receiving increased attention.

A unique aspect of the casualty insurance industry is what is often described as the "long tail" that characterizes the industry's claims reporting, processing, and payment structure.[26] Whereas life insurance is heavily oriented toward products sold to or for individuals, commercial customers account for a very large portion of the total casualty insurance market. The long tail nature of many types of liability (both individual and commercial) and casualty insurance claims arises from the fact that months and years may pass between the date of the occurrence and reporting of the claim and the actual payment of a settlement to a policyholder. Many casualty industry claims are the subject of lawsuits to determine settlement amounts. Furthermore, some of these claims require expert evaluation to determine the extent of the damages—for example, a fire in a major manufacturing plant or damage to an oceangoing vessel. Thus, the liability structure of a casualty insurance company is very much a function of the products that it sells and the claims reporting and settlement process for those types of products.

From an asset/liability management perspective, most casualty insurance companies traditionally have been classified as having relatively short-term liabilities, even though the spectrum of casualty insurance policies covers a wide range of liability durations. One of the primary factors that limits the duration of a non-life company's assets is the so-called **underwriting (profitability) cycle**, generally averaging three to five years. These cycles typically result from adverse claims experience and/or periods of extremely competitive pricing. They often coincide with general business cycles and, in the low part of the cycle, frequently require companies to liquidate investments to supplement cash flow shortfalls.

Estimating the duration of a casualty insurance company's liabilities introduces a different set of issues than with life insurance liabilities. Using multiscenario and multifactor models, casualty actuaries attempt to capture 1) the underwriting cycle, 2) the liability durations by product line, and 3) any unique cash outflow characteristics. For non-life companies, business cycles and not

---

[26] "Long tail" refers to the possibly long time span between the liability-triggering event and the filing of a claim related to it.

interest rate cycles, per se, determine a company's need for liquidity through appropriate durations and maturities of assets.

4.2.1 Risk Objectives

Like life insurance companies, casualty insurance companies have a quasi-fiduciary role; thus the ability to meet policyholders' claims is a dominant consideration influencing investment policy. The risks insured by casualty companies, however, are less predictable. In fact, for companies exposed to catastrophic events—such as hurricanes, tornadoes, and explosions—the potential for loss may be significantly greater. Furthermore, casualty policies frequently provide replacement cost or current cost coverage; thus inflation adds to the degree of risk. In setting risk objectives, casualty companies must consider both cash flow characteristics and the common stock to surplus ratio.

▶ **Cash flow characteristics.** Not surprisingly, cash flows from casualty insurance operations can be quite erratic. Unlike life insurance companies, which historically have been able to project cash flows and make forward commitments, casualty companies must be prepared to meet operating cash gaps with investment income or maturing securities. Therefore, for the portion of the investment portfolio relating to policyholder reserves, casualty companies have low tolerance for loss of principal or diminishing investment income. Investment maturities and investment income must be predictable in order to directly offset the unpredictability of operating trends.

Interestingly, no regulations require casualty insurance companies to maintain an asset valuation reserve, although risk-based capital requirements have been established in the United States. Regulators and rating agencies closely monitor the ratio of a casualty insurance company's premium income to its total surplus. Generally, this ratio is maintained between 2-to-1 and 3-to-1.

▶ **Common stock to surplus ratio.** Inflation worldwide has further reduced investment risk tolerance among many casualty insurers. In fact, volatile stock market conditions in the 1970s persuaded many casualty companies to reduce the percentage of surplus invested in common stock. Until then, it was not uncommon for a casualty insurance company to hold common stock investments equal to or greater than its total surplus. Regulators in the United States forced several major companies to liquidate large portions of their common stock holdings near the end of the 1974 bear market because of significant erosion of surplus. This liquidation impaired these companies' ability to increase volume and, in some cases, their ability to provide sufficient financial stability for existing volume of business.

Essentially, the regulators gave such companies the option of reducing common stock holdings or of temporarily ceasing or curtailing the issuance of new policies. Needless to say, this experience reduced casualty companies' risk tolerance for the portion of the investment portfolio related to surplus. Unlike the life insurance industry, the casualty industry has almost no absolute limits imposed by regulation (in the United States, some states do limit commons stocks as a percentage of surplus). However, many casualty companies have adopted self-imposed limitations restricting common stocks at market value to some significant but limited portion (frequently one-half to three-quarters) of total surplus. During the bull market of the 1990s, many companies modified those self-imposed limits. Nevertheless, the attention paid to stock market risk exposure has prevented a repeat of the mid-1970s experience.

4.2.2 *Return Objectives*

Historically, most casualty insurance companies have not implicitly taken investment earnings into account when calculating premiums, in striking contrast to the accumulation rates long factored into life insurance premiums. For this reason, casualty insurance companies were once thought to be operating as if they were two separate organizations—an insurance company and an investment company operating a balanced fund (a fund holding a mixture of bonds and stocks). However, times have changed and the investment and operating functions are much more closely coordinated now. Factors influencing return objectives include competitive pricing policy, profitability, growth of surplus, tax considerations, and total return management.

► **Competitive policy pricing.** Low insurance policy premium rates, due to competition, provide an incentive for insurance companies to set high desired investment return objectives. The flip side is that high investment returns may induce insurance companies to lower their policy rates, even though a high level of returns cannot be sustained. In the late 1970s and early 1980s, for example, many casualty insurance companies, especially the larger ones, took advantage of the high interest rates being earned on new investments to lower insurance premiums or to delay the normal passthrough of cost increases to their customers. As a result of this strategy, casualty insurance premiums lagged the otherwise high rate of inflation that characterized the early 1980s. Once interest rates began to fall, projections of high investment returns became suspect. The operating margin decline that many casualty insurance companies experienced in the mid-1980s resulted, in part, from the mispricing of their products because of expected returns that did not materialize. The low interest rate and weak stock market environment of 2000–2002 reinforced the perception that insurers cannot rely on investment returns to cover underwriting losses and that underwriting quality and profitable pricing are important. Thus any influence of competitive policy pricing on a casualty company's return objectives needs to be assessed in light of well-thought-out capital market assumptions and the insurance company's ability to accept risk.

► **Profitability.** Investment income and the investment portfolio return are primary determinants of continuing profitability for the typical casualty company and, indeed, the industry. The underwriting cycle influences the volatility of both company and industry earnings. Return requirements for casualty companies are not framed in reference to a crediting rate for their policies; rather, casualty insurance portfolios are managed to maximize return on capital and surplus to the extent that prudent asset/liability management, surplus adequacy considerations, and management preferences will allow.

Given the underwriting uncertainties inherent in the casualty insurance business, investment income obviously provides financial stability for the insurance reserves. In fact, investment earnings are expected to offset periodic underwriting losses (claims and expenses in excess of premium income) from the insurance side of the company. Most casualty insurance products are priced competitively, and thus casualty premium rates are generally not sufficiently ample or flexible to eliminate the loss aspects of the underwriting cycle. The insurance industry measures underwriting profitability using the "combined ratio," the percentage of premiums that an insurance company spends on claims and expenses. Over the past 25 years, the combined ratio for U.S.-based non-life insurance companies has been above 100 percent, reflecting underwriting losses, in over 60 percent of the years.

► **Growth of surplus.** An important function of a casualty company's investment operation is to provide growth of surplus, which in turn provides the opportunity to expand the volume of insurance the company can write. As mentioned earlier, the risk-taking capacity of a casualty insurance company is measured to a large extent by its ratio of premiums to capital and surplus. Generally, companies maintain this ratio between 2-to-1 and 3-to-1, although many well capitalized companies have lower ratios. Casualty companies have invested in common stocks, convertible securities, and alternative investments to achieve growth of surplus. These investments' return and marketability characteristics fit well within the industry's underwriting cycles.

► **Tax considerations.** Over the years, non-life insurance companies' investment results have been very sensitive to the after-tax return on the bond portfolio and to the tax benefits, when they exist, of certain kinds of investment returns. In the United States, these returns have included dividend income (through the exclusion of a portion of the dividends received by one corporation on stock issued by another corporation), realized long-term capital gains, and tax-exempt bonds. U.S. casualty insurance companies have historically favored the latter, especially when underwriting is profitable, to achieve the highest after-tax return. For many casualty companies, the flexibility to shift between taxable and tax-exempt bonds has long been an important consideration as a key element of managing and optimizing after-tax income through the operating loss carryback and carryforward provisions of the U.S. tax code. Most companies have maintained some balance of taxable and tax-exempt bonds in their portfolios, shifting that mix as tax considerations warranted. Recent changes in the tax laws have diminished most of the tax benefits available to casualty insurance companies. Outside of the United States, tax-exempt securities for insurance companies either do not exist or are more limited in supply. For non-U.S. insurance companies, therefore, taxes are even more of a constraint.

► **Total return management.** Active bond portfolio management strategies designed to achieve total return, rather than yield or investment income goals only, have gained popularity among casualty insurance companies, especially large ones. Because GAAP and statutory reporting require that realized capital gains and losses flow through the income statement, the decline in interest rates and increase in bond prices since 1982 have encouraged casualty insurance portfolio managers to trade actively for total return in at least some portion of their bond portfolios.

One of the most interesting characteristics of casualty insurance companies is that their investment returns vary significantly from company to company. This variation reflects 1) the latitude permitted by insurance regulations; 2) differences in product mix, and thus in the duration of liabilities; 3) a particular company's tax position; 4) the emphasis placed on capital appreciation versus the income component of investment return; and 5) the strength of the company's capital and surplus positions. Exhibit 6 illustrates this contrast.[27]

---

[27] Because insurers' portfolios are heavily weighted toward fixed income, the variation in yields for four major companies shown in Exhibit 6 provides evidence for variation in total returns (data for which are not readily available).

EXHIBIT 6	Pretax Portfolio Yields of U.S. Casualty Insurance Companies: Selected Years, 1975–2004			
	Allstate (%)	CNA Financial (%)	State Farm (%)	Travelers (%)
1975	5.1	5.3	5.5	7.3
1985	6.8	9.7	8.2	7.2
1995	6.0	6.4	5.7	5.9
2000	5.5	6.4	6.0	6.8
2004	5.3	4.3	4.6	5.5

Source: Best's Insurance Reports (2005).

4.2.3 Liquidity Requirements

Given the uncertainty of the cash flow from casualty insurance operations, liquidity has always been a paramount consideration for non-life companies, in sharp contrast with life insurance companies which face relatively certain cash flows, excluding policy loans and surrenders. In addition to its use in meeting cash flow needs, liquidity has also been a necessary adjunct of a casualty company's variable tax position. Historically, casualty companies have found it necessary to liquidate portions of their bond portfolios to increase tax-exempt income during periods of underwriting profits and to increase taxable income during periods of underwriting losses. Liquidity remains a necessity for casualty companies, providing portfolio flexibility under changing tax, underwriting, and interest rate conditions.

To meet its liquidity needs, the typical casualty company does several things related to the marketability and maturity schedule of its investments. Quite often it maintains a portfolio of short-term securities, such as commercial paper or Treasury bills, as an immediate liquidity reserve. In addition, it may also hold a portfolio of readily marketable government bonds of various maturities; maintain a balanced or laddered maturity schedule to ensure a sufficient rollover of assets; match some assets against seasonal cash flow needs; or concentrate some portion of its bond portfolio in higher-quality bonds that are generally more marketable. Needless to say, such attention to maturity and marketability complements the limited risk tolerance and further modifies the return objectives of casualty insurers.

4.2.4 Time Horizon

The time horizon of casualty insurance companies is a function of two primary factors. First, the durations of casualty liabilities are typically shorter than those of life insurance liabilities. Second, underwriting cycles affect the mix of taxable and tax-exempt bond holdings. Because the tax-exempt **yield curve** in the United States tends to be more positively sloped than the taxable curve, casualty companies find that they must invest in longer maturities (15 to 30 years) than the typical life company to optimize the yield advantage offered by tax-exempt securities (see Exhibit 7).

	Comparison of Average Maturity of Bond Portfolios of Selected U.S. Non-Life and Life Insurance Companies: Year-End 2004
EXHIBIT 7	

Company	Average Maturity of Bond Portfolio (Years)
Casualty	
Allstate	13
CNA Financial	14
State Farm	7
Travelers	7
Life	
AXA Equitable-NY	11
Lincoln National	9
Prudential	8

Source: *Best's Insurance Reports* (2005).

Differences in the average maturity of bond portfolios between casualty and life insurance companies may also reflect the companies' willingness to accept interest rate risk via asset/liability duration mismatches and trade at least some portion of their portfolios through a market or underwriting cycle.

In terms of common stock investments, casualty companies historically have been long-term investors, with growth of surplus being the primary return objective of their portfolios' stock portion. As noted earlier, realized gains and losses flow through the income statement. Currently, the long-term equity investor status of the industry has been modified by objectives related to current reported earnings that have in turn led to some additional turnover in the common stock portfolio and more active management of the total portfolio.

4.2.5 Tax Concerns

Tax considerations are a very important factor in determining casualty insurance companies' investment policy. Prior to changes in the tax law in 1986, U.S. casualty insurance companies operated under a relatively simple and straightforward set of tax provisions. Under those laws, their investment policy was directed toward achieving the appropriate balance between taxable and tax-exempt income on one hand, and taking advantage of the lower capital gains tax rate and corporate dividend exclusion, where possible, on the other.

As a result of the 1986 changes, tax-exempt bond income became subject to tax for U.S. casualty insurance companies. Applying the current tax provisions requires a series of calculations to determine the net tax being levied on tax-exempt bond income. Because the equations must factor in both the operating profit or loss characteristics of the casualty company and alternative minimum tax provisions of the code, a computer model is generally needed to determine the appropriate asset allocation, if any, between tax-exempt and taxable securities for both new purchases and existing holdings. The complexities and implications of the taxation of tax-exempt bond income for casualty companies are beyond the scope of this reading.

As in the life insurance industry, casualty insurers are likely to be subjected to further tax code modification, which increases uncertainty for the investment manager as to the tax consequences of certain portfolio activities or alternatives when measured over a long time horizon. Tax considerations also shape the investment policy of non-U.S. casualty insurance companies. Portfolio managers typically work closely with the companies' tax advisors to measure and monitor the tax implications of various portfolio strategies.

4.2.6 Legal and Regulatory Factors

Although the insurance industry in general is heavily regulated, casualty company investment regulation is relatively permissive. On the one hand, classes of eligible assets and quality standards for each class are specified just as they are for life companies. In the United States, New York state law, which is considered the most restrictive, requires that assets equal to 50 percent of unearned premium and loss reserves combined be maintained in "eligible bonds and mortgages." Beyond these general restrictions, however, casualty insurance companies are permitted to invest the remainder of their assets in a relatively broad array of bonds, mortgages, stocks, and real estate, without restriction as to the amount invested in any particular asset class (except in certain states that limit common stock and/or real estate holdings).

A casualty company is not required to maintain an asset valuation reserve. In essence, then, the surplus of a casualty company reflects the full impact of increases and decreases in the market value of stocks. The United States, however, has recently established risk-based capital regulations for the casualty industry. U.S. risk-based capital regulations for casualty insurers specify the minimum amount of capital that an insurer must hold as a function of the size and degree of the asset risk, credit risk, underwriting risk, and off-balance sheet risk that the insurer takes.[28]

4.2.7 Determination of Portfolio Policies

As in the case of life insurance companies, casualty companies' limited investment risk tolerance is the dominant factor in determining their investment policy. Because of contractual liabilities and difficulty in forecasting the cash flow from insurance operations, casualty companies seek some degree of safety from the assets offsetting insurance reserves. Indeed, casualty companies' willingness to assume investment risk with the assets offsetting surplus has been moderated, or is at least subject to more careful management, as a result of market volatility in recent years.

Over and above liquidity needs, which are clearly important, casualty insurance companies develop a significant portfolio of stocks and bonds and generate a high level of income to supplement or offset insurance underwriting gains and losses. Capital appreciation also builds the surplus base and supports additional investment in the business. The structure of a casualty company's

[28] Asset risk addresses fluctuation in market value. **Credit risk** addresses probability of default. Underwriting risk arises from underestimating liabilities from business already written or inadequately pricing current or prospective business. Off-balance sheet risk addresses the risk from items not reflected in the balance sheet.

bond portfolio between taxable and tax-exempt securities depends on the company's underwriting experience and current tax policy. A casualty company's investment and business operating policies and strategies must be closely coordinated given the volatility of both the capital markets and the casualty insurance markets.

To conclude, we provide a sample investment policy statement. The format and content of investment policy statements are of course unique to each insurance company; however, Example 15 details an investment policy statement for a typical casualty insurance company.

EXAMPLE 15

Investment Policy Statement for a Casualty Insurance Company

Cornish Casualty Insurance Company ("the Company") underwrites auto and homeowners insurance. The company is licensed to do business in all 50 U.S. states. In recent years, the Company's business has been growing steadily, and its board of directors has approved a strategic plan for increasing its growth rate and profitability. The Company's total assets exceed $5 billion, and its surplus approaches $2 billion. The company is facing increased competition in its markets from companies selling auto and homeowners insurance through the Internet, as well as from other direct sellers. This competitive environment has focused the board and management's attention on increasing the after-tax return on the bond portfolio and enhancing the growth of surplus. The company's chief investment officer has been asked to revise the Company's investment policy statement to reflect the changes that will be necessary to meet the new growth targets. The CIO has revised the return and risk objectives for the overall portfolio and various portfolio segments. Following are the investment objectives and constraints under which the Company's investment portfolio will be managed.

Investment Philosophy

The assets of the Company should be invested to provide for the payment of all contractual obligations to policyholders and to contribute to the growth of surplus over the long-term. Therefore, the investment strategy will be based on prudent investment principles within the context of applicable insurance regulations. The strategy will seek to achieve the appropriate balance among the following: providing investment income to enhance profitability; maintaining liquidity and generating cash flow to meet all obligations; and growing the value of assets over time, thereby contributing to the Company's ability to write additional business and grow premium income.

Investment Goals, Objectives, and Constraints

The Company's investment goals and objectives will be stated in terms of return expectations and requirements and risk tolerance. The constraints under which the investment portfolio will be managed include liquidity considerations, time horizon, regulatory restrictions, tax considerations and unique requirements.

Return Objectives

The return objectives of the Company are threefold: a) earn a sufficient return to fund all policyholder liabilities, b) support the competitive pricing of all products, and c) contribute to the growth of surplus through capital appreciation. The return objectives will be measured in terms of meeting or exceeding projections of investment income and total return.

Risk Tolerance

The risk tolerance of the Company is based on the competitive requirements of various product lines, risk-based capital considerations, and the responsibility to fulfill all short-term and long-term obligations to policyholders. Credit (default) risk and stock market risk need to be monitored and managed so as to support the competitive position of the Company while providing for its long-term viability.

Investment Constraints

The Company's investment constraints can be defined in terms of the following factors.

Liquidity. The portfolio will be managed to meet the liquidity requirements to pay all benefits and expenses in a timely manner. Investment cash flows will be a primary source of liquidity, to minimize lower yielding cash reserves. In addition, publicly traded securities will provide an important additional source of liquidity.

Time Horizon. The Company is a long-term investor but will adjust the average maturity of the bond portfolio in line with the relative attractiveness of the after tax return on taxable versus tax-exempt bonds.

Tax. Tax considerations determine the optimal allocation within the bond portfolio between taxable and tax-exempt bonds. Tax considerations may also play a role in the realization of gains and losses for both the bond and stock portfolios.

Regulatory. All investments must qualify under the insurance law of the state in which the Company is domiciled.

Unique Circumstances. Private placement bonds are not authorized and investments in commercial mortgage loans and real estate are limited, due to liquidity considerations.

Review Schedule

This policy statement will be reviewed at least annually by the Board of Directors and is subject to modification based on significant changes in insurance or tax regulations as well as significant changes in the Company's financial position and/or capital or insurance market conditions.

[Other parts of the investment policy statement are omitted.]

5   BANKS AND OTHER INSTITUTIONAL INVESTORS

The final type of institutional investor that we discuss in detail is banks.

5.1 Banks: Background and Investment Setting

Banks are financial intermediaries involved in taking deposits and lending money. Nearly everywhere, however, the scope of banks' activities has evolved and widened over time, although distinct regional and national traditions remain. Western Europe and Canada follow the model of universal banking, in which traditional banking (involving deposit-taking and lending), securities underwriting, and insurance (in Europe) are organized under one corporate roof.[29] In this universal banking model, banks can provide one-stop shopping for financial services. In contrast to this model, in the 20th century the United States and Japan evolved regulatory separations between commercial banking and investment banking (security underwriting) activities. Gradually, this separation has eroded in the United States, as highlighted by the 1998 merger of Citicorp (a holding company that included Citibank) and Travelers Group (a holding company that included Travelers Insurance and Salomon Smith Barney) and by the Gramm–Leach–Bliley Act of 1999, which permits affiliations under a financial holding company structure. Nevertheless, important differences in regulatory constraints and business structures persist among banks internationally.

Banks' liabilities consist chiefly of time and demand deposits[30] (as much as 90 percent of total liabilities and capital for smaller banks) but also include purchased funds and sometimes publicly traded debt. The asset side of the balance sheet consists of loan and securities portfolios as well as an assortment of other assets. For Federal Deposit Insurance Corporation insured U.S. commercial banks as of the end of 2002, loans and leases represented on average 58 percent of assets. Loans may include real estate, commercial, individual, and agricultural loans. Securities represented 19 percent of total assets; other assets (trading accounts, bank premises and fixed assets, and other real estate owned) were 14 percent; and cash and Federal funds represented 5 and 4 percent, respectively.

Traditionally, a bank's portfolio of investment securities has been a residual use of funds after loan demand has been met. The securities portfolio nevertheless plays a key role in managing a bank's risk and liquidity positions relative to its liabilities. Consequently, a bank's asset/liability risk management committee (ALCO) is generally in charge of overseeing the bank's securities portfolio. Exhibit 8 sets a context for understanding a bank's ALCO's concerns. Although banks have fee and other non-interest sources of income, and, of course, non-interest expenses, interest revenues and costs are the chief

---

[29] **Bancassurance** is the term that has developed to describe the sale of insurance by banks. As of 2004, more than 50 percent of life insurance is sold through banks in Spain, France, and Italy, and about 20 percent is sold through banks in the United Kingdom and Germany. Although banks in Japan have been permitted to sell insurance products since 2002 and in the U.S. since 1999, banks constitute a minor share of the insurance market in these countries.

[30] A **time deposit** is a deposit requiring advance notice prior to a withdrawal; a **demand deposit** is one that can be drawn upon without prior notice, such as a checking account.

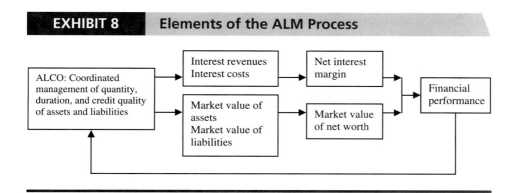

EXHIBIT 8 **Elements of the ALM Process**

financial variables affecting bank profitability. The quantity, duration, and credit quality of both the loan and securities portfolio affects a bank's interest revenues. On the market-value balance sheet, interest rate risk affects the market value of net worth representing the value of equity claims on the bank. Observing the bank's financial performance, the ALCO can make needed changes in assets and liabilities.

Some more detail is helpful. Among the profitability measures that the ALCO will monitor are the following:

▶ The **net interest margin**, already mentioned, equals net interest income (interest income minus interest expense) divided by average earning assets. Net interest margin is a summary measure of the net interest return earned on income-producing assets such as loans and bonds.[31]

▶ The **interest spread** equals the average yield on earning assets minus the average percent cost of interest-bearing liabilities. The interest spread is a measure of the bank's ability to invest in assets yielding more than the cost of its sources of funding.

Because both interest income and interest expense fluctuate in response to interest rate changes, net interest margin and interest spread are key indicators of a bank's ability to profitably manage interest rate risk. Among the risk measures the ALCO will monitor are the following:

▶ The **leverage-adjusted duration gap** is defined as $D_A - kD_L$, where D_A is the duration of assets, D_L is the duration of liabilities, and $k = L/A$, the ratio of the market value of liabilities (L) to the market value of assets (A). The leverage-adjusted duration gap measures a bank's overall interest rate exposure. For a positive interest rate shock (unexpected increase in rates), the market value of net worth will decrease for a bank with a positive gap; be unaffected for a bank with a zero gap (an immunized balance sheet); and increase for a bank with a negative gap.[32]

---

[31] Earning assets include all assets that generate explicit interest income (plus lease receipts) but exclude discount instruments such as acceptances.

[32] The change in the market value of net worth for an interest rate shock is approximately equal to the leverage-adjusted duration gap times the size of the bank (measured by A) times the size of the interest rate shock. Bankers also use other gap concepts in measuring interest rate risk. See Koch and MacDonald (2003).

► Position and aggregate **Value at Risk (VAR)** are money measures of the minimum value of losses expected over a specified time period (for example, a day, a quarter, or a year) at a given level of probability (often 0.05 or 0.01). As a result of risk-based capital regulatory initiatives internationally, nearly all banks track this measure of exposure to large losses.

► Credit measures of risk may include both internally developed and commercially available measures such as CreditMetrics.

A bank's securities portfolio plays an important role in achieving its financial performance objectives. According to one survey, banks' objectives in managing securities portfolios include the following, listed in order of importance:[33]

► **To manage overall interest rate risk of the balance sheet.** In contrast to business, consumer, and mortgage loans, bank-held securities are negotiable instruments trading in generally liquid markets that can be bought and sold quickly. Therefore, securities are the natural adjustment mechanism for interest rate risk. For example, if the duration of equity is higher than desired, a bank can shorten it by shortening the maturity of its securities portfolio.

► **To manage liquidity.** Banks use their securities portfolios to assure adequate cash is available to them. The rationale for selling securities to meet liquidity needs is again the ready marketability of securities.

► **To produce income.** Banks' securities portfolios frequently account for a quarter or more of total revenue.

► **To manage credit risk.** The securities portfolio is used to modify and diversify the overall credit risk exposure to a desired level. Banks frequently assume substantial credit risk in their loan portfolios; they can balance that risk by assuming minimal credit risk in their securities portfolio. Additionally, they can use the securities portfolio to diversify risk when the loan portfolio is not adequately diversified.

Banks also use their securities portfolios to meet other needs. For example, in the United States, banks must hold (pledge) government securities against the uninsured portion of deposits (an example of a **pledging requirement**—i.e., a required collateral use of assets).

Just as a bank's liabilities are interest-rate sensitive (as is its loan portfolio, on the asset side), a bank's security portfolios consist almost exclusively of fixed-income securities. This characteristic, as well as the bias toward low-credit risk holdings, is reinforced by regulatory constraints on securities holdings. Exhibit 9 gives the average asset class weights of U.S. commercial banks' securities portfolios (because of rounding weights they do not sum to exactly 100). We note that Exhibit 9 does not show off-balance-sheet derivatives used to manage interest rate and credit risk.

The major trend in banks' securities holdings during the last 10 years or more has been the decline in holdings of tax-exempt bonds and the increase in holdings of mortgage-backed securities, which are included under corporate securities in Exhibit 9.

---

[33] BAI Foundation (1995).

EXHIBIT 9	U.S. Commercial Banks: Investment Securities Weights (Trading Account Not Included): Year-End 2003

Asset Class	All Commercial Banks (%)
U.S. Treasury securities	5.2
U.S. government agency and corporate securities	68.8
Municipal securities	8.3
Other domestic debt securities	10.6
Non-U.S. debt securities	5.2
Equities	1.8

Source: www.financialservicesfacts.org.

5.1.1 Risk Objectives

As already emphasized, banks' risk objectives are dominated by ALM considerations that focus on funding liabilities. Therefore, risk relative to liabilities, rather than absolute risk, is of primary concern. Although banks would like to earn high interest margins, they must not assume a level of risk that jeopardizes their ability to meet their liabilities to depositors and other entities. Overall, banks have below-average risk tolerance as concerns the securities portfolio.

5.1.2 Return Objectives

A bank's return objectives for its securities portfolio are driven by the need to earn a positive return on invested capital. For the interest-income part of return, the portfolio manager pursues this objective by attempting to earn a positive spread over the cost of funds.

5.1.3 Liquidity Requirements

A bank's liquidity position is a key management and regulatory concern. Liquidity requirements are determined by net outflows of deposits, if any, as well as demand for loans.

5.1.4 Time Horizon

A bank's time horizon for its securities portfolio reflects its need to manage interest rate risk while earning a positive return on invested capital. A bank's liability structure typically reflects an overall shorter maturity than its loan portfolio, placing a risk management constraint on the time horizon length for its securities portfolio. This time horizon generally falls in the three- to seven-year range (intermediate term).

5.1.5 Tax Concerns

Banks' securities portfolios are fully taxable. In the United States prior to 1983, the full amount of interest used to finance the purchase of tax-exempt securities was tax deductible, and banks were major buyers of municipal bonds. Since 1986, such deductions have been completely disallowed for the purchase of most municipal bonds, and U.S. banks' portfolios have been concentrated in taxable securities. In the United States since 1983 securities gains and losses affect net operating income. Thus realized securities losses decrease reported operating income, while securities gains increase reported operating income. According to some observers, this accounting treatment creates an incentive not to sell securities showing unrealized losses, providing a mechanism by which earnings can be managed.

5.1.6 Legal and Regulatory Factors

Regulations place restrictions on banks' holdings of common shares and below-investment-grade risk fixed-income securities. To meet legal reserve and pledging requirements banks may need to hold substantial amounts of short-term government securities. Risk-based capital (RBC) regulations are a major regulatory development worldwide affecting banks' risk-taking incentives. RBC requirements restrain bank risk-taking by linking the formula for required capital to the credit risk of the bank's assets, both on and off balance sheet. To illustrate this type of regulation, following the Basel Accord, since 1993 bank assets have been placed in one of four risk categories involving risk weights of 0%, 20%, 50%, and 100%, respectively.[34] A risk weight of 100, for example, applies to most bank loans. That weight means that 100 percent of the loan is subject to the baseline minimum 8 percent capital requirement. Under Basel II, proposed for implementation in 2006, banks will place assets in risk-exposure categories involving weights of 0%, 20%, 50%, 100%, and 150%, respectively. In contrast to the original Basel Accord, Basel II accounts for credit-quality differences within a given security type.

5.1.7 Unique Circumstances

There are no common unique circumstances to highlight relative to banks' securities investment activities. That situation stands in contrast to banks' lending activities, in which banks may consider factors such as historical banking relationships and community needs, which may be viewed as unique circumstances.

Example 16 excerpts the investment policy statement of a hypothetical small commercial bank. We incorporated this reading's investment objectives and constraints framework in its format, and we included a section on authorized investments that typically is found in such documents. The IPS excerpts cover many of the major topics that would be included in an IPS for a typical U.S. commercial bank (referred to as the "Bank").

---

[34] The Basel Accord, sponsored by the Bank for International Settlements, applies to the banks of a group of major industrialized countries.

EXAMPLE 16

Investment Policy Statement for a Commercial Bank

A. Purpose

The purpose of the investment policy statement (IPS) is to set forth the policies and procedures that govern the administration of all the Bank's investment activities. The Bank's Money Market Account is subject to additional constraints set forth in a later section of the IPS.

B. Responsibility

The Bank's Board of Directors (the "Board") is responsible for formulating and implementing investment policies. The Board delegates authority for making specific investments to the Bank's officers ("Management") designated in Exhibit A attached to this IPS, for investments consistent with this IPS. The Board also appoints an Investment Committee (the "Committee") to act as a liaison between the Board and Management and to carry out the following functions:

1. Monitor and review all investment decisions for compliance with the IPS and with federal and state regulations.

2. Review the IPS and recommend changes to it to the Board when appropriate.

C. Investment Objectives and Constraints

The primary purposes of the investment portfolio are to provide liquidity and to control the overall interest rate and credit risk exposures of the Bank. The portfolio will convert excess cash resulting from net deposit inflows and/or slack loan demand into earning assets. The portfolio will be drawn down when needed to meet net deposit outflows, loan demand, or other contingencies.

Return Requirements

The Bank will attempt to earn an average positive spread over the cost of funds.

Risk Objectives

- ► Because of the need to be able to satisfy depositor and other liabilities at short notice and taking account of the typical characteristics of its loan portfolio, the Bank's tolerance for interest rate, credit, and liquidity risk in its securities portfolio is below average.
- ► The yield on investments is secondary to liquidity and safety of principal.
- ► To limit the risk of loss as a result of an individual issuer default, the Bank will maintain adequate diversification in its holdings.

Tax

As a taxable corporation the Bank will appraise taxable and tax-exempt investments on an after-tax basis.

Regulatory

All investments must qualify under state and federal banking regulations governing the investment activities of the Bank.

Unique Circumstances

None.

D. Authorized Investments

The following investments are legally permitted by Federal Regulations and authorized by the Board.

1. U.S. Treasury securities
2. U.S. government agency and agency-guaranteed securities
3. Certificates of deposit and bankers acceptances

   a. Insured CDs. Negotiable and nonnegotiable CDs of any domestic commercial bank or savings and loan association may be purchased.

   b. Uninsured CDs. Investment in excess of $100,000 in the CDs of a single domestic bank may be made only in those banks shown on the Approved List (Exhibit B).

   c. Eurodollar CDs. Investments may be made only in such CDs issued by banks on the Approved List.

   d. Yankee CDs. Investments may be made only in such CDs issued by banks on the Approved List.

   e. Banker's acceptances. Investments are limited to accepting banks on the Approved List.

   f. Federal funds sold. Sales of federal funds may be made only to those institutions on the Approved List.

   g. Repurchase agreements (repos).

      i. The term shall not exceed 30 days, although a continuous agreement (remaining in effect until cancelled) is allowed.

      ii. The securities acceptable for purchase under a repo are those issued by the U.S. Treasury and agencies of the U.S. government.

      iii. The institutions with which repos may be made are limited to those on the Approved List.

   h. Reverse repurchase agreements (reverse repos). Reverse repos may be used so long as no more than 40 percent of the funds so obtained are used to purchase additional securities.

E. Maturity of Investments

To control the risk of loss resulting from an increase in the level of interest rates, Management is restricted to investments that mature within five years. This restriction does not apply to securities repurchased under the provisions of a repurchase agreement.

F. Diversification Requirements

1. U.S. Treasury and agency securities. These may be held in unlimited quantities.

2. Securities not guaranteed by the U.S. Government, its agencies, or instrumentalities are subject to an overall maximum 10% commitment at cost.

G. Unauthorized Transactions

1. Short sales.

2. Adjusted Trades. The Bank may not hide an investment loss by an adjusted trade—that is, selling a security at a fictitiously high price to a dealer and simultaneously buying another overpriced security from the same dealer.

[Exhibits and other sections omitted.]

5.2 Other Institutional Investors: Investment Intermediaries

As we define the term, institutional investors are financial intermediaries in various legal forms with relatively large amounts of money to invest. The institutional investors previously discussed in this reading (pension plans, foundations, endowments, insurance companies, and banks) have well-defined purposes besides investing. Banks take deposits and make loans, for example; pension plans have the specific purpose of providing retirement income.

Investment companies constitute another type of institutional investor that is important in financial markets. Investment companies include such investment vehicles as mutual funds (open-end investment companies), closed-end funds (closed-end investment companies), unit trusts, and exchange-traded funds. All these vehicles represent pooled investor funds invested in equity and fixed-income markets. Investment companies are pure investment vehicles in the sense that they have no other corporate purpose besides investing. We might aptly call them investment intermediaries. Each investment company selects its specific investment objectives and describes objectives, constraints, and costs in legally prescribed formats (e.g., a prospectus) and draws in funds from investors who are attracted to it for various portfolio purposes. Commodity pools serve similar purposes, but in futures rather than equity and fixed-income markets. Hedge funds are another type of investment vehicle that falls under the rubric of institutional investors. Hedge funds differ from investment companies in that they market to other institutional investors and to high-net-worth individuals exclusively; in addition, they are subject to fewer regulations.

One cannot generally characterize the investment objects and constraints of a given type of investment intermediary with the expectation that it will apply to all members of the group. Mutual funds, for example, cover the range of equity and fixed-income investment styles; one cannot characterize the return requirement and risk tolerance of "a mutual fund" in general, as we have done for other institutional investors such as life insurers. Readers who may be involved in managing equity or fixed-income mutual funds will find relevant guidance in the readings on equity portfolio management and fixed-income portfolio management, respectively.

Nonfinancial corporations (i.e., businesses), although not financial intermediaries, are major investors in **money markets** (markets for fixed-income securities with maturities of one year or less) to manage their cash positions. "Cash," of course, includes "liquid cash" such as funds held in demand deposits and very short-term money market securities, and "long-term" or "core" cash, which is invested in longer-term money market instruments. These investments are part of the corporate function of cash management, which typically falls under the responsibilities of an organization's corporate treasurer. For most companies, liquidity and safety of principal are paramount investment considerations in cash management. Companies with very large cash positions will actively manage the composition of the cash position relative to anticipated cash needs (including seasonal needs), nondomestic currency needs, and tax concerns. Cash management is an important function for all the institutional investors previously discussed as well as for governmental units.[35]

---

[35] See Kallberg and Parkinson (1993) for more on cash management.

SUMMARY

This reading has described the investment contexts in which institutional investors operate. Our chief focus has been the development of an investment policy statement for defined-benefit pension plans, defined-contribution pension plans, endowments, foundations, life insurance companies, non-life insurance companies, and banks. We have discussed the specific considerations that enter into the development of appropriate return and risk objectives. We then addressed liquidity requirements, time horizon, tax concerns, legal and regulatory factors, and unique circumstances.

► The two major types of pension plan are defined-benefit (DB) plans and defined-contribution (DC) plans. A defined-benefit plan specifies the plan sponsor's obligations in terms of the benefit to plan participants. In contrast, a defined-contribution plan specifies the sponsor's obligations in terms of contributions to the pension fund rather than benefits to participants.

► DB pension assets fund the payment of pension benefits (liabilities). The investment performance of a DB plan should be judged relative to its adequacy in funding liabilities even if it is also judged on an absolute basis. The funded status of a DB plan is the relationship of the plan assets to the present value of plan liabilities, and is usually measured with respect to the projected benefit obligation (PBO) definition of plan liabilities.

► In setting a risk objective, DB plan sponsors need to consider plan funded status, sponsor financial status and profitability, sponsor and pension fund common risk exposures, plan features (such as provision for lump-sum distributions), and workforce characteristics.

► A DB pension plan's broad return objective is to achieve returns that adequately fund its pension liabilities on an inflation-adjusted basis. An appropriate return requirement for a fully funded plan is the discount rate applied to pension liabilities. The pension fund's stated return desire may be higher and may reflect considerations relating to reducing pension contributions or increasing pension income.

► For DB plans, liquidity requirements relate to the number of retired lives, the size of contributions in relation to disbursements, and plan features. Factors affecting the time horizon length include whether the plan is a going concern, the age of the workforce, and the proportion of retired lives.

► Defined-contribution plans fall into two types: those in which the plan sponsor sets investment policy, and those in which the plan participants individually set policy. The investment process for the sponsor-directed plans is a simpler version of the process for DB plans.

► For participant-directed DC plans, the principal issues are offering participants sufficient investment choices and avoiding inadequate diversification because of holdings of the sponsor company's stock.

► Hybrid pension plans combine features of DB and DC plans. A cash balance plan is a hybrid plan in which the promised benefit is shown as a balance in a participant-individualized statement. Another important type of hybrid plan is the Employee Stock Ownership Plan (ESOP), a type of DC plan entirely or primarily invested in the employer's stock.

► Foundations are grant-making institutions. Private foundations are typically subject to a payout requirement that specifies a minimum level of spending. Endowments are generally not subject to a legal spending requirement.

Endowments typically provide vital support of ongoing operations and programs of institutions such as universities, hospitals, museums, and religious organizations.

▶ The return objective for most foundations (and endowments) can be stated as the sum of the annual spending rate, the cost of generating returns (managing assets), and the expected inflation rate. A multiplicative formulation of the components is more precise than an additive one in specifying the return level that should allow the foundation or endowment to preserve the inflation-adjusted value of assets over many periods.

▶ A foundation's investment policy can often be more risk tolerant than the investment policy of DB plans because foundation assets need not be managed with respect to a stream of legal liabilities, in general. Endowment risk tolerance often depends on the importance of the endowment to the supported institution's operating budget as reflected in the spending rate, and the use of a smoothing rule for spending, which dampens the portfolio's sensitivity to short-run volatility.

▶ A foundation or endowment's liquidity requirements come from both anticipated and unanticipated cash needs in excess of contributions received. Anticipated needs are captured in the periodic distributions prescribed by a foundation's or endowment's spending rate. Generally time horizons are long. A variety of legal and regulatory issues can affect a foundation or endowment's investment activities.

▶ Insurance companies play a role in absorbing personal and business risks. Insurers are broadly divided into life insurers and non-life insurers (casualty insurers); the two groups have distinct investment concerns.

▶ Historically, return requirements for life insurers have been tied to the interest rates used by actuaries to determine policyholder reserves or accumulation rates for the funds being held by a company for future disbursement. Actual return objectives have been less clearly defined but may relate to an interest rate spread concerning liabilities.

▶ Insurers have moved towards segmenting their portfolios in relation to associated liabilities and setting return objectives by major line of business. The result is that a single company's investment policy may incorporate multiple return objectives. Furthermore, many companies have established separate investment policies, and strategies, for each segment of their portfolios.

▶ Because of public policy concerns related to payment of insurance benefits, insurer portfolios are viewed as quasi-trust funds from a public policy perspective. As a result, conservative fiduciary principles limit the risk tolerance of both life and non-life insurers.

▶ As one consequence of the need for managing risk with respect to their contractual liabilities, insurers use a variety of asset/liability management techniques.

▶ Life insurance companies have valuation concerns (related to prescribed valuation reserves), reinvestment risk, credit risk, and cash flow volatility.

▶ The liquidity concerns associated with disintermediation of cash value policies, asset/liability mismatch, and asset marketability risk have increased insurers' traditionally relatively minimal liquidity requirements.

▶ Life insurers have been viewed as the classic long-term investor. As a result of portfolio segmentation, life insurers may establish relatively shorter time horizons for some portfolio segments (e.g., group annuities).

▶ As a regulated industry, life insurers face many regulatory and legal constraints including those relating to eligible investments, the prudent investor rule, and valuation methods.

▶ In contrast to life insurers, non-life insurers typically have shorter-term liabilities. The underwriting (profitability) cycle may require non-life insurers to liquidate investments to supplement cash flow shortfalls. For both of these reasons, non-life insurers have much shorter investment time horizons than do life insurers.

▶ Return requirements reflect competitive pricing policy, profitability concerns, and the requirement for a growing surplus to support the writing of new business.

▶ A bank's portfolio investments are a residual use of funds after loan demand has been met. The portfolio's overall objectives are to manage the interest rate risk of the balance sheet, manage liquidity, produce income, and manage credit risk. The bank's return objective is to earn a positive spread over the cost of funds. Banks typically have below-average risk tolerance, and liquidity is a key concern. Bank investment is subject to a range of legal and regulatory factors.

▶ Investment companies such as mutual funds as well as commodity pools and hedge funds are institutional investors that function as investment intermediaries. In contrast to other types of institutional investors, one cannot generalize about the investment objectives and constraints of these types of investors.

▶ Among institutional investors, ALM considerations are particularly important for DB pension funds, insurance companies, and banks.

1. *Worden Technology, Inc.*

Based in London, Worden Technology, Inc. is an established company with operations in North America, Japan, and several European countries. The firm has £16 billion in total assets and offers its employees a defined-benefit pension plan.

Worden's pension plan currently has assets of £8.88 billion and liabilities of £9.85 billion. The plan's goals include achieving a minimum expected return of 8.4 percent with expected standard deviation of return no greater than 16.0 percent. Next month, Worden will reduce the retirement age requirement for full benefits from 60 years to 55 years. The median age of Worden Technology's workforce is 49 years.

Angus Williamson, CFA, manages the pension plan's investment policy and strategic asset allocation decisions. He has heard an ongoing debate within Worden Technology about the pension plan's investment policy statement. Exhibit 1 compares two IPSs under consideration.

EXHIBIT 1	Investment Policy Statements	
	IPS X	**IPS Y**
Return requirement	Plan's objective is to outperform the relevant benchmark return by a substantial margin.	Plan's objective is to match relevant benchmark return.
Risk tolerance	Plan has a high risk tolerance because of the long-term nature of the plan and its liabilities.	Plan has a low risk tolerance because of its limited ability to assume substantial risk.
Time horizon	Plan has a very long time horizon because of its infinite life.	Plan has a shorter time horizon than in the past because of plan demographics.
Liquidity requirement[a]	Plan has moderate liquidity needs to fund monthly benefit payments.	Plan has minimal liquidity needs.

[a] Assume Worden will not contribute to its pension plan over the next several years.

Identify which investment policy statement, X or Y, contains the appropriate language for each of the following components of Worden Technology's pension plan:

    i. Return requirement.

    ii. Risk tolerance.

    iii. Time horizon.

    iv. Liquidity.

Justify your choice in each instance.

2. *LightSpeed Connections*

Hugh Donovan is chief financial officer of LightSpeed Connections (LSC), a rapidly growing U.S. technology company with a traditional defined-benefit pension plan. Because of LSC's young workforce, Donovan believes the pension plan has no liquidity needs and can thus invest aggressively to maximize returns. He also believes that U.S. Treasury bills and bonds, yielding 5.4 percent and 6.1 percent, respectively, have no place in a portfolio with such a long time horizon. His strategy, which has produced excellent returns for the past two years, has been to invest the portfolio as follows:

▶ 50 percent in a concentrated pool (15 to 20 stocks) of initial public offerings in technology and Internet companies, managed internally by Donovan;

▶ 25 percent in a small-capitalization growth fund;

▶ 10 percent in a venture capital fund;

▶ 10 percent in an S&P 500 index fund; and

▶ 5 percent in an international equity fund.

Working with LSC's Investment Committee, the firm's president, Eileen Jeffries, has produced a formal investment policy statement, which reads as follows:

"The LSC Pension Plan's return objective should focus on real total returns that will fund its long-term obligations on an inflation-adjusted basis. The "time-to-maturity" of the corporate workforce is a key element for any defined pension plan; given our young workforce, LSC's Plan has a long investment horizon and more time available for wealth compounding to occur. Therefore, the Plan can pursue an aggressive investment strategy and focus on the higher return potential of capital growth. Under present U.S. tax laws, pension portfolio income and capital gains are not taxed. The portfolio should focus primarily on investments in businesses directly related to our main business to leverage our knowledge base."

A. Evaluate Donovan's investment strategy with respect to its effect on each of the following:

 i. LSC's pension plan beneficiaries.

 ii. Managing pension assets in relation to LSC's corporate strength.

B. Evaluate LSC's investment policy statement in the context of the following:

 i. Return requirement.

 ii. Risk tolerance.

 iii. Time horizon.

 iv. Liquidity.

3. *Gwartney International*

U.S.-based Gwartney International (GI) is a financially healthy, rapidly growing import/export company with a young workforce. Information regarding GI's defined-benefit pension plan (which is subject to ERISA) appears in Exhibits 2 and 3.

EXHIBIT 2

Asset Class	Actual and Target Allocation (%)	Prior-Year Total Return (%)
Large-capitalization U.S. equities	35	10.0
Small-capitalization U.S. equities	10	12.0
International equities	5	7.0
Total equities	50	
U.S. Treasury bills (1-year duration)	10	4.5
U.S. intermediate-term bonds and mortgage-backed securities (4-year duration)	17	1.0
U.S. long-term bonds (10-year duration)	23	19.0[1]
Total fixed income	50	
Total	100	10.0

[1] Income element 7.0%; price gain element 12.0%.

EXHIBIT 3

Present value of plan liabilities	$298 million
Market value of plan assets	$300 million
Surplus	$2 million
Duration of liabilities	10 years
Actuarial return assumption	7.0%
GI board's long-term total return objective	9.0%

In accordance with GI policy, the plan discounts its liabilities at the market interest rate for bonds of the same duration. GI's risk objectives include a limitation on volatility of surplus.

Giselle Engle, the newly appointed chief financial officer, must explain to the board of directors why the surplus declined in a year when the actual investment return was 100 basis points more than the long-term objective stated by the board.

A. Explain how the plan surplus could decline in a given year despite an actual return in excess of the long-term return objective.

B. Explain the importance of an appropriate investment time horizon when setting investment policy for GI's corporate pension plan.

C. Discuss the risk tolerance of GI's corporate pension plan.

4. *Food Processors, Inc.*

Food Processors, Inc. (FPI) is a mature U.S. company with declining earnings and a weak balance sheet. Its defined-benefit pension plan (which is subject to ERISA) has total assets of $750 million. The plan is underfunded by $200 million by U.S. standards—a cause for concern by shareholders, management, and the board of directors.

The average age of plan participants is 45 years. FPI's annual contribution to the plan and the earnings on its assets are sufficient to meet pension payments to present retirees. The pension portfolio's holdings are equally divided between large-capitalization U.S. equities and high-quality, long-maturity U.S. corporate bonds. For the purpose of determining FPI's contribution to the pension plan, the assumed long-term rate of return on plan assets is 9 percent per year; the discount rate applied to determine the present value of plan liabilities, all of which are U.S.-based, is 8 percent. As FPI's Treasurer, you are responsible for oversight of the plan's investments and managers and for liaison with the board's Pension Investment Committee.

At the committee's last meeting, its chair observed that both U.S. stocks and U.S. bonds had recorded total returns in excess of 12 percent per year over the past decade. He then made a pointed comment: "Given this experience, we seem to be overly conservative in using only a 9 percent future return assumption. Why don't we raise the rate to 10 percent? This would be consistent with the recent record, would help our earnings, and should make the stockholders feel a lot better."

EXHIBIT 4	Capital Markets Data			
Asset Class	**Total Return 1929–1993 (%)**	**Total Return 1984–1993 (%)**	**Annualized Monthly Standard Deviation 1984–1993 (%)**	**Consensus Forecast Total Return 1994–2000 (%)**
U.S. Treasury bills	3.7	6.4	2.2	3.5
Intermediate-term Treasury bonds	5.3	11.4	5.6	5.0
Long-term Treasury bonds	5.0	14.4	11.7	6.0
U.S. corporate bonds (AAA rated)	5.6	14.0	8.9	6.5
U.S. common stocks (S&P 500)	9.5	14.9	18.0	8.5
U.S. inflation rate (annual rate)	3.2	5.5	N/A	3.3

You have been directed to examine the situation and prepare a recommendation for next week's committee meeting. Your assistant has provided you with the background information shown in Exhibit 4.

Assume that consensus forecast total returns for bonds are at least approximately equal to the bonds' yields.

A. Explain what is meant when a pension plan is said to be "underfunded" and use FPI to illustrate.

B. Discuss the risk–return dilemma that FPI faces.

C. Explain a rationale for reducing the discount rate from its current level of 8 percent.

D. Explain how the underfunded condition of FPI's plan would be affected if the discount rate were reduced to 7 percent from the current 8 percent.

5. *Medical Research Foundation*

The Medical Research Foundation (MRF), based in the United States, was established to provide grants in perpetuity. MRF has just received word that the foundation will receive a $45 million cash gift three months from now. The gift will greatly increase the size of the foundation's endowment from its current $10 million. The foundation's grant-making (spending) policy has been to pay out virtually all of its annual net investment income. Because its investment approach has been conservative, the endowment portfolio now consists almost entirely of fixed-income assets. The finance committee understands that these actions are causing the real value of foundation assets and the real value of future grants to decline because of inflation effects. Until now, the finance committee believed it had no alternative to these actions, given the large immediate cash needs of the research programs being funded and the small size of the foundation's capital base. The foundation's annual grants must at least equal 5 percent of its assets' market value to maintain MRF's U.S. tax-exempt status, a requirement that is expected to continue indefinitely. The foundation anticipates no additional gifts or fundraising activity for the foreseeable future.

Given the change in circumstances that the cash gift will make, the finance committee wishes to develop new grant-making and investment policies. Annual spending must at least meet the 5 percent of market value requirement, but the committee is unsure how much higher spending can or should be. The committee wants to pay out as much as possible because of the critical nature of the research being funded; however, it understands that preserving the real value of the foundation's assets is equally important in order to preserve its future grant-making capabilities. You have been asked to assist the committee in developing appropriate policies.

A. Identify and discuss the three key elements that should determine the foundation's grant-making (spending) policy.

B. Formulate and justify an investment policy statement for the foundation.

6. *James Children's Hospital*

The James Children's Hospital (JCH), based in Washington, DC, has an operating budget of $15 million and has been operating at a budget surplus for the last two years. JCH has a $20 million endowment (JCHE) whose sole purpose is to provide capital equipment for the hospital. The endowment's long-term expected total return is 8.6%, which includes a 3.3% income component. JCHE has no minimum payout requirement and expects no future contributions. Traditionally, the JCHE board of directors has determined the annual payout based on current needs. Payouts have been rising steadily—to $1,375,000 two years ago and to $1,400,000 last year.

Michelle Parker, chief financial officer of JCHE, has asked the board's guidance in establishing a long-term spending policy for JCHE. She has received $1,600,000 in requests to buy equipment and is concerned about the inflation rate for medical equipment prices, which is 4%, versus 2.5% for the U.S. Consumer Price Index.

A. Discuss the implications of the current pressure on JCHE to increase spending.

B. Discuss how JCHE's time horizon affects its risk tolerance.

C. Determine a long-term spending policy for JCHE, including a spending rate as a percentage of assets, and justify the policy.

7. *Donner Life Insurance*

Susan Leighton, treasurer for U.S.-based Donner Life Insurance, has just joined the board of a charitable organization that has a large endowment portfolio. She is researching how the investment policy for an endowment differs from that of life insurance companies and has thus far reached the following conclusions:

1. Both endowments and life insurance companies have aggressive return requirements.

2. Endowments are less willing to assume risk than life insurance companies because of donor concerns about volatility and loss of principal.

3. Endowments are less able to assume risk than life insurance companies because of expectations that endowments should provide stable funding for charitable operations.

4. Endowments have lower liquidity requirements than life insurance companies because endowment spending needs are met through a combination of current income and capital appreciation.

5. Both endowments and life insurance companies are subject to stringent legal and regulatory oversight.

Evaluate each of Leighton's statements in terms of accuracy and justify your conclusions.

8. *Hannibal Insurance Company*

U.S.-based Hannibal Insurance Company sells life insurance, annuities, and guaranteed investment contracts (GICs) and other protection-based and savings-based products. The company has traditionally managed its investments as a single portfolio, neither segmenting the assets nor segregating the surplus. The following data describe the portfolio:

EXHIBIT 5	Hannibal Insurance Portfolio Data	
	Four Years Ago	**Last Year**
Assets (reserves and surplus portfolio)	$450 million	$500 million
Duration of assets	6.0 years	6.0 years
Liabilities	$390 million	$470 million
Estimated duration of liabilities	5.5 years	4.0 years

The company attributes the decline in the duration of its liabilities to increases in interest rates and the passage of time.

Hannibal's chief financial officer (CFO) has instructed the portfolio manager as follows: "The rapidly increasing popularity of our two-year fixed rate GIC product has increased our asset base substantially during the last year. Interest rates have been rising and will probably rise another 100 basis points this year. You should continue to take advantage of this situation by investing in higher-yielding, investment-grade, longer-duration bonds in order to maximize our spread and maintain a constant duration of the assets. This strategy will ensure the delivery of a competitive return to our customers."

A. Judge the appropriateness of Hannibal's investment strategy as stated by the CFO. Prepare two arguments that support your position.

B. Evaluate two factors that would affect liability duration for a life insurance company other than changes in interest rates and the passage of time. Relate the two factors to the specific situation at Hannibal. Assume stable mortality rates.

C. Determine the suitability of the segmentation approach to portfolio management at Hannibal Insurance Company. Prepare three arguments that support your position.

D. Contrast the return requirement of the surplus portfolio to the return requirement of policyholder reserves, in regard to U.S. life insurance companies in general.

9. *Winthrop Bank*

Winthrop Bank is a commercial bank with operations in North America. Evaluate the effect of each of the following scenarios on the bank's investment objectives, constraints, or risk-taking ability.

A. The target average maturity of loans is increased, with overall risk tolerance unchanged.

B. The ALCO decides to increase Winthrop Bank's credit standards for loans although Winthrop Bank's overall risk tolerance is unchanged.

C. Winthrop decides to sell its mortgage loans as soon as they are booked.

D. More opportunities exist for expanding net interest margins with low risk in Winthrop's loan portfolio than in its securities portfolio.

SOLUTIONS FOR READING 20

1. *Worden Technology, Inc.*

IPS Y and IPS X offer different components that are appropriate for Worden Technology's pension plan:

i. *Return requirement.* IPS Y has the appropriate return requirement for Worden's pension plan. Because the plan is currently underfunded, the manager's primary objective should be to make it financially stronger. The risk inherent in attempting to maximize total returns would be inappropriate.

ii. *Risk tolerance.* IPS Y has the appropriate risk tolerance for Worden's plan. Because of its underfunded status, the plan has a limited risk tolerance; a substantial loss in the fund could further jeopardize payments to beneficiaries.

iii. *Time horizon.* IPS Y has the appropriate time horizon for Worden's plan. Although going-concern pension plans usually have long time horizons, the Worden plan has a comparatively short time horizon because of the company's reduced retirement age and relatively high median age of its workforce.

iv. *Liquidity.* IPS X has the appropriate liquidity constraint for Worden's plan. Because of the early retirement feature starting next month and the age of the workforce (which indicates an increasing number of retirees in the near future), the plan needs a moderate level of liquidity to fund monthly payments.

2. *LightSpeed Connections*

A. **i.** Concentrating LSC's pension assets as Donovan has done subjects the plan beneficiaries to an extraordinarily high level of risk because of the high correlation between the market values of the portfolio and LSC's business results.

ii. By concentrating the pension assets heavily in technology and Internet companies, Donovan has increased the company's risk as the pension plan's sponsor. LightSpeed now faces the prospect of having to provide additional funding to the pension plan at a time when the company's own cash flow and/or earnings position may be weakened. A more prudent approach would be to invest in assets expected to be less highly correlated with the company's market value, so in the event additional funding for the pension plan becomes necessary, it will be less likely to occur when LSC is in a weakened financial position.

B. **i.** The IPS drafted by Jeffries and the investment committee correctly identifies that the return requirement should be total return, with a need for inflation protection that is sufficient to fund the plan's long-term obligations. The IPS is weak in that it neglects to state a specific return requirement.

ii. The IPS fails to address the pension plan's risk tolerance, one of the two main objectives of a complete investment policy statement. Consequently, the IPS does not provide the guidance on risk tolerance that would highlight the potential risk to the beneficiaries and the company of LSC's current aggressive investment strategy.

      iii. The IPS correctly addresses the time horizon constraint by stating that the assets are long-term in nature, both because of LSC's young workforce and the normal long-term nature of pension investing.

      iv. The IPS fails to address the liquidity constraint; although liquidity is a minimal concern in this case, the IPS should nonetheless address that fact.

3. *Gwartney International*

    A. The amount of surplus will decline when the present value of plan liabilities rises faster than the market value of the assets. According to the information provided, GI's liabilities have a duration of 10 years, the same as U.S. long-term bonds which returned a total of 19% for the previous year (7% income, 12% from capital gains associated with a decline in interest rates for the period). The decline in interest rates for long-term bonds translates into a lower discount rate for the plan's liabilities. The 12% gain in bonds implies that the plan's liabilities would have increased by the same amount. The combination of a 12% gain in liabilities and a 10% return on assets resulted in a decrease in the pension plan's surplus.

    B. Investment time horizon is a primary determinant of an investor's risk tolerance. GI has a young workforce with many years until retirement, indicating a long time horizon. GI should thus adopt a long investment horizon, allowing investment in higher-risk, higher-expected-return asset classes.

    C. The plan's risk tolerance embodies the plan sponsor's ability and willingness to absorb the consequences of adverse investment outcomes and/or prolonged subpar investment performance (i.e., its sensitivity to the possibility of being required to increase contributions at unpredictable times and intervals). The less risk an investor can tolerate, the less return will be achieved in the long run.

        GI is financially healthy and growing. Given its financial health, the company has the ability to increase contributions when necessary. Because of GI's young workforce, the pension plan has a long time horizon, allowing for investment in riskier assets. The plan is also currently fully funded, and GI is financially strong. All these considerations point to GI having an above-average risk tolerance.

4. *Food Processors, Inc. (FPI)*

    A. In the United States, every ERISA-qualified defined-benefit pension plan has a projected benefit obligation, which represents the discounted present value of the retirement benefits that the plan is obligated by law to make, given certain assumptions about future rates of pay and workforce factors. If the plan assets at fair market value exceed the PBO, the plan is said to be overfunded. Conversely, if the value of the plan assets falls short of the PBO, the plan is said to be underfunded. Given that FPI's plan is underfunded by $200 million and its assets total $750 million, its PBO must be $950 million.

    B. FPI faces a dilemma. On the one hand, it needs to improve returns in order to "catch up" on its underfunding; this necessity implies that more risk should be taken. On the other hand, FPI cannot afford to have the underfunding become worse, which it would if FPI incurs more risk that does not produce higher returns in the short run. Alternatively, the company might be tempted, as the chair suggests, to raise the actuarial assumption of what future return levels will be, thereby making the asset base automatically more productive simply by declaring it to be so. Future returns, however, are generated not by actuaries or other individuals but by markets, by asset-class exposures within markets, and by long-term relationships between economic and market factors—all taking place in the context of funding, allocation, and payout decisions unique to FPI's pension plan.

Of primary importance is that the return expected must be consistent with the return the various alternative investment instruments available to the plan can reasonably offer in the long term.

C. A U.S. pension plan's discount rate is the rate applied in determining the present value of its pension obligations. Because pension liabilities are typically long term, the discount rate should bear some rational relationship to the long-term interest rates in the marketplace at the time of the calculation. The usual model for the discount rate is the rate at which high-quality, long-term bonds such as the long Treasury bond are quoted, reflecting consensus expectations of long-run inflation plus a real rate of return. Thus, a manager may decide to reduce the discount rate based on capital market conditions reflecting a decline in long-term interest rates, as seen in Exhibit 4. Based on the consensus forecasts for long-term Treasury bonds and inflation shown in Exhibit 4, a discount rate of 6 to 7 percent would be reasonable. FPI is currently using an 8 percent discount rate, which is out of line with current capital market conditions. FPI should thus consider adopting a lower discount rate.

D. Reducing the discount rate applied to FPI's PBO would have the effect of increasing the present value of FPI's pension benefit obligations. Because the market value of the assets available to liquidate this obligation remains unchanged, the underfunded situation would be made worse by a reduction in the discount rate. The size of the gap between the PBO and the value of the assets, now $200 million, would increase.

5. *Medical Research Foundation*

A. Key elements that should determine the foundation's grant-making (spending) policy are as follows:

▶ average expected inflation over a long horizon;

▶ average expected nominal return on the endowment portfolio over the same long horizon; and

▶ the 5 percent of asset value payout requirement imposed by the tax authorities as a condition for ongoing tax exemption.

To preserve the real value of its assets and to maintain its spending in real terms, the foundation cannot pay out more, on average over time, than the average real return it earns from its portfolio net of investment management expenses. The portion of the total return representing the inflation rate must be retained and reinvested if the foundation's principal is to grow with inflation. Because of the minimum 5 percent spending policy mandated by tax considerations, the real return of the portfolio will have to equal or exceed 5 percent plus the cost of earning investment returns in order to preserve the foundation's tax-exempt status and maintain its real value of principal and future payouts.

B. The new IPS should include the following components:

▶ *Return objective.* A total return approach is recommended to meet the foundation's objective of maintaining real value after grants.

The required annual return shall be the sum of the spending rate plus the expected inflation rate.[1]

▶ *Risk tolerance.* The adoption of a clear-cut spending policy will permit cash flows to be planned with some precision, adding stability to annual budgeting and reducing the need for liquidity. Based on its long time horizon, low liquidity needs, and (now) ample assets, the foundation's risk tolerance is above average.

▶ *Liquidity requirements.* Based on asset size and the predictable nature of cash payouts, liquidity needs are low.

▶ *Time horizon.* The foundation, with an unlimited lifespan, has a very long time horizon.

▶ *Tax considerations.* The foundation is tax-exempt under present U.S. law as long as the annual minimum payout of 5 percent is met.

▶ *Legal and regulatory constraints.* The foundation is governed by the Uniform Management of Institutional Funds Act (UMIFA) as well as IRS regulations.

▶ *Unique circumstances.* None apply, other than those previously discussed.

6. *James Children's Hospital (JCH)*

A. The current spending request of $1,600,000 represents $1,600,000/$20,000,000 = 0.08 or 8% of the value of the endowment. This level of spending is high given the endowment's long-term expected total return of 8.6 percent per year (in nominal terms) and expected 4 percent inflation rate for medical equipment prices. If such spending is permitted, the current beneficiaries of the JCHE (for example, the patients of JCH) may receive benefits at the expense of future beneficiaries, because the endowment is unlikely to be able to maintain its value in inflation-adjusted terms.

B. JCHE has a perpetual time horizon; it can thus tolerate a higher risk level (in terms of volatility of returns) than a fund with a shorter time horizon. The higher risk tolerance results from the longer period available to make up for any market downturns. With a higher risk tolerance, JCHE can target a higher expected return.

C. JCHE's long-term spending policy should balance the needs of current and future beneficiaries. Its spending policy should balance income needs and the need to build the payout stream to preserve purchasing power. JCHE balances these conflicting objectives only when future beneficiaries receive the same inflation-adjusted distribution that current beneficiaries receive. With zero real growth, intergenerational neutrality exists. Because market returns are variable, JCHE should use a smoothing mechanism that will apply the spending rate to a moving average of market value:

Expected total return	8.6%
− Inflation	−4.0
Real expected return	4.6
− Spending rate	−4.6
Expected real growth	0.0%
Recommended spending rate	4.6%

---

[1] This additive return objective is easy to understand; as discussed in the reading, a multiplicative return objective would be more precise.

7. *Donner Life Insurance*

Leighton made both incorrect and correct statements about life insurance and endowment portfolios:

1. *Both endowments and life insurance companies have aggressive return requirements* is an inaccurate statement. The return requirements of life insurance companies are first and foremost liability driven, matching assets with fixed obligations, and must be consistent with their conservative stance toward risk. Life insurance companies' return requirements also include, as an objective, the earning of a competitive return on the assets that fund surplus.

  The return requirements of endowments, although subject to a range of risk tolerances, are driven by the endowment's spending rate, the need to preserve purchasing power, and the need to provide a growing financial contribution to the endowed organization.

2. *Endowments are less willing to assume risk than life insurance companies because of donor concerns about volatility and loss of principal* is an inaccurate statement. Life insurance companies tend to have a lower tolerance for risk than endowments do. Confidence in a life insurance company's ability to pay its benefits (obligations) as they come due is a crucial element in the industry's financial viability. Life insurance companies thus are sensitive to the risk of any significant chance of principal loss or any significant interruption of investment income.

  Endowments, by contrast, tend to have a higher tolerance for risk. Their long-term time horizons and predictable cash flows, relative to their spending rate requirements, enable them to pursue more aggressive strategies than life companies can.

3. *Endowments are less able to assume risk than life insurance companies because of expectations that endowments should provide stable funding for charitable operations* is an inaccurate statement. Life insurance companies' ability to assume risk is circumscribed by their need to ensure the funding of liabilities to policyholders. The ALM focus of life insurance companies typically requires major holdings of bonds to offset the interest-sensitive nature of most life insurance liabilities. Regulations, including risk-based capital requirements, generally constrain the ability of life insurance companies to invest in higher risk assets.

  In contrast, the main risk facing an endowment is loss of purchasing power over time. Endowments have very long time horizons and are not focused on funding liabilities. Therefore, endowments should be able to accept higher volatility than life insurance companies in the short term to maximize long-term total returns.

4. *Endowments have lower liquidity requirements than life insurance companies because endowment spending needs are met through a combination of current income and capital appreciation* is an accurate statement. Life insurance companies face the need for liquidity as a key investment constraint, because life insurance products are promises to pay money depending on certain expected or unexpected events.

  Endowments typically have low liquidity needs, except to fund periodic distributions and to cover emergency needs. Distributions are usually foreseeable and can usually be met from a combination of investment income and the sale of readily marketable securities.

5. *Both endowments and life insurance companies are subject to stringent legal and regulatory oversight* is an inaccurate statement. Life insurance companies are subject to relatively rigorous legal and/or regulatory oversight with respect to their portfolio composition and investment strategies.

In contrast, endowments are relatively unburdened with legal and/or regulatory restraints, at least at the federal level in the United States, although some states do have specific rules and regulations regarding management of endowment assets.

8. *Hannibal Insurance Company*

A. The investment strategy of Hannibal Insurance Company is inappropriate, because the company is ignoring interest rate risk and the strategy threatens both the surplus and policyholder reserves.

Hannibal's investment strategy has three key negative consequences. First, the company faces major interest rate risk, as evidenced by the duration mismatch. Second, a focus on short-duration products will accelerate the mismatch. Finally, the company has not generated sufficient reserves and surplus relative to liabilities, given the risks it faces; thus it is increasing its risk of insolvency.

Given the interest rate sensitivity of many life insurance products, controlling interest rate risk is one of the most challenging tasks facing portfolio managers in the insurance industry. Although tolerance for interest rate risk, or level of mismatch, varies from company to company, duration mismatch can become an acute problem in periods of rising interest rates. Meeting the return objective of earning a significant spread is important, but assets and liabilities must be managed in a way that offsets the effects of changes in interest rates.

Confidence in an insurance company's ability to meet its obligations is so vital to the company's survival that special care must be taken to avoid any significant losses of principal. Hannibal has taken on a substantial amount of interest rate risk in recent years. Continuing a spread-maximization strategy in the face of rising interest rates threatens the firm's financial stability.

The mismatch must be corrected. Continuing along the path outlined by the CFO will magnify the interest rate risk, which the CFO is ignoring because of the "increasing popularity" of a short-duration product. As the duration of the assets is held steady through the CFO's urging to invest in higher-yielding, longer-duration bonds, the duration of the liabilities will shrink. The CFO is focusing on a spread-maximization strategy and mistakenly relying on investment-grade securities to provide policyholder security. The real danger lies in another direction—namely the potential forced sale of assets, with sizable losses resulting from interest rate increases, to pay off short-duration liabilities.

The company has a relatively small surplus portfolio. Surplus is an indicator of an insurance company's financial health and is vital to expansion of the business. If interest rates continue to rise as expected, the market value of the portfolio assets will decline, which may wipe out the surplus and a portion of policyholder reserves. With the company unable to expand or meet its obligations, its viability becomes questionable.

B. Two additional factors that affect liability duration for a life insurance company are 1) the duration of products sold and 2) policy surrenders and/or loans.

▶ The *duration of products sold* is a main driving force influencing the overall duration of liabilities. The extent to which a company directs marketing efforts toward short- or long-duration products will tilt overall duration. In this case, the company is placing a heavy emphasis on a two-year guaranteed investment contract product. The duration of this product will be much shorter than that of the overall portfolio. Management indicates that this product is popular, with sales increasing in recent years. This increase, all else being equal, will contribute to a decline in the duration of liabilities.

▶ Duration of liabilities is also driven by *policy surrender and/or loans*, either of which can be triggered by interest rate changes. Surrender rates triggered by interest rate changes are more difficult to predict than mortality rates and have become a critical variable for many life insurance companies. During periods of rising interest rates, policyholder redemptions accelerate as policyholders seek the most competitive rate. Such behavior would be typical in an environment in which "interest rates are rising and are expected to rise another 100 basis points." Accelerating surrenders could also influence an actuary to reduce the assumed duration of a company's liabilities.

C. Because of the varied features in life and annuity contracts, most life insurance companies segment their portfolios to group liabilities with similar interest-rate-sensitivity characteristics. Portfolios are then constructed by segment in such a way that the most appropriate securities fund each product segment. This practice also recognizes that particular product lines have unique time horizons and return objectives and should be managed accordingly.

Segmentation would be appropriate at Hannibal because of the problems arising from the popularity of a short-duration product. The portfolio manager could construct a portfolio targeted to the liabilities created by this product. Three arguments for the segmentation approach could be chosen from the following. Segmentation:

▶ aids in managing liabilities of similar characteristics;

▶ assists in the selection of the most appropriate assets to fund product segments (liabilities);

▶ aids in the management and/or measurement of interest rate risk and duration mismatch by product line;

▶ provides a framework for meeting return objectives by product line;

▶ provides for accurate measurement of the profitability of product lines and/or manager performance;

▶ provides for the allocation of investment income by line of business;

▶ provides for the measurement of risk-adjusted returns; and

▶ facilitates accountability and allays regulatory concerns.

D. The focus of the return requirement for policyholder reserves is on earning a competitive return on the assets used to fund estimated liabilities. Life insurance companies are considered spread managers, in that they manage the difference between the return earned on investments and the return credited to policyholders. Spread management can take various forms, such as a yield approach versus a total-return approach, but the objective remains the same.

The focus of the return requirement for the surplus is on long-term growth. An expanding surplus is an important indicator of financial stability and the base for building the lines of business. When selecting investments for the surplus portfolio, managers typically seek assets with the potential for capital appreciation, such as common stocks, venture capital, and equity real estate.

9. *Winthrop Bank*

A. Because the loan portfolio is now subject to greater interest rate risk, although overall risk tolerance has not changed, the target maturity of the securities portfolio must be reduced to offset the loan portfolio's greater risk.

B. Winthrop Bank should have more leeway to invest in below-investment-quality debt in its bond portfolio as a result.

C. Winthrop's decision decreases the need for liquidity in its securities portfolio.

D. The development suggests taking less risk in its securities portfolio.

LINKING PENSION LIABILITIES TO ASSETS

by Aaron Meder and Renato Staub

LEARNING OUTCOMES

The candidate should be able to:	Mastery
a. contrast the assumptions concerning pension liability risk in asset-only and liability-relative approaches to asset allocation;	☐
b. discuss the fundamental and economic exposures of pension liabilities and identify asset types that mimic these liability exposures;	☐
c. compare pension portfolios built from a traditional asset-only perspective to portfolios designed relative to liabilities and discuss why corporations may choose not to implement fully the liability mimicking portfolio.	☐

Pension assets exist to defease* the benefit promises made by plan sponsors to participants and beneficiaries—the pension liability. It follows that pension investment policies should be set in a way that explicitly integrates the exposures of the pension liability. Excluding the liability's exposures from the analysis is like setting a soccer team's starting lineup without fully considering the opposing team. This is analogous to the traditional approach to pension investing, which has resulted in portfolios that may be appropriate in an asset-only framework but are exposed to unrewarded risk when evaluated relative to liabilities. Efficient investment policies can be designed and thus unrewarded risk avoided if the exposures of the liability are explicitly integrated into the investment framework.

The intent of this reading is twofold:

► Provide insight into modeling the pension liability, focusing on which fundamental and economic factors influence its evolution.

---

*Render void; offset.

445

► Using the fundamental and economic factors that influence both assets and the pension liability we provide a framework to model assets and liabilities consistently.

While we focus on pension plans, the general framework put forth to link assets and liabilities via fundamental and economic factors is applicable to many situations where assets are set aside to defease a future obligation that has market related exposures. Thus, the framework can be generalized to insurance products, postretirement health benefits, or college savings plans.

1   INTRODUCTION

Some pension sponsors have not explicitly integrated the pension liability's fundamental and economic exposures into the investment policy decision. Instead, their process has focused on setting appropriate "asset-only" portfolios. Such a process may be the current paradigm because the plan's contribution requirement, accounting cost, and balance sheet are all currently based on a smoothed relationship between assets and liabilities, mitigating the impact of a mismatch between the two. Thus, many plan managers select portfolios from the asset-only efficient frontier, relying on the actuarial and accounting smoothing to keep the relationship between assets and liabilities relatively stable over the short horizon.

Selecting portfolios from an asset-only perspective implicitly assumes that the liability has no risk at all; at least none that is market related. By 'market related' we mean that the exposure is influenced by market related factors such as interest rates, inflation, or economic growth. However, pension liabilities, representing the present value of deferred wages, by their very nature are driven by economics and have many market related exposures. Not integrating these exposures can result in inefficient investment policies when measured versus liabilities, as they may be exposed to excessive and unrewarded risk relative to liabilities. Such unrewarded risk was masked by the bull market of the 1990s and subsequently unmasked by the storm of falling equity markets and interest rates that plagued the industry at the turn of the millennium. Couple this with the global pension regulatory environment trending towards unsmoothing pension assets and liabilities, and there is an increasing incentive to design investment policies that better integrate assets and liabilities.

Hence, in our investment framework, we allow for an *economic* liability.[1] This framework fundamentally changes the picture in that assets that mirror the economic liability (which becomes the investment benchmark), are considered low risk. Table 1 summarizes the fundamental difference between designing policies with an asset-only perspective versus a liability-relative perspective.

Clearly, in liability relative space the liability now takes center stage. Unfortunately, there is no investable asset that perfectly mimics the exposures of a pension liability. As a result, we must create the investment benchmark by constructing a portfolio of assets that best mimics the liability.

---

[1] The concept of an economic liability is not new. There is much literature in support of an economic view of the liability. [9] Treynor, et al., (1976), [2] Bookstaber and Gold (1988), [1] Arnott and Bernstein (1988), [7] Ryan and Fabozzi (2002) and most recently [10] Waring (2004) are examples.

TABLE 1	Asset-Only and Liability-Relative Perspectives	
	Asset Only	**Liability Relative**
Liability exposures	None	Term structure, inflation, growth
Risk-free investment/ Benchmark	Cash	Liability mimicking asset portfolio
Low risk investments	Low correlation with assets	High correlation with liability

HOW TO DEFINE RISK?   2

Developing the appropriate investment benchmark depends on the relevant investment horizon for defining investment risk.

If the plan sponsor defines risk as the risk that assets will not hedge the liability *over the next year*, then we must focus on short-term market-related liability exposures. This has been the focus of most advisors by using a portfolio of long duration bonds to proxy the liability. This approach captures the liability's exposure to short-term changes of the term structure.

However, modeling the term structure exposure only captures part of the liability risk. Arnott and Bernstein (1988) state that "the size of pensions the corporation pays in future years will have little to do with today's level of long-term interest rates" and Bookstaber and Gold (1988) say "those who act as if the world were defined only by cash flows and interest rate exposure, duration and dedication, see only part of the asset/liability picture." Rather, in order to see the full picture of pension fund investment risk, one must also focus on the volatility of the estimated benefit payments themselves and how they change over time. An emphasis only on the short-term liability may be sensible for the relatively few financially weak companies with poorly funded plans. However, most companies are relatively healthy with well funded ongoing plans and have the ability to focus on both long and short horizons.

For the relatively healthy company with an ongoing plan, risk is both the short-term volatility of plan costs and the long-term risk of pension assets being insufficient to defease the liability. Hence, liability modeling must deal with both horizons, and in particular, it must address the question of what the liabilities will look like in the future and how can we best hedge them as they evolve.

PENSION LIABILITIES DECOMPOSED   3

Again, pension liabilities vary in value like assets, and in order to measure investment risk relative to liabilities, we must understand how assets and liabilities are related. To put our approach in perspective, we will focus on a hypothetical defined benefit plan of People Corporation Inc., which has a typical liability profile and typical plan provisions.

As for assets, the value of a liability can be determined in two steps:

▶ estimating the expected benefit payments, i.e., the future cash outflows; and

▶ discounting them. That is:

$$V_L = \sum_t \frac{B_t}{(1 + r_t)^t} \qquad \text{(1)}$$

where V_L is the market value of the pension liability, B_t the benefit payment at time t, and r the appropriate discount rate. Liability risk is the volatility of its value and can be attributed to volatility in the discount rate and estimated benefit payments.

Consistent with asset pricing, the discount rate used for the economic liability must reflect the market related exposures of the benefit payments. For example, if the benefit payments increase with inflation then the investment benchmark would have a real rate bond component, and accordingly, the applicable discount rate should reflect the real rate bond risk premium used by the market to discount inflation linked cash flows.

Thus, we turn our attention to modeling the benefit payments and understanding their inherent fundamental and economic exposures, as these are what drive the interest rate used for discounting. Pension benefits are not known with certainty. They exhibit volatility attributable to volatility in wages, inflation, and many non-market-related factors; or growth attributable to future service costs, new entrants and other non-market-related factors.

The extent and causes of the uncertainty in pension benefits vary greatly by demographic group. Thus, modeling the variations in estimated benefits is easiest by decomposing the benefits into demographic groups whose benefit levels are driven by different exposures. These exposures are either market related or not. We address each in turn.

Market Related Exposures

1. Inactive Participants

These are the benefits attributable to participants currently receiving pension payments (retirees), or participants who are no longer working for the firm and are owed a benefit, but have not yet started receiving benefit payments (deferreds). The estimated benefit payments to this group are fixed, in a market related sense, unless they are indexed with inflation in order to protect the retiree's standard of living. Exhibit 1 shows People Corporation's estimated future inactive benefit payments.

EXHIBIT 1   Inactive Benefits

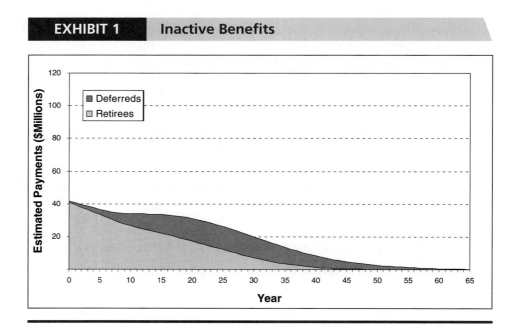

People Corporation's plan does not provide inflation indexing. Therefore the inactive benefit payments are fixed and hence the value of these benefit payments very "bond like" with the only market exposure being the exposure to the term structure. The portfolio of assets that best mimics such a liability is a bond portfolio whose cash flows match the estimated benefit payments. On the other hand, if the benefit payments are indexed with inflation, the benefit payments and thus the value of the liability will vary with the level of inflation. In this case, the investment benchmark is a mixture of real rate bonds and nominal bonds. If the plan provides full one for one inflation indexation the benchmark for this portion of the liability is 100% inflation linked bonds.

2. *Active Participants*

These are the estimated benefit payments associated with currently active employees. When modeling these benefit payments we slice the estimated benefit payments into two components: benefits attributable to past service rendered and wages earned (accrued benefits) and benefits attributable to future service and wages (future benefits).

2.1 Accrued Benefits These are benefits attributable to past service rendered and past wages earned. Like inactive benefits, they are fixed in a market related sense unless they are indexed with inflation in order to protect the participant's standard of living. Consistent with People Corporation's inactive benefits, there is no inflation indexation and therefore the investment benchmark will consist of nominal bonds. The present value of these benefits plus the inactive benefits represents the plan's liability attributable to "accrued benefits." Exhibit 2 shows People Corporation's estimated benefit payments attributable to accrued benefits.

| EXHIBIT 2 | Accrued Benefits |

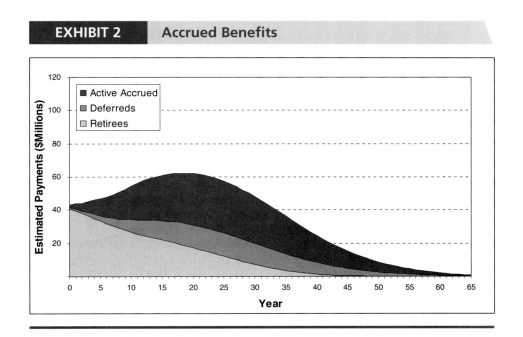

2.2 Future Benefits Future benefits are benefits attributable to future wages to be earned, future service to be rendered, and future new entrants into the plan. These benefits drive the evolution of the liability over the long term, but they will have very little impact on the pension plan's overall liability in the short term. For many plans, these benefits will dominate the liability in 20 years. Therefore, to the extent that these benefits are funded (and therefore at risk of becoming unfunded) and capital market driven (hedgeable), they need to be considered today when determining the investment benchmark.

For frozen pension plans, the liability attributable to future benefits is zero and therefore doesn't need to be considered.[2] That is, for frozen plans the accrued benefit liability is the ultimate liability of the plan and has market exposures that are best mimicked by a combination of nominal and index-linked bonds.

2.2.1 Future Wages   People Corporation's plan, along with many other plans, provides wage-related benefits. Assuming a certain rate of future wage increases, the actuary provides an estimate of benefit payments attributable to future wage increases. We will call the present value of these estimated benefit payments the "future wage liability." In many countries, the funding target is set equal to the accrued benefit liability plus future wage liability and therefore is the relevant investment benchmark. Using accounting nomenclature the accrued benefit liability plus the future wage liability is analogous to the projected benefit obligation in the U.S. under FAS 87 and the defined benefit obligation internationally under IAS19.

People Corporation assumes future wage increases of 4% per annum. These wage increases and the corresponding benefits are attributable to two economic forces: wage inflation and real wage growth. People Corporation assumes 2% wage inflation and 2% real wage growth. Exhibit 3 shows its estimated cash flows attributable to accrued benefits plus the future wage increases, split between future wage inflation and future real wage growth.

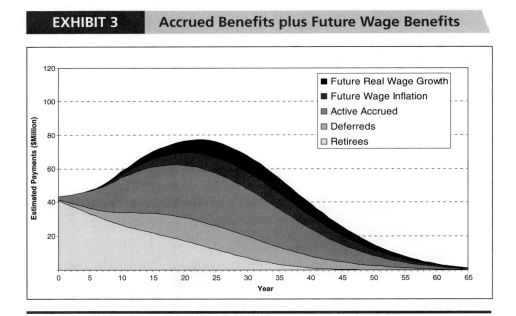

EXHIBIT 3   Accrued Benefits plus Future Wage Benefits

2.2.1.1 Future Wage Inflation   There is a long-term relationship between general inflation and wage inflation. Thus, cash flows of real rate bonds will vary similarly to the variations in the estimated benefit payments attributable to future wage inflation. However, People Corporation's wage inflation benefits for each

---

[2] These are plans where the accrued benefits are frozen and no future accruals will be granted.

active employee are only exposed to inflation until retirement. After retirement these benefit payments are fixed and no longer exposed to changes in inflation. As a result, a combination of real rate bonds and nominal bonds will be the investment benchmark for People Corporation's wage inflation liability.

2.2.1.2 Future Real Wage Growth   Real wage growth is linked with economic growth through labor's share of productivity increases. There is strong evidence for a stable share of labor in national income.[3] In other words, the real wage growth is linked with productivity increases. Dividends are also related to economic growth; therefore we expect a stable long-term relationship between the stock market and the GDP.[4] In order to portray this relationship, we regress the real U.S. GDP on the real S&P 500 and find:[5]

EXHIBIT 4	GDP Regressed on the S&P 500

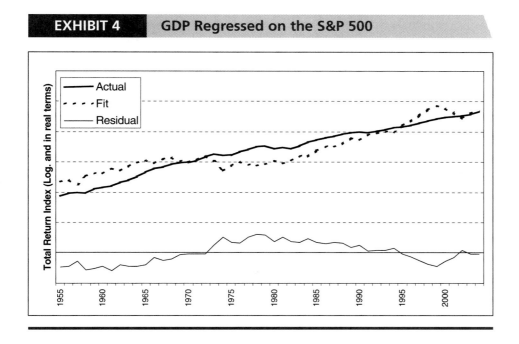

Very high t-statistics of 14 for the intercept and 27 for the slope, and an R^2 of 92% are evidence for a strong *long-term* relationship. However, this is not striking news, as there is much literature in support of this.[6]

Just like People Corporation's wage inflation benefits, its real wage growth benefits for each active employee are only exposed to real wage growth until retirement. After retirement these benefit payments are fixed and no longer exposed to changes in growth. As a result a combination of equities and nominal bonds will be the investment benchmark for People Corporation's real wage growth liability.

2.2.2 Future Service Rendered   To the extent that it is funded and hedgeable, we can expand our definition of the liability by including the benefit payments attributable to future service rendered. These are shown for People Corporation in Exhibit 5.

---

[3] See [8] Singer and Terhaar, p. 19.

[4] More precisely, we expect the stock market to anticipate the economy.

[5] The data series consists of annual observations.

[6] See for instance [3] Campbell, Lo, and MacKinlay, or [5] Fama and French.

EXHIBIT 5	Estimated Benefit Payments: Accrued Benefits plus Future Wages plus Future Service

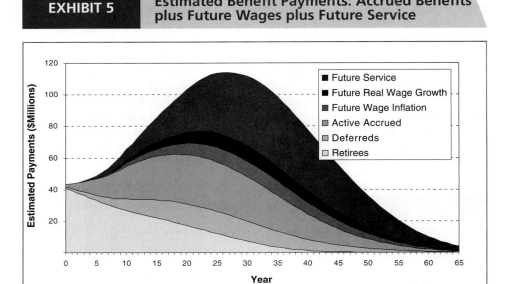

Just like the volatility of future wage benefits, the volatility of future service benefits is linked to wage growth. As wages grow, the service accruals granted will be based on higher wages, and thus the corresponding benefit payment will be higher. But in reality this portion of the liability is often not included in the funding target and relatively uncertain. Hence, it should be excluded from the investment benchmark.

3. Future Participants

Finally, if appropriate, we can fully expand our definition of the liability and include the estimated benefits attributable to future new entrants. For a plan closed to new entrants, this liability is zero and for an ongoing plan this portion of the liability is rarely funded to any extent, and the corresponding benefits are the most uncertain of all the benefits we've discussed. As a result, they should be excluded from the investment benchmark.

For People Corporation, the relevant investment benchmark is the accrued benefit liability plus the future wage liability. Table 2 summarizes the market related exposures for each portion of this benchmark along with the corresponding liability mimicking assets.

TABLE 2	Market Related Exposures and Liability Mimicking Assets	
Portion of the Investment Benchmark	**Market Related Exposures**	**Liability Mimicking Assets**
Inactive	Term structure	Nominal bonds
Active—accrued	Term structure	Nominal bonds
Active—future wage	Inflation	Real rate bonds
	Growth	Equities
	Term structure	Nominal bonds

Non-Market Related Exposures: Liability Noise

As mentioned above, the estimated benefit payments have both market related and non-market related exposures. We call the uncertainty in benefit payments attributable to non-market related exposures "liability noise." There are two components of liability noise:

► plan demographic experience differing from the actuary's model given that the underlying probabilities are certain; and

► model uncertainty—the fact that the underlying probabilities are not certain (e.g., mortality rate change due to medical innovations).

If the probabilities underlying the actuary's model are certain, the main factor that drives liability noise is the number of participants. Statistical methods can be used to estimate this component of noise; the larger the plan's population the more closely experience will track the model.[7] By its very nature, however, model uncertainty is difficult to estimate. The extent and causes of the liability noise vary greatly by demographic groups. We address inactive participants and then active participants.

1. Inactive Participants

For retirees, liability noise is attributable to one major source. Embedded within the actuarial projection of benefit payments is a mortality assumption about the length of people's lives and hence the duration they will be receiving benefits. To the extent that mortality experience differs from what was assumed, the benefit payments will vary accordingly. If people live longer than assumed, benefit payments will be larger and vice versa. At this point in time there are few liquid assets whose cash flows are linked with mortality. Thus, mortality exposure is currently difficult to hedge. However, there are bonds under development where the coupons are inversely linked to mortality, and an index linked to U.S. life expectancy has recently been developed.

In addition to longevity risk, a deferred's estimated benefits are based on an assumption about when the participant will retire and start receiving benefits. The sooner the participant elects to receive benefits the smaller the annual benefit the plan provides, as the participant is expected to receive it for a longer time. Thus, the uncertainty regarding the timing and amount of benefits coupled with mortality risk result in deferred liabilities being noisier and less hedgeable than retirees' liabilities.

2. Active Participants

In addition to a mortality assumption, active employees' estimated benefit payments are embedded with assumptions of withdrawal, disability, and retirement, and therefore are embedded with a large amount of uncertainty, much more so than those of retirees or deferreds. The estimated benefit payments for an employee who is many years away from retirement are based on a long string of probabilities and represent the actuary's best estimate regarding the plan's future obligation. Although we cannot hedge the noise, the greater the relative size of liability noise, the less hedgeable the liability.[8]

---

[7] [6] Leibowitz, et al., (1991) estimates that this component of liability noise "would range from 2% to 3% for a small group ($10-million liability) to just a small fraction of 1% for a liability of $1 billion."

[8] [6] Leibowitz, et al., (1991) claims that liabilities with noise in excess of 10% "offer little practical assistance in surplus management."

4   LINKING ASSETS AND LIABILITIES VIA FUNDAMENTAL FACTORS

As suggested above, pension liabilities have many market related and nonmarket related exposures. Based on the discussed exposures, we hypothesize that People Corporation's investment benchmark is some combination of nominal bonds, real rate bonds and equities. These are the cornerstone liability mimicking assets. The crucial question is: what is their appropriate combination? Using the economic and fundamental factors that underlie asset and liability values, we can formally link liabilities and assets and determine the investment benchmark.

We have demonstrated that the accrued benefit liability has primarily market related exposures to shifts in the discount rate, and thus the relevant factor is the term structure which entails the real rate, inflation, and a nominal bond premium. Further, the future wage liability is exposed to the change in wage level and thus economic growth and inflation. To the extent that the future wage liability is linked with economic growth, equity growth is a relevant factor as well. Finally, if the plan provides for some inflation indexation, the liability has some similarity with real rate bonds and thus is exposed to changes in the real rate bond premium.

On the other hand, the economic and fundamental factors underlying the cash flows provided by the assets are the real risk-free rate of return, the rate of inflation, the corresponding risk premia, and, in the case of equity, the rate of growth.

With these factors in mind we are ready for factor modeling. In a first step to that end, we determine the factors involved. The *Capital Asset Pricing Model* (CAPM) holds that an asset's fair return (expected return) entails the risk-free rate of return as a compensation for consumption deferral plus a risk premium commensurate with the asset's risk. Further, the risk-free rate can be disaggregated into the compensation for inflation and the real risk-free rate of return.

In practice, inflation is proxied by the change of the consumer price index (CPI), and the real risk-free rate is proxied by the T-bill return minus the inflation proxy. With regard to the risk premium, historical analysis, often combined with a forward-looking adjustment, helps to determine the risk premium as the difference between the asset's total return and the risk-free rate. Further, with regard to growth, we believe in a long-term relationship between the overall economy and the stock market.

Since assets and liabilities represent economic values, they can be modeled with the same underlying factors, as the above description implies. Table 3 shows our suggested factor covariance matrix, disaggregated into a correlation matrix and a column of standard deviations, i.e., it describes the relationships between the factors.[9]

Setting Asset and Liability Sensitivities

The next step in the process requires setting the *sensitivities* of assets and liabilities versus the factors. The sensitivities describe how much the value of the assets and liabilities move in response to a move in the corresponding factor.

---

[9] For a discussion of the parameters, see Appendix 21.

TABLE 3	Factor Covariance Matrix						
	Risk	Real Rate	Inflation	Growth	Equity Premium	Nominal Bonds Premium	Real Bonds Premium
Real Rate	0.80%	1.00		0.20	0.10	0.05	0.05
Inflation	0.80%		1.00	−0.10	0.20	0.20	
Growth	1.00%	0.20	−0.10	1.00	−0.10	0.10	0.05
Equity Premium	1.00%	0.10	0.20	−0.10	1.00	0.40	0.30
Nominal Bonds Premium	0.66%	0.05	0.20	0.10	0.40	1.00	0.85
Real Bonds Premium	0.40%	0.05		0.05	0.30	0.85	1.00

1. Assets

When determining the sensitivities of bonds it is useful to set up a model:

$$V_B = \sum_t \frac{CF_t}{(1 + r_t)^t} \qquad (2)$$

where CF are the cash flows and r is the discount rate. To the extent that the cash flows are fixed (as in the case of a nominal bond), the value is sensitive to changes in the real rate, inflation, and the nominal bond premium. If the cash flows are inflation linked as is the case with real rate bonds, then the bond will not be sensitive to changes in inflation since inflation affects the numerator and denominator in an offsetting way.

When modeling equities we utilize dividend discount models. For instance, according to the *Gordon Growth Model*, the intrinsic value of equity is:

$$V_E = \frac{D}{r - g} \qquad (3)$$

where D is the annual dividend payment, r the discount rate, and g the growth rate of the dividends.

From these valuation formulas, we can derive the sensitivities versus the underlying factors. As an example, consider bonds with a maturity of five years and a par yield of 5.5%. If the actual short-term risk-free rate moves by 100 basis points, the yield of a 5-year bond usually moves by less since:

▶ the 5-year yield is a function of the *actual* short-term risk-free rate and all expected *future* short-term rates (i.e., the forward rates); and

▶ there is no information about the future short-term rates, as they are further out. Hence, the market assumes they are close to their average, i.e., it anticipates *mean-reversion*.

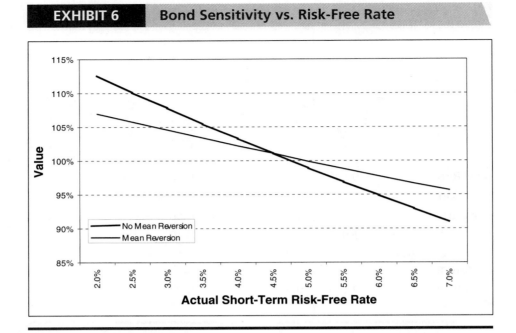

EXHIBIT 6   Bond Sensitivity vs. Risk-Free Rate

In Exhibit 6, the first case assumes that all expected future short-term rates move exactly by the same amount as the actual short-term risk-free rate, while the second case assumes that they still move in the same direction but by a decreasing amount the further out they are.

Specifically, the second case assumes mean reversion, while the first case does not. Since mean reversion mitigates the impact of a move of the actual short-term risk-free rate on the resulting discount rate, the corresponding bond value function is flatter than in the case of no mean reversion: we infer a decrease in bond value of approximately 2% in response to a 1% increase of the short term rate.

2. Liabilities

Since People Corporation's plan does not provide for inflation indexation, the accrued benefit liabilities' cash flows will be fixed in a market related sense. Visually the model for this portion of the liability looks identical to a bond.

$$V_{L-AB} = \sum_t \frac{B_t}{(1 + r_t)^t} \tag{4}$$

Essentially, we deal with a very long-term bond and hence, the key risk is a change in the discount rate.

People Corporation's future wage benefits are completely driven by wage inflation and real wage growth. In the case of s years till retirement, d years till demise and subsequent termination of the obligation, the intrinsic value of our future wage liability[10] is

$$V_{L-FW} = \frac{B}{r - g} \cdot \frac{((1 + g)^s - 1) \cdot ((1 + r)^{d-s} - 1)}{(1 + r)^d} \tag{5}$$

---

[10] For the derivation of Formula 5, see Appendix 21.

where r is the discount rate of the liability, and g the rate of growth. Comparing this with the present value of equity (Equation 3), one will notice that the liability has the same core structure as equity but also includes a correction factor.

As mentioned earlier, future wage benefits can be bifurcated into two components—future wage inflation and future real wage growth. In a market-related sense, the future wage inflation is completely driven by the actual inflation between now and each active employee's retirement. If People Corporation's plan provided for inflation indexation, the cash flow stream would almost exactly mimic the cash flow stream of real rate bonds. But inflation linkage only exists between now and retirement. Therefore, for active participants the closer to retirement they are the more certain and similar to nominal bonds are the cash flows. We approximate the active population's time to retirement by using the average future service calculated by the actuary; for People Corporation's plan it is 11 years. Any change in inflation from the assumed rate (2% in People Corporation's case) would compound itself on average for 11 years if the change in inflation persisted that long. However, our model assumes that the market anticipates inflation to revert over the medium term, that is, in less than 11 years. Based on our model, inflation changes have very little impact on this portion of the liability.

Just like the future wage inflation, cash flows are not driven indefinitely by inflation. Future real wage growth only applies until retirement. Again, we use the average future service to approximate the sensitivity of these cash flows to changes in future real wage growth. The key difference here is that we expect changes in growth to persist longer than we assume for inflation, and this expectation is mirrored in a higher sensitivity.

With regard to the discount rate, we recognize that the cash flows in the case of future real wage growth are equity linked prior to retirement and fixed thereafter. As a result, the cash flows are similar to both equities and bonds, and thus their corresponding discount rate should reflect both the bond premium and the equity premium.

The sensitivity matrix turns out to be:

TABLE 4 Sensitivity Matrix

	Real Rate	Inflation	Growth	Equity Premium	Nominal Bonds Premium	Real Bonds Premium
Liability—Accrued Benefit	−200%	−200%			−1000%	
Liability—Wage Inflation	−200%				−500%	−500%
Liability—Wage Growth	−200%	−200%	1500%	−600%	−600%	
Equity	−500%	−200%	1000%	−1000%		
Nominal Bonds	−200%	−200%			−550%	
Real Bonds	−200%					−450%

The final piece of information we need is an estimate of the residual risks, liability noise in the case of liabilities. When estimating liability noise, we know that the accrued benefit is less noisy than the future wage liability and thus more hedgeable. However, the focus of the paper is not on quantifying the liability noise and for this example we assume People Corporation's liabilities have no residual risk.[11]

Results

At this point, we have all necessary ingredients to calculate the risks of assets and liabilities and their mutual correlations. Based on our parameters, we find:

TABLE 5 Derived Covariance Matrix

	Risk	Liability— Accrued Benefit	Liability—Wage Inflation	Liability—Wage Growth	Equity	Nominal Bonds	Real Bonds
Liability—Accrued Benefit	7.4%	1.00	0.94	0.32	0.31	0.98	0.73
Liability—Wage Inflation	5.4%	0.94	1.00	0.27	0.26	0.90	0.88
Liability—Wage Growth	17.6%	0.32	0.27	1.00	0.92	0.32	0.16
Equity	15.5%	0.31	0.26	0.92	1.00	0.35	0.25
Nominal Bonds	4.6%	0.98	0.90	0.32	0.35	1.00	0.75
Real Bonds	2.5%	0.73	0.88	0.16	0.25	0.75	1.00
Real Estate	9.2%	0.16	0.14	0.42	0.48	0.21	0.21

Most important, as the derived covariance matrix demonstrates, while the accrued benefit liability is highly correlated with nominal and real bonds, the future wage liability is highly correlated with equity. This is in line with our previous recommendation: accrued benefits can be hedged best with a combination of nominal and real bonds, and the most appropriate hedge for benefits due to future wages is dominated by equity; the reason for this is the joint growth component.

Recombining the decomposed liability and the corresponding mimicking assets we get the following liability mimicking asset portfolio for People Corporation's pension fund.

	Nominal Bonds	Real Rate Bonds	Equities
Liability mimicking asset portfolio	85%	5%	10%

---

[11] [4] Ezra (1991) estimates the noise for a liability consisting of accrued benefits and future wages to be 7%. This estimate is attained by modeling the liability as a bond.

The allocation of People Corporation's liability mimicking asset portfolio is representative of their typical pay related liability profile. However, the resulting allocation is sensitive to many liability structural factors including the proportion of the future wage liability to the overall liability, the degree of inflation indexation, and the status of the plan (e.g., ongoing, closed, or frozen). For example, if the fund was less mature and/or had a higher proportion of future wage liability there would be a higher allocation to equities. If the plan offered full one-for-one inflation indexation via a cost of living allowance (COLA), you would see the nominal bonds replaced with real rate bonds. And, if the plan was frozen and therefore no longer had any exposures to future wage growth, there would be no real rate bonds or equities, only nominal bonds.

Designing Investment Policies Relative to Liabilities

People Corporation could invest in this liability mimicking portfolio and this would be the low risk investment. This means that investing in this portfolio results in the best chance of tracking the liability as it grows and evolves over time. In addition, this is also the appropriate investment benchmark. If the return on the fund's assets beats the return on the liability mimicking asset portfolio, all stakeholders should be satisfied since the pension promises will be paid.

However, by definition, investing in the liability mimicking portfolio will not provide an expected return in excess of the liability and therefore future service benefits and benefits earned by future participants would be defeased by future cash contributions.

Often, this low risk strategy will be too expensive for plan sponsors to maintain over the long run. Therefore, in most cases, we do not recommend investing in the low risk portfolio, but only measuring investment risk against it. The challenge is to find the most efficient way to allocate more assets to "higher returning" asset classes such as equities while minimizing the amount of unrewarded risk taken versus the liability. This can be approached in two steps.

1. Hedge the liability. Derivatives can be used to synthetically represent the market-related exposures of the liability mimicking asset portfolio. For example, interest rate derivatives can be used to mimic the term structure exposure of the liability—the liability's largest risk factor. And, utilizing derivatives to hedge requires far less capital than cash investment, thus, freeing up capital to be invested in "higher returning" assets.

2. Focus the remaining capital on efficient return generation. This can be done within asset-only space because once the liability has been hedged assets should not be given "credit" for further hedging.

This liability relative approach often leads to different investment policies than the traditional asset-only approach. The traditional approach typically leads to 60%–70% equities with the remainder in short and immediate duration nominal bonds. The liability relative approach, on the other hand, leads to investing in long duration nominal bonds, real rate bonds, equities and derivatives to hedge the liability, with the remainder invested in well-diversified return focused component.

CONCLUSION   5

The recent poor performance of pension plan assets versus liabilities has called into question the traditional approach to measuring investment performance—the asset only framework. This has brought about an increasing emphasis on measuring pension fund performance relative to what really matters—the plan's liabilities. Utilizing this framework can help plans avoid unrewarded investment risk like that experienced at the beginning of the decade.

Measuring risk relative to liabilities requires modeling of the liability and understanding the liability's market related exposures. Many practitioners to date have taken an overly simplistic approach by modeling the liability as a short position in a long duration bond. Such an approach focuses on short-term changes in the term structure used to discount the expected benefit payments, but does not capture the expected benefit payments exposures to inflation and economic growth.

Given the long-term relationship between equity and the GDP, appropriate hedging of the obligation requires some equity exposure as well. Without a doubt, stock markets and the GDP do not constantly move in line, as the stock market is much more cyclical, but the cyclicality is around the GDP, and this is why we stress the long-term nature of this relationship.

The long-term relationship between the GDP and the equity market is important for considerations such as pension fund liabilities. Since pension liabilities represent deferred wages, the future value of benefit payments is exposed to future economic growth and inflation. Therefore, for the majority of plans, we believe that the low risk investment benchmark consists of mostly nominal and real rate bonds with the remainder in equities.

Capturing the liabilities' beta exposures to inflation and economic growth can be accomplished by employing a multifactor approach consistently to both assets and liabilities.

Ultimately, a liability is indeed more complicated than a long duration bond and factoring in exposures to economic growth and inflation allows for a more robust measurement of liability relative to investment risk and performance.

And, when most sponsors take investment risk relative to liabilities, this can be done most efficiently by first hedging the liability with the aid of derivatives and then focusing on efficient return generation.

APPENDIX 21

Derivation of Formula 5

Assume the accrued benefit equals B, but grows in line with economic growth of g. Further, there are s years till retirement and d years till demise and termination of the obligation.

Then the present value of an eternal benefit obligation attributable to future wage growth (this does not include the accrued benefit portion of the liability) starting in s years equals

$$V_{Ls} = \frac{B}{r - g} \cdot \frac{(1 + g)^s - 1}{(1 + r)^s}$$

(1)

Next, the present value of the same eternal benefit obligation attributable to future wage growth (this does not include the accrued benefit portion of the liability) for s years till retirement but starting in d years equals

$$V_{Ld} = \frac{B}{r - g} \cdot \frac{(1 + g)^s - 1}{(1 + r)^d}$$

(2)

The present value of a benefit obligation attributable to future wage growth, starting in s years and ending in d years equals the difference between 1 and 2.

$$V_L = V_{Ls} - V_{Ld}$$

or

$$V_{L-FW} = \frac{B}{r - g} \cdot \frac{((1 + g)^s - 1) \cdot ((1 + r)^{d-s} - 1)}{(1 + r)^d}$$

REFERENCES

1. Arnott, Robert D., and Peter L. Bernstein. "The Right Way to Manage Your Pension Fund." *Harvard Business Review*, January–February 1988.

2. Bookstaber, Richard, and Jeremy Gold. "In Search of the Liability Asset." *Financial Analysts Journal*, January/February 1988.

3. Campbell, John Y., Andrew W. Lo, and A. Craig MacKinlay. *The Econometrics of Financial Markets*. Princeton University Press, 1997. Chapter 7.

4. Ezra, D. Don. 1991. "Asset Allocation by Surplus Optimization," *Financial Analysts Journal*, January–February.

5. Fama, Eugene, and Kenneth French. "Dividend Yields and Expected Stock Returns," *Journal of Financial Economics*, 22, 1988.

6. Leibowitz, Martin L., Stanley Kogelman, and Lawrence Bader. "Asset Performance and Surplus Control: A Dual Shortfall Approach." Salomon Brothers Inc., July 1991.

7. Ryan, Ronald J., and Frank J. Fabozzi. "Rethinking Pension Liabilities and Asset Allocation." *Journal of Portfolio Management*, Summer 2002.

8. Singer, Brian D., and Kevin Terhaar. 1997. "Economic Foundations of Capital Market Returns." Research Foundation of the Institute of Chartered Financial Analysts.

9. Treynor, Jack L., Patrick Regan, and William W. Priest, Jr. The Financial Reality of Pension Funding Under ERISA. Dow Jones-Irwin, Homewood, IL: 1976.

10. Waring, M. Barton. "Liability-Relative Investing II." *Journal of Portfolio Management*, Fall 2004.

PRACTICE PROBLEMS FOR READING 21

The following information relates to Questions 1–6[1]

Gabriela Cardoso, CFA, is the managing director of the pension plan for Farima Bank (the "Company"). Headquartered in São Paulo, Brazil, it is the largest bank in South America. Cardoso has recently hired Paulo Silva to assist her in reevaluating the pension plan's investment portfolio.

In the past, the pension plan's investment portfolio has been constructed based on an asset-only framework rather than a liability-relative approach. In a discussion on switching to a liability-relative approach, Cardoso asks Silva to list the assumptions of an asset-only approach. Silva states the following are assumptions of an asset-only framework:

Assumption 1: There is no market-related liability risk.

Assumption 2: Liability exposures are limited to the term structure of interest rates.

Assumption 3: Low risk investments are those that have high correlations to liabilities.

Silva asks the Company's actuaries to develop an estimate of the Company's future pension payments. Currently, the Company pays a cost of living adjustment (COLA) on retiree pension payments, which is based on the local consumer price index (CPI). In order to reduce current costs, the Company is considering limiting the COLA to only payments to those who have already retired. Cardoso tells Silva to factor the COLA limitation into his estimate of the benefit payment that will be made 15 years from now.

Silva presents Exhibit 1, noting that approximately half of the future wage inflation liability is assumed to correlate closely to CPI and half of the future real wage growth is assumed to correlate closely with domestic equities:

EXHIBIT 1	Components of Estimated Future Benefit Payments in Year 15
Liability Exposure	**Amount of Payment (in R\$[2] Millions)**
Retirees	10
Deferreds	5
Active Accrued	9
Future Wage Inflation	6
Future Real Wage Growth	2

---

[1]Developed by Bill Akmentins, CFA (Dallas, Texas).

[2]Brazilian real.

End-of-reading problems and solutions copyright © CFA Institute. Reprinted with permission.

Cardoso next asks Silva to develop a liability mimicking portfolio based on the liability exposures for all future estimated pension payments in Year 15. She also asks him to identify the non-market factors that could have an impact on the Company's pension liability in Year 15. Silva lists the following non-market factors that he believes would be difficult if not impossible to mimic in an investment portfolio:

Factor 1:   An increase in the Company retirees' savings rate.
Factor 2:   A decrease in the number of participants versus projections.
Factor 3:   Medical innovations resulting in changes to the mortality rate.

Cardoso notes the following characteristics of a low-risk investment for a pension fund:

Characteristic 1:   A high correlation to pension liabilities.
Characteristic 2:   A low correlation to other investment assets.
Characteristic 3:   A low correlation to the term structure of interest rates.

Cardoso has one final request for Silva: develop strategies that will fully hedge the Company's market-related pension liability and reduce the expected cost of the plan to the Company (i.e., lower pension plan contributions in the future).

1. Which assumption of an asset-only approach stated by Silva is *most likely* correct?
   A. Assumption 1.
   B. Assumption 2.
   C. Assumption 3.

2. Based on Exhibit 1, in a liability-mimicking portfolio, which of the following amounts is *closest* to the pension payments in Year 15 that could best be mimicked using real (inflation-indexed) bonds?
   A. R$10 million.
   B. R$12 million.
   C. R$13 million.

3. Based on Exhibit 1, in a liability-mimicking portfolio, which of the following amounts is *closest* to the pension payments in Year 15 that could best be mimicked using nominal bonds?
   A. R$13 million.
   B. R$14 million.
   C. R$18 million.

4. Which of the non-market factors listed by Silva would *least likely* have an impact on the Company's pension liability?
   A. Factor 1.
   B. Factor 2.
   C. Factor 3.

5. Which of the characteristics of a low risk investment listed by Cardoso fits *most closely* to a liability-relative approach?
   A. Characteristic 1.
   B. Characteristic 2.
   C. Characteristic 3.

6. Which of the following strategies will *most likely* satisfy Cardoso's final request? The Company should:

   A. use derivatives to hedge the market-related pension liability and invest the remaining cash using an asset-only approach.

   B. use real and nominal bonds to hedge the market-related pension liability and invest the remaining cash in a well-diversified return-generating portfolio.

   C. use derivatives to hedge severe declines in the equity and bond markets and invest the remaining cash in a well-diversified return-generating portfolio.

SOLUTIONS FOR READING 21

1. A is correct. An asset-only approach assumes there is no market-related liability risk. An asset-only approach focuses only on the return and risk of the investment portfolio.

2. C is correct. All of the retiree benefits of R$10 million can be mimicked using real bonds to account for the CPI COLA as well as half of the R$6 million of future wage inflation [R$10 + (R$6 × 0.50) = R$13]. Only some of the future wage inflation is exposed to inflation because after retirement those benefit payments are fixed and no longer exposed to changes in inflation. Silva states that about half of the future wage inflation is assumed to correlate with CPI and thus can be mimicked using inflation-protected (real) bonds.

3. C is correct. All of the deferred benefits of R$5 million plus all of the active accrued benefits of R$9 million plus half of the future wage inflation and half of the real future wage growth can best be mimicked using nominal bonds whose cash flows match the estimated benefit payments. [R$5 + R$9 + (R$6 × 0.5) + (R$2 × 0.5)] = R$18.

4. A is correct. Changes in the retirees' savings rate have no impact on the Company's pension liability.

5. A is correct. The higher the correlation the investment has to the Company's pension liability, the more likely the Company will be to meet its pension obligations.

6. A is correct. The pension liability is fully hedged using derivatives (the first criterion) and the remaining cash is invested according to an asset-only approach that maximizes return while minimizing volatility with the expectation that the resulting return would be higher than the cost of the derivatives and thereby reduce the amount of future pension plan contributions (cost) by the Company (the second criterion).

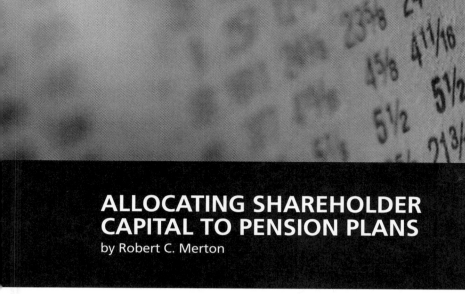

ALLOCATING SHAREHOLDER CAPITAL TO PENSION PLANS

by Robert C. Merton

LEARNING OUTCOMES

The candidate should be able to:	Mastery
a. compare and contrast funding shortfall and asset/liability mismatch as sources of risk faced by pension plan sponsors;	☐
b. explain how the weighted average cost of capital for a corporation can be adjusted to incorporate pension risk and discuss the potential consequences of not making this adjustment;	☐
c. explain, in an expanded balance sheet framework, the effects of different pension asset allocations on total asset betas, the equity capital needed to maintain equity beta at a desired level, and the debt-to-equity ratio.	☐

INTRODUCTION

Good evening, it's a pleasure to be here and thank you all for coming. It will not come as news to any of you that adequate provision for retirement through a combination of state, employer, and personal savings is a worldwide concern. It's a major concern in Asia and South America, in the U.S. and continental Europe, and, of course, here in the U.K. For corporations with defined benefit (DB) pension plans, the problem has manifested itself in a funding shortfall between pension assets and pension liabilities. The shortfall is a consequence of the large decline in equities in the first three years of this decade, in combination with drops in interest rates that have raised the value of the liabilities. The falling stock prices during that period also coincided with—and

This is an edited transcript of a speech delivered in London on October 21, 2004 at a conference on pensions sponsored by BNP Paribas. Some events that have occurred since that time are reflected in the footnotes.

"Allocating Shareholder Capital to Pension Plans," by Robert C. Merton, reprinted from *Journal of Applied Corporate Finance,* winter 2006. Copyright © 2006. Reprinted with permission from Blackwell Publishing.

467

indeed reflected—reductions in the companies' earnings and hence in their ability to fund their shortfalls out of business operations.

The new accounting treatment of pensions in the U.K.—a version of which is now being considered by the FASB in the U.S.—will make these shortfalls more transparent to interested parties, particularly investors, rating agencies, and regulators. And as the new rules come into force, they are likely to have real effects, such as limiting dividends and other distributions to shareholders. Some companies are responding by capping or shutting down their DB plans, and then creating defined contribution (DC) plans.[1]

There are of course multiple facets to this very important issue. My remarks this evening will focus primarily on the corporate challenge of providing retirement income to employees while limiting the costs and risks of retirement plans to the firms, and ensuring that investors and rating agencies understand both the risks and corporate efforts to deal with them. My main focus throughout will be on the real economic import and consequences of such issues and not how they are reflected on financial statements. This is not to suggest that accounting issues are unimportant, only that accounting is not my expertise—and because I value the time you are spending with me, I will concentrate on what I know a bit more about.

In the rest of this talk I will address five questions:

▶ What are the major issues and challenges surrounding pensions? We all know that the shortfall has been the focus of attention. However, I will make a case that while the gap between assets and liabilities is important, of far greater concern for the future is the risk mismatch between pension assets and pension liabilities. Most U.K. and U.S. companies have been funding debt-like liabilities with investments in equity-heavy asset portfolios.[2]

▶ To what extent do the equity market and equity prices reflect the shortfall in pension funding and the mismatch in risk? Do the markets see through the smoothing of pension earnings by accounting convention and consider pension shortfalls and mismatch risks in valuing the equity? What does the evidence tell us? Moreover, even if the market appears capable of reflecting pension risk, is it possible that analysts' P/E multiples and management's assessments of cost of capital are distorted by failure to take full account of the risks associated with pension assets?

---

[1] IBM's recent announcement of its shift to a DC plan could turn out to be a watershed event that precipitates the unraveling of the DB system. If healthy and employee-centric companies are getting rid of DB plans even for existing employees, what kind of companies are going to pay ever larger premiums to remain part of the system insured by the Pension Benefit Guaranty Corporation?

[2] One notable difference between U.S. and U.K. companies is that the latter provide workers with inflation-indexed benefits, and such benefits can be immunized with inflation-linked "Gilts."

► How should management analyze and formulate strategic solutions? I will offer no specific solutions tonight because each firm faces somewhat different circumstances and no one prescription fits all. Nevertheless, I do want to lay out a framework for analyzing the problem from a strategic perspective that can be used in formulating a company's pension policy. In particular, I will recommend that companies take an integrated perspective that views pension assets and liabilities as parts of their economic value and risk balance sheets—and one that accordingly treats the pension asset allocation decision as a critical aspect of a corporate-wide enterprise risk management program. Finally, I will offer the concept of a *risk budget*— basically, a list of all of a company's major exposures along with an estimate of the amount of equity capital necessary to support each one. One important use of such a risk budget is to enable management to address the question of how much equity capital must be allocated to the risk positions, or risk mismatches, that are created by asset allocation decisions in DB pension plans.

► The fourth question has to do with issues of implementation. If a company chooses to make a major change in its pension policy, such as a partial or complete immunization accomplished by substituting bonds for stocks, how would you communicate the risk implications of the new policy to the rating agencies and investors? How would your approach be affected by whether your plan is fully funded, underfunded, or overfunded? If underfunded, should one borrow to fully fund the plan?

► The fifth and final section discusses the challenges associated with moving from a DB plan to a defined contribution, or DC, plan. What are the major issues to be thinking about when contemplating such a change?

I will confess to you at the outset that most of the examples I will discuss come from the U.S. rather than the U.K. The only defense I offer for such provincialism is to plead my own familiarity with U.S. companies and numbers. But let me suggest that most of the U.S. cases I will present have rough counterparts in the U.K.—and that if you make some effort to translate the numbers and the circumstances into a U.K. context, I think you will find that the main issues that I raise tonight apply, with roughly equal force, to U.K. companies.

THE APPARENT ISSUE—FUNDING SHORTFALL   1

The funding shortfall has been the focus of analysts, the rating agencies (which have treated the shortfall as a form of debt for at least a decade), and regulators. You heard the numbers in my introduction; these are big numbers and the problem needs to be addressed. But I have no magic solution if you are under-funded by $1 billion; I cannot tell you how to wave a wand or give you a strategy that makes the underfunding disappear in true economic terms. And just to be clear, when I say "underfunded," I mean that the current marked-to-market value of the pension assets is less than the current marked-to-market value of the pension liabilities.

Underfunding has long been a problem, though it was largely hidden in the 1990s. This was partly driven by a mistaken tendency to equate higher *expected* returns with higher *realized* returns. Like most economists, I agree that equity returns in general are expected to be higher than fixed-income returns. However, the concept of higher expected equity returns has been translated, thanks to a misapplication of actuarial science, into the statement, "For companies with a long enough time horizon, higher expected returns can be assumed to imply higher realized returns for certain." And from there it is a short step to the idea that $1 invested today in stocks is worth more than $1 invested in bonds. This mistaken way of thinking,[3] which is effectively embedded in pension accounting and actuarial smoothing of pension returns, has been a major driver of corporate pension allocations. What such thinking ignores, of course, are the very different levels of risk associated with the higher expected returns on equities, a reality that became very clear during the market experience of 2000–2002.

The Real Issue—Risk Mismatch

But, again, I believe that the biggest pension problem facing Corporate America and its investors is not the shortfall, but the risk mismatch between pension assets and liabilities. Suppose you were looking at two companies. For Company A, the ratio of its pension assets and liabilities on a marked-to-market basis is 1.0. For Company B, the ratio of assets to liabilities is 1.05 to 1.0. Which company should we be more worried about? With no other information about the companies or their plans, common sense of course says that the firm that is 5% overfunded is in a better position.

But let me now give you the rest of the story. Company A's allocation of pension assets is to choose 100% bonds with the same duration as its pension liabilities. Company B has 85% of its pension asset portfolio in equities. Now, which of the two should you watch more closely? The point I'm making with this simple example is that balance sheet numbers, whether marked-to-market or not, are *static* and therefore of limited use. They are a picture of where the firm and its assets and liabilities are right now. They reveal nothing about the risk that those two numbers may change, either by how much or with what likelihood.

In the first case, as long as Company A maintains its policy, even though the plan is just fully funded, that funding will be completely adequate; you do not need to be overfunded if you always hold assets that precisely hedge the risk of the liabilities. In the second case, however, even a funding ratio of 1.05 is probably not sufficient. While it is quite true that the company's funding ratio could jump from 1.05 to 1.20 in a year's time, it could just as quickly fall to 0.85. The balance sheet numbers that purport to measure a pension surplus or deficit give no indication of risk.

---

[3] The fallacy of treating expected stock returns as risk free has been demonstrated by Paul Samuelson in several of his writings: "Lifetime Portfolio Selection by Dynamic Stochastic Programming," *Review of Economics and Statistics* 51 (1969); and "The Long-Term Case of Equities and How It Can Be Oversold," *Journal of Portfolio Management* (Fall, 1994); and, more recently, by Zvi Bodie, in "On the Risk of Stocks in the Long Run," *Financial Analysts Journal* (May–June, 1995). Still another way of demonstrating this fallacy is to note that a 40-year return asset return swap in which one receives the cumulative total return on the S&P 500 over 40 years and pays the cumulative return on either UST bills (rolled over) or UST 10-year bonds can be purchased for $0.

The risk mismatch is likely to be of greatest concern in cases where the ratio of pension assets to the market capitalization of equity is high. For publicly traded U.S. companies with DB pension plans near the end of 2001, the median ratio of pension assets to the market cap of equity for the top quintile of firms (ranked by that ratio) was 2 to 1.[4] That underscores the point that pension assets are not small relative to the total equity of the firm. Moreover, it is typical to have 60% to 70% of the pension assets in equities. This means that for at least 20% of the companies in this sample, the equities holdings in their pension portfolios are larger than the entire market cap of the firm's equity (60% of 2.0 is 1.2).

Take the case of General Motors, which has the largest corporate pension fund in the U.S., with total assets of approximately $90 billion. If we assume that 65% of those assets are devoted to equities—which, again, is standard U.S. corporate practice—that means the company has approximately $60 billion invested in equities. At the moment, GM has a market cap of approximately $22 billion, which means that it may well have almost three times its own market cap invested in the equities of other companies.[5] Even for large firms, if you are thinking in terms of the size of the pension investment versus such things as the amount of equity capital, this is quite considerable. We need to be aware of that in our thinking.

Now consider a corporate balance sheet that includes $60 billion of equity on the asset side and a $60-billion liability that is perfectly matched in terms of value but not risk. This mismatched combination of assets and liabilities would not show up any differently on accounting statements—even under the new IAS rule—than $60 billion of debt assets that were perfectly matched in risk to the pension liability. The first of these two combinations is equivalent to making a $60-billion bet on the stock market and financing it with $60 billion of fixed-rate, long-term debt. For those of you who are familiar with derivatives, this is equivalent to entering into a $60-billion asset return swap where you pay a fixed rate of interest in return for receiving the total realized market return on equities.

Recognizing the Risk

As you know, when a swap is first done on standard terms, it has essentially no value; in terms of the balance sheet, it thus has no entry. What about its risk? Would you say there is a fair amount of risk if you bought $60 billion of equity and financed it with $60 billion of fixed-rate debt? That is a huge risk position. I am not saying that risk-taking is wrong, but failing to recognize the size of that risk position is a mistake. Imagine a CEO, accompanied by his or her CFO or finance director, announcing to an audience of shareholders, creditors, and other stakeholders, "Our current market capitalization is $15 billion. Our strategy for the coming year is to buy $60 billion of equities and finance the purchase with $60 billion of long-term fixed-rate debt." I think that recommendation would evoke a considerable amount of discussion.

---

[4] For the pension quintile ratios of pension assets to market cap, I am indebted to a presentation by Michael Gilberto of J.P. Morgan Chase at a JPM Investment Management Conference on October 4, 2001.

[5] Although GM recently reported that the 2005 gains in its pension fund have given it a pension surplus of some $6 billion, the economic reality—again based on the assumption that 60% of the fund is in equities—is that the VaR or equity capital necessary to support that risk exposure is several times the firm's current (January 24, 2006) equity market cap of $13 billion.

And this brings me to the issues of transparency and framing. I am not suggesting that companies are consciously attempting to mislead investors about their pension policies. What I am trying to emphasize is the importance of acknowledging the economic reality that the pension assets *are* the shareholders' assets, and then framing the risks accordingly. Pension assets are "encumbered" assets in the sense that there is a lien against them by the pensioners in the plan, but the residual gains and losses from that pension asset portfolio basically flow to the shareholders.

Now, there is one important exception to this rule—namely, companies with pension deficits facing a significant probability of default and bankruptcy. Since the pension losses of such firms are likely to end up being borne by the Pension Benefit Guaranty Corporation in the U.S.—and by the Pension Protection Fund in the U.K.—the value-maximizing strategy may well be to maintain and even enlarge the risk mismatch of their pensions in the hope that large pension gains can help rescue the firm by covering the shortfall and limiting future contributions to the plan. But, for reasonably healthy companies, pension assets are effectively (though not institutionally) assets of the corporation, and pension liabilities are liabilities of the corporation, no matter what happens to the pension assets. It is an obligation of the corporation, much like payments of interest and principal on its debt.

In this sense, then, pension risks *are* corporate risks. And as I discuss in more detail later, how one frames the risks in corporate DB plans will affect corporate decisions to continue or modify such plans as well as the choice of assets to fund them. When you consider the magnitude of the total value changes stemming from the mismatch of risk, it becomes very clear that the mismatch is a bigger problem than the current shortfall in funding. For companies with large DB plans, the impact on corporate values of a recession-induced drop in equities combined with a drop in interest rates—a combination similar to what we saw during the first years of this decade—could end up dwarfing the effects of a downturn on the operating businesses. The risks associated with today's pension asset-liability mismatches are very big risks indeed.

2   ACCOUNTING FOR VALUE MISMATCH AND RISK

My second major point has to do with how the markets seem to take account of both the value mismatch—that is, the size of any pension surplus or shortfall—and the risk mismatch. In terms of value, research done over a decade ago at the National Bureau of Economic Research on U.S. companies—and I have no reason to think it would be materially different for U.K. companies—supports the idea that share prices do in fact reflect the value of pension surpluses or shortfalls. In particular, companies with large pension deficits appear to trade at lower P/E multiples and price-to-book ratios than firms with fully or overfunded DB plans.[6]

This finding did not come as a surprise. But I have to confess to some surprise at the findings of some recent work I did with colleagues Zvi Bodie and Li Jin on the value effects of pension risk mismatch.[7] And let me remind you once

---

[6] See, for example, Martin Feldstein and Stephanie Seligman, "Pension Funding, Share Prices, and National Savings," *Journal of Finance,* Vol. 4, No. 36 (1981).

[7] See Li Jin, Robert C. Merton, and Zvi Bodie, "Do a Firm's Equity Returns Reflect the Risk of Its Pension Plan?" forthcoming *Journal of Financial Economics.*

more of the proposition we were testing: You could have a pension plan in which pension assets and pension liabilities are roughly equal in value, meaning there is no shortfall or surplus. But if the pension assets were largely in equities and the liability is largely fixed-rate debt, the risk exposure would be huge. And the question we were attempting to answer in our study was: Does the market capture that risk? Given the arcane accounting and institutional separation between the pension plan and the rest of the business, I did not think the market would take it into account.

But our results suggest that, during the period of our study[8]—1993 to 1998—the U.S. stock market did a pretty good job of picking up the differences in risk. More specifically, a company with a larger fraction of equity in its pension portfolio tended, all other things equal, to have a larger "beta"—a widely used measure of risk that reflects, among other things, the "systematic-risk" volatility of the stock price itself. In other words—and this is simplifying things a bit—the greater risk associated with equity-heavy pension plans seemed to show up in more volatile stock prices.

What's especially interesting to me about these findings is that they apply to a period that preceded the large market decline that started in 2000. It's relatively easy to see how investors could become sensitized to the possibility of pension losses during a market downturn. But the evidence of our study seems to show that share prices do take account of pension risk, even when most pensions are in surplus—and when the risk shows up nowhere on the accounting balance sheet. And to the extent the marketplace charges firms for bearing that added pension risk, our findings have some important implications for corporate policy and investment decisions that I will discuss later.

To repeat my point, then, our evidence comes not from surveying analysts but from looking at what actually happens to share prices. And this, of course, is supportive of the idea of an efficient stock market. But we are not out of the woods yet. It is entirely possible that some equity analysts do not pay much attention to pension risk when assessing P/E multiples and comparing companies. It's also possible that some corporate managers may not be taking account of the contribution of pension risk to overall corporate risk when making major capital allocations among their different businesses. And, as discussed below, the result could be distortions of both analysts' valuations and strategic corporate business decisions.

Calculating the Weighted Average Cost of Capital

To illustrate this point, let's say you are a corporate executive considering a decision to expand into more or less the same business you are in now. In that case, the standard capital budgeting approach is to estimate the expected future cash flows and then discount those flows at the firm's weighted average cost of capital (WACC). How do you get estimates of your WACC? If you are a publicly traded company, you can typically observe the historical movement of your share prices, and then estimate the beta of the share returns. When you do this, you are really assuming that the historical volatility of the stock is a reliable proxy for its risk—and, in this sense, beta is a wholly *market-based* measure of risk. The market may be completely wrong about this, but this is how investors perceive the risk of your stock.

---

[8] In 1993, companies were required for the first time to report ERISA form 5500, which provides a list of the firm's pension holdings as of year end.

Now, in valuing a project, unless the firm is financed entirely with equity, you cannot simply take the firm's beta and come up with a cost of equity capital. You have to take account of the use of debt in the firm's capital structure. To do that, you "de-leverage" the equity to come up with the WACC, which is an average of your debt and equity rates; you get the equity rates from the riskiness measured historically. Your debt rates are your observed debt rates. That is standard procedure for estimating WACC.

But the use of WACC to evaluate this project is based on a couple of important premises. First, as mentioned, the project in question should have roughly the same operating risk and be able to support the same leverage ratio as the rest of the firm's assets. Second, the calculation of the firm's leverage ratio should reflect all senior corporate obligations, not just on balance-sheet debt.[9]

Incorporating Pension Risk into WACC

Given our focus on pension assets and liabilities, this suggests there may be a problem with this standard procedure for estimating WACC: its failure to take account of the risk of other important assets that are not reflected on GAAP balance sheets. As we have already seen, pension assets can be a significant fraction of total corporate assets. And for companies with large DB plans, an equity-heavy asset portfolio can be one of the main sources of total volatility on the left side of the balance sheet—in some cases as large as the operating business itself.

On the other side of the balance sheet, pension liabilities are missing from the standard procedure as well. Pension liabilities are debt. Though collateralized by the pension assets, they are an obligation of the firm and thus part of the leverage or gearing of the firm.

By failing to take account of their pension assets and pension liabilities when estimating their cost of capital, companies are probably distorting their measures of operating, or project, risk in two ways. First, they are effectively assigning the firm's total risk to its business operations, when a potentially significant part of that risk could in fact come from the pension fund assets. Second, because the standard analysis does not take account of the pension liabilities, it understates the firm's leverage ratio.

The typical effect of these two distortions is to overstate WACC for an operating project. If our analysis instead used a pension-adjusted leverage ratio and included the pension assets on the left-hand side of the balance sheet, the resulting estimates of "unleveraged" operating beta for most companies with large DB plans would fall.

To sum up, then, if management estimates WACC by the standard method, it can lead to a major distortion of the capital allocation decision. It means applying too high a hurdle rate to projects, which means the firm may not undertake all the projects that are expected to increase its value. Taken by itself, it does not imply anything about the optimal asset allocation in the pension fund plan, but it is one possible consequence of not taking account of it.

---

[9] For illustrative purposes, all the calculations of the effect of the pension plan on beta estimates for WACC are based on the assumption that corporations do not pay income taxes. In practice, companies need to incorporate into their WACC analysis an estimate of the company's marginal corporate tax rate. If the company is and expects to be fully taxable at all times, a portion of the value of the pension assets and the pension liabilities are "owned" by the government and so therefore are their risks. But that computation is very firm-specific and not required for the level of demonstration here.

TABLE 1	Errors in Estimates of Weighted Average Cost of Capital: Examples						
	Pension Assets ($bn)	Pension Liabilities ($bn)	Pension Surplus/ Deficit ($bn)	Market Cap ($bn)	Book Value of Debt ($bn)	Standard WACC[a]	WACC Adjusted for Pension Risks[a]
Boeing	33.8	32.7	1.1	30.9	12.3	8.80%	6.09%
DuPont	17.9	18.8	(0.9)	42.6	6.8	9.44%	8.15%
Eastman Kodak	7.9	7.4	0.5	8.6	3.2	9.75%	7.47%
Textron	4.5	3.9	0.6	5.9	7.1	7.98%	6.81%

[a] WACC numbers are based on a risk-free rate of 5% and a market-risk premium of 7%.

Source: "The Real Problem with Pensions," *Harvard Business Review*, December 2004.

Illustrations

To give you an idea of how big that distortion could be for some real companies, let's look at four examples: Boeing, DuPont, Eastman Kodak, and Textron.[10] As shown in Table 1, all but DuPont have pension surpluses. And DuPont's pension shortfall is tiny compared to both its total liabilities and assets and to its market cap. These are financially healthy companies; they are surely not high on anyone's list of the type of pension issues that normally concern us.

Calculating a standard WACC, which fails to take account of the risk of the pension assets and the gearing of the pension liabilities, leads to an estimated cost of capital for Boeing of 8.8%. But when we make an adjustment for the company's pension risk that reflects the extent of its asset–liability mismatch—and take account of the size of the pension liabilities, which changes the firm's leverage ratio—Boeing's estimated WACC drops to about 6%, implying an overstatement of almost 300 basis points by the standard methods. That is the extreme case in the sample, but estimates of the overstatements for all four firms exceed 100 basis points.

This is not to say that the managements of these four companies are actually making this mistake; I have not worked with any of these companies and have no knowledge of their capital budgeting process. What I am saying is that if they follow the standard textbook procedure for estimating WACC, without adjusting for the risk and size of the pension fund, they could be materially overstating their cost of capital. And since we know that stock-price multiples are roughly inversely related to required returns or cost of capital, analysts who are overstating the estimates of cost of capital are also likely to be underestimating the multiples of the companies they cover.

In sum, pension decisions in terms of both asset size and allocation have the potential to affect the management of the entire firm at the most fundamental level. Strategic investment and risk-management decisions can be affected by the allocation of pension assets. And for reasons I've just illustrated, the failure of corporate managements to view pension assets and liabilities as part of the firm may well be leading to underinvestment in the operating part of the business.

---

[10] These examples appear in Lin, Merton, and Bodie, forthcoming *JFE*, cited above.

3   STRATEGIC ANALYSIS AND POLICY DEVELOPMENT

My third major point is about strategic analysis and working toward developing a pension plan policy. I hope the preceding remarks have demonstrated the need for an integrated enterprise-wide approach, one that views pension assets and liabilities as parts of the firm's comprehensive economic and risk balance sheets. To evaluate their sources and impact at the strategic level, pension risks should be evaluated not only in terms of implementation of the pension plan, but within the context of the firm's other objectives, risks, and strategic plans, including effects on credit ratings.

Or to turn this thought upside down, all of a company's major business and financing decisions should be informed by a well-structured analysis that views capital allocation, capital structure, *and* pension plan decisions as parts of an integrated strategy. Much of my emphasis to this point has been on the potential effects of pension asset allocation on corporate capital allocation and capital structure choices. It is precisely because of these effects—of this linkage between the pension and the operating business—that pension asset allocation should be considered a strategic issue, one that is overseen at the highest level of corporate decision-making.

But if we continue to view the pension fund as an off-balance sheet entity with no ties to the firm, our decision-making will likely also continue to be distorted by the higher expected returns on equities, even if the new accounting rules force us to report actual rather than expected returns in our financial statements. After all, shifting pension assets from equities to bonds will lower the expected returns on our asset portfolio and raise the contributions needed, at least in the near-term, to meet plan obligations. And that sounds like a bad thing, a value-reducing proposition—until one begins to consider the effect on risk. When you look at the whole picture, lowering the expected returns on the assets also lowers the risk of the entire firm. And by lowering risk, you create the capacity for the firm to take other risk—core operating risks, if you will, that are likely to add more value than passive equity investments in other companies.

That brings me to the concept of a "risk budget" I mentioned earlier. I find it useful to think of companies as having risk budgets that are very much analogous to their capital budgets. Reducing risk in one place releases capacity to increase risk elsewhere without having to add more equity capital to the firm. And this means that the total opportunity created by reducing risks in the pension fund is to enable the firm to take more risk in its operating businesses, which is presumably where it is most likely to find positive net present value opportunities. The expected net effect of such changes is an increase in firm value. Although you reduce the expected return on your pension assets, you gain more from the new operating assets that you are now able to hold without additional equity capital—all of which is made possible by the reduction of risk in the pension fund.

Having said this, let me also hasten to add that 100% bonds will not be the optimal pension portfolio for all DB plans. But the possibility for such gains from reducing pension risk is a good reason to view your pension assets and liabilities as part of an enterprise-wide risk framework. As with any other decision that affects corporate balance sheets or income statements, changes in pension strategy and risk are bound to show up somewhere else. And, as I said a moment ago, it is because of their effects on the rest of the firm that pension

TABLE 2   Effect of Pension Asset Risk Mismatch on Equity Risk and Cost of Capital: LT Corporation (with Fully Funded Pension Plan)

	Standard Balance Sheet Estimates				
	Value ($bn)	Risk (Beta)		Value ($bn)	Risk (Beta)
Operating Assets	$40	1.05	Debt	$19	0.00
			Equity	$21	2.00
Total Assets	**$40**	**1.05**	**Total L&E**	**$40**	**1.05**

Estimated WACC Operating Assets = 12.35%.

decisions must be overseen by decision-makers at high levels in the corporate organization, people entrusted with managing the risks and maximizing the value of the entire enterprise.

An Illustration

As a hypothetical illustration of how to evaluate the risk of a company's operating assets *and* its pension plan, let's take the case of a company called LT. Table 2 provides standard balance sheet estimates of operating asset risk and WACC, without considering the pension plan. All numbers are market values, not book values. We arrived at the value of the operating assets by taking the market value of equity and the market value of debt—$21 billion and $19 billion, respectively—and adding those up to arrive at $40 billion, which is equal to the value of total assets.

To do a conventional calculation of WACC for LT, we began by estimating its beta from historical market returns—and our estimate turned out to be 2.0. Then, taking account of the firm's debt and its level of risk, we determined that the weighted risk of debt and equity results in an "unleveraged" or "asset" beta of 1.05. If LT's management team were using this method to evaluate a project similar to the company's other operations, the project would be valued using a WACC based on a risk factor of 1.05. Using a risk-free rate of 5% and a market-risk premium of 7%, we would come up with a WACC of around 12%.

In Table 3, we show what happens when you adjust the conventional analysis to incorporate a full economic balance sheet—one that takes account of risk as well as value and so includes the pension assets and pension liabilities. The pension plan is fully funded—$46 billion of assets and $46 billion of liabilities—and since there is no surplus or shortfall, there is no entry on the traditional balance sheet. Since 60% of the pension assets are invested in equities, LT does have a significant risk exposure to equities, but, again, that exposure is not recorded on its GAAP balance sheet. When we expand the balance sheet to include the pension assets and liabilities, we have a much larger company—$86 billion of total assets instead of $40 billion, and $65 billion of total debt instead of $19 billion. We can easily estimate the risk of the pension asset portfolio—a well-diversified portfolio of equities and debt—just by looking at its composition: If we assume that the stocks have a beta of 1.0 and the bonds have a beta of 0, a portfolio with 60% equities can be assumed, pretty much by definition, to have a beta of 0.60.

TABLE 3   Effect of Pension Asset Risk Mismatch on Equity Risk and Cost of Capital: LT Corporation (with Fully Funded Pension Plan)

Full Economic Balance Sheet Estimates

	Value ($bn)	Risk (Beta)		Value ($bn)	Risk (Beta)
Operating assets	$40	0.36	Debt	$19	0.00
Pension assets	$46	0.60	Pension liabilities	$46	0.00
			Equity	$21	2.00
Total Assets	**$86**	**0.49**	**Total L&E**	**$86**	**0.49**

Estimated WACC Operating Assets = 7.52%.

The next step, then, using the firm's equity beta of 2.0, is to use LT's leverage ratio and its pension assets and liabilities to "back out" the firm's operating asset risk, which turns out to be 0.36. In this particular case, then—perhaps an extreme one, but useful in making my point—the operating assets actually have a materially lower systematic risk than the pension fund assets![11] Moreover, when we evaluate the total asset risk, which includes the risk of both the operating assets and the pension assets, we get 0.49, which is less than half the estimate we came up with—1.05—doing the analysis the conventional way.

But for purposes of project valuation and capital budgeting, the relevant comparison for LT's management in this case is not between 1.05 and 0.49 but between 1.05 and 0.36. If we were to do a capital budgeting analysis of contemplated projects for LT's core business, we would use 0.36 in calculating WACC, and if we did so, the cost of capital would fall from over 12% to 7.5% (5% + {0.36 × 7.0}). For projects with an expected life of ten years, the effect of overestimating the discount rate by some 450 basis points can be an underestimation of project values on the order of 30–40%. And as this example is meant to suggest, neglecting the risk of the pension plan can lead to major distortions of the capital budgeting process.

Besides improving capital allocation decisions, use of this expanded balance sheet approach provides a better picture of your firm in terms of its value and risk allocations between your operating businesses and other activities such as pension asset investments, which are largely passive investments. Your pension plan may make use of active fund managers, but unless you are a financial firm, managing financial assets is probably not part of your core business. Use of an expanded risk balance sheet can give top management a better picture of the composition and risk character of the firm.

Considering Alternative Pension Policies

Now I will try to show how the economic and risk balance sheets from Table 3 can be used to explore alternative pension asset allocation policies and their implications for capital structure and firm risk. Before I go any further, let me

---

[11] This is in fact not uncommon for the kind of companies that have DB plans—in many cases, basic industrial companies with relatively low betas.

TABLE 4	Effect of Pension Fund Asset Allocation on Asset and Equity Risk: LT Corporation		
Fraction of Pension Assets in Equities	**Pension Asset Beta**	**Total Asset Beta**	**Firm Equity Beta**
0.00	0.00	0.17	0.70
0.25	0.25	0.30	1.23
0.60	**0.60**	**0.49**	**2.00**
0.75	0.75	0.57	2.34
1.00	1.00	0.70	2.88

warn you that I'm not offering a specific policy recommendation for LT or any other firm. What I'm presenting is a framework for thinking about the effects of different asset allocation on the risk of the enterprise.

The conventional analysis of a change in pension asset allocation—say, a major shift from stocks to bonds—focuses mainly on the effects of the change in expected return on corporate balance sheets and income statements. At least from the vantage point of GAAP—though less so with the new UK standard—the primary effect of such a change is to reduce reported earnings.[12] In addition to such accounting effects, conventional analysis also takes account of any effects on the stand-alone risk of the pension fund.

The main focus of economic analysis, however, begins with the changes in risk. When a company alters the mix of its pension assets between fixed-income and equities, it changes its equity risk and the risk of the overall firm. For example, as can be seen in Table 4, if LT were to raise its pension allocation of equities from 60% to 100%, our analysis suggests that the firm's total asset risk factor would increase from 0.49 to 0.70—a significant increase in the risk of the total company. And the beta of the firm's equity is estimated to jump from 2.0 to 2.88—though, again, I ask you not to take the precision of these numbers seriously. In this case, you see nearly a 50% increase in the risk of the firm's equity. Investors require a higher expected return for this kind of increase in risk.

Now, let me also say that such an increase in risk is not inherently bad. What is important, however, is to understand the change and any possible firm-wide effects.

A decision to go to 100% equities, though not necessarily a bad idea for all companies, does mean a higher return requirement by your equity holders. When you think of the higher expected return on the equities in your pension fund, the good news is that you can indeed expect them to produce higher returns, at least over a sufficiently long time horizon. The bad news, however, is that because of the risk associated with your pension assets, your own shareholders will demand a higher return than they did before and lower the P/E multiple on your stock. So, even if your future pension contributions turn out to be lower and your reported earnings higher as a consequence of an all-equity pension, the reduction in your multiple may leave your stock price unaffected or even lower than otherwise.

---

[12] But if the firm also maintains its total risk posture by simultaneously issuing new debt and using the proceeds to buy back stock, the effect on EPS is not clear; EPS could increase.

But, again, I am not offering a specific prediction or recommendation here. My purpose is simply to show how overall firm risk and its equity risk are influenced by pension asset allocation and to note that such changes could end up increasing the firm's cost of capital and lowering its multiple. Neither of these effects is necessarily bad, but you should prepare yourself for the probable changes.

Effects of Pension Change on Optimal Capital Structure

As we change the pension asset allocation, what are the implications for the capital structure or the amount of equity capital required to keep the risk of our equity unchanged? Let's return to the case of LT and assume that the company's management and shareholders are comfortable with their current equity risk factor of 2.0. Let's further assume that one of the firm's key risk management objectives is to maintain the beta risk of its equity at that level.

As we saw in Table 4, an increase in the allocation of pension asset to equities increases the risk of the total assets. And if we increase the risk on the left-hand side of the balance sheet, in order to keep the risk of our equity unchanged we have to reduce leverage or gearing. If you increase asset risk and leave the capital structure unchanged, equity risk goes up. Another way of saying this is that, for your creditors and equityholders to be as comfortable as they were before the pension change, any increase in asset risk will have to be offset by taking less risk with your capital structure. There is no free lunch in that sense.

Table 5 provides an indication of how much equity capital the firm would need to maintain an equity risk of 2.0 for a range of pension asset allocation choices. We begin with the assumption that LT's management and shareholders are comfortable with the status quo, at least in the sense that the combination of a 60% pension equity allocation with $21 billion of shareholders' equity meets the firm's risk management criterion of maintaining an equity beta of 2.0. But, according to Table 5, if management took the extreme step of increasing the pension allocation to 100% equities, the firm would have to issue $9 billion of new equity in order to maintain the same risk for LT's equity holders. In other words, to keep its equity risk the same, the firm would have to deleverage or reduce the gearing by $9 billion, and, as shown in Table 5, its debt-to-equity ratio would drop from 0.9 to 0.33. At the other extreme, if the firm were to shift the entire pension into bonds that perfectly match the pension liabilities, the amount of equity capital needed to keep the equity risk at 2.0 would fall to $7 billion from $21 billion—and the debt-to-equity ratio would rise above 4.0.

TABLE 5   Tradeoff between Pension Asset Allocation and Firm Capital Structure

Fraction of Pension Assets in Equities	Total Asset Beta	Firm Equity Beta	Equity Capital ($bn)	Debt/Equity Ratio
0.00	0.17	2.00	7.3	4.48
0.25	0.30	2.00	12.9	2.10
0.60	**0.49**	**2.00**	**21.0**	**0.90**
0.75	0.57	2.00	24.5	0.63
1.00	0.70	2.00	30.1	0.33

Cushioning Your Risks with Capital

Tables 4 and 5 provide just two illustrations of how, once you have set the analysis up correctly, you can begin to discuss pension asset allocation in an integrated way, taking into account the impact you are having on the capital structure and risk of the business. You can use this tool to ask how much capital you are holding in the firm to cushion the risk mismatch of the pension fund versus the amount needed to support the risk of the operating businesses.

You are not going to trade on the precision of these numbers, but the magnitudes and implications here are essentially valid and will stand up to more sophisticated applications. In fact, my firm IFL has done this kind of analysis for clients who were surprised to discover how much of their total risk, and therefore the total amount of capital allocation, had to do with the risk mismatch in their pension fund.

Does this say that all companies should immunize their pension liabilities and thus avoid a risk mismatch in your pension fund? The answer is no.[13] Our

---

[13] Immunization of the pension liabilities, although the value-maximizing approach in many cases, will not *always* be the optimal solution. The problem with current immunization practices, or those that now go under the name "LDI," is that they apply ALM only with respect to the pension assets and pension liabilities alone instead of considering ALM with respect to the assets and liabilities of the *entire* corporation.

When determining an optimal policy, one must define the objectives and conditions under which you are assessing alternative pension fund policies. If you frame the problem as: What provides the maximum assurance to plan participants of the benefits that they have accrued in a plan that is currently fully funded (to the level of the ABO at true marked-to-market valuations) and that *will continue* to be fully funded as future benefits accrue *pari passu* with the existing benefits of the plan, the answer is indeed immunization. This particular framing takes as given the amount and terms of the promised benefits and *assumes* that the firm cannot in the future "dilute" the security of the current beneficiaries' claims by either promising additional benefits in the future without immediately fully funding them or by changing the investment policy of the fund. To my knowledge, neither of these future financing and investment conditions is set either by employee contract or by ERISA law for typical U.S. DB plans.

From a general equilibrium perspective, pension asset optimization should consider the perspective of the firm and its shareholders as well as the beneficiaries of the plan in terms of the "bargain" between the two since the equilibrium level of promised pension benefits the firm will agree to is determined in part by the cost of providing those benefits, which in turn depends on the terms of the arrangement between the firm and its beneficiaries. I believe that over the past two decades, firms did not recognize how costly the benefits they offered were at the time they agreed to them, but they do now; and as we see everywhere, they are rapidly closing their DB plans for new members and freezing them for existing members.

No insurance company offers full-faith and credit of the U.S. government for its retirement annuity liabilities, even though very large AAA companies can be downgraded (AIG). In principle, the market could provide full-faith and credit annuities with individual segregated accounts for each of its annuity participants. But it doesn't, and I suspect that few customers would be so risk averse as to be willing to pay the high incremental cost to move from AA-rated commingled funds of regulated insurers to segregated full-faith and credit asset accounts. That is, for the bulk of retirees, the competitive market equilibrium is probably not at that "corner solution" of extreme risk aversion.

To return to my original point, when one views the pension allocation decision in the context of *all* the firm's assets and *all* its liabilities—that is, when one practices ALM for the *entire firm*—one can surely imagine a solution in which the optimal asset risk position in the pension fund is not complete immunization and thus zero correlation with the exposure of the firm's net operating assets. In some cases, the optimal asset exposure could turn out to be one that is *negatively correlated* with the operating assets of the firm, which in turn would reduce the entire risk of the corporate asset base and improve the (implied) credit rating of the pension liabilities more effectively than simply holding debt securities with match duration to the pension liabilities.

The limitation of immunization, then, is not that matching pension assets and liabilities will fail to add value but that it may not be the value-maximizing strategy. Since returns on equities, in the vast majority of cases, will be positively correlated with a firm's operating assets, holding equities in the pension fund is not likely to be an outcome of the firm-wide analysis recommended here. Immunization-like positions in bonds or long-dated fixed rate swaps will be an important part of the portfolio composition. However, when optimal tax, liquidity considerations, and hedge accounting rules are taken into account, it is entirely possible that the optimal pension asset mix could include

(Note continued on next page . . .)

analysis says only that you should understand how much risk your shareholders are bearing as a result of the mismatch, how much capital you are using to support it, and how your cost of capital is affected by it. An integrated approach requires you to look at all of these factors and consider all the choices that can be made. And when you do that, you are in a position to make an informed strategic decision.

4   IMPLEMENTATION

When you have done this analysis and decided on a pension policy, you then have to decide how to communicate that policy to the rating agencies, to your shareholders, to analysts, and to others. We believe that a good way to do that is to provide a full reasoned analysis in support of your new policy, one that includes a demonstration of how much risk-reduction credit you expect to get from changing a 60% equity allocation to, say, one of 25%. If you accept the numbers in the LT example, for example, you could eliminate almost $8 billion in equity.

But that estimate would simply provide a starting point for your discussion. You would then have to see how much the rating agencies would actually allow you to reduce equity without affecting the rating when you show them how much risk you are taking out on a permanent basis. This is an unsettled question, and the answer to it can be expected to change over time as the rating agencies and credit markets develop greater understanding of pension risk and its effect on overall firm risk. But to repeat my point: effective communication is an important element of the implementation.

Underfunding

The LT case is an example of a fully funded plan with no surplus or deficit. If the firm were underfunded, what might you want to consider? One possibility is to issue debt to fund the plan if you can. I'm not going to comment on whether that's the best strategy; the only answer I can give is that it depends on the firm and its circumstances. In making such a decision, some of the big issues will include taxes, whether you are a profitable firm, and how your communication with the rating agencies goes. Funding the plan may well be the optimal decision—or you may choose to fund the plan while making a change in the asset mix of the pension. And, of course, debt and equity are not the only possibilities for pension assets; there are other assets, including all variety of derivatives.

Overfunding

If you have a surplus, what do you do? Even if you want to match-fund the risk of what you owe, do you take risk with the surplus and, if so, what kinds of risk? Those are all part of the equation of what you need to analyze when thinking about and implementing a policy. There is no single answer for all cases.

---

significant holdings of alternatives like true "zero-beta" hedge funds (which are often highly taxed if held on the corporate balance sheet) and long-dated, illiquid equity put warrants on selected industries as well as interest rate, currency, credit default swaps to offset "passive" exposures of the operating businesses. (See my article, "You Have More Capital than You Think," *Harvard Business Review* 83, No. 11 (November 2005), 84–94.)

In sum, I do not believe that in 2006 the optimal pension asset allocation decision should be reduced to the "one size fits all" prescription of complete immunization.

MOVING FROM A DB TO A DC PLAN   5

To those of you who decide that the answer is to end your DB plan and start a DC plan, I offer some observations. Suppose that an employee, upon retirement, would like to receive a stream of income comparable to the one earned in the latter part of his or her working life in order to maintain more or less the same standard of living. Although some plans are more generous than others, the basic idea of a DB plan is that it provides something near to one's final income, perhaps scaled down somewhat. When this arrangement works, it's wonderful because the employees do not need to know anything; they simply have to believe it will happen, and the benefits have to materialize at the appointed time.

With a DC plan, life becomes simpler for the corporation in some ways. The moment it pays its fraction of income into the plan, it has seemingly carried out all of its obligations. The problem, however, is that in making this change, you are now putting your employees in the position of having to make some quite complex investment decisions. Imagine if you were approached by a 42-year-old who told you he wanted to retire at 67, and to have an income during retirement that was roughly equal to 70% of his average earnings between the ages of 62 and 67. What would you tell him he had to invest in and how much he should be contributing in order to hit that target? We do not even know today what that person will be making in 20 years' time, so this is quite a complex problem.

We do not ask people to do their own medical surgery or other kinds of important activities which require a great deal of specialization. Yet, when addressing one of the most important challenges in their lives, funding their retirements, employees in DC plans are essentially forced to obtain advice that is typically based in large part on the assumption that history will simply repeat itself. However, a reasonable question for any of us as consumers to ask is, "What happens if history does not repeat itself?"

What other major product do consumers buy where they allow someone to hand them the product, tell them this is an important part of their lives, and then warn them that "If it does not work, it is your problem"? I am not just pointing fingers, because I am also in this business. I do not know the optimal solution, but I know that we can do better than simply leave individuals to make these complex decisions about risks.

That does not mean that DC plans are bad. What it does suggest, however, is that DC plans as they are commonly carried out today, particularly in the U.S., are not the long-run answer. We have to design a product that works institutionally from a DC plan but has an output that looks more like a DB plan. This kind of product is on the drawing board.

CONCLUSION   6

Corporations today face huge challenges in managing DB plans, and, if we go to the DC plans, there are huge challenges there as well. When I worked at a large investment bank, we had a focus group that aimed to design a great financial product for retired people. Focus groups were held all over the U.S., and participants included non-profit institutions as well as private corporations. The most common response from participants when asked what they thought of our product proposals was that "the products are too good to be true; we do not believe it can happen." But once we suggested that such products might be made available through their employers, their response was quite different: "Anything offered through the employer plan has been scrubbed; it has been studied by financial experts and lawyers. We trust our employers."

I cannot imagine that the response would be much different here in the UK. Consumers everywhere are looking for solutions they can trust—and, by and large, they seem to trust their employers. It is important to recognize that, with a DC plan, the firm may eliminate—at least on paper—a lot of risks and future obligations, but keep in mind that once you change the plan to a DC, your employees will expect you to have done a great job for them. If lots of people do not receive in the future what they were promised, companies may find themselves making good, either voluntarily or otherwise, on what prove to be the implicit obligations associated with being a long-lived institution.

Robert C. Merton is a co-founder and Chief Science Officer of Integrated Finance Limited (IFL), a strategic advisory and pension-solutions firm, as well as John and Natty McArthur University Professor at the Harvard Business School. He was awarded the 1997 Nobel Prize in Economics for his contributions to modern finance, particularly in the area of option pricing.

PRACTICE PROBLEMS FOR READING 22

The following information relates to Questions 1–6[1]

Chiming Lee, CFA, was recently appointed Investment Strategist for Southern Star (the "Company"), a large publicly traded pharmaceutical company focused on cancer treatment. The Company is considering expanding the Research and Development division and a key decision that needs to be made is whether to raise capital by issuing equity or debt. The Company's equity beta (β) is 1.2 and its debt beta is 0.0. The Company has a defined benefit pension plan.

The Chief Financial Officer (CFO) asks Lee to perform an analysis of the Company's equity and debt structure with the consideration of the pension plan. The pension plan is fully funded with assets equal to $14 billion (market value). Currently there are approximately 12,000 retired employees, and 20,000 current employees who are expected to retire within the next few years. The Company does not impose a mandatory retirement age; however, most employees elect to retire when they reach the age of 62. Lee starts the analysis by gathering the Company's Standard Balance Sheet Estimates displayed in Exhibit 1. All data are in U.S. dollars and marked-to-market.

EXHIBIT 1	Standard Balance Sheet Estimates (in $U.S. Billions)		
Assets		**Liabilities & Shareholders' Equity**	
Operating Assets	$17	Liabilities	$7.6
		Shareholders' Equity	$9.4
Total Assets	$17	Total Liabilities and Shareholders' Equity	$17

The Company traditionally estimates the weighted average cost of capital (WACC) based only on the data in Exhibit 1 and assuming a risk-free rate of 3% and a market-risk premium of 6%.

However, Lee is concerned about the impact that the pension plan would have on the WACC estimate. The asset allocation of the pension plan includes two asset classes: seventy percent of the pension assets are invested in large cap equities, and thirty percent are in fixed income securities. The pension plan's equities have a beta of 1.0 and the fixed income securities and pension liabilities have a beta of 0.0. Lee decides to view the pension plan assets and liabilities as a part of the Company and to recalculate the WACC for the Operating Assets by including the pension assets and liabilities.

The CFO states that while the ratio of pension plan assets to the Company's market capitalization of equity is high, since the pension plan is fully funded there are virtually no risks involved with the pension plan. Lee is not sure about

---

[1]Developed by Pamela Yang, CFA (Boston, Massachusetts).

End-of-reading problems and solutions copyright © CFA Institute. Reprinted with permission.

the CFO's statement and considers the effect of lowering the equity allocation of the pension plan from 70% to 60% on the Company's total asset beta, while maintaining the operating asset risk.

1. Based on Exhibit 1, the beta for total (operating) assets is *closest* to:
   A. 0.32.
   B. 0.36.
   C. 0.66.

2. The beta for total (operating) assets, *including* the pension plan assets and liabilities is *closest* to:
   A. 0.32.
   B. 0.36.
   C. 0.66.

3. The WACC for the operating assets including the pension plan assets and liabilities is *closest* to:
   A. 3.52%.
   B. 5.18%.
   C. 6.98%.

4. In what way would Lee's idea of changing the pension plan's equity allocation *most likely* affect the Company's total asset beta?
   A. Decrease.
   B. No change.
   C. Increase.

5. If Lee decides to reduce the pension plan's equity allocation from 70% to 60%, assuming a constant operating asset beta, the total asset beta would be *closest* to:
   A. 0.09.
   B. 0.32.
   C. 0.60.

6. If the Company decides to implement Lee's idea of lowering the pension plan's equity allocation, the Company's debt/equity ratio will *most likely*:
   A. decrease.
   B. not change.
   C. increase.

SOLUTIONS FOR READING 22

1. C is correct. Equity and liabilities without consideration of pension debt are $17: ($9.4 + $7.6). Beta ($\beta$) for Shareholder Equity and Liabilities is ($9.4 / $17) $\times$ 1.2 + ($7.6 / $17) $\times$ 0 = 0.6635.

2. B is correct. Total assets including pension assets for the company are $31: ($17 + $14), and the total debts including pension obligations are $21.6 ($7.6 + $14). The beta for total assets is: ($9.4 / $31) $\times$ 1.2 + ($21.6 / $31) $\times$ 0 = 0.3639.

3. A is correct. Including the pension assets, total asset beta is 0.364: ($9.4 / $31 $\times$ 1.2), and pension assets beta is 0.7: (70% $\times$ 1). Based on the ratio of each asset category versus total assets, operating asset beta is backed out as 0.087: $14 / $31 $\times$ 0.7 + $17 / $31 $\times$ operating asset beta = 0.364, therefore, operating asset beta is 0.087. WACC = 3% + 0.087 $\times$ 6% = 3.52%.

4. A is correct. Decreasing equity holdings will lower risk associated with the pension plan assets. If the operating risks remain the same, total asset risk will decrease from 0.364 to 0.32. Pension assets' beta now becomes 0.6: (1 $\times$ 0.6), and the operating assets' beta remains at 0.087, therefore total risk beta = 0.087 $\times$ $17 / $31 + 0.6 $\times$ $14 / $31 = 0.32.

5. B is correct. The pension assets beta now becomes 0.6: (1 $\times$ 0.6), and the operating assets beta remains at 0.087, therefore the total asset beta = 0.087 $\times$ $17 / $31 + 0.6 $\times$ $14 / $31 = 0.32.

6. C is correct. Lowering equity holdings in the pension means higher fixed income, and this will increase the ratio.

$4\frac{5}{8}$ $4\frac{11}{16}$ — $\frac{3}{8}$

$5\frac{1}{2}$ $5\frac{1}{2}$ — $\frac{3}{8}$

$20\frac{5}{8}$ $21\frac{13}{16}$ — $\frac{1}{16}$

$17\frac{3}{8}$ $18\frac{1}{8}$ + $\frac{7}{8}$

$13\frac{1}{2}$ $6\frac{1}{2}$ — $\frac{1}{2}$

$7\frac{1}{4}$ $6\frac{1}{2}$

$31\frac{1}{32}$ — $\frac{1}{8}$

$\frac{15}{16}$

$\frac{9}{16}$ $\frac{9}{16}$

$\frac{9}{16}$

$\frac{13}{32}$

$7\frac{13}{16}$ $7\frac{15}{16}$

$7\frac{15}{16}$

$2\frac{5}{8}$ $2\frac{11}{32}$ $2\frac{1}{2}$ +

$2\frac{3}{4}$ $2\frac{1}{4}$ $2\frac{1}{4}$

$12\frac{1}{16}$ $11\frac{3}{8}$ $11\frac{3}{4}$ +

$33\frac{3}{4}$ 33 $33\frac{1}{16}$ —

$25\frac{5}{8}$ $24\frac{9}{16}$ $25\frac{1}{8}$ +

12 $11\frac{5}{8}$ $11\frac{7}{8}$ +

16 $10\frac{1}{2}$ $10\frac{1}{2}$ $10\frac{1}{8}$ —

78 $15\frac{7}{8}$ $15\frac{13}{16}$ $15\frac{1}{8}$ —

$9\frac{1}{16}$ $8\frac{1}{4}$ $8\frac{1}{8}$ +

$11\frac{1}{4}$ $10\frac{1}{8}$

10-year moving average price/earnings A price-to-earnings ratio in which the numerator (in a U.S. context) is defined as the real S&P 500 price index and the denominator as the moving average of the preceding 10 years of real reported earnings on the S&P 500.

Absolute return objective A return objective that is independent of a reference or benchmark level of return.

Absolute-return vehicles Investments that have no direct benchmark portfolios.

Accounting risk The risk associated with accounting standards that vary from country to country or with any uncertainty about how certain transactions should be recorded.

Accreting swap A swap where the notional amount increases over the life of the swap.

Accrual equivalent after-tax return The tax-free return that, if accrued annually, produces the same after-tax accumulation as the taxable portfolio.

Accrual equivalent tax rate A method of measuring tax drag that finds the annual accrual tax rate that would produce the same after-tax accumulation as a tax system based in whole or in part on deferred realized gains.

Accrual taxes Taxes that are levied and paid on a periodic basis, usually annually.

Accumulated benefit obligation (ABO) The present value of pension benefits, assuming the pension plan terminated immediately such that it had to provide retirement income to all beneficiaries for their years of service up to that date.

Accumulated service Years of service of a pension plan participant as of a specified date.

Active investment approach An approach to portfolio construction in which portfolio composition responds to changes in the portfolio manager's expectations concerning asset returns.

Active management An approach to investing in which the portfolio manager seeks to outperform a given benchmark portfolio.

Active return The portfolio's return in excess of the return on the portfolio's benchmark.

Active risk A synonym for tracking risk.

Active/immunization combination A portfolio with two component portfolios: an immunized portfolio which provides an assured return over the planning horizon and a second portfolio that uses an active high-return/high-risk strategy.

Active/passive combination Allocation of the core component of a portfolio to a passive strategy and the balance to an active component.

Active-lives The portion of a pension fund's liabilities associated with active workers.

Actual extreme events A type of scenario analysis used in stress testing. It involves evaluating how a portfolio would have performed given movements in interest rates, exchange rates, stock prices, or commodity prices at magnitudes such as occurred during past extreme market events (e.g., the stock market crash of October 1987).

Ad valorem fees Fees that are calculated by multiplying a percentage by the value of assets managed; also called assets under management (AUM) fees.

Add-on interest A procedure for determining the interest on a bond or loan in which the interest is added onto the face value of a contract.

Adverse selection risk The risk associated with information asymmetry; in the context of trading, the risk of trading with a more informed trader.

After-tax asset allocation The distribution of asset classes in a portfolio measured on an after-tax basis.

Algorithmic trading Automated electronic trading subject to quantitative rules and user-specified benchmarks and constraints.

Allocation/selection interaction return A measure of the joint effect of weights assigned to both sectors and individual securities; the difference between the weight of the portfolio in a given sector and the portfolio's benchmark for that sector, times the difference between the portfolio's and the benchmark's returns in that sector, summed across all sectors.

Alpha Excess risk-adjusted return.

Alpha and beta separation An approach to portfolio construction that views investing to earn alpha and investing to establish systematic risk exposures as tasks that can and should be pursued separately.

Alpha research Research related to capturing excess risk-adjusted returns by a particular strategy; a way investment research is organized in some investment management firms.

Alternative investments Groups of investments with risk and return characteristics that differ markedly from those of traditional stock and bond investments.

American option An option that can be exercised on any day through the expiration day. Also referred to as *American-style exercise*.

Amortizing and **accreting swaps** A swap in which the notional principal changes according to a formula related to changes in the underlying.

Amortizing swap A swap where the notional amount declines over the life of the swap.

Anchoring trap The tendency of the mind to give disproportionate weight to the first information it receives on a topic.

Angel investor An accredited individual investing chiefly in seed and early-stage companies.

Appraisal data Valuation data based on appraised rather than market values.

Arbitrage The condition in a financial market in which equivalent assets or combinations of assets sell for two different prices, creating an opportunity to profit at no risk with no commitment of money. In a well-functioning financial market, few arbitrage opportunities are possible. Equivalent to the *law of one price*.

Arrears swap A type of interest rate swap in which the floating payment is set at the end of the period and the interest is paid at that same time.

Ask price (or ask, offer price, offer) The price at which a dealer will sell a specified quantity of a security.

Ask size The quantity associated with the ask price.

Asset allocation reviews A periodic review of the appropriateness of a portfolio's asset allocation.

Asset covariance matrix The covariance matrix for the asset classes or markets under consideration.

Asset location The choice of accounts in which specific assets are placed.

Asset swap A swap, typically involving a bond, in which fixed bond payments are swapped for payments based on a floating rate.

Asset/liability management The management of financial risks created by the interaction of assets and liabilities.

Asset/liability management approach In the context of determining a strategic asset allocation, an asset/liability management approach involves explicitly modeling liabilities and adopting

G-1

the allocation of assets that is optimal in relationship to funding liabilities.

Asset-only approach In the context of determining a strategic asset allocation, an approach that focuses on the characteristics of the assets without explicitly modeling the liabilities.

Assurity of completion In the context of trading, confidence that trades will settle without problems under all market conditions.

Assurity of the contract In the context of trading, confidence that the parties to trades will be held to fulfilling their obligations.

Asynchronism A discrepancy in the dating of observations that occurs because stale (out-of-date) data may be used in the absence of current data.

At the money An option in which the underlying value equals the exercise price.

AUM fee A fee based on assets under management; an ad valorem fee.

Automated trading Any form of trading that is not manual, including trading based on algorithms.

Average effective spread A measure of the liquidity of a security's market. The mean effective spread (sometimes dollar weighted) over all transactions in the stock in the period under study.

Back office Administrative functions at an investment firm such as those pertaining to transaction processing, record keeping, and regulatory compliance.

Backtesting A method for gaining information about a model using past data. As used in reference to VAR, it is the process of comparing the number of violations of VAR thresholds over a time period with the figure implied by the user-selected probability level.

Back-to-back transaction A transaction where a dealer enters into offsetting transactions with different parties, effectively serving as a go-between.

Backwardation A condition in the futures markets in which the benefits of holding an asset exceed the costs, leaving the futures price less than the spot price.

Balance of payments An accounting of all cash flows between residents and nonresidents of a country.

Bancassurance The sale of insurance by banks.

Barbell portfolio A portfolio made up of short and long maturities relative to the investment horizon date and interim coupon payments.

Basis The difference between the cash price and the futures price.

Basis point value (BPV) Also called *present value of a basis point* or *price value of a basis point* (PVBP), the change in the bond price for a 1 basis point change in yield.

Basis risk The risk that the basis will change in an unpredictable way.

Basis swap A swap in which both parties pay a floating rate.

Bear spread An option strategy that involves selling a put with a lower exercise price and buying a put with a higher exercise price. It can also be executed with calls.

Behavioral finance An approach to finance based on the observation that psychological variables affect and often distort individuals' investment decision making.

Benchmark Something taken as a standard of comparison; a comparison portfolio; a collection of securities or risk factors and associated weights that represents the persistent and prominent investment characteristics of an asset category or manager's investment process.

Best efforts order A type of order that gives the trader's agent discretion to execute the order only when the agent judges market conditions to be favorable.

Beta A measure of the sensitivity of a given investment or portfolio to movements in the overall market.

Beta research Research related to systematic (market) risk and return; a way investment research is organized in some investment management firms.

Bid price (or bid) The price at which a dealer will buy a specified quantity of a security.

Bid size The quantity associated with the bid price.

Bid–ask spread The difference between the current bid price and the current ask price of a security.

Binary credit options Options that provide payoffs contingent on the occurrence of a specified negative credit event.

Binomial model A model for pricing options in which the underlying price can move to only one of two possible new prices.

Binomial tree A diagram representing price movements of the underlying in a binomial model.

Block order An order to sell or buy in a quantity that is large relative to the liquidity ordinarily available from dealers in the security or in other markets.

Bond option An option in which the underlying is a bond; primarily traded in over-the-counter markets.

Bond-yield-plus-risk-premium method An approach to estimating the required return on equity which specifies that required return as a bond yield plus a risk premium.

Bottom-up Focusing on company-specific fundamentals or factors such as revenues, earnings, cash flow, or new product development.

Box spread An option strategy that combines a bull spread and a bear spread having two different exercise prices, which produces a risk-free payoff of the difference in the exercise prices.

Broad market indexes An index that is intended to measure the performance of an entire asset class. For example, the S&P 500 Index, Wilshire 5000, and Russell 3000 indexes for U.S. common stocks.

Broker An agent of a trader in executing trades.

Brokered markets Markets in which transactions are largely effected through a search-brokerage mechanism away from public markets.

Brokers See *Futures commission merchants.*

Bubbles Episodes in which asset market prices move to extremely high levels in relation to estimated intrinsic value.

Buffering With respect to style index construction, rules for maintaining the style assignment of a stock consistent with a previous assignment when the stock has not clearly moved to a new style.

Build-up approach Synonym for the risk premium approach.

Bull spread An option strategy that involves buying a call with a lower exercise price and selling a call with a higher exercise price. It can also be executed with puts.

Bullet portfolio A portfolio made up of maturities that are very close to the investment horizon.

Business cycle Fluctuations in GDP in relation to long-term trend growth, usually lasting 9–11 years.

Business risk The equity risk that comes from the nature of the firm's operating activities.

Butterfly spread An option strategy that combines two bull or bear spreads and has three exercise prices.

Buy side Investment management companies and other investors that use the services of brokerages.

Buy-side analysts Analysts employed by an investment manager or institutional investor.

Buy-side traders Professional traders that are employed by investment managers and institutional investors.

Calendar rebalancing Rebalancing a portfolio to target weights on a periodic basis; for example, monthly, quarterly, semiannually, or annually.

Calendar-and-percentage-of-portfolio rebalancing Monitoring a portfolio at regular frequencies, such as quarterly. Rebalancing decisions are then made based upon percentage-of-portfolio principles.

Call An option that gives the holder the right to buy an underlying asset from another party at a fixed price over a specific period of time.

Calmar ratio The compound annualized rate of return over a specified time period divided by the absolute value of maximum drawdown over the same time period.

Cap A combination of interest rate call options designed to hedge a borrower against rate increases on a floating-rate loan.

Cap rate With respect to options, the exercise interest rate for a cap.

Capital adequacy ratio A measure of the adequacy of capital in relation to assets.

Capital allocation line A graph line that describes the combinations of expected return and standard deviation of return available to an investor from combining an optimal portfolio of risky assets with a risk-free asset.

Capital flows forecasting approach An exchange rate forecasting approach that focuses on expected capital flows, particularly long-term flows such as equity investment and foreign direct investment.

Capital market expectations (CME) Expectations concerning the risk and return prospects of asset classes.

Caplet Each component call option in a cap.

Capped swap A swap in which the floating payments have an upper limit.

Carried interest A private equity fund manager's incentive fee; the share of the private equity fund's profits that the fund manager is due once the fund has returned the outside investors' capital.

Carry Another term for owning an asset, typically used to refer to commodities. (See also *carry market*.)

Carry market A situation where the forward price is such that the return on a cash-and-carry is the risk-free rate.

Cash balance plan A defined-benefit plan whose benefits are displayed in individual recordkeeping accounts.

Cash flow at risk A variation of VAR that measures the risk to a company's cash flow, instead of its market value; the minimum cash flow loss expected to be exceeded with a given probability over a specified time period.

Cash flow matching An asset/liability management approach that provides the future funding of a liability stream from the coupon and matured principal payments of the portfolio. A type of dedication strategy.

Cash price or **spot price** The price for immediate purchase of the underlying asset.

Cash settlement A procedure used in certain derivative transactions that specifies that the long and short parties engage in the equivalent cash value of a delivery transaction.

Cause-and-effect relationship A relationship in which the occurrence of one event brings about the occurrence of another event.

Cautious investors Investors who are generally averse to potential losses.

Cell-matching technique (stratified sampling) A portfolio construction technique used in indexing that divides the benchmark index into cells related to the risk factors affecting the index and samples from index securities belonging to those cells.

Centralized risk management or **companywide risk management** When a company has a single risk management group that monitors and controls all of the risk-taking activities of the organization. Centralization permits economies of scale and allows a company to use some of its risks to offset other risks. (See also *enterprise risk management*.)

Chain-linking A process for combining periodic returns to produce an overall time-weighted rate of return.

Cheapest to deliver A bond in which the amount received for delivering the bond is largest compared with the amount paid in the market for the bond.

Cherry-picking When a bankrupt company is allowed to enforce contracts that are favorable to it while walking away from contracts that are unfavorable to it.

Civil law A legal system derived from Roman law, in which judges apply general, abstract rules or concepts to particular cases. In civil systems, law is developed primarily through legislative statutes or executive action.

Claw-back provision With respect to the compensation of private equity fund managers, a provision that specifies that money from the fund manager be returned to investors if, at the end of a fund's life, investors have not received back their capital contributions and contractual share of profits.

Clearinghouse An entity associated with a futures market that acts as middleman between the contracting parties and guarantees to each party the performance of the other.

Closed-book markets Markets in which a trader does not have real-time access to all quotes in a security.

Closeout netting In a bankruptcy, a process by which multiple obligations between two counterparties are consolidated into a single overall value owed by one of the counterparties to the other.

Cobb-Douglas production function (**Cobb-Douglas model**) A production function (model for economic output) based on factors of labor and capital that exhibits constant returns to scale.

Coincident economic indicators A set of economic variables whose values correlate with current economic activity.

Collar An option strategy involving the purchase of a put and sale of a call in which the holder of an asset gains protection below a certain level, the exercise price of the put, and pays for it by giving up gains above a certain level, the exercise price of the call. Collars also can be used to provide protection against rising interest rates on a floating-rate loan by giving up gains from lower interest rates.

Collateral return (or collateral yield) The component of the return on a commodity futures contract that comes from the assumption that the full value of the underlying futures contract is invested to earn the risk-free interest rate.

Collateralized debt obligation A securitized pool of fixed-income assets.

Combination matching (or horizon matching) A cash flow matching technique; a portfolio is duration-matched with a set of liabilities with the added constraint that it also be cash-flow matched in the first few years, usually the first five years.

Commingled real estate funds (CREFs) Professionally managed vehicles for substantial commingled (i.e., pooled) investment in real estate properties.

Commitment period The period of time over which committed funds are advanced to a private equity fund.

Commodities Articles of commerce such as agricultural goods, metals, and petroleum; tangible assets that are typically relatively homogeneous in nature.

Commodity forward A contract in which the underlying asset is oil, a precious metal, or some other commodity.

Commodity futures Futures contracts in which the underlying is a traditional agricultural, metal, or petroleum product.

Commodity option An option in which the asset underlying the futures is a commodity, such as oil, gold, wheat, or soybeans.

Commodity spread Offsetting long and short positions in closely related commodities. (See also *crack spread* and *crush spread*.)

Commodity swap A swap in which the underlying is a commodity such as oil, gold, or an agricultural product.

Commodity trading advisors Registered advisors to managed futures funds.

Common law A legal system which draws abstract rules from specific cases. In common law systems, law is developed primarily through decisions of the courts.

Community property regime A marital property regime under which each spouse has an indivisible one-half interest in property received during marriage.

Completeness fund A portfolio that, when added to active managers' positions, establishes an overall portfolio with approximately the same risk exposures as the investor's overall equity benchmark.

Confidence band With reference to a quality control chart for performance evaluation, a range in which the manager's value-added returns are anticipated to fall a specified percentage of the time.

Confidence interval An interval that has a given probability of containing the parameter it is intended to estimate.

Confirming evidence trap The bias that leads individuals to give greater weight to information that supports an existing or preferred point of view than to evidence that contradicts it.

Consistent growth A growth investment substyle that focuses on companies with consistent growth having a long history of unit-sales growth, superior profitability, and predictable earnings.

Constant maturity swap or **CMT swap** A swap in which the floating rate is the rate on a security known as a constant maturity treasury or CMT security.

Constant maturity treasury or **CMT** A hypothetical U.S. Treasury note with a constant maturity. A CMT exists for various years in the range of 2 to 10.

Constant returns to scale A characteristic of a production function such that a given percentage increase in capital stock and labor input results in an equal percentage increase in output.

Constraints 1) Restricting conditions; 2) Relating to an investment policy statement, limitations on the investor's ability to take full or partial advantage of particular investments. Such constraints are either internal (such as a client's specific liquidity needs, time horizon, and unique circumstances) or external (such as tax issues and legal and regulatory requirements).

Contango A condition in the futures markets in which the costs of holding an asset exceed the benefits, leaving the futures price more than the spot price.

Contingent claims Derivatives in which the payoffs occur if a specific event occurs; generally referred to as options.

Contingent immunization A fixed-income strategy in which immunization serves as a fall-back strategy if the actively managed portfolio does not grow at a certain rate.

Continuous auction markets Auction markets where orders can be executed at any time during the trading day.

Continuous time Time thought of as advancing in extremely small increments.

Contrarian A value investment substyle focusing on stocks that have been beset by problems.

Controlled foreign corporation A company located outside a taxpayer's home country and in which the taxpayer has a controlling interest as defined under the home country law.

Convenience yield The nonmonetary return offered by an asset when the asset is in short supply, often associated with assets with seasonal production processes.

Conversion factor An adjustment used to facilitate delivery on bond futures contracts in which any of a number of bonds with different characteristics are eligible for delivery.

Convexity A measure of how interest rate sensitivity changes with a change in interest rates.

Convexity adjustment An estimate of the change in price that is not explained by duration.

Cooling degree day The greater of i) 65 degrees Fahrenheit minus the average daily temperature, and ii) zero.

Core capital The amount of capital required to fund spending to maintain a given lifestyle, fund goals, and provide adequate reserves for unexpected commitments.

Core-plus A fixed-income mandate that permits the portfolio manager to add instruments with relatively high return potential to core holdings of investment-grade debt.

Core-satellite A way of thinking about allocating money that seeks to define each investment's place in the portfolio in relation to specific investment goals or roles.

Core-satellite portfolio A portfolio in which certain investments (often indexed or semiactive) are viewed as the core and the balance are viewed as satellite investments fulfilling specific roles.

Corner portfolio Adjacent corner portfolios define a segment of the minimum-variance frontier within which portfolios hold identical assets and the rate of change of asset weights in moving from one portfolio to another is constant.

Corner portfolio theorem In a sign-constrained mean–variance optimization, the result that the asset weights of any minimum-variance portfolio are a positive linear combination of the corresponding weights in the two adjacent corner portfolios that bracket it in terms of expected return (or standard deviation of return).

Corporate governance The system of internal controls and procedures used to define and protect the rights and responsibilities of various stakeholders.

Corporate venturing Investments by companies in promising young companies in the same or a related industry.

Cost basis The amount paid to acquire an asset.

Cost of carry The costs of holding an asset.

Cost of carry model A model for pricing futures contracts in which the futures price is determined by adding the cost of carry to the spot price.

Country beta A measure of the sensitivity of a specified variable (e.g., yield) to a change in the comparable variable in another country.

Covariance A measure of the extent to which the returns on two assets move together.

Coverage Benchmark coverage is defined as the proportion of a portfolio's market value that is contained in the benchmark.

Covered call An option strategy involving the holding of an asset and sale of a call on the asset.

Covered interest arbitrage A transaction executed in the foreign exchange market in which a currency is purchased (sold) and a forward contract is sold (purchased) to lock in the exchange rate for future delivery of the currency. This transaction should earn the risk-free rate of the investor's home country.

Crack spread The difference between the price of crude oil futures and that of equivalent amounts of heating oil and gasoline.

Credit default swap A swap used to transfer credit risk to another party. A protection buyer pays the protection seller in return for the right to receive a payment from the seller in the event of a specified credit event.

Credit derivative A contract in which one party has the right to claim a payment from another party in the event that a specific credit event occurs over the life of the contract.

Credit event An event affecting the credit risk of a security or counterparty.

Credit forwards A type of credit derivative with payoffs based on bond values or credit spreads.

Credit method When the residence country reduces its taxpayers' domestic tax liability by the amount of taxes paid to a foreign country that exercises source jurisdiction.

Credit protection seller With respect to a credit derivative, the party that accepts the credit risk of the underlying financial asset.

Credit risk or **default risk** The risk of loss caused by a counterparty's or debtor's failure to make a timely payment or by the change in value of a financial instrument based on changes in default risk.

Credit spread forward A forward contract used to transfer credit risk to another party; a forward contract on a yield spread.

Credit spread option An option based on the yield spread between two securities that is used to transfer credit risk.

Credit spread risk The risk that the spread between the rate for a risky bond and the rate for a default risk-free bond may vary after the purchase of the risky bond.

Credit swap A type of swap transaction used as a credit derivative in which one party makes periodic payments to the other and receives the promise of a payoff if a third party defaults.

Credit VAR A variation of VAR related to credit risk; it reflects the minimum loss due to credit exposure with a given probability during a period of time.

Credited rates Rates of interest credited to a policyholder's reserve account.

Credit-linked notes Fixed-income securities in which the holder of the security has the right to withhold payment of the full amount due at maturity if a credit event occurs.

Cross hedging With respect to hedging bond investments using futures, hedging when the bond to be hedged is not identical to the bond underlying the futures contract. With respect to currency hedging, a hedging technique that uses two currencies other than the home currency.

Cross-default provision A provision stipulating that if a borrower defaults on any outstanding credit obligations, the borrower is considered to be in default on all obligations.

Cross-product netting Netting the market values of all contracts, not just derivatives, between parties.

Crush spread The difference between the price of a quantity of soybeans and that of the soybean meal and oil that can be produced by those soybeans.

Currency forward A forward contract in which the underlying is a foreign currency.

Currency option An option that allows the holder to buy (if a call) or sell (if a put) an underlying currency at a fixed exercise rate, expressed as an exchange rate.

Currency return The percentage change in the spot exchange rate stated in terms of home currency per unit of foreign currency.

Currency risk The risk associated with the uncertainty about the exchange rate at which proceeds in the foreign currency can be converted into the investor's home currency.

Currency swap A swap in which the parties make payments based on the difference in debt payments in different currencies.

Currency-hedged instruments Investment in nondomestic assets in which currency exposures are neutralized.

Current credit risk (or jump-to-default risk) The risk of credit-related events happening in the immediate future; it relates to the risk that a payment currently due will not be paid.

Cushion spread The difference between the minimum acceptable return and the higher possible immunized rate.

Custom security-based benchmark A custom benchmark created by weighting a manager's research universe using the manager's unique weighting approach.

Cyclical stocks The shares of companies whose earnings have above-average sensitivity to the business cycle.

Daily settlement See *Marking to market.*

Data-mining bias Bias that results from repeatedly "drilling" or searching a dataset until some statistically significant pattern is found.

Day traders Traders that rapidly buy and sell stocks in the hope that the stocks will continue to rise or fall in value for the seconds or minutes they are prepared to hold a position. Day traders hold a position open somewhat longer than a scalper but closing all positions at the end of the day.

Dealer (or market maker) A business entity that is ready to buy an asset for inventory or sell an asset from inventory to provide the other side of an order.

Decentralized risk management A system that allows individual units within an organization to manage risk. Decentralization results in duplication of effort but has the advantage of having people closer to the risk be more directly involved in its management.

Decision price (also called arrival price or strike price) The prevailing price when the decision to trade is made.

Decision risk The risk of changing strategies at the point of maximum loss.

Dedication strategies Specialized fixed-income strategies designed to accommodate specific funding needs of the investor.

Deduction method When the residence country allows taxpayers to reduce their taxable income by the amount of taxes paid to foreign governments in respect of foreign-source income.

Deemed dispositions Tax treatment that assumes property is sold. It is sometimes seen as an alternative to estate or inheritance tax.

Deemed distribution When shareholders of a controlled foreign corporation are taxed as if the earnings were distributed to shareholders, even though no distribution has been made.

Deep in the money Options that are far in-the-money.

Deep out of the money Options that are far out-of-the-money.

Default risk The risk of loss if an issuer or counterparty does not fulfill its contractual obligations.

Default risk premium Compensation for the possibility that the issue of a debt instrument will fail to make a promised payment at the contracted time and in the contracted amount.

Default swap A contract in which the swap buyer pays a regular premium; in exchange, if a default in a specified bond occurs, the swap seller pays the buyer the loss due to the default.

Defaultable debt Debt with some meaningful amount of credit risk.

Deferred swap A swap with terms specified today, but for which swap payments begin at a later date than for an ordinary swap.

Deferred taxes Taxes that are postponed until some future date.

Defined-benefit plan A pension plan that specifies the plan sponsor's obligations in terms of the benefit to plan participants.

Defined-contribution plan A pension plan that specifies the sponsor's obligations in terms of contributions to the pension fund rather than benefits to plan participants.

Deflation A decrease in the general level of prices; an increase in the purchasing power of a unit of currency.

Delay costs (or slippage)   Implicit trading costs that arise from the inability to complete desired trades immediately due to order size or market liquidity.

Delivery   A process used in a deliverable forward contract in which the long pays the agreed-upon price to the short, which in turn delivers the underlying asset to the long.

Delivery option   The feature of a futures contract giving the short the right to make decisions about what, when, and where to deliver.

Delta   The relationship between the option price and the underlying price, which reflects the sensitivity of the price of the option to changes in the price of the underlying.

Delta hedge   An option strategy in which a position in an asset is converted to a risk-free position with a position in a specific number of options. The number of options per unit of the underlying changes through time, and the position must be revised to maintain the hedge.

Delta-normal method   A measure of VAR equivalent to the analytical method but that refers to the use of delta to estimate the option's price sensitivity.

Demand deposit   A deposit that can be drawn upon without prior notice, such as a checking account.

Demutualizing   The process of converting an insurance company from mutual form to stock.

Derivative   A financial instrument that offers a return based on the return of some other underlying asset.

Derivatives dealers   The commercial and investment banks that make markets in derivatives. Also referred to as market makers.

Descriptive statistics   Methods for effectively summarizing data to describe important aspects of a dataset.

Deteriorating fundamentals sell discipline   A sell discipline involving ongoing review of holdings in which a share issue is sold or reduced if the portfolio manager believes that the company's business prospects will deteriorate.

Diff swap   A swap in which payments are based on the difference in floating interest rates on a given notional amount denominated in a single currency.

Differential returns   Returns that deviate from a manager's benchmark.

Diffusion index   An index that measures how many indicators are pointing up and how many are pointing down.

Direct commodity investment   Commodity investment that involves cash market purchase of physical commodities or exposure to changes in spot market values via derivatives, such as futures.

Direct market access   Platforms sponsored by brokers that permit buy-side traders to directly access equities, fixed income, futures, and foreign exchange markets, clearing via the broker.

Direct quotation   Quotation in terms of domestic currency/ foreign currency.

Discount interest   A procedure for determining the interest on a loan or bond in which the interest is deducted from the face value in advance.

Discounted cash flow (DCF) models   Valuation models that express the idea that an asset's value is the present value of its (expected) cash flows.

Discrete time   Time thought of as advancing in distinct finite increments.

Discretionary trust   A trust structure in which the trustee determines whether and how much to distribute in the sole discretion of the trustee.

Disintermediation   To withdraw funds from financial intermediaries for placement with other financial intermediaries offering a higher return or yield. Or, to withdraw funds from a financial intermediary for the purposes of direct investment, such as withdrawing from a mutual fund to make direct stock investments.

Distressed debt arbitrage   A distressed securities investment discipline that involves purchasing the traded bonds of bankrupt companies and selling the common equity short.

Distressed securities   Securities of companies that are in financial distress or near bankruptcy; the name given to various investment disciplines employing securities of companies in distress.

Diversification effect   In reference to VAR across several portfolios (for example, across an entire firm), this effect equals the difference between the sum of the individual VARs and total VAR.

Dividend recapitalization   A method by which a buyout fund can realize the value of a holding; involves the issuance of debt by the holding to finance a special dividend to owners.

Dollar duration   A measure of the change in portfolio value for a 100 bps change in market yields.

Downgrade risk   The risk that one of the major rating agencies will lower its rating for an issuer, based on its specified rating criteria.

Downside deviation   A measure of volatility using only rate of return data points below the investor's minimum acceptable return.

Downside risk   Risk of loss or negative return.

Due diligence   Investigation and analysis in support of an investment action or recommendation, such as the scrutiny of operations and management and the verification of material facts.

Duration   A measure of the approximate sensitivity of a security to a change in interest rates (i.e., a measure of interest rate risk).

Dynamic approach   With respect to strategic asset allocation, an approach that accounts for links between optimal decisions at different points in time.

Dynamic hedging   A strategy in which a position is hedged by making frequent adjustments to the quantity of the instrument used for hedging in relation to the instrument being hedged.

Earnings at risk (EAR)   A variation of VAR that reflects the risk of a company's earnings instead of its market value.

Earnings momentum   A growth investment substyle that focuses on companies with earnings momentum (high quarterly year-over-year earnings growth).

Econometrics   The application of quantitative modeling and analysis grounded in economic theory to the analysis of economic data.

Economic exposure   The risk associated with changes in the relative attractiveness of products and services offered for sale, arising out of the competitive effects of changes in exchange rates.

Economic indicators   Economic statistics provided by government and established private organizations that contain information on an economy's recent past activity or its current or future position in the business cycle.

Economic surplus   The market value of assets minus the present value of liabilities.

Effective capital gain tax rate   A rate that adjusts the capital gains tax rate to reflect previously taxed dividends, income, or realized capital gains.

Effective duration   Duration adjusted to account for embedded options.

Effective spread   Two times the distance between the actual execution price and the midpoint of the market quote at the time an order is entered; a measure of execution costs that captures the effects of price improvement and market impact.

Efficient frontier   The graph of the set of portfolios that maximize expected return for their level of risk (standard deviation of return); the part of the minimum-variance frontier beginning with the global minimum-variance portfolio and continuing above it.

Electronic communications networks (ECNs) Computer-based auctions that operate continuously within the day using a specified set of rules to execute orders.

Emerging market debt The sovereign debt of nondeveloped countries.

Endogenous variable A variable whose values are determined within the system.

Endowments Long-term funds generally owned by operating non-profit institutions such as universities and colleges, museums, hospitals, and other organizations involved in charitable activities.

Enhanced derivatives products companies (or special purpose vehicles) A type of subsidiary separate from an entity's other activities and not liable for the parent's debts. They are often used by derivatives dealers to control exposure to ratings downgrades.

Enterprise risk management An overall assessment of a company's risk position. A centralized approach to risk management sometimes called firmwide risk management.

Equal probability rebalancing Rebalancing in which the manager specifies a corridor for each asset class as a common multiple of the standard deviation of the asset class's returns. Rebalancing to the target proportions occurs when any asset class weight moves outside its corridor.

Equal weighted In an equal-weighted index, each stock in the index is weighted equally.

Equitized Given equity market systematic risk exposure.

Equitizing cash A strategy used to replicate an index. It is also used to take a given amount of cash and turn it into an equity position while maintaining the liquidity provided by the cash.

Equity forward A contract calling for the purchase of an individual stock, a stock portfolio, or a stock index at a later date at an agreed-upon price.

Equity-indexed annuity A type of life annuity that provides a guarantee of a minimum fixed payment plus some participation in stock market gains, if any.

Equity options Options on individual stocks; also known as stock options.

Equity q The ratio of a company's equity market capitalization divided by net worth measured at replacement cost.

Equity risk premium Compensation for the additional risk of equity compared with debt.

Equity swap A swap in which the rate is the return on a stock or stock index.

ESG risk The risk to a company's market valuation resulting from environmental, social, and governance factors.

Estate All of the property a person owns or controls; may consist of financial assets, tangible personal assets, immovable property, or intellectual property.

Estate planning The process of preparing for the disposition of one's estate (e.g., the transfer of property) upon death and during one's lifetime.

Eurodollar A dollar deposited outside the United States.

European option An option that can be exercised only at expiration. Also referred to as *European-style exercise*.

Eurozone The region of countries using the euro as a currency.

Ex post alpha (or Jensen's alpha) The average return achieved in a portfolio in excess of what would have been predicted by CAPM given the portfolio's risk level; an after-the-fact measure of excess risk-adjusted return.

Excess capital An investor's capital over and above that which is necessary to fund their lifestyle and reserves.

Excess currency return The expected currency return in excess of the forward premium or discount.

Exchange A regulated venue for the trading of investment instruments.

Exchange fund A fund into which several investors place their different share holdings in exchange for shares in the diversified fund itself.

Exchange for physicals (EFP) A permissible delivery procedure used by futures market participants, in which the long and short arrange a delivery procedure other than the normal procedures stipulated by the futures exchange.

Execution uncertainty Uncertainty pertaining to the timing of execution, or if execution will even occur at all.

Exemption method When the residence country imposes no tax on foreign-source income by providing taxpayers with an exemption, in effect having only one jurisdiction impose tax.

Exercise or **exercising the option** The process of using an option to buy or sell the underlying.

Exercise rate or **strike rate** The fixed rate at which the holder of an interest rate option can buy or sell the underlying.

Exogenous shocks Events from outside the economic system that affect its course. These could be short-lived political events, changes in government policy, or natural disasters, for example.

Exogenous variable A variable whose values are determined outside the system.

Expiration date The date on which a derivative contract expires.

Explicit transaction costs The direct costs of trading such as broker commission costs, taxes, stamp duties, and fees paid to exchanges; costs for which the trader could be given a receipt.

Externality Those consequences of a transaction (or process) that do not fall on the parties to the transaction (or process).

Factor covariance matrix The covariance matrix of factors.

Factor push A simple stress test that involves pushing prices and risk factors of an underlying model in the most disadvantageous way to estimate the impact of factor extremes on the portfolio's value.

Factor sensitivities (also called factor betas or factor loadings) In a multifactor model, the responsiveness of the dependent variable to factor movements.

Factor-model-based benchmark A benchmark that is created by relating one or more systematic sources of returns (factors or exposures) to returns of the benchmark.

Fallen angels Debt that has crossed the threshold from investment grade to high yield.

Family offices Entities, typically organized and owned by a family for its benefit, that assume responsibility for services such as financial planning, estate planning, and asset management.

Fed model An equity valuation model that relates the earnings yield on the S&P 500 to the yield to maturity on 10-year U.S. Treasury bonds.

Federal funds rate The interest rate on overnight loans of reserves (deposits) between U.S. Federal Reserve System member banks.

Fee cap A limit on the total fee paid regardless of performance.

Fiduciary A person or entity standing in a special relation of trust and responsibility with respect to other parties.

Fiduciary call A combination of a European call and a risk-free bond that matures on the option expiration day and has a face value equal to the exercise price of the call.

Financial capital As used in the text, an individual investor's investable wealth; total wealth minus human capital. Consists of assets that can be traded such as cash, stocks, bonds, and real estate.

Financial equilibrium models Models describing relationships between expected return and risk in which supply and demand are in balance.

Financial futures Futures contracts in which the underlying is a stock, bond, or currency.

Financial risk Risks derived from events in the external financial markets, such as changes in equity prices, interest rates, or currency exchange rates.

Fiscal policy Government activity concerning taxation and governmental spending.

Fixed annuity A type of life annuity in which periodic payments are fixed in amount.

Fixed trust A trust structure in which distributions to beneficiaries are prescribed in the trust document to occur at certain times or in certain amounts.

Fixed-income forward A forward contract in which the underlying is a bond.

Fixed-rate payer The party to an interest rate swap that is obligated to make periodic payments at a fixed rate.

Floating supply of shares (or free float) The number of shares outstanding that are actually available to investors.

Floating-rate loan A loan in which the interest rate is reset at least once after the starting date.

Floating-rate payer The party to an interest rate swap that is obligated to make periodic payments based on a benchmark floating rate.

Floor A combination of interest rate options designed to provide protection against interest rate decreases.

Floor broker An agent of the broker who, for certain exchanges, physically represents the trade on the exchange floor.

Floor traders or **locals** Market makers that buy and sell by quoting a bid and an ask price. They are the primary providers of liquidity to the market.

Floored swap A swap in which the floating payments have a lower limit.

Floorlet Each component put option in a floor.

Forced heirship rules Legal ownership principles whereby children have the right to a fixed share of a parent's estate.

Formal tools Established research methods amenable to precise definition and independent replication of results.

Forward contract An agreement between two parties in which one party, the buyer, agrees to buy from the other party, the seller, an underlying asset at a later date for a price established at the start of the contract.

Forward curve The set of forward or futures prices with different expiration dates on a given date for a given asset.

Forward discount (or forward premium) The forward rate less the spot rate, divided by the spot rate; called the forward discount if negative, and forward premium if positive.

Forward hedging Hedging that involves the use of a forward contract between the foreign asset's currency and the home currency.

Forward price or **forward rate** The fixed price or rate at which the transaction scheduled to occur at the expiration of a forward contract will take place. This price is agreed on at the initiation date of the contract.

Forward rate agreement (FRA) A forward contract calling for one party to make a fixed interest payment and the other to make an interest payment at a rate to be determined at the contract expiration.

Forward strip Another name for the *forward curve*.

Forward swap A forward contract to enter into a swap.

Foundations Typically, grant-making institutions funded by gifts and investment assets.

Fourth market A term occasionally used for direct trading of securities between institutional investors; the fourth market would include trading on electronic crossing networks.

Front office The revenue generating functions at an investment firm such as those pertaining to trading and sales.

Front-run To trade ahead of the initiator, exploiting privileged information about the initiator's trading intentions.

Full replication When every issue in an index is represented in the portfolio, and each portfolio position has approximately the same weight in the fund as in the index.

Fully funded plan A pension plan in which the ratio of the value of plan assets to the present value of plan liabilities is 100 percent or greater.

Functional (or multifunctional) **duration** The key rate duration.

Fund of funds A fund that invests in a number of underlying funds.

Fundamental law of active management The relation that the information ratio of a portfolio manager is approximately equal to the information coefficient multiplied by the square root of the investment discipline's breadth (the number of independent, active investment decisions made each year).

Funded status The relationship between the value of a plan's assets and the present value of its liabilities.

Funding ratio A measure of the relative size of pension assets compared to the present value of pension liabilities. Calculated by dividing the value of pension assets by the present value of pension liabilities. Also referred to as the funded ratio or funded status.

Funding risk The risk that liabilities funding long asset positions cannot be rolled over at reasonable cost.

Futures commission merchants (FCMs) Individuals or companies that execute futures transactions for other parties off the exchange.

Futures contract An enforceable contract between a buyer (seller) and an established exchange or its clearinghouse in which the buyer (seller) agrees to take (make) delivery of something at a specified price at the end of a designated period of time.

Futures exchange A legal corporate entity whose shareholders are its members. The members of the exchange have the privilege of executing transactions directly on the exchange.

Futures price The price at which the parties to a futures contract agree to exchange the underlying.

Gain-to-loss ratio The ratio of positive returns to negative returns over a specified period of time.

Gamma A numerical measure of the sensitivity of delta to a change in the underlying's value.

Global custodian An entity that effects trade settlement, safekeeping of assets, and the allocation of trades to individual custody accounts.

Global investable market A practical proxy for the world market portfolio consisting of traditional and alternative asset classes with sufficient capacity to absorb meaningful investment.

Global minimum-variance portfolio The portfolio on the minimum-variance frontier with smallest variance of return.

Gold standard currency system A currency regime under which currency could be freely converted into gold at established rates.

Gordon (constant) **growth model** A version of the dividend discount model for common share value that assumes a constant growth rate in dividends.

Government structural policies Government policies that affect the limits of economic growth and incentives within the private sector.

Grinold–Kroner model An expression for the expected return on a share as the sum of an expected income return, an expected nominal earnings growth return, and an expected repricing return.

Gross domestic product (GDP) The total value of final goods and services produced in the economy during a year.

Growth in total factor productivity A component of trend growth in GDP that results from increased efficiency in using capital inputs; also known as technical progress.

Growth investment style With reference to equity investing, an investment style focused on investing in high-earnings-growth companies.

Guaranteed investment contract A debt instrument issued by insurers, usually in large denominations, that pays a guaranteed, generally fixed interest rate for a specified time period.

H-model A variant of the two-stage dividend discount model in which growth begins at a high rate and declines linearly throughout the supernormal growth period until it reaches a normal growth rate that holds in perpetuity.

Hague Conference on Private International Law An intergovernmental organization working toward the convergence of private international law. Its 69 members consist of countries and regional economic integration organizations.

Heating degree day The greater of i) the average daily temperature minus 65 degree Fahrenheit, and ii) zero.

Hedge funds A historically loosely regulated, pooled investment vehicle that may implement various investment strategies.

Hedge ratio The relationship of the quantity of an asset being hedged to the quantity of the derivative used for hedging.

Hedged return The foreign asset return in local currency terms plus the forward discount (premium).

Hedging A general strategy usually thought of as reducing, if not eliminating, risk.

High yield A value investment substyle that focuses on stocks offering high dividend yield with prospects of maintaining or increasing the dividend.

High-water mark A specified net asset value level that a fund must exceed before performance fees are paid to the hedge fund manager.

High-yield investing A distressed securities investment discipline that involves investment in high-yield bonds perceived to be undervalued.

Highest-in, first-out (HIFO) A concept related to tax loss harvesting in which investors are allowed to sell the highest cost basis lots first, which defers realizing the tax liability associated with lots having a lower cost basis.

Historical method A method of estimating VAR that uses data from the returns of the portfolio over a recent past period and compiles this data in the form of a histogram.

Historical simulation method The application of historical price changes to the current portfolio.

Holdings-based style analysis An approach to style analysis that categorizes individual securities by their characteristics and aggregates results to reach a conclusion about the overall style of the portfolio at a given point in time.

Homogenization Creating a contract with standard and generally accepted terms, which makes it more acceptable to a broader group of participants.

Human capital or **net employment capital** An implied asset; the present value of expected future labor income.

Hybrid markets Combinations of market types, which offer elements of batch auction markets and continuous auction markets, as well as quote-driven markets.

Hypothetical events A type of scenario analysis used in stress testing that involves the evaluation of performance given events that have never happened in the markets or market outcomes to which we attach a small probability.

Illiquidity premium Compensation for the risk of loss relative to an investment's fair value if an investment needs to be converted to cash quickly.

Immunization An asset/liability management approach that structures investments in bonds to match (offset) liabilities' weighted-average duration; a type of dedication strategy.

Immunization target rate of return The assured rate of return of an immunized portfolio, equal to the total return of the portfolio assuming no change in the term structure.

Immunized time horizon The time horizon over which a portfolio's value is immunized; equal to the portfolio duration.

Implementation shortfall The difference between the money return on a notional or paper portfolio and the actual portfolio return.

Implementation shortfall strategy (or arrival price strategy) A strategy that attempts to minimize trading costs as measured by the implementation shortfall method.

Implicit transaction costs The indirect costs of trading including bid–ask spreads, the market price impacts of large trades, missed trade opportunity costs, and delay costs.

Implied repo rate The rate of return from a cash-and-carry transaction implied by the futures price relative to the spot price.

Implied volatility The volatility that option traders use to price an option, implied by the price of the option and a particular option-pricing model.

Implied yield A measure of the yield on the underlying bond of a futures contract implied by pricing it as though the underlying will be delivered at the futures expiration.

Income tax structure How and when different types of income are taxed.

Incremental VAR A measure of the incremental effect of an asset on the VAR of a portfolio by measuring the difference between the portfolio's VAR while including a specified asset and the portfolio's VAR with that asset eliminated.

Index amortizing swap An interest rate swap in which the notional principal is indexed to the level of interest rates and declines with the level of interest rates according to a predefined schedule. This type of swap is frequently used to hedge securities that are prepaid as interest rates decline, such as mortgage-backed securities.

Index option An option in which the underlying is a stock index.

Indexing A common passive approach to investing that involves holding a portfolio of securities designed to replicate the returns on a specified index of securities.

Indirect commodity investment Commodity investment that involves the acquisition of indirect claims on commodities, such as equity in companies specializing in commodity production.

Individualist investors Investors who have a self-assured approach to investing and investment decision making.

Inferential statistics Methods for making estimates or forecasts about a larger group from a smaller group actually observed.

Inflation An increase in the general level of prices; a decrease in the purchasing power of a unit of currency.

Inflation hedge An asset whose returns are sufficient on average to preserve purchasing power during periods of inflation.

Inflation premium Compensation for expected inflation.

Information coefficient The correlation between forecast and actual returns.

Information ratio The mean excess return of the account over the benchmark (i.e., mean active return) relative to the variability of that excess return (i.e., tracking risk); a measure of risk-adjusted performance.

Information-motivated traders Traders that seek to trade on information that has limited value if not quickly acted upon.

Infrastructure funds Funds that make private investment in public infrastructure projects in return for rights to specified revenue streams over a contracted period.

Initial margin requirement The margin requirement on the first day of a transaction as well as on any day in which additional margin funds must be deposited.

Initial public offering The initial issuance of common stock registered for public trading by a formerly private corporation.

Input uncertainty Uncertainty concerning whether the inputs are correct.

Inside ask (or market ask) The lowest available ask price.

Inside bid (or market bid) The highest available bid price.

Inside bid–ask spread (also called market bid–ask spread, inside spread, or market spread) Market ask price minus market bid price.

Inside quote (or market quote) Combination of the highest available bid price with the lowest available ask price.

Institutional investors Corporations or other legal entities that ultimately serve as financial intermediaries between individuals and investment markets.

Interest rate call An option in which the holder has the right to make a known interest payment and receive an unknown interest payment.

Interest rate cap or **cap** A series of call options on an interest rate, with each option expiring at the date on which the floating loan rate will be reset, and with each option having the same exercise rate. A cap in general can have an underlying other than an interest rate.

Interest rate collar A combination of a long cap and a short floor, or a short cap and a long floor. A collar in general can have an underlying other than an interest rate.

Interest rate floor or **floor** A series of put options on an interest rate, with each option expiring at the date on which the floating loan rate will be reset, and with each option having the same exercise rate. A floor in general can have an underlying other than the interest rate.

Interest rate forward See *Forward rate agreement*.

Interest rate management effect With respect to fixed-income attribution analysis, a return component reflecting how well a manager predicts interest rate changes.

Interest rate option An option in which the underlying is an interest rate.

Interest rate parity A formula that expresses the equivalence or parity of spot and forward rates, after adjusting for differences in the interest rates.

Interest rate put An option in which the holder has the right to make an unknown interest payment and receive a known interest payment.

Interest rate risk Risk related to changes in the level of interest rates.

Interest rate swap A contract between two parties (counterparties) to exchange periodic interest payments based on a specified notional amount of principal.

Interest spread With respect to banks, the average yield on earning assets minus the average percent cost of interest-bearing liabilities.

Internal rate of return The growth rate that will link the ending value of the account to its beginning value plus all intermediate cash flows; money-weighted rate of return is a synonym.

Intestate Having made no valid will; a decedent without a valid will or with a will that does not dispose of their property is considered to have died intestate.

In-the-money Options that, if exercised, would result in the value received being worth more than the payment required to exercise.

Intrinsic value or **exercise value** The value obtained if an option is exercised based on current conditions.

Inventory cycle A cycle measured in terms of fluctuations in inventories, typically lasting 2–4 years.

Inverse floater A floating-rate note or bond in which the coupon is adjusted to move opposite to a benchmark interest rate.

Investment objectives Desired investment outcomes, chiefly pertaining to return and risk.

Investment policy statement (IPS) A written document that sets out a client's return objectives and risk tolerance over a relevant time horizon, along with applicable constraints such as liquidity needs, tax considerations, regulatory requirements, and unique circumstances.

Investment skill The ability to outperform an appropriate benchmark consistently over time.

Investment strategy An investor's approach to investment analysis and security selection.

Investment style A natural grouping of investment disciplines that has some predictive power in explaining the future dispersion in returns across portfolios.

Investment style indices Indices that represent specific portions of an asset category. For example, subgroups within the U.S. common stock asset category such as large-capitalization growth stocks.

Investor's benchmark The benchmark an investor uses to evaluate performance of a given portfolio or asset class.

Irrevocable trust A trust arrangement wherein the settlor has no ability to revoke the trust relationship.

J factor risk The risk associated with a judge's track record in adjudicating bankruptcies and restructuring.

J-curve The expected pattern of interim returns over the life of a successful venture capital fund in which early returns are negative as the portfolio of companies burns cash but later returns accelerate as companies are exited.

Joint ownership with right of survivorship Jointly owned; assets held in joint ownership with right of survivorship automatically transfer to the surviving joint owner or owners outside the probate process.

Justified P/E The price-to-earnings ratio that is fair, warranted, or justified on the basis of forecasted fundamentals.

Key rate duration A method of measuring the interest rate sensitivities of a fixed-income instrument or portfolio to shifts in key points along the yield curve.

Lagging economic indicators A set of economic variables whose values correlate with recent past economic activity.

Law of one price The condition in a financial market in which two financial instruments or combinations of financial instruments can sell for only one price. Equivalent to the principle that no arbitrage opportunities are possible.

Leading economic indicators A set of economic variables whose values vary with the business cycle but at a fairly consistent time interval before a turn in the business cycle.

Legal and regulatory factors External factors imposed by governmental, regulatory, or oversight authorities that constrain investment decision-making.

Legal/contract risk The possibility of loss arising from the legal system's failure to enforce a contract in which an enterprise has a financial stake; for example, if a contract is voided through litigation.

Leverage-adjusted duration gap A leverage-adjusted measure of the difference between the durations of assets and liabilities which measures a bank's overall interest rate exposure.

Leveraged floating-rate note or **leveraged floater** A floating-rate note or bond in which the coupon is adjusted at a multiple of a benchmark interest rate.

Liability As used in the text, a financial obligation.

Life annuity An annuity that guarantees a monthly income to the annuitant for life.

Lifetime gratuitous transfer A lifetime gift made during the lifetime of the donor; also known as *inter vivos* transfers.

Limit down A limit move in the futures market in which the price at which a transaction would be made is at or below the lower limit.

Limit move A condition in the futures markets in which the price at which a transaction would be made is at or beyond the price limits.

Limit order An instruction to execute an order when the best price available is at least as good as the limit price specified in the order.

Limit up A limit move in the futures market in which the price at which a transaction would be made is at or above the upper limit.

Linear programming Optimization in which the objective function and constraints are linear.

Liquidity The ability to trade without delay at relatively low cost and in relatively large quantities.

Liquidity event An event giving rise to a need for cash.

Liquidity requirement A need for cash in excess of new contributions (for pension plans and endowments, for example) or savings (for individuals) at a specified point in time.

Liquidity risk Any risk of economic loss because of the need to sell relatively less liquid assets to meet liquidity requirements; the risk that a financial instrument cannot be purchased or sold without a significant concession in price because of the market's potential inability to efficiently accommodate the desired trading size.

Liquidity-motivated traders Traders that are motivated to trade based upon reasons other than an information advantage. For example, to release cash proceeds to facilitate the purchase of another security, adjust market exposure, or fund cash needs.

Locked limit A condition in the futures markets in which a transaction cannot take place because the price would be beyond the limits.

Locked up Said of investments that cannot be traded at all for some time.

Lock-up period A minimum initial holding period for investments during which no part of the investment can be withdrawn.

Logical participation strategies Protocols for breaking up an order for execution over time. Typically used by institutional traders to participate in overall market volumes without being unduly visible.

London Interbank Offer Rate (LIBOR) The Eurodollar rate at which London banks lend dollars to other London banks; considered to be the best representative rate on a dollar borrowed by a private, high-quality borrower.

Long The buyer of a derivative contract. Also refers to the position of owning a derivative.

Longevity risk The risk of outliving one's financial resources.

Long-term equity anticipatory securities (LEAPS) Options originally created with expirations of several years.

Low P/E A value investment substyle that focuses on shares selling at low prices relative to current or normal earnings.

Lower bound The lowest possible value of an option.

M^2 A measure of what a portfolio would have returned if it had taken on the same total risk as the market index.

Macaulay duration The percentage change in price for a percentage change in yield. The term, named for one of the economists who first derived it, is used to distinguish the calculation from modified duration. (See also *modified duration*.)

Macro attribution Performance attribution analysis conducted on the fund sponsor level.

Macro expectations Expectations concerning classes of assets.

Maintenance margin requirement The margin requirement on any day other than the first day of a transaction.

Managed futures Pooled investment vehicles, frequently structured as limited partnerships, that invest in futures and options on futures and other instruments.

Manager continuation policies Policies adopted to guide the manager evaluations conducted by fund sponsors. The goal of manager continuation policies is to reduce the costs of manager turnover while systematically acting on indications of future poor performance.

Manager monitoring A formal, documented procedure that assists fund sponsors in consistently collecting information relevant to evaluating the state of their managers' operations; used to identify warning signs of adverse changes in existing managers' organizations.

Manager review A detailed examination of a manager that currently exists within a plan sponsor's program. The manager review closely resembles the manager selection process, in both the information considered and the comprehensiveness of the analysis. The staff should review all phases of the manager's operations, just as if the manager were being initially hired.

Mandate A set of instructions detailing the investment manager's task and how his performance will be evaluated.

Margin The amount of money that a trader deposits in a margin account. The term is derived from the stock market practice in which an investor borrows a portion of the money required to purchase a certain amount of stock. In futures markets, there is no borrowing so the margin is more of a down payment or performance bond.

Market bid The best available bid; highest price any buyer is currently willing to pay.

Market fragmentation A condition whereby a market contains no dominant group of sellers (or buyers) that are large enough to unduly influence the market.

Market impact (or price impact) The effect of the trade on transaction prices.

Market integration The degree to which there are no impediments or barriers to capital mobility across markets.

Market microstructure The market structures and processes that affect how the manager's interest in buying or selling an asset is translated into executed trades (represented by trade prices and volumes).

Market model A regression equation that specifies a linear relationship between the return on a security (or portfolio) and the return on a broad market index.

Market on open (close) order A market order to be executed at the opening (closing) of the market.

Market order An instruction to execute an order as soon as possible in the public markets at the best price available.

Market oriented With reference to equity investing, an intermediate grouping for investment disciplines that cannot be clearly categorized as value or growth.

Market resilience Condition where discrepancies between market prices and intrinsic values tend to be small and corrected quickly.

Market risk The risk associated with interest rates, exchange rates, and equity prices.

Market segmentation The degree to which there are some meaningful impediments to capital movement across markets.

Market timing Increasing or decreasing exposure to a market or asset class based on predictions of its performance; with reference to performance attribution, returns attributable to shorter-term tactical deviations from the strategic asset allocation.

Market-adjusted implementation shortfall   The difference between the money return on a notional or paper portfolio and the actual portfolio return, adjusted using beta to remove the effect of the return on the market.

Market-not-held order   A variation of the market order designed to give the agent greater discretion than a simple market order would allow. "Not held" means that the floor broker is not required to trade at any specific price or in any specific time interval.

Marking to market   A procedure used primarily in futures markets in which the parties to a contract settle the amount owed daily. Also known as the *daily settlement*.

Mass affluent   An industry term for a segment of the private wealth marketplace that is not sufficiently wealthy to command certain individualized services.

Matrix prices   Prices determined by comparisons to other securities of similar credit risk and maturity; the result of matrix pricing.

Matrix pricing   An approach for estimating the prices of thinly traded securities based on the prices of securities with similar attributions, such as similar credit rating, maturity, or economic sector.

Maturity premium   Compensation for the increased sensitivity of the market value of debt to a change in market interest rates as maturity is extended.

Maturity variance   A measure of how much a given immunized portfolio differs from the ideal immunized portfolio consisting of a single pure discount instrument with maturity equal to the time horizon.

Maximum loss optimization   A stress test in which we would try to optimize mathematically the risk variable that would produce the maximum loss.

Mega-cap buy-out funds   A class of buyout funds that take public companies private.

Methodical investors   Investors who rely on "hard facts."

Micro attribution   Performance attribution analysis carried out on the investment manager level.

Micro expectations   Expectations concerning individual assets.

Middle-market buy-out funds   A class of buyout funds that purchase private companies whose revenues and profits are too small to access capital from the public equity markets.

Midquote   The halfway point between the market bid and ask prices.

Minimum-variance frontier   The graph of the set of portfolios with smallest variances of return for their levels of expected return.

Missed trade opportunity costs   Unrealized profit/loss arising from the failure to execute a trade in a timely manner.

Model risk   The risk that a model is incorrect or misapplied; in investments, it often refers to valuation models.

Model uncertainty   Uncertainty concerning whether a selected model is correct.

Modern portfolio theory (MPT)   The analysis of rational portfolio choices based on the efficient use of risk.

Modified duration   An adjustment of the duration for the level of the yield. Contrast with *Macaulay duration*.

Monetary policy   Government activity concerning interest rates and the money supply.

Money markets   Markets for fixed-income securities with maturities of one year or less.

Moneyness   The relationship between the price of the underlying and an option's exercise price.

Money-weighted rate of return   Same as the internal rate of return; the growth rate that will link the ending value of the account to its beginning value plus all intermediate cash flows.

Monitoring   To systematically keep watch over investor circumstances (including wealth and constraints), market and economic changes, and the portfolio itself so that the client's current objectives and constraints continue to be satisfied.

Monte Carlo simulation method   An approach to estimating VAR that produces random outcomes to examine what might happen if a particular risk is faced. This method is widely used in the sciences as well as in business to study a variety of problems.

Mortality risk   The risk of loss of human capital in the event of premature death.

Multifactor model   A model that explains a variable in terms of the values of a set of factors.

Multifactor model technique   With respect to construction of an indexed portfolio, a technique that attempts to match the primary risk exposures of the indexed portfolio to those of the index.

Multiperiod Sharpe ratio   A Sharpe ratio based on the investment's multiperiod wealth in excess of the wealth generated by the risk-free investment.

Mutuals   With respect to insurance companies, companies that are owned by their policyholders, who share in the company's surplus earnings.

Natural liquidity   An extensive pool of investors who are aware of and have a potential interest in buying and/or selling a security.

Net interest margin   With respect to banks, net interest income (interest income minus interest expense) divided by average earning assets.

Net interest spread   With respect to the operations of insurers, the difference between interest earned and interest credited to policyholders.

Net worth   The difference between the market value of assets and liabilities.

Net worth tax or **net wealth tax**   A tax based on a person's assets, less liabilities.

Netting   When parties agree to exchange only the net amount owed from one party to the other.

Nominal default-free bonds   Conventional bonds that have no (or minimal) default risk.

Nominal gross domestic product (nominal GDP)   A money measure of the goods and services produced within a country's borders.

Nominal risk-free interest rate   The sum of the real risk-free interest rate and the inflation premium.

Nominal spread   The spread of a bond or portfolio above the yield of a Treasury of equal maturity.

Nondeliverable forwards (NDFs)   Cash-settled forward contracts, used predominately with respect to foreign exchange forwards.

Nonfinancial risk   Risks that arise from sources other than the external financial markets, such as changes in accounting rules, legal environment, or tax rates.

Nonparametric   Involving minimal probability-distribution assumptions.

Nonstationarity   A property of a data series that reflects more than one set of underlying statistical properties.

Normal backwardation   The condition in futures markets in which futures prices are lower than expected spot prices.

Normal contango   The condition in futures markets in which futures prices are higher than expected spot prices.

Normal portfolio   A portfolio with exposure to sources of systematic risk that are typical for a manager, using the manager's past portfolios as a guide.

Notional amount The dollar amount used as a scale factor in calculating payments for a forward contract, futures contract, or swap.

Notional principal amount The amount specified in a swap that forms the basis for calculating payment streams.

Objective function A quantitative expression of the objective or goal of a process.

Off-market FRA A contract in which the initial value is intentionally set at a value other than zero and therefore requires a cash payment at the start from one party to the other.

Offsetting A transaction in exchange-listed derivative markets in which a party re-enters the market to close out a position.

Open market operations The purchase or sale by a central bank of government securities, which are settled using reserves, to influence interest rates and the supply of credit by banks.

Open outcry auction market Public auction where representatives of buyers and sellers meet at a specified location and place verbal bids and offers.

Operations risk or **operational risk** The risk of loss from failures in a company's systems and procedures (for example, due to computer failures or human failures) or events completely outside of the control of organizations (which would include "acts of God" and terrorist actions).

Opportunistic participation strategies Passive trading combined with the opportunistic seizing of liquidity.

Opportunity cost sell discipline A sell discipline in which the investor is constantly looking at potential stocks to include in the portfolio and will replace an existing holding whenever a better opportunity presents itself.

Optimization With respect to portfolio construction, a procedure for determining the best portfolios according to some criterion.

Optimizer A heuristic, formula, algorithm, or program that uses risk, return, correlation, or other variables to determine the most appropriate asset allocation or asset mix for a portfolio.

Option A financial instrument that gives one party the right, but not the obligation, to buy or sell an underlying asset from or to another party at a fixed price over a specific period of time. Also referred to as contingent claims.

Option price, option premium, or **premium** The amount of money a buyer pays and seller receives to engage in an option transaction.

Option-adjusted spread (OAS) The current spread over the benchmark yield minus that component of the spread that is attributable to any embedded optionality in the instrument.

Options on futures (futures options) Options on a designated futures contract.

Options on physicals With respect to options, exchange-traded option contracts that have cash instruments rather than futures contracts on cash instruments as the underlying.

Order-driven markets Markets in which transaction prices are established by public limit orders to buy or sell a security at specified prices.

Ordinary income Earnings from employment.

Ordinary life insurance (also whole life insurance) A type of life insurance policy that involves coverage for the whole of the insured's life.

Orphan equities investing A distressed securities investment discipline that involves investment in orphan equities that are perceived to be undervalued.

Orphan equity Investment in the newly issued equity of a company emerging from reorganization.

Out-of-the-money Options that, if exercised, would require the payment of more money than the value received and therefore would not be currently exercised.

Output gap The difference between the value of GDP estimated as if the economy were on its trend growth path (potential output) and the actual value of GDP.

Overall trade balance The sum of the current account (reflecting exports and imports) and the financial account (consisting of portfolio flows).

Overconfidence trap The tendency of individuals to overestimate the accuracy of their forecasts.

Overnight index swap (OIS) A swap in which the floating rate is the cumulative value of a single unit of currency invested at an overnight rate during the settlement period.

Pairs trade (or pairs arbitrage) A basic long–short trade in which an investor is long and short equal currency amounts of two common stocks in a single industry.

Panel method A method of capital market expectations setting that involves using the viewpoints of a panel of experts.

Partial correlation In multivariate problems, the correlation between two variables after controlling for the effects of the other variables in the system.

Partial fill Execution of a purchase or sale for fewer shares than was stipulated in the order.

Participate (do not initiate) **order** A variant of the market-not-held order. The broker is deliberately low-key and waits for and responds to the initiatives of more active traders.

Passive investment approach An approach to portfolio construction in which portfolio composition does not react to changes in capital market expectations; includes indexing and buy-and-hold investing.

Passive management A buy-and-hold approach to investing in which an investor does not make portfolio changes based upon short-term expectations of changing market or security performance.

Passive traders Traders that seek liquidity in their rebalancing transactions, but are much more concerned with the cost of trading.

Payer swaption A swaption that allows the holder to enter into a swap as the fixed-rate payer and floating-rate receiver.

Payment netting A means of settling payments in which the amount owed by the first party to the second is netted with the amount owed by the second party to the first; only the net difference is paid.

Payoff The value of an option at expiration.

Pension funds Funds consisting of assets set aside to support a promise of retirement income.

Pension surplus Pension assets at market value minus the present value of pension liabilities.

Percentage-of-portfolio rebalancing Rebalancing is triggered based on set thresholds stated as a percentage of the portfolio's value.

Percentage-of-volume strategy A logical participation strategy in which trading takes place in proportion to overall market volume (typically at a rate of 5–20 percent) until the order is completed.

Perfect markets Markets without any frictional costs.

Performance appraisal The evaluation of portfolio performance; a quantitative assessment of a manager's investment skill.

Performance attribution A comparison of an account's performance with that of a designated benchmark and the identification and quantification of sources of differential returns.

Performance evaluation The measurement and assessment of the outcomes of investment management decisions.

Performance guarantee A guarantee from the clearinghouse that if one party makes money on a transaction, the clearinghouse ensures it will be paid.

Performance measurement A component of performance evaluation; the relatively simple procedure of calculating an asset's or portfolio's rate of return.

Performance netting risk For entities that fund more than one strategy and have asymmetric incentive fee arrangements with the portfolio managers, the potential for loss in cases where the net performance of the group of managers generates insufficient fee revenue to fully cover contractual payout obligations to all portfolio managers with positive performance.

Performance-based fee Fees specified by a combination of a base fee plus an incentive fee for performance in excess of a benchmark's.

Periodic (or batch) **auction markets** Auction markets where multilateral trading occurs at a single price at a prespecified point in time.

Permanent income hypothesis The hypothesis that consumers' spending behavior is largely determined by their long-run income expectations.

Personality typing The determination of an investor's personality type.

Plain vanilla swap An interest rate swap in which one party pays a fixed rate and the other pays a floating rate, with both sets of payments in the same currency.

Plan sponsor An enterprise or organization—such as a business, labor union, municipal or state government, or not-for-profit organization—that sets up a pension plan.

Pledging requirement With respect to banks, a required collateral use of assets.

Point estimate A single-valued estimate of a quantity, as opposed to an estimate in terms of a range of values.

Policy portfolio A synonym of strategic asset allocation; the portfolio resulting from strategic asset allocation considered as a process.

Policyholder reserves With respect to an insurance company, an amount representing the estimated payments to policyholders, as determined by actuaries, based on the types and terms of the various insurance policies issued by the company.

Political risk (or geopolitical risk) The risk of war, government collapse, political instability, expropriation, confiscation, or adverse changes in taxation.

Portable Moveable. With reference to a pension plan, one in which a plan participant can move his or her share of plan assets to a new plan, subject to certain rules, vesting schedules, and possible tax penalties and payments.

Portable alpha A strategy involving the combining of multiple positions (e.g., long and short positions) so as to separate the alpha (unsystematic risk) from beta (systematic risk) in an investment.

Portfolio implementation decision The decision on how to execute the buy and sell orders of portfolio managers.

Portfolio management process An integrated set of steps undertaken in a consistent manner to create and maintain an appropriate portfolio (combination of assets) to meet clients' stated goals.

Portfolio optimization The combining of assets to efficiently achieve a set of return and risk objectives.

Portfolio segmentation The creation of subportfolios according to the product mix for individual segments or lines of business.

Portfolio selection/composition decision The decision in which the manager integrates investment strategies with capital market expectations to select the specific assets for the portfolio.

Portfolio trade (also known as program trade or basket trade) A trade in which a number of securities are traded as a single unit.

Position a trade To take the other side of a trade, acting as a principal with capital at risk.

Position trader A trader who typically holds positions open overnight.

Positive active position An active position for which the account's allocation to a security is greater than the corresponding weight of the same security in the benchmark.

Post-trade transparency Degree to which completed trades are quickly and accurately reported to the public.

Potential credit risk The risk associated with the possibility that a payment due at a later date will not be made.

Potential output The value of GDP if the economy were on its trend growth path.

Preferred return With respect to the compensation of private equity fund managers, a hurdle rate.

Pre-investing The strategy of using futures contracts to enter the market without an immediate outlay of cash.

Premium Regarding life insurance, the asset paid by the policy holder to an insurer who, in turn, has a contractual obligation to pay death benefit proceeds to the beneficiary named in the policy.

Prepackaged bankruptcy A bankruptcy in which the debtor seeks agreement from creditors on the terms of a reorganization before the reorganization filing.

Prepaid swap A contract calling for payment today and delivery of the asset or commodity at multiple specified times in the future.

Present (price) value of a basis point (PVBP) The change in the bond price for a 1 basis point change in yield. Also called *basis point value* (BPV).

Present value distribution of cash flows A list showing what proportion of a portfolio's duration is attributable to each future cash flow.

Pretrade transparency Ability of individuals to quickly, easily, and inexpensively obtain accurate information about quotes and trades.

Price discovery Adjustment of transaction prices to balance supply and demand.

Price improvement Execution at a price that is better than the price quoted at the time of order placement.

Price limits Limits imposed by a futures exchange on the price change that can occur from one day to the next.

Price risk The risk of fluctuations in market price.

Price uncertainty Uncertainty about the price at which an order will execute.

Price weighted With respect to index construction, an index in which each security in the index is weighted according to its absolute share price.

Priced risk Risk for which investors demand compensation.

Primary risk factors With respect to valuation, the major influences on pricing.

Prime brokerage A suite of services that is often specified to include support in accounting and reporting, leveraged trade execution, financing, securities lending (related to short-selling activities), and start-up advice (for new entities).

Principal trade A trade with a broker in which the broker commits capital to facilitate the prompt execution of the trader's order to buy or sell.

Private equity Ownership interests in non-publicly-traded companies.

Private equity funds Pooled investment vehicles investing in generally highly illiquid assets; includes venture capital funds and buyout funds.

Private exchange A method for handling undiversified positions with built-in capital gains in which shares that are a component of an index are exchanged for shares of an index mutual fund in a privately arranged transaction with the fund.

Private placement memorandum A document used to raise venture capital financing when funds are raised through an agent.

Probate The legal process to confirm the validity of a will so that executors, heirs, and other interested parties can rely on its authenticity.

Profit-sharing plans A defined-contribution plan in which contributions are based, at least in part, on the plan sponsor's profits.

Projected benefit obligation (PBO) A measure of a pension plan's liability that reflects accumulated service in the same manner as the ABO but also projects future variables, such as compensation increases.

Prospect theory The analysis of decision making under risk in terms of choices among prospects.

Protective put An option strategy in which a long position in an asset is combined with a long position in a put.

Proxy hedging Hedging that involves the use of a forward contract between the home currency and a currency that is highly correlated with the foreign asset's currency.

Prudence trap The tendency to temper forecasts so that they do not appear extreme; the tendency to be overly cautious in forecasting.

Psychological profiling The determination of an investor's psychological characteristics relevant to investing, such as his or her personality type.

Public good A good that is not divisible and not excludable (a consumer cannot be denied it).

Purchasing power parity The theory that movements in an exchange rate should offset any difference in the inflation rates between two countries.

Pure sector allocation return A component of attribution analysis that relates relative returns to the manager's sector-weighting decisions. Calculated as the difference between the allocation (weight) of the portfolio to a given sector and the portfolio's benchmark weight for that sector, multiplied by the difference between the sector benchmark's return and the overall portfolio's benchmark return, summed across all sectors.

Put An option that gives the holder the right to sell an underlying asset to another party at a fixed price over a specific period of time.

Put–call parity An equation expressing the equivalence (parity) of a portfolio of a call and a bond with a portfolio of a put and the underlying, which leads to the relationship between put and call prices.

Put–call–forward parity The relationship among puts, calls, and forward contracts.

Quality control charts A graphical means of presenting performance appraisal data; charts illustrating the performance of an actively managed account versus a selected benchmark.

Quality option (or swap option) With respect to Treasury futures, the option of which acceptable Treasury issue to deliver.

Quoted depth The number of shares available for purchase or sale at the quoted bid and ask prices.

Quote-driven markets (or dealer markets) Markets that rely on dealers to establish firm prices at which securities can be bought and sold.

Rate duration A fixed-income instrument's or portfolio's sensitivity to a change in key maturity, holding constant all other points along the yield curve.

Ratio spread An option strategy in which a long position in a certain number of options is offset by a short position in a certain number of other options on the same underlying, resulting in a risk-free position.

Real estate Interests in land or structures attached to land.

Real estate investment trusts (REITs) Publicly traded equities representing pools of money invested in real estate properties and/or real estate debt.

Real option An option involving decisions related to tangible assets or processes.

Real risk-free interest rate The single-period interest rate for a completely risk-free security if no inflation were expected.

Rebalancing Adjusting the actual portfolio to the current strategic asset allocation because of price changes in portfolio holdings. Also: revisions to an investor's target asset class weights because of changes in the investor's investment objectives or constraints, or because of changes in capital market expectations; or to mean tactical asset allocation.

Rebalancing ratio A quantity involved in reestablishing the dollar duration of a portfolio to a desired level, equal to the original dollar duration divided by the new dollar duration.

Re-base With reference to index construction, to change the time period used as the base of the index.

Recallability trap The tendency of forecasts to be overly influenced by events that have left a strong impression on a person's memory.

Receiver swaption A swaption that allows the holder to enter into a swap as the fixed-rate receiver and floating-rate payer.

Recession A broad-based economic downturn, conventionally defined as two successive quarterly declines in GDP.

Reference entity An entity, such as a bond issuer, specified in a derivatives contract.

Regime A distinct governing set of relationships.

Regulatory risk The risk associated with the uncertainty of how a transaction will be regulated or with the potential for regulations to change.

Reinvestment risk The risk of reinvesting coupon income or principal at a rate less than the original coupon or purchase rate.

Relative economic strength forecasting approach An exchange rate forecasting approach that suggests that a strong pace of economic growth in a country creates attractive investment opportunities, increasing the demand for the country's currency and causing it to appreciate.

Relative return objective A return objective stated as a return relative to the portfolio benchmark's total return.

Relative strength indicators A price momentum indicator that involves comparing a stock's performance during a specific period either to its own past performance or to the performance of some group of stocks.

Remaindermen Beneficiaries of a trust; having a claim on the residue.

Replacement value The market value of a swap.

Repurchase agreement A contract involving the sale of securities such as Treasury instruments coupled with an agreement to repurchase the same securities at a later date.

Repurchase yield The negative of the expected percent change in number of shares outstanding, in the Grinold–Kroner model.

Required return (or return requirement) With reference to the investment policy statement, a return objective relating to the level of return that will be adequate to satisfy a need.

Resampled efficient frontier The set of resampled efficient portfolios.

Resampled efficient portfolio An efficient portfolio based on simulation.

Residence jurisdiction A framework used by a country to determine the basis for taxing income, based on residency.

Residence–residence conflict When two countries claim residence of the same individual, subjecting the individual's income to taxation by both countries.

Residence–source conflict   When tax jurisdiction is claimed by an individual's country of residence and the country where some of their assets are sourced; the most common source of double taxation.

Residue   With respect to trusts, the funds remaining in a trust when the last income beneficiary dies.

Retired-lives   The portion of a pension fund's liabilities associated with retired workers.

Return objective   An investor objective that addresses the required or desired level of returns.

Returns-based benchmarks   Benchmarks that are constructed using 1) a series of a manager's account returns and 2) the series of returns on several investment style indexes over the same period. These return series are then submitted to an allocation algorithm that solves for the combination of investment style indexes that most closely tracks the account's returns.

Returns-based style analysis   An approach to style analysis that focuses on characteristics of the overall portfolio as revealed by a portfolio's realized returns.

Reverse optimization   A technique for reverse engineering the expected returns implicit in a diversified market portfolio.

Revocable trust   A trust arrangement wherein the settlor (who originally transfers assets to fund the trust) retains the right to rescind the trust relationship and regain title to the trust assets.

Rho   The sensitivity of the option price to the risk-free rate.

Risk aversion   The degree of an investor's inability and unwillingness to take risk.

Risk budget   The desired total quantity of risk; the result of risk budgeting.

Risk budgeting   The establishment of objectives for individuals, groups, or divisions of an organization that takes into account the allocation of an acceptable level of risk.

Risk exposure   A source of risk. Also, the state of being exposed or vulnerable to a risk.

Risk governance   The process of setting overall policies and standards in risk management.

Risk management   The process of identifying the level of risk an entity wants, measuring the level of risk the entity currently has, taking actions that bring the actual level of risk to the desired level of risk, and monitoring the new actual level of risk so that it continues to be aligned with the desired level of risk.

Risk objective   An investor objective that addresses risk.

Risk premium approach   An approach to forecasting the return of a risky asset that views its expected return as the sum of the risk-free rate of interest and one or more risk premiums.

Risk profile   A detailed tabulation of the index's risk exposures.

Risk tolerance   The capacity to accept risk; the level of risk an investor (or organization) is willing and able to bear.

Risk tolerance function   An assessment of an investor's tolerance to risk over various levels of portfolio outcomes.

Risk-neutral probabilities   Weights that are used to compute a binomial option price. They are the probabilities that would apply if a risk-neutral investor valued an option.

Risk-neutral valuation   The process by which options and other derivatives are priced by treating investors as though they were risk neutral.

Roll return (or roll yield)   The component of the return on a commodity futures contract that comes from rolling long futures positions forward through time.

Rolling return   The moving average of the holding-period returns for a specified period (e.g., a calendar year) that matches the investor's time horizon.

Sample estimator   A formula for assigning a unique value (a point estimate) to a population parameter.

Sandwich spread   An option strategy that is equivalent to a short butterfly spread.

Savings–investment imbalances forecasting approach   An exchange rate forecasting approach that explains currency movements in terms of the effects of domestic savings–investment imbalances on the exchange rate.

Scalper   A trader who offers to buy or sell futures contracts, holding the position for only a brief period of time. Scalpers attempt to profit by buying at the bid price and selling at the higher ask price.

Scenario analysis   A risk management technique involving the examination of the performance of a portfolio under specified situations. Closely related to *stress testing*.

Seats   Memberships in a derivatives exchange.

Secondary offering   An offering after the initial public offering of securities.

Sector/quality effect   In a fixed-income attribution analysis, a measure of a manager's ability to select the "right" issuing sector and quality group.

Security selection   Skill in selecting individual securities within an asset class.

Security selection effect   In a fixed-income attribution analysis, the residual of the security's total return after other effects are accounted for; a measure of the return due to ability in security selection.

Segmentation   With respect to the management of insurance company portfolios, the notional subdivision of the overall portfolio into sub-portfolios each of which is associated with a specified group of insurance contracts.

Sell side   Broker/dealers that sell securities and make recommendations for various customers, such as investment managers and institutional investors.

Sell-side analysts   Analysts employed by brokerages.

Semiactive management (also called enhanced indexing or risk-controlled active management)   A variant of active management. In a semiactive portfolio, the manager seeks to outperform a given benchmark with tightly controlled risk relative to the benchmark.

Semiactive, risk-controlled active, or enhanced index approach   An investment approach that seeks positive alpha while keeping tight control over risk relative to the portfolio's benchmark.

Semivariance   A measure of downside risk. The average of squared deviations that fall below the mean.

Separate property regime   A marital property regime under which each spouse is able to own and control property as an individual.

Settlement date or **payment date**   The designated date at which the parties to a trade must transact.

Settlement netting risk   The risk that a liquidator of a counterparty in default could challenge a netting arrangement so that profitable transactions are realized for the benefit of creditors.

Settlement period   The time between settlement dates.

Settlement price   The official price, designated by the clearinghouse, from which daily gains and losses will be determined and marked to market.

Settlement risk   When settling a contract, the risk that one party could be in the process of paying the counterparty while the counterparty is declaring bankruptcy.

Settlor (or **grantor**)   An entity that transfers assets to a trustee, to be held and managed for the benefit of the trust beneficiaries.

Shari'a   The law of Islam. In addition to the law of the land, some follow guidance provided by Shari'a or Islamic law.

Sharpe ratio (or reward-to-variability)   A measure of risk-adjusted performance that compares excess returns to the total risk of the account, where total risk is measured by the account's standard deviation of returns.

Short The seller of a derivative contract. Also refers to the position of being short a derivative.

Shortfall risk The risk that portfolio value will fall below some minimum acceptable level during a stated time horizon; the risk of not achieving a specified return target.

Shrinkage estimation Estimation that involves taking a weighted average of a historical estimate of a parameter and some other parameter estimate, where the weights reflect the analyst's relative belief in the estimates.

Shrinkage estimator The formula used in shrinkage estimation of a parameter.

Sign-constrained optimization An optimization that constrains asset class weights to be nonnegative and to sum to 1.

Single-payment loan A loan in which the borrower receives a sum of money at the start and pays back the entire amount with interest in a single payment at maturity.

Situational profiling The categorization of individual investors by stage of life or by economic circumstance.

Smart routing The use of algorithms to intelligently route an order to the most liquid venue.

Smoothing rule With respect to spending rates, a rule that averages asset values over a period of time in order to dampen the spending rate's response to asset value fluctuation.

Socially responsible investing (ethical investing) An approach to investing that integrates ethical values and societal concerns with investment decisions.

Soft dollars (also called soft dollar arrangements or soft commissions) The use of commissions to buy services other than execution services.

Sole ownership Owned by one person; assets held in sole ownership are typically considered part of a decedent's estate. The transfer of their ownership is dictated by the decedent's will through the probate process.

Solow residual A measure of the growth in total factor productivity that is based on an economic growth model developed by economist Robert M. Solow.

Sortino ratio A performance appraisal ratio that replaces standard deviation in the Sharpe ratio with downside deviation.

Source jurisdiction or **territorial tax system** A framework used by a country to determine the basis for taxing income or transfers. A country that taxes income as a source within its borders imposes source jurisdiction.

Source–source conflict When two countries claim source jurisdiction of the same asset; both countries may claim that the income is derived from their jurisdiction.

Sovereign risk A form of credit risk in which the borrower is the government of a sovereign nation.

Spontaneous investors Investors who constantly readjust their portfolio allocations and holdings.

Spot return (or price return) The component of the return on a commodity futures contract that comes from changes in the underlying spot prices via the cost-of-carry model.

Spread An option strategy involving the purchase of one option and sale of another option that is identical to the first in all respects except either exercise price or expiration.

Spread duration The sensitivity of a non-Treasury security's price to a widening or narrowing of the spread over Treasuries.

Spread risk Risk related to changes in the spread between Treasuries and non-Treasuries.

Stack and roll A hedging strategy in which an existing stack hedge with maturing futures contracts is replaced by a new stack hedge with longer dated futures contracts.

Stack hedge Hedging a stream of obligations by entering futures contracts with a *single* maturity, with the number of contracts selected so that changes in the *present value* of the future obligations are offset by changes in the value of this "stack" of futures contracts.

Stale price bias Bias that arises from using prices that are stale because of infrequent trading.

Standard deviation The positive square root of variance.

Stated return desire A stated desired level of returns.

Static approach With respect to strategic asset allocation, an approach that does not account for links between optimal decisions in future time periods.

Static spread (or zero-volatility spread) The constant spread above the Treasury spot curve that equates the calculated price of the security to the market price.

Stationary A series of data for which the parameters that describe a return-generating process are stable.

Status quo trap The tendency for forecasts to perpetuate recent observations—that is, to predict no change from the recent past.

Sterling ratio The compound annualized rate of return over a specified time period divided by the average yearly maximum drawdown over the same time period less an arbitrary 10 percent.

Stock companies With respect to insurance companies, companies that have issued common equity shares.

Stock index futures Futures contracts on a specified stock index.

Storage costs or **carrying costs** The costs of holding an asset, generally a function of the physical characteristics of the underlying asset.

Straddle An option strategy involving the purchase of a put and a call with the same exercise price. A straddle is based on the expectation of high volatility of the underlying.

Straight-through processing Systems that simplify transaction processing through the minimization of manual and/or duplicative intervention in the process from trade placement to settlement.

Strangle A variation of a straddle in which the put and call have different exercise prices.

Strap An option strategy involving the purchase of two calls and one put.

Strategic asset allocation 1) The process of allocating money to IPS-permissible asset classes that integrates the investor's return objectives, risk tolerance, and investment constraints with long-run capital market expectations. 2) The result of the above process, also known as the policy portfolio.

Stratified sampling (or representative sampling) A sampling method that guarantees that subpopulations of interest are represented in the sample.

Stress testing A risk management technique in which the risk manager examines the performance of the portfolio under market conditions involving high risk and usually high correlations across markets. Closely related to *scenario analysis*.

Strike spread A spread used to determine the strike price for the payoff of a credit option.

Strip An option strategy involving the purchase of two puts and one call.

Strip hedge Hedging a stream of obligations by offsetting each individual obligation with a futures contract matching the maturity and quantity of the obligation.

Structural level of unemployment The level of unemployment resulting from scarcity of a factor of production.

Structured note A variation of a floating-rate note that has some type of unusual characteristic such as a leverage factor or in which the rate moves opposite to interest rates.

Style drift　Inconsistency in style.

Style index　A securities index intended to reflect the average returns to a given style.

Stylized scenario　A type of analysis often used in stress testing. It involves simulating the movement in at least one interest rate, exchange rate, stock price, or commodity price relevant to the portfolio.

Sunshine trades　Public display of a transaction (usually high-volume) in advance of the actual order.

Surplus　The difference between the value of assets and the present value of liabilities. With respect to an insurance company, the net difference between the total assets and total liabilities (equivalent to policyholders' surplus for a mutual insurance company and stockholders' equity for a stock company).

Surplus efficient frontier　The graph of the set of portfolios that maximize expected surplus for given levels of standard deviation of surplus.

Survey method　A method of capital market expectations setting that involves surveying experts.

Survival probability　The probability an individual survives in a given year; used to determine expected cash flow required in retirement.

Survivorship bias　Bias that arises in a data series when managers with poor track records exit the business and are dropped from the database whereas managers with good records remain; when a data series as of a given date reflects only entities that have survived to that date.

Swap　A contract calling for the exchange of payments over time. Often one payment is fixed in advance and the other is floating, based upon the realization of a price or interest rate.

Swap rate　The interest rate applicable to the pay-fixed-rate side of an interest rate swap.

Swap spread　The difference between the fixed rate on an interest rate swap and the rate on a Treasury note with equivalent maturity; it reflects the general level of credit risk in the market.

Swap tenor　The lifetime of a swap.

Swap term　Another name for *swap tenor*.

Swaption　An option to enter into a swap.

Symmetric cash flow matching　A cash flow matching technique that allows cash flows occurring both before and after the liability date to be used to meet a liability; allows for the short-term borrowing of funds to satisfy a liability prior to the liability due date.

Synthetic call　The combination of puts, the underlying, and risk-free bonds that replicates a call option.

Synthetic forward contract　The combination of the underlying, puts, calls, and risk-free bonds that replicates a forward contract.

Synthetic index fund　An index fund position created by combining risk-free bonds and futures on the desired index.

Synthetic put　The combination of calls, the underlying, and risk-free bonds that replicates a put option.

Tactical asset allocation　Asset allocation that involves making short-term adjustments to asset class weights based on short-term predictions of relative performance among asset classes.

Tactical rebalancing　A variation of calendar rebalancing that specifies less frequent rebalancing when markets appear to be trending and more frequent rebalancing when they are characterized by reversals.

Tail value at risk (or conditional tail expectation)　The VAR plus the expected loss in excess of VAR, when such excess loss occurs.

Target covariance matrix　A component of shrinkage estimation; allows the analyst to model factors that are believed to influ-ence the data over periods longer than observed in the historical sample.

Target semivariance　The average squared deviation below a target value.

Target value　The value that the portfolio manager seeks to ensure; the value that the life insurance company has guaranteed the policyholder.

Tax alpha　The value created by using investment techniques that effectively manage tax liabilities.

Tax avoidance　Developing strategies that minimize tax, while conforming to both the spirit and the letter of the tax codes of jurisdictions with taxing authority.

Tax concerns　Concerns related to an investor's tax position.

Tax drag　The negative effect of taxes on after-tax returns.

Tax efficiency　The proportion of the expected pretax total return that will be retained after taxes.

Tax evasion　The practice of circumventing tax obligations by illegal means such as misreporting or not reporting relevant information to tax authorities.

Tax loss harvesting　The practice of realizing a loss to offset a gain or income, thereby reducing the current year's tax obligation.

Tax premium　Compensation for the effect of taxes on the after-tax return of an asset.

Tax risk　The uncertainty associated with tax laws.

Tax structures　The specifics of how governments collect taxes.

Taylor rule　A rule linking a central bank's target short-term interest rate to the rate of growth of the economy and inflation.

Tenor　The original time to maturity on a swap.

Term life insurance　A type of life insurance policy that provides coverage for a specified length of time and accumulates little or no cash values.

Termination date　The date of the final payment on a swap; also, the swap's expiration date.

Testamentary gratuitous transfer　The bequeathing or transfer of assets upon one's death. From a recipient's perspective, it is called an inheritance.

Testator　A person who makes a will.

Theta　The change in price of an option associated with a one-day reduction in its time to expiration; the rate at which an option's time value decays.

Tick　The smallest possible price movement of a security.

Time deposit　A deposit requiring advance notice prior to a withdrawal.

Time horizon　The time period associated with an investment objective.

Time to expiration　The time remaining in the life of a derivative, typically expressed in years.

Time value or **speculative value**　The difference between the market price of the option and its intrinsic value, determined by the uncertainty of the underlying over the remaining life of the option.

Time value decay　The loss in the value of an option resulting from movement of the option price toward its payoff value as the expiration day approaches.

Time-period bias　Bias that occurs when results are time-period specific.

Time-series estimators　Estimators that are based on lagged values of the variable being forecast; often consist of lagged values of other selected variables.

Time-weighted average price (TWAP) strategy　A logical participation strategy that assumes a flat volume profile and trades in proportion to time.

Time-weighted rate of return　The compound rate of growth over a stated evaluation period of one unit of money initially invested in the account.

Timing option With respect to certain futures contracts, the option that results from the ability of the short position to decide when in the delivery month actual delivery will take place.

Tobin's q An asset-based valuation measure that is equal to the ratio of the market value of debt and equity to the replacement cost of total assets.

Top-down Proceeding from the macroeconomy, to the economic sector level, to the industry level, to the firm level.

Total factor productivity A variable which accounts for that part of Y not directly accounted for by the levels of the production factors (K and L).

Total future liability With respect to defined-benefit pension plans, the present value of accumulated and projected future service benefits, including the effects of projected future compensation increases.

Total rate of return A measure of the increase in the investor's wealth due to both investment income (for example, dividends and interest) and capital gains (both realized and unrealized).

Total return The rate of return taking into account capital appreciation/depreciation and income. Often qualified as follows: **Nominal** returns are unadjusted for inflation; **real** returns are adjusted for inflation; **pretax** returns are returns before taxes; **post-tax** returns are returns after taxes are paid on investment income and realized capital gains.

Total return analysis Analysis of the expected effect of a trade on the portfolio's total return, given an interest rate forecast.

Total return swap A swap in which one party agrees to pay the total return on a security. Often used as a credit derivative, in which the underlying is a bond.

Tracking risk (also called tracking error, tracking error volatility, or active risk) The condition in which the performance of a portfolio does not match the performance of an index that serves as the portfolio's benchmark.

Trade blotter A device for entering and tracking trade executions and orders to trade.

Trade settlement Completion of a trade wherein purchased financial instruments are transferred to the buyer and the buyer transfers money to the seller.

Trading activity In fixed-income attribution analysis, the effect of sales and purchases of bonds over a given period; the total portfolio return minus the other components determining the management effect in an attribution analysis.

Transaction exposure The risk associated with a foreign exchange rate on a specific business transaction such as a purchase or sale.

Transcription errors Errors in gathering and recording data.

Translation exposure The risk associated with the conversion of foreign financial statements into domestic currency.

Transparency Availability of timely and accurate market and trade information.

Treasury spot curve The term structure of Treasury zero coupon bonds.

Treynor ratio (or reward-to-volatility) A measure of risk-adjusted performance that relates an account's excess returns to the systematic risk assumed by the account.

Turnover A measure of the rate of trading activity in a portfolio.

Twist With respect to the yield curve, a movement in contrary directions of interest rates at two maturities; a nonparallel movement in the yield curve.

Type I error With respect to manager selection, keeping (or hiring) managers with zero value-added. (Rejecting the null hypothesis when it is correct.)

Type II error With respect to manager selection, firing (or not hiring) managers with positive value-added. (Not rejecting the null hypothesis when it is incorrect.)

Unconstrained optimization Optimization that places no constraints on asset class weights except that they sum to 1. May produce negative asset weights, which implies borrowing or shorting of assets.

Underfunded plan A pension plan in which the ratio of the value of plan assets to the present value of plan liabilities is less than 100 percent.

Underlying An asset that trades in a market in which buyers and sellers meet, decide on a price, and the seller then delivers the asset to the buyer and receives payment. The underlying is the asset or other derivative on which a particular derivative is based. The market for the underlying is also referred to as the spot market.

Underwriting (profitability) **cycle** A cycle affecting the profitability of insurance companies' underwriting operations.

Undisclosed limit order (reserve, hidden, or iceberg order) A limit order that includes an instruction not to show more than some maximum quantity of the unfilled order to the public at any one time.

Unhedged return A foreign asset return stated in terms of the investor's home currency.

Unique circumstances Internal factors (other than a liquidity requirement, time horizon, or tax concern) that may constrain portfolio choices.

Universal life insurance A type of life insurance policy that provides for premium flexibility, an adjustable face amount of death benefits, and current market interest rates on the savings element.

Unrelated business income With respect to the U.S. tax code, income that is not substantially related to a foundation's charitable purposes.

Unstructured modeling Modeling without a theory on the underlying structure.

Uptick rules Trading rules that specify that a short sale must not be on a downtick relative to the last trade at a different price.

Urgency of the trade The importance of certainty of execution.

Valuation The process of determining the value of an asset or service.

Valuation reserve With respect to insurance companies, an allowance, created by a charge against earnings, to provide for losses in the value of the assets.

Value The amount for which one can sell something, or the amount one must pay to acquire something.

Value at risk (VAR) A probability-based measure of loss potential for a company, a fund, a portfolio, a transaction, or a strategy over a specified period of time.

Value investment style With reference to equity investing, an investment style focused on paying a relatively low share price in relation to earnings or assets per share.

Value weighted (or market-capitalization weighted) With respect to index construction, an index in which each security in the index is weighted according to its market capitalization.

Value-motivated traders Traders that act on value judgments based on careful, sometimes painstaking research. They trade only when the price moves into their value range.

Variable annuity A life annuity in which the periodic payment varies depending on stock prices.

Variable life insurance (unit-linked life insurance) A type of ordinary life insurance in which death benefits and cash values are linked to the investment performance of a policyholder-selected pool of investments held in a so-called separate account.

Variable prepaid forward A monetization strategy that involves the combination of a collar with a loan against the value of the underlying shares. When the loan comes due, shares are sold to pay off the loan and part of any appreciation is shared with the lender.

Variable universal life (or flexible-premium variable life)   A type of life insurance policy that combines the flexibility of universal life with the investment choice flexibility of variable life.

Variance   The expected value of squared deviations from the random variable's mean; often referred to as volatility.

Variation margin   Additional margin that must be deposited in an amount sufficient to bring the balance up to the initial margin requirement.

Vega   A measure of the sensitivity of an option's price to changes in the underlying's volatility.

Venture capital   The equity financing of new or growing private companies.

Venture capital firms   Firms representing dedicated pools of capital for providing equity or equity-linked financing to privately held companies.

Venture capital fund   A pooled investment vehicle for venture capital investing.

Venture capital trusts   An exchange-traded, closed-end vehicle for venture capital investing.

Venture capitalists   Specialists who seek to identify companies that have good business opportunities but need financial, managerial, and strategic support.

Vested   With respect to pension benefits or assets, said of an unconditional ownership interest.

Vintage year   With reference to a private equity fund, the year it closed.

Vintage year effects   The effects on returns shared by private equity funds closed in the same year.

Volatility   Represented by the Greek letter sigma (σ), the standard deviation of price outcomes associated with an underlying asset.

Volatility clustering   The tendency for large (small) swings in prices to be followed by large (small) swings of random direction.

Volume-weighted average price (VWAP)   The average price at which a security is traded during the day, where each trade price is weighted by the fraction of the day's volume associated with the trade.

Volume-weighted average price strategy   A logical participation strategy that involves breaking up an order over time according to a prespecified volume profile.

Wealth relative   The ending value of one unit of money invested at specified rates of return.

Weather derivative   A derivative contract with a payment based on a weather-related measurement, such as heating or cooling degree days.

Wild card option   A provision allowing a short futures contract holder to delay delivery of the underlying.

Will (or testament)   A document associated with estate planning that outlines the rights others will have over one's property after death.

Within-sector selection return   In attribution analysis, a measure of the impact of a manager's security selection decisions relative to the holdings of the sector benchmark.

Worst-case scenario analysis   A stress test in which we examine the worst case that we actually expect to occur.

Yardeni model   An equity valuation model, more complex than the Fed model, that incorporates the expected growth rate in earnings.

Yield beta   A measure of the sensitivity of a bond's yield to a general measure of bond yields in the market that is used to refine the hedge ratio.

Yield curve   The relationship between yield and time to maturity.

Yield curve risk   Risk related to changes in the shape of the yield curve.

Yield spread   The difference between the yield on a bond and the yield on a default-free security, usually a government note, of the same maturity. The yield spread is primarily determined by the market's perception of the credit risk on the bond.

Yield to worst   The yield on a callable bond that assumes a bond is called at the earliest opportunity.

Zero-cost collar   A transaction in which a position in the underlying is protected by buying a put and selling a call with the premium from the sale of the call offsetting the premium from the purchase of the put. It can also be used to protect a floating-rate borrower against interest rate increases with the premium on a long cap offsetting the premium on a short floor.

Zero-premium collar   A hedging strategy involving the simultaneous purchase of puts and sale of call options on a stock. The puts are struck below and the calls are struck above the underlying's market price.